This bo
written
each of
The firs
justice
adminis
and acc
deals wi
adminis
justice p
tinctive
final pa
conclud

The
chapter
political
ogy, as
are pra
particul
particul
manage

Administrative Justice in Context

Edited by
Michael Adler

·HART·
PUBLISHING
OXFORD AND PORTLAND, OREGON
2010

Published in the United Kingdom by Hart Publishing Ltd
16C Worcester Place, Oxford, OX1 2JW
Telephone: +44 (0)1865 517530
Fax: +44 (0)1865 510710
E-mail: mail@hartpub.co.uk
Website: http://www.hartpub.co.uk

Published in North America (US and Canada) by
Hart Publishing
c/o International Specialized Book Services
920 NE 58th Avenue, Suite 300
Portland, OR 97213-3786
USA
Tel: +1 503 287 3093 or toll-free: (1) 800 944 6190
Fax: +1 503 280 8832
E-mail: orders@isbs.com
Website: http://www.isbs.com

British Library Cataloguing in Publication Data
Data Available

ISBN: 978-1-84113-928-9

Typeset by Compuscript, Shannon
Printed and bound in Great Britain by
TJ International Ltd, Padstow, Cornwall

ACKNOWLEDGEMENTS

I should like to acknowledge my gratitude to the ESRC for the award a seminar grant; to Dr Richard Whitecross and Dr Jackie Gulland, who helped me to organise the seminar series; to those who gave papers, acted as respondents, chaired sessions, took part in the seminars and made the series such a success; and to everyone who has contributed to this book. I should also like to acknowledge my gratitude to the Leverhulme Trust for the award of an Emeritus Fellowship, which has enabled me to undertake the task of editing and see the book through to publication.

TABLE OF CONTENTS

LIST OF CONTRIBUTORS

From 1996–2007, **Michael Adler** was Professor of Socio-legal Studies at the University of Edinburgh, where he is now Emeritus Professor and holder of a Leverhulme Emeritus Fellowship. He convened the ESRC Seminar Series on 'Administrative Justice: Current State and Future Prospects', which gave rise to this book. He is the author (with Christopher Farrell, Steven Finch, Jane Lewis, Sue Morris and Dan Philo) of *Administrative Grievances: a Development Study* (National Centre for Social Research, 2006) and is currently writing up research (funded by the ESRC) comparing the experiences of represented and unrepresented tribunal users.

Patrick Birkinshaw is Professor of Public Law at the University of Hull. His many publications include *Grievances, Remedies and the State*, 2nd edn (Sweet & Maxwell, 1994), *European Public Law* (Cambridge University Press, 2003), and *Freedom of Information: The Law, The Practice and The Ideal*, 4th edn (Cambridge University Press, 2010). He has acted as a special adviser on two occasions to the Public Administration Select Committee of the House of Commons.

John Clarke is Professor of Social Policy at the Open University. He has had a long-standing interest in the roles of managerialism and consumerism in reshaping social welfare. He has written several books, including (with Janet Newman, Nick Smith, Elizabeth Vidler and Louise Westmarland) *Creating Citizen-Consumers: Changing publics and changing public services* (Sage, 2007) and (with Janet Newman) *Publics, Politics and Power: Remaking the public in public services* (Sage, 2009).

Robin Creyke holds the Alumni Chair of Administrative Law at the Australian National University and has recently been appointed as a Senior Member of the Commonwealth Administrative Appeals Tribunal. She is a member of the Commonwealth Administrative Review Council, which is currently focusing its research on access to justice issues, and recently edited *Tribunals in the Common Law World* (The Federation Press, 2008). With Dennis Pearce and John McMillan (Commonwealth Ombudsman), she has undertaken empirical research into the impact and outcomes of court and tribunal review on government.

Patrick Dunleavy is Professor of Political Science and Public Policy at the London School of Economics and Political Science and Chair of LSE Public Policy Group (PPG), which has a long track record of working with the National Audit Office and government departments on improving the interfaces between citizens and public policy. With colleagues in PPG and Helen Margetts (see below), he co-authored the 2005 NAO report *Citizen Redress: What citizens can do if things go wrong with public services*. A wider research project, funded by the Nuffield Foundation, on citizen redress but covering all levels of UK government, is currently being written up. His co-authors (**Simon Bastow**, **Jane Tinkler**, **Sofia Goldchluk** and **Ed Towers**) are all members of PPG.

David Feldman is Rouse Ball Professor of English Law and a Fellow of Downing College in the University of Cambridge. He is also a Fellow of the British Academy and a Judge of the Constitutional Court of Bosnia and Herzegovina and, from 2000 to 2004, was Legal Adviser to the Parliamentary Joint Select Committee on Human Rights. Among many publications on constitutional and administrative law and criminal procedure, his books include *Civil Liberties and Human Rights in England and Wales*, 2nd edn (Oxford University Press, 2002) and, as editor and contributor, *English Public Law*, 2nd edn (Oxford University Press, 2009).

Andrew Gamble is Professor of Politics and a Fellow of Queens' College in the University of Cambridge, and currently Head of the Department of Politics and International Studies. He is also a Fellow of the British Academy and joint editor of *The Political Quarterly*. His research interests lie in political economy, political theory and British politics, and his books include *Between Europe and America: The Future of British Politics* (Palgrave Macmillan, 2004) and *The Spectre at the Feast: Capitalist Crisis and the Politics of Recession Politics* (Palgrave Macmillan, 2009). In 2005, he received the Isaiah Berlin Prize from the Political Studies Association for lifetime contribution to political studies.

Jackie Gulland is Lecturer in Sociology at the University of Stirling. She has a particular interest in informal dispute resolution mechanisms and recently completed a PhD on complainants' experiences of local authority complaints procedures, entitled *Complaining, Appealing or Just Getting it Sorted Out: Complaints procedures for community care service users* (University of Edinburgh, 2007).

Simon Halliday is Professor of Law at the University of Strathclyde and Conjoint Professor of Law at the University of New South Wales (Australia). With Colin Scott, he has recently completed a conceptual study of administrative justice and feedback mechanisms (funded by the Nuffield Foundation) and a study of public sector liability risk management (funded by the ESRC and the IRCHSS). He is the author of *Judicial Review and Compliance with Administrative Law* (Hart Publishing, 2004) and (with David Cowan) *The Appeal of Internal Review: Law, Administrative Justice and the (Non)-Emergence of Disputes* (Hart Publishing, 2003).

Carsten Henrichsen is Professor of Administrative Law at the University of Copenhagen (Denmark) and head of the research group on administrative law in the Faculty of Law. He has a long-standing interest of combining legal studies of public administration with empirical insights drawn from political science, organisational theory and systems theory. He has published several interdisciplinary studies, including *Administrative Justice and Modern Administration* (Academic Publishers, 1997) and *Public Administration*, 2nd edn (Thomson Publishers, 2006).

Marc Hertogh is Professor of Socio-Legal Studies at the University of Groningen (The Netherlands). With Simon Halliday, he has written on the impact of administrative courts and the ombudsman and edited *Judicial Review and Bureaucratic Impact* (Cambridge University Press, 2004). He has also published several theoretical and empirical studies on legal consciousness. He recently edited *Living Law: Reconsidering Eugen Ehrlich* (Hart Publishing, 2009).

Robert A Kagan is Professor of Political Science and Emanuel S. Heller Professor of Law at the University of California, Berkeley (USA). He is the author of *Regulatory Justice* (Russell Sage Foundation, 1978), *Adversarial Legalism: The American Way of Law* (Harvard University Press, 2001), (with Eugene Bardach) *Going by the Book: The Problem of Regulatory Unreasonableness*, reprinted (Transaction Books, 2002), and (with Neil Gunningham and Dorothy Thornton) *Shades of Green: Business, Regulation and Environment* (Stanford University Press, 2003).

Irvine Lapsley is Professor of Accounting and Director of the Institute of Public Sector Accounting Research at the University of Edinburgh Business School. He is editor of *Financial Accountability & Management*, a journal devoted to accountability and financial management in public sector and nonprofit organisations. He is Chair of the Scientific Committee of the EIASM Public Sector Conference, a co-chair of the EIASM research workshop on the Third Sector, and co-chair of the New Public Sector Seminar, which has been supported by BAA, CIMA and ESRC. He has published widely on public sector financial management issues and been an advisor to the Finance and Health Committees in the Scottish Parliament.

Jeremy Lonsdale is Director-General, Value for Money Audit at the National Audit Office. Together with Marie-Louise Bemelmans-Videc and Burt Perrin, he is the editor of *Making Accountability Work: Dilemmas for Evaluation and for Audit* (Transaction Publishers, 2007).

Morag McDermont is Senior Lecturer in Law at the University of Bristol and Programme Director of the MSc in Socio-Legal Studies. She is currently carrying out research into applicants' experiences of the Employment Tribunal system. Her book, *Governing, Independence and Expertise: the Business of Housing Associations* (Hart Publishing) will be published in 2010.

Helen Margetts is Professor of Society and the Internet at the Oxford Internet Institute (OII) and Fellow of Mansfield College in the University of Oxford. A political scientist specialising in politics and government on the Internet, she has authored and co-authored a wide range of books and articles as well as a series of policy reports for the National Audit Office, including (with Patrick Dunleavy and others) *Digital Era Governance* (Oxford University Press, 2006); (with Christopher Hood) *Tools of Government in the Digital Age* (Palgrave Macmillan, 2007); and

Government on the Internet (a joint LSE-OII study for the NAO, 2007). She is editor of the new journal *Policy and Internet*.

Walter Merricks has recently been appointed Chair of the Office of Health Professions Adjudicator, having previously been Chief Ombudsman for the Financial Ombudsman Service (from 1999–2009). From 2001–04, he was Chairman of the British and Irish Ombudsman's Accociation (BIOA).

Tom Mullen is Professor of Law at the University of Glasgow and was a Member of the Administrative Justice Steering Group in Scotland. He wrote AJSG's second report *Administrative Justice in Scotland—The Way Forward* (Consumer Focus Scotland, 2009).

Janet Newman is Professor of Social Policy and Director of the Publics Research Programme in the Centre for Citizenship, Identities and Governance at the Open University. Her research centres on new formations of governance, professional and organisational change, and the transformations of notions of 'publics' and 'publicness'. Her recent publications include *Publics, Politics and Power* (Sage, 2009) and other books with John Clarke (see above), and *Power, Participation and Political Renewal* (Policy Press, 2007), written with Marian Barnes and Helen Sullivan.

Dawn Oliver is Emeritus Professor of Constitutional Law at University College London. She has written extensively on the public law private law divide and (with Jørg Fedtke) edited *Human Rights and the Private Sphere* (Routledge Cavendish, 2007).

Martin Partington is Emeritus Professor of Law and Senior Research Fellow at the University of Bristol. In 2000–01, he was a Consultant to the Leggatt Review of Tribunals. From 2001–05, he was a Law Commissioner and was subsequently a Special Consultant to the Law Commission. He organised of the Bristol Conference on Administrative Justice in 1997 and, with Michael Harris, edited *Administrative Justice in the 21st Century* (Hart Publishing, 1999).

Ko de Ridder is Professor of Public Administration at the University of Groningen (The Netherlands). With KJ de Graaf, JH Jans and AT Marseille, he recently edited *Quality of Decision-Making in Public Law: Studies of Administrative Decision-Making in the Netherlands* (Europa Law Publishing, 2007).

Colin Scott is Professor of EU Regulation and Governance at University College Dublin and a Research Associate of the ESRC Centre for Analysis of Risk and Regulation at LSE. He has recently completed two pieces of work with Simon Halliday (see above) and is additionally engaged in research projects on 'Reflexive Governance in the Public Interest' (funded by the EC under the 6th Framework Programme of Research), the mapping of the central state administration in Ireland (funded by the IRCHSS) and transnational private regulation (with Fabrizio Cafaggi and Linda Senden, and funded by the Hague Institute for the Internationalisation of Law).

Robert Thomas is Senior Lecturer in Administrative Law at the University of Manchester. He has recently completed an empirical study of asylum appeals funded by the Nuffield Foundation and is the author a forthcoming book entitled *Administrative Justice and Asylum Appeals* (Hart Publishing, 2010).

Brian Thompson is Senior Lecturer in Law at the University of Liverpool and Member of the Administrative Justice and Tribunals Council. With Richard Kirkham and Trevor Buck, he conducted a study of public services ombudsmen in the UK, Ireland, Australia and New Zealand, which was funded by the Economic and Social Research Council. It has been written up for publication as *The Ombudsman Enterprise and Administrative Justice* (Ashgate, 2010).

Albertjan Tollenaar is Assistant Professor of Administrative Law and Public Administration at the University of Groningen (The Netherlands). He wrote his PhD dissertation (in Dutch) on internal policy rules in municipalities and their effect on the quality of decision making.

Introduction

MICHAEL ADLER

Administrative Justice in the UK Emerges from the Shadows

The terms 'civil justice' and 'criminal justice' are both familiar and reasonably well understood. The former refers to the provision by the state for all its citizens of the 'means by which they can secure the just and peaceful settlement of disputes between them as to their respective legal rights'[1] and 'a remedy for the adverse effects of a breach of public duty'.[2] The latter refers, on the one hand, to the means for 'convicting and punishing the guilty and helping them to stop offending' and, on the other, for 'protecting the innocent',[3] but also covers the means for detecting crime and bringing it to justice; and for carrying out the orders of the court, such as collecting fines, and supervising community and custodial punishment. In the mid-1990s, Lord Woolf carried out a review of civil justice in England and Wales and his two reports (Woolf 1995, 1996) gave rise to a wide-ranging programme of reform. Criminal justice has been under almost constant review and has been the subject of legislative reform at regular intervals.[4] By comparison, the term 'administrative justice' has, until recently, been shrouded in obscurity and has not been a concept with which many people—except perhaps a few academics and researchers—were familiar. Recent developments suggest that this looks set to change. The White Paper *Transforming Public Services: Complaints, Redress and Tribunals* (Department for Constitutional Affairs 2004), which was written in response to the Leggatt Report,[5] *Tribunals for Users* (Leggatt 2001), which had proposed a series of reforms to the organisation of tribunals, was considerably more ambitious than Leggatt in that it did not just deal with tribunals but aimed to improve the entire system of administrative justice. It devoted a chapter (chapter 3) to 'The Administrative Justice Landscape' and recommended, inter alia, that the Council on Tribunals should be replaced by an Administrative Justice Council, with a correspondingly wider remit of keeping

[1] Lord Diplock in *Bremer v South India Shipping Corp Ltd* (1981) AC909, 917, cited (with approval) in Woolf (1995: ch 1, para 2).

[2] Woolf (1995: ch 1, para 2).

[3] 'Aims and Objectives of the Criminal Justice System', available at http://www.cjsonline.gov.uk/the_cjs/aims_and_objectives/index.html.

[4] Most recently the Crime and Public Order Act 1994, the Criminal Justice and Police Act 2001, the Criminal Justice Act 2003 and the Criminal Justice Act 2006.

[5] Commissioned by the then Lord Chancellor, Lord (Derry) Irvine in 2000.

under review the performance of the administrative justice system as a whole and advising government on changes in legislation, practice and procedure that would improve the ways in which it works. This change was implemented by the Tribunals, Courts and Enforcement Act (TCEA) 2007, which placed the new two-tier Tribunals Service and the Administrative Justice and Tribunal Council[6] on a statutory footing.

TCEA has brought in numerous changes. It enables judicial review cases, over which the superior courts formerly had exclusive jurisdiction, to be heard in the second-tier or Upper Tribunal, and has made the Tribunals Service, like the Court Service, into an executive agency of the Ministry of Justice, with a much-enhanced status, and has given the Administrative Justice and Tribunal Council, which formerly had oversight over tribunals, oversight over complaints procedures, ombudsmen and redress mechanisms as well. Change is in the air. Since TCEA was concerned with those tribunals that had a UK and GB remit, it obviously had implications for 'devolved tribunals' in Scotland, Wales and Northern Ireland and these are now being addressed. Administrative justice is, indeed, emerging from the shadows.[7]

Background Developments

The sense that administrative justice was an idea whose time was about to come provided the motivation for an application to the Economic and Social Research Council (ESRC) under its Seminars Competition for a grant to support a series of seminars on the topic. In my application to the ESRC, I noted that research on administrative justice was, at that stage, characterised by an institutional division of labour. Those who had undertaken research on particular forms of resolving disputes between the citizen and the state, such as complaints procedures, ombudsmen, administrative tribunals and judicial review, were familiar with research in that field but not necessarily with research in other, related fields. One aim of the seminars was therefore to bring together academics who had undertaken research on these sub-divisions of administrative justice in the expectation that it would lead to a cross-fertilisation of ideas and lead to a greater understanding of 'administrative justice' as a whole. Another aim of the seminars was to encourage communications among academics in different disciplines, in particular law, political science, public policy, sociology, social policy and accounting, and between academics on the one hand and representatives of the various stakeholders in the field on the other. There are a large number of stakeholders in central and local government, in the various sub-divisions of administrative

[6] The change of name took account of the fact that Employment Tribunals, which fall under the remit of the Council, do not hear disputes between the citizen and the state and are not part of the administrative justice landscape.

[7] These are most advanced in Scotland. See Administrative Justice Steering Group (2008, 2009).

justice referred to above, and among organisations representing the public, and, I argued, a serious effort needed to be made to ensure that these stakeholders took an active part in the seminar series. At the time, relations between academics and stakeholders were cordial but not particularly close, although past experience suggested that many stakeholders would be keen to take part.

The specialised nature of research on administrative justice was something of a disappointment in light of the very similar concerns that motivated researchers in the different sub-divisions of administrative justice and the fact that, over the previous 25 years, several attempts had been made to bring them together and create a more coherent research community. In 1985, the Social Sciences and the Law Committee of the Economic and Social Research Council (ESRC) commissioned Richard Rawlings to undertake a review of socio-legal research on aspects of administrative justice. The review, entitled *The Complaints Industry* (Rawlings 1985) focused on grievance mechanisms, that is, on mechanisms for 'wrong-righting' the activities of administrators and their surrogates, and holding them to account.

Although Rawlings recognised that grievance mechanisms were only one means of achieving fair procedures and just outcomes in administrative decision making, his report, nevertheless, focused on them. It did not attempt to analyse the concept of administrative justice as such and had little to say about first-instance administrative decision making. For various reasons, it did not attempt to review research on judicial review, regulation or managerial techniques (such as accounting and audit procedures) for holding first-instance decision makers to account, and focused on administrative tribunals, public inquiries, ombudsmen, MPs and councillors, and internal complaints procedures. This 'institutional' approach had some beneficial consequences in that it facilitated cross-sectoral comparisons between examples of the same institution in different sectors or fields, for example, between different tribunals or different ombudsmen. However, it was probably not the most intellectually exciting of approaches, and helped to perpetuate the division of the field into a number of institutional sub-fields.

In light of the Rawlings Report, the ESRC launched a small initiative on 'Citizens Grievances and Administrative Action'. However, if one of the aims of this initiative was to provide an intellectual impetus for further socio-legal research on administrative justice, it was not particularly successful. Although Rawlings' innovative textbook (written with Carol Harlow), *Law and Administration* (Harlow and Rawlings 1984, 1997, 2009) has undoubtedly been very influential, it did not itself lay the foundation for a wide-ranging socio-legal research agenda. A considerable volume of socio-legal research continued to be undertaken within each of the institutional sub-divisions that were reviewed in the Rawlings Report—and within several of the institutional sub-divisions that were not considered—but the extent of intellectual cross-fertilisation and the number of attempts to make sense of developments in administrative justice as a whole in light of the major changes in the nature of the state that have taken place in recent years was very limited. *Grievances, Remedies and the State* (Birkinshaw 1985, 1994), *Grievances, Complaints and Local Government*: (McCarthy, Simpson and Hill 1992) and *When*

Citizens Complain: Reforming Justice and Administration (Birkinshaw and Lewis 1993) represent the only attempts to analyse the different mechanisms for obtaining redress of grievances against a wide range of government departments and public bodies. However, they are largely descriptive and do not refer to the term 'administrative justice'.

In light of this generally negative assessment, it is important to acknowledge one successful initiative, which was intended to draw attention to the importance of administrative justice in the UK. This was the 'International Conference on Administrative Justice', organised by Martin Partington at the University of Bristol in November 1997. This conference, which was supported by the (then) Lord Chancellor's Department, brought together large numbers of academics with an interest in administrative justice and practitioners in the field. Some 50 papers were presented, 33 of which were subsequently published in a book entitled *Administrative Justice in the 21st Century* (Harris and Partington 1999). The discussions that took place were extremely lively and informative, and the papers that were published provide evidence of the quality and quantity of research on administrative justice that was being undertaken in the UK.

Unlike the Rawlings Review, the Bristol Conference did attempt to raise some theoretical questions about the nature and scope of administrative justice. However, there was only one invited paper on this subject—a very sceptical paper by the Canadian academic Terence Ison (1999)—and the other papers that addressed the issue did so from the perspective of the institutional sub-division in which their authors worked. The editors of the book provided a very helpful summary of the key questions that emerged from the published papers (ibid p 4). They included:

— How can a system of administrative justice best ensure the existence of an appropriate quality of administrative decision making at the initial stage?
— What is the significance of the development of new procedures for the review of administrative action?
— What are the practical and constitutional problems posed by the emergence of regulatory agencies in response to privatisation?
— What are the insights provided by empirical research into the operation of particular aspects of the administrative justice system?
— What are the implications of the UK assuming human rights obligations, domestically, supranationally and internationally, for the operation of administrative justice?
— What is the role and efficacy of mechanisms designed to monitor the processes of administrative justice?
— What should be the means of providing an overview and evaluation of recent, as well as potential future, models of administrative adjudication and review?

Although the Conference led to the establishment of the Bristol Centre of Administrative Justice, the very full research agenda it set out was not really taken forward.

In these circumstances, and in light of clear evidence that the government was committed to administrative justice reform, I concluded that a seminar programme would provide a very appropriate and much needed means of addressing these and related problems. Socio-legal research on redress mechanisms and forms of accountability had, until this point, paid scant attention to theoretical work on the nature of administrative justice or to the changing nature of the state and its implications for administrative decision making. In the proposed seminar programme, it was proposed that these weaknesses should be addressed by prioritising these two topics and by making them the starting point for subsequent discussions. However, although the seminar series would have a theoretical starting point, it would have some rather more practical end points in that it would conclude by considering how administrative justice could most effectively be enhanced and by developing a research agenda which identified the most important questions relating to administrative justice that needed to be addressed.

As indicated above, the White Paper (Department for Constitutional Affairs 2004) marked a great step forward in recognising administrative justice as a concept and in taking a holistic approach to mechanisms of redress or forms of accountability that was designed to ensure that citizens are treated fairly by government departments and public bodies. Written in response to the recommendations of the Leggatt Report (Leggatt 2001), which proposed a series of reforms to the organisation of tribunals, it was considerably more ambitious than Leggatt in that it did not just deal with tribunals but aimed to improve the entire system of administrative justice. Although Leggatt referred, in passing, to the need to improve first-instance decision making, he focused on tribunals because this was what he was asked to do. The White Paper took Leggatt's concerns very seriously but placed them in a wider administrative justice context by considering them alongside other systems of redress, such as complaints procedures, ombudsmen and judicial review. It pointed out (Department for Constitutional Affairs 2004: para 3.5) that '[e]ach route to redress has its advantages and disadvantages' and argued that 'our task is to find ways of combining the strengths of all the redress methods so as to give people real choice and a genuinely responsive service'. Its strategy (ibid: para 2.2) 'turns on its head the Government's traditional emphasis first on courts, judges and court procedure, and second on legal aid to pay mainly for litigation lawyers'. The aim was to develop a range of policies and services that, so far as possible, would help people to avoid problems and legal disputes in the first place; and where this was not possible, provide tailored solutions to resolve the dispute as quickly and cost-effectively as possible without necessarily seeking redress from a tribunal. Thus, it favoured attempts to resolve cases—through reconsideration, negotiation, early neutral evaluation, mediation or conciliation—prior to a tribunal hearing.

The White Paper raised a large number of questions to which, when the seminar series was planned, there were no clear answers. Although the main aim of this seminar series was not to provide answers to these questions—the parallel series of seminars funded by the Nuffield Foundation (Sunkin 2006) focused more closely on policy issues than this one did—it was hoped that the exchange of ideas which these seminars were intended to generate, and their effects on the thinking of those who attended, would encourage discussion and debate and contribute to the process of finding answers to such questions.[8]

The ESRC Seminar Series

The application to the ESRC was successful and a grant of £15,000 made it possible to plan a series of five seminars on administrative justice. These seminars took place between March 2006 and June 2007. The main aims of the seminar series were:

— to review the current state of theoretical work on administrative justice, broadly defined as work concerned with the justice and fairness of administrative procedures;
— to consider recent changes in the nature of the state and recent developments in public administration, in the UK and elsewhere and to assess their implications for administrative justice;
— to assess the current state of administrative justice in the UK, in particular the balance between external and internal forms of accountability and the degree of co-ordination between them, and consider how administrative justice might be enhanced;
— to bring together academics who undertake research in different sub-divisions of administrative justice and practitioners who work in different sub-divisions of administrative justice in order to facilitate dialogue and address these tasks; and
— to develop a research agenda that focuses on some of the most important questions that still need to be addressed.

Five seminars were held over a 15 month period between March 2006 and June 2007.[9] A total of 15 papers were presented at the five seminars. In addition, at the final seminar, there were four 'round table discussions' (one each for academics, users, stakeholders and funding bodies) at which research priorities were discussed.

Each of the 15 papers was circulated in advance in order to ensure that participants had read it beforehand. The session at which it was discussed was introduced

[8] Following on from the seminars, the Nuffield Foundation launched a new research initiative on administrative justice. Projects have been funded in four areas: pathways from initial handling and filtering to sorting and settlement; feedback mechanisms and administrative justice; choice of redress mechanisms; and quality of decision making in redress.

[9] The seminars were hosted by seminar participants at the University of Edinburgh, the University of York, the University of Liverpool, Queen's University, Belfast and the University of Edinburgh (again). Two of them (the York seminar and the second Edinburgh seminar) were two-day events and the other three (the first Edinburgh seminar, the Liverpool seminar and the Belfast seminar) were one-day events. Attendances at the five seminars were 38 (Edinburgh I), 36 (York), 30 (Liverpool), 40 (Belfast) and 50 (Edinburgh II).

by two discussants with the author being given an opportunity to respond to their comments and those of other participants. This formula worked well at the first seminar and was adopted throughout the series.

Participants included academics from a variety of disciplines (including law, political science, public policy, sociology, social policy, accounting and IT), policy makers in government and public sector organisations; members of the tribunals judiciary and ombudsmen; and representatives of the regulatory bodies that oversee their activities, for example, the Administrative Justice and Tribunals Council.[10]

Although it is hard to judge the 'success' of a seminar series, the quality of most of the papers was very good indeed, the respondents succeeded in identifying points for discussion, and the ensuing discussions were extremely lively. Those in one branch of administrative justice learned from those in other branches, academics learned from practitioners and vice versa. Participants spoke with increasing confidence and authority about the concept of administrative justice.

A number of interesting ideas for future research were raised in the round-table discussions at the final seminar. Those that generated most support involved the need for:

- more comparative research—in which comparisons are made between different policy areas, different redress mechanisms and different countries;
- research on the nature and incidence of administrative grievances, in different policy areas;
- research on ways of improving the justice and fairness of first-instance decision making;
- research on the effectiveness of feedback from redress mechanisms to first-instance decision makers;
- research on trust in administration and the relationship between trust and complaining or appealing;
- research on 'paths to administrative justice', analogous to the extremely influential studies of 'paths to civil justice' carried out by Professor Dame Hazel Genn (Genn 1999; Genn and Paterson 2001);
- research on overlaps between complaints systems and appeal mechanisms suggested by the National Audit Office report on *Citizen Redress: What citizens can do if things go wrong with public services* (NAO 2005); and
- research on the desirability and feasibility of proportionate (appropriate) dispute resolution and on the relationship between choice and justice.

A short account of the seminar series (Adler 2007) was published in *Tribunals*, a journal published by the Tribunals Committee of the Judicial Studies Board (JSB).

[10] Two groups were unfortunately under-represented: groups providing advice and representation and postgraduate research students. In both cases, considerable efforts were made to recruit members of these groups by publicising the seminars and offering to meet the travel and subsistence costs of those who took part. The main reasons for non-attendance given by those providing advice and representation was 'pressure of work' and the difficulties involved in taking time off from their 'primary' activities. In the case of postgraduate research students, the main problem was our inability to identify those who were working in the field.

The range and quality of the papers presented during the seminar series was of such a high standard that it seemed appropriate to use them as the basis for an edited book on administrative justice, which would reflect the current state of thinking on administrative justice as it emerges from the shadows and moves centre stage.

From the Seminar Series to the Book

In proceeding from the seminar papers to the book, it was clear that there were some important gaps which needed to be filled. For example, among the contextual developments considered in the second seminar, insufficient attention had been paid to developments in human rights and their implications for administrative decision making. And, as a counterbalance to the emphasis on theoretical work in seminar series, there needed to be a more sustained assessment of recent policy developments in the UK. In addition, although there had been some notable seminar contributions from international scholars, it was felt that the concerns addressed in the seminar series were perhaps too parochial and that the book should have more of a comparative or international flavour. This meant that, in addition to contributions that were based on seminar papers that their authors had already presented, an edited book would be strengthened if it were to include some additional contributions. A number of additional contributions were commissioned and their inclusion has undoubtedly strengthened the collection.

The book is divided into five groups of chapters, each of which reflects a particular set of concerns. Since administrative justice is not a set of normative principles that exist in splendid isolation and the context in which administrative decision making takes places imposes constraints on the actual and potential achievement of administrative justice, the first group deals with the impact on administrative decision making of five of the most important 'contextual changes'. A number of the chapters in this group have been jointly authored by those who presented papers at one of the seminars and those who acted as respondents to them. These chapters comprise those by: **Andrew Gamble** and **Robert Thomas** on changes in governance and public administration, which analyses the rise of the regulatory state, the development of multi-level governance and new techniques of public administration, such as the New Public Management (NPM), contracting-out, and the increased use of private companies in the delivery of public services; **John Clark, Morag McDermont** and **Janet Newman** on changes in management and service delivery, which explores the contested logics of consumer choice and administrative justice in the governance of public services; **Irvine Lapsley** and **Jeremy Lonsdale** on changes in audit and accounting, which argues that the growth in audit has been accompanied by a high degree of scepticism about whether assessments accurately reflect performance and about whether the performance movement is good for democracy; and **Helen Margetts** and **Martin Partington** on changes in information technology, which outlines the development of e-government in the UK and identifies those areas in which its implications for administrative justice are most important. This group of chapters also contains a newly-commissioned chapter by **David Feldman** on the implications of developments in human rights and, in particular, the stronger protection for human rights in the UK that resulted from the passage of the Human Rights Act 1998, for administrative decision making.

The second group of chapters deals with conceptual issues and analytic approaches and contains four chapters. The first, by **Michael Adler**, argues that administrative justice is an 'essentially contested concept', identifies three 'competing conceptions' and commends the approach which now appears to be in the ascendancy in the UK. The second, by **Bob Kagan**, analyses the roles of trust, and mistrust, in shaping the way administrative decision systems are organised. He argues that when political parties, interest groups, legal experts, or political leaders distrust the competence, political neutrality, and fairness of bureaucrats, they are inclined to demand stricter control of administrative discretion through detailed rules, rights to participate in administrative decision making processes, more formal and adversarial legal procedures, and searching judicial review of administrative decisions and that, when this occurs, administrative systems are driven or at least 'nudged' toward more formal, bureaucratic and adversarial modes of structuring the processes for deciding individual cases. When this happens, the administrative process becomes more formal and less reliant on professional judgment in dealing with hard cases, while individual officials become more likely to be pressured toward a legalistic style of applying rules and deciding cases. The third, by **Simon Halliday** and **Colin Scott**, criticises these two approaches and puts forward a cultural typology of administrative justice, based on 'grid-group cultural theory', originally developed by the anthropologist Mary Douglas. The fourth chapter in this group, by **Marc Hertogh**, applies the concept of 'legal consciousness' to front-line decision makers, suggesting that public officials can be characterised as 'legalists', 'loyalists', 'cynics', or 'outsiders' and discusses the ways in which a focus on legal consciousness can contribute to the study of administrative justice.

The third group of chapters deals with the application of administrative justice principles to private law disputes and includes two chapters, one by **Dawn Oliver** and the other by **Walter Merricks.** Dawn Oliver discusses the potential for developing the 'horizontal effect' of administrative justice and considers the scope for extending both human rights protection and the substantive grounds for judicial review (irrationality, procedural impropriety and illegality) to purely private activity. Walter Merricks explores the place of private sector ombudsman schemes (and in particular the Financial Ombudsman Service) in the world of administrative justice; and the extent to which they contribute to the notion, explored in Dawn Oliver's paper, of a horizontal effect of administrative justice principles.

The fourth group contains three chapters on administrative justice in other countries. The first chapter, by **Robin Creyke**, identifies the distinctive features of administrative justice in Australia and asks how the expression 'administrative justice' has been used, how embedded it is in administrative culture and whether administrative justice has been achieved in Australia. The second chapter, by **Albertjan Tollenaar** and **Ko de Ridder**, approaches the concept of administrative justice from a Continental European point of view, .argues that, in the Netherlands, court and complaints procedures do not provide comparable levels of protection to their counterparts in the common-law countries, and that, in the wake of New Public Management (NPM), more and more managerial instruments for improving administrative decision making, such as benchmarking and certification, are now being used to improve 'administrative quality'. The third chapter, by **Carsten Henrichsen**, charts the evolution of the 'law state' of the nineteenth century into the 'social state' of the twentieth century and argues that, since the end of the twentieth century, two tendencies have emerged, one leading to a 'market state' and the other to what he calls a 'milieu state', each of these four states being associated with a different conception of administrative justice. Henrichsen identifies the different forms of administrative justice in each of these four states and concludes that the choice between the 'market state' and the 'milieu state' will, in the end, be a political choice.

The final set of chapters deals with current developments in the UK. The first chapter, by **Patrick Birkinshaw**, reviews the development of grievance mechanisms and remedies against the state in the UK over the last 30 years, covering courts, tribunals and ombudsmen, and including an analysis of the EU dimension and alternative dispute resolution. 30 years ago, according to Birkinshaw, effective means of ventilating complaints and grievances was often lacking; in the intervening period, there has been considerable progress. Today, there are different forms of exclusion, in many cases the result of governmental decision making. Thus, there are whole areas, for example, in respect of surveillance, foreign policy and government contracting, where decisions and their impact are secreted from public scrutiny and complaint. The second chapter, by **Tom Mullen** identifies the defining characteristics of the four main institutions and procedures for dealing with citizen versus state disputes in the UK (associated with courts mainly offering formal/adversarial adjudication; tribunals offering informal/enabling adjudication; ombudsman operating thoroughly inquisitorial methods leading to recommendations; and external review operating thoroughly inquisitorial methods. He notes the extent to which, in recent years, there has been a degree of convergence between them and concludes that, although the boundaries between them may need to be shifted, the institutional structure should be retained. Thus, there would continue to be four main institutions and styles of decision making. The third chapter, by **Patrick Dunleavy** and his colleagues in the LSE Public Policy Group, is based on the study they carried out for the National Audit Office (NAO 2005). It argues that the redress mechanisms that are available for UK citizens are poor in avoidable ways, especially if their substantial annual costs are considered and suggests that the government should commit itself to achieving and maintaining a 'low complaints' regime and to getting better value for money from the ways in which redress mechanisms are organised. It concludes by making a number of recommendations for achieving these ends. The last two chapters, by **Jackie Gulland** and **Brian Thompson**, deal with recent legislative and policy developments in the UK. Jackie Gulland's chapter focuses on complaints and ombudsmen, while Brian Thompson's focuses on tribunals and the courts.

The general approach of the book is both socio-legal and interdisciplinary. Thus, many of the authors use one or other of the social sciences in an attempt to throw light on the concept of administrative justice. A few of the chapters adopt a (more or less) doctrinal approach but others, in particular those which deal with the impact of societal developments on administrative justice, explicitly adopt a 'law in context' approach. Although most of the contributors are academics, some are practitioners. As a result, the book should not only be of interest to lawyers, particularly those with interests in administrative law, but should also be of interest to social scientists, particularly those with interests in public administration, public policy and public management.

References

Adler, M (2007) 'From Concepts to Consensus' *Tribunals* 3.

Administrative Justice Steering Group (2008) *Options for the Future Administration and Supervision of Tribunals in Scotland* (Glasgow, Consumer Focus Scotland) available at http://www.ajtc.gov.uk/docs/Tribunals_in_Scotland.pdf.

—— (2009) *Administrative Justice in Scotland—The Way Forward* (Glasgow, Consumer Focus Scotland.

Birkinshaw, P (1985, 1994) *Grievances, Remedies and the State* (London, Sweet & Maxwell).

Birkinshaw, P and Lewis, N (1993) and *When Citizens Complain: Reforming Justice and Administration* (Buckingham, Open University Press).

Department for Constitutional Affairs (2004) *Transforming Public Services: Complaints, Redress and Tribunals.* Cm 6243 (Norwich, The Stationery Office), available at www.dca.gov.uk/pubs/adminjust/transformfull.pdf.

Genn, H (1999) *Paths to Justice* (Oxford: Hart Publishing).

Genn, H and Paterson, A (2001) *Paths to Justice Scotland* (Oxford: Hart Publishing).

Harlow, C and Rawlings, R (1984) *Law and Administration,* 1st edn (London: Weidenfeld and Nicolson).

Harlow, C and Rawlings, R (1997) *Law and Administration,* 2nd edn (London: Butterworth).

Harlow, C and Rawlings, R (2009) *Law and Administration,* 3rd edn (Cambridge: Cambridge University Press).

Harris, M and Partington, M (eds) (1999) *Administrative Justice in the 21st Century* (Oxford, Hart Publishing).

Ison, T (1999) 'Administrative Justice: Is it such a good idea?' in M Harris and M Partington (eds), *Administrative Justice in the 21st Century* (Oxford, Hart Publishing).

Leggatt, Sir Andrew (2001) *Tribunals for Users: One System; One Service* (London, Lord Chancellor's Department) available at http://www.tribunals-review.org.uk/.

McCarthy, P, Simpson, B and Hill, M (1992) *Grievances, Complaints and Local Government* (Aldershot, Avebury).
National Audit Office (2005) *Citizen Redress: What citizens can do if things go wrong with public services* HC 24 (London, The Stationary Office).
Rawlings, R (1985) *The Complaints Industry* (London, ESRC).
Sunkin M (2006) 'Keep up the Momentum' *Tribunals* 9.
Woolf, LJ (1995) *Access to Justice: Interim Report on the Civil Justice System in England and Wales* (London, Lord Chancellor's Department).
—— (1996) *Access to Justice: Final Report on the Civil Justice System in England and Wales* (London, Lord Chancellor's Department).

Part 1

Contextual Changes and Their Implications for Administrative Decision Making

1

The Changing Context of Governance: Implications for Administration and Justice

ANDREW GAMBLE AND ROBERT THOMAS

Introduction

Recent decades have witnessed enormous changes in the nature of governance and public administration which have affected virtually every aspect of how people are governed. These changes have included the rise of the regulatory state; the development of the multi-layered polity, in which power is now exercised both above and below the level of the state; and new techniques of public administration, such as the new public management, contracting-out, and the increased use of private companies in the delivery of public services. These developments have exerted profound changes in how the business of governing is now undertaken; they have come about against the backdrop of, and have also largely inspired, changes in how to understand and comprehend the way in which we are governed, in particular the 'governance' turn. The complexity of contemporary governance means that the individual is now placed in the hitherto unprecedented position of not being able easily to understand or appreciate the governing environment to which she is subject. Furthermore, as states have undergone such changes in the process of governing, they have also sought to renew and modernise their constitutional arrangements.

This chapter examines these changes and considers some of their implications for administrative decision making. This examination proceeds by first discussing the different meanings attached to the notion of governance, and then considering the traditional model of governance developed in the United Kingdom, the Westminster model. The chapter then examines the challenges to this model that have arisen in the last thirty years, in particular the changing context of governance, both transnational and European, the rise of the regulatory state, and the modernisation of the constitution. The argument of the chapter is that Britain has passed through not one but two major modernising revolutions in governance since the 1970s that have transformed and are still transforming its governance, the first associated with the Conservative Government (between 1979 and 1997) and the second with the Labour Government (since 1997). Finally, the chapter offers some brief reflections on the implications of these changes for administrative decision making and administrative justice.

The Meaning of Governance

At the heart of the notion of governance is a very simple idea—that the process of *governing* is separate from the particular bodies and agencies that comprise the *government.* Government is only an aspect of governance, although a very important one. As Peters and Pierre (2000) have explained, governance refers to the steering capacities of a political system, the institutions and structures that determine the forms of governing and shape its outcomes. It is an open question as to which particular agents are responsible for the steering. To be concerned with governance is to be concerned with what Michael Mann (1986) has called 'infrastructural power' and, as such, governance is not optional but integral to the functioning of any social system.

Governance has three main dimensions. First, there are the ordering principles, such as the market, or bureaucracy or networks, which provide the constitutional framework for governing; the fundamental laws, rules, and standards, which determine such things as the locus of decision making, the limits within which power is exercised, and the boundary between the public and the private. Secondly, governance involves a set of levels, sites and locations, for example global, regional, national and local. Thirdly, it entails a set of techniques that determine such questions as how power is exercised, how rights are defined and protected, and how interests are represented.

The Westminster Model

The form of governance that became established in the UK was the Westminster Model. For a long time this was a highly successful form of governance, resting on what David Marquand (1988) has called 'club government', a set of informal networks which prized personal connection, authority, expertise and secrecy, and sought to deflect democratic pressures for more open and accountable government.

At the heart of the Westminster model is the doctrine of parliamentary sovereignty, Crown-in-Parliament, laid out in its clearest form by Dicey (1885) at the end of the nineteenth century. In this doctrine, sovereignty is undivided and unlimited. There is no authority higher than the Crown-in-Parliament to which an appeal can be made. There is no separation of powers, which means that the courts are in a subordinate position to Parliament. They can interpret decisions of the Parliament in various ways but they cannot formally overturn or block them. There is no codified constitutional document to which the courts can refer to reject a particular piece of legislation. The constitution is a matter of conventions and precedents, the latter established by acts of Parliament. But no Parliament can bind its successors, there is no entrenchment and, in principle, any Parliament can reverse whatever legislation it chooses and can also legislate retrospectively.

This doctrine of parliamentary sovereignty derived from a particular understanding of the power of the Crown in England, and the emergence of a highly centralised, unitary state in the early modern period, which successfully subordinated all other powers within its territory to its authority, including most notably the transnational Church. The absolutist power of the monarchy was challenged successfully in the seventeenth century, and the supremacy of Parliament established. But many royal prerogative powers never came under the control of Parliament, and this meant that power remained centralised and concentrated, increasingly wielded by the leadership group, acting in the name of the monarch, that could command a majority in Parliament. This oligarchic power was then tempered by the gradual extension of democracy, so that the parliamentary elites were obliged to form mass party organisations outside Parliament and seek the endorsement of the electorate.

The coming of mass democracy greatly altered the way politics was conducted but it did not much alter the forms of governance in the British polity. The powers of the House of Lords were curtailed, but there was no new constitutional settlement and the centralised character of the British state, and the oligarchic and secretive structures through which it operated, were left largely in place. Even the election of majority Labour Governments did not much disturb them, since Labour was only too happy to make full use of the unfettered executive powers which a parliamentary majority conferred on them. The creation of the welfare state through the twentieth century was effected largely through the powers of the executive.

Since Parliament was the ultimate source of sovereignty all other branches of the state were deemed to be subordinate to it. All the departments and agencies which made up the state were subject to the will of Parliament and were obliged to enforce its decisions. In the democratic era the party that won a majority of parliamentary seats in a general election formed the government, and decided policy, which all parts of the state bureaucracy were obliged to carry out as the expression of the will of the people. An important part of the Westminster model was that the civil service was neutral, offering policy advice and implementing the policy choices of the government of the day on a strictly non-partisan basis. Ministers were accountable to Parliament and to the electorate for the policies of their departments.

The Revolution in Governance

The Westminster model was at its height in the first half of the twentieth century. It belongs to an era of strong, powerful nation-states which were rapidly expanding both their spending and their functions. The British state was not unusual in this respect. It became an extended state, both through warfare and through welfare, but where it stood out from many other states was that much of Britain's extended state was still encased in traditional state forms. The Westminster model celebrated a particular Whig interpretation of British history, which emphasised that the right balance had to be struck between representative and responsible government, and treated the development of British institutions as the story of liberty and progress. But while democracy conferred legitimacy on the British state, and allowed the executive to claim that it had a popular mandate for its policies, the actual delivery of these policies was through traditional means. There was little attempt to modernise the way in which the state was organised, or how it operated. The term 'state' itself was little used in discussions of British politics and British institutions. The relationship between the state and its citizens was conceived as a partnership, in which the process of democratic election conferred legitimacy on the government and obligations on citizens to obey the laws that it passed. If citizens disliked these laws they could vote for other parties to overturn them, or even start their own.

It is this world of clear territorial borders, jurisdiction within a defined territory, national legitimacy, and a strong link between citizens and the state through participation in national elections and party affiliation which has been so much eroded. Since the 1970s a revolution in governance has been taking place. Government is certainly not disappearing in the UK or anywhere else, but the context in which governments operate has been transformed, as they grapple with profound challenges arising from globalisation, Europeanisation, the modernisation of the administration and organisation of government, and an evolving constitution. As a result of these changes, governance is becoming more fragmented and diversified, and as a result it is much harder for both politicians and citizens to understand the process of governing. The Westminster model although it always contained much that was illusory, did provide clarity about governance and public administration, and about the role of politicians and citizens, which was reassuring and fostered a climate of relative stability and certainty. One of the distinctive features of contemporary governance arrangements is that nobody seems to be in control any more, and it has become increasingly hard to pinpoint who has responsibility, who is accountable, or where policies come from. This is because decisions are now taken at so many different levels and by so many different bodies. There are no longer single but multiple points of decision making, and lines of accountability and responsibility have become blurred. The old levers of power no longer work in the way they used to do, so that operating in this new world requires different skills and capacities. One of the paradoxes of the new governance regime is that governments have never been so intrusive yet, at the same time, never so lacking in the capacity to formulate and implement coherent policies. Increased complexity is one of the most striking characteristics of contemporary governance.

The extent of these changes should not be exaggerated. They are also not of one piece. The changes have different logics, they operate at different speeds, and they often conflict. But together they have forced a reassessment of the way government is perceived. Governance in the UK can no longer be analysed as though the UK was a single-level polity, or a self-contained nation-state. No state by itself has the resources or the capacities to exercise control across all areas of public policy (Wallace 1996). In an important sense they never did, but for much of the twentieth century the illusion was created that single-level, self-contained nation-states were not just the core units of the international system, but were masters of their fate. National electorates, by choosing between the programmes which parties put before them, could decide the direction of policy and the character of the society in which they lived.

The idea that each country could be self-governing and relatively self-contained represented a particular flowering of the modern liberal ideal of national self-determination. Governance was always more complex than this and, in the nineteenth century in particular, the importance of global markets and global capital accumulation in shaping modern societies was much emphasised, rather than the power of governments. But the growth in the scope and scale of the modern state in the twentieth century, fuelled by warfare and welfare, also encouraged new ideologies about the capacity and desirability of the state controlling and planning society in the interests of all its citizens (Mannheim 1940). This desire to erect forms of governance centred on the nation-state was further enhanced by the destruction of so much of the international political and economic system by the effects of two world wars and the Great Depression. The regime of governance that became established was one of national protectionism rather than international liberalism, and it ushered in a world of blocs, and separate jurisdictions. The UK model of governance, the Westminster Model, was one of the distinctive national variants that flourished at this time. Since Britain escaped both invasion and occupation, it enjoyed institutional continuity, unlike most other countries, which meant that at no point was a new regime and a new constitution installed. This allowed the survival of many archaic features of British government and public administration until the crisis of the 1970s (although then many of the constitutional changes did not take place until the 1990s). Although there had been significant modernisation in the nineteenth century, in the twentieth century the pace slowed and a highly durable system of club government was perfected which successfully resisted pressures for greater openness and democratic participation (Moran 2003).

The UK model of governance was eventually undermined because so many of the conditions which had sustained it gradually disappeared. In place of a single-level polity of a centralised nation-state, a multi-level polity has emerged, which has made the centralism which is still a marked feature of British government increasingly anachronistic. A multi-level polity and multi-level governance apply in two senses. The first conception of the multi-level polity recognises that governance, even within the frame of the nation-state, has to be conceived as comprising several overlapping levels, rather than a simple hierarchy of levels. Applied regionally, it means that a novel political arrangement like the EU can be conceived as a multi-level polity (Bache and Flinders 2004), although it is unclear whether the policy process within the EU is best understood as an inter-state or intra-state process (Hix 1994). The second conception of the multi-level polity sees it in global terms as an emerging framework for transnational governance, growing out of an increasingly inter-connected global economy and transnational civil society (Rosenau 1995). It recognises that the international system is both an inter-state system, which has national governments at its core, and a transnational system, which permits many kinds of connections between organisations and networks beyond the control of national governments.

From a national governance perspective, recent changes in governance and public administration in the UK have created a multi-level polity with policy-making systems at local, regional, national and supranational levels. Alongside the traditional executive and legislative institutions at Westminster, since 1997 Scotland, Wales and Northern Ireland have acquired devolved institutions; there has been some experimentation with City Mayors (notably in London), and some plans (currently on hold) for devolution of powers to English regions. The old informal arrangements for devolution of powers from the centre have been replaced by a much more formal arrangement and are still evolving. The other great change has been due to the effects of membership of the EU, which has led to many areas of policy, particularly in the economic sphere, being determined at the European level rather than at Westminster. The sovereignty of Westminster has been pared away from two sides.

From a transnational governance perspective, the changes are more radical still. The governance of the UK can be viewed from the standpoint of the global economy and transnational civil society, and accordingly the specific arrangements in the UK can be viewed as part of a system of transnational governance. There are continual tensions between the increasingly connected character of the global economy and transnational society, and the fragmented and territorial nature of political authority in the inter-state system. An increasingly interconnected global economy has created many global public goods, including energy, water, protection of the biosphere, security, and human rights (Kaul, Grunberg and Stern 1999). Since national governments cannot deliver these on their own, international co-operation becomes essential for creating the international institutions and agencies at the global level that can formulate and implement solutions to cope with these problems. But, despite some successes, the extent of co-operation is usually seriously inadequate, even at the EU level. At the global level, the problem is far worse, since we are a long way from a global government with the capacity and resources to impose solutions or broker compromises in the way that national governments do. What exists is an embryonic state operating in a multi-level polity, but with very loose connections between the levels. The policy process takes place at many different levels and sites, and with many different authorities, from key supranational agencies like the World

Trade Organisation (WTO), the International Monetary Fund (IMF), and the World Bank, to regional governments without statehood like the EU, traditional nation-states, as well as many non-state actors, including transnational companies and transnational social movements. In this highly complex and fragmented world, many policies are still decided at the national level through national political institutions, and nation-states remain key brokers between institutions at different levels of the international system. But few policy issues can any longer be dealt with solely within a domestic policy process. Solutions to policy problems increasingly require forms of international co-operation and agreement, which inevitably means that sovereignty is pooled and shared (Cerny 1991).

If the nation-state is no longer the exclusive focus either of legitimacy or of policy capacity, how are the different policy competences, which are all concentrated in one place in a single-level polity, shared out between the different levels? The framework which Theodore Lowi (1972) developed for understanding the US federal policy process has been adopted by William Wallace for analysing the policy process in the EU. Lowi distinguishes four major types of policy: constituent policies which determine the fundamental rules and priorities of the political system; redistributive policy which challenge the structural distribution of costs and benefits between citizens and regions; distributive policies which allocate resources through government-funded programmes; and regulatory policies, which provide rules governing particular sectors. The first two are the focus of much political argument and struggle, since they concern the fundamentals of the social and economic order, while the second two are the heart of the contemporary extended state.

For Britain, most constituent issues are now decided at supranational levels through various treaties and agreements, for example on security, trade, and the environment, which British Governments have signed, and which have created a number of international institutions and agencies. The major constituent issues at the level of the British polity itself centre on questions of the internal constitution of the British state, particularly devolution, electoral reform, human rights and civil liberties, freedom of information, as well as whether Britain should cede further sovereign powers to the EU (such as joining the euro) (Gamble 2006). Many of the constituent issues of the past, such as whether the economy should be organised on capitalist or socialist principles, are no longer live ones. In the present circumstances of the international political economy, even with the fallout from the global financial crisis of 2008, there no longer appears a choice at the national level.

Redistributive issues are important at the EU level, particularly for matters concerning the budget, farm subsidies and regional aid. They are also increasingly important at the global level, in debates on world poverty and the impact of world trade rules; for instance, the current impasse in the negotiations at the WTO between rich and poor states, and between the US and EU. The problem for groups in transnational civil society seeking to put such issues on transnational government agendas is finding arenas where they can do so, and getting access to agencies which have the capacity or the will to act. At the national level redistributive issues have declined greatly in importance, but have not disappeared altogether.

Distributive issues remain very important at the national level, because the British government is still responsible for many major spending programmes. The scope for distributive politics at the EU level is extremely limited because the budget remains so small (still only 1 per cent of EU GDP). Devolution within the UK transfers responsibility for many distributive issues and programmes to the new regional institutions. In all cases, distributive policies are associated with policy networks and policy communities, and the creation of strong links between them and relevant government departments in order to facilitate both formulation and implementation of policy.

Regulatory issues have assumed increasing importance at global and EU levels, but also at the national level, as British governments have sought to move away from the politics of distribution and redistribution, The rise of a regulatory state has been a strong trend in recent decades, related to the doctrines of the new public management, which has changed the scope and instruments of government through outright privatisation, as well as the use of specialist agencies, outsourcing and public–private partnerships for the delivery of government-funded public services. As the number of service providers has increased, so the need for regulation and new forms of accountability has grown. In the EU, the process is complicated by the need to harmonise different national regulatory styles.

Different policy issues increasingly relate to different levels, and this is not a static picture but one that is constantly evolving. Trade issues, for example, are now handled by the EU, which negotiates on behalf of all its members with the WTO. What drives transnational policy agendas are the requirements of an open liberal economic order, and this agenda is promoted both by the international agencies themselves and by transnationally oriented companies, trade unions, media and think tanks as well as political parties.

Nation-states remain the pivot of this system, but recognising the gains from co-operation in an interdependent world, national governments have been prepared to give up sovereignty or to pool it, and to accept the jurisdiction of international and regional bodies. In the case of the UK the most striking instance of this has been its membership of the EU, and its acceptance (reluctant at times) of the various treaties which have deepened the process of European integration. The British courts have acknowledged that, by virtue of their incorporation into national law, the Treaties give the European Court of Justice jurisdiction over Britain and, in appropriate cases, can over-rule British judicial decisions. On many questions policy agendas now have to be formed at the European level, and lobbying to influence that agenda has to take place in Brussels.

The EU is not developing into a United States of Europe on federal lines; rather, it is still very much at best at a confederal stage, consisting of a set of supranational institutions created to fulfil particular purposes and functions. The policy agendas of the EU revolve around questions such as agriculture, competition policy and regional aid, and in recent years increasingly the question of enlargement, the single market, foreign and defence policy, social policy, and economic and monetary union. The policy process in the EU has different characteristics from the policy process in Britain. It is more open, there are many more points of access, and it makes greater use of regulation and law. It is also much more fragmented, prone to deadlock and therefore much less able to provide binding decisions. The policy agendas of the EU are heavily influenced by the interests of the European states through the Council of Ministers, but they are also driven by the policy entrepreneurship of the Commission. The European Parliament is gradually assuming a larger role, but European public opinion is not yet effectively organised. Business interests and trade unions are, however, well organised at the European level, and lobbying organisations have sprung up to service them. In addition there are many networks of experts and professionals who seek to influence the agendas that are formed.

Modernising the British State

The New Public Management

Changes in the global and regional pattern of governance have been very important in reshaping the context of UK governance. They have done this by acting as a spur for a far-reaching overhaul of the British state. This has come in two successive waves since the 1970s, first the Thatcher Governments of the 1980s, many of whose reforms were consolidated and extended under the Major Government, and secondly by Labour Governments since 1997, which again built on and extended the Thatcher–Major legacy, but also launched a new programme of constitutional reform, which the Conservatives had fiercely resisted.

The new regulatory state that was established under Thatcher did not mean that before Thatcher there was no regulatory state in Britain. However, what Thatcher did was to break decisively with the traditional forms of the British state and create the space in which new forms of governance became established. This did not happen all at once, and it certainly did not happen according to any preconceived plan—there were many experiments and false starts. But partly because the Conservatives governed for so long (18 years), it meant that there was time for cumulative, incremental change, so that by the time the Conservatives left office, many of the changes were deeply embedded and would have been very hard for any successor government to change, even if had wanted to.

The changes introduced by the Thatcher Governments initially caused some misunderstanding because the main thrust of the policy appeared to be its monetarist and economic liberal reform programme that aimed to reverse Britain's relative economic decline. Government rhetoric was about deregulation of industry, shrinking the size of the state, privatising state industries, removing subsidies and feather-bedding, weakening employment protection and trade unions and, in general, ending government intervention and rolling back the state. But this was never simply a laissez-faire programme in the sense of withdrawing the state and allowing civil society to flourish. It also involved opening up the private and public sectors to competition and pressure from the global market, breaking the hold of established professional groups and trade unions, and introducing new forms of impersonal regulation and public accountability to replace the forms of self-regulation and club government which had predominated in Britain (Moran 2003).

The apparent paradox of 'the free economy and the strong state' (Gamble 1994) was not really a paradox, since, in order to create or recreate the free economy, Thatcher's ministers found they needed to extend the state in novel ways to create new forms of accountability, monitoring, and audit. Dispensing with self-governing professional associations meant that different, and more objective, independent measures of performance were needed to make sure that both private and public services were as efficient as they could be, and as well adapted as they could be to the demands of the global economy. Only those sectors which could become and stay internationally competitive were worth preserving, but in order to make sure they were internationally competitive, the Government accepted that new forms of regulation were necessary. One of the best examples of this process was the financial services industry, which was transformed from a typical example of a traditional self-regulating sector to one of the three major financial centres in the new global economy (Moran 2003). Similar transformations were applied to many of the old nationalised industries. They were turned into new international businesses under tough regulatory regimes that monitored performance and had powers to intervene if necessary. The private sector acquired greater freedoms under the Thatcher reforms, not least because of tax reductions and the weakening of unions, but it also became subject to more impersonal and comprehensive regulation to ensure that it remained competitive.

The same has been even truer of the public sector. The Thatcher Government did succeed in redrawing the boundaries between the public and the private sectors by privatising most of the public utilities, but it made much slower progress with its plans to reshape the welfare state. After some false starts and false hopes, the strategy that eventually emerged was aimed at changing the way in which the public sector was organised and managed, rather than transferring it wholesale to the private sector by making individuals pay for health and education. In order to achieve this the Government borrowed heavily from experience and practice in the United States and introduced many of the forms of public administration that had been pioneered there, in particular setting up agencies that were independent of central government departments to deliver services, using internal markets, targets, and audit, bringing about the split between providers and purchasers, implementing public–private partnerships and much more. These changes have been extensively mapped and analysed (Rhodes 1997; Pollitt, Girre, Lonsdale and Mul 1999; Vincent-Jones 2006). What they represent is a revolution in the way

Britain is governed. The new public management has spread its tentacles into every part of the public sector, and has led to the rise of a new managerial class of executives and consultants, inspectors and accountants, to run it. Far from the state being rolled back, it has become much more intrusive and interventionist in many spheres that were formerly administered by professionals themselves.

These changes are often swept up into the general category of neo-liberalism, but this formulation is unhelpful unless care is taken to distinguish between different aspects and phases of neo-liberalism (Gamble 2006b). In the 1980s and 1990s there was much discussion of different national models of capitalism, in which the British model was contrasted (usually unfavourably) with developmental state models found in Europe and East Asia, or the welfare state models found in Scandinavia (Hutton 1995). What the debate ignored in relation to Britain was that the Thatcherite reforms laid the foundation for a British version of the developmental state or competition state, only fully realised under the Blair Government, which achieved sufficient economic success to make the British economy the best performing in the OECD. What this British model did not involve was any permanent down-sizing in the importance of government—instead, government expanded its reach considerably, and under the Blair Government also raised substantially its spending as a share of GDP. The aim of the Blair Government was to invest heavily in human capital and in infrastructure while promoting a flexible, open and competitive economy. While this had erased the image of the British economy from the 1970s as one in terminal decline, it was undertaken within the mantras and rules of the new public management, so that many of the policies were strongly criticised by those on the Left.

The Constitution

The second wave of modernisation was the constitutional reform programme of the Blair Government. Although, as many observers have noted, this programme has been piecemeal, fragmented, incoherent, and often improvised, its overall effect has been substantial. Although disappointing the hopes of many constitutional reformers for a single comprehensive package of reform, including a written constitution, the reform programme nevertheless adds up to the most far-reaching set of changes to the British state since the seventeenth century (Hazell 1999). What is also clear is that the programme is unfinished, and that there will have to be many adjustments and further changes in the future, as the implications of the changes already made sink in, and as new anomalies and inconsistencies arise (HM Government 2007).

There is also the question of whether the constitutional reform programme has actually changed any of the fundamentals of the UK model of governance. Critics note that British Government remains highly centralised, and that many of the practices of a dominant executive, supine legislature, weak judiciary remain, along with excessive secrecy and lack of accountability. They say that the changes are just cosmetic and have not been really radical, but are easily assimilated into existing constitutional practice. Although many of these criticisms are true, but they ignore how much has changed in the last few years, and how much more may change in the years to come, and just what a break has occurred in the customary constitution (Johnson 2004). Three specific changes in particular are worth highlighting—devolution, integrity, and judicial review.

Devolution has created a quasi-federal polity in the UK, replacing the informal arrangements of the territorial constitution with formal devolution of powers, an elected Assembly in Wales and an elected Parliament in Scotland. Already a new Bill has been introduced to extend the Welsh Assembly's powers to bring them more in line with those of Scotland, and further changes may take place in the years ahead. This is a fundamental break in the governance model that was established at the time of the Act of Union in 1707. It raises serious political questions about the status of England, about the desirability of an English Parliament, of devolution to the English regions, and of the breakup of the UK altogether. If the UK does hold together, then it is likely that the quasi-federal arrangements that have come into being will, at some stage, be further formalised, accepting the multi-level nature of the polity, and defining more closely the powers of the different levels. So long as there is no devolution to the English regions and no English Parliament, the elision of the UK Parliament with the English Parliament perpetuates the idea that the old centralist UK state is still in business. But its foundations are now cracked, and the logic of the multi-level polity is that this at last becomes recognised as new forms of local and regional government are instituted.

One of the major constitutional changes has been the enhancement of the integrity arm of government. There has been considerable progress in establishing bodies to monitor the behaviour of civil servants, ministers, advisers, and agencies. The Freedom of Information Act has made a start at making access to official information easier, and a number of channels have been opened up that make it easier to hold Ministers to account and to redress citizens' grievances. Many reformers are again dissatisfied with what has been achieved, but the direction of travel is plain enough, and British Government has become more open than it was. The checks on ministerial and MPs behaviour are fairly stringent, and even minor infractions get considerable publicity. Changes in one area have often created pressure for further change. A recent example is the legislation requiring political parties to list all their donations. This did not cover political loans, but, when it was discovered that the political parties had been exploiting this loophole, proposals were quickly brought forward to close it. The setting up of permanent watchdogs like the Electoral Commission has meant that regulation in these areas becomes cumulative and is difficult for those who are subject to it to control it.

A third area of major change is judicial review. As noted above, the position of the judiciary in the UK has been greatly strengthened in relation to the executive because of the signing of the European treaties, and more recently the incorporation of the European Convention of Human Rights into UK law. The doctrine of unlimited parliamentary sovereignty has been qualified, and many observers of the constitution have pointed to a class of measures, like devolution and the ECHR, which appear to entrench certain constitutional arrangements. For that reason, they also allow the judiciary greater scope for challenging Ministers' decisions and challenging legislation. As quasi-federalism develops so the judiciary may well acquire a role there as well. One consequence is that judicial review appears to be increasing, and at the expense of elected politicians. Some regret this and argue that most decisions are best left to democratic representatives to decide in Parliament (Waldron 2006; Bellamy 2007). But this is not what is happening, and the courts are beginning to become more assertive, while politicians are beginning to tailor legislation to ensure that it is ECHR compatible and therefore safe from being struck down by judges.

The State and the Citizen

A number of problems are associated with the recent changes in governance that have already been identified for the relationship between the state and the citizen. The first of these is the trend towards disengagement of citizens from formal politics. The basic problem is this: do most voters still relate to politics as active citizens, concerned to share in collective decision making as an important part of their self-identity, or have they become instead passive consumers of politics? Are they prepared to exercise their options for 'voice' through the political system rather than their options for 'exit'—by switching parties or by not bothering to vote at all? If they no longer regard themselves as citizens, then they may not feel the need to be represented by political parties, or to identify with any particular one, and will act instrumentally towards voting and participating, disengaging unless they have some direct interest in a particular election or decision.

Advocates of democracy had expected that rising levels of education would produce an electorate that was able and keen to make informed choices between political programmes and political leaders. But those in charge of contemporary political campaigns have found that treating voters as consumers, and campaigning as a branch of marketing, is generally more effective in winning elections than treating voters as informed citizens, and this has made electoral politics increasingly a competition of brands, styles and personalities. In response, the parties have begun to shed their mass character, and much of their internal democracy, in order to make themselves more effective competitors in the political market place. Political careers have been professionalised, and an increasing emphasis has come to be placed upon the presentation rather than the substance of policy. The ideological gap between the parties has substantially narrowed, leading to what Mair and Katz (1995) have called, the rise of the 'cartel party'. Many voters have become disconnected from the formal political process, and this has not so far been remedied by the many constitutional reforms introduced in recent years. A well-functioning constitution requires institutions and mechanisms that make it easy for citizens to participate, and help to sustain a vigorous civil society, and the concept of a 'public sphere', which is separate from both the family and the market (Marquand 2004; Ginsborg 2005).

A second big challenge which contemporary governance poses is how to ensure that government still has the capacity to deliver for its citizens. The idea of responsible government is that a government takes responsibility for its actions and is accountable for them to its electorate. The Government has the constitutional power to take initiatives and propose new measures, and it does so mindful of its overall responsibility for the public interest and public welfare. Can national governments any longer be held accountable for their actions, or to put it another way, are national governments becoming accountable for less and less?

The present phase of globalisation, which first appeared in the early 1970s, and became more fully established in the 1990s, has been accompanied by new kinds of political fragmentation, which have made the task of national government more complicated. There has been a proliferation of new supranational bodies with overlapping jurisdictions. Nation-states have become less self-contained, as international regimes of various kinds have been established to cope with the problems arising from the growing economic and political interdependence of the world economy. There are now many issues which are settled by transnational and supranational bodies, and which only come to national parliaments for ratification. The European Union is one of the most prominent examples of this. Under the Single European Act and other Treaties, there are many areas of policy in which the majority of legislation originates at the EU level, and is passed down to member states for implementation.

This presents a particular challenge to the relationship between a national government and its citizens. The more matters are transferred to subordinate or superior bodies, the less national government can claim to be responsible for what the government does. This tends to undermine the government's legitimacy in the eyes of voters. If there is no longer any very clear locus of decision making, and if governments no longer seem to be in charge, then the danger exists that voters will react accordingly, and lose trust in the governments they elect to promote the public interest or to protect the private interests of the citizens. At the extreme this can contribute to increasing distrust of the formal mechanisms of representative democracy.

One of the most difficult issues for constitutional government is how to adapt to a world of multi-level and transnational governance where it is hard to pin down exactly where decisions are taken. To some extent there has always been multi-level governance—federalist constitutions require it—but in the case of the UK, a new dimension has been added by accession to the EU and internal devolution. There is widespread ignorance about who is responsible for which policy, and naturally numerous opportunities for ministers to absolve themselves of responsibility by claiming that the decision which is being objected to has come from somewhere else. This ability to put the blame on some other tier of government has become endemic, and is corrosive of constitutional government, because national governments are still symbolically looked to as the protectors of the national interest and the public interest. Huge expectations about the competence and capacity of governments to deliver outcomes which voters want still abound, and politicians themselves, particularly at election time, do little to damp down those expectations. Since they are competing with other parties for votes the temptation is always to claim much greater competence than they really have. In government, politicians often find that the levers they need to achieve the things they have promised do not exist.

This is not just the fault of a system in which certain powers and functions have been transferred from the nation-state, but it is certainly a factor. In a system of multilateral governance, and still more of transnational governance, it can be hard for the voters to understand where a particular decision comes from, and who is imposing it. Decisions by the EU Commission, by the European Court, by the WTO, and by the numerous boards which are busy standardising such things as accounting rules and carbon emissions, often constrain what national politicians can do. Many matters are clearly no longer a matter for national decision. National politicians are increasingly forced to provide accounts that justify the arrangements of pooled sovereignty, but by definition this can make them appear weak, especially if they face any kind of populist challenge calling for the repatriation of powers and the withdrawal from international treaties. The framework of international governance that has been erected is quite vulnerable to these kinds of challenge, since governments generally fail most tests of accountability, transparency and legitimacy. All that national politicians can do is to claim influence over decisions, but such influence often looks weak when measured against full-blooded assertions of the national interest.

The constitutional challenge is how to bring transparency to the governing process. National governments remain crucial to the way societies are governed, but the structures of accountability and the lines of responsibility have become blurred. A more precise definition of powers and where and how they are exercised has become necessary, with appropriate channels for scrutiny and reporting. Government has a solidity which governance lacks. There are now many forms of governance, including networks and markets, which cannot be controlled or corralled by governments. But this does not mean that government is dissolving into governance, only that to understand the new processes of governance, including globalisation, we need to see how they provide a new context for government, one that departs from the old bureaucratic, top-down, hierarchical models of government that were once so common.

The third challenge posed by recent changes in governance is related to the other two, and is perhaps more fundamental than either of them. The disengagement of citizens has undermined representative democracy, and the shift to new patterns of governance has undermined responsible government. The growth of complexity, however, threatens to undermine participative democracy, by taking many areas of policy out of politics altogether, as politicians divest themselves of the responsibility for making hard choices, encouraging the rise of a managerial and technocratic style of politics over which citizens can have no influence.

Government in the past, of course, has often been secretive and opaque, and this still continues, but to a lesser extent. Modern governments are probably now more open than they have ever been, aided by freedom of information acts and a more intrusive media. The change does not arise so much from the amount of knowledge available to citizens, as from the nature of contemporary knowledge and the process by which it is produced.

As with the other trends already examined, the extent of this trend towards greater complexity is controversial, and certainly uneven, and some of the wilder claims that are made need qualifying. There are, however, some solid grounds for thinking that complexity is increasing in contemporary societies, as a result of the processes that have expanded the division of labour and the division of knowledge. It is not something that has suddenly occurred, but it has gradually emerged over a long period. It is associated with new kinds of risk, and with new ways of managing risk, and creates some major new dilemmas for policy.

The rise in new forms of governance is one of the sources of complexity, as is the greater cultural diversity of modern societies, and the consequences of individualism for the way people live. But the principal source of increased complexity, and the new forms of risk, lies in the technologies that have become available in recent decades. Industrial societies have reached the point where economic and technological developments have become so rapid and so continuous that they are constantly revolutionising lifestyles and behaviour (Beck 1992). Established political and constitutional processes provide politicians with little control over these developments, yet they have to deal with their unintended consequences, particularly the new risks and new dangers that they produce. But, because of the trends towards citizen disengagement from representative politics and declining trust in politicians and in government, as well as the shrinking capacity of the state in relation to the tasks it faces, governments appear increasingly ill-equipped to handle the problems that technological development throws up, not least because so many of these developments pose fundamental moral and political challenges to the way people live, and even to the fixity of some of the constants of human life itself (such as extending its span).

One of the obvious consequences of these developments is an increasing dependence on expertise of various kinds, since many of the issues, from climate change to nuclear energy, and from GM foods to genetic selection, and the effects of new drugs, are such that only experts could possibly offer an informed opinion. But experts' own knowledge is limited, experts often disagree and science deals in probabilities not certainties—all of which contributes to the feeling that a growing number of problems are insoluble, and yet everyone agrees that they have to be solved. Since politics is a practical activity aimed at finding pragmatic solutions to everyday problems, this is not good news for politicians, could be created. The problem that contemporary governance regimes have to wrestle with is therefore how to open up new spaces for politics, how a new kind of public domain that reinvigorates both representative and participative democracy, empowering citizens and enabling them to participate in policy discussion and secure their rights in new ways. The instinct of politicians is increasingly to 'depoliticise' decisions by setting up boards and committees of experts to take the decisions on their behalf, and remove them from any political process, whether representative or participative. But this means that increasing areas of public life are subject to only very indirect accountability to the people. Politicians retreat to dealing with those few areas where their decisions can make a difference, or where there is high symbolic value in them being involved. For the rest they invoke terms like governance and globalisation to suggest that there are no alternatives to the courses they are pursuing, and that the constraints on policy making are so tight that there is only one possible course of action.

As politicians are blamed more and more for what goes wrong in government, and the media portrays every branch of government as incompetent, chaotic, indecisive, and corrupt, it is not surprising that politicians increasingly seek to divest themselves of the necessity of actually taking decisions in difficult areas. These are devolved to the appropriate experts. But politicians still tend to get blamed for anything that goes wrong, and ignored when things go well, even though they have less and less control over what actually happens. This trend toward de-politicisation and charismatic, celebrity politics threatens to undermine attempts to create more participative forms of democracy, as well as schemes for empowering citizens, and to rebuild trust in representative democracy. Clearly a healthy governance regime would require all three. But it would need to find ways to resist the present trends that are pushing citizens and politicians further apart and creating policy structures that, for all the talk of consultation, often make it harder for genuine participation to take place.

Implications for Administrative Decision Making and Administrative Justice

So, what are the implications of all this for administrative decision making and the project of administrative justice? At the centre of the idea of administrative justice is the concept of accountability: individuals affected by decisions should have the ability to call to account those responsible for those decisions. Administrative justice concerns the extent to which individuals affected by decisions are treated fairly and have the ability to ensure adequate redress of grievances. Calling decision makers to account has the dual purpose of ensuring that individuals are afforded what they are due and also ensuring, through proper feedback mechanisms, better standards of public service and administration.

Many of the changes in governance and public administration that have been identified in this chapter place demands on administrative justice in terms of its ability to secure effective accountability for individuals affected by the administration of public policy. If the Westminster model is no longer an adequate way of describing our governance arrangements, then administrative justice needs to respond to challenges posed by examining how to secure effective accountability, questioning how existing processes need to be reformed in order to achieve this, and assessing the potential of alternative forms of accountability. Take, for instance, the prevalence of governance through networks and markets, privatisation, and contracting-out. The exercise of public power through such means requires consideration of the extent to which administrative justice principles can be extended to purely private decision making and how to secure and understand effective accountability when power is exercised by non-state regulatory agencies (discussed by Oliver in this volume). Similarly, the development of non-state regulatory regimes poses difficult challenges concerning their accountability (see chapter by Black in this volume).

Moreover, as noted above, the diffusion of power and decision making upward to bodies above the level of national government and downward to subordinate bodies can lead to increasing levels of distrust by citizens toward government. A major task for administrative justice is to consider how public expectations for justice can be organised so as to restore trust (see chapters by Kagan and Hertogh in this volume). This complexity and diffusion of public power also requires administrative justice redress mechanisms to be designed firmly with the perspective of the user firmly in mind (Leggatt, 2001). The rationalisation of administrative justice around the concept of citizen redress, rather than around institutional dichotomies such as the distinction between complaints and appeals (see chapter by Dunleavy in this volume), and the adoption of a holistic approach to administrative justice, need to be explored.

Finally, the changes in governance and public administration highlight the complex environment in which public action is now conducted and the nature of the competing accountability processes which need to be enveloped within the administrative justice project. The concept of accountability is itself multi-faceted and governance presupposes a variety of different forms of accountability mechanisms—political, legal, managerial, financial, market-based—each of which focuses on different end-goals (Day and Klein 1987; Mulgan 2003; Mashaw 2006). A public agency is politically accountable to ministers and elected representatives to ensure that it follows the policies that those democratically elected representatives chose in the interests of social well-being. The agency will itself also have its own internal and managerial mechanisms of accountability to ensure that front-line staff are both competent and operationally effective in carrying out their tasks and responsibilities. Furthermore, the agency will be legally accountable to individuals who complain that their rights or interests have been adversely affected and seek redress through the variety of administrative justice redress mechanisms (internal review, complaints procedures, ombudsmen investigations, appeals to tribunals and judicial review by the courts). Furthermore, the rise of the audit society (Power 1997; Lapsley and Lonsdale in this volume) and the marketisation of public services have provided the impetus for recognising the importance of financial accountability and scrutiny of the effective use of available resources.

As Scott (2000) has noted, the transformations of public administration have made more transparent the dense networks of accountability within which public power is now exercised. Clearly, these accountability processes will sometimes, if not frequently, place competing demands on governmental institutions. Given the competing demands on governance structures, it is usually difficult if not impossible to satisfy fully each demand for accountability. The questions for government and also commentators is then: how should such organisations and governance arrangements be best organised and designed in order to attempt to reconcile the competing accountability demands placed upon them? Which types of accountability work best in which particular contexts? And to what extent does enhancing one form of accountability entail and justify sacrificing another?

To illustrate the point, consider immigration bureaucracies in the UK, and also elsewhere, which are responsible for managing migration. These agencies are subjected to strong impulses from elected officials to manage and administer immigration policy effectively to secure the security of the state's borders. At the same time, as immigration decision making profoundly affects individuals, such agencies are normally subjected to a high volume of legal challenges both via specialist tribunals and the courts (Thomas 2005). The tension for the bureaucracy is to meet the competing accountability challenges effectively so as to ensure that it is both managerially effective and that it enables proper and adequate redress by which individuals can challenge adverse decisions, while at the same time being politically responsive to elected politicians and the public. Competing accountabilities pressures, such as financial accountability, increase the difficulty of the task because government often seeks efficiency savings.

Given the range of different and often competing accountability mechanisms in which governance regimes operate, the broader task for administrative justice is then to assess and evaluate how these different accountability processes can be reconciled and how best to manage their competing tensions. The changes in governance and public administration clearly make the task of both examining and achieving administrative justice highly complex. Nevertheless, if administrative justice is to be secured in the changing environment of public administration, then broadening its focus beyond that of seeking redress for grievances toward the organisation of governance regimes that operate under competing accountability mechanisms seems necessary.

References

Bache, I and Flinders, M (eds) (2004) *Multi-Level Governance* (Oxford, Oxford University Press).

Beck, U (1992) *Risk Society: Towards a New Modernity* (London, Sage).

Bellamy, R (2007) *Political Constitutionalism: A Republican Defence of the Constitutionality of Democracy* (Cambridge, Cambridge University Press).

Cerny, P (1991) *The Changing Architecture of Politics: Structure, Agency, and the Future of the State* (London, Sage).

Day, P and Klein, R (1987) *Accountabilities: Five Public Services* (London, Tavistock).

Dicey, AV (1885) *Introduction to the Study of the Law of the Constitution* (London, Macmillan).

Gamble, A (1994) *The Free Economy and the Strong State: the politics of Thatcherism* (London, Macmillan).

—— (2006a) 'The European Disunion' 8 *British Journal of Politics and International Relations* 34.

—— (2006b) 'Two Faces of Neo-liberalism' in R Robison (ed) *The Neo-Liberal Revolution: Forging the Market State* (London, Palgrave-Macmillan).

Ginsborg, P (2005) *The Politics of Everyday Life* (New Haven, Yale University Press).

Greenleaf, WH (1983) *The British Political Tradition: The Rise of Collectivism* Volume I (London, Methuen).

Hazell, R (1999) *Constitutional Futures: A History of the Next Ten Years* (Oxford, Oxford University Press).

Hix, S (1994) 'The Study of the European Community: the challenge to European politics' 17 *West European Politics* 1.

HM Government (2007) *The Governance of Britain* CM 7170 (London, The Stationery Office).

Hutton, W (1995) *The State We're In* (London, Cape).

Johnson, N (2004) *Reshaping the Constitution* (London, Palgrave-Macmillan).

Kaul, I, Grunberg, I and Stern, M (1999) (eds) *Global Public Goods: International cooperation in the twenty first century* (Oxford, Oxford University Press).

Leggatt, A (2001), *Tribunals for Users—One System, One Service* (London, Lord Chancellor's Department).

Lowi, T (1972) 'Four Systems of Policy, Politics and Choice' 32 *Public Administration Review* 298.

Mair, P and Katz, R (1995) 'Changing models of party organisation and party democracy: the emergence of the cartel party' 1 *Party Politics* 28.

Mann, M (1986) *The Sources of Social Power* (Cambridge, Cambridge University Press).

Mannheim, K (1940) *Man and Society in an Age of Reconstruction* (London, Routledge Kegan and Paul).

Marquand, D (1988) *The Unprincipled Society: New Demands and Old Politics* (London, Cape).

—— (2004) *Decline of the Public* (Cambridge, Polity).

Mashaw, J (2006) 'Accountability and Institutional Design: Some Thoughts on the Grammar of Governance' in M Dowdle (ed), *Public Accountability: Designs, Dilemmas and Experiences* (Cambridge, Cambridge University Press).

Moran, M (2002) *The British Regulatory State* (Oxford, Oxford University Press).

Mulgan, R (2003) *Holding Power to Account: Accountability in Modern Democracies* (London, Palgrave-Macmillan).

Peters, G and Pierre, J (2000) *Governance, Politics and the State* (London, Palgrave-Macmillan).

Pollitt, C, Girre, X, Lonsdale, J and Mul, R (1999) *Performance or Compliance? Performance Audit and Public Management in Five Countries* (Oxford, Oxford University Press).

Power, M (1997) *The Audit Society: Rituals of Verification* (Oxford, Oxford University Press).

Rhodes, R (1997) *Understanding Governance: Policy Networks, Governance, Reflexivity and Accountability* (Buckingham, Open University Press).
Rosenau, J (1995) 'Governance in the Twenty-First Century' 1 *Global Governance* 13.
Scott, C (2000) 'Accountability in the Regulatory State' 27 *Journal of Law and Society* 38.
Thomas, R (2005) 'Evaluating Tribunal Adjudication: Administrative Justice and Asylum Appeals' *Legal Studies* 462.
Vincent-Jones, P (2006) *The New Public Contracting: Regulation, Responsiveness, Relationality* (Oxford, Oxford University Press).
Waldron, J (2006) 'The Core of the Case against Judicial Review', 115 *Yale Law Journal* 1346.
Wallace, W (1996) 'Government without Statehood', in W Wallace and H Wallace (eds), *Policy-Making in the European Union* (Oxford, Oxford University Press).

2

Delivering Choice and Administering Justice: Contested Logics of Public Services

JOHN CLARKE, MORAG MCDERMONT
AND JANET NEWMAN

Introduction

In this chapter we examine what happens when the logic of administrative justice encounters public service reforms based on different logics: in particular the commitment to consumer or user choice as an organising principle for the provision of public services. Since the 1980s, successive UK governments have sought to reform public services by challenging the bureaucratic and professional frameworks for the allocation and delivery of services in ways that promote the principle of user or consumer choice. These range from the 'right to buy' and 'choice-based letting' in public or social housing, through parental choice in education and personalised budgets in social care, to patient choice in health care.

Choice based reforms were developed alongside other strategies—for example, processes of marketisation and privatisation, or the installation of managerialism as the preferred mode of organisational governance. As Clarke and Newman (1997) argue, managerialism challenged the combination of bureaucratic and professional logics (bureau-professionalism) that dominated British public service provision. In some senses, managers were supposed to serve as a proxy for marketisation and privatisation, given the identification of managers with making organisations think and behave in more 'business-like' ways. Managers were also expected to make public organisations more 'customer-focused'. Nevertheless, the rise of the principle of choice and the associated idea of addressing users of public services as consumers, or citizen-consumers, emerged as a central, if not dominant, logic in the last decade, with former Prime Minister Tony Blair arguing that:

> In reality, I believe people do want choice, in public services as in other services. But anyway, choice isn't an end in itself. It is one important mechanism to ensure that

> citizens can indeed secure good schools and health services in their communities. Choice puts the levers in the hands of parents and patients so that they as citizens and consumers can be a driving force for improvement in their public services. We are proposing to put an entirely different dynamic in place to drive our public services; one where the service will be driven not by the government or by the manager but by the user—the patient, the parent, the pupil and the law-abiding citizen.[1]

Not even managers, it seemed, could bring about the necessary reforms in public services. Only by placing consumer/user choice at the heart of the system could the ideas of quality, responsiveness, innovation and improvement be guaranteed. As an organisational logic for public services, however, choice generates a number of political, policy and practice difficulties (Clarke, Smith and Vidler 2006, Clarke et al 2007). In particular, it imposes a framework for decision making that—at best—runs counter to the principles and normative framework of administrative justice. Each of these logics defines particular sorts of subjects (citizens, members of the public, consumers, etc) and particular sorts of relationships between them and public institutions (service providing organisations, the government, etc). Choice and justice both attempt to inscribe those understandings—those imagined subjects and relationships—into organisational practices. In what follows, our intention is to examine these two different logics and ask what happens when they come together—how can choice and justice be articulated, combined or reconciled?

In developing this analysis, however, we will also draw attention to how these different organisational logics are articulated with political discourses, in particular the apparently shared discourse of equality as a foundational value for public provision. Both consumer choice and administrative justice are legitimated as organising logics in terms of their capacity to express and enact equality. What then becomes visible is the mutability of equality as a legitimating concept: the logics of consumer choice and administrative justice express and enact very different meanings of equality. This ambiguity adds to the political, policy and practical strains of trying to reconcile their claims to govern the realm of public service provision. In the course of the chapter, we examine the two logics, drawing out the ways in which consumer choice and administrative justice conceive of the public and how it is to be served. We pay particular attention to how each logic is understood to express and enact equality. Although we have stressed the ways in which the logic of consumer choice has challenged and displaced bureaucratic and professional frameworks for governing public services (including their adoption of justice as a principle to be administered in bureaucratic and professional practices), administrative justice remains a salient logic. Later in the chapter we consider moments at which these logics come into renewed contact: for example in appeal processes about the exercise of choice in public services (parental choice, housing allocation and so on).

[1] Tony Blair, quoted in *Guardian* (London 24 June 2004) 1.

Logics of Choice and Justice

In this chapter, we consistently refer to consumer choice and administrative justice as logics, and think it is appropriate to say something about our preference for this term (over other possibilities such as principles, models or ideal types). The language of 'logics' allows us to explore the implicit principles, norms or rules that give legitimacy to decisions and actions of those involved in policy and delivery (see March and Olsen 1989). We want to make the concept do rather more than that. As we hinted at the introduction to the chapter, logics bring to bear social imaginaries: they identify a cast of characters, and specify the sorts of conditions and patterns of relationship in which those characters interact. In Foucault's terms, logics also organise the ways in which knowledge and power are articulated (Foucault 1981; for a discussion of knowledge-power knots, see Clarke et al 2007: 114–17). The logic of consumer choice, for instance, identifies user-consumers and service providers (borrowing from the public choice theory distinction between producers and consumers). It specifies the conditions in which self-directing consumers encounter service providers—and valorises the expectation that their wishes will be satisfied. In the process it re-imagines the power relations of public service—and the sorts of knowledge that matter. Consumers may be intrinsically knowledgeable (knowing about their own needs/desires/wants) or may be helped to become 'well informed' consumers. Consumers are the empowered agents of the consumer choice logic while 'service providers' (a genericising term) are subordinated to their demands.

Borrowing from Foucault in this way points to how such logics attempt to govern 'conduct'—the conduct of particular sort of actors and the practices of the organisational settings that these actors inhabit. The logic of consumer choice is very clearly exemplified in the claim by Harry Cayton (then the 'Patient Tsar' at the Department of Health) that the National Health Service must change from dealing with 'the lying down patients of the past' to engaging with 'the standing up consumers of the future' (Cayton 2003). Here we can see the process of imagining new subjects and the new field of relationships—especially organisational relationships—in which they are to be empowered. We think this view of logics is rather different from the abstraction of principles, models or types. In particular, it enables us to sidestep some of the difficulties about the relationship between normative and empirical aspects of such abstractions. Ideal types—of both consumer choice and administrative justice—tend to conceal their normative character, and deal with empirical instances as the accretion of impurities. For example, market models of choice explain empirical problems (such as market failure, or inappropriate consumer behaviour) as revealing imperfections in reality, rather than in the model. In contrast, we understand logics to be normative projects—they actively invent their ideals, turn them into programmatic statements and into policies, guidelines, training programmes and practices of identity formation. They organise—or attempt to organise—people, places, objects, signs, styles and symbols. That is, in Foucault's phrase, they try to assemble and align all those elements needed to ensure the 'conduct of conduct'.

There are several other points to emphasise about these logics. The first is that logics are almost always plural: politics, policy, organisations and occupations are sites that are typically characterised by the presence of heterogeneous logics, rather than being constituted by a single logic. This heterogeneity is not simple pluralism: such sites do not just contain different logics. They are traversed by contentious and contested logics involved in struggles for domination of the site (and the ways in which it is linked to other sites). So the logic of consumer choice does not just sit alongside the logic of administrative justice (or welfare professionalism). It is, on the contrary, the focus of efforts to displace, subordinate or residualise the other logics. It is also the focus of efforts to connect different sites—here politics, policy networks, organisations and occupations—through the principle and practice of choice-making. As a result, encounters between the logic of consumer choice and the logic of administrative justice are unlikely to be comfortable ones.

Second, this view of contested logics opens up the possibility of studying the ways in which different logics interact, producing tensions in particular sites or dilemmas for particular groups of actors. What logic is supposed to govern encounters between 'service users' and 'service providers'? How do would-be service users approach service providers—as rights-bearing citizens; as service users (or clients) engaged with bureau-professional rules; as supplicants to knowledgeable and powerful professions, or as sovereign consumers expecting to be served? Similar dilemmas exist for service providers (as organisations, as occupations and as individual workers): what is their mode of interaction with users? What has happened to the 'knowledge power knots' that organised public service professionalism? And even the issue of what to call the service user has become problematic: are they a patient, client, user, citizen, consumer or a customer? We have discussed these issues extensively elsewhere (eg, Clarke et al 2007, Clarke 2007, Clarke and Newman 2007). But our point here is that public services have become the site of 'unstable encounters' as the logics of choice and administrative justice struggle to govern them.

Third, this focus on logics enables us to pay attention to how logics make their way between sites—or more precisely, how they become translated from one location to another (Lendvai and Stubbs 2007). Our reference here to translation reflects a certain frustration with models of policy transfer. Translation draws attention to active processes through which logics move—for example, from US public choice theory to 'choice-centred' policy networks to governmental programmes to legislation and guidance to specific organisations and occupations. Translation points to the connective work that has to be done—by active agents—to articulate and align logics, practices and agents (see also Smith 2005, on 'institutional ethnography'). In these processes of translation—from place to place and from site to site—logics get developed, revised, reassembled, and reworked to 'fit' new locations. Installing consumer choice in public services, for instance, required translations to the diverse formations and trajectories of different public services (in different places): there is no generic public service to which the logic of consumer choice could be applied. We say a little more about this below.

Finally, looking at public services through the lens of logics enables us to see the ways in which specific logics are contestable. We emphasise three ways in particular here. Each logic is intrinsically imperfect—it is necessarily incomplete or unfinished, even as it lays claim to grand principles (justice, equality, etc). The processes of translation—and the encounters with other already established logics—make the installation of a logic a contingent, conditional and potentially unstable process. As such, a logic is usually contestable in its own terms: its incompleteness creates the conditions—and the language—of challenge. Justice is always subject to challenges on the grounds of unfairness, about miscarriages (of justice), or about exclusions and omissions. Similarly, choice is always subject to challenge on the grounds of unfairness, exclusions and omissions, and the conditions of choice (the 'small print'). Each logic, secondly, can be challenged from other existing logics: the installation of the logic of consumer choice provoked extensive criticism that drew, in part, on the discourse of justice. Justice itself may be challenged by other discourses, particularly those about the situational superiority of other forms of knowledge, such as scientific, expert or professional knowledge. Professional judgement may then override the abstract logics of justice. The third aspect of contestation that is important for us here revolves around the borrowings that such logics make. They are themselves assemblages, articulating other valued terms, principles and commitments into a (more or less) coherent programme of governing specific sites and agents. But such borrowings carry with them other meanings or inflections that may not be suppressed or silenced in their new articulation. In what follows, we point to how both the logic of consumer choice and the logic of administrative justice attempt to borrow and realise the idea(l) of equality. Each gives it a specific articulation, but neither, we suggest, manages to fix or stabilise its meaning to the exclusion of other possibilities. Equality, then, both forms a key term for these two logics—and a key term for those seeking to challenge them.

Imagining Choice

Choice operates as a term that can condense and contain a variety of meanings, motivations and possibilities. It can mobilise or give voice to very different aspirations or desires. We suggest that this indeterminacy of meaning gives the idea of choice a capacity to 'speak for' diverse concerns in relation to public services. These include a desire for greater control of one's situation, an aspiration to define one's own needs, and a wish to shape some or all of the following—outcomes, processes, relationships, and patterns of interaction. In the context of public services, choice provides a means of representing the desire to be heard ('voice'), to be recognised or taken seriously ('respect'), and to feel a part of processes and institutions ('membership' or 'partnership'). It certainly runs well beyond the simple image of a wish to be 'satisfied'. Grasping this variety of meanings and motivations is, we think, important for avoiding too quick a collapse into the market logic of consumer choice. Idea(l)s of choice speak to, and for, many desires.

The indeterminacy of choice makes possible this condensation of many meanings and motivations—but it also makes choice a focus for a range of doubts and anxieties. In the context of public services, choice appears to both address—and evoke—anxieties about standards in public services; about relationships of trust and interdependency; about formations of power and powerlessness in the interactions between members of the public and public organisations; about the experience of being subordinated or demeaned; and about the (in)equity of public processes and institutions. Choice is also a focus for anxieties about exacerbated individuation, fragmentation and disconnectedness. In particular, many respondents in the study of citizen-consumers (Clarke et al 2007) were at pains to indicate that using public services was 'not like shopping'. This finding is echoed in the study by Rosen, Curry and Florin (2005: 7), who argue that 'The majority of participants perceived important differences between choices about health and health care and other consumer-type choices'. They also note (ibid: 8) that there is 'scepticism about the value of choice and its effectiveness at improving services.' We can think of few words that condense such a rich and powerful mix of aspirations and anxieties.

It is precisely the indeterminacy of choice (its relative emptiness and openness) that enables the term to carry such an excess of meaning. As we hinted above, the problems with choice are not about its abstract multi-faceted desirability: after all, who could be against choice? Rather the problems of choice emerge as it becomes specified, detailed and concretised—when a particular model of choice (lifted wholesale from market imagery) comes to mean choice in practice. At that point, doubts, uncertainties and anxieties come to the fore: can it work? Can it deliver all those aspirations? What conditions are needed to make it work? What might it displace or diminish that we also value?

This perspective on choice as a condensate offers one way of explaining the popularity of what we might call 'choice-in-general' (rather than particular mechanisms or practices). Choice—from this perspective—looks uncannily like what the marketing industry understands as a brand: it is a focus of affective, as well as instrumental, identifications. More generally, this view of choice as a condensate explains something of its potency in public discourse about public services. At the same time, however, choice has been the object of sustained criticism in the UK and beyond (eg, Needham 2003 and 2007, Furnell et al 2008, Somers 2008). It is viewed as producing inequality in that the middle class has proved to be rather more adept in pursuing their preferences. It is viewed as reducing relationships to a series of transactions between provider and user. It is constitutive of individualised forms of reasoning and action that bracket away ethical forms of reasoning and judgement. And this individualism undermines the collective purpose of public services. As we noted above, there is a persistent reluctance to view public services as commodified or as quasi-commercial exchanges—the desire of many users is for sustained and personal relationships with service providers rather than a series of individuated transactions (Clarke et al 2007).

Despite its limitations and its susceptibility to critique, choice remains attractive to both governmental actors and some service users for a number of reasons. First, it offers a break with the paternalism of welfare providers, and the potential to unlock the knowledge power knot of professional practice (Clarke et al 2007). As such it is aligned with notions of service-user empowerment and has been associated with the claims of particular social movements and groups (eg, of those with physical or learning disabilities). Second, it is in line with 'modernised' political notions of equality as fairness. A choice for the many, rather than the few, emerged as an anchoring point for the argument about inequality. New Labour argued that, by extending choice to active consumers of public services, equity would be enlarged. While promising to reform and modernise public services, New Labour could not avoid addressing issues of equality, not least since it had to continue to speak to its traditional electoral supporters as well as win over liberal/progressive sections of the middle classes. 'Welfarism' has often been associated—albeit loosely—with social democratic or reformist images of social change, improvement and progress. To some extent, this implied mitigating the effect of social inequalities. New Labour systematically residualised the concern with inequality as 'old-fashioned': a hang-over from older ways of thinking. Instead, it offered an abbreviated concern with 'equity' as the guiding principle of social progress. In New Labour terms, a consumer-centred model of public services would both promote equity and overcome the problems of inequality associated with 'old' public services:

> Those on the left who defend the status quo on public services defend a model that is one of entrenched inequality. I repeat: the system we inherited was inequitable. It was a two-tier system. Our supposedly uniform public services were deeply unequal as league and performance tables in the NHS and schools have graphically exposed. … The affluent and well educated … had the choice to buy their way out of failing or inadequate provision—a situation the Tories' 'opting out' reforms of the 1980s encouraged. It was a choice for the few, not for the many. (Blair 2003)

Critics of the choice agenda in public services were confronted by a characteristic New Labour device, the charge of elitism: 'It is frequently asserted—often by those who have a good deal of choice in their own lives—that users of public services do not in fact want choice' (Ministers of State 2004: 4). The idea of 'choice for the many, not the few' emerged as an anchoring point for the second argument about inequality: that by extending choice to active consumers of public services, equity would be enlarged:

> Extending choice—for the many, not the few—is a key aspect of opening up the system in the way we need. Not choice for a small minority … because it boosts equity. It does so for three reasons. First, universal choice gives poorer people the same choices available only to the middle-classes. It addresses the current inequity where the better off can switch from poor providers. But we also need pro-active choice (for example, patient

> care advisers in the NHS) who can explain the range of options available to each patient. Second, choice sustains social solidarity by keeping better off patients and parents within the NHS and public services … Third, choice puts pressure on low quality providers that poorer people currently rely on. It is choice with equity we are advancing. Choice and consumer power as the route to greater social justice not social division. (Blair 2003)

Equity here became a matter of dealing with forms of unequal access to, or treatment by, public services. This was a rather limited view of the relationship between public services and inequality, since it ignored the longer political debate about whether public services should remedy, rather than reproduce, patterns of social inequality. The challenge for New Labour was to continue to draw on the language of equality but to redefine this for the 'modern' conception of nation and people by a focus on 'equity', 'opportunity' and 'choice'. This was accomplished by the transformation of 'diversity' in New Labour discourse. For the most part, New Labour treated equality struggles as belonging to an earlier era—and viewed them as having produced successful outcomes. Instead a more 'person-centred' view of diversity replaced the list of categorical differences. Although forms of socio-demographic difference were sometimes referred to (a list of women, minority ethnic communities, young people, old people and the 'hard to reach', for example), these were rarely seen as sites of structural inequalities. The dominant meaning of diversity in the New Labour lexicon was of a nation rich in individual differences of needs, wants and expectations. It was this diversity that must motivate public services.

> Since every person has differing requirements, their rights will not be met simply by providing a 'one size fits all' service. The public expects diversity of provision as well as national standards. (Office of Public Services Reform 2002: 13)

This conception of diversity flattened structured difference (and its inequality-producing effects) into a field of idiosyncratic and individualised wants, needs and desires. These individuated members of the public closely resembled the individuals-as-consumers imagined in neo-classical economics. What located or motivated their differences did not matter—what did matter were the desires that they brought to market (and the money needed to satisfy them).

This egalitarian entitlement of everyone to choice was to be secured by New Labour acting as the 'people's champions' against 'producer power' (Clarke 1997). This voicing also picks up on 'fairness' (since it promotes equity) and implies an engagement with improving the quality of services (since poorer people are served by poorer providers). Choice is a principle of demotic (rather than democratic) populism, in the sense that everyone is—or ought to be—entitled to choice.

Delivering Choice

Here we turn from the 'generic' logic of consumer choice to consider briefly how consumer-oriented policies are being translated and enacted in different public services. As we noted earlier, while there might be a general logic of consumer choice, there is no generic public service: each service involves specific forms of relationship between providers, the public and individual users. Each specific service has, then, been the focus of intensive work of translation and articulation as choice gets turned into the 'small print' of legislation, guidelines, service design, staff training and development and more. The New Labour governments after 1997 inherited a variety of consumerist developments from their Conservative predecessors.

The consumer-choice link was a potent feature of several aspects of Thatcherism's remaking of the welfare state and public services in the UK during the 1980s. Most notable were the creation of the 'right-to-buy' for council house tenants in the Housing Act of 1980 and the creation of a 'quasi-market' to enable school 'choice' in the Education Reform Act of 1988 (see, for example, Gewirtz, Ball and Bowe 1995, Forrest and Murie 1991). Choice was the defining characteristic of the consumer's relation to public services and had a complex relationship to 'marketising' processes (see, inter alia, Bartlett, Roberts and Le Grand 1998). The 'right to buy' in housing (partially) dissolved the distinction between the public and private sector by shifting public resources (at a subsidised price) into private ownership. 'Choice' in schooling gave parents (as the proxy consumers of education) the non-cash mediated right to choose schools for their children. More precisely, it gave parents the right to *express a preference* about schools for their children (even though the practice is widely referred to as 'parental choice'). As a result, parents attempted to choose schools—and schools got to choose children (and their parents). Elsewhere, 'market stimulation' was intended to involve spending public money on creating a market of competing providers (eg, in the field of domiciliary and residential care after the 1990 NHS and Community Care Act). However in most public services 'choice' was mediated by managerial and/or bureau-professional decision making: in health care, GPs mediated patient choices; in social care, social service assessments (of need and budgets) mediated user choice and so on.

Subsequently, a consumer model of choice has been further extended into public services in ways that try to mimic market exchange. For example, health care has been at the centre of debates about 'choice' that have focused on the 'expert patient' and the de-centring of medical knowledge (Newman and Vidler 2006). Policing involves a distinctively 'authoritative' relationship between the service and the public, based in and involving the exercise of the law. Nevertheless, the process of moving from Police Force to Police Service has been associated with re-thinking the relationships between the police and the public (Westmarland and Smith 2004, Westmarland and Clarke 2009, Clarke 2009). While social care for older people has historically been viewed as a 'Cinderella service', the combination of demographic changes, the challenges to institutional care and especially the movements of disabled peoples made it a publicly and politically more visible domain of policy in which choice has been promulgated (Clarke, Smith and Vidler 2006). Social housing has been the focus of attempts to extend both 'choice' and 'voice'—through processes of tenant empowerment and the policy of 'Choice based Lettings' (for example, see McKee and Cooper 2007, Cowan and McDermont 2006, Cowan and Marsh 2004). Each of these services is 'in transition'—engaged in the process of negotiating shifting conditions, pressures, demands and expectations. Each service has its own distinctive institutional history and trajectory. They are located differently in constitutional and governance formations. They have different organisational histories, cultures and capacities. They are also inhabited by different occupational or professional formations embodying distinctive notions of expertise, autonomy and discretion. But each of them has encountered the translation of the logic of choice into the institutional arrangements of service production and delivery. Each of them has, indeed, been marked by the attempt to install the logic of choice as the dominant institutional logic—shaping the conduct of organisations, of managers, of staff and, not least, of those using the service.

Imagining Justice

Just as choice operates as a term that can condense and contain a variety of meanings, so does justice. Like choice, we expect justice to do a lot of work. Also like choice, justice has a certain indeterminancy. Turning to a dictionary we find that justice can have meanings such as 'integrity; impartiality; rightness; the awarding of what is due'; justice is associated with the qualities of being righteous, upright, fair, impartial, giving someone their due, making decisions in accordance with facts.[2] Such is the strength of the idea of justice as a 'common sense' understanding, that we seldom define *justice* in studies of administrative justice. Hazel Genn's (1999) study of the everyday perceptions of seeking justice, *Paths to Justice: What people do and think about going to law*, is silent about the meaning of justice. Nevertheless, its subtitle links (unquestioningly) the idea of seeking justice with 'going to law', that is, with the use of legal mechanisms. This version of common sense might not have been recognisable in the eighteenth and nineteenth centuries: for example, Hutton (1787: 6) commented that '[t]he straight, the easy, the concise road to justice is blocked up, and the traveller is led through the dark, long, and intricate windings of law'.

The logics of administrative justice are said to provide a set of 'principles that can be used to evaluate the justice inherent in administrative decision-making'. Here again, we find that such 'principles' must contain a great deal, encompassing both 'procedural fairness' and 'substantive justice' (Adler 2003: 323–24). We expect justice, like choice, to address concerns that our side of the story should be heard, that we should be treated with respect, and that we should be able to call

[2] *Chambers Twentieth Century Dictionary* (Edinburgh, Chambers, 1983).

officials to account for decisions made about us. But we also expect it to deliver a form of social justice, a more 'equal society' (Weir 2006: ix).[3]

The logic of administrative justice leads to a set of procedural rights, encapsulated (in a lawyerly way of talking) in the title of Galligan's book, *Due Process and Fair Procedures* (1996). To legal scholars this idea(l) of being treated fairly can mean many things: that the decision maker should take account of all the facts; that there should be a right to be heard; that the outcome of decision making should be predictable and that decision makers should give reasons for their decisions; that those not satisfied about a decision have the right to appeal; and a right to be heard before a neutral and independent judge. These concepts, when set out as a series of 'rights', can seem obvious and incontestable—although they are anything but. Take the 'right to be heard'—what is it that must be heard? For the lawyer, what must be uncovered is whether the correct procedures were followed; but for the claimant denied welfare benefits what they want heard is their pain, or their hunger, that has resulted from a denial of benefit (see Sarat 1990). The lawyer wants to keep to the 'facts', silencing the claimant's emotion in the process.

In the government's White Paper, *Transforming Public Services: Complaints, Redress and Tribunals* (DCA 2004) administrative justice is taken as a normative expectation of citizens:

> We are all entitled to receive correct decisions on our personal circumstances; where a mistake occurs we are entitled to complain and to have the mistake put right with the minimum of difficulty; where there is uncertainty we are entitled to a quick resolution of the issue, and we are entitled to expect that, where things go wrong, the system will learn from the problem and will do better in the future. (DCA 2004: para 1.5)

In this imagining, administrative justice means correctness in decision making—encapsulated in the White Paper's slogan 'getting it right first time'—resolution of uncertainty and learning from mistakes. But what can come to be claimed as an individual 'mistake' is more often than not the effect of larger dynamics or forces, from a failure to invest resources (in training, consultation, in scrutiny and review: Galligan 1996: 112–22) to, more fundamentally, a belief in the minimisation of procedural controls. Alan Greenspan may have been able to write off the crisis in credit as resulting from a mistaken faith in bankers—millions might question whether the language of 'mistake' trivialises the outcome.

Here we can see that our expectations of administrative justice are inextricably connected to the delivery of substantive justice. In doing so, we are insisting that the bureaucratic and legal technologies of administrative justice deliver some form of 'equality'. But the indeterminacy of administrative justice becomes ever more apparent: 'judicial review provides only partial redress for those who believe their socio-economic rights have been violated' (Weir 2006: xiii). For administrative justice to enter this arena mixes up bureaucratic and legal decision making

[3] Social justice is ranked second only to freedom as a quality of a democratic society that we expect in the UK (Dunleavy et al 2005).

with politics: politicians consider social justice as a matter of policy; courts are reluctant to intervene in decisions that are seen as political.[4] If judges (and other adjudicators) see themselves as having a role in delivering social justice, it lies confined within rights and obligations set out in existing legislation, and their role becomes one of translation (with frequent battles between government ministers and judges as to what counts as translation and what as new policy). Just as significantly, the logic of justice often requires this process of translation to abstract legal subjects from their social conditions or circumstances. Only by losing their social character can they become individuals in law (Edelman 2006). All of these demands combine to produce a recurrent tension between 'justice' and 'social justice'.

Regardless of the lack of specificity of the idea(l) of administrative justice, it could be said to have reached a certain level of understanding in the popular consciousness of law in the proposal for a 'right to administrative justice' to be included in a British Bill of Rights and Responsibilities (AJTC 2008). Rights, it seems, are the 'modern' way to understand the delivery of justice—but does a 'right' to administrative justice compete with our right to choose? In this next section we consider what happens when the logics of administrative justice clashes with the logics of choice.

Justice Meets Choice

In an earlier section, we used the idea that choice-in-general acts as a condensate for a wide range of individual aspirations and political goals. In this section, we argue that it is at the point of moving to choice-in-particular that choice clashes with administrative justice. Choice in public service delivery can never be pure 'consumer' choice because public services are always enmeshed in calculations and decisions about the allocation of resources that are simultaneously scarce and valued. Choice as a programme for resource allocation, where the number of 'customers' exceeds the available resources, produces practices that 'sift' this demanding public in order to manage the organisational dilemma. In current public service systems, the task of balancing demands and resources is typically devolved to the organisational level. Just as past systems of philanthropic welfare and bureau-professional welfare found ways of distinguishing between the deserving and the undeserving, or the genuinely needy and the others, so too choice-driven welfare must construct distinctions and priorities. As a result, a whole array of techniques and technologies must come into play: exclusion lists, timing-out of chances to choose (choice must be exercised within a given

[4] Take for example the right to care services, as set against the role of local government to set its own budgets: *R v Gloucestershire CC, ex p Barry* [1997] AC 584.

time-frame), and sets of rules that prioritise certain customers over others. Such rules may be formalised in regulations or concealed within other practices of selection (the identification by schools of pupils and parents with desirable characteristics, for example). Choice, in other words, must be managed; but is not 'managed choice' a contradiction in terms?

When choice becomes specified, managed and mediated in these institutional settings of public services, it also creates a terrain of perceived unfairness and injustice. At that moment, the frustrated consumer may become the aggrieved citizen—expecting and demanding that principles of justice and fairness be upheld. In this section we use two examples to examine such clashes between the logics of choice and administrative justice: parental choice in schools, and the allocation of social housing through choice-based lettings schemes.

Parental Choice in the Allocation of Places to Secondary School

Blair's 1997 election slogan was the prioritisation of 'Education, Education, Education'. As choice became adopted as the mantra of New Labour, nothing was more central than parents being allowed to choose which school their children attended. The process of choosing a secondary school can become of overwhelming importance to final-year primary school pupils and their parents, occupying much of the year from receiving information about schools at the beginning of the school year, to school visits and the submission of choice forms to the local authority, to the communication to parents of the outcome (Wilkins 2009: chapter 2).[5] Moreover, the process may not end there, as for many the allocated school is not the school of their choice.[6] Dissatisfied parents can pursue their school of choice through the statutory school admission appeals procedure.[7]

According to the DCSF website, 'well-informed choice' is the ultimate aim of school selection, and the Childcare Act 2006 places a legal duty on local authorities to ensure that 'all parents have access to high quality, accurate and timely information' (DCSF 2008a: 1.8). Where the allocation of public services was the job of 'street-level bureaucrats' (Lipsky, 1980), rules and procedures were directed at front-line staff and managers to guide and constrain bureaucratic discretion. Now, in the framework of choice, it is the customer—the parent—who must be serviced with appropriate information, for they have

[5] This section draws extensively on the doctoral study of parental choice by Andrew Wilkins at the Open University. We are grateful to him for sharing his work, and for commenting on our use of it.

[6] In 2008, it was estimated that 120,000 children out of 560,000 in England and Wales were not allocated their first choice school, estimated at 20,000 more than in the previous year (Curtis and Lipsett 2008).

[7] The Department for Children, Schools and Families (DCSF) was one of two departments that replaced the Department for Education and Skills (DfES) in June 2007. The other, the Department for Innovation, Universities and Skills (DIUS), is responsible for further- and higher education.

become the decision makers. But, as Blair said, choice must be 'pro-active', and even the government acknowledges that the process of choosing is not without difficulty. For those deemed unable to 'navigate the system' (DfES 2005: 3.11) on their own, there are Choice Advisers whose role is to advise on this process of navigation. In compulsory education at secondary level everyone is eligible to take part—and therefore to choose. But it may be possible to divide off those deemed 'unable or unwilling' to engage with choice (typically families living in 'the most deprived communities'), and guide these parents by 'independently' interpreting the information for them (DCSF 2006: 2–9). So choice for these families becomes mediated through the eyes of professionals. Here we see a set of old welfarist categories and concepts revitalised—given new life and new affectivity within the logic of consumer choice. This management of choice for the most 'deprived' is one mechanism by which the schools choice system attempts to reconcile an ideologically driven agenda with the idea(l) that all must be given an 'equal' chance to participate, a gesture to justice perhaps? So the role of the choice advisor includes drawing upon information about schools (performance and value-added data, admission policies, oversubscription data, special needs policy and provision, uniform policy, and so on) and 'interpret[ing] the data and information independently and in a way that meets a family's needs' (DCSF 2006: 9).

The second encounter between choice and justice arises in the established system of appeals. Although School Admission Appeal Panels are not meant to be formal legalistic forums, they lay claim to being 'independent' bodies of 'lay' members (ie, people without personal experience in the management or provision of education in any school) and 'persons with experience in education' (ie, people who are acquainted with educational conditions in the area and are often former teachers) (DCSF 2008b: 1.4). They are expected to perform in a judicial way, considering all relevant guidelines, including the Code of Practice on School Admissions, and applying the law to the facts of the case (DCSF 2008b: 1.7).[8] In general, most parents represent themselves.[9] These appeal panels, however, have bred a new type of expert—consultants, like Chris Woodhead (former Chief Inspector of Schools and former Head of Ofsted) who advise parents on how to approach the panel. Some warn against using 'vague emotional arguments' (Blinkhorn and Griffiths 2008; also see Rooney 2007), insisting instead that parents present arguments about the processes and procedures of decision making, such as contesting the methods used to measure the distance from

[8] According to the Code of Practice (DCSF 2008b: 4.71), appeals must follow a two-stage decision-making process. First, the panel should assess whether admitting an additional pupil would cause prejudice to efficient education or the efficient use of resources ('prejudice'). If the panel finds that admission of the appellant would not cause such prejudice, then the appeal should be upheld. Second, if the panel decides that admission of additional children would result in prejudice, it should consider whether the parent's grounds for their child to be admitted to the school outweigh such prejudice.

[9] Parents may, if they wish, be accompanied by a friend or a representative (DCSF 2008b: 4.35). Legal representation is both discouraged and infrequent.

home to the school of choice. This elaborate appeals system is a recognition of the managed nature of school choice. The central role that bureaucratic discretion continues to play in administering parental choice is an acknowledgement that, at the end of the day, bureaucratic rules still count.

The appeals system can be seen as an example of the failure of choice policy and practice to cope with the allocation of scarce resources. In the end, the demands of justice require choice to acknowledge administrative and, if necessary, legal mechanisms. This process of appeal is itself resource-intensive: every year around 10 per cent of all admissions are appealed. The system of parental choice fails to achieve the promise of combining choice and equity in other ways too: it is open to manipulation, for example, from parents who rent flats or buy houses within the catchment area of the school of their choice, or use the address of a grandparent or other relative, in order to get their child into that school. The system of parental choice may attempt to achieve procedural justice or 'due process' justice through the appeals system, but it does not have the resources to seek out and 'prosecute' illegalities. Far more critically, it does not have the ability to deliver 'social justice'. Middle-class parents have the economic and cultural capital to manipulate the system by moving into the catchment area of 'good' schools and to represent themselves and their children as 'subjects of value' to these schools. The problems associated with parental choice of school have led one education authority (Brighton and Hove City Council in Sussex) to reject parental choice as an acceptable system for allocating children to schools outside their catchment area and to adopt a lottery system instead. When parents, aggrieved at this change in direction, launched a legal challenge, the Office of the Schools Adjudicator[10] ruled in favour of the proposed lottery system, arguing it would give 'a greater degree of justice' (Lipsett 2007). Indeed, the Brighton and Hove story demonstrates the difficulty of combining procedural justice and social justice, not least because there are so many divergent (if not conflicting) claims to justice. In conflicts over parental choice of school, we can trace different conceptions of justice and injustice: the injustices of 'postcode lotteries'; the injustices of social advantage (in the forms of economic, social or cultural capital); the injustices of spatial effects; and the injustices of specific allocations (particularly those that fail, or are seen to fail, to reward people for acting like a 'good parent').

The Case of Social Housing and Choice-based Lettings

In the provision of social housing, as in other areas of public service delivery, much has been done to attempt to turn the tenant into a customer, not, however, without considerable resistance (Marston 2004; also see the periodic success of

[10] The Office of the Schools Adjudicator was set up under the School Standards and Framework Act 1998 to adjudicate disputes arising from proposed changes in admission arrangements for schools.

campaigners against the quasi-privatisation of council housing in proposals for the 'voluntary' transfer of council housing to housing associations). In a development similar to the parental choice of school agenda, choice-based lettings (CBL) appeared as an alternative scheme for allocating social housing, apparently shifting the decision making from professional housing managers to tenants-as-consumers. It first appeared as government policy in the Housing Green Paper 2000 (DETR/DSS 2000; see Cowan and McDermont 2006). The benefits of CBL over previous systems of bureaucratic allocation, usually involving a 'points' system, were said to be many. Households would have a longer-term commitment to the locality of their choice; it would promote 'more sustainable communities' and 'increase personal well-being'. It was even claimed that CBL would 'help to reduce anti-social behaviour, crime, stress and educational under-achievement' (DETR/DSS 2000, para 9.7).

In choice-based letting households on housing waiting lists would not have to wait to be allocated a property by housing managers, rather they would bid for properties advertised by local authorities and registered social landlords. CBL was said to be more transparent than the old 'points systems' operated by local authorities and some housing associations for allocating households to properties because it would be much simpler for applicants to understand. More critically, it involved an ideological shift from passive households being *allocated* a property to 'active homeseekers' to whom a property is *let* (see Cowan and Marsh 2005).

However, choice based letting of social housing, like parental choice of school, became problematic because it was concerned with the allocation of scarce resources, a particular issue (in social housing) in relation to homelessness. Households accepted by local authorities as homeless become a particular financial burden on local government, because they come to occupy temporary accommodation which is expensive (and paid for by the local authority). For this group of housing occupiers, 'pro-active' choice could become coerced choice if they did not bid within a prescribed time limit. Here, the budgetary constraints on the local authority—the need to reduce spending on expensive temporary accommodation—could lead a housing officer making bids on applicants' behalf (Cowan, McDermont and Morgan 2007).

It is in the arena of homelessness that the logic of the choice agenda in social housing has so publicly come into conflict with the logic of administrative justice. A number of successful court appeals against the London Borough of Lambeth have called into question whether CBL can sit comfortably alongside established principles of 'housing need', principles that are concerned with (the now old-fashioned?) attempts to produce social justice in housing.

Existing case law on housing allocation schemes has established that local authorities must give 'reasonable reference' to households with greater housing need. This imposes on CBL schemes a certain degree of complexity and sophistication. There are a number of divergent schemes in operation across the country, many taking as their starting point an approach of banding households according to levels of need (Cowan and Marsh 2004). It is these schemes for prioritising households under CBL that have led to largely successful challenges in the courts. The basic argument put forward in the courts has been that, by lumping together households with varying degrees of need into one band, households with greater need are not given a 'reasonable preference' as required by the Housing Acts.

In *R(A) v Lambeth BC; R(Lindsay) v Lambeth BC*,[11] the CBL schemes were found unlawful because Lambeth's scheme had nine bands into which all households on the waiting list were placed. This included around four per cent of households which were not entitled to reasonable preference. As these households were able to 'compete on equal terms' with households entitled to preference placed in the same band, the scheme was held to be invalid. Lambeth's scheme was also found to be unlawful because it was too simplistic in another attribute: it did not allow for the fact that households could have composite assessments of housing need which would make their need greater relative to those households with only one 'level' of need.

Lambeth argued that with the CBL scheme in place they had fewer refusals of property, leading to reduced rent loss, properties empty for shorter times and therefore more sustainable communities. The judge was unconvinced: the success of the scheme, in his view, was not down to choice itself

> but [to] greater knowledge of what an applicant was prepared to accept. Furthermore, in many ways, the policy provides the antithesis of choice. A realisation that what would otherwise be regarded as substandard accommodation in an unwanted area can be the only way of avoiding an unacceptably long wait is hardly what most would regard as a real choice.[12]

Choice-in-practice thus clashes with administrative law. The simplicity needed to make CBL transparent led to an inability to address the issues of complex housing need—what might be termed the 'social justice' element—and so they were considered illegal. The court's argument should, one would have thought, have put a brake on the rush to promote choice in social housing—at least in areas of high demand. The simplicity required for choice in incompatible with the delivery of some form of 'social justice' to the most vulnerable of families, those without a home.

However, what this particular element of our story forces us to question is how the principles of administrative justice can be played out in the knowledge-power game of choice. In the long run, did it make any difference that the courts found CBL schemes to be illegal? The policy agenda was not brought to a halt. Policy-makers and practitioners continue to tinker with the technologies at their disposal, choice continues to be the dictating factor, and administrative justice, in many respects, remains at the margins.

[11] [2002] HLR 57.
[12] Ibid (Collins J), para 13.

John Clarke, Morag McDermont and Janet Newman

Conclusion: Contested Logics

In this chapter, we have explored the contested logics of consumer choice and administrative justice in the governance of public services. We have used the concept of logics to explore how the conduct of public services is governed, and what happens when emergent logics—such as the logic of consumer choice—are used to displace or subordinate older logics. In the case of consumer choice and administrative justice, the contestation takes on a distinctive quality because the two logics share a commitment to deliver fairness and equality. The meanings and ways of enacting these two concepts are however very different. Equality or fairness comes to be specified in particular and narrow ways—as well as in rather different ways—within the two logics. Translated into the 'small print' of choice within specific services or within specific administrative procedures, the delivery of fairness and equality may often disappoint.

Nevertheless, British governments have remained committed to the concept and logic of consumer choice in public services over the last three decades despite political, academic, professional and popular reservations. Choice—as the governing logic—promises much: popular engagement, the disciplining of recalcitrant public servants, the combination of cost reduction and quality improvements and more. It also promises to disperse or diffuse the 'responsibility of government'—if services are to be delivered (or even co-produced) in the encounter between active consumers and customer-centred service providers, then responsibility for the outcomes must rest there. Attractive though the logic of consumer choice is, it seems difficult to imagine a process of governing public services in which the logic of administrative justice does not play at least a supporting role. To the extent that public services continue to be associated with promises of fairness, equality, equity and justice, choice cannot provide the only governing logic.

Choice is, as we have seen, susceptible to problems of mediation and management in a public service context, particularly where the available resources and level of demand remain out of balance. The mediation of choice leads to the recurrence of two problems. On the one hand, public service choices will be perceived as not like 'real choices' (those conducted through market exchange and only mediated by the cash nexus). People differ as to whether public service choices should be like 'real choices' and market exchange is often perceived as unjust or unequal (producing or reproducing material inequalities). On the other hand, the mediation of choice means that the promised transparency of choice cannot be delivered: something always stands between choice and outcome. As we argued, this is a landscape of potential frustration, mistrust and perceived unfairness and injustice. Here the logic of administrative justice is summoned to restore the promise of equity and fairness.

In the end, we think there are three critical points to make about the involvement of these two governing logics in public services. Their contested co-existence produces instabilities, dilemmas and tensions for those involved in public services (as providers, users, managers, regulators and more) because they carry very different conceptions of the public, of how it is to be served, and of how equality, equity, fairness or justice might be realised. Second, they are not the only governing logics 'in play' in the world of public services. They have to jostle for position not only with each other, but with other logics that claim to be authoritative—forms of professional, scientific or legal expertise (in the case of policing, for example). Finally, it is their capacity to mobilise meanings and motivations that makes them potent logics—and at the core of those meanings is the imagery of equality. For the present, public services are still tangled with concerns about equality—and these two logics have to engage with those imaginings of fairness and justice, and try to manage the gaps between promises and practice.

References

Adler, M (2003) 'A socio-legal approach to administrative justice' 25 *Law and Policy* 323.

AJTC (Administrative Justice and Tribunals Council) (2008) 'British Bill of Rights and Responsibilities: A Right to Administrative Justice', available at www.ajtc.gov.uk/adjust/articles/ajtc_bill_rights.htm.

Bartlett, W, Le Grand, J and Roberts, J (eds) (1998) *A Revolution in Social Policy: Quasi-market reforms in the 1990s* (Bristol, The Policy Press).

Blair, T (2003) *Progress and Justice in the 21st Century*, Fabian Society Annual Lecture, 17 June, available at www.politics.guardian.co.uk/speeches/story/0,11126,979507,00.html.

Blinkhorn, A and Griffiths, S (2008) 'I won't send my child to a sink school' *Sunday Times, News Review*, 23 March, 12.

Cayton, H (2003) *Trust Me, I'm A Patient: Can Healthcare Afford the Informed Consumer?* Speech Delivered to the Royal College of Physicians, BUPA Health Debate, 2 September, London.

Clarke, J (1997) 'Capturing the Customer: Consumerism and Social Welfare.' 1 *Self, Agency and Society* 55.

—— (2007) 'It's not like shopping: relational reasoning and public services', in M Bevir and F Trentman (eds), *Governance, Citizens and Consumers: agency and resistance in contemporary politics* (Basingstoke, Palgrave Macmillan).

—— (2009) 'The People's Police? Citizens, Consumers and Communities' in R Simmons, M Powell and I Greener (eds), *The Consumer in Public Services* (Bristol: The Policy Press).

Clarke, J and Newman, J (1997) *The Managerial State: Power, Politics and Ideology in the Remaking of Social Welfare* (London, Sage).

Clarke, J, Newman, J, Smith, N, Vidler, E and Westmarland, L (2007) *Creating Citizen-Consumers: Changing Publics and Changing Public Services* (London, Sage).

Clarke, J, Smith, N and Vidler, E (2006) 'The Indeterminacy of Choice: political, policy and organisational dilemmas' 5 *Social Policy and Society* 1.

Cowan, D and Marsh, A (2004) 'From Need to Choice: *R(A) v Lambeth LBC; R(Lindsay) v Lambeth LBC*' 67 MLR 478.

—— (2005) 'From need to choice, welfarism to advanced liberalism? Problematics of social housing allocation' 25 *Legal Studies* 22.

Cowan, D and McDermont, M (2006) *Regulating Social Housing: Governing Decline?* (London, Glasshouse).

Cowan, D, McDermont, M and Morgan, K (2008) *Problematic Allocations*, Final Report to the ESRC, available at www.bris.ac.uk/law/research/centres-themes/nominations/nominationsreport.pdf.

Curtis, P and Lipsett, A (2008) 'Fewer parents getting secondary school of their choice for children' *Guardian*, 4 March, available at www.guardian.co.uk/education/2008/mar/04/schools.publicschools.

Department for Children, Schools and Families (DCSF) (2006) *Choice Advice: Guidance for Local Authorities* (Norwich, The Stationary Office).

—— (2008a) *Duty to provide information, advice and assistance: Guidance for local authorities* (Nottingham, DCSF Publications).

—— (2008b) *School Admission Appeals Code* (Norwich, The Stationery Office).

Department for Education and Skills (DfES) (2005) *Higher Standards, Better Schools for All* (London, The Stationery Office).

Department of the Environment, Transport and the Regions (DETR) (2000) *Quality and Choice: A Decent Home for All* (London, DETR).

Forrest, R and Murie, A (1991) *Selling the Welfare State: The Privatisation of Welfare Housing* (London, Routledge).

Foucault, M (1981) *The History of Sexuality: Volume One* (Harmondsworth: Penguin Books).

Galligan, D (1996) *Due Process and Fair Procedures* (Oxford, Clarendon Press).

Gewirtz, S, Ball, S and Bowe, R (1995) *Markets, Choice and Equity in Education* (Buckingham, Open University Press).

Greener, I (2003) 'Who choosing what? The evolution and impact of "choice" in the NHS, and its importance for New Labour' in C Bochel, N Ellison and M Powell (eds), *Social Policy Review* (Bristol, The Policy Press).

Hutton, W (1787) *Courts of Requests: Their Nature, Utility and Powers* (Birmingham, Pearson and Rollason).

Jordan, B (2006) 'Public services and the service economy: individualism and the choice agenda' 35 *Journal of Social Policy* 143.

Lendvai, N and Stubbs, P (2007) 'Policies as translation: situating transnational social policies', in S Hodgson and Z Irving (eds), *Policy Reconsidered: meanings, politics and practices* (Bristol, Policy Press).

Lipsett, A (2007) 'Brighton's school lottery backed by ruling', *Guardian*, 13 July, available online at www.guardian.co.uk/education/2007/jul/13/schools.uk2.

Lipsky, M (1980) *Street-Level Bureaucracy: Dilemmas of the Individual in Public Services* (New York, Russell Sage).

Marston, G (2004) 'Managerialism and Public Housing Reform' 19 *Housing Studies* 5.

McKee, K and Cooper, V (2007) 'The Paradox of Tenant Empowerment: Regulatory and Liberatory Possibilties' December *Housing, Theory and Society* 1.

Ministers of State for Department of Health, Local and Regional Government, and School Standards (2004) *The Case for User Choice in Public Services.* A Joint Memorandum to the Public Administration Select Committee Inquiry into Choice, Voice and Public Services.

Needham, C (2003) *Citizen-consumers: New Labour's marketplace democracy* (London, The Catalyst Forum).
—— (2007) *The reform of public services under New Labour: Narratives of consumerism* (Basingstoke: Palgrave).
Newman, J and Clarke, J (2009) *Publics, Politics and Power: remaking the public in public services* (London, Sage).
Newman, J and Vidler, E (2006) 'Discriminating customers, responsible patients, empowered users: consumerism and the modernisation of health care' 35 *Journal of Social Policy* 193.
Office of Public Services Reform (2002) *Reforming our Services: Principles into Practice* (London, Office of Public Services Reform).
Rooney, B (2007) *How to Win Your School Appeal: Getting your child into the school of your choice*, 2nd edn (London, A and C Black).
Sarat, A (1990) '"The law is all over": Power, Resistance and the Legal Consciousness of the Welfare Poor' 2 *Yale Journal of Law and Humanities* 343.
Somers, M (2008) *Genealogies of Citizenship: Markets, Statelessness, and the Right to Have Rights* (Cambridge, Cambridge University Press).
Westmarland, L and Clarke, J (2009) 'Awkward customers? Policing in a consumer age' in M Barnes and D Prior (eds), *Subversive Citizens: power, resistance and agency in public services* (Bristol: The Policy Press).
Westmarland, L and Smith, N (2004) 'From scumbags to consumers: customer service and the commodification of policing'. Paper presented at the British Criminological Society annual conference, July.
Wilkins, A (2009) *The Slippery Dynamics of School Choice: A Discursive Approach* (PhD thesis, The Open University).

3

Developments in E-government

HELEN MARGETTS AND MARTIN PARTINGTON

Introduction: Contextual Changes and their Implications for Administrative Decision Making

From the 1950s onwards, organisations of all kinds have adopted an increasingly sophisticated array of digital technologies, with profound consequences for organisational decision making and operations. During the first decade of the Millennium, the Internet transformed the way in which many UK citizens interacted with banks, shops, travel companies, airlines, the media, and each other. This paper examines the extent to which a similar change has taken place with respect to technological change in government (known as e-government) and interactions between citizens and government, and considers the implications for administrative justice.

E-government may be defined as the use by government of information technology internally and to interact with citizens, businesses, voluntary organisations and other governments. Defined in this way, e-government has been developing in Britain for the last 50 years, since the first computers entered the 'back office' of large transaction processing departments (such as the Post Office) in the 1950s. From that time on, most departments and agencies became increasingly reliant on complex networks of information technology systems. Administrative decision making is crucially dependent on these systems and so is policy making, as these systems have been shown to be policy critical and technological innovation opens up new potential for policy innovation (Margetts 1999). But these earlier information systems were largely internally facing, with few implications for how citizens interacted with government, because they were based on technologies used by government but not by citizens. In contrast, the Internet offered real potential for transformation of government's interactions with the outside world, because of its widespread use throughout social, political and economic life. Whereas in 1995 the Internet had barely touched either UK society or government, a decade later virtually all government departments and agencies and local governments had a website. The UK government was maintaining literally thousands of websites and, for many people, this electronic front end or 'window' on government was the first place they would look when needing to undertake some kind of interaction with government.

The governments of most developed countries have put considerable resources into developing e-government. E-government is big business in the twenty-first century, amounting to over one per cent of GDP in most industrialised nations and around £14 billion annually in the UK according to recent estimates (Cabinet Office 2005). Particularly ambitious (and expensive) plans include the £12 billion dedicated to the NHS IT strategy and the Home Office's proposed identity card scheme including a national identity register, at an estimated cost of around £5 billion (Home Office 2008).

So e-government, including the new electronic 'front-end' on government and the connected information systems threaded throughout administrative operations, changes the context of administrative justice. This chapter outlines the development of e-government in the UK, identifying the areas where the implications for administrative justice could be most important. In simple terms, administrative justice can be deemed to comprise:

— getting decisions right first time and, where errors do occur, correcting them as soon as possible;
— enabling people to understand better their rights and obligations;
— an overall commitment to fairness.

This chapter considers these three dimensions in turn. The first section looks at the context for administrative decision making and 'getting things right' by considering how digital technologies have been incorporated into government (the supply side of e-government). The accuracy of administrative decision making and the capacity to recognise and correct errors relies crucially on the information held by government in information systems in the 'back office' of e-government. So this section investigates the organisational changes that have taken place during the last decade to develop and manage the UK e-government effort and drive forward the agenda. These changes have taken place at the centre of government, in central agencies; at the level of departments and agencies; and through widespread contracting out of the IT function to private sector computer services providers.

The second section of the paper considers the context of 'enabling people to better understand their rights and obligations' by evaluating how and how much citizens are using e-government at the 'front-end' (the 'demand' side of e-government). Research has shown that for e-government, just as for e-commerce, information seeking has moved online for those citizens who use the Internet. So the quality of government's online presence is crucial in enabling people to understand better their rights and obligations. This section covers both the extent to which citizens are using e-government, and the nature of that use, using an experimental investigation into how citizens look for government-related information on the Internet.

The third section considers how e-government might affect the 'overall fairness' of governmental administration. In particular, while the Internet may radically enhance the capacity of some citizens to determine their rights and obligations, what of those people who do not have access to the Internet and how can government reach out to them? Furthermore, the section considers the effect of e-government on government's 'nodality', one of the four 'tools' of government policy identified by Christopher Hood in 1983 and discussed in the context of the digital age by Hood and Margetts in 2006 (Hood 1983; Hood and Margetts 2007). Hood described nodality as the characteristic of being at the centre of social and informational networks; most public policies involve government using its capacity to disseminate to and collect information from citizens in some way and some policies are based entirely on the use of nodality. Of the four 'tools' of government (the others are authority, treasure and organisation), nodality is the most economical in terms of governmental effort and minimising 'trouble, vexation and oppression' on the citizenry. So both governments and citizens could have much to gain in administrative justice terms from the potential for government to increase nodality via the use of digital technologies.

The Development of E-government in the UK

In common with most advanced industrialised nations, the UK government has put considerable organisational resources into e-government over the past decade. Of course, as noted earlier, e-government in the sense of the use of IT inside organisations to aid or replace administrative processes has been part of UK government for much longer than a decade with the first computers entering government in the 1950s (Lamb 1973; Margetts 1999). By the 1990s, the UK government bureaucracy was entirely reliant on a complex network of information systems, with virtually no department or agency 'technology free'. These systems received little public or political attention (except when they went wrong) until the rise of the Internet. Gradually, as e-commerce started to take off in the 1990s and Internet penetration crept up, policy-makers started to realise the potential of new web-based technologies. In part, the impetus came from overseas, particularly from Australia, which developed a reputation as a world leader in e-government that peaked in 1999, and the USA, where Vice-President Al Gore made the 'information superhighway' a corner stone of his and President Clinton's administrative reform programme (the National Performance Review) in the mid 1990s.

Central Organisation of E-government

Political attention was accompanied by organisational and financial resources. Until the late 1990s the network of information systems and computers that was the precursor to e-government, was managed by the central computer and telecommunications agency, the CCTA, which until 1984 'owned' all the computers in British central government. The agency was passed from Cabinet Office to Treasury and back again, finally meeting its demise in 1999, when e-government finally caught the attention of politicians, with ministers from both the larger political parties promising to be the British Al Gore in the run up to the 1997 election. The Conservative government created the Central Information Technology Unit inside the Cabinet Office, an elite group which took over any residual strategic activities from the CCTA (which was exiled to Norwich and eventually completely run down). From 1999, the UK's policy-making apparatus was 'strengthened considerably' (Dunleavy et al 2007). The Office of the e-Envoy (OeE) replaced the CITU in the Cabinet Office and was given the lead role, with a core policy objective of achieving a target for electronic service delivery by making all government services available electronically by 2005, as well as wider 'e-society' aims of making the UK the best environment in the world for e-commerce by 2002 and ensuring that everyone who wanted it had access to the Internet by 2005. At its peak in 2001, the agency employed around 250 staff and incurred annual running costs of around £50 million. The office closed down the CCTA's initial government portal (the optimistically named open.gov.uk) and replaced it with a new central government website in 2001 (www.ukonline.gov.uk), which was the centrepiece of the government's investment programme.

By 2002, the UK was committing more resources centrally to promoting the development of electronic public services than other similar countries and the Office of the e-Envoy was visited by envious officials from countries such as the Netherlands and Australia. But the outcomes were somewhat mixed. A National Audit Office report in 2002 found that although the 2005 target regime had been a useful incentive for encouraging departments to offer services electronically, a focus on availability rather than take-up meant that the take up of e-government was disappointing and there was 'relatively little up to date and good quality information about the development of central government on the web' (Dunleavy et al 2002: 3). The ukonline portal had been dismantled and replaced by www.direct.gov.uk, an expensive initiative with many critics, some of whom created a parody site www.directionlessgov.com to illustrate how the by-now ubiquitous search engine Google was a better tool for finding government information than the official government portal. By 2004, conveniently timed for the 2005 targets, the Office of the e-Envoy was no more and had been replaced by an e-Government Unit also in the Cabinet Office, but with a rather different remit and a far smaller budget. In November 2005, the e-Government Unit announced its latest e-Government strategy under the title *Transformational Government*, based around the three key themes of citizen-centric government, the development of shared services, and IT professionalism (Cabinet Office 2005). The strong welcome they received from across the IT industry indicated that the early hopes of e-government had not, as yet, reached fruition.

By 2007, responsibility for the development of e-government rested with the Delivery and Transformation Group (formerly the e-Government Unit) in the Cabinet Office, working with the Chief Information Officer's Council with the brief to drive forward the Government's strategy for IT-enabled change in the provision of public services; to review delivery of departments' programmes for making efficiency savings through e-enablement; and to make recommendations as necessary to the Committee on Public Services and Public Expenditure. The government programme was overseen by the PSX (E) Cabinet sub-committee, chaired by the Chief Secretary to the Treasury. The total annual IT expenditure for central government was around £6.5 billion (Dunleavy et al 2007). Within that figure, the cost of directly running government websites was around £208 million (ibid: 23).

At this point, policy took a strongly centralised position. The aim was to reduce the number of government websites (of which there were by this time 2,500, according to the Transformational Government report, although earlier drafts of the report suggested 4,000), mainly by moving principal service delivery and related information provision functions over time to two government 'super sites': Directgov, oriented towards citizens; and businesslink.gov.uk, oriented towards firms and enterprises. Departments would retain their own 'corporate sites', containing chiefly departmental information for professional audiences, policy documents and reports. The process of transition was scheduled for the period up to 2011. It is notoriously difficult to measure the size of a domain, but a National Audit Office report in 2007 suggested that the UK government domain (ie, every website with an address ending in '.gov.uk', which includes both local and central government) amounted to well over 10 million pages (Dunleavy et al 2007). The new strategy would involve moving a significant proportion of this content over to Directgov. The 2007 NAO report on *Government on the Internet* (ibid) identified a number of risks with this strategy, particularly that one central site could not fulfil the information needs of the customers of all departments, and that, with such centralised provision of information, the remaining corporate sites would tend to stagnate and become out of date, meaning information on specific policy areas would actually be harder to find than before. At the time of writing it was too early to say whether these risks had materialised, but Directgov grew rapidly from a relatively small site of 4,000 pages in 2007 to 20,000 pages in 2009 with 1.8 million 'in-links' from other sites.

An important question that needs to be asked in the context of administrative justice is whether it is advisable to have government as the sole or principal source of information about rights and entitlements. One of the principles that lawyers bring to justice systems generally is that of independence. It is perfectly proper for governments to seek to explain the rules and practices they adopt in the delivery of the wide range of social policies that they offer to the public. But it is also important that there are available to the public independent and authoritative accounts of those policies which highlight the difficult problems of implementation and interpretation which government websites may be tempted to gloss over. The suggestion for a Google Rights service, somewhat analogous to Google Maps, is one that should be explored further (Taghioff 2007: 28).

Supplying E-government at the Organisational Level

E-government is not, of course, supplied from the centre alone. Every government department and agency must to some extent tackle the challenges of the digital age. For organisations of all kinds, information technology has necessitated completely new skills, of which four types may be distinguished (OECD 2004: 209). First, from the 1960s onwards, when systems first spread throughout government, any medium-to-large agency has required IT specialists, who have the ability to develop, operate and maintain IT systems. Second, many organisations require at least some 'advanced users': competent users of advanced and often sector-specific, software tools. Third, since the spread of personal computers across the desktops of administrative organisations, most white-collar workers are required to be 'basic users' of generic tools, such as word processing, spreadsheet packages and the Internet. Fourth, in the private sector the rise of e-commerce has led to the need for e-business skills, that is, for those skills that are needed to exploit new business opportunities provided by IT, particularly the Internet, at the highest organisational levels, particularly since the Internet has been shown to play an increasingly important role in a company's competitiveness (OECD 2004). It can be argued that IT is equally important for contemporary policy making and that government officials too need such skills.

All of these new skills requirements have posed distinct challenges to government organisations, but the first was particularly challenging as it necessitated the establishment and rapid growth of a new 'IT profession', rather than the re-training of existing generalist staff. Universal shortages of the requisite skills meant that government agencies have often had to compete with the commercial world to attract staff. In the early days of government IT, when the UK government had a reputation as an IT innovator, it was easier to tempt staff at the cutting edge of the new profession into government. Departments started to build up information technology divisions that could build, maintain and develop their mainframe accounting and transaction processing systems. In those days, such projects were so large, the technology so expensive and the required expertise so specialised, that governments were more likely than commercial firms to be able to afford the necessary investment in infrastructure and training. As information systems spread across government, the need for IT staff in government was massive; in the UK by 1993, £500 million was being spent annually on information technology staff costs across central government departments, that is, 22 per cent of IT expenditure (Kable 1994: 16). Meanwhile, commercial firms had overtaken governments in terms of innovation, and were offering more interesting work, at far higher salaries than government agencies constrained by public sector pay scales. The demand accelerated as information technology in general and the Internet in particular became increasingly associated with competitiveness and productivity. Continual competition for technically skilled personnel posed a major challenge to most governments and in the UK, the supply of IT staff was recognised as a 'recurrent problem' as early as 1978 (Civil Service Department 1978: 50).

In the last decade, the fourth of the skills requirements generated by IT has also proved particularly important in the UK: the requirement for officials at departmental and agency level to realise the potential of e-government. From the supply side perspective, a number of cultural barriers to e-government have been identified (Margetts and Dunleavy 2002). What might be thought of as defining features of UK administrative culture—hierarchy, uniformity and solemnity—can all work against the development of new internet-based ways of working. And channel rivalry, where government officials lack the interest or incentives to create new internet-based channels which replace traditional ways of working, can also slow progress on e-government. For example, channel rivalry can lead to a tendency to find reasons for inaction and for exaggerated risk-averse behaviour on e-government issues. This is due to an unwillingness to divert resources away from established ways of doing things towards developing internet communications or transactions and a tendency to regard putting services on the Internet as something that must be added on to all the activities that the agency does already. It can also lead to the attitude that no e-government innovation at all can be responsibly entered into until a clear financial case for it has been made, and a high rate of return established, but without making any effort to map the consequences of not developing internet-based interactions, to calculate the risk of growing obsolescence in the agency's IT infrastructure or methods of working, or to recognise that a reluctance to develop e-government can lead to a cumulative lag in the agency's progress (Margetts and Dunleavy 2002).

The creation of a new service or agency can provide significant opportunities for the development of new processes that embrace the potential use of Information Technology. In the administrative justice context, this is clearly evident in the recent establishment of the Tribunals Service, which offers considerable scope for the use of the Internet not only to provide information to citizens about what tribunals do, but also to facilitate the ways in which citizens can carry out the interactions with the Service in pursuing their appeals. For example, the Internet can enable citizens to lodge appeals online, to discover the progress of their appeal, and even obtain a determination of the appeal. The Parking Appeals Service, for example, undertakes all its business online. The Internet also has great potential to help individual appellants—who often lack legal (or other) representation in presenting their cases—understand how tribunals and other decision-taking processes work. It could also and in appropriate contexts, facilitate different forms of complaints handling—for example, through online mediation.

Government Under Contract

In fact, the private sector has played a major role in taking on the challenge of supplying e-government, as the last decade has seen the finishing touches to a development that started to spread across UK government in the 1980s—the outsourcing of government information technology. By 1995, virtually every department and agency was involved in a major relationship with at least one major computer services provider (Margetts 1999). These corporations play an ever increasing role in shaping e-government.

In the UK, the market of firms providing computer services for government has grown enormously in the last twenty years. By 1993, 23 per cent of IT expenditure was spent on commercial services, rising to 30 per cent in 1995 (Margetts 1999). The market in the UK was shaped by the distinctive characteristics of public management reform that took place concurrently, in which contracting out played a central part. Centralised contracting out strategies under the auspices of new public management during the 1980s and early 1990s (formalised under Market Testing and Compulsory Competitive Tendering) and distinctive models of contract financing in the 1990s (the Private Finance Initiative) led to a particularly radical form of IT outsourcing (or 'totalsourcing'), in which government agencies retained very little expertise internally. Agencification, through the Next Steps programme, also played a role, as in some departments the information technology divisions were made into executive agencies (such as the information technology arm of the Department of Transport, the DVOIT) and then tendered for contracts. Progressively throughout the 1990s, government contracts became so large that only the largest companies could tender for them, meaning that the market of firms providing computer services for government became increasingly centralised. By the early 2000s the UK market was distinctly oligopolistic, with the top five companies holding around 90 per cent of large government IT contracts in terms of contract value and one company in particular, Electronic Data Systems, holding over 60 per cent of contract value up until 2004 (Dunleavy et al 2006).

In this way, as large scale IT divisions have been progressively replaced by contract relationships, UK e-government has taken a different organisational 'shape' from earlier forms of government administration, with these relationships playing an important role. Research has shown this pattern is quite distinctive in the UK compared with other industrialised nations. In the US, for example, a tighter regulatory regime, as well as legislation specifically geared at involving smaller firms, has led to a less oligopolistic market, where the top five companies hold only around 20 per cent of government business (in comparison to the 80 per cent figure for the UK noted above). In Canada, Japan and the Netherlands, domestic companies hold larger shares of the government IT services market than in the UK, ranging from a mixed market in Canada to an almost wholly domestic market in Japan. In Canada, Denmark and the Netherlands—all with reputations for success in the e-government field—governments outsource lower proportions of their information technology; indeed in Canada, representatives of computer services providers described the federal government as their 'greatest competitor' (Dunleavy and Margetts et al 2007).

In the UK, the Private Finance Initiative was abandoned for IT projects in 2004, with the Treasury admitting 'difficulties with achieving appropriate risk transfer in IT PFI' (HM Treasury 2003) and announcing a return to 'conventional procurement methods'. However, the legacy is there in a number of long-term high-value partnerships between UK government departments and their suppliers. PFI fuelled the existent trends for UK government IT contracts to increase in size, and for the distinctive shape of the UK contracting market, meaning that large-scale long-term contracts will be a feature of UK government IT contracting for decades to come and these companies will continue to shape the future of government administration in general as well as e-government specifically.

Digital Era Governance

By 2004, some commentators were beginning to suggest that digital technologies were so central to governmental operations and policy making that 'digital era governance' could be regarded as a new 'paradigm' for public administration (Dunleavy and Margetts et al 2005, 2006), replacing the former dominance of the so-called 'New Public Management' (NPM) (Barzelay, 2000; Hood, 1985, 1994; Pollit et al 2007) as a model for public management reform. Digital era governance includes a range of information technology-centered changes, involving the re-integration of governmental processes and organisations, a more holistic approach to treating citizens and increasingly radical forms of digitalisation.

Reintegration includes: reversing fragmentation caused by 20 years of 'new public management reform', in which hundreds of central government and micro-local agencies were created; 'joining up' governmental departments and agencies; and partnership, working across organisational boundaries. As noted above, the creation of the new Tribunals Service provides a significant opportunity for such re-integration in the administrative justice sphere, bringing together, as it does, a range of disparate appeal systems.

Needs-based Holism includes: refocusing organisational structures and processes around clients; paying attention to the end-to-end redesign of processes; 'one-stop' processes that allow citizens to initiate or complete several dealings with government with one interaction.

Digitalisation includes: electronic service delivery; new forms of automation that can lead to disintermediation or 'zero-touch' services, where no public service official need touch a transaction; and new forms of 'open-book' governance, where digital applications allow the revealing of government decision making and processes and increasing transparency in government.

The combination of these changes could bring far more radical change to the context of administrative decision making than earlier moves towards e-government, some of which are discussed below. Under Digital era governance, organisational change will take place to the extent where governmental organisations will 'become' their websites, the organisation just a support structure for the online presence, the information architecture and connected 'customer management' systems. But Digital era governance is a potential model for public service reform, an ideal type that is developing to greater or lesser extent across developed countries. There are alternative scenarios as to how far Digital era governance will be recognised as a coherent phenomenon and implemented successfully. The danger in the UK must be that the way in which IT has been outsourced actually cuts across much of the Digital era governance agenda, with large long term single agency contracts working against re-integration of fragmented departments. Another possible scenario is that managers and political elites, long educated in the NPM School, will find it difficult to change direction and will allow state agencies to fall behind the curve of rationalisation and innovation processes, leaving the government sector tending to residualise as a laggard sector.

Administrative Justice Implications of E-government

So how does e-government measure up in the UK and what of its potential to enhance administrative decision making? One challenge here is the reliability of large government IT systems, which has been a problematic area for government information technology in the UK. Here it is difficult to record any major success in the last decade, although at the sub-national level in London, the Congestion Charge (introduced in 2003) and the Oyster Card ticketing scheme (2004) provide notable exceptions. The comment of one opposition politician that 'government plus IT equals disaster'[1] and the depressingly frank comment made by then UK Trade Secretary, Patricia Hewitt, on the BBC programme *Question Time* (25th September, 2003), that 'Great big IT projects, databases and the rest of it have a horrible habit of going wrong' still hold an element of truth in the UK context. In every year over the last two decades, it would be possible to find press reports of at least one deeply troubled government IT project.[2] Examples of government agencies which have suffered major and costly failure of information systems or projects include the Passports Agency (in 2001, when a new system for allocating passports was paralysed); the Contributions Agency (with the second version of the National Insurance Recording System); the Child Support Agency (in 2002, when a new system rocketed to £200 million, £50 million over budget, and in 2005, when it was estimated that the agency spent more on administration than it collected in maintenance from absent fathers); and the Immigration and Naturalisation Directorate (left with 12,000 letters unanswered after a new system was delayed and finally abandoned in 2001). Research evidence suggests that the UK compares badly against the USA, Japan, Australia, Canada, New Zealand and the Netherlands in the 'scrap rate' of government IT projects in a seven-country study funded by the UK Economic and Social Research Council (Dunleavy et al 2006).

Most projects do, however, eventually result in the creation or development of information systems, and there is no doubt that the context in which government attempts to 'get decisions right first time and where errors do occur, correct

[1] Comment made by Richard Allen, MP at IPPR seminar, Westminster House, London, March 2004.

[2] See Margetts and Willcocks (1993) for a summary of notorious IT project failures prior to the 1990s and Organ (2003: 32) for a list of 15 more recent disasters.

them as soon as possible' is heavily shaped by a myriad of large scale information systems and databases, created over decades. A recent report identified over 40 large scale data holdings of personal data about citizens across central government (Anderson et al 2009). The report was controversial because of the allegations it made about the legality of some of these data holdings in terms of data privacy. But this and other work have clearly shown both the scale and importance of these databases, and what has become to be known as the 'identity management' of citizens' personal information in administrative decision making. The Department for Work and Pensions (DWP), for example, maintains over 150 separate systems feeding into the processing and payments of benefits. The five largest systems include the *Customer Information System*, described by DWP as 'one of the largest databases in Europe', which will eventually hold 85 million records and transfer data from existing sources into a centralised database that is available over secure channels to 80,000 members of DWP staff, 60,000 users from seven other government departments and over 445 local authorities. The *Customer Management System*, which supports Jobcentre Plus, is used for processing benefit applications, gathering information and evidence to support claims for Income Support, Jobseekers Allowance, Incapacity Benefit and other JCP benefits. Another system, the *Customer Account Manager* was introduced by the Pension Service in 2003 to administer the Pension Credit benefit, allowing application information to be collected, decisions to be made and benefits awarded and paid, as well as passing on information collected on Housing and Council Tax benefits to the relevant Local Authority. Meanwhile a range of legacy systems use software dating back to the 'Operational Strategy' systems developed in the 1980s (see Margetts 1999). They store basic customer information and details on payments and are used by Benefit Decision Centres to decide on and register decisions on applications for Job Seekers' Allowance, a benefit for people of working age who are seeking work. Most of DWP's interactions with citizens and most of their administrative decision making rely on a complex mesh of inputs and outputs to more than one of these systems. Several systems are unable to interact with each other. Some processes are greatly hampered by the lack of an overall screen for data input, so the official must view many screens and will have to manually check personal details against the paper application and the electronic details, to spot a change of circumstances, for example. Failure to make effective two-way links between systems can have vital implications for citizens' circumstances; for example, when citizens are withheld Job Seekers' Allowance because of failure to attend an interview at a Job Centre, local benefits relating to housing and Council Tax may be withdrawn due to an automatic data feed between systems, even though they may in fact still be eligible for these benefits even when JSA is withdrawn (see Dunleavy et al 2009).

This brief snapshot of DWP provides a sense of the complexity of the 'identity management' of citizens in UK government and its importance for administrative decision making. In 2002, the Home Office developed a National Identity Scheme, originally intended to replace the current 'mosaic' of documents with which citizens prove their identities (driving licences, passports, etc.) but also a major rationalisation of government's holding of personal data, through a central database of identity information (the National Identity Register) to underpin the provision of a wide range of services and for intelligence and law enforcement purposes. The original plans were greatly scaled down in response to widespread criticism of the costs and risks of the programme and in the revised plan the National Identity Register was intended only to store basic biographical information such as names, addresses and dates of birth and National Insurance numbers. Plans for a 'gold standard' identity database were shelved, with the existing Department for Work and Pensions Customer Information System being used as the basis for the National Identity Register. The Scheme was to be delivered 'collaboratively' with a 'wide range of other Government departments' described as 'partners' and including the Identity and Passport Service, the Foreign and Commonwealth Office, and the new Border Agency. In 2009, even this revised plan looked unlikely to survive; both the opposition Conservative party and ministers within the Labour administration pledged to abandon the scheme due to its cost and unproven benefits and the 2008 delivery plan was removed from the Home Office web site. But clearly the development of some form of modern system for managing citizens' identities will be a crucial challenge for any incoming government in 2010.

Citizens' Interactions with E-government

A key indicator of the likely impact of e-government on administrative justice must be the extent to which citizens are using it and how they are doing so. For these citizens, e-government has great potential to enhance their access to governmental information and their rights and obligations, the second dimension of administrative justice noted above. This extends not just to ways in which citizens interact with government at their first point of contact, but also if and when they seek to complain about or challenge a decision or the way in which it has been taken.

This subsection covers two ways of considering how citizens use e-government to access government-related information of this kind, first by looking at the available evidence on the extent to which citizens are using the Internet to interact with government and second, by looking at some experimental evidence on how citizens actually experience e-government when they use the Internet to look for government-related information.

Usage of E-government

With respect to usage e-government in the UK got off to a slow start. In 2005, the Oxford Internet Survey (Dutton et al 2005) found that only 24 per cent of respondents reported some kind of e-government interaction in the previous 12 months, up only marginally on 2003. These figures for usage of e-government contrasted strongly for other online activities such as e-commerce and e-travel; the same survey found that 87 per cent of users used the Internet to look up product information, 66 per cent used the Internet to search for information about local events, and 61 per cent used it to access current news bulletins. When it comes to interactions other than information seeking, the differences between use of the Internet for non-governmental and governmental activities were still starker. While only 6 per cent of users had used the Internet to pay for government services, taxes, fines and licences, 71 per cent had used it to book travel, 54 per cent had used it download or listen to music, and 48 per cent had used it to play games and 45 per cent had used it to bank online.

However, by 2007 these figures started to shift. In the 2007 survey, of the 67 per cent of the population who used the Internet, 46 per cent had interacted with government electronically during the previous year. But they still lagged behind the 90 per cent of Internet users who had sought product information and the 79 per cent who had bought products online (Dutton and Helsper 2007). And, according to cross-national data, the usage of e-government in the UK remained low in comparison with other European Countries. In 2008, Eurostat found that 26 per cent of UK citizens had 'interacted with public authorities online' in the last three months, compared with nearly 50 per cent in the Netherlands and 41 per cent in France.

In 2009, the same survey showed a sharper increase in e-government usage: 59 per cent of users undertook at least one e-government activity online, compared to 46 per cent in 2007 and 39 per cent in 2005. This increase was significant across all the measured interactions with government. Information seeking was still the most common citizen-government interaction and the most common information seeking activities were looking for information about local council services (35 per cent of users) and central government services (33 per cent), followed by looking for information on schools and education (27 per cent). Most other activities were undertaken online by between one-tenth and one-fifth of users (13 per cent to 20 per cent). Thus, finally, the frequency of online transactions, such as paying for government services, taxes, fines and licences, was starting to catch up with information seeking, having increased more dramatically than information seeking in the previous two years.

The figures cited above show an apparently modest demand for e-government in the UK, in comparison with other countries and in comparison with the demand for e-commerce and e-banking. But the potential for change—rather than the reality—is shown clearly by the responses to other questions in the Oxford Internet Survey. Respondents are asked 'where they would go to first' if they needed to find out various pieces of information or undertake certain activities and were offered a range of choices for their response such as a book or directory, the telephone or visiting a local office or shop. In 2007, nearly half of all respondents said that they would go to Internet first to 'find the name of your MP' if they didn't know it already, while over half said that they would go to the Internet first if they were planning a journey or booking a holiday. A more modest 40 per cent said that they would go to the Internet first if they needed to find information about their taxes, suggesting perhaps that UK Internet users have lower expectations of the online presence of governments than than of other organisations. By 2009 these figures had risen again, with 56 per cent of citizens saying they would go to the Internet first to find the name of their MP and 48 per cent saying they would do so to get information about their taxes.

These figures suggest that a significant proportion of the population (around 50 per cent and growing) interact with government online as far as possible and indeed do not expect to do so in any other way. For this group, the potential for e-government is unlimited. For the remainder of Internet users, there is clearly potential for using e-government although it is not their first 'port of call'.

Experiencing E-government: Experimental Evidence

Another way of determining the extent to which e-government is helping citizens to determine their rights and obligations is to look at actual behaviour on the Internet and how easy it is to find government-related information. Detailed data on how people actually use the Internet is difficult to obtain, being a carefully guarded secret of key gate-keeping corporations such as Google. It is particularly difficult with respect to government due to the small proportion of people's time spent online that relates to government. But a research team led by the first author of this chapter has used a range of user experiments to assess how Internet users experience government's online provision when they look for government-related information, particularly information about their rights to benefits and services. The experiments were carried out in OXLAB, an experimental laboratory developed by the first author in Oxford. Subjects were provided with a number of questions to answer, the relevant information for which we knew to be available on one or more government sites (in particular, the UK government portal, www.direct.gov.uk). Subjects were given an hour to answer as many questions as possible and were incentivised via a turn-up fee and a small additional fee for each question correctly answered. We carried out two series of experiments. The first set was conducted for a National Audit Office study of UK *Government on the Internet* (Dunleavy et al 2007) for which the first author was part of the research team. These experiments explored behaviour under two treatments: in one group subjects were allowed to use any method they liked to find the information, while the subjects were directed to use the UK government portal, the cross-government site www.direct.gov.uk and could use internal but not external search engines. In the second experiment carried out in July 2007, there were also two treatments: one the same as in the first experiments, where subjects could use any method they liked including search engines, and second, where subjects could do what they like but were given a 'tip' directing them to a government website that contained the relevant information (such as Directgov itself, the parliament site or the European Union site). We wanted to use these different treatments to assess the effect of government strategies to direct citizens towards their sites (through a cross-government portal, or through directing citizens to the official source of information) on the ease with which they were able to answer a number of government-related questions.

These experiments (reported in full in Dunleavy et al 2007 and in Escher et al 2008) revealed a number of findings about how people look for and find government-related information, some of which are particularly pertinent for administrative justice. First, most citizens use search engines to find what they want to know and Google is overwhelmingly the search engine of choice. Secondly, our subjects only rarely searched beyond the first ten results. Even where subjects were offered a 'tip' (ie, the name of the government site where such information could be found), people who followed the tip would use a search engine significantly less often but, interestingly, even if they did, in 60 per cent of cases they did not find the tip helpful or felt it would have been quicker to use Google. They also exhibited a surprisingly wide variety of search strategies, suggesting that search behaviour could be quite difficult for government organisations to predict and highlighting the need for detailed analysis of browser-based usage statistics.

The experiments also revealed the difficulty of directing citizens to government information. As noted above, current UK government strategy is that all citizens using or looking for government information should be directed to the site www.direct.gov.uk. Yet, in our experiments, this site was hardly used where people could choose. The information was on the site, but was not easily visible to users of other routes that Google suggested would be quicker. In our first experiment, for those people who could choose their sources of information freely in the open search treatment, Directgov was rarely used to answer the questions. On average, about one out of seven questions (15 per cent) in this treatment was answered by accessing information from Directgov at some point. In our second experiment, subjects who did not use the tip accessed Directgov on average for only one question in ten.

We also found a lot of competition for visibility: for many subjects, we found that non-governmental sources were often the preferred choice. In our first experiment, for those subjects who were free to use open search, almost half the questions (44 per cent) were answered using non-governmental sources. Even in our second experiment, where some subjects were pointed towards government sites, of all questions, less than half (47 per cent) were using the website of a governmental or quasi-governmental body. For obvious reasons (all of our tips were governmental sites), people who followed our tip used significantly more governmental sites (59 per cent versus 41 per cent). However, even for those people who followed the tip, about 40 per cent of the questions were answered using non-governmental sites.

We found a high variation in the ease with which questions were answered, but in general neither the 'tip' of an official source, nor the use of the government portal, meant that they were answered more easily. For four questions, the tip made little difference but, for four others, the subjects who followed the tip took significantly longer than those who did not. Only for two questions did using the tip save time. In our first experiment, our subjects spent on average about 30 seconds more on answering a question in the cross-government site treatment before answering it (or deciding to skip it) than subjects in the open search treatment (Dunleavy et al 2007: 2).

Perhaps most importantly for the purposes of this chapter, some of the rights-based questions were among the most difficult to answer. We asked five questions that required subjects to look for information about their rights, such as the right to free prescriptions, a minimum wage, the right to appeal against a school that had been allocated, and the right to complain against a public or private decision. Two questions served as good examples of how government can use the Internet to provide rights information for citizens in an easily accessible way: questions on school admissions appeals and on the minimum wage were answered quickly, with few clicks, and predominantly from government sources. But the other questions posed serious problems, with a third of subjects being unable to answer them correctly and quite often skipping them completely. The EU site in particular offered very little help for our subjects on airline delay compensation. What is more, it emerged that even those who used the site had trouble in finding the correct information for this question, as it was obviously difficult to understand (both on the EU as well as the airline's site). There were also no alternative governmental sources that could be substituted for the unhelpful EU site. For the other two questions, there were a number of governmental sources in place (Directgov and NHS respectively) but they were not easy to find with Google. A question about how to complain to HSBC bank was particularly difficult: many people who did not use the tip had trouble finding complaints information on the HSBC website and about a third answered incorrectly or just skipped the question. This is clearly an area where government sites should be more visible, as banks such as HSBC may not be forthcoming with information on how to appeal against their decisions. But it is not only the low visibility on Google that causes problems: it is also hard to find the information once one is on the correct site as even half of those who used our tip eventually consulted a search engine to find a suitable site. Prescription information was especially hard to locate on the site as people spent a longer time answering when they did not use Google straight away.

An Overall Commitment to Fairness in E-government?

As noted in the introduction, e-government has the potential to affect the overall fairness of governmental administration. In particular, while the previous section discussed the behaviour of users of the Internet, the fact that a significant proportion of UK citizens still does not use the Internet has implications for equality in government treatments, given that online channels have received so much attention and resources in recent years.

'Digital Divides' in the Demand for E-government

So what of those citizens who do not use the Internet? The 'digital divide' between those who have access to the Internet and those who do not is often quoted as a reason why e-government cannot become universal and other channels have to be kept open. The Oxford Internet Survey (2003, 2005, 2007 and 2009) has shown a slow and steady increase in Internet penetration in the UK throughout the 2000s, from 58 per cent in 2003 to 70 per cent in 2009 (Dutton et al 2009). By 2009, 70 per cent of Britons were using the Internet. Of the 30 per cent who did not use the Internet, one-fifth (21 per cent) planned to get access during the following year and there was a stable group of households (around 6 per cent of the total) who had had access to the Internet in the past but did not currently have access to it. The percentage of Britons who have never used the Internet decreased from 35 per cent in 2003 to 23 per cent in 2009. In contrast to other countries, where many users of the Internet do so in Internet cafes or other external locations, in Britain Internet use is almost synonymous with home access: only 4.5 per cent of Internet users do not have home access (Dutton et al 2009).

There is evidence to suggest that digital 'exclusion' is related to various other kinds of social disadvantage, such as social and economic exclusion. Research suggests that people who suffer deep social exclusion are four times more likely to be disengaged from the Internet (Helsper 2008). The Oxford Internet surveys show that non-users of the Internet continued to be differentiated in terms of their age, income and education, particularly in terms of their age. Only 34 per cent of retired people used the Internet in 2009 (up from 22 per cent in 2003, but fairly static between 2005 and 2009), compared with 86 per cent of employed people and 100 per cent of students. Among people with basic education (up to secondary school level) only 49 per cent use the Internet while most of those (93 per cent) with university education did so (Dutton et al 2009). The gap in Internet usage between those with basic and higher education is increasing. Similarly, those in the highest income category are more than twice as likely to use the Internet as those in the lowest income category.

The figures have implications for administrative justice in the digital era. As shown in the previous section, citizens who use the Internet are likely to spend less time and to experience lower transaction costs finding information, including information about their rights and obligations, than those who do not. Those who do not use the Internet are less likely to have easy access to this information, particularly as online channels become the principal way in which the government disseminates information to citizens. They are likely to be most disadvantaged in social, economic and educational terms, and probably more likely to be in need of such information. In this sense, digital exclusion can have a 'reinforcing' detrimental effect on fairness, as those most in need of services and information online may be the least likely to access it. For example, although finding online health information is the fastest growing area of Internet use (Dutton and Helsper 2007), in 2009 only 41 per cent of people with a health or disability problem used the

Internet, significantly less than the proportion of people without a health problem (Dutton et al, 2009).

It also needs to be remembered that the vast majority of websites currently providing information about rights and entitlements do so primarily through the provision of written information. Thus 'digital exclusion' may not just be a question of the accessibility of people to the hardware required to access the Internet. There may also be significant problems of illiteracy or inability to use or understand English that also have the effect of excluding citizens from the services available on the Internet. Of course, the Internet provides limitless opportunities for providing information in other ways—visual and audio, and in varieties of language. But these approaches need to become a central feature of website design.

For government, there may be a way around this tendency to unfairness in the digital era, due to evidence suggesting that even non-users may be able to access e-government indirectly. The 2007 Oxford Internet Survey found that 73 per cent of non-users thought that, if they needed to use the Internet, they 'definitely' or 'probably' knew someone who would be able to access it for them. For lapsed users this figure was even higher (88 per cent), suggesting perhaps that lapsing from Internet use could be a rational time-saving response. The data is displayed in Figure 1.

These figures, combined with data presented in the previous section, suggest a more nuanced version of the digital divide than is usually presented, with UK citizens as a whole falling into four key groups, shown in Figure 2.

Figure 1: Availability of Proxy-Users to Ex-Users and Non-Users: responses to the question 'if you needed to use the Internet to send an e-mail or something, do you know someone who could do this for you?'

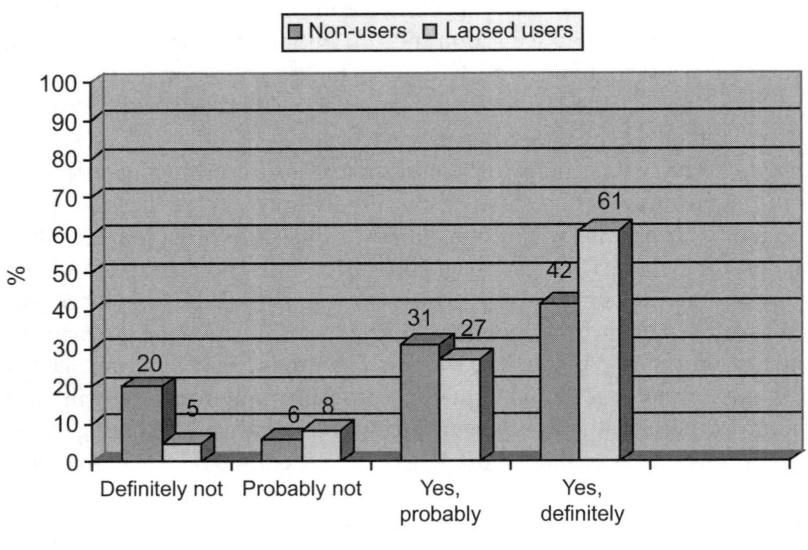

Source: Oxford Internet Survey 2007

Figure 2: Digital Divides in E-government Use 2007

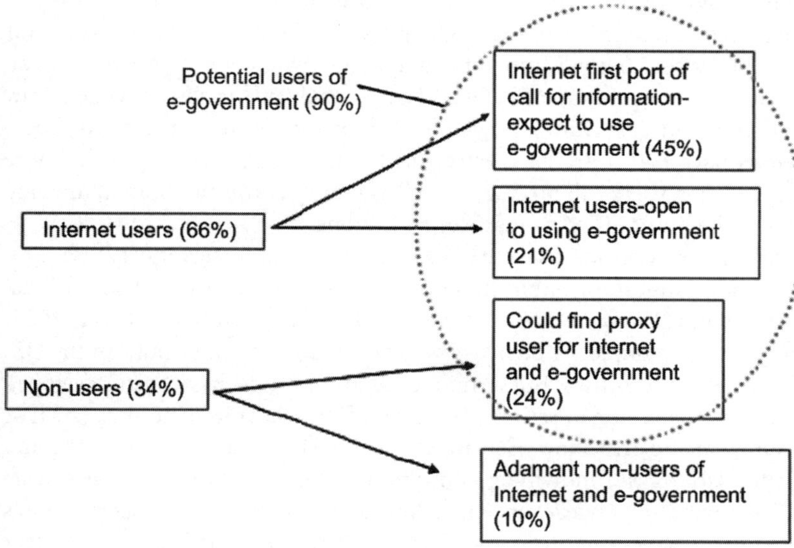

First, there are *avid internet users*, who will consider the Internet as the first port of call for any Internet interactions. As noted above, this group is nearing one-half of the population (with some variations that might be attributable to the supply side of e-government, which government agencies themselves will have to work to overcome). Second, there are *less enthusiastic internet users*, who nonetheless could probably be persuaded to interact online. Third, there are *non-users*, who are reasonably confident of finding an intermediary who could access the Internet for them. If government wishes to target these with e-government initiatives they will need to focus on intermediaries, such as voluntary organisations, carers or family members. Indeed, in the specific context of administrative justice, organisations such as Citizens' Advice are key potential intermediaries. The fourth group of *adamant non-users* of e-government are going to be very difficult to reach online, and other strategies will have to be carefully targeted. The figures are, of course, very approximate (and continually changing) but the figure gives a general picture of hope for those wishing to drive up the usage of e-government.

Technological Developments: Administrative Justice 2.0

From the mid-2000s, newer forms of web-based technologies started to offer new possibilities for citizen interactions with government, reinforcing the 'digital-era' trends noted above in the discussion of digital era governance. So-called 'Web 2.0' technologies allow users of websites to generate content themselves, for example through posting comments, photos or videos. Famous applications include social networking sites (such as Facebook, LinkedIn and MySpace); photo and video-sharing sites such as YouTube, Flickr and I-Tunes; discussion and comment sites such as Twitter; the user written encyclopaedia Wikipedia; and sites where consumers may leave feedback, such as Tripwise (for holidays) and Amazon (for books). Other Web 2.0 applications include blogs (where any internet user can create their own online space for news and comment) and 'mash-ups' which draw in information and data from a range of other sites, often user-generated. These applications have had a dramatic effect on Internet usage, making it far more likely that internet users will produce as well as merely consume content, drawing citizens into the 'front office' of many organisations.

If these types of applications were to be adopted by public sector organisations, they could have important implications for administrative justice. The National Audit Office report *Government on the Internet* (Dunleavy and Margetts et al 2007) found hardly any examples of their use by governmental organisations in the UK, or indeed in other countries. But a number of applications have been developed by non-governmental organisations. For example, social enterprise sites (such as www.Iwantgreatcare.org) allow users to rate hospitals, primary care providers and even (in the latter case) individual consultants. The more controversial private sector US site www.ratemyteachers.com allows pupils and parents to score schools and individual teachers. In 2007 the Cabinet Office published an independent report by Steinberg and Mayo (2007), entitled *The Power of Information*, which promoted government development of user-generated websites, and by 2009 it was possible to point to some examples initiated by government organisations. The NHS has invested substantially in the NHS Choices site, which provides users a chance to rate and rank hospitals and the healthcare that they have received. In 2009, the government announced that it was planning to extend these types of opportunities for user feedback, ranking and posting comments across other sectors such as education, and the Conservative opposition was equally enthusiastic about the possibilities offered by these technologies.

If these types of application extend across the public sector, they could provide a real 'citizen voice' in many areas of administrative decision making, generating new types of information previously unavailable to public sector officials with clear benefits for government and citizens in administrative justice terms. The rapid development and uptake of these technologies by private sector and non-governmental organisations, however, increases the pressure on government organisations to innovate, and also drives up the competition that government faces for public attention, noted in the previous section.

Conclusion: Administrative Justice in the Digital Era

Governmental use of digital technologies has clearly developed considerably in the last decade. The UK government has placed e-government higher up the policy agenda than it has ever been before, with a renewed organisational push from the centre and a massive influx of resources to departments and agencies. Policy makers have embraced the topic for the first time. In the eyes of some commentators 'digital era governance' has overtaken previous administrative reforms to become the new 'paradigm' for the reform of government, with major implications for the nature of governmental administration. Newer web-based technologies and the people who use them are poised to take forward the digital era governance agenda.

However, at the departmental level, a number of organisational barriers to e-government remain, particularly shortage of information technology expertise and a residual reluctance of public officials to fully embrace internet-based ways of working. The key organisational change has been large scale outsourcing which has drawn a number of huge global computer services providers into government. The slow and piecemeal development of e-government has led to a highly complex system of 'identity management' in UK government, which pulls government organisations back from being able to develop the full potential of digital era governance. The information architecture and customer management systems of most government departments are decades behind those maintained by many supermarkets or banks. All these factors contribute to a technological context for administrative decision making that is not necessarily guaranteed to enhance government's capacity to get things right or to correct them when they go wrong.

From the citizens' perspective, new technologies offer great opportunities to enhance their ability to understand their rights and obligations and to obtain redress when things go wrong, the second dimension of administrative justice examined here. Use of e-government in the UK has lagged behind other countries and sectors, but the gap is, at last, beginning to narrow. However, experimental evidence of how people actually experience government's online presence suggests that government organisations face considerable competition to stay visible in the online world, and citizens can struggle to find government-related information. It is difficult to direct Internet users to government sources: the days when people would automatically phone or visit their town hall if they needed information are gone. Online users search, they look at the top ten results and the information that government wants them to have needs to be there in those top ten results in easily accessible form. There is early information to suggest that government organisations have some work to do in this area: the Internet is an excellent place to provide information about rights—but this type of information can be the most difficult to find and to understand.

To some extent government faces greater competition for visibility and public attention on the Internet than it ever has off-line. If someone wishes to find out something about their immediate locality, they are probably more likely to turn to the private sector site www.upmystreet.com than to a governmental site. This competition does not necessarily derive from the inadequacy of government information; indeed upmystreet.com was originally founded using publicly available government information alone and was created to highlight the lack of visibility of government on the web (as was, more recently, the spoof government portal www.directionlessgov.com, which highlighted the weaknesses of the official portal www.direct.gov.uk). The problem is lack of competitiveness in the online environment, in comparison with other organisations which employ more sophisticated strategies to make sure they get noticed online and, for example, push themselves to the top of search engine listings.

Government does not just face competition from the commercial world; it also faces competition from voluntary organisations and from other governments. During the terrible aftermath of the tsunami of 26th December, 2004, citizens from all around the world were desperate to find out what had happened to friends and relatives caught up in the disaster. The UK government was (with the Swedish government) strongly criticised for its response. Eventually it was travel organisations (such as Lonely Planet) and charitable organisations (such as the International Red Cross) which set up the most successful bulletin boards for enabling lost relatives to make contact. After the terrorist attacks in Bali in 2005, the UK government was again criticised for having inadequate information on the Foreign and Commonwealth Office website, in comparison with the Australian equivalent, which warned its citizens not to travel to Bali.

Governments also face competition from a myriad of 'cyber crime' organisations or individuals, who are quite sophisticated in maximising their online presence. Hackers even maximise their own nodality by advertising their skills on websites, while operating outside the jurisdiction in which their presence is most obvious. Various 'underground' sites give rankings to an astonishing range of illegal products and services, such as hacking devices, password breakers and credit card generators (it takes only five minutes to learn how to generate valid credit card details from such a site, according the Head of the US FBI's cybercrime unit). So, for example, if someone is seeking information on 'stun guns' on the web in the UK, the first site to appear on a search engine listing will be a site offering to sell one, rather than any authoritative information. Likewise, a recent scam was run successfully in Ireland by an organisation offering to apply for a European Health Insurance Card on behalf of any Irish citizens who intended to travel in the EU, at the cost of £15, when in fact the service was available online and free-of-change on the Health and Safety Executive's website. By obtaining good rankings in the search engine listings, the site was able to 'beat' the official site and many citizens ended up paying for a service they could easily have had without charge.

With regard to the 'overall fairness' of government in this changed technological context, widespread use of the Internet offers new dangers of unfairness and inequality, as some types of digital exclusion can have a reinforcing effect on social and economic exclusion. But many of the digitally excluded appear to have access to intermediaries who can use the Internet on their behalf. To reach these people, as well as other sub-sets of the population, the government needs to develop a segmentation strategy, recognising differential behaviour among both Internet users and non-internet users. For those who use the Internet, there are some people who automatically expect to deal with government online, and others who will have to be encouraged to do so. For non-users, government needs to develop a strategy for identifying and communicating with intermediaries who can access the Internet on behalf of those who cannot do so themselves, and a concerted outreach strategy for those who have no contact with the Internet at all.

In this context, it is important to remember that there could be a better use of older technologies to facilitate online use. For example, the Financial Services Ombudsman (FSO) has sought to improve citizen access to its services by a better use of telephone services. It has sought to reduce significantly the extent to which people have to draft and submit complaints forms themselves. Thus FSO staff help people complete their applications online (for more details, see Merrick's chapter in this volume). Similar steps have been taken by some government departments. Here again Government is effectively replicating what consumers have come to expect from a wide range of consumer providers in the private sector, for example, from insurance companies where customers can receive telephone assistance to complete online applications.

Finally, the Internet and digital technologies may also have an impact on 'overall fairness' in policy terms, through their impact upon government's nodality, defined in the introduction as government's centrality in social and informational networks. From its very name, we might expect information technology to have a beneficial effect on nodality, by providing government with more strategies than ever before for disseminating information to and collect information from citizens. However, the evidence outlined in this chapter shows how government can face increased competition for nodality from other sources in the online world. These forms of competition can weaken the government's own ability to give out information to citizens and can mean that government suffers a net loss of nodality online. The danger here is that if nodality is weakened as a policy tool, the government could be forced to turn to more costly tools in terms of expenditure and policy instruments which cause more 'trouble, vexation and oppression' (Hood 1983; Hood and Margetts 2007) for its citizens.

Acknowledgements

This chapter draws heavily upon joint work with Professor Patrick Dunleavy, Jane Tinkler, Simon Bastow from LSE Public Policy Group, and Tobias Escher and Stephane Reissfelder from the Oxford Internet Institute, University of Oxford, including research carried out for several NAO reports including *Government on the Internet* (National Audit Office 2007) and *Department for Work and Pensions: Communicating with Customers* (National Audit Office, 2009) and the book *Digital Era Governance: IT Corporations, the State and e-Government* (Oxford University Press), by Patrick Dunleavy, Helen Margetts, Simon Bastow and Jane Tinkler. This chapter reflects entirely the views and opinions of the authors. It does not in any way represent the views of the National Audit Office.

References

Anderson, R, Brown, I, Dowty, T, Inglesant, P, Heath, W and Sasse, A (2009) *Database State* (York, Joseph Rowntree Reform Trust).

Barzelay, M (2000) *The new public management: Improving research and policy dialogue* (Berkeley, CA, University of California Press).

Cabinet Office (2005) *Transformational Government: Enabled by Technology*, Cm 6683 (London: The Stationary Office) available at http://www.cabinetoffice.gov.uk/media/141734/transgov-strategy.pdf.

Civil Service Department (CSD) (1978) *Longer Term Review of Administrative Computing in Central Government* (London, HMSO).

Dunleavy, P, Margetts, H, John, S and McCarthy, D (1999) *Government on the Web* HC 87 Session 1999–2000 (London, The Stationery Office), available at www.governmentontheweb.org/downloads/report_1999/990087app2.pdf.

Dunleavy, P, Margetts, H, Bastow, S, Callaghan, R and Yared, H (2002) *Government on the Web 2*, HC 764 Session 2001–02 (London, The Stationery Office), available at www.nao.org.uk/publications/0102/government_on_the_web_ii.aspx.

Dunleavy, P, Margetts, H, Bastow, S and Tinkler, J (2005) 'New Public Management is Dead—Long Live Digital-Era Governance' 16 *Journal of Public Administration Research and Theory* 467–94.

Dunleavy, P, Margetts, H, Bastow, S and Tinkler, J (2006) *Digital Era Governance: IT Corporations, the State and e-Government* (Oxford, Oxford University Press).

Dunleavy, P, Margetts, H, Bastow, S, Pearce, O and Tinkler, J (2007) *Government on the Internet* (London, The Stationery Office), available at www.nao.org.uk/publications/nao_reports/06-07/0607529.pdf.

Dutton, WH, di Gennaro, C and Millwood, A (2005) *The Internet in Britain: The Oxford Internet Survey (OxIS) 2005* (Oxford, Oxford Internet Institute).

Dutton, WH and Helsper, E (2007) *The Internet in Britain: The Oxford Internet Survey (OxIS) 2007* (Oxford, Oxford Internet Institute).

Dutton, WH, Helsper, E and Gerber, M (2009) *The Internet in Britain: The Oxford Internet Survey (OxIS) 2009* (Oxford, Oxford Internet Institute).

Helsper, E (2008) *Digital Inclusion: An Analysis of Social Disadvantage and the Information Society* (London: (London, Communities and Local Government), available at www.communities.gov.uk/documents/communities/pdf/digitalinclusionanalysis.

HM Treasury (2003) *PFI: Meeting the Investment Challenge* (London, HMSO), available at www.hm-treasury.gov.uk/pfi.htm.

Home Office (2008) *National Identity Scheme Delivery Plan*, available at www.ips.gov.uk/cps/files/ips/live/assets/documents/Doc_D__IPS_delivery_report_8.pdf.

Hood, C (1983) *The Tools of Government* (Basingstoke, Macmillan).

—— (1985) Contemporary public management: A new global paradigm? 10 *Public Policy and Administration* 104–17.

—— (1994) *Explaining economic policy reversals* (Buckingham, Open University Press).

Hood, C and Margetts, H (2007) *The Tools of Government in the Digital Age* (Houndmills, Palgrave Macmillan).

Kable (1994) Market Profile: Civil Service IS 1994/5 (London).

Lamb, C (1973) *Computers in Government* (London, Allen and Unwin).

Margetts, H (1999) *Information Technology in Government: Britain and America* (London, Routledge).

Margetts, H and Dunleavy, P (2002) *Cultural Barriers to E-Government*, Academic Article published by the National Audit Office 4 April 2002 (HC 704-III) in conjunction with the Value for Money report 'Better Public Services Through E-Government' (HC 704), available at www.governmentontheweb.org.

Margetts, H and Willcocks, L (1993) 'Information Technology in Public Services: Disaster Faster?' 13 *Public Money and Management* 49–56 (for a summary of some notorious IT project failures prior to the 1990s).

Mayo, E and Steinberg, T and Mayo, E (2007) *The Power of Information: an independent review* (London, Cabinet Office).

National Audit Office (2009) *Department for Work and Pensions: Communicating with Customers*, HC 421 Session 2008–09 (London: The Stationery Office), available at www.nao.org.uk/publications/0809/communicating_with_customers.aspx.

OECD (2004) *Information Technology Outlook 2004* (Paris, Organization for Co-operation and Development).

Organ, J (2003) 'The Coordination of e-Government in Historical Context', 18 *Public Policy and Administration* 21–36.

Petricek, V, Esher, T, Cox, I and Margetts, H (2005) 'The Web Structure of E-Government—Developing a Methodology for Quantitative Evaluation', paper submitted to the World Wide Web conference, Edinburgh 2006, available at www.governmentontheweb.org.

Pollitt, C, Van Thiel, S, and Homburg, V (eds) (2007) *The New Public Management in Europe* (London, Palgrave Macmillan).

Taghioff, D (2007) *Advicenow guides: helping advisors and advice service users. An evaluation of Advicenow's internet-based information guides* available at www.asauk.org.uk/fileLibrary/pdf/Adnwevrpt.pdf.

4

The Audit Society: Helping to Develop or Undermine Trust in Government?

IRVINE LAPSLEY AND JEREMY LONSDALE

Introduction

This chapter examines the audit function and, in particular, the changes in public audit and the debate over its significance in contemporary society. The particular lens adopted is the manner and nature of the ways in which public sector audit aids (or is intended to aid) citizens by influencing aspects of their everyday lives. In recent years, the scope of audit has gone beyond examining whether taxes are spent properly and into questions of whether, for example, the hospitals people use are clean, schools perform well, or the relevant authorities are capable of keeping them safe from terrorist threats or natural disasters. We approach this subject in six stages. First, we examine the changing nature of audit. Secondly, we explore the importance of performance measurement in contemporary society and its implications for audit. Thirdly, we consider the thesis that audit has become so significant that it shapes crucial aspects of the society in which we live. Fourthly, we examine evidence of this 'Audit Society'. Fifthly, we address an issue which has not received much attention to date, namely the impact of concerns about the growth of audit on the auditor. Finally, we reflect on whether, despite all the manifest changes in the roles and expectations of the auditor, this function is (or can be) an essential mechanism for building and maintaining trust in government amongst citizens.

What Audit Is, and Is Becoming

Traditionally, audit has been seen as a technical activity, involving the checking of adherence to rules and regulations, the identification of administrative weaknesses, and the collection of evidence to form judgments about the accuracy of sets of accounts. It has an image of sobriety, impartiality and absence of emotion, with auditors engaged, as one observer put it, 'in a kind of perpetual inquest on …

in efficiency and profligacy' (Hennessy 1996). Auditors work to professional guidelines and operate within statutory powers. They are not expected to comment on the merits of policy or engage in partisan debate or speculation, yet the importance of their findings on topical issues may place them firmly within policy debates.

There are strong connections between audit and the theme of this book of treating citizens fairly. In democratic countries, all public organisations are subject to audit, which is a basic means of ensuring that they are spending money raised from taxpayers in line with formal (often legal) requirements and, more recently, assessing whether they are providing services to citizens in line with published targets and standards. As one writer has put it:

> Public auditors are important to mitigate the agency problem between citizens and government institutions and to improve transparency. They analyse the official financial statements and evaluate accuracy and compliance of these statements with laws and regulations. Furthermore, some auditing institutions are endowed with competencies to conduct performance audits of policy programs. All these audits are important in order to inform citizens about the accuracy of the financial statements, to provide insights into the state of public finances, and to fight corruption, waste and misappropriation of public funds. (Schelker 2007: 39–40)

In many settings, for example, parliamentary committees, audit findings constitute the basis of a key element of democratic accountability, through which those with responsibility in public organisations are required to explain to elected representatives of the people how they have conducted their affairs.

The relationship between citizens and audit is rarely direct, however, although there are some exceptions. In the United States, official auditors at local level are directly elected, and in some Swiss communes, audit court members are chosen in elections in the municipal assembly and there is some evidence that high levels of audit court autonomy encourage greater intensity of citizen political discussion (Torgler and Schaltegger 2005). Usually though there is little or no public involvement in shaping audit work, and citizens show very little interest in its findings or may be unaware of them, unless the audit report is dealing with high profile events in the public gaze. At times, efforts are made by audit bodies to consult with representative organisations on the subjects to examine, and occasionally audits may be identified as a result of promptings from members of the public, but often there is little transparency about how topics are prioritised and chosen. In a number of countries, including the United Kingdom and Australia, audit bodies have been accorded a 'whistleblower' role, whereby concerned citizens can report instances where they consider public money might be at risk. This helps to give more substance to the argument made by many senior audit officials (Black 2000, Bourn 2007) that they conduct their work in the 'public interest'.

As Gamble and Thomas have argued in this volume, the relationship between the citizen and the state in the United Kingdom has changed in many ways in the last two decades. Of particular relevance to this chapter, we have seen provision of much larger amounts of performance information, sometimes in more accessible forms such as league tables (Hood 2007); the development of 'customer' charters promising certain service standards (Pollitt and Bouckaert 2004); consultation exercises around policy changes or as a way of eliciting views; and the opening up of decision making to greater participation by the public (Newman 2001). At the same time, however, the period has also been characterised by what many see as a decline in trust in government amongst citizens (O'Neill 2002). This can be seen in the development of scepticism over published performance claims, fears of little genuine holding to account of officials and ministers, some evidence of dishonesty and manipulation of performance data (eg, hospital waiting lists), and a lack of understanding of complex rules and expectations amongst the general public, for example, in respect of tax credits. To some, the decline in trust and the rise in audit are closely connected, scrutiny processes being 'low trust/high cost models for controlling public services ... shaped by centralist assumptions and orientations' (Clarke 2003).

Our interest in this chapter is in whether the development of what Power (1997) has described as an 'audit society', has helped ensure that citizens are treated more fairly, or whether, as has been stated elsewhere 'scrutiny processes are likely to remain a site of potential tension in the relationships between governments, public services organizations and the public' (Clarke 2003). We argue that the enthusiasm for audit in its widest sense as a form of control and as a driver for anticipated performance improvement in public services remains undiminished. We also suggest that the 'audit society' is more complex than has been considered hitherto, particularly with regard to the role of the auditor in society and against a background of major developments in government. This chapter suggests that there is evidence of some adaptation of practice amongst auditors in the light of concerns at the expansion of scrutiny work. This shift of emphasis includes auditors taking more account of the treatment of citizens by public bodies and focusing their work more on the interests of citizens. The chapter ends by arguing that, notwithstanding these developments, auditors need to do more to fulfil the democratic potential of their work and be a more effective force for ensuring the state uses its resources effectively in the interests of citizens.

A Crucial Issue: Audit and Performance Measurement

The last 25 years are widely associated with the expansion in the role of scrutiny, checking, regulation and verification (Power 1997; Hood et al 1999; Moran 2001; Power 2003; Hood et al 2004; Gray and Jenkins 2007). It has been suggested that 'The growth of scrutiny is a striking feature of late twentieth century bureaucratic life ... New ways of holding bodies to account are a growth business; there is more information available and more people involved in scrutinising others.' (Lonsdale and Bemelmans-Videc 2007). Such developments can also be seen in the increase in the budgets of audit offices (Martin 2005), the expansion of performance measurement, target setting and reporting practices (Wilkinson 2005), and the extension of audit bodies into a growing range of areas such as issuing good practice guidance and reporting on the credibility of government data (Wilkins and Lonsdale 2007). Such developments are not part of a careful plan, one review noting that '[e]xisting external scrutiny arrangements have evolved to serve Government intentions at particular points in time' (Crerar 2007).

The audit practices of the public sector have been shaped by the demands of public accountability. For decades, they were influenced by issues of probity and regularity; the need to account properly for all public monies expended by public sector institutions. In addition, from the inception of his office in 1866, the Comptroller and Auditor General, the head of the National Audit Office (prior to 1984 the Exchequer and Audit Department) has also pursued more in-depth investigations of specific topics (Normanton 1966). The extension of this activity, now known as 'value-for-money' auditing, has spread across the public sector and become enshrined in statute. The National Audit Act 1983 gave the Comptroller and Auditor General the legal powers to do this work in central government. Value-for-money auditing was introduced for local government in England and Wales when the Audit Commission was created in 1983 under the Local Government Finance Act 1982 (Campbell-Smith 2008). In Scotland, the Accounts Commission has had similar responsibilities for value-for-money audits in local authorities since the Local Government (Scotland) Act 1972. The Accounts Commission was merged with that part of the National Audit Office located in Scotland to create a unified public sector audit body, Audit Scotland, which has undertaken scrutiny studies across the entire public sector in Scotland since it was formed in 1999. The enduring nature of this practice of value-for-money audits is a central feature of the accountability of public services.

Alongside developments in audit, we have seen the creation of much more extensive performance measurement regimes in both local and central government (Wilkinson 2005). Local government has had the Best Value regime and Comprehensive Performance Assessments, and central government, the Public Service Agreement regime since 1998. Hood (2007) has noted that 'managing government and public services by numbers that describe outputs, outcomes, inputs and throughputs—that is, quantitative indicators—is commonly said to be a central theme of contemporary public service reformers'. He sees quantification as at the heart of New Public Management (NPM), with management by numbers coming in three major forms—target systems, ranking systems and 'intelligence' systems. Government departments and local authorities now publish performance against targets in their annual reports. This shift of focus from bureaucratic procedures to a managerial emphasis in which results are of paramount importance has accentuated performance measurement in public services.

The development of performance measurement has attracted considerable publicity, particularly where there is an evident link to the levels of resources made available or where it affects service delivery. A classic case of this is the 'star' system for hospitals in England, in which hospitals were rated from zero to four stars, depending on their performance against targets. This information was placed in the public domain, a device to reward success and shame poorly performing hospitals. For successful hospitals, one benefit was more autonomy; for poorly performing hospitals, the management faced the threat of removal. However, Bevan and Hood (2006) analysed the 'performance' of this performance system and reported examples of data manipulation to achieve targets, although there were also benefits in terms of responsiveness to patient needs. Despite such benefits, the star system was abandoned in 2005, after five years. This is a high profile example of a performance measurement system with distinct benefits and unintended outcomes—including, in this case, its own demise. The major reasons for the failure of the star system were its inability to grade hospital performances robustly enough to be captured in a simple four-star classification system and the attendant disputes over outcomes. Indeed, it is evident that the agency established to undertake the star system was itself becoming somewhat disillusioned with the merits of this system, as evidenced in the writing of Bevan, a former chair of the Commission of Health Improvement (Bevan and Hood 2006).

The significance of performance measurement in public services can be seen from two different perspectives. First, there has been considerable effort expended on the development of performance measures by government, audit and oversight bodies, as well as by researchers, into the issues surrounding their development, yet its impact is still to be determined. Johnsen (2005) observes that, notwithstanding the continual criticism (even ridicule) of performance measurement, there has been a proliferation of performance indicators and the emergence of a *performance measurement industry*. Yet despite these efforts, there is little evidence of great interest amongst those at whom much of the information is aimed—politicians—who get most of their information in other ways such as talking to senior people (Pollitt 2006; Johnson and Talbot 2007), and limited evidence that it has added to the quality of democratic debate or to the ability of citizens to make choices (Pollitt 2006).

A second perspective is the manner in which new techniques, notably benchmarking (Bowerman et al 2001) and the Balanced Scorecard (Aidemark 2001), have been adopted by public service organisations, and yet do not resolve performance measurement dilemmas. Benchmarking, for example, hinges crucially on comparing different organisations or parts of organisations, but genuine comparability can prove elusive (Bowerman et al 2001). Also, while the popularity of the Balanced Scorecard is evident, it is not without difficulties. It does make different components of performance measurement more explicit, but there are issues over the measurement of components and the nature of their relationship (Aidemark 2001).

Modell (2004) depicts these different developments in performance measurement as *myths*, including the initial reliance on quantification (especially accounting numbers), given its lack of demonstrable success, and the current focus on a multi-dimensional approach to performance measurement. While recognising that the idea of tightly coupling organisational strategy and performance measures is not new, Modell claims that considerable research is necessary to demonstrate the nature of the 'new wave' performance measurement models and specifically, the Balanced Scorecard. But, in the absence of detailed empirical support, Modell (2004) sees this as yet another 'myth' in performance measurement.

These observations present a fundamental challenge to practitioners of performance measurement in Johnsen's 'performance measurement industry'. In essence, the 'mythical' status accorded to much performance measurement by Modell alleges that it fails to achieve its purpose. The difficulties to which Modell alludes can also be assessed indirectly. Lonsdale (1999), for example, in attempting to assess the impact of national auditors, ultimately struggles to do so because of the difficulties over the availability of appropriate measures of the performance of these oversight bodies. This raises the fundamental question that, while managers and professionals may benefit from sophisticated performance systems, the major difficulty is the availability of robust measures that ultimately inhibits the realisation of this objective.

Despite all of these difficulties and cautionary remarks, given the centrality of the role of measurement and scrutiny to NPM, its future seems assured. Policymakers *expect* functioning performance measurement systems to exist, and continuing development and investment in them looks likely to follow, as the least effective elements are removed. Observers of performance management have come to similar conclusions. Although there is considerable literature highlighting the problems, Bouckaert and Halligan (2008) have concluded that '[i]t is almost certain that "performance" will remain as a focus of public management and policy … [although] the way in which it will continue is uncertain.' Travers (2007) has argued that '[a] steady stream of theorists and commentators has written about managerialism and the consequences of over-regulation, but no-one in government has taken this seriously', whilst a major review of audit and inspection in Scotland considered that 'although the public have limited awareness of scrutiny processes, there is a clear public expectation that there is and should be external scrutiny of services provided to them, or on their behalf' (Crerar 2007). These observations place performance measurement and audit at the heart of accountability mechanisms for the delivery of public services, notwithstanding their limitations.

The Audit Society: Some Evidence For and Against

A major challenge for managers of public sector organisations is the need to make sense of their environment, and an increasingly important element of this has been the auditability of management actions. The impact of audit on management actions in public services is explored in this section. At first sight, the connection between 'management' and 'audit' may seem uni-dimensional: managers act, and auditors investigate and report on the financial results of these management actions. However, in his influential book *The Audit Society* (1997), Michael Power argues that many aspects of life are increasingly subject to audit. He summarises this phenomenon (ibid: 3), as follows:

> During the late 1980s and early 1990s, the word 'audit' began to be used in Britain with growing frequency in a wide variety of contexts. In addition to the regulation of private company accounting by financial audit, practices of environmental audit, value for money audit, management audit, forensic audit, data audit, intellectual property audit, medical audit, teaching audit, and technology audit emerged, and, to varying degrees, acquired a degree of institutional stability and acceptance. Increasing numbers of individuals and organisations found themselves subject to new or more intensive accounting and auditing requirements. In short, a growing population of 'auditees' began to experience a wave of formalised and detailed checking up on what they do.

The argument is that the impact of this phenomenon may be so pervasive that it could alter the uni-dimensional nature of the relationship between management (actions) and auditors (verifiers of the financial consequences of these management actions). Specifically it has been suggested that audit, instead of providing an ex post evaluation of financial transactions, creates a framework against which broader management actions can be evaluated. In this way, auditing may shape the behaviour of managers, making them act in a way in which their actions are rendered verifiable by auditors (Power 1997).

We have already identified manifestations of this 'audit society'. In addition to conventional financial audit, there is a widespread and heavy emphasis on value for money (VFM) audit within the public sector, often involving professional accounting firms, many of whom undertake work on behalf of the audit bodies. Forms of audit are penetrating many others aspects of organisations (eg, clinical audit of hospital work) and in increasingly diverse parts of society. For example, it was reported that the Equality Commission envisaged compulsory inspections of companies in a bid to reduce the gap in wages earned by male and female workers—a so-called 'gender audit' (Prosser 2005)—whilst police forces in Scotland faced the possibility of a 'religious audit' (Howie 2006) to determine whether there is sectarianism.

All of the above forces combine to create what Power (1994) has called an 'audit explosion' (Power 1994). Trying to put some scale on this development, Martin (2005: 498) reported that

> Between 1997 and 2003 [New Labour] created nine major new inspectorates and greatly expanded the reach and remit of at least eight other inspection services. Reflecting this rapid growth in scale and scope, the cost of external inspection of UK public services rose steeply from £250 million in 1997/8 to £550 million in 2002/3. (OPSR 2003)

In Scotland, 11 completely new bodies were created between 1999 and 2007 to perform scrutiny functions not previously carried out by other bodies, and new bodies were created to carry out previous roles, but with extended powers (Crerar 2007). The cost of the education inspectorate OFSTED more than doubled, and the Audit Commission's workforce increased by 90 per cent between 1997 and

2003. The number of reports produced by the NAO for Parliament increased from 45 to 60 around 2004, as the parliamentary committee to which it reports expanded its programme of hearings. In Scotland, direct scrutiny costs increased by 55 per cent between 2002–03 and 2005–06, although the proportion of direct scrutiny costs was 0.18 per cent of overall public sector expenditure, compared with 0.2 per cent in England. In contrast to the degree of precision around direct costs, the cost of compliance with audit and inspection is not known because little effort has been made to capture the details.

As Power (2003) elaborates, the audit explosion is a convergence of financial and non-financial audit and inspection practices, often informed by ideas of quality assurance, rather than simply accounting or financial auditing practices. The emergence of the audit explosion is located by Power (2003: 191) firmly within the broader framework of New Public Management. This phenomenon is not unproblematic. Power (2003) identifies outcomes such as the elevation of audit to a management style, and the elevation of auditors to 'all-purpose solution agents' (ibid: 191), with attendant elaborate compliance games. In terms of audit practice, it is suggested that VFM-type audits are increasingly difficult, as VFM auditors move on from straightforward studies of efficiency of operations (eg, laundry, catering) to more complex, higher level activities, often with significant interdependencies, for which 'VFM' is not obvious (Lapsley and Pong 2000, Ling 2007).

These particular dimensions of the audit society may influence the behaviour of management in public sector organisations in deleterious ways. The power and influence attributed to audits (Power 2003) may distort the behaviour of managers as they seek to be seen to be discharging their duties appropriately. The lack of objective measures of performance for novel areas of audit investigation (Lapsley and Pong 2000) attenuates the auditability of the management function, with likely attendant defensive behaviour by managers of public sector organisations. One particular side effect of such an outcome could be the adoption of a 'tick box' attitude on the part of managers in seeking to achieve compliance with audit templates. Some have also argued that scrutiny arrangements are 'difficult to adapt to forms of network and partnership working: producing problems of overlap, integration and multiple 'ownership' (Newman 2001).

The 'burden of compliance' is also an issue. In evidence to the 2007 Crerar Review—itself a response to the growth of scrutiny arrangements in Scotland—many service providers complained of the burden of external scrutiny. As the final report commented:

> The point was made particularly strongly by local government, but health boards, registered social landlords and care establishments all felt that the volume of performance reporting and external scrutiny had become disproportionate to the benefit delivered and to the risk it was set up to overcome, and was distracting resources from front-line delivery. (Crerar 2007: 40)

The central assumptions of the audit society thesis are, however, not without their critics. The declaration that this phenomenon exists has been criticised by some as a misinterpretation, or overstatement, of the influence of audit (Humphrey and Owen 2000). To these authors, the idea has become powerful by default, through a decline in other values and modes of organisation. Others—taking a highly empirical approach—have also questioned whether the expansion of scrutiny activity is ultimately as pervasive as has been suggested, a point which Power accepts (Power 2005). Hood et al (2004: 185) describe as a 'folk tale' the idea

> that oversight and audit activity of various kinds over public services has grown dramatically over the last two decades or so, representing a new 'age of inspection' (Day and Klein 1990:4). There are cases and places that undoubtedly fit that pattern, as we have shown. But this study also shows that any such development has not been uniform across countries and policy sectors.

Hood et al cite the example of the university sector in the UK, which has seen 'particularly dramatic rises in external oversight from a very low base', in contrast to the higher levels of the civil service, where it has been less pronounced.

Other doubts have been expressed. Talbot (2009) has expressed some scepticism, noting 'Some academics joined the fray, pointing to possible perverse effects from "gaming" and measurement problems of targets, performance indicators and inspection regimes. Actual evidence and serious analysis of benefits and problems was harder to come by.' Examining the criticisms of the development of quality assurance regimes, Travers (2007: 172) also notes that

> [o]ne can also see, however, that the critics (of over-regulation) are vulnerable to the charge that they are simply defending the traditional economic interests and privileges of the professions. It is hard to criticise the idea that doctors or teachers should listen to the views of patients and students (increasingly described as 'consumers' rather than 'clients') without sounding arrogant or elitist.

Indeed, the shift from a 'producer orientation' and the reconstruction of the citizen as a 'consumer' can be seen as a central tenet of many public service reforms of the 1980s and 1990s in the UK. From this perspective, audit is a way of providing evidence that consumers' needs have been met. Linked to this, in a paper entitled 'There is no such thing as audit society', Maltby (2008) argues that the general public has been forgotten in Power's analysis, along with the possibility that an effective audit would be welcomed, even though Maltby notes that charities, pressure groups and trade unions regularly demand environmental, ethical and social audits (further prima facie evidence of Power's 'audit explosion'). She adds that the most vocal critics are the 'experts' and concludes that:

> [t]he Audit Society and its progeny, Power's own papers and the wail of unhappy academics and doctors and civil servants, are ultimately not a protest about the creation of an iron cage around society. They are the stifled chorus of fury at being made accountable.

Also linked to this is the question of whether the concerns about the impact of accountability mechanisms, expressed by professionals, accord with the views of the wider population. Whilst some at the sharp end of accountability regimes have criticised the way they are handled, Pollitt, in response to Behn (2001), has commented:

> I can detect little public (or indeed political) sentiment in favour of mutual, non-punitive accountability for public programmes. … On the contrary, the tendency (amplified by the mass media) seems to be to intensify the transparency and hierachical accountability of both ministers and public managers. And this may not be an entirely bad thing. In the not too distant past it seemed that ministers and senior public servants were rather easily able to conceal and cover up incompetence and wrong doing.' (Pollitt 2003: 94)

The danger also is that the Audit Society debate ignores the legitimate views of elected representatives. Although some at the receiving end of strong questioning from parliamentarians have complained about the approach (Landers 1999), the Chairman of the House of Commons Committee of Public Accounts commented in 2009 that his committee members ask the questions that their constituents would ask if they were in their place (Hansard 2009), for example, expressing incredulity at the scale of losses on IT or defence projects or scepticism about the way in which senior officials seem to avoid the consequences of policy failure.

There are further concerns about the Audit Society thesis. The first is that, by lumping together anything which involves checking or uses the word 'audit', we risk losing sight of the varied justifications for different types of work, their differing places on what has been referred to as the accountability/learning continuum (Lonsdale and Bemelmans-Videc 2007), and the varied degree of involvement of, and consultation with, those subject to the work. In addition, some scrutiny is externally imposed (eg, parliamentary committees), elements of the way in which government is held to account, whilst some are means by which government chooses to impose control on different parts of itself (eg, internal audit). Some such as financial audits have detailed and widely accepted rules and standards, whilst other, such as performance measurement, less so. The differences in process and status lead to significant differences in tone, formality (including the scope for punishment or publicising adverse findings) and what has been described elsewhere as 'relational distance' (Hood et al 1999).

The Impact of the Audit Society

We now turn to consider the evidence on the influence of the audit society on government, and whether it has helped or hindered the improvement of administration on behalf of citizens. We can examine the evidence from three different perspectives. These are the impact of the expansion of audit activities:

— on improving the performance of government;
— on improving the accountability of government; and
— on innovation and risk taking in government.

The first argument is that the expansion of the audit society has damaged—or at least, not improved—the performance of government. The evidence is mixed. Van Thiel and Leeuw (2002) have written of a 'performance paradox', whereby the expansion of output measurement in the public sector has led to unintended consequences including ossification, a lack of innovation, tunnel vision and sub-optimisation, which can jeopardise the efficiency and effectiveness of policy implementation. The paradox is the weak correlation between performance indicators and performance itself, with a range of dysfunctional consequences including perverse learning (focusing on what gets measured).

Considering the evidence, Peters (2005: 171) has argued that:

> transformation in governance [which includes accountability mechanisms] has, to some extent, enhanced the capacity of government to perform its tasks but in the process these changes have exacerbated the familiar problems of co-ordination and altered the ways in which accountability can be enforced. There is little doubt that government in 2004 is more efficient in a strictly economic sense than it was in 1984, or 1994, or even the late 1990s. Likewise, many of the changes in government that have been implemented during the reform process have enhanced public participation, especially the involvement of clients of programmes. … Further, there is some evidence that the public is now more satisfied with the individual services provided by the public sector.

More specifically, some have argued that there is evidence that the Best Value regime 'yielded positive benefits in terms of service responsiveness, efficiency, effectiveness, accountability and quality' (Higgins, James and Roper 2004) and 'increased self-awareness and understanding' amongst local authorities which were prompted to give attention to longstanding problems (Gray and Jenkins 2004). There is also some evidence from interviews with leaders and elected mayors of councils whose performance improved dramatically following poor performance in their comprehensive performance assessments. The inspection process, although seen as too prescriptive and onerous, was considered to be a 'wake up' call, without which the impetus for dramatic radical improvement would have been much weaker (IDeA 2009). A review of the use of targets in executive agencies (James, 2005) also suggests they 'do seem to have contributed to furthering progress towards the majority of agency specific goals in the majority of executive agencies.'

However, there is also evidence of the Best Value regime affecting performance adversely. In England and Wales a review of Best Value found that complying with the requirements of the audit process placed significant new administrative burdens on local authorities and the growth of inspection consumed large amounts of time, effort and funding (Centre for Local and Regional Government Research 2006). In Scotland, a review of its Best Value framework found that local authorities reported that this exercise took up a great deal of time and felt that they were over inspected and that it placed an unnecessary burden on them (Grace et al 2007). Furthermore, a study by Arnaboldi and Lapsley (2008) found evidence of compliance with Best Value Audit as a legitimating activity, with little evidence of achieving the Best Value aim of culture change. This resonates with Power's (1997) prediction that so called 'culture changes' would be short lived, if they occurred at all. Also, Grace et al (2007) reported limited benefits of Best Value processes and procedures on citizens and users of services.

Other studies have questioned whether developments have helped government performance. Sanderson (2001) concludes that performance measurement systems have limitations as drivers of change and improvement, especially when externally imposed, whilst Peters (2005) has argued that the benefits of changes in governance have been achieved at the cost of poor co-ordination and accountability problems. Other problems include public sector externalities (James, 2005); imposition of unnecessary administrative costs and having an adverse effect on resource allocation (Higgins, James and Roper 2004).

A second perspective might be called the 'accountability paradox'. The argument here is that, despite the expansion in the means of holding people to account through the increase in scrutiny, audit and inspection, and the greater amount of performance data, the public, media and Parliament see little sign that public organisations and the people who run them are made accountable. The problems have been described elsewhere (Lonsdale and Bemelmans-Videc 2007: 8):

> The shortcomings are various. Some see the rendering of accounts as too slow to allow for adequate corrective measures at a time when they could be most effective, too compromised and lacking in independence, or too much under the control of professionals and technocrats. Some consider the processes for questioning those responsible for government activities too polite and lacking in rigour, insufficiently supported by expert assistance, and thus lacking in real bite. Others see those providing the basis for holding to account as too cautious and hesitant in their conclusions and the outcome of their efforts doing too little to prevent repeated occurrences of similar problems. To others, put simply, the problem is that people don't get fired for failure in the public sector as they do in the business world.

Again, the evidence of the impact of audit regimes on improving or hindering accountability is mixed. Much of the benefit of audit and inspection regimes has been in terms of increasing transparency and providing assurance about the reliability of data. There is little doubt that more performance information is available now than was the case in the past, that it is more accessible to a range of users, particularly, via the Internet, and that it is in many formats (eg, league tables, summary leaflets about council performance, websites etc). Crerar (2007: para 3.4) has pointed out that '[t]he public is the ultimate beneficiary of all scrutiny and should be able to take assurance that public money is being used properly and that services are well provided'. He also noted that ministers use scrutiny to account to the public, Parliament uses scrutiny processes to hold ministers and others to account for their performance, and elected members hold officials to account through scrutiny arrangements.

The impact of the use of audit for accountability purposes varies, however. In some cases it forms part of the sanctioning and reward arrangements. Under CPA (Comprehensive Performance Assessment), well-performing local authorities secured exemptions from future inspections, removal of council tax caps and less ring fencing of grants. Poor performers received a tighter regime, more frequent inspections and, possibly, the imposition of external monitoring boards

(McLean, Haubrich and Gutierrez-Romero 2007). While there is no doubt that some are punished for not meeting targets, it can also be argued that other regimes often have only limited bite. In other cases, for example, Public Service Agreements (PSAs)—the government's main performance targets—there appear to be less direct effects. PSAs have frequently been changed or dropped after limited discussion, raising doubts about their ability to drive performance. More generally, the Treasury has recognised that, at times, there has been insufficient implementation of recommendations made by the PAC and new instructions have been circulated to departments (HM Treasury 2008).

A third argument is that the expansion of scrutiny has acted as a barrier to innovation and risk taking in government (Cabinet Office 2000). From one perspective, the evidence for this seems weak because at a high level, the last 15–20 years—the period of the perceived growth of the 'audit society'—can be seen as the time of the most rapid transformation of government, some of the most extensive innovations—the introduction of private finance and private sector delivery of public services, the harnessing of IT, partnership working, tailored services and new types of provision (Pollitt and Bouckaert 2004). Indeed, it can be argued that the period has been one of hyper-activity, with evidence of government willing to try to tackle complex problems—obesity, climate change, computerisation of the NHS—with new and (possibly over) ambitious approaches.

A good case can also be made that audit has in fact been supportive of change and innovation. Some have argued, for example, that the changing role of the Audit Commission has meant that it became 'an agency of policy and organisational innovation, prescribing best practice, identifying dangerous deviations and divergences, advising on the most effective organizational systems, structures and cultures, and propounding the need for better management of public services' (Clarke 2003). In 2009, the NAO published its second report identifying barriers to change and highlighting stories of successful innovation. It even went so far as to acknowledge that failure was acceptable, as long as it was carefully managed and the failing project closed down quickly once identified (National Audit Office, 2009). Indeed, perhaps the most significant criticism of the NAO has been, not that it has criticised some of the most significant (and arguably risky) innovations of recent decades—the Private Finance Initiative or the NHS IT transformation—but that it has been too supportive (Collins 2007). Reports by the NAO have in fact been generally positive about many of the innovations of the last decade or more including the use of private finance, service transformations such as NHS Direct, policy developments such as 'Modernising Government', 'joined up' government, regional development agencies and a host of other initiatives. Instead, many of its most critical reports—and those of the Committee of Public Accounts that it supports—have been about traditional failings such as weak project management or process failings. And it is not clear that those bodies under review consider audit itself an hindrance to innovation. An NAO survey in 2008 (perhaps not an entirely unbiased tool) found that more than 80 per cent of central government departments considered an external review by the NAO a 'major' or 'minor' help, or neither (National Audit

Office, 2009). In contrast, around 60 per cent of departments considered a PAC hearing (based on an NAO report) a hindrance or neutral in its effects.

On the other hand, concerns about the impact of audit on innovation have been raised for some time. A number of observers have repeated the observation, raised in one review (Cabinet Office 2000), 'There is a widely held perception, for example, that auditors and scrutiny bodies will criticise departments for undertaking new and risky policies.' Seven years later, Crerar raised similar concerns, and Gray and Jenkins (2004) concluded that these regimes 'imposed a very real constraint on the freedom and capacity to innovate and deliver added value in the interests of preventing failure and, when it occurred, finding scapegoats'. It is hard to prove one way or another, although we are aware of examples of cases where officials have been advised that particular actions are risky because 'the auditors won't like it'. At the very least, there is a risk that audit and scrutiny can reinforce the existing conservatism of organisations which are aware of the unsympathetic political and media responses to perceived failure. Fear of criticism and assumptions and 'myths' about how auditors will respond are aspects of the 'audit society'.

The Impact of the Audit Society on Audit and Auditors

The attention of much of the discussion around the audit society has focused on the impact of audit on those who are audited, whilst relatively little attention has been given to how auditors themselves have responded to the criticisms of their work. In recent years, there have been many technical and organisational developments affecting the public sector audit and accounting professions. These have included the introduction of commercial-style accounting in the public sector (in the 1990s for executive agencies and 2001 for central government departments), the creation of devolved audit bodies in Scotland and Wales, which have subsequently adopted new approaches to audit, the speeding up of public sector audit timetables requiring faster, more efficient working, the Gershon review of efficiency and the Comprehensive Spending Review 2007, which has helped to focus government departments first on 'efficiency' and then on 'value for money' issues, the fall-out from the Enron and Worldcom scandals, and the introduction of reviews of departmental capability in 2006.

Although Travers (2007) suggests that no-one in government has taken over-regulation seriously, there is evidence that the debate about the audit society has in fact shaped how auditors have acted in a number of ways. These can be summarised as attempts to:

- be responsive to requests to do new work;
- make greater efforts to identify and publicise the perceived benefits of their work;

- seek to address 'audit burden' concerns, for example, through better co-ordination and changes to working practices;
- seek to take a more citizen-focused perspective in their work; and
- maintain a strong critique of excessive regulation and inadequate performance measurement regimes.

First, although it might be assumed that the 'audit society' would be driven by auditors who were keen to extend their empires, much of the expansion of the audit role has been *instigated by governments*—often the same ones that have criticised the impact of audit at other times. Elected governments have introduced new forms of audit, often in response to specific perceived needs, and auditors have been keen to respond. In 1997, for example, the Chancellor of the Exchequer invited the NAO to audit the 'assumptions' made in the Budget (Heald 2003); in 2002 the NAO was invited, in response to strong parliamentary pressure, to examine—on a regular basis—the systems underpinning PSA targets; and—at various times—the NAO has been asked by government to examine the accuracy of asylum statistics (2004), the implications of changes in taxation regimes for pensions (2004) and the robustness of efficiency savings claims (2008). None of these pieces of work was initiated by auditors, in keeping with Hood's observation (2007) that one of the distinctive features of the development of quantified performance indicators in England, compared to other countries, is the 'degree to which such uses of performance measures have been dominated by the executive rather than the legislature. For example, the central performance measurement systems in Japan, France and the USA have all been legislatively based, while that applying to England owes little to parliamentary initiative or specific legislation.'

Wilkins and Lonsdale (2007) have highlighted how the stimulus for developments has varied. Looking at the UK and Australia, where new roles have been given to audit institutions over the last 20 years, they note that several of these new roles have been instigated by the executive, but amongst those they identified, were some which arose from legislative pressure as elected representatives sought greater transparency from government. Wilkins and Lonsdale (ibid) acknowledge that auditors have usually been only too willing to assist, noting that 'Audit institutions exist in a public sector environment where there is continuous pressure to demonstrate relevance and value to the community. Thus, when requests arise they are usually interpreted as opportunities to demonstrate the capabilities and value of the audit role'. This suggests that audit bodies have been adept at making themselves useful. As Martin (2005) put it, they have 'consistently come up with uncomplicated and timely advice about "what works", combined with an uncanny ability to anticipate the next twist in the government's thinking'. This picture of the auditor as willing collaborator in the creation of an audit society is rather more complex than Martin suggests and we revisit it below.

Secondly, auditors have—perhaps inevitably—been more confident than other observers about the beneficial effects of their work and have increasingly sought to publicise them. Funkhouser (2005) provides a well-argued practitioner riposte to the critiques of those, such as Behn and Dubnick, who have argued that auditors only pounce on small errors, undermine trust in government and pursue 'aggressive, adversarial strategies'. Funkhouser—himself the elected City Auditor of Kansas City, Missouri for 18 years—argues that there is plenty of evidence that performance auditing plays 'a critical role in effective democratic governance by strengthening accountability and improving performance', citing statistics and anecdotal evidence from specific audits in the United States. Audit bodies themselves have sought to publicise examples of their impact in their annual reports. In 2008, for example, the NAO reported that its work had generated £656 million of financial impacts (National Audit Office 2008a), whilst Audit Scotland noted how others saw it: 97 per cent of local bodies and 86 per cent of central government bodies thought it provided a high quality audit service (Audit Scotland 2008). There have also been attempts by auditors to maximise the value of their work, holding conferences and seminars around specific reports, disseminating new products arising from audits such as toolkits, briefings and guidance, and working with departmental audit committees to help them increase their effectiveness and ensure robust risk management (Lonsdale, 2007; Bouckaert and Halligan 2008).

Thirdly, efforts appear to have been made by audit bodies to reduce the impact of their work on the organisations audited, and practitioners would argue that they are far more attuned to the risks than they were a decade ago. In 1998, the Public Audit Forum was set up to provide a setting in which thinking about audit amongst all the UK audit bodies and others could take place. A number of key publications have been issued reflecting the change of thinking, most notably a guide to what audited bodies could expect from their auditors (Public Audit Forum 2000). This highlighted the need for mutual understanding in the audit planning process; better use of the work of others; reporting in a fair, appropriate and timely manner; adding value; and observing professional ethics. In 2003, an Audit Liaison Group was established for central government, chaired by the Permanent Secretary of the Treasury and the Comptroller and Auditor General, designed to facilitate government-auditor discussion of strategic issues affecting audit. Both initiatives have been intended to better co-ordinate and oversee the way in which audit is organised in order to maximise the potential benefits of the work and minimise the downsides.

Methodological developments in audit have also been seen designed to limit audit effort or make it more effective. For example, since the late 1990s auditors at the NAO have reduced the amount of sample testing—the most intrusive element of audit work—undertaken as part of a rationalisation of audit work and a shift to a more risk focused approach. Efforts have been made in some sectors—in particular, the NHS—to share data and co-ordinate audit and inspection visits to hospitals under a 2004 concordat between 20 audit and inspection bodies. The Concordat's website (www.concordat.org.uk) lists key achievements, including the Audit Commission's requirement on its auditors to consider the cost of their recommendations. Collaborative work has taken place between the NAO and Audit Commission (for example, on public sector delivery chains cutting through both central and local government), although not perhaps as extensively as some consider it should have done. To better execute performance measurement work, the Performance Information Panel was established by the Treasury, involving representatives of the Cabinet Office, NAO, the Office of National Statistics and the Audit Commission. A manual for performance measurement was developed and issued jointly in 2001 (Bouckaert and Halligan 2008). For value for money audit work, there is a lot more consultation at various stage with those being examined—about methods, about existing data sources, about involvement on reference panels and contractors, and about emerging findings (National Audit Office 2008). The audit process has tended to be a lot less confrontational in the work than it used to be, and there has been greater willingness on the part of the senior management of organisations to suggest areas for examination, closer contact between auditors and senior officials—for example, through audit committees, which have grown in the public sector—and greater commonality of training and experience; all central government finance directors now need to be professionally qualified. In addition, there have also been technical improvements in audit and performance measurement which arguably should make it more useful. These included the development of standards for performance measurement, and the integration of a wider range of social science and evaluation methods into VFM work (Lonsdale, 2008).

There are also signs that audit has wanted to be seen to respond to the needs of citizens. This can be seen, for example, in the language used by the Audit Commission, which has increasingly talking about taking a 'citizen perspective' in its reports (Clarke 2003). Steve Bundred, Chief Executive of the Audit Commission, stated in 2008 that the new inspection regime and the reporting should 'resonate with the public', adding that:

> We want to ensure that the public is more engaged with the CAA [*Comprehensive Area Assessment*] than it has been with the CPA. The CPA has been a powerful driver of improvement in local government, but I can't honestly say they talk of little else in my local pub. We want the CAA to be used more like Trip Adviser [sic], and some of the websites that people do use. (Klaushofer, 2008: 18)

Other developments point to greater attention being paid to citizens. Auditors argue that they select topics of importance to citizens or take a client-focused perspective—based either on their own analysis of pertinent issues or arising from forms of consultation (Audit Scotland 2008). They also highlight efforts to involve citizens—or more likely, bodies representing citizens—in their work, for example, in focus groups or consultations, or to sit on reference panels to advise on the audit. There have also been attempts to look at social exclusion and scrutinise the accessibility of service provision, for example, in work on the accuracy of benefits literature, on the accessibility of government websites, on the roll-out of digital television, and on 'postcode lotteries' in health provision. In addition, there are examples of encouraging informed public discussion through the dissemination of findings beyond the formal accountability processes to which audit contributes (for example, accessible guidance on how to fulfil their role was issued to governors of 23,000 schools following an audit of school performance in 2007, or leaflets on how to choose between utility suppliers). Finally, many audit reports have examined and reported on the quality of interactions between the citizen and the state, assessing for example, whether the demands on citizens are reasonable (for example, in terms of providing information), whether redress and compensation mechanisms are effective or whether citizens have been disadvantaged by inadequate 'joining-up' of service provision. However, there is still some way to go. Crerar (2007) notes that service users are not always referred to in the organisational aims of external scrutiny bodies, and that there is still uncertainty as to how to weigh user evidence against that of professionals.

Auditors have also argued that much of the focus of their work is on the public interest—defined in terms of the common interests of citizens—and, in particular, on ensuring that the public interest is not subverted in a range of ways. In *extremis*, this means helping to guard against corruption and fraud; more mundanely by helping to prevent errors and mistakes that undermine confidence in public provision. It also means highlighting the risk of conflicts of interest—particularly important where so much public work is done under contract—or where overwhelming complexity jeopardises effective administration.

Finally, auditors have not been uncritical supporters of performance measurement regimes, and have maintained a critical eye over them, and over regulatory bureaucracy and its inadequacies. The NAO's regular report to Parliament on Public Service Agreement (PSA) systems has repeatedly highlighted weaknesses in data systems and urged more effective setting of targets to make them more useful (National Audit Office 2007). In 2003, the Chairman of the Audit Commission told a parliamentary committee that targets can be 'a very distracting add-on and irritant', as well as 'real obstacles for change'. He added that 'slavish devotion to the universal meeting of targets, many of which have not been set very intelligently, is a sure-fire way of not improving public services' (Select Committee on Public Administration 2003). Similarly, the Chief Executive of the Audit Commission said publicly that the Comprehensive Performance Assessment did not capture very well the complexity of local authorities (Gray and Jenkins 2004). The NAO has also been critical of poorly designed or implemented regulations, and ineffective regulators, whose weaknesses fail to protect consumers. It reports annually to Parliament on the Administrative Burdens Reduction Programme, designed to reduce the burden of complying with regulations. This draws on an annual perception survey of 2,000 businesses (National Audit Office 2008b) designed to track views over time.

Conclusion: Audit as Supporting Trust in Government?

This chapter has argued that the expanded role played by audit—in terms of scale and reach—remains a major characteristic of modern government and shows no signs of disappearing. This can be interpreted as a continuation of the audit explosion and the growing faith in quantification, despite the emerging problems and shortcomings. However, the development of audit over recent years is a complex issue. The expansion of audit scrutiny is not as uniform as might have been expected, whilst concerns that the expansion of audit has undermined innovation and change in government fail to explain how it has coincided with a period of major change in the way public services are delivered. We have also shown how the 'audit society' debate itself has had an impact on the way in which auditors conduct their work, in particular, that they have sought to make their work more focused on the needs of citizens, even though, to most people, the activity remains technical and opaque. In addition, we have highlighted the fact that, despite the growth of available audited performance information, there is little evidence that citizens make extensive use of it, except in direct and personal ways, such as in the form of school league tables. Moreover, their representatives do so less than might be expected. Instead, a feature of the Audit Society, despite, the attempts to offer assurance about reported performance, is a high degree of scepticism about whether assessments accurately reflect performance (Wilson 2004) and uncertainty about whether the performance movement will be as good for democracy as had been hoped (Talbot 2005).

Nevertheless, we conclude by outlining how audit might be better harnessed for the benefits of citizens and to achieve its democratic potential. Ultimately, the role of audit should be to give citizens grounds for having confidence in the legitimacy, honesty and responsibility of government, and whether they are getting services which provide value for money and are efficient and responsive. It must also be about explaining why—where appropriate—such confidence is unfounded. At other times, the purpose of the information is to inform political, policy and management debates (van der Knaap 2006) and play an enlightenment role. In each of these ways, audit can contribute to the development of trust in government and can help to ensure that citizens and their interests are treated fairly. This is important because as Mulgan (2006: 26) has put it 'Governments need trust not just to survive, but also to do their day-to-day work. Without it laws will more often be evaded and broken, taxes will be harder to raise, and information will be harder to gather'. However, trust will not emerge spontaneously, and the evidence of recent years indicates that governments find it hard to generate it on their own. Trust needs to be nurtured and sustained, which raises the role of third-party involvement. It is here that there is a role for audit. Audit offices are generally trusted organisations, with well qualified staff. They are generally seen as taking a balanced, non-partisan approach to reporting on government performance, and attempting—often successfully—to do so in ways designed to be understood by the non-specialist. They are independent—so they can 'speak truth unto power'—and have powers of access to information, which others do not have.

Thus, the expansion of audit as an activity and the development of new and arguably more ambitious approaches to analysing and presenting performance information that are characteristic of the last 20 years—the more positive aspects of the 'Audit Society'—offer the prospect of giving citizens greater insight into government. However, to play a valuable role, audit must address a number of factors that help to reduce its effectiveness. Auditors must gain a better understanding of their impact and effect, and of the costs of compliance, eliminate overlaps and duplication between themselves and others, protect their independence to avoid 'regulatory capture' and accusations of bias or partiality to particular interests and policies, constantly develop its approaches to take account of technical developments that will make it more effective, and use its privileged position effectively. Audit must also avoid overstretching itself and taking on roles and responsibilities that it is ill-equipped to fulfil (Ling 2007), and must recognise that greater involvement in performance evaluation risks narrowing the distance between evaluation and government, allowing some to challenge its independence (Clarke 2003).

To do this, public auditors need to develop traditional scrutiny and attest functions in a number of ways. These include:

Focusing on problems and issues stretching beyond individual organisations and programmes—in order to pick up, for example, the collaborative and cross-government issues that governments have sought to tackle;

Contributing to well informed debate—for example, by producing work that helps improve citizens' understanding of where taxes are spent and how different levels of government fit together, and by explaining systems and processes that currently confuse and alienate;

Supporting democratic citizenship—through the generation of public discourse around public performance by interpreting data, encouraging objective analysis, disseminating findings widely and involving citizens in its work, making performance information more intelligible;

Synthesising its own work—by drawing out themes and wider lessons from a range of individual reports to provide an overview, make links, and take a cross-government perspective;

Asking inconvenient questions to keep government responsive to citizens—in a world of news management the ability to bring difficult issues to public attention is a crucial, if at times uncomfortable, one to be used wisely;

Championing transparency—for example, by producing information that is value added, pushing for maximum information to be published, challenging unnecessary use of confidentiality provisions, and writing reports in language that can be understood;

Contributing to the creation of an environment in which proper debate about performance—for example, maximising the benefit from developments such as resource accounts and reporting against targets, as well as encouraging a mature debate about the causes of failure in government.

In doing this, auditors must be seen to retain their traditional values of independence in making judgements. However, the manner in which government auditors are drawn into policy issues (Gendron et al 2007) may eclipse the traditional role of the government auditor. In seeking to push the envelope of possibilities for accountability and scrutiny, the well intentioned interventions of government auditors may reinforce the reliance governments and citizens place on auditors in contemporary society.

References

Aidemark, L (2001) 'The Meaning of Balanced Scorecards in the Health Care Organisation' 17 *Financial Accountability and Management* 23.

Arnaboldi, M and Lapsley, I (2008) 'Making Management Auditable: The Implementation of Best Value in Local Government' 44 *Abacus* 22.

Audit Commission, Commission for Social Care Inspection, Healthcare Commission, HM Inspectorate of Constabulary, HM Inspectorate of Prisons, HM Inspectorate of Probation and Ofsted (2008) *An Approach to Assessing the Equality Impact of Comprehensive Area Assessment (CAA)* (London) available at www.audit-commission.gov.uk/SiteCollectionDocuments/Downloads/EqualityImpactAssessment.pdf+An+Approach+to+Assessing+the+Equality+Impact+of+Comprehensive+Area+Assessment&hl=en&gl=uk.

Audit Scotland (2008) *Annual Report 2007–08*, available at www.audit-scotland.org.uk.

Behn, R (2001) *Rethinking Democratic Accountability* (Washington, DC, Brookings Institution Press).

Bevan, G and Hood, C (2006) 'Have Targets Improved Performance in the English NHS?' 332 *British Medical Journal* 419.

Black, RW (2000) *Supporting Democratic Scrutiny by Public Audit* (London, Public Management and Policy Association, PMPA).

Bouckaert, G and Halligan, J (2008) *Managing Performance: International Comparisons* (London, Routledge).

Bowerman, M, Ball, A and Francis, G (2001) 'Benchmarking as a Tool for the Modernisation of Local Government' 17 *Financial Accountability and Management* 321.

Bourn, J (2007) *Public Sector Audit: Is it Value for Money?* (London, John Wiley).

Cabinet Office (2000) *Wiring it Up: Whitehall's Management of Cross-Cutting Policies and Services*, Performance and Innovation Unit report (London), available at www.opensigle.inist.fr/handle/10068/401613

Campbell-Smith, D (2008) *Follow the Money: The Audit Commission, Public Money and the Management of Public Services (1983–2008)* (London, Allen Lane).

Centre for Local and Regional Government Research, Cardiff University (2006) *The Long term Evaluation of the Best Value Regime: Final Report* (London, Communities and Local Government).

Clarke, J (2003) 'Scrutiny through inspection and audit: Policies, structures and processes' in T Bovaird and E Loffler (eds), *Public Management and Governance* (London, Routledge).

Collins, T (2007) 'Channel 4 Dispatches—Is the National Audit Office a mere critical friend to government?' 26 September *Computer Weekly.*

Crerar, L (2007) *Report of the Independent Review of Regulation, Audit, Inspection and Complaints Handling of Public Services in Scotland* (Edinburgh, Scottish Government), available at www.scotland.gov.uk/Resource/Doc/82980/0053065.pdf.

Funkhouser, M (2005) 'Accountability, Performance and Performance Auditing: Reconciling the Views of Scholars and Auditors' *Paper to the Accountable Governance: An International Research Colloquium*, 20–22 October, Belfast.

Gendron, Y, Cooper, DJ and Townley, B (2007) 'The construction of auditing expertise in measuring government performance' 32 *Accounting, Organizations and Society* 101.

Grace, C, Nutley, S, Downe, J and Martin, S (2007) *Decisive Moment. The Independent Review of the Best Value Audit Process. Final Report to the Accounts Commission and Audit Scotland* (Edinburgh, Audit Scotland).

Gray, A and Jenkins, B (2004) 'Government and Administration: Too Much Checking, Not Enough Doing?' 57 *Parliamentary Affairs* 269.

—— (2007) 'Checking Out? Accountability and Evaluation in the British Regulatory State' in M-L Bemelmans-Videc, J Lonsdale and B Perrin (eds), *Making Accountability Work: Dilemmas for Evaluation and for Audit* (Somerset, NJ, Transaction Publishers).

Hansard (2009) *House of Commons Hansard Debates*, 12 March, Col 481, available at www.services.parliament.uk/hansard/Commons/ByMonth/0903/index.html

Heald, D (2003) 'Fiscal Transparency: Concepts, Measurement and UK Practice' 81 *Public Administration* 723.

Hennessy, P (1996) *Muddling Through: Power, Politics and the Quality of Government in Post-war Britain* (London, Victor Gollancz).

Higgins, P, James, P and Roper, I (2004) 'Best Value: Is it Delivering?' 24 *Public Money and Management* 251.

Hood, C (2007) 'Public Service Management by Numbers: Why Does it Vary? Where has it Come From? What Are the Gaps and the Puzzles?' 27 *Public Money and Management* 95.

Hood, C, Scott, C, James, O, Jones, G and Travers, T (1999) *Regulation inside Government: Waste-Watchers, Quality Police and Sleaze-Busters* (Oxford, Oxford University Press).

Hood, C, James, O, Peters, B Guy, Scott, C (eds) (2004) *Controlling Modern Government: Variety, Commonality and Change* (Cheltenham, Edward Elgar).

Howie, M (2006) 'Police Officers Face Religion Survey to Test Claims of Bias', *The Scotsman,* 3 June.

Humphrey, C and Owen, D (2000) 'Debating the 'Power' of Audit, 4 *International Journal of Auditing* 29–50.

HM Treasury (2008) *Dear Accounting Officer Letter 'Following up PAC reports'*, DAO(GEN)03/08, available at www.hm-treasury.gov.uk/d/dao0308.pdf.

IDeA (2009) *Looking back, moving forward: accounts of council improvement by leading politicians* (London, Local Government Association), available at www.idea.gov.uk.

James, O (2005) 'Performance Targets for Executive Agencies and Public Sector Externalities in the UK' in G Drewry, C Greve and T Tanquerel (eds), *Contracts, Performance Measurement and Accountability in the Public Sector* (Amsterdam, IOS Press).

Johnsen, A (2005) 'What does 25 years of experience tell us about the state of performance measurement in public policy and management?' 25 *Public Money and Management* 9.

Johnson, C and Talbot, C (2007) 'The UK Parliament and performance: Challenging or challenged?' 73 *International Review of Administrative Sciences* 113.

Klaushofer, A (2008) 'We know where you live' *Public Finance*, 5–11 December, 18.

Landers, B (1999) 'Encounters with the Public Accounts Committee: A Personal Memoir' 77 *Public Administration* 195.

Lapsley, I and Pong, C (2000) 'Modernisation v Problematisation: Value—for—money audit in public services' 9 *European Accounting Review* 541.

Ling, T (2007) 'New Wine in Old Bottles? When Audit, Accountability and Evaluation Meet' in M-L Bemelmans-Videc, J Lonsdale and B Perrin (eds), *Making Accountability Work: Dilemmas for Evaluation and for Audit* (Somerset, NJ, Transaction Publishers).

Lonsdale, J (1999) 'Impacts' in C Pollitt, X Girre, J Lonsdale, R Mul, H Summa and M Waerness (eds), *Performance or Compliance?: Performance audit and public management in five countries* (Oxford, Oxford University Press).

—— (2007) 'Helping Government to be responsive, responsible and respected: a reaction to Jocelyne Bourgon' 73 *International Review of Administrative Sciences* 31.

—— (2008) 'Balancing Independence and Responsiveness: A Practitioner Perspective on the Relationships Shaping Performance Audit' 14 *Evaluation* 227.

Lonsdale, J and Bemelmans-Videc, M-L (2007) 'Accountability—The Challenges for Two Professions' in M-L Bemelmans-Videc, J Lonsdale and B Perrin (eds), *Making Accountability Work: Dilemmas for Evaluation and for Audi.,* (Somerset, NJ, Transaction Publishers).

McLean, I, Haubrich, D and Gutierrez-Romero, R (2007) 'The perils and pitfalls of performance measurement: the CPA regime for local authorities in England' 27 *Public Money and Management* 111.

Maltby, J (2008) 'There is no such thing as audit society' *Paper presented at the Conference of Practical Criticism in the Managerial Social Sciences*, Leicester University Management School, 15–17 January.

Martin, S (2005) 'Evaluation, Inspection and the Improvement Agenda: Contrasting Fortunes in an Era of Evidence-Based Policy-Making' 11 *Evaluation* 496.

Modell, S (2004) 'Performance Measurement Myths in the Public Sector: A Research Note' 20 *Financial Accountability and Management* 39.

Moran, M (2001) 'The Rise of the Regulatory State in Britain' 54 *Parliamentary Affairs* 19.

Mulgan, G (2006) *Good and Bad Power* (London, Allen Lane).

National Audit Office (2007) *Fourth Validation Compendium Report* London, available at www.nao.org.uk/publications/0708/fourth_validation_compendium_r.aspx.

—— (2008a) *Annual Report* London, available at www.nao.org.uk/publications/0708/nao_annual_report_2008.aspx.

—— (2008b) *The Administrative Burdens Reduction Programme* London, available at www.nao.org.uk/publications/0708/administrative_burdens.aspx.

—— (2009) *Innovation across central government* London, available at www.nao.org.uk/publications/0809/innovation_across_government.aspx.

Newman, J (2001) *Modernising Governance: New Labour, Policy and Society* (London, Sage Publications).

Normanton, E (1966) *The Audit and Accountability of Governments* (Manchester, Manchester University Press).

O'Neill, O (2002) *A Question of Trust: 2002 BBC Reith Lectures* (Cambridge, Cambridge University Press).

Peters, BG (2005) 'Squaring Several Circles: Co-ordination, Performance and Accountability' in G Drewry, C Greve and T Tanquerel (eds) *Contracts, Performance Measurement and Accountability in the Public Sector* (Amsterdam, IOS Press).
Pollitt, C (2003) *The Essential Public Manager* (Maidenhead and Philadelphia, PA, Open University Press).
—— (2006) 'Performance information for democracy: The Missing Link?' 12 *Evaluation* 38.
Pollitt, C and Bouckaert, G (2004) *Public Management Reform* (Oxford, Oxford University Press).
Power, M (1994) *Audit Explosion* (London, Demos).
—— (1997) *The Audit Society: Rituals of Verification* (Oxford, Oxford University Press).
—— (2003) 'Auditing and the Production of Legitimacy' 28 *Accounting Organizations and Society* 379.
—— (2005) 'The Theory of the Audit Explosion' in E Ferlie, L Lynn and C Pollitt (eds), *The Oxford Handbook of Public Management* (Oxford, Oxford University Press).
Prosser, M (2005) Chair, UK Women and Work Commission, EU Gender Equality Conference, Birmingham, 7–8 November.
Public Audit Forum (2000) What Public Bodies Can Expect from Their Auditors', available at www.public-audit-forum.gov.uk/publicat.htm.
Sanderson, O (2001) 'Performance Management, Evaluation and Learning in "Modern" Local Government' 79 *Public Administration* 297.
Schelker, M (2007) 'Public Auditors: Empirical Evidence from the United States' Working Paper, available at www.ssrn.com/abstract=957528.
Select Committee on Public Administration, House of Commons. Minutes of Evidence, 9 January 2003, question 538.
Talbot, C (2005) 'Performance Management' in E Ferlie, L Lynn and C Pollitt (eds), *The Oxford Handbook of Public Management* (Oxford, Oxford University Press).
Travers, M (2007) *The New Bureaucracy: Quality assurance and its critics* (Bristol, Policy Press).
Torgler, B and Schaltegger, C (2005) 'The Determinants of Political Discussion: How Important are audit courts and local autonomy?' Working Paper Series, Berkeley Program in Law and Economics, University of California, Berkeley.
Van der Knaap, P (2006) 'Responsive Evaluation and Performance Management' 12 *Evaluation* 278.
Van Thiel, S and Leeuw, F (2002) 'The Performance Paradox in the Public Sector' 25 *Public Performance and Management Review* 267.
Wilkins, P and Lonsdale, J (2007) 'Public Sector Auditing for Accountability: New Directions, New Tricks?' in M-L Bemelmans-Videc, J Lonsdale and B Perrin (eds), *Making Accountability Work: Dilemmas for Evaluation and for Audit* (Somerset, NJ, Transaction Publishers).
Wilkinson, J (2005) 'The Growth of Performance Measurement: Help or Hindrance?' in G Drewry, C Greve and T Tanquerel (eds), *Contracts, Performance Measurement and Accountability in the Public Sector* (Amsterdam, IOS Press).
Wilson, J (2004) 'Comprehensive Performance Assessment—Springboard or Dead-Weight?' 24 *Public Money and Management* 63.

5

Changes in Human Rights

DAVID FELDMAN

The Background to the Changes: Human Rights Before the 1998 Legislation

Over the past decade, developments in human rights have changed the legal framework for administrative justice in the UK. Before that, international human rights law had already acquired limited significance for policy making and legislation. In particular, the European Convention for the Protection of Human Rights and Fundamental Freedoms (ECHR) had had some influence, because judgments of the European Court of Human Rights bound the UK in international law, and policies or processes sometimes had to be changed or new legislation had to be enacted in order to meet requirements flowing from those judgments. Yet human rights law generally had had little direct impact on administrative decision making, because international treaties are not directly applicable in domestic law in the United Kingdom unless legislation is passed to give effect to them, and there had been no such legislation. Whilst courts usually interpreted legislation on the assumption that it did not contravene the United Kingdom's international obligations, express provisions could easily displace that assumption. The House of Lords had firmly rejected the notion that a public body would be acting unreasonably, and therefore unlawfully, if it failed to protect or at least consider the implications of rights under the ECHR for its decisions: judges would not take it on themselves to incorporate the ECHR into domestic law by a side wind.[1]

Nevertheless, fundamental rights had made some impression through the common law. Judges were developing the idea that there are some rights which are fundamental as a matter of common law, including the right of access to a court to determine legal rights and obligations, the right not to be left destitute and homeless, the right to confront one's accusers in criminal proceedings, a convict's right to communicate with an investigative journalist in order to campaign to reverse his (or her) conviction, and the right to be free of a real likelihood of

[1] *R v Secretary of State for the Home Department, ex p Brind* [1991] 1 AC 696 (HL).

death, torture or inhuman or degrading treatment.[2] This indication of changing judicial attitudes was symbolically important, but its practical effects were relatively limited, except in two fields.

First, courts assumed that legislation did not breach (or authorise a breach of) those rights unless it did so clearly by express, unequivocal words or necessary implication.[3] However, they often undermined the potential of this assumption by treating very general words as clear and unambiguous even when they were not specific or concrete.

Secondly, in reviewing some administrative decisions on removing illegal immigrants and failed asylum-seekers from the country, unequal treatment of heterosexual and homosexual armed services personnel, and treatment of patients in the NHS, some judges said that the decisions had to be subjected to particularly anxious scrutiny (rather than the usual test of unreasonableness derived from *Wednesbury*) if they threatened fundamental rights.[4] However, there seems to be only one reported case in which a court, having decided that a party's right required anxious scrutiny of a decision, went on to quash the decision. That case concerned the location of a hearing as part of a public inquiry, not a normal administrative decision, and there is no certainty that the challenged decision would have survived scrutiny on the ordinary test of *Wednesbury* unreasonableness.[5] In other cases, anxious scrutiny appears to have had no practical effect on the result.

Meanwhile, fundamental rights were becoming increasingly important in EU law. The Court of Justice of the European Communities accepted that certain fundamental rights were part of the general principles of Community law, derived from the common constitutional traditions of the member states (where they can be identified), and from international treaties to which member states have contributed. They therefore include the rights under the ECHR.[6] In EU law they have constitutional force, binding the organs of the EU and those of states when acting to give effect to EU law, even when implementing obligations under public international law which are potentially incompatible with the fundamental

[2] See respectively the discussions in *R v Lord Chancellor, ex p Witham* [1998] QB 575 (DC); *R v Secretary of State for Social Security, ex p Joint Council for the Welfare of Immigrants* [1997] 1 WLR 275 (CA); *R v Davis* [2008] UKHL 36, [2008] AC 1128 (HL); *R v Secretary of State for the Home Department, ex p Simms* [2000] AC 115 (HL); *Bugdaycay v Secretary of State for the Home Department* [1987] AC 514 (HL); and *A v Secretary of State for the Home Department (No 2)* [2005] UKHL 71, [2006] 2 AC 221 (HL).

[3] *R v Eastbourne (Inhabitants)* (1803) 4 East 103, 107 (Lord Ellenborough CJ); *R v Secretary of State for Social Security, ex p Joint Council for the Welfare of Immigrants* [1997] 1 WLR 275 (CA).

[4] See *Bugdaycay v Secretary of State for the Home Department* (n 2 above); *R v Ministry of Defence, ex p Smith* [1996] QB 517 (CA).

[5] *R v Lord Saville of Newdigate, ex p A* [2000] 1 WLR 1855. I am grateful to Ms Lisa Hirsowitz for drawing my attention to the significance of this decision.

[6] See eg Case T-177/01 *Jégo-Quéré et Cie v Commission* [2002] ECR II-2365, [2003] QB 854 (CFI); Case C-50/00P *Unión de Pequeños Agricultores v Council of the European Union* [2002] ECR I-6677, [2003] QB 893 (ECJ).

rights.[7] These rights are now incorporated in the Treaties by what is now Article 6(2) of the Treaty on European Union.[8] The Maastricht Treaty also incorporated a Social Chapter, giving additional rights in employment and certain other rights, to which the Labour government, which was elected in 1997, subsequently acceded. Alongside this, an EU Charter of Fundamental Rights, proclaimed in December 2000, lists a wide range of social and economic rights as well as those derived from the ECHR. It is not directly enforceable, but is used by the European Court of Justice as an aid to interpreting EU law, including the rights recognised in Article 6(2), and applies to EU institutions and to institutions in member states when implementing Community law.

The Arrival of Domestic Human Rights Legislation

The relative weakness of legal protection for human rights in the UK was a target of the constitutional reforms brought forward by the Labour government after its election victory in 1997. In 1998 and 1999, devolution legislation came into force under which it was outside the powers of the devolved executive and legislative bodies established in Wales, Scotland and Northern Ireland to act in a manner incompatible with most of the rights under the ECHR which bound the UK in international law ('Convention rights'), or with EU law (including fundamental rights recognised by the Court of Justice).[9] The Human Rights Act 1998 (HRA), which came fully into force on 2 October 2000, then additionally required all public authorities in the United Kingdom to act in a way compatible with Convention rights unless prevented by primary legislation from doing so, and provided that all legislation was to be read and given effect so far as possible in a manner compatible with Convention rights.

As a result, for the first time it became possible to bring domestic legal proceedings to enforce those rights under the ECHR that the United Kingdom had bound itself in international law to secure to everyone within its jurisdiction, and also to use those rights by way of defence in legal proceedings. This potentially affects all action and decision making by public authorities, and administrative justice as it relates to their activities.[10] As the HRA is of general rather than geographically

[7] Joined Cases C-402/05 P and C-415/05 P *Kadi and Al Barakaat International Foundation v Council and Commission* [2008] ECR I-6351.

[8] Formerly Art F2 of the Maastricht Treaty.

[9] The relevant provisions of the Government of Wales Act 1998 came into force on 1 December 1998, those of the Scotland Act 1998 on 1 July 1999, and those of the Northern Ireland Act 1998 on 2 December 1999.

[10] For an outline of the principles involved see Feldman (2009, ch 7). More detailed treatments are provided by Beatson, Grosz, Hickman, Singh and Palmer (2008); Clayton and Tomlinson (2009), Lester, Pannick and Herberg (2009) and Wadham, Mountfield, Edmundson and Gallagher (2007).

limited effect across the United Kingdom, this chapter concentrates on it rather than the devolution legislation.

Convention Rights and Their Impact

The rights from the ECHR which became part of domestic law, the 'Convention rights' listed in section 1 of the HRA, are currently:

the right to life (Article 2);
the right to be free of torture and inhuman or degrading treatment or punishment (Article 3);
the right to be free of slavery and forced labour (Article 4);
the right not to be deprived of liberty (Article 5);
the right to a fair hearing in the determination of criminal charges and civil rights and obligations (Article 6);
the right to be free of retrospectively imposed criminal liability, including penalties (Article 7);
the right to respect for private and family life, home and correspondence (Article 8);
the right to freedom of conscience, belief and religion (Article 9);
the right to freedom of expression (Article 10);
the right to freedom of association and peaceful assembly (Article 11);
the right to marry and found a family (Article 12);
the right to be free of discrimination on various grounds in relation to the enjoyment of other Convention rights (Article 14);
the right to property (Protocol 1, Article 1);
the right to education (Protocol 1, Article 2);
the right to free elections (Protocol 1, Article 3);
the right not to be subjected to the death penalty (Protocol 13, Article 1).

The rights have three important characteristics which have emerged from the case-law of the European Court of Human Rights, the final and authoritative arbiter of the interpretation and application of the rights. First, the Convention is regarded as a living instrument, with the capacity to develop organically by interpretation in response to changing social and moral ideas, conditions and needs. The intentions or understandings of the framers and drafters of the Convention do not exercise a stranglehold over the development of the rights. As a result, the scope of some rights has expanded beyond all recognition as a result of interpretation by the Court. For example, Article 8 now applies to a wide range of interests including storage of and access to personal data, environmental threats to homes, sleep, sexual orientation and activity, recognition of reassigned gender, adoption, child-care decision making, photography in public and private places, and the level of damages in domestic law for invasion of privacy.

Secondly, despite being phrased mainly negatively as freedoms from interference, many Convention rights are interpreted as imposing obligations on the state and its agencies to offer assistance to people in protecting their rights.[11] This is derived from the state's obligation under ECHR Article 1 to *secure* the rights to everyone within its jurisdiction, not merely to refrain from violating them. Thus the right to life under Article 2 goes beyond a right not to be arbitrarily deprived of life, and imposes obligations on the state to take such steps as are reasonable in the circumstances to protect people whom a state body knows (or should have known) to be identifiably at risk of immediate and serious harm from other people.[12] This is in addition to an obligation to take adequate steps to prevent people being killed by the activities of state authorities themselves.[13] There are further duties in respect of the investigation of suspicious deaths and prosecution of offenders, including cases in which state agents may be implicated.[14] Positive obligations in respect of rights extend the scope of rights such as those under articles 2, 3, 8, 10, 11, and Protocol 13, Article 1.

The third characteristic of the rights is that they, and the ECHR itself as a whole, fall to be interpreted as part of the matrix of international law, including other human rights obligations of states.

In consequence, the scope of the rights is often considerably more extensive than might be expected from the bare text of the ECHR. At the same time, there are several kinds of limit on the rights. First, there is the natural limit imposed by the definition or scope of each right. Secondly, most rights are qualified: they may be restricted (though not entirely abrogated) by measures which meet criteria set out in the ECHR and interpreted by the European Court of Human Rights. Typically, a restriction must be prescribed by law (importing general requirements derived from the idea of the rule of law), pursue a legitimate purpose (usually specified in the relevant article), and be necessary in a democratic society for that purpose (typically requiring a pressing social need for interference with the right, as limited an interference as possible, and a rational and proportionate relationship between the aim and the interference). Thirdly, under the Act a public authority does not act unlawfully in violating a Convention right if the authority can rely on a requirement in primary legislation as permitting the violation. The implications of the second and third limits are explained below.

The legal requirements do not exhaust the potential impact of human rights. There has been a good deal of talk about creating a culture of human rights in public administration, incorporating the values which lie behind human rights

[11] The fullest analysis is provided by Mowbray (2004).

[12] *Osman v UK* App No 23452/94, (1998) 29 EHRR 245 (ECtHR).

[13] *McCann v UK* App No 18984/91, (1995) 21 EHRR 97 (Eur Ct HR); *LCB v UK* App No 23413/94, (1998) 27 EHRR 212 (ECtHR).

[14] See, eg, *Kaya v Turkey* App No 22729/93, (1998) 28 EHRR 1 (ECtHR); *Edwards v United Kingdom* App No 46477/99, (2002) 35 EHRR 19 (ECtHR); *R (Amin) v Secretary of State for the Home Department; R (Middleton) v Her Majesty's Coroner for West Somersetshire* [2003] UKHL 51, [2004] 1 AC 653 (HL).

as well as the legal requirements of the ECHR.[15] The process would also allow standards from other international human rights instruments, including those dealing with social, economic and cultural rights, to be made a part of administrative decision making, thus greatly expanding the range of considerations which are relevant. This could affect a vast range of areas of administration and policy, including childcare, health care, social welfare, immigration and deportation, housing, education, environmental protection, taxation, the arts and culture more generally, in policy making as well as individualised decision making.

Implementing Convention Rights in Administrative Systems

Some public authorities were outstandingly well prepared to implement the Act in 2000, and took the opportunity to reflect on their practices and ethos and develop them in line with the values underpinning Convention rights. The country's police forces were an excellent example of this, with the Association of Chief Police Officers providing leadership. Police training stressed the common-sense nature of most of the requirements of Convention rights, and showed how the values underpinning the rights—dignity, fairness, rationality in decision making, equality, pluralism, autonomy, responsibility and tolerance, among others—were consistent with the values of modern policing. Central government offered very useful guidance on the way public bodies are affected by the rights, promoting understanding of the relevant principles, in a series of valuable publications.[16]

However, another possible but less satisfactory approach is to skimp on principled training for front-line staff, under pressure of limited budgets and other demands on time and resources. In some fields, central government tried to secure compliance among front-line staff by issuing circulars and other written guidance based on legal advice, emphasising the risk of legal liability and stressing what not to do, rather than concentrating on the congruence between human rights principles and professional values and objectives. This can generate defensive, bureaucratic arrangements which do little to encourage humane decision making or improve practice. It can also lead managers and policy-makers to relegate responsibility for human rights within the organisation to their legal departments, where they become the preserve solely of lawyers instead of engaging all staff. In October 2003, the Audit Commission, having conducted a survey of public authorities, noted that human rights could bring benefits to users of public services, but reported that

> 58 per cent of public bodies surveyed still have not adopted a strategy for human rights. In many local authorities the Act has not left the desks of the lawyers. In health,

[15] See eg Klug (2000).

[16] The rights are integrated in the advice contained in Treasury Solicitor (2006), and excellent accounts of the rights and their impact are offered in Department for Constitutional Affairs (2006a), aimed at public authorities, and (2006b), aimed at the general public.

> 73 per cent of trusts are not taking action. … In the criminal justice sector the initial flurry of activity has stopped.

Furthermore, only 39 per cent of public bodies were taking action to ensure that contractors and partners were taking reasonable steps to comply with Convention rights.[17] Even the Parliamentary and Health Service Ombudsman currently promulgates sets of principles for good administration, handling complaints and remedying maladministration which make no express reference to the Act or human rights, although several of the principles refer to standards such as proportionality which are consistent with human rights thinking.[18]

These tendencies were visible in the approach taken to school education by both central government and local education authorities. Head teachers and school governors were bombarded with circulars detailing things to avoid and were given very little guidance on how to use Convention rights positively as a framework for good educational practice. As a result, some schools adopted a defensive stance, restricting the freedom of pupils and their families (eg, by forbidding photography at school events) and formalising interaction between staff, pupils and families. While this often avoided a (usually tiny) risk of violating rights, it did so at the cost of changing educational relationships in ways which were out of step with the values which both human rights and education are supposed to embody and advance.

Even where human rights are portrayed positively within organisations and front-line staff are encouraged to make them part of their everyday professional thinking in the implementation of the Act, Convention rights could often slip down the list of training and managerial priorities once the initial process had been completed, as the Audit Commission (above, note 17) observed in the criminal justice system. Public authorities face many competing demands. While their objectives may be clear at a high level of generality, deciding on the relative priority to be accorded to each in particular circumstances requires an exercise of judgement. Initially, political pressure made implementing the HRA a high priority. Later, attention had to shift to other targets, such as efficiency or other standards for delivering services, leaving the lawyers to deal with any difficulties arising under the Act.

Equally significantly, giving effect to human rights is usually not one of the core objectives of a public authority. For reasons which will be explored further below, Convention rights normally operate as constraints on the ways in which an authority is allowed to pursue its objectives and meet its responsibilities, rather than as organisational objectives of the institution. If pressure from government, regulators, 'stake-holders', funding bodies or consumers forces the authority to concentrate on value for money, transparency, democratic accountability, quantifiable service standards or policy goals, the authority may, entirely rationally,

[17] Audit Commission (2009: paras 3, 12–13).

[18] Parliamentary and Health Service Ombudsman (2009a, 2009b, 2009c).

come to treat understanding of and respect for human rights as a relatively low priority or even an inconvenience.

Nevertheless, legislation and the legal sanctions which it provides have made Convention rights a more powerful consideration for decision makers than ever before, to be kept in the back, and sometimes at the front, of their minds. In an administrative context human rights can have one or more of four effects: (i) limiting the range of things which public authorities may do, that is, ruling certain activities or objectives out entirely and demanding others; (ii) limiting the means by which or circumstances in which public authorities may pursue their objectives; (iii) requiring public authorities to adjust their decision-making procedures to ensure that there is adequate protection for rights and that the procedures are fair; and (iv) limiting the range of justifying reasons that can be lawfully deployed if the decision is challenged.

In relation to (i), this depends on the nature of the right. Absolute rights are capable of making it impossible to implement certain policies, for example, policies relating to deportation or extradition. By contrast, (ii), (iii) and (iv) are concerned with justifications for interfering with non-absolute rights. It has been said that the HRA has introduced a culture of justification, and that is often true.

The impact of this on administrative justice depends not only on the rights but also on distinctive features of administrative justice. It is essentially concerned with decision making in relation to identified people, and, although it is a contested concept, any model of administrative justice turns on the values which are central to shaping the process of either making or reviewing decisions affecting people. Mashaw has outlined three competing models of administrative justice (bureaucratic rationality, professional treatment, and moral judgement), whose legitimating values are respectively accurate and efficient administration (the needs of the organisation), serving clients (meeting their needs as fully as possible) and promoting fairness (resolving disputes about rights, that is, about benefits and burdens).[19] What roles do human rights play in these models? So far as rights prohibit or demand particular actions or outcomes, they are potentially relevant to all three models. They tend to restrict the range of acceptable answers to questions about substantive fairness (moral judgement), and constrain discretion in identifying and meeting people's needs (professional treatment). Where they limit the means by which a public authority can pursue its objectives or require fair procedures before people can be subjected to disadvantageous treatment, they also affect the extent to which the systematic, bureaucratic needs of the organisation can form the primary focus for decision making, although that does not mean that requirements of human rights are always, or even usually, at odds with bureaucratic rationality. In so far as the Act limits or focuses the admissible types of justification for infringing rights, it is relevant to all three models, and the models themselves may affect the application of the right, since (depending on

[19] Mashaw (1983: 25–31).

the right in question) it may be possible to justify an infringement by reference, for example, to the public interest in good administration by having clear, bright-line rules (bureaucratic rationality), in meeting the needs of the person affected by relying on extensive professional discretion (professional treatment) or in adjudicating between competing individual rights or interests by insisting on independent adjudication procedures (moral judgment).

Adler has extended Mashaw's models by adding three additional 'ideal types': managerialism (pursuing improved performance through good management); consumerism (maximising participation by and satisfaction of those who benefit from services and facilities); and markets (allowing free play to market forces, on the assumptions that people are the best judges of what they want and that markets tend to be economically efficient).[20] They reflect different (though potentially complementary) views of the roles of the state and consumers respectively in deciding what services should be provided and how.

At this macro-administrative level, managerialism allows the state to set objectives, but allows relatively low-level managers a good deal of freedom to decide how to give effect to them. Managers might choose (in Mashaw's terms) a bureaucratically rational, professional treatment or moral judgment approach, and be assessed by their superiors by reference to their success in achieving the objectives set. Consumerism also allows public administrators to decide how to organise services, but has a different criterion for accountability after the event: performance is assessed principally by reference to the degree of satisfaction among those who receive the services, rather than compliance with centrally promulgated standards or targets.

By contrast, commitment to markets reflects suspicion of any claim on the part of official decision makers to know what is good for people. The role of public administrators is seen as being to give people the opportunity to vote for goods, services and so on by participating in a market, where competition between goods and providers allows people to choose for themselves. This replaces an emphasis on giving people a 'voice' within the administrative system with the ideal of allowing or requiring people to 'exit' from it as far as possible.[21]

The effect of Convention rights on these methods of organising public services is relatively straightforward. As we shall see, they are usually concerned with outcomes and justifications, putting limits on the range of acceptable outcomes and justifications rather than dictating them. That can affect bureaucratic rationality and managerial efficiency by making some otherwise sensible procedures or outcomes unacceptable. In relation to consumerism, people's perceptions of their human rights may influence their sense of satisfaction with the way administrators treat them. Markets may operate alongside either managerialism (with the role of management being to secure goods or services rather than to provide them directly) or consumerism (where the market is a way of allowing people to obtain

[20] Adler (2003).

[21] See the discussion in Halliday (2004: ch 6).

the services they want through choices between opportunities). Convention rights cannot dictate how markets operate, but some economic rights, such as the right to property or the right to exploit one's own labour, are preconditions for the operation of markets.

More controversial is the relationship between markets and other rights such as a right to freedom of expression, to participate in the cultural life of the community, to benefit from the fruits of development or science, and to participate in a democratic political system. For example, within those international systems devoted to world economic development on a market model (such as the WTO and the World Bank), it has usually been thought that human rights are likely to interfere with the economic self-interest of participants in the market on which its operation depends. It has recently been powerfully argued that fundamental rights and capitalist economic globalisation are not contradictory forces, but can accommodate each other.[22] But whether or not human rights and markets can co-exist happily, the 'hidden hand' of a traditional market cannot be relied on as a way of producing respect for human rights. Even free-market economists do not usually claim that markets dependably produce benefits beyond economic efficiency.

This suggests that human rights may perhaps help in advancing bureaucratic rationality and may provide one measure for assessing desert in relation to Mashaw's 'moral judgment' model. They are also capable of assisting assessments which have to be made in the professional treatment model. Their main impact, however, is likely to be as side-constraints both on the range of values which can be pursued through any model, on the methods which can be used to pursue them, on the types of accountability which are required, and on the range of justifications which are admissible in relation to infringements of the rights. In this way, legal sanctions to protect rights can be seen as increasing the weight attributable to rights in comparison with bureaucratic rationality, markets, and so on.

Key Questions for Administrative Justice

Against this background we can turn to examine a number of key questions which Convention rights, through the mechanism and structure of the HRA, pose for practitioners of administrative justice.

The introduction of a legal requirement to act compatibly with Convention rights raises a number of questions for institutions and individuals in the administrative justice process. Some of these relate to all personnel whether engaged as primary decision makers, as reviewers or as appellate bodies. Others are relevant

22 Kinley (2009).

only to reviewing or appellate bodies. We shall deal with the following five issues:

1. What is the effect of the Convention rights on legality?
2. Does the HRA apply to private bodies delivering public services? (For a further discussion of this question, see Oliver's chapter in this volume.)
3. Who has to decide whether a decision is Convention-compatible and what consequences flow from incompatibility?
4. Does a decision maker have to adopt the sort of reasoning which a court would adopt in a human rights case?
5. What is required by way of fair procedures?

What Is The Effect of the Convention Rights on Legality?

Section 6(1) of the HRA states: 'It is unlawful for a public authority to act in a way which is incompatible with a Convention right.' However, section 6(2) provides that a public authority which acts incompatibly with a Convention right does not act unlawfully if:

> (a) as the result of one or more provisions of primary legislation, the authority could not have acted differently; or
> (b) in the case of one or more provisions of, or made under, primary legislation which cannot be read and given effect in a way which is compatible with the Convention rights, the authority was acting so as to give effect to or enforce those provisions.

This clearly protects public authorities against liability under the HRA when they act in compliance with a duty imposed by primary legislation expressly, or by necessary implication from the express terms of the legislation. For example, the Inland Revenue Commissioners were held to have no power to make an extra-statutory concession allowing widowers to claim a statutory bereavement allowance, which was restricted in a discriminatory way to widows only, in order to pursue equality between men and women, rather than deal pragmatically with hardship or transitory anomalies or make policy in the interstices of tax legislation, so their refusal to make such a concession was protected by section 6(2)(a).[23] In another case, the Secretary of State had given effect to legislation entitling a widow, but not a widower, to certain payments on the death of her spouse, and had refused to make equivalent payments to widowers *ex gratia*. The House of Lords held that the legislation was incompatible with the right to be free of discrimination under ECHR Article 14 taken together with Article 1 of Protocol 1, but the majority concluded that the Secretary of State was protected by section 6(2)(b), as he had been giving effect to the statutory scheme.

[23] *R (Wilkinson) v Inland Revenue Commissioners* [2005] UKHL 30, [2005] 1 WLR 1718 (HL) [20]–[23] (Lord Hoffmann, with whom Lords Nicholls, Hope, Scott and Brown agreed on this point). The Strasbourg Court has, as a result, since held that there was a violation of Art 14 ECHR: *Hobbs v UK* (2006) 44 EHRR 1113.

The claimants' argument would have turned a discretion to make *ex gratia* payments into an obligation.[24]

It is right to protect the responsible public authorities if they are simply complying with an obligation set out in clear terms in primary legislation which cannot be read and given effect in a Convention-compatible manner. However, some Law Lords have treated section 6(2) as creating a wider exception from liability, protecting public authorities when they are exercising a power or discretion which could have been used in a Convention-compatible way, and whenever they are acting to give effect to a statutory scheme, whether or not the particular act or decision which violates a Convention right is required or even authorised by the statute.

In *Doherty v Birmingham City Council*[25] the Council had statutory power to manage a caravan site of which it was the occupier. In doing so, it exercised its common law power to serve notice on gipsies to leave the site where they had been living for about 17 years, and brought county court proceedings for possession. The gipsies wanted to argue that the possession proceedings violated their right to respect for their home under ECHR Article 8, and that the county court should therefore exercise its discretion against making a possession order. In the House of Lords, Lord Hope, with whom Lords Rodger and Walker agreed, held that section 6(2)(b) protected a public authority which 'is doing what it has been authorised to do by the primary legislation' even if it was actually exercising a common law power but in a statutory framework.[26]

If this were correct, it would leave virtually no room for the obligation of public authorities under section 6(1) to act in a manner compatible with Convention rights where a public authority is exercising a function which is in any way affected by statute. If the statute compels the authority to violate a Convention right, or a duty to act compatibly with a right, would effectively make the legislative provision in question otiose, the authority would of course be protected by s 6(2)(a). But even where the authority has a discretion which could be exercised compatibly with the right, it could claim to be giving effect to the provisions of the statute in the very wide sense advanced by Lord Hope in *Doherty*. It makes no sense to apply section 6(2), designed to protect parliamentary sovereignty, to acts and decisions under common law powers and to statutory powers or obligations which could quite sensibly have been exercised in a Convention-compliant manner.

Lord Mance in *Doherty* took a narrower view of section 6(2) which, it is submitted, is far more persuasive. His Lordship pointed out that nothing in the relevant legislation made it improper for the council to take account of Convention rights, so there was no reason to allow the authority to violate a right without liability

[24] *R (Hooper) v Secretary of State for Work and Pensions* [2005] UKHL 29, [2005] 1 WLR 1681 (HL) [6] (Lord Nicholls), [48]–[52] (Lord Hoffmann), [72]–[75], [82] (Lord Hope).

[25] *Doherty v Birmingham City Council* [2008] UKHL 57, [2008] 3 WLR 636 (HL).

[26] Ibid at [21]. Lord Rodger at [89] and Lord Walker at [97]–[104 agreed.

when statute had not required that outcome.[27] Lord Mance's approach avoids the risk of emasculating the rights, and hence s 6(1) of the HRA 1998, whenever a public authority is acting within a statutory framework.[28]

It would be unsafe for administrators and those reviewing or deciding appeals against their decisions to assume that the new Supreme Court will in future uncritically follow the view of Lord Hope in *Doherty*. Unless required by statute to do so, public authorities should not act incompatibly with Convention rights, and should be prepared for their decisions to be quashed and liability to follow if they do so.

Does the HRA Apply to Private Bodies Delivering Public Services?

The focus of section 6(1) is clearly on bodies which are clearly public authorities, particularly those exercising the power of the state. However, section 6(3)(b) complicates matters by including within the category of public authorities 'any person certain of whose functions are functions of a public nature …', although section 6(5) establishes that this does not apply in relation to acts the nature of which is private.

The need for a category of partly public, partly private bodies results from changes in the way the state does its business. For more than two decades the private and voluntary sectors have acquired an increasingly important role in the provision of public services and facilities through privatisation of formerly state-owned corporations, statutory requirements or permissions for public bodies to contract out the provision of services or the management of public assets, and different forms of private financing initiatives and public–private partnerships (for a further discussion of this topic, see Gamble and Thomas's chapter in this volume). Patterns of private involvement and the terms on which the private sector offers facilities and services to the public instead of or on behalf of public institutions vary across the country. One might think that it would be invidious were the Convention rights of people who use facilities and receive services for which the public sector is ultimately responsible to depend on the particular form of the arrangements for providing them in different localities. Section 6(3)(b) recognises that private persons and bodies often exercise public functions, and ought to make it possible for those who are affected by the functions to assert Convention rights in relation to them no matter who actually does the work or makes the facilities available.

[27] Ibid at [141]–[53].

[28] For an example of the difficulty, see the somewhat unconvincing attempt by Baroness Hale in *Huang v Secretary of State for the Home Department* [2007] UKHL 11, [2007] 2 AC 167 (HL) [17] to justify not applying the wide interpretation of s 6(2)(b) to the review of immigration decisions, on the ground that immigration legislation, unlike housing legislation, had merely conferred discretion on officers rather than imposed Parliament's own assessment of the balance between rights and public interests in the form of a set of bright-line rules.

However, in practice the interpretation of section 6(3)(b) has been bedevilled by the reluctance of some judges to saddle the private and voluntary sectors with obligations under the HRA which, they think, should lie only on the public sector. This has sometimes led to a very narrow view of this 'hybrid', part public and part private, category of public authorities. Yet it is a matter of impression and approach. Instead of developing a definitive test for a public function, the courts have identified the following factors as indicating (although not conclusively) that a private body is performing a public function:

— where the body has statutory powers or duties in respect of the exercise of the function;[29]
— where the body performs a governmental function, which would otherwise have been exercised by a central or local governmental body, or is acting on behalf of such a body for that purpose;[30]
— where the body is funded or subsidised by a governmental body out of public funds;[31]
— where the body provides a service to the public, or one which it is in the public interest to have provided;[32]
— where the body is performing a function and the state assumes responsibility for the subject-matter of the function in question, bearing in mind that the functions for which the state accepts responsibility change over time;[33]
— where the state has an extensive interest in and effective machinery for regulating and overseeing the discharge of the function;[34]
— where a failure to exercise the function properly would give rise to a significant risk to Convention rights (for which the state could be liable in Strasbourg).[35]

The lack of a clear test often makes it difficult for people in private and voluntary organisations, who are providing services and facilities for members of the public pursuant to a duty imposed by statute on some person or body, to know whether they are bound by the obligation to act compatibly with Convention rights. This affects people concerned with administrative justice in those organisations, including, for example, those who have to deal with disciplinary

[29] *Aston Cantlow and Wilmcote with Billesley Parochial Church Council v Wallbank* [2003] UKHL 37; [2004] 1 AC 546 (HL) [12] (Lord Nicholls); *YL v Birmingham City Council (Secretary of State for Constitutional Affairs intervening)* [2007] UKHL 27, [2008] 1 AC 95 (HL) [8] (Lord Bingham), [26] (Lord Scott), [69] (Baroness Hale, especially if the powers are coercive), [102] ff (Lord Mance), [150] (Lord Neuberger).

[30] *Aston Cantlow* above [10], [12] (Lord Nicholls), [49] (Lord Hope), [88] (Lord Hobhouse), [159] (Lord Rodger); *YL* above [102] (Lord Mance), [159] (Lord Neuberger).

[31] *Aston Cantlow* [12] (Lord Nicholls); *YL* [10] (Lord Bingham), [26] (Lord Scott), [68] (Baroness Hale), [103] (Lord Mance), [148] (Lord Neuberger).

[32] *Aston Cantlow* [12] (Lord Nicholls); *YL* [67] (Baroness Hale), 103 (Lord Mance).

[33] *YL* [7] (Lord Bingham), [66] (Baroness Hale), [114]–[15] (Lord Mance).

[34] *YL* [9] (Lord Bingham).

[35] *YL* [11] (Lord Bingham).

matters in privately run prisons and people deciding whether to exclude tenants from social housing provided or managed by housing associations.

The first question is whether the body's functions are public.[36] Other matters, such as the institutional relationship between the body and government agencies, are not relevant.[37] Judges have distinguished between a 'function' and an 'act'. A function signifies generalised, goal-directed activity. Exercising a function may involve many acts, and the issue is the nature of the function, not of individual acts.[38]

However, it may not be easy to distinguish functions from acts. For example, in *YL v Birmingham City Council (Secretary of State for Constitutional Affairs intervening)*, the claimant resided in a nursing home run by a private company under a contract between the company and the claimant. The company had a contractual arrangement with the Council to accept people in need of care and attention in respect of whom the Council had an obligation under section 21 of the National Assistance Act 1948 to make arrangements, and those to whom the social services department had obligations in respect of registered nursing needs, which the local NHS primary care trust had to assess and provide for. Under the contract between the company and the Council, the company agreed to provide residential care for patients placed in its homes by the Council in accordance with the Council's care plan for each patient, to be paid for by the Council, and to provide nursing care assessed to be needed by each patient and paid for by the NHS primary care trust. The company agreed with the Council to act compatibly with Convention rights. The question was whether the company owed a duty directly to the patient under the HRA to comply with the patient's Convention rights, or only a duty to the Council under the company's contract with the Council. The company would owe a duty directly to the patient only if the company was exercising a public function. This required clarification of what the relevant 'function' was.

A majority of the House of Lords held that the company's function was providing residential and nursing services as a commercial organisation in a commercial market, and that this was a private function, even though the services were provided to people who were vulnerable and for whom the Council and NHS primary care trust would otherwise have had to care by virtue of their statutory duties under the 1948 Act.

However, there is a philosophical division within the judiciary. Not all judges regard it as clear that one should focus on the nature of the job being done rather than the reasons why it needs to be done when considering whether a person or body is exercising a public function. This reflects a sense that private bodies

[36] *Aston Cantlow* [6] (Lord Bingham, dissenting).

[37] *YL* [61] (Baroness Hale, dissenting), 87 (Lord Mance, disapproving the approach in *Poplar Housing and Regeneration Community Association v Donoghue* [2001] EWCA Civ 595, [2002] QB 48 (CA)).

[38] *YL* [129] (Lord Neuberger).

should have to act compatibly with Convention rights when they are acting to allow a public authority (which would be bound by the HRA) to discharge its functions by providing services or facilities to the public.

The difficulties which these differences generate, and the implications of a decision one way or the other, can be seen by contrasting *YL*, above, with a more recent case in which the Court of Appeal struggled to work out the implications of *YL*. In *R (Weaver) v London & Quadrant Housing Trust (Equality and Human Rights Commission intervening)*,[39] the only questions were whether the Trust, a registered social landlord that provided housing at less than market rents to people who could not satisfy their housing needs in the open market, exercised a function of a public nature so as to be a 'hybrid' public authority under section 6(3)(b) of the HRA, and, if so, whether the act of terminating the tenancy of a social tenant was an act of a private nature within the meaning of section 6(5). The Trust conceded that it was a hybrid public authority because, as a registered social landlord, it had statutory power (shared with local authorities but not with private landlords) to apply for anti-social behaviour orders and parenting orders against people occupying its houses. Registered social landlords also have special statutory powers to demote an assured tenant to the status of a 'demoted tenant' with reduced security of tenure and to grant 'family intervention tenancies' to occupiers who are on behaviour support programmes. But the Trust argued that granting, managing and terminating tenancies in the course of managing its housing stock did not involve a public function, and that in any event terminating a tenancy was a private act, regulated by public law. Accordingly it denied that it was obliged to act compatibly with tenants' Convention rights in relation to the management of tenancies.

Elias LJ held that the relevant function (as distinct from act) of the Trust was providing housing for people unable to provide for themselves in the open market, and that this was a public function. Elias LJ tested the function against four indicative factors identified by Lord Nicholls in an earlier House of Lords decision:[40] 'the extent to which in carrying out the relevant function the body is publicly funded, or is exercising statutory powers, or is taking the place of central government or local authorities, or is providing a public service.' The Trust benefited substantially from government grants and transfers of housing from local authorities to maintain its housing stock so that it could pursue publicly valuable objectives; it had a statutory duty to co-operate closely with local authorities to help them perform their statutory duties and achieve their objectives; its work in providing cheap housing, below market cost, for people who could not afford market rents could properly be regarded as governmental, as subsidising poor sections of the public is a role commonly though not exclusively performed by governmental bodies; and the Trust acted in the public interest, in a

[39] *R (Weaver) v London & Quadrant Housing Trust (Equality and Human Rights Commission intervening)* [2009] EWCA Civ 587, [2010]1 WLR 363 (CA).

[40] *Aston Cantlow*, n 29 above, at [12].

non-commercial way, and was regulated by a public body (the Housing Corporation) within a statutory framework to secure the objectives of government policies, with restricted powers of alienation and management of its houses. Cumulatively (though not separately), Elias LJ decided, these factors made the function of providing social housing a public function.[41]

Elias LJ went on to hold that the act of terminating a tenancy for non-payment of rent was not an act of a private nature, because, whilst the right to terminate flowed from private law, the act of termination was inextricably bound up and necessarily involved in the Trust's public function of providing and managing social housing, not merely incidental or supplementary to it.[42]

Lord Collins of Mapesbury did not find it necessary to decide whether providing and managing social housing is a public function. Once it had been conceded that the Trust was a hybrid public authority within section 6(3)(b), albeit for reasons peripheral to the provision and management of houses, the only remaining question was whether that provision and management was an act of a private nature within section 6(5) so as to exclude it from the application of Convention rights. On this latter point, his Lordship agreed with Elias LJ.[43]

By contrast, Rix LJ, dissenting, after exhaustively analysing earlier case-law, concluded that the allocation and management of social housing by the Trust fell outside the 'public function' category of section 6(3)(b) and was in any event an 'act of a private nature' so that section 6(5) excluded the applicability of Convention rights.[44]

The disagreements in this case show how uncertain the law now is. All one can say is that the view of the majority in *YL* protects private and voluntary providers of housing, but the majority decision of the Court of Appeal in *London & Quadrant Trust* shows that *YL* has done nothing to simplify the task of decision makers in organisations (public and private), which provide that and other services, who need to know when they are bound by Convention rights.

Who Has to Decide Whether a Decision Is Convention-Compatible and What Consequences Flow From Incompatibility?

Ultimately the compatibility of any rule, decision or action with Convention rights is a matter for courts and tribunals. However, administrators have a number of responsibilities of their own. The main one applies where action is governed by legislation, whether primary or subordinate. Section 3(1) of the HRA requires everyone (not only courts and tribunals) to read and give effect to all legislation in a manner compatible with Convention rights so far as it is possible to do so. This presents two problems for administrative organisations. First,

[41] *London & Quadrant*, n 39 above, [68]–[72].
[42] Ibid at [76].
[43] Ibid at [101]–[02].
[44] Ibid at [161].

it is unrealistic to expect administrators with little or no legal training, let alone expertise in human-rights law, to decide reliably whether legislation is compatible with Convention rights, save in the most obvious cases. Secondly, if an administrator decides that a legislative provision is incompatible with a Convention right, it is far from clear what he or she can be expected to do about it within a framework of administrative consistency and managerial control.

Take, for example, review of decisions concerning applications to the Social Fund for discretionary payments.[45] The Social Fund is a cash-limited fund, currently administered through Jobcentre Plus (part of the Department for Work and Pensions), from which are made two classes of payments: mandatory payments in respect of maternity, funeral and cold weather heating expenses; and discretionary payments in respect of a person's urgent needs for basic items which cannot be met from other sources.[46] The Secretary of State for Work and Pensions controls the amount of money paid into the Fund,[47] and (by linking allocations to particular purposes and by giving legally binding directions to the appropriate officers) the aggregate amount which each local office can use on discretionary payments of a particular description in a given period.[48] Discretionary payments may, and usually do, take the form of loans, although grants are possible in some cases.[49]

The Social Fund was first established in the 1980s in an attempt to control the huge increase in the number and cost of single payments in the supplementary benefits scheme. As originally conceived, decisions made by a social fund officer might be reviewed by that officer or a more senior officer in the same office, but there was to be no provision for independent appeal or review (except by way of judicial review). This caused disquiet in Parliament, and the legislation ultimately included a statutory right both to an internal review within the local office[50] and a further review by independent Social Fund Inspectors, appointed by the Social Fund Commissioner and operating in the Birmingham office of the Independent Review Service for the Social Fund. The Inspectors are appointed and their work is monitored by the Commissioner, who has no decision-making function but gives general advice and assistance and reads a sample of decisions.[51] The importance of this independent review is shown by the fact that Social Fund Inspectors vary or reverse decisions of officers in over 50 per cent of the cases reviewed, and random checks on officers' decisions have revealed a similar rate of errors in cases where applicants have not sought a further review by an Inspector, leading the

[45] The description which follows relates to arrangements in England, Wales and Scotland. Separate but similar legislation applies in Northern Ireland.

[46] Social Security Contributions and Benefits Act 1992 ss 138, 140(3).

[47] Social Security Administration Act 1992 s 167(3).

[48] Social Security Administration Act 1992 s 168(3), (3A); Social Security Contributions and Benefits Act 1992 s 140(3).

[49] Social Security Contributions and Benefits Act 1992 s 139(3). For a thorough and up-to-date account of the operation of the Fund, see Buck (2009).

[50] See now Social Security Administration Act 1992 s 66(1), (2).

[51] See now Social Security Administration Act 1992 ss 65, 66.

Commissioner, Sir Richard Tilt, to make critical comments about the quality of primary decision making by officers of Jobcentre Plus,[52] a part of the Department for Work and Pensions.

People in such need that they have to apply to the Social Fund are specially likely to be at risk of being unable to enjoy at least two Convention rights: the right not to be subjected to degrading treatment under ECHR Article 3; and, most frequently, the right to respect for private and family life and home under Article 8. Officers dealing with applications have to comply with several layers of legislation: the Act of Parliament establishing the Fund and authorising the making of subordinate legislation; subordinate legislation in the form of general directions issued by the Secretary of State, binding on officers and Inspectors; and guidance which is to be taken into account by but does not technically bind officers,[53] although it would be a brave official at the front line who would ignore guidance from the Secretary of State.

If an officer or Inspector considers that a direction or guidance on its normal reading produces a result incompatible with a Convention right, what is he or she to do? One possibility would be to try to find a Convention-compatible reading, and give effect to it if one is available. This would be consistent with the obligation imposed by section 3(1) of the HRA, but if the individual officer acts without reference to the views of other officials in the organisation or to consistency of practice it is likely to lead to inconsistency and confusion. There is an even greater difficulty if the decision maker concludes that no compatible reading is available. In that case the direction, as subordinate legislation, may well be invalid by reason of the incompatibility (subject to section 6(2) of the HRA, discussed above). If the official decides that his or her duty is therefore to disregard the direction and act as necessary to achieve compatibility with the right, the risk of administrative disorder increases. Either way, the organisation as a whole will find it hard to stay within budgetary limits if predictability is undermined.

Another possibility would be to follow the direction and institutional practice, hoping that the outcome would later be held to be compatible with the right. This, however, would fail to take seriously the statutory requirement in section 3(1) of the HRA and the explicit statement in section 6(1) of the general rule that an act incompatible with a Convention right is unlawful.

In practice, the senior officials of the Independent Review Service for the Social Fund considered the matter at a series of internal meetings and seminars involving outside experts, and developed a compromise that the Commissioner embodied in an Advice Note, which was agreed at the Service's Quality Forum in September 2002 together with Support Notes to the Advice Note, and came into effect on 1 April 2003.[54] The Commissioner has a statutory duty 'to monitor the quality of decisions

[52] See Tilt (2007).

[53] Social Security Contributions and Benefits Act 1992 s 140(2); Social Security Administration Act 1992 s 66(7).

[54] *Commissioner's Advice on the Human Rights Act 1998* and *Support Notes on Commissioner's Advice on the Human Rights Act 1998*, available at www.irs-review.org.uk/infocent/commad/commad.htm.

of social fund inspectors and give them such advice and assistance as he thinks fit to improve the standard of their decisions',[55] and therefore considers that the inspectors are required to follow his general advice.[56] Whether or not this is correct as a matter of law, it is in line with bureaucratic rationality and managerialism within an institution which values consistency. It might pose a risk to the Service's independence of government if the Commissioner were in thrall to the Secretary of State (who appoints him), but the Commissioner has successfully maintained a distance from and high level of independence of government. The Support Notes, by contrast, are not in any way binding on Inspectors, but are likely to be taken very seriously by them and are another instrument for achieving consistency of approach.

The Advice and Support Notes recognise both the significance of the statutory duty under section 3(1) of the HRA to read and give effect to all legislation in a Convention-compatible manner if possible, and the risk of invalidity flowing from applying a direction or guidance which is ultra vires on account of being incompatible and incapable of being read or applied in a compatible manner. At the same time, in the interests of consistency and sound management, it places institutional constraints on the freedom of individual Inspectors to adopt new interpretations of legislation (primary or subordinate) or to refuse to apply subordinate legislation.

The Notes explain that Inspectors should first decide cases on the basis of ordinary domestic law. They should then consider whether the result would violate a Convention right. Section 4B of the Support Notes draws a number of important considerations to the attention of Inspectors. First, a decision relating to the Fund will only an be unlawful under the HRA if the Fund is the state body responsible for helping with the kind of need in question. If the responsibility lies on a social services department, it will not violate a Convention right to refuse a payment. Secondly, if a grant is not available it might be possible to interpret the legislation as allowing the Inspector to order a loan, which could meet the state's obligations under the ECHR sufficiently to avoid a violation of the right. The decision here is clearly one for the Inspector alone.[57]

However, the Notes impose two limitations on what the Inspector may properly do. The Support Notes contain the following instruction in bold type:

> In the interests of consistency, if an Inspector considers that a decision on a case under domestic law, without regard to Convention rights, might lead to the violation of a Convention right, he must consult the R & D Team before proceeding.[58]

[55] Social Security Administration Act 1992 s 65(5)(a).

[56] 'As the purpose of my statutory duty to give advice to Inspectors is to improve the standards of their decision-making, it is implicit that Inspectors must act on that advice. I should perhaps say that I do not generally give advice on individual cases. Instead my advice focuses on the principles and approach to take in relation to matters such as interpretation of the law and evaluation of evidence. However if I see a case when case-reading that I think has been unsatisfactorily handled I will refer it back to another Inspector for a fresh review.' Tilt, n 52 above, reply to question 7.

[57] *Support Notes on Commissioner's Advice on the Human Rights Act 1998*, n 54 above, p 3.

[58] Ibid. The R & D (Research and Development) Team, among other things, helps the Commissioner to perform his duty to give advice and to monitor the quality of review.

This does not relieve the Inspector of responsibility for deciding the case, but ensures that appropriate advice is available and that lessons learned from novel cases can be shared with other Inspectors. Next, the Advice and Support Notes deal with the situation where subordinate legislation, such as a direction, would lead to a violation of a Convention right and cannot be read and given effect in a Convention-compatible manner. Such a direction is ultra vires unless primary legislation, which cannot be read and given effect in a Convention-compatible manner, prevents the removal of the incompatibility. As the Secretary of State has a fairly wide power to make or revoke directions, the primary legislation will nearly always allow the removal of the incompatibility. That being so, one might expect the Inspector not to apply the invalid direction. However, the Advice says, 'In such circumstances the appropriate course will usually be to raise the matter with the Secretary of State, who may issue a revised direction, and/or seek a declaration from the High Court, which could quash the relevant direction.'[59]

This shows how the legal requirements of the HRA may be moderated in the interests of demands of consistent decision making taking account of the institutional context and organisational structure in which decisions are taken. In Mashaw's terms, human rights, which operate predominantly within a 'moral judgement' model of administrative justice, are recognised, but where they directly conflict with rules promulgated administratively with binding force they are restricted by the needs of bureaucratic rationality. To put it another way, practical realism imposes limits on the theoretical force of Convention rights within the administrative setting.

Does A Decision Maker Have to Adopt the Sort of Reasoning Which a Court Would Adopt in a Human Rights Case?

The next question concerns the type of analysis and reasoning which the law expects of an administrative decision maker where a Convention right is engaged. In *R (SB) v Governors of Denbigh High School*,[60] school governors decided to adopt a uniform code for pupils and not to exempt a girl who, adhering to a minority but firmly and conscientiously held view of the requirements of Islam relating to women's dress, wanted to wear a *jilbab* (a long black gown concealing the shape of her body) at school. The school's uniform code allowed a *shalwar kameez* (a sleeveless dress with a square neck-line worn over loose trousers tapering to the ankles) with a shirt, school tie and school pullover. When she arrived at school for the start of the year wearing a *jilbab* she was sent away and told to change into a *shalwar kameez* before returning. Instead of going back, she challenged the

[59] *Commissioner's Advice on the Human Rights Act 1998*, n 54 above, p 5, s 4E. The Support Notes provide an example of a case in which this is thought to be the appropriate response: *Support Notes*, n 54 above, p 6, s 6, Example 1.

[60] *R (SB) v Governors of Denbigh High School* [2005] EWCA Civ 199, [2005] 1 WLR 3372 (CA); [2006] UKHL 15, [2007] 1 AC 100 (HL).

decision by way of judicial review, arguing that she had been unlawfully excluded from school and that her right to manifest her religious belief under ECHR Article 9 and her right to education under Article 2 of Protocol No 1 had been violated.

The first instance judge, Bennett J, held that she had not been excluded from school, and so had not suffered a violation of Protocol No 1, Article 2. He also rejected the claim under Article 9. On appeal, the Court of Appeal decided that she had been excluded and that the uniform code restricted her freedom of religion, so both articles were engaged. The Court considered whether the interference with the rights could be justified, and held that, although the code and the requirement to comply with it might well have been reasonable and, indeed, correct in the circumstances, the Governors had failed to make out a justification because they had not shown that they had analysed the girl's request by reference to the ECHR and its case-law. Decision makers, the Court said, had to give reasons for decisions which engaged Convention rights in a form which addressed the human rights justifications for interfering with the right.

This would have placed a substantial burden on non-lawyers to justify in terms of human rights law every decision which interfered with a Convention right. School education constantly gives rise to issues concerning freedom of belief, freedom of expression, respect for private life and the right to education. Requiring each decision to be explicitly justified in terms of human rights law would have been, as one commentator said, formalistic and would tend to judicialise education (and, by extension, all areas of public service and administration) to an undesirable extent.[61] The school governors therefore appealed to the House of Lords, and the Secretary of State for Education and Skills intervened to argue that the Court of Appeal's reasoning had been based on a fundamental misunderstanding of the HRA.

The House of Lords agreed, and reversed the decision of the Court of Appeal's decision. A majority held that there had been no interference with the claimant's Convention rights, because it would have been possible for her without undue hardship to attend another school at which she would have been permitted to wear a *jilbab*.[62] Nevertheless, all five Law Lords considered whether, if there was an interference, it was justified, and concluded that it was. Their Lordships made it clear that the HRA, and for most purposes the substantive Convention rights, require that the outcome of a decision or act be compatible with Convention rights, but do not require a particular form of reasoning to justify the decision. If the decision is substantively compatible with the right, an administrator's failure to justify it in terms of human-rights case-law would not vitiate it. In

[61] Poole (2005: 691–95). This was cited with approval by Lord Bingham of Cornhill in the House of Lords: [2006] UKHL 15, [2007] 1 AC 100, [31].

[62] [2006] UKHL 15, [2007] 1 AC 100, [21]–[25] (Lord Bingham), [50]–[55] (Lord Hoffmann), [88]–[90] (Lord Scott of Foscote). Lord Nicholls at [41] and Baroness Hale at [92]–[93] thought that there had been an interference with the rights.

the vast majority of cases, substance, not form, is the significant matter.[63] As Lord Hoffmann said, the only way in which analysing an issue in terms of the Convention jurisprudence would help to protect a decision from challenge under the HRA would be that a public authority, by doing so, 'may help to persuade a judge that its answer fell within the area of judgment accorded to it by the law.'[64]

That might seem to cast doubt on the importance of an understanding of human rights to an administrative decision maker, or the value of attempting to analyse issues in terms of Convention rights. However, such doubts would be misplaced, for two reasons.

First, decisions are more likely to be compatible in substance with Convention rights if the person taking them considers the significance of the rights (alongside other relevant matters) when making the decision. This can be done on the basis of broad principles if the decision maker is aware of the relevant principles. Indeed, as human rights are to a considerable extent a distillation of common sense and common humanity, taking account of them will probably help to secure a high-quality decision. (There is a problem, of course, if decision makers in some areas of public administration have not been introduced to the principles. As noted earlier, the education service has suffered from this. In the Court of Appeal in *SB*, Brooke and Mummery LJJ pleaded for head teachers and governors to receive what Mummery LJ called 'clear, constructive and practical advice on how to anticipate and prepare for problems, how to spot them as and when they arise and how to deal with them properly.'[65] The value of an awareness of these matters, at the level of general principles, is reduced but not eliminated by the reversal of the Court of Appeal's decision.)

Secondly, giving reasons, which include an assessment of matters relevant to compatibility with Convention rights, will usually make it more likely that the decision will be upheld on review or appeal. Whilst it is true (as noted above) that providing reasons for decisions with human-rights implications will not make lawful a decision which is in substance incompatible with a right, it is also true that reasons, when given, will be given significant weight by reviewing bodies in relation to some grounds of review.

As questions of compatibility with Convention rights, including legitimacy of aims and proportionality of response, are issues going to the legality of the decision or measure, a reviewing court or tribunal must make its own assessment, and is not allowed simply to rely on the primary decision maker's view subject only to the application of the test of *Wednesbury* unreasonableness. This has been made clear in a number of cases in judicial statements of the highest authority.[66]

[63] Ibid at [29]–[31] (Lord Bingham), [41] (Lord Nicholls), 68 (Lord Hoffmann), [91] (Lord Scott) and [95] (Baroness Hale).

[64] Ibid at [68].

[65] [2005] EWCA 199, [2005] 1 WLR 3372, [82] (Brooke LJ), [89] (Mummery LJ).

[66] See, eg *SB*, n 60 above, at [30] (Lord Bingham) and [68] (Lord Hoffmann). The position is even clearer in relation to appellate authorities (rather than reviewing bodies): see *Huang v Secretary of State for the Home Department* [2007] UKHL 11, [2007] 2 AC 167 (HL).

As Baroness Hale has said, if one asks who is to decide whether or not a claimant's Convention rights have been infringed,

> [t]he answer is that it is the court before which the issue is raised. The role of the court in human rights adjudication is quite different from the role of the court in an ordinary judicial review of administrative action. In human rights adjudication, the court is concerned with whether the human rights of the claimant have in fact been infringed, not with whether the administrative decision-maker properly took them into account.[67]

Nevertheless, a primary decision maker's reasons may carry weight in several ways. If the decision maker is particularly well placed to make a difficult assessment, or has particular expertise in the subject-matter to which the decision relates, or has special constitutional responsibility for and authority in the field, a reviewing body (at least if it lacks similar or greater expertise and constitutional authority) will be slow to conclude that the primary decision maker's conclusion was erroneous. For this reason, in *SB* the conclusion that any interference by the school's uniform policy with the pupil's Convention right to manifest her religion was proportionate to a legitimate aim was influenced by the fact that the school's governors and head teacher had made considerable efforts to obtain well informed advice from Muslim religious leaders about the religious acceptability of different forms of dress and had framed the code in the light of that advice, being sensitive to the need to respect the widely differing religious beliefs and cultural traditions of pupils at the school, particularly as the head teacher and governors were very well qualified by experience and law to decide how best to accommodate them.[68] Moreover, if there is a question as to whether a decision is within the area of judgement accorded to decision makers in relation to such matters as proportionality, the way in which a decision maker approached the problem may, as we have seen, help to persuade the reviewer that it is within the area.[69]

Appellate bodies usually have less freedom than reviewing bodies to take into account the primary decision maker's reasoning in relation to Convention rights. The House of Lords held in *Huang v Secretary of State for the Home Department*[70] that an appellate tribunal must make its own assessment of the justifiability of any infringement of a Convention right, and is not permitted merely to accept the view of the primary decision maker as to (for example) whether an infringement of a right is a proportionate means of pursuing a legitimate objective. However, even appellate bodies may be influenced by primary decision makers' findings of fact which are relevant to such matters. Furthermore, it is probably true that, psychologically speaking, people are more likely to be persuaded that a decision is proportionate if the primary decision maker has given reasons for concluding that it is proportionate than if no such reasons are given.

67 *Belfast City Council v Miss Behavin' Ltd* [2007] UKHL 19, [2007] 1 WLR 1420 (HL) [31].

68 See *SB*, n 60 above, especially at [34] (Lord Bingham), [65] (Lord Hoffmann) and [98] (Baroness Hale).

69 See text at n 64 above.

70 [2007] UKHL 11, [2007] 2 AC 167 (HL).

For these reasons, while an absence of reasons or bad reasons will not make unlawful a decision which is substantively compatible with Convention rights, a reasoned justification when offered may not be irrelevant to the decision of either an appellate or, more particularly, a reviewing body. To quote Baroness Hale again in a case concerning the licensing of sex shops:

> the court has to decide whether the authority has violated the Convention rights. In doing so, it is bound to acknowledge that the local authority is much better placed than the court to decide whether the right of sex shop owners to sell pornographic literature and images should be restricted—for the prevention of disorder or crime, for the protection of health or morals, or for the protection of the rights of others. But the views of the local authority are bound to carry less weight where the local authority has made no attempt to address that question. Had the Belfast City Council expressly set itself the task of balancing the rights of individuals to sell and buy pornographic literature and images against the interests of the wider community, a court would find it hard to upset the balance which the local authority had struck. But where there is no indication that this has been done, the court has no alternative but to strike the balance for itself, giving due weight to the judgments made by those who are in much closer touch with the people and places involved than the court could ever be.[71]

The vexed question of the weight which a reviewing body should attach to the views of a primary decision maker is sometimes put in terms of deference, but this is unhelpful in practical terms. Deciding that X should (or should not) accept Y's conclusion on an issue is the conclusion of a process of assessment. Saying that X should (or should not) defer to Y does not help to explain why that should or should not happen. Deference is therefore not a legal principle, and can never be more than a descriptive umbrella hiding a variety of complex institutional and constitutional evaluations. For instance, judges may probe but will not ultimately reject a clear opinion from the Foreign Secretary as to the impact on the UK's relations with other states of a decision requiring a specific piece of information to be divulged or an investigation to be carried out.[72] The reason is that the Foreign Secretary is uniquely well placed to make such judgements. Institutionally, the Foreign and Commonwealth Office has better access to relevant information and experience than any other body. Constitutionally,

[71] *Belfast City Council v Miss Behavin' Ltd*, n 67 above, at [37].

[72] *R (Corner House Research) v Director of the Serious Fraud Office (JUSTICE intervening)* [2008] UKHL 60, [2008] 3 WLR 568 (HL) (Director entitled to accept assessment of Ministers and civil servants that continuing inquiry would be likely to lead Saudi Arabian government to withdraw cooperation with the UK on anti-terrorist intelligence, and to discontinue investigation; court could not question the correctness of that assessment); *R (Bancoult) v Secretary of State for Foreign and Commonwealth Affairs* [2008] UKHL 61, [2008] 3 WLR 955 (HL) (Foreign Secretary entitled to exclude inhabitants of British dependency from vicinity of their islands to protect strategic interests asserted by USA in respect of their military base on the islands); *R (Binyam Mohamed) v Secretary of State for Foreign and Commonwealth Affairs* [2010] EWCA Civ 65 (decision to restore to open judgment redacted material which, according to the Foreign Secretary, might, if restored, lead the USA to refuse to cooperate with the UK on security matters in future, and so would damage the UK's national security, 10 February 2010).

the Foreign Secretary is responsible for acting on behalf of the Crown to conduct the UK's foreign relations, and is accountable to one or other of the Houses of Parliament for that activity.

By contrast, decisions of less elevated executive and administrative bodies give rise to fewer issues of constitutional authority. Whilst a body may have some claim to expertise (although, as the *ProLife Alliance* case shows,[73] sometimes courts are too ready to attribute expertise to bodies which in reality have no specialist understanding of the matter in question, such as offensiveness in relation to broadcasting), the constitutional position of officials in central and, to an even greater degree, local government and quangos presents few, if any, reasons for a court to decline to review their conclusions.

What is Required By Way of Fair Procedures?

Many Convention rights carry with them requirements of procedural fairness which must be observed if an interference with the right is to be justifiable. For example, a deprivation of liberty can be justified under Article 5 only if the person detained is able to test the legality of detention promptly in a fair hearing before an independent and impartial tribunal. No hearing can be fair unless the detainee is given enough information about the reasons for detention to allow him or her to mount an effective defence.[74] The same applies to control orders made against suspected international terrorists, which severely restrict civil rights and infringe the right to respect for private and family life under ECHR Article 8.[75] Social workers who take a child into care to protect him or her against a suspected danger from a member of the family must give the family a fair chance to respond to the allegations and to participate in planning to reintegrate the family.[76]

Where a public authority exercises a power or duty which involves the determination of civil rights and obligations, those affected have a right under ECHR Article 6.1 to a fair hearing within a reasonable time before an independent and impartial tribunal. 'Independent' means independent of the state and of the original decision maker. An in-house review by an official lacks the necessary quality of independence to meet the requirements of Article 6.1. There is also a lack of the necessary independence if the reviewer can be removed by a minister without an independent procedure for establishing on the merits whether there are good grounds for removal,[77] if a minister can give binding directions to reviewers in

[73] *R (ProLife Alliance) v British Broadcasting Corporation* [2003] UKHL 23, [2004] 1 AC 485 (HL).

[74] ECHR Art 5.4 as interpreted by the ECtHR in *A v UK* (App No 3455/05) ECtHR 19 February 2009.

[75] ECHR Art 6.1; *Secretary of State for the Home Department v AF (No 3)* [2009] UKHL 28, [2009] 3 WLR 74 (HL).

[76] *W v UK* App No 9749/82, (1987) 10 EHRR 29 (ECtHR).

[77] *R (Brooke) v Parole Board* [2008] EWCA Civ 29 (CA).

individual cases,[78] or if a reviewing panel includes a member of the body which made the original decision.[79]

However, the European Court of Human Rights has interpreted Article 6.1 as permitting administrative decision makers to determine civil rights as long an aggrieved party has access to review by a court of 'full jurisdiction'. The meaning of this term is itself open to interpretation. In essence, a lack of independence can be remedied if there is an appeal to or opportunity for external review by an independent and impartial body which can apply an appropriate rigorous standard of scrutiny to significant findings and assessments. The process of decision making is examined in the round.[80]

It is not always necessary for the independent tribunal to make its own independent assessment of all matters raised by a case. Sometimes it can rely on the assessment of administrators earlier in the process, subjecting it to normal principles of judicial review, including *Wednesbury* unreasonableness. Lord Hoffmann has said that full jurisdiction in this context means 'full jurisdiction to deal with the case as the nature of the decision requires.'[81] Some decisions call for expert judgement best offered by specialist administrative officers. If the procedure followed by those officers is fair, it is not necessary or proper for a reviewing court to extend its own supervisory functions. It has been held that the sufficiency of review by the independent tribunal depends on (among other things) the subject matter of the decision, the manner in which it was reached, and the content of the dispute, including desired and actual grounds of appeal.[82] On the other hand, where an administrative decision engages Convention rights such as the right to respect for private life under Article 8, the independent tribunal must be able to quash the decision if not satisfied that it is a necessary and proportionate way of responding to a pressing social need to pursue an aim which is capable of forming the basis for a justification for interfering with the particular right.[83]

The difficulty which this presents for decision makers is that it is not always possible to say whether a decision-making procedure meets the required standard of fairness until it has run its course. A few examples illustrate the complexity arising in different factual circumstances.

[78] *R (Girling) v Parole Board* [2006] EWCA Civ 1779, [2007] QB 783 (CA); *R (Brooke) v Parole Board*, above.

[79] *R (Bewry) v Norwich City Council* [2001] EWHC 657 (Admin), [2002] HRLR 2 (housing benefit review board including councillors); *R (Smith) v Lincoln Crown Court* [2001] EWHC 928 (Admin), [2002] 1 WLR 1332 (member of licensing committee sitting in Crown Court on appeal from decision of licensing justices forming part of the same committee).

[80] See further Bailey (2009: paras 12.30–12.34).

[81] *R (Alconbury Developments Ltd) v Secretary of State for the Environment, Transport and the Regions* [2001] UKHL 23, [2003] 2 AC 295 (HL) [87].

[82] *Bryan v UK* App No 19178/91, (1995) 21 EHRR 342, [45]; *Runa Begum v Tower Hamlets LBC (First Secretary of State intervening)* [2003] UKHL 5, [2003] 2 AC 430, [5]–[7] (Lord Bingham), [51]–[54] (Lord Hoffmann).

[83] See eg *Lustig-Prean and Beckett v UK* (1999) 29 EHRR 548 (ECtHR).

Any power to prevent people from working in a role where they might harm people, such as teaching, medicine, or as a carer, involves a determination of civil rights and so attracts the right to in the determination of civil rights under ECHR Article 6.1. However, the need to protect vulnerable people may limit the extent to which a person must be given a hearing before being suspended, but in such cases it will violate Article 6 if there is any significant delay between the decision and a hearing before an independent tribunal.[84]

Housing cases are particularly sensitive, because they involve not only the right of the person wanting to be housed but also the property rights of the owner of the premises (whether in the public or the private sector) and, in relation to public sector housing, the competing needs and rights of other people with claims on the housing stock. Nevertheless, where administrative decisions effectively determine civil rights and obligations, they engage the right to a fair hearing by an independent tribunal under ECHR Article 6.1. In housing matters, the House of Lords has provisionally accepted that decisions relating to housing may be treated as determining civil rights, on the understanding that the procedural requirements of Article 6.1 must be given effect sufficiently flexibly to accommodate the administrative needs of housing authorities.[85] If housing legislation makes an administrative body the final arbiter of factual matters and allows an appeal to or review by a court only on points of law, the decision-making process would not be sufficiently independent to satisfy Article 6.1. Section 3 of the HRA may then require courts to act as courts of 'full jurisdiction' so as to provide effective review, even if an appeal to the court under the statute lies only on a point of law. In effect, issues necessary to the decision are 'jurisdictional facts', which in terms of ordinary administrative law are treated as questions of law, and so normally within the remit of courts on judicial review.[86]

It can thus be seen that Convention rights can have a significant impact on the procedural obligations of administrative decision makers and also on the extent of external review by tribunals or courts.

Conclusions

We have seen how Convention rights affect administrative justice as side-constraints. To some extent they affect procedure. In particular, ECHR Article 6.1 and other rights, which include due-process entitlements, can both structure

[84] See *R (Wright) v Secretary of State for Health* [2009] UKHL 3, [2009] 2 WLR 267 (HL).

[85] *Runa Begum v Tower Hamlets LBC* [2003] UKHL 5, [2003] 2 AC 430, HL; *Tomlnison* but see now *Birmingham City Council* [2010] UKSC 8, 17 February 2010.

[86] *Adan v Newham LBC* [2001] EWCA 1916, [2002] 1 WLR 2120 (CA). The actual outcome reached in *Adan* was disapproved by the House of Lords in *Runa Begum*, n 85 above, but the principle (as opposed to its application to the facts) is consistent with, and seems to be required by, the ratio of the House in *Runa Begum*. See further *R (Gilboy) v Liverpool City Council* [2008] EWCA Civ 751, [2009] 3 WLR 300 (CA).

decision-making procedures and impose enhanced review obligations on courts and tribunals. There may also be advantages to considering Convention rights expressly in the course of an administrative decision. But Convention rights under the HRA focus mainly on the substance of decisions, and on the balance between the responsibilities of administrative decision makers and those of courts and tribunals in appeal and review proceedings. We have also seen how the needs of consistent and efficient decision making may themselves require the legal status and implementation of Convention rights to be subject to compromise in practice to allow effective management of a complex programme such as the Social Fund.

The courts are still at an early stage in the process of developing a jurisprudence on human rights. Important questions concerning the structure and interpretation of the HRA, including the scope of section 6(2) of the HRA and the extent of the category of public authorities, have not yet been satisfactorily answered. As a result, there are major areas in which administrative decision makers face significant uncertainty. Nevertheless, the basic principles of the Convention rights are not complicated, and with appropriate training any intelligent decision maker should be able to grasp their connection with principles of good administration, including fairness and treating people with dignity, concern and respect, and ensuring that any infringement of a right is justified.

References

Adler, M (2003) 'A Socio-legal Approach to Administrative Justice' 25(4) *Law and Policy* 323.

Audit Commission (2003) *Human Rights: Improving Public Service Delivery*, available at http://www.justice.gov.uk/about/docs/acrep03.pdf.

Bailey, S (2009) 'Due Process Rights' in D Feldman (ed), *English Public Law*, 2nd edn (Oxford, Oxford University Press), ch 12.

Beatson, J, Grosz, S, Hickman, T, Singh, R and Palmer, S (2008) *Human Rights: Judicial Protection in the United Kingdom* (London, Sweet & Maxwell).

Buck, T (2009) *The Social Fund: Law and Practice*, 3rd edn (London, Sweet & Maxwell).

Clayton, R and Tomlinson, H (2009) *The Law of Human Rights*, 2nd edn (Oxford, Oxford University Press).

Department for Constitutional Affairs (2006a) *Human Rights: Human Lives—A Handbook for Public Authorities*, available at www.justice.gov.uk/guidance/humanrights.htm.

—— (2006b) *A Guide to the Human Rights Act 1998*, 3rd edn, available at www.justice.gov.uk/guidance/humanrights.htm.

Feldman, D (2009) 'Standards of review and human rights in English law' in D Feldman (ed), *English Public Law*, 2nd edn (Oxford, Oxford University Press), ch 7.

Halliday, S (2004) *Judicial Review and Compliance with Administrative Law* (Oxford, Hart Publishing).

Kinley, D (2009) *Civilising Globalisation: Human Rights and the Global Economy* (Cambridge, Cambridge University Press).

Klug, F (2000) *Values for a Godless Age: The Story of the United Kingdom's New Bill of Rights* (London, Penguin).

Lester of Herne Hill, Lord, Pannick, Lord, and Herberg, J (eds) (2009) *Human Rights Law and Practice*, 3rd edn (London, Butterworths).

Mashaw, JL (1983) *Bureaucratic Justice: Managing Social Security Disability Claims* (New Haven, Yale University Press).

Mowbray, A (2004) *The Development of Positive Obligations under the European Convention on Human Rights by the European Court of Human Rights* (Oxford, Hart Publishing).

Parliamentary and Health Service Ombudsman (2009a) *Principles of Good Administration*, available at www.ombudsman.org.uk/improving_services/principles/index.html.

—— (2009b) *Principles for Remedy*, available at www.ombudsman.org.uk/improving_services/principles/index.html.

—— (2009c) *Principles of Good Complaint Handling*, available at www.ombudsman.org.uk/improving_services/principles/index.html.

Poole, T (2005) 'Of headscarves and heresies: the *Denbigh High School* case and public authority decision making under the Human Rights Act' PL 685.

Tilt, Sir R (2007) 'Comment', in *Adjust*, the newsletter of the Council on Tribunals, April, available at www.council-on-tribunals.gov.uk/adjust/item/comment_sfcomm.htm.

Treasury Solicitor's Department (2006) *The Judge Over Your Shoulder*, 4th edn, available at www.tsol.gov.uk/Publications/judge.pdf.

Wadham, J, Mountfield, H, Edmundson A and Gallagher, C (2007) *Blackstone's Guide to the Human Rights Act 1998*, 3rd edn (Oxford, Oxford University Press).

Part 2

Conceptual Issues and Analytic Approaches

6

Understanding and Analysing Administrative Justice

MICHAEL ADLER

Introduction

In this chapter, it is argued that what lies at the heart of justice, namely that 'everyone should receive what is due to them', applies just as much to procedures as to outcomes. The meaning of administrative justice, defined as the justice inherent in administrative decision making, is then analysed. It is argued that, like legal justice and social justice, administrative justice has procedural and substantive dimensions. Thus, it is concerned with the fairness of the ways in which people are treated as well as the justice of what they receive or contribute.

In support of the claim that administrative justice has procedural and substantive dimensions, reference is made to research, which shows that people attach importance to the fairness of the procedures to which they are subjected whether or not they work to their advantage and independently of their assessment of the justice of the outcome.

In order to achieve administrative justice, it is argued that, in addition to external forms of accountability, internal procedures are required. An approach to the justice of administrative decision making, which sees it in terms of the 'trade-offs' between a number of competing conceptions of administrative justice and embraces procedural fairness as well as substantive justice, is developed and outlined, and its potential assessed.

The chapter concludes by commending the approach to administrative justice promoted by the UK Government in its 2004 White Paper 'Transforming Public Services: Complaints, Redress and Tribunals' (Cm 6243, 2004) and expressing the hope that it will go some way towards ensuring that everyone receives what is due to them, both in terms of how they are treated by administrative agencies and in terms what they receive from or contribute to them.

Michael Adler

The Concept of Justice

The Meaning of Justice

Miller (1976: 19–20) asserts that 'the subject matter of justice is the manner in which benefits and burdens are distributed among men [and women] whose qualities can be investigated' and 'the just state of affairs is one in which each individual has exactly those benefits and burdens which are due to him [or her] by virtue of his [or her] personal characteristics and circumstances'. Although there is considerable disagreement about the scope of justice claims and the priority that should be given to them, justice is widely recognised as a principle of wide application and considerable importance. Some scholars contend that it is all-important, Rawls (1972) in particular asserting that it is the primary criterion by which the basic structure of society should be judged: 'the first virtue of social institutions, just as truth is of systems of thought' (ibid: 3).

Rawls distinguishes between the *concept* of justice, which refers to 'a proper balance between competing claims', and competing *conceptions* of justice, each of which expresses a different set of 'principles for identifying those considerations which determine this balance' (ibid: 10). The coexistence of a single concept and several competing conceptions suggests that justice is, like many other important social and political ideals, *essentially contested* (Gallie 1964). As such, it can be defined in a fairly uncontroversial way (in this case as 'a proper balance between competing claims') but the terms in which it is defined (ie, what constitutes 'a proper balance' and even what is to count as a 'claim') are the subject of considerable disagreement. These disagreements are not random but are associated with differences in personality, gender, class, culture and ideology, and vary across time and space.

Legal Justice and Social Justice

It has become commonplace to distinguish between different subdivisions of justice in terms of their fields of application. Thus, Honoré (1970) points out that, while *restorative justice* is concerned with compensation for harm or injury (in civil matters), *punitive justice* is concerned with the punishment of wrongdoing (in criminal matters). Together these two subdivisions of justice comprise *legal justice*, which is a major concern of the legal system, ie of litigation and the courts. *Social justice*, on the other hand, is concerned with how benefits and burdens, or what Miller (1999: 1) calls 'the good and bad things in life', should be distributed among individuals and groups in society. As such, it is the subject matter of social, economic and fiscal policy, which are concerned with the distribution of 'primary goods' such as income, wealth, health and education. It is a major concern of government, in particular of those government departments that are responsible for devising and implementing programmes of taxation and public expenditure.

Other institutions in civil society, such as private and non-profit organisations, are also concerned with social justice but are not dealt with here.

Two caveats need to be made at this point:

- Because reparation and punishment have been included in the domain of legal justice, the burdens (or 'bad things') which are included here refer to other disadvantages, such as the taxes that are needed to finance the public provision of benefits and services.
- Although social justice usually refers to the allocation of material benefits and burdens, the 'primary goods' with which it is concerned also include intangible (non-material) resources, eg consideration and respect.

Although social justice can be distinguished from legal justice, some of the same moral considerations apply to them both. Likewise, although legal justice is obviously bound up with the legal system, it is important to recognise that this is also true of social justice—legal justice and social justice are merely concerned with different aspects or areas of law.

Procedural Fairness and Substantive Justice

A distinction can also be made between *procedural fairness*, which I take to be synonymous with *procedural justice* and is concerned with 'process' (Richardson 1984), and *substantive justice*, which is concerned with 'outcomes'. Procedural fairness focuses on how individuals are treated while substantive justice focuses on what they end up with. Both the sub-divisions referred to above, ie legal justice and social justice, have procedural and substantive dimensions. In the case of legal justice, procedural fairness includes the rules of evidence and procedure which govern proceedings in the criminal and civil courts, while substantive justice refers to the outcomes of criminal and civil actions; in the case of social justice, procedural fairness includes the administrative rules which govern decision making by government departments and other official bodies while substantive justice refers to the allocation of benefits, the delivery of services, the award of licences, the imposition of taxes and so on.

It is, of course, possible to take issue with the distinction made above on the grounds that treating people fairly should itself be regarded as an outcome of the decision-making process. However, if it is an outcome, it is clearly a different kind of outcome from most of the outcomes that the procedures are established to achieve. If the latter is referred to as a *primary outcome*, the former may be referred to as a *secondary outcome*. The primary outcome of criminal procedures in the courts is to determine guilt and court procedures can be judged by how effectively they do so, ie by the proportion of 'guilty people' who are acquitted and the proportion of 'innocent people' who are convicted. Likewise the primary outcomes of administrative procedures are to confer entitlements, impose obligations or regulate activities, and they may likewise be judged by the proportion of false negatives and false positives they produce. Criminal courts and administrative agencies should both aim to treat people fairly but that is not their primary purpose. Even if treating people fairly is regarded as an outcome, a distinction can be made between the just outcomes which the procedures are intended to deliver and the fairness of the ways in which the procedures deal with people.

The idea of *procedural fairness* suggests that a concern with 'ensuring that everyone receives their due' can be applied to procedures and that a procedurally just state of affairs is one in which individuals are treated in a manner that reflects what is due to them in light of their personal characteristics and circumstances.

There have been various attempts to specify the requirements of procedural fairness. Thus, in legal justice, reference is made to a fair trial (in the case of criminal prosecutions) and to fair proceedings (in civil matters). In a criminal prosecution, the procedural requirements reflect the rights and duties of the accused and the state. What these ought to be are matters of ongoing debate but there is wide agreement that accused persons should be entitled to know the case against them, to be legally represented, to plead not guilty and, if they do so, to be treated as innocent until found guilty. The evidence against them must stand up and the case for the prosecution must be established 'beyond reasonable doubt'. Likewise, in a civil action, where the outcome is decided 'on the balance of probabilities', there are procedural requirements, which reflect the rights and duties of the parties in dispute, that are also matters of ongoing debate.

Procedural considerations are also an important component of social justice and how administrative agencies should treat individuals is not a settled matter. However, there would appear to be a fair measure of agreement that, in applying policies to individuals, like cases should be dealt with alike, policies should not be applied retrospectively (unless it is to the advantage of the individuals concerned to do so), people should be shown respect, their circumstances should be investigated thoroughly, and their claims should be decided impartially and expeditiously, irrespective of the outcome.

The Relationship between Procedural Fairness and Substantive Justice

There are basically two approaches to understanding the relationship between procedural fairness and substantive justice. The first approach, which is clearly an instrumental one, asserts that fair procedures can be identified in terms of their contribution to the outcome of the decision. Thus fair procedures are those which lead to correct, and in that sense, just decisions. The second, non-instrumental approach asserts that fair procedures are important for their own sake, because they reflect and protect beliefs about how people should be treated, whether or not they result in just outcomes.

Procedural Fairness Is Instrumental to Substantive Justice

The first approach emphasises the link between process and outcome. Thus, assuming it is possible to identify a 'correct' outcome, a given procedure is justified to the extent that it results in such an outcome. However, as Richardson (1984: 111) points out, there are a number of problems with this approach. First, there may be no uniquely correct outcome—while the facts may be agreed, the precise implications of law or policy in relation to them may be hotly contested. Second, even if there is a uniquely correct outcome, it may be very difficult to specify those procedures that are most likely to deliver it. Third, procedures are not free and, if efficiency is taken into account, the optimum level of procedural protection will be that which minimises both the costs of the procedure (*direct costs*) and the costs of reaching an incorrect decision (*error costs*). While the identification of direct costs may be relatively straightforward (since it involves identifiable items like the salaries paid to those involved and associated overhead costs), the calculation of error costs (the cost to the individual of a wrongful prosecution, of failure in an action where they had a legitimate claim or of wrongly denying someone what they are entitled to) can be exceedingly difficult to calculate. This problem will be revisited later in the chapter.

Substantive Rights Call For Procedural Protection

Dworkin (1986: 80) introduces another element into the calculation of error costs. Using the criminal law as an example, he distinguishes between two types of harm: *bare harm* and *moral harm*. The innocent suspect who is mistakenly convicted and punished suffers bare harm in being sent to prison from the suffering, frustration, pain and failure to satisfy his or her desires that are associated with imprisonment. In addition, he or she suffers moral harm in being wrongly deprived of the right not to be punished when innocent. These additional moral costs stem from the infringement of a right and, according to Dworkin, justify greater expenditure on procedures designed to avoid wrongful convictions than on procedures designed to avoid wrongful acquittals. For Dworkin, having a substantive right triggers a secondary right to procedural protection. This does not only apply in relation to the criminal law but applies equally in relation to civil law (ibid: 92) and, by extension, to administrative law. Although the distinction which Dworkin makes enhances the attractiveness of the instrumental approach, the downside is that, where there are no substantive rights, it would seem to follow from his argument that individuals have no enforceable claim to any specific form of procedural protection, and that procedural fairness is essentially a matter of policy.

Perfect, Imperfect and Pure Forms of Procedural Justice

In dealing with the relationship between procedural fairness and substantive justice, Rawls (1972: 85–86) makes a distinction between *perfect*, *imperfect* and *pure* forms of procedural justice.

Perfect procedural justice has two characteristic features. First, there is an independent criterion for determining what a fair division is; and, second, it is possible to devise a procedure that is certain to have this result.

Imperfect procedural justice has only the first of these features. While there is an independent criterion for determining what the outcome should be, there is no way of specifying a procedure which will always produce this result. However, some procedures may be regarded as more likely than others to produce the right outcomes or to do so in more cases.

Pure procedural justice has neither of these features. There is no independent criterion for determining the right outcome: instead there is a correct or fair procedure such that the outcome of applying it, whatever that may be, should be regarded as correct or fair provided that it has been properly followed. In this kind of procedural justice, the justice of any outcome is founded on the fairness of the institutional arrangements from which it arises.

Since procedures which always lead to just outcomes can rarely, if ever, be devised, perfect procedural justice has little practical relevance. Imperfect procedural justice is exemplified by existing criminal, civil and administrative procedures, although there will always be arguments about whether or not they actually minimise the number of false positives and false negatives and thereby facilitate the attainment of correct outcomes.[1] Pure procedural justice is exemplified by a lottery or a 'free market', although, in developing his contractual theory of justice—based on the principles of justice people would choose if they chose them 'under a veil of ignorance', that is, ignoring everything they already know about themselves and the society in which they happen to live—Rawls (1972: 201) argues, in effect, that just outcomes will result from the adoption of fair procedures.[2]

Procedures Are Primarily Instrumental But Also Reflect Authoritative Standards

According to Galligan (1996: 6), procedures are purposive and the first and primary concern of procedures is to lead to desired outcomes. However, a second concern is to ensure that what he calls 'contextual values' are respected. While one sense of fairness consists in achieving the outcomes required by law, a second sense of fairness is linked to these other values and is satisfied when they are respected. Within different legal procedures, Galligan lists dealing with a matter according to legal standards, deciding as an official thinks best, reaching agreement between the parties, investigating a situation and reporting on the results, and adopting a framework based on participation where no precise standards are laid down in advance. He claims (ibid: 54) that there are authoritative standards based on tiers of values which constitute the standards of fair treatment, so that a person treated in accordance with them is treated fairly and the procedures are fair to the degree

[1] Barry (1965: 102, fn 4) argues that the dovetailing of fair procedures and just outcomes is not an accident, since procedures are usually selected with an eye to such dovetailing, and that there is no analytic connection between fair procedures and just outcomes such that either one entails the other.

[2] Rawls (1972: 201) concedes that fair procedures can result in a range of outcomes, all of which are just. He refers to this situation as *quasi-pure procedural justice.*

that they have this result. The first tier consists of the standards of the particular area of criminal law, civil law or administrative law, which dictate the basic legal objectives that apply in the case in question and are directed towards achieving particular outcomes. The second tier comprises standards from cognate sources, for example the common law, neighbouring statutes or policy imperatives, which qualify, modify or augment the first tier of outcome-based standards. The third tier is even more general and draws on social principles, which include but go beyond legal principles. Some standards have an impact on outcomes, directly or indirectly; others place constraints on the course of action that leads to outcomes, while a few may be entirely independent of outcomes. Procedures are thus contingent on serving some end, purpose or value and are therefore neither intrinsically fair nor intrinsically unfair.

Procedures Reflect Values Which Are Independent of Outcomes

The claim is often made, for example by Tribe (1988: 666), that the need to provide procedural fairness springs from the obligation to respect a person's dignity and autonomy as a human being. However, Bayles (1990: 11) argues that process values are not derived solely from the dignity and autonomy of individuals but are what, following Rawls, 'rational persons would accept for use in a society in which they expected to live'. Examples of such values are participation, equal treatment, intelligibility, timeliness and confidence in the decision-making process. Although some of the procedures which give effect to these values may promote accuracy, Bayles argues that they should be assessed independently of such effects. It follows (ibid: 115–139) that procedures should not be evaluated solely in terms of the extent to which they minimise the sum of direct costs plus error costs (arising from false positives and false negatives) but should also take into account process benefits, that is, the positive benefits which follow from giving effect to process values. He also argues (ibid: 163–189) that procedural principles are not relevant across the board and that their appropriateness depends on the characteristics of the decision-making process in question. He distinguishes between adversary adjudication, bureaucratic investigation, directorship, professional service and negotiation, specifies when each is appropriate, and identifies which principles of procedural justice apply in each case.

Although there is much to commend in Bayles' approach, not least his acceptance of the relative autonomy of procedural values, his contention that principles derived from adversarial proceedings in the courts may not be appropriate in all contexts and, more generally, that different principles apply to different types of decision making, is clearly problematic. It is not clear, in the same way as it is not clear with Rawls' account of the 'original position', why rational people would all choose the same set of principles; and, even if they did, it is not clear that they would order these principles in the same way. Bayles does not deal with the issue of ordering, and this is a major shortcoming since many of the principles are competitive, that is, the more you have of one, the less you can have of another. This can be illustrated by means of an example. The greater the emphasis on participation, the harder it will be to reach decisions quickly, on the other hand, the greater the emphasis on speed, the less likely that individuals will be able to participate fully in the decision-making process. The principles of procedural justice not only compete with each other but have a price tag attached to them, which means that they compete with other principles such as efficiency. Unfortunately Bayles does not consider such issues.

Although it can be argued that considering a principle like efficiency involves appealing to a concept unrelated to justice, it is clearly unrealistic to ignore the issue of costs. Allocating additional resources to the decision-making process can be expected to enhance the probability of achieving a correct outcome but no society can be expected to devote all its resources to enhancing its decision-making procedures. Trade-offs are required.

Conclusions

It has been argued in this section that procedural considerations apply to social justice in the same way as they apply to legal justice. The relationship between process and outcome, that is, between procedural fairness and substantive justice, has been examined, and a number of different positions identified. Some of the problems associated with a purely instrumental view of procedures were identified and Dworkin's view that substantive rights call for procedural protection considered. Although it constitutes an important advance, I do not think it goes far enough. Two non-instrumental views were then considered: Galligan's view that, although the primary function of procedures is to lead to desired outcomes, a secondary function is to reflect 'authoritative standards based on tiers of values' which include but go beyond legal principles, and Bayles' view that process values, which are independent of outcomes, and are what 'rational persons would accept for use in a society in which they expected to live', provide the basis for evaluating procedures. Although there are differences in emphasis between these two views, they both recognise that, although procedural fairness can contribute to substantive justice, it does not only have instrumental value but can be justified in its own terms. Moreover, they both recognise that a uniform set of procedural principles does not apply across the board and that the appropriateness of any set of procedural principles depends on the characteristics of the decision-making process in question.

The Social Psychology of Procedural Justice

Early Studies: Thibaut and Walker

Some 35 years ago, two American social psychologists, Thibaut and Walker (1975), attempted to define and clarify the nature of procedural justice through the application of social psychological methods to courtroom disputes. They hypothesised that litigants' satisfaction with dispute resolution outcomes would be independently influenced by their assessments of the fairness of the dispute resolution process.

Thibaut and Walker distinguished between *process control* (control over the opportunity to present evidence) and *decision control* (control over the final decision), and used experimental methods to test their hypothesis experimentally. Their results showed that the method of reaching a decision, as well as the outcomes it generates, is important in determining perceptions of fairness and satisfaction, and that people prefer adversarial procedures to inquisitorial ones, mainly because they give the parties greater control over the decision-making process. On this basis, they concluded that procedures that are high in process control should be used in disputes dominated by conflicts of interest because, in spite of the fact that information gathering is biased, such procedures are most likely to ensure the consideration of individual circumstances that is needed to maximise fairness.

Subsequently another American social psychologist, Leventhal (1980), using an approach based on 'equity theory', put forward a model which can be applied to a wide range of non-legal contexts. He identified six justice rules (consistency, bias suppression, accuracy of information, correctability, representation and ethicality) and, although he did not carry out any empirical research himself, subsequent research confirmed the importance of four of them, namely consistency, accuracy, bias suppression and representation, indicating that there are four potential underlying dimensions of procedural justice.

In the course of a review of social psychological studies of procedural justice, Lind and Tyler (1988: 133–135) claimed that Leventhal overestimated the impact of favourable outcomes, that is, of distributive justice, on judgments of justice and concluded that the most serious flaw in his work was his belief that procedures are of less importance than outcomes in determining judgments of overall fairness.

More Recent Studies: Tyler

Tyler set out to test the importance of criteria of procedural justice that he derived from the theories of Thibaut and Walker, and Leventhal. As he points out (Tyler 1988: 105), Thibaut and Walker's two categories (process control and decision control) map on to Leventhal's representation category but Leventhal's other categories do not have any equivalents in Thibaut and Kelly's study. His research set out to test the importance of a composite set of categories and to determine whether Thibaut and Walker's empirical findings are specific to courtroom settings or can be generalised across a wider range of contacts with legal authorities, whether they apply when the contact is voluntary as well as when it is involuntary, and whether the meaning of fairness varies with sex, age, race, education, income and 'liberalism'.

Tyler's sample comprised 652 persons who had personal experience of the police and/or the courts in the previous 12 months. *Process control* was measured in terms of how much opportunity respondents had to present their problem or case to the authorities before decisions were made; *decision control* by how much control they had over the decision made by the authorities. *Consistency* involved comparisons with previous experience, prior expectations, what they thought happened to others or the experiences of friends, family or neighbours. *Impartiality* was measured by combining responses to two questions: whether the authorities did anything that was 'improper' or 'dishonest' and whether officials had lied to respondents, and also by asking respondents how hard the police or judge had tried to be fair. *Accuracy* was also measured by combining the responses to two questions: whether the authorities had the information they needed about how to make good decisions and how to handle the problem; and whether they had tried to bring the problem into the open so that it could be solved. *Correctability* was measured by asking respondents whether they knew of an organisation to which they could have complained about unfair treatment. Finally, *ethicality* was measured by combining responses to two questions: whether the authorities had been polite to the respondents and showed concern for their rights. Respondents were also asked how fair the procedures used by the organisation were and how fairly they had been treated, with both answers rated on a four-point scale. The results were as follows:

- Process and outcome, that is, procedural fairness and substantive justice, were strongly related.
- Seven aspects of process made *independent* contributions to the assessment of procedural fairness: the effort of the authorities to be fair; their honesty; whether their behaviour was consistent with ethical standards; whether opportunities for representation were given; the quality of decisions made; whether opportunities to appeal decisions existed; and whether the behaviour of authorities showed bias.
- Contrary to expectations, consistency between the ways in which respondents were treated, their previous experiences, prior expectations and their perceptions of the ways in which others were treated, were not important; but ethicality was.
- The criteria used to assess the fairness of an experience were similar to those used to assess the fairness of the authorities involved. In both cases, the effort to be fair, ethicality, honesty and representation were important.
- Individuals judge procedural fairness by using a variety of positively interrelated criteria. Factor analysis suggests that there are two underlying factors: the first factor includes assessments of the nature of the experience itself (ie, opportunities for representation, impartiality and the quality of the decisions made); the second factor includes assessments that compare the experience to external standards (ie, consistency and ethicality).

— In different situations (voluntary v involuntary contact, favourable v unfavourable outcomes), individuals judge the fairness of procedures using different criteria.
— There was no evidence that different types of people judge the fairness of procedures differently.

Tyler concludes (ibid: 128) that his findings strongly support previous research in demonstrating that a key determinant of reactions to encounters with legal authorities is the person's assessment of the fairness of the procedures which are used. As far as the meaning of procedural fairness is concerned, people's judgments are clearly complex and multifaceted. Although people pay attention to seven criteria, the major ones are linked to outcome (ethicality, honesty and the effort to be fair) rather than consistency with other outcomes, and Tyler speculates that this may be because people lack the information to make judgments of consistency. Representation is only one of a number of concerns that influence people's judgments and how hard authorities try to be fair appears to be the key overall factor. However, concern with ethicality (politeness and a concern with rights) is also important.

In a more recent review of psychological research on perceptions of justice and fairness, Tyler (2000:121) concludes that the following four factors contribute to perceptions of procedural fairness: opportunities for participation (voice), the neutrality of the forum, the trustworthiness of the authorities and the degree to which people are treated with dignity and respect.

Galligan's Critique

Galligan (1996: 93) has subjected Tyler's earlier study to some strong criticism, on the grounds that Tyler misunderstands the relationship between procedures and outcomes and fails to appreciate that the primary significance of procedural notions (like hearing and bias) is in upholding normative expectations relating to outcomes. Galligan concedes that procedures are particularly salient where normative expectations regarding outcomes are uncertain. However, he goes on to say that, even in such circumstances, procedures are still justified as a means to the achievement of certain outcomes and to argue that empirical research should take account of this, since failure to do so leads to the unwarranted conclusion that procedures have their own normative foundations and that people assess fairness in terms of these norms.

Galligan concludes (ibid: 94–95) that Tyler's research, and that of other psychologists, is based on an unsatisfactory theoretical framework and a misunderstanding of the relationship between normative expectations in relation to procedures and normative expectations in relation to outcomes. He claims that the theoretical framework which informs these studies assumes what it purports to demonstrate, namely that procedures have their own normative foundation and that people assess fairness primarily on that basis. According to him, empirical research based on such a framework is defective and conclusions that are derived from it must therefore be questioned. He then goes on to outline an alternative approach which seeks to identify, within a given context, standards of fair treatment without insisting on a strict division between those relating to outcomes and those relating to procedures. The result of such research would, he claims, point to a cluster of values and standards of different kinds, each of which contributes an element to an overall sense of fair treatment. It follows from this that fair procedures are simply those procedures that lead to fair treatment according to authoritative standards.

Is Galligan's criticism fair? I think not. Tyler's findings, and those of others who work in the same tradition, are, of course, shaped by their a priori theorising about the relationship between process and outcome, and thus between procedural fairness and substantive justice. However, the models that inform their work are not especially prescriptive and the conclusions from Tyler's study, and indeed from other studies, that people assess the fairness of procedures independently from the fairness of outcomes, are based on the results of carefully documented empirical research. As Lind and Tyler (1988: 29) demonstrate, Thibaut and Walker's early research findings that the achievement of just outcomes in conflicts of interest is best achieved by vesting control with the parties in dispute have been replicated and extended in other studies and the gist of subsequent work has been that vesting control with the parties enhances procedural fairness whether or not it promotes just outcomes. Lind and Tyler go on to claim (ibid: 92) that the picture that seems to be emerging is that people are rather more concerned with process and rather less concerned with outcomes than one might have supposed. Moreover, they point out (ibid: 212–213) that more recent studies have broadened the scope of procedural justice research to include the study of allocation procedures and that such research indicates that procedural concerns are important when allocation decisions are being made and when organisational policies are being determined. Against the weight of empirical evidence that perceptions of procedural fairness exercise an independent effect on responses to favourable and unfavourable outcomes and on perceptions of distributive justice, it is not clear how damaging Galligan's criticisms are or how much weight should be given to them.

Conclusions

Two important conclusions can be drawn from the body of social psychological research reviewed above. First, empirical research in a variety of settings has repeatedly demonstrated that perceptions of procedural fairness exercise an independent effect on responses to favourable or unfavourable outcomes and on perceptions of distributive justice. Second, people use different criteria to judge procedural fairness in different decision-making contexts. However, notwithstanding the reference to recent research on allocation procedures, it should be noted that the studies on which these conclusions are based were all carried out in the field of criminal justice. Whether or not they apply to other areas of law, that is, to civil and administrative law, has still to be demonstrated.

It is, of course, important to ask whether procedural fairness and substantive justice can be studied in terms of the perceptions of those who are subject to official decision making, and what studies of perceptions of justice tell us about justice itself. The well-known maxim 'justice must not only be done but must also be seen to be done' suggests that perceptions of justice are very important. In addition, although the research referred to in this section of the chapter does not settle the matter, it provides strong support for the claim that procedural fairness should not be seen in purely instrumental terms. Procedural fairness can contribute to substantive justice[3] but is also important in its own right.

External and Internal Approaches to Procedural Fairness

Two Approaches to Procedural Fairness

One approach to the achievement of procedural fairness emphasises principles that are imposed on the administration by institutions that are *external* to it, in particular by the courts but also by agencies like 'ombudsmen', as a result of an individual challenging an administrative decision. Another approach emphasises principles that are put into place *internally*, that is, by the administration itself, perhaps as a result of some internal monitoring of administrative decisions. The distinction is an analytic one and, in practice, the two approaches may be combined. Each of them is considered in turn.

External Approaches

Procedural Protection for 'Adjudicative' Decisions

As Harlow and Rawlings (1997: 495) note, there has been a general tendency for the courts to model the administrative process in their own adjudicative image. Fuller (1978: 353) identified the distinguishing characteristic of adjudication as being to confer 'on the affected person a peculiar kind of participation in the decision, that of presenting proofs and reasoned arguments for a decision in his favour'. This implies that, for a decision to be adjudicatory, certain procedural constraints must be placed on the decision maker. The model of procedure which facilitates the presentation of 'proofs and reasoned arguments' is exemplified by the criminal and civil courts, but it is also found in other settings, such as tribunal

[3] As Rothstein (1999: 3) points out, if the implementation of a policy is regarded as unfair, it will undermine the legitimacy of the policy in question.

proceedings, which share some of the same features. Actual decision making may have all or some or none of the characteristics of adjudication and Harlow and Rawlings (1997: 496) conceive of a sliding scale: the closer to the ideal type outlined above, the more judicialised the process and the more the courts will insist on applying the principles of 'natural justice'; the further away, the less judicialised the process and the less the courts will insist on applying such principles.

The principles of 'natural justice' seek to ensure a degree of procedural fairness and include the so-called 'rule against bias', which stipulates that decisions should be made by an impartial judge and that they must be set aside where there are reasonable grounds for suspecting bias, and the 'right to a hearing', which stipulates that each party should have the opportunity of knowing the case against him and stating his own case. In common law jurisdictions, they comprise the unwritten rules enunciated by judges in the superior courts.

The Donoughmore Committee on Ministers' Powers (1932), sought to distinguish three categories of decision making, namely 'judicial', 'quasi-judicial' and 'administrative' decision making, each of which was based on a different type of dispute, but, according to Harlow and Rawlings (1997: 33) their thinking was crude and their arguments circular. The Committee's approach has some attractions for 'green light theorists', who assume that the state is the only effective guarantor of individual freedom and emphasise the role of legislation and regulation rather than the use of the courts, because it serves to insulate administrative decisions from legal scrutiny. However, it has been criticised on the grounds that it has proved to be very difficult (if not impossible) in practice to separate these three types of functions, and because one effect of applying it would be to deprive large numbers of decisions of any procedural protection on the grounds that they are 'administrative'. The Committee's approach had little attraction for 'red light theorists', who assume that the state is a threat to the freedom of the individual and favour a strong role for the courts in scrutinising the legality of administrative decisions (ibid: 499).[4]

More Flexible Approaches

Exponents of 'flexible' protection claim that it provides a way round the problems of classifying disputes, of applying the rules of natural justice to those that are classified as 'adjudicatory' and offering no protection at all to those that are classified as 'administrative'. Mullan (1975: 281, cited in Harlow and Rawlings 1997: 504) has argued that different types of decision making have different procedural requirements, that the more closely they resemble 'straight law/fact determinations resulting in serious consequences for those concerned, the more legitimate is the demand for procedural protection, while the more closely they resemble broad, policy-orientated decisions, the less they are in need of such protection'. Although this approach avoids the problems of classification, and

[4] For a full account of 'red light' and 'green light' theories, see Harlow and Rawlings (1997: chs 2–4).

claims to recognise that different types of decision require different forms of procedural protection, it operates with only one model of procedural fairness and cannot provide any protection for decisions that involve the application of policy. A further problem is that the optimum degree of protection is not instantly recognisable and that a fair measure of discretion is required.

This position has led Harlow and Rawlings (1997: 514) to question how far it is the court's job to pursue the optimum form of procedure for different kinds of decision. They doubt whether judges have the information or the expertise needed to determine the particular form of procedural protection that is appropriate for different types of decision and, even, whether such an activity is consistent with the rule of law. Leaving these normative issues aside, they claim (ibid: 516) that there has been a measure of increased activism and of greater flexibility of response.

Judicial review can only be used when all other mechanisms for challenging an administrative decision have been exhausted. Its function is to determine whether or not the decision of a public body (or a private body acting under public law) is lawful, that is, whether or not the authority had exceeded its legal powers, abused its discretionary powers, failed to perform a statutory duty or breached the requirements of natural justice. It is used relatively infrequently: in 2005 (the last year for which statistics are available), there were 5,382 applications for judicial review in England and Wales.[5] Compared with the number of questionable administrative decisions, this is a miniscule number. Of this total, permission to seek judicial review was granted in only 733 cases (14 per cent of applications), 281 cases were actually heard, and, of these, 118 were allowed (House of Commons Library: Tables 1–3). These cases comprised 42 per cent of cases that were heard but only 2 per cent of applications.

These statistics do not suggest that judicial review provides a very effective check on routine administrative decision making. Nor do data covering the period 2000–05 support Harlow and Rawlings' contention that there has been an increase in judicial activism. On the contrary, the number of successful judicial reviews decreased each year over this five-year period, from a 'high' of 782 in 2000 to a 'low' of 118 in 2005 (ibid). Of course, the availability of judicial review may serve to make administrators more careful that the decisions they make are in accordance with the law,[6] and judicial review decisions may have a 'radiating effect' (Galanter 1983). However, because first-instance decision makers in administrative agencies may not know about relevant court decisions or feel any

[5] In addition, there were 229 judicial review actions in Scotland (Scottish Civil Courts Review 2007: Table 8).

[6] The Cabinet Office issues a pamphlet entitled *The Judge over Your Shoulder: Judicial Review of Administrative Decisions* for 'reasonably well-informed and interested junior administrators whose task is to make decisions affecting members of the public, or to prepare the material to enable others to make such decisions'. Its stated aim is 'to inform and improve the quality of administrative decision-making and, by so doing, make decisions less vulnerable to Judicial Review'. It is now in its fourth edition.

commitment to applying them, let alone the principles underlying them, this is likely to be quite limited.

Halliday (2004) has argued that judicial review must meet several conditions for it to have an impact on first-instance decision makers. They must be knowledgeable, conscientious and competent, the organisation for whom they work must give priority to compliance with the law over other considerations, and the law itself must be clear and consistent. As Halliday (ibid: 168) points out, 'the extent to which these conditions are fulfilled will vary according to context'. However, it is probably quite rare for all of them to be met simultaneously and, if this is the case, it must inevitably limit the effectiveness of judicial review as a check on routine administrative decision making.

In the United Kingdom, disputes between the citizen and the state are more likely to be heard by a tribunal than by a court. 50 years ago, the Franks Committee on Tribunals and Inquiries (1957: para 42) enunciated three principles—*openness, fairness and impartiality*—that were to apply to tribunal decision making. Openness requires publicity for the proceedings and knowledge of the essential reasoning underlying the decision; fairness requires the adoption of clear procedures which enable the parties to understand their rights, present their case fully and know the case which they have to meet; while impartiality requires freedom from the influence, real or apparent, of the department that is responsible for the decision that is subject to appeal. However, it should be noted that these principles were to apply to tribunals which hear appeals from first instance administrative decisions and not to the decisions themselves and that, in any case, they represented 'good practice' and were not enforceable. Although the role of the Council on Tribunals, set up under the Tribunals and Enquiries Act 1959, was to keep the constitution and working of tribunals under review, its powers and resources were quite limited (Harlow and Rawlings, 1997: 471).

The number of administrative decisions that are appealed to a tribunal is substantial and dwarfs the numbers that are subject to judicial review. This is partly because those who appeal to a tribunal are not subject to any charges and it costs a great deal to bring an action of judicial review in the High Court or Court of Session, and partly a question of proportionality (see Adler 2008a). In 2005, when 281 judicial review cases were heard in England and Wales, 732,947 cases were decided by the tribunals and inquiries that fell within the jurisdiction of the Council on Tribunals.[7] While the function of a judicial review is to determine whether or not an administrative decision is lawful, the function of an appeal to a tribunal is rather broader than this. Although few tribunals can question the merits of an administrative decision where this involves the correct application of

[7] More than 90 per cent of these cases involved appeals against administrative decisions while the remainder involved *party v party* disputes. The largest category of *party v party* disputes (40,571 in 2005/2006) were employment disputes (Council on Tribunals 2006: 75). In 2007/2008, the last year for which statistics are available), there were 670,781 tribunal hearings (Administrative Justice and Tribunals Council 2008: 66).

law, most tribunals can question the facts on which the administrative decision was based and can make a new decision based on facts that the administrative decision maker may not have been aware of but which the tribunal has accepted. However, on the basis of research into the effectiveness of representation in four tribunals, Genn (1994) concluded that there are considerable limits to tribunals' effectiveness as a check on administrative decision making. According to Genn (ibid: 284), these limits are based on the mismatch between the claim that tribunals are relatively informal and free from technicality and the reality that they have to make decisions in accordance with complicated regulations, statute and case law, on low levels of representation (by lawyers or lay advocates) in many tribunals, and on the fact that unrepresented parties in tribunal proceedings were much less likely to be successful. Although that may have been true in the recent past, evidence from a recent study of four tribunals (Adler 2009) indicates that tribunals have become more 'active', 'interventionist' and 'enabling', and that unrepresented appellants are much less disadvantaged than was previously the case.[8]

Although tribunal decisions can and do benefit appellants, they have a rather limited impact on first instance decision makers. In a study of decision making in social security (Baldwin, Wikeley and Young 1992), over half (52.6 per cent) of the adjudication officers[9] who were interviewed claimed that, in making decisions, they were 'not at all influenced' by a tribunal's likely response to an appeal. This compares to a quarter (25.0 per cent) of officers who claimed that tribunals had a procedural effect in that the prospect of an appeal led them to be more thorough and document their decisions more fully. However, it should be noted that the tribunals referred to here were first-tier tribunals and that the Social Security Commissioners, which were a second-tier tribunal, undoubtedly had a greater impact on first-instance decision makers. However, as a means of enhancing the quality of first-instance decision making, these fin dings indicate that tribunals are not particularly effective.

Procedural Protection for Administrative Decisions

Because the courts hear such a small number of cases of judicial review, and because, in any case, natural justice embodies a very restricted conception of procedural fairness, the courts provide little procedural protection for administrative decisions. To deal with this and to provide better protection for those who think they have been treated unfairly, the Parliamentary Commissioner for Administration (PCA), or Parliamentary Ombudsman, was appointed in 1967 to deal with grievances from individuals who felt they had suffered an injustice arising from maladministration by a central government department against

[8] Especially if they had received advice before the hearing.

[9] Civil servants appointed by the Secretary of State to determine claims for benefit independently of the Minister (Baldwin, Wikeley and Young: 29). The Social Security Act 1998 abolished adjudication officers and claims to benefit are now made by civil servants working for the Department for Work and Pensions or one of its executive agencies.

which there was no available remedy. 'Maladministration' was not defined in the Parliamentary Commissioner Act 1967 that established the PCA, although the Leader of the House of Commons (Richard Crossman) described it as including bias, neglect, inattention, delay, incompetence, ineptitude, perversity, turpitude, arbitrariness and so on.[10]

Subsequently, a Parliamentary Commissioner (Sir William Reid) elaborated on Crossman's list by giving more examples of what the term covers.[11] 'Injustice' was likewise not defined in the Act but, for a complaint to be upheld, the PCA must conclude that the individual has suffered some kind of loss or harm that would otherwise not have occurred. Thus, in light of the distinction made in Part 1 above, it is clear that the PCA adopts an instrumental rather than a non-instrumental approach to procedural fairness since redress is only available if maladministration has a deleterious effect on the person concerned.[12]

A number of other ombudsmen were subsequently established to deal with complaints about services in the public sector that fell outside the PCA's remit. In addition, there are also ombudsmen covering various private sector services but, with the exception of the Legal Services Ombudsmen for England and Wales and for Scotland, and the Financial Services Ombudsman, these do not have statutory powers.

Ombudsmen use inquisitorial methods to investigate allegations that maladministration has given rise to injustice. Where a complaint that maladministration has given rise to injustice is upheld, they may recommend *remedial action* on the organisation that was the subject of the complaint; suggest that the organisation pays *compensation* to the complainant; or propose that the organisation issues an *apology*.[13] Thus, in addition to providing remedies for those who complain, ombudsmen may order the organisation complained of to modify its

[10] Hansard (754 HC Official Report col 51 (18 October 1966) (RHS Crossman MP)).

[11] Reid's list of examples comprised rudeness (though that is a matter of degree); unwillingness to treat the claimant as a person with rights; refusal to answer reasonable questions; neglecting to inform a complainant on request of his or her rights or entitlement; knowingly giving advice which is misleading or inadequate; ignoring valid advice or overruling considerations which would produce an uncomfortable result for the over-ruler; offering no redress or manifestly disproportionate redress; showing bias, whether because of colour, sex, or any other grounds; omission to notify those who thereby lose a right of appeal; faulty procedures; failure by management to monitor compliance with adequate procedures; cavalier disregard of guidance which is intended to be followed in the interest of equitable treatment of those who use a service; partiality; and failure to mitigate the effects of rigid adherence to the letter of the law where that produces manifestly unequal treatment. See 'Annual Report of the Council on Tribunals' HC (1993) 290 [7].

[12] It is, of course, possible for maladministration to occur without the complainer suffering any injustice. In such a case, the complainer would not be entitled to any redress.

[13] Remedial action involves correcting the injustice caused by the maladministration and reversing the decision made because of it; compensation can cover direct and indirect losses resulting from maladministration; and an apology would normally come from the head of the organisation complained of. It should be noted that remedial action is not always feasible and that compensation may be appropriate when remedial action is not. However, where the losses caused by maladministration are psychological rather than material, it may be difficult to put a monetary value on them. In Great Britain, but not in Northern Ireland, Ombudsmen can only recommend a remedy and remedies are not legally enforceable.

administrative procedures. However, although an organisation may wish to do so to avoid more complaints in the future, there is, in general, no systematic check on whether or not it has done so.

Although complainants are expected to have exhausted any internal complaint procedures beforehand, it does not cost them anything to take their complaint to an ombudsman. Ombudsmen are independent of the organisation against which the complaint is made and no legal (or other) representation is required, Independence should, in theory, guarantee impartiality but this may be compromised where the ombudsman's staff are drawn from, and subsequenty return to, organisations that can be the subject of a complaint. In addition, except for the CLA in Northern Ireland, ombudsmen's remedies are not legally enforceable.

A successful complaint to an ombudsman, like a successful application for judicial review, can make a difference for the individual who uses it to redress a grievance. However, although ombudsmen are used more frequently than judicial review, the number of complaints to an ombudsman is relatively modest. In 2005, 1,715 cases were reported to the Parliamentary Ombudsman (PO), 1,891 to the Health Services Ombudsman (HSO) and 18,321 to the Local Government Ombudsman (LGO) for England and Wales.[14] 31 per cent of complaints to the PO and 41 per cent to the HSO were upheld in full while 31 per cent of complaints to the PO and 23 per cent to the PO and 36 per cent to the HSO were upheld in part.[15] These are clearly not trivial figures but, because the complaints usually relate to quite specific sets of circumstances and because the findings do not carry the force of precedent, it is unlikely that they provide a very effective check on routine administrative decision making. The impact of the LGO on local authority decision making was clearly less than this—although complaints to the ombudsman led to local settlements in 2,842 cases, the LGO issued only 120 reports alleging maladministration.[16] There has, as far as I am aware, been no attempt to assess the wider impact of ombudsman decisions on first-instance decision makers.

Internal Approaches

Mashaw's Approach

Although it has been conventional to look to courts and tribunals, and to other forms of accountability, such as ombudsmen, that are external to the locus of organisational decision making, as the means of achieving either procedural fairness or substantive justice, the available evidence does not suggest that this approach is very effective. It is for this reason that Mashaw (1974) argued that additional safeguards, such as internal quality controls and quality assurance systems, are needed to ensure

[14] Statistics taken from Parliamentary and Health Services Ombudsman (2006: Figs 10 and 12) and Local Government Ombudsman (2006: App 2b). In addition, there were 1,724 complaints to the Scottish Public Services Ombudsman.

[15] Ibid.

[16] In addition, there were 1,724 complaints to the Scottish Public Services Ombudsman (SPSO).

that the process of decision making is fair. Recruitment procedures, induction and training programmes, and appraisal systems are also important.

In two recent publications (Adler 2003, 2006), I have extolled the virtues of Mashaw's subsequent book, *Bureaucratic Justice* (Mashaw 1983), which comprises a detailed empirical study of administrative decision making in the American Disability Insurance (DI) Scheme and uses this case study to develop an approach to administrative justice that claims to have wide, general application. Instead of approaching administrative justice through a 'legal prism' by focusing on the relatively small number of decisions made by the courts in those cases that are the subject of an appeal, Mashaw approaches it directly by focusing on the vast number of first-instance decisions and shows how the justice that inheres in these decisions can be understood and enhanced. He defines 'administrative justice' in terms of 'those qualities of a decision process that provide arguments for the acceptability of its decisions' (ibid: 24), identifies three 'competing' models of administrative justice, which he associates with *bureaucratic rationality*, *professional treatment* and *moral judgment*, characterises these three models in terms of their *legitimating values*, *primary goals*, *organisational structures* and *cognitive techniques*, and argues that administrative justice results from the 'trade-offs' that are made between the three models in particular instances (ibid: 31).

Taking Mashaw's approach as my starting point, I have attempted in my own work to modify and extend it in a number of ways. I re-named Mashaw's three models (referring to them as *bureaucratic*, *professional* and *legal* models), added three more (*managerial*, *consumerist* and *market* models) to reflect some very important developments in the management of public services that have taken place since the publication of *Bureaucratic Justice* in 1983, and characterised them rather differently (in terms of their characteristic *mode of decision making*, their *legitimating values*, their characteristic *mode of accountability* and *mode of redress*) One important advantage of this characterisation over Mashaw's is that it includes external as well as internal accountability mechanisms.[17] Sainsbury (2008: 327) takes issue with my reference to external modes of accountability, on the grounds that 'for example, it is not clear how administrative review can form part of an argument for the acceptability of front-line decisions' but the fact that decision makers can be, and sometimes are, held accountable in this way seems to me to contribute to the acceptability of their decisions. Similarly Cane (2009: 216) argues that 'the provision of redress cannot be a criterion of acceptability because it assumes that the effected person (rightly) considers the decision unacceptable', but the fact that decisions can be, and sometimes are, challenged in this way likewise seems to me to contribute to their acceptability. As Sainsbury (2008: 327)

[17] Mashaw is, in my view, too negative about the contribution of external forms of accountability to the achievement of administrative justice. While it may be true that what he calls front-line administrators 'continually face decisions for which external standards provide no binding, perhaps no relevant, guidelines' (Mashaw 1983: 16), it does not follow that external standards play no part at all in setting standards for decision makers.

himself put it, 'the acceptability of front-line decisions is enhanced if a remedy exists, in other words, having some form of redress mechanism would add to the justice argument for any particular decision process'.

The latest version of my fully-elaborated representation of administrative justice, which results from the trade-offs that are made between the six normative models, is set out in Table 1 below.[18]

Note that I have characterised the third model in Table 1 in terms of 'legality', since characterising it in terms of 'fairness', as Mashaw does, would appear to beg the question.[19]

My extended model of administrative justice has not been immune to criticism. Sainsbury (2008: 326) is not convinced that I have identified three new 'decision processes', which can be used as the basis for new models of administrative justice. Instead of depicting managerialism, consumerism and the market as separate models of administrative justice, Halliday (2004: 121) argues that they are not 'as distinct and robust as those of Mashaw' and that they are the constituents of

Table 1: Six Normative Models of Administrative Justice

Model	Mode of Decision making	Legitimating Goal	Mode of Accountability	Mode of redress
Bureaucratic	Applying rules	Accuracy	Hierarchical	Administrative review
Professional	Applying knowledge	Public service	Interpersonal	Second opinion or complaint to a professional body
Legal	Asserting rights	Legality	Independent	Appeal to a court or tribunal (public law)
Managerial	Managerial autonomy	Improved performance	Performance indicators and audit	None, except adverse publicity or complaints that result in sanctions.
Consumerist	Consumer participation	Consumer satisfaction	Consumer Charters	'Voice' and/or compensation through Consumer Charters
Market	Matching supply and demand	Economic efficiency	Competition	'Exit' and/or court action (private law)

[18] This table differs in a number of minor ways from earlier versions that appeared in Adler (2003) and Adler (2006). It provided a framework for analysing the impact of computerisation on decision making in social security in 14 OECD countries (Adler and Henman 2008). The results are summarised in Adler (2003) and Adler (2006).

[19] For a helpful discussion of legality, which is a synonym for 'the rule of law', see Selznick (1980: 11–18).

a single model of administrative decision making, now widely known as the 'New Public Management' or NPM (Hood 1991 and Hood 1996). And, although Cane (2009: 216) is prepared to accept that the market is a model of administrative justice insofar as it provides a criterion for judging the acceptability of administrative decisions, he does not regard managerialism and consumerism as models of administrative justice in this sense.

I am not persuaded by Cane's claim that 'managerialism' does not provide a criterion for judging the acceptability of administrative decisions. The theory and practice of management, as taught in Business and Management Schools and implemented in myriad organisations around the world, are based on the premise that it does not provide such a criterion, and I believe that it does. Equally, I am not persuaded by his claim that it 'would make managerialism a *cause* of injustice rather than a *criterion* of justice'(emphasis added). Mashaw's *Bureaucratic Justice* makes it clear that there are competing conceptions of administrative justice and that what is 'just' in terms of one conception may be 'unjust' in terms of another. Thus, I do believe that there is a managerialist conception of justice although what is just from the perspective of that conception would be unjust from the perspective of other conceptions. Likewise, I am not persuaded by Cane's argument that 'consumerism' is an aspect of what Mashaw calls 'moral judgment' and what I prefer to call 'legality'. Although 'consumerism' and 'legality' are both 'bottom-up' conceptions of administrative justice, in that they put the consumer or the citizen into the driving seat, they seem to me to be conceptually distinct, since political means are central to the former while legal techniques are central to the latter.

In response to Halliday, I would argue that, although NPM is a composite form, it is best understood as a 'trade-off' between the managerialist, consumerist and market models referred to above, which are analytically distinct and can exist on their own. Thus, each can sometimes be encountered in the absence of either one or both the others. I would also argue, in response to Sainsbury and Cane, the each of the three additional models of administrative justice, characterised as I have characterised them, constitutes an argument for the acceptability of front-line decisions. Thus, if the decision is made in accordance with the tenets of, say, managerialism or consumerism, it can, from that perspective, be regarded as acceptable.

In addition to modifying and extending Mashaw's approach to take account of recent developments in the management of public services, I have also sought to respond to two specific criticisms that can be made of his work. The first of these criticisms is that, in assessing the relative influence of the different models of administrative justice, Mashaw ignored their absolute strengths. Consider two situations in which the strengths of three models are given weights of 30, 20 and 10 units and 3, 2 and 1 units respectively; although the relative strengths of the three models are identical in both situations, their absolute strengths are clearly very different. In the first situations, the three models are all 'strong' whereas, in the second situation, they are all 'weak'. As far as administrative justice is concerned, trade-offs between 'strong' models are very different from trade-offs between 'weak' ones. Although Mashaw does not, in my view, give sufficient attention to the absolute strengths of the competing models of administrative justice, I have attempted to do so in my own work.

A second criticism of Mashaw's approach is that he took the policy context for granted. However, just as different orientations to administration, that is, to how programmes should be run, can be understood in terms of a number of normative models which are in competition with each other, so, at least in theory, different orientations to policy, that is, to what programmes aim to achieve, can also be understood in this way. In a study of administrative decision making in prisons (Adler and Longhurst 1994)[20], I attempted to identify competing models of policy and to combine them with competing models of administration. The resulting 'two-dimensional' model was necessarily more complex, but its characteristics were similar in that, with this model, it was possible to understand the trade-offs that were made between different combinations of policy and administration in particular cases and to see what different sets of trade-offs might have been more desirable. Since the models of policy refer to outcomes while the models of administration refer to process, the two-dimensional model provides a way of combining procedural fairness with substantive justice.

Finally, in my work, I have attempted to be more explicit than Mashaw about the ways in which the trade-offs between the different models are accomplished. Developing an approach derived from the work of Mannheim (1952), it became clear to me that the trade-offs that are made, and likewise those that could be made, between the different models of administrative justice reflect the concerns and the bargaining strengths of those institutional actors who have an interest in promoting each of them, typically civil servants and officials in the case of the bureaucratic model; professionals and 'street level bureaucrats' (Lipsky 1980) in the case of the professional model; lawyers, court and tribunal personnel in the case of the legal model; management consultants in the case of the managerial model; consumers and members of the public in the case of the consumerist model; and private sector owners, managers and shareholders in the case of the market model. The outcome of the power struggle between these institutional actors determines the trade-offs between the different models of administrative justice with which they are associated. These trade-offs vary between organisations and, within a given organisation, between those parts responsible for the implementation of different policies, and between the different stages of policy implementation. In addition, they also vary over time and between countries.

The Nature of Administrative Justice

It is argued here that administrative justice, ie the justice inherent in administrative decision making, like legal justice and social justice, has procedural and substantive dimensions and that, for this reason, the 'two-dimensional' model

[20] The results are likewise summarised in Adler (2003) and Adler (2006).

outlined above represents a particularly successful means of representing and analysing administrative justice.

This approach would not commend itself to those, like Galligan (1996), who associate administrative justice with the legal model of decision making and assert its moral superiority. Galligan claims that the great range of administrative processes can be divided into three groups: processes of a routine nature, decisions requiring distinct elements of inquiry and judgment, and discretionary processes of a policy kind (ibid: 229–40). At one end of the spectrum, routine administration involves the almost mechanical application of a set of standards to a simple and easily established set of facts; at the other end of the spectrum, decisions about how to treat an individual involve the exercise of strong discretion and are substantially governed by policy considerations; but, within the middle ground, two normative models of decision making compete with each other. He calls the first of these models *bureaucratic administration* and the second *administrative justice*, and the association of this term with one of these models is particularly significant. According to Galligan, the goal of bureaucratic administration is to maximise the common good by means of 'accurate and proper' decision making and 'individual cases are significant only as elements in achieving acceptable aggregates'. On the other hand, administrative justice seeks to treat each person fairly. In this model, the accurate and proper application of authoritative standards is still important, but the emphasis is on fair treatment of the individual, ie on the accuracy and propriety of the individual decision, not just of decisions in the aggregate. Although Galligan accepts that the bureaucratic administration model is the 'natural and dominant' model, he argues that efforts should be made to curb its natural hegemony in order to support the (morally superior) administrative justice model. His approach is not followed here because of its normative commitment to one, among several, competing conceptions of administrative justice and because of its failure to recognise the opportunity costs associated with its realisation.

Normative Theorising

One of the attractions of Mashaw's approach is that it enables us to see both what trade-offs are made between various justice models in particular instances and what different sets of trade-offs might be more desirable, not merely for the institutional actors who have an interest in promoting each of the models in play but for all concerned, that is, in some overall sense. However, the attempt to arrive at a 'better' balance between the different models in play and identify a different set of trade-offs that will enhance 'the public interest' raises a number of problems. Since there is no 'magic formula', this exercise necessarily involves the exercise of judgment. Of course, this does not make it an arbitrary exercise. It is one which can, and should, be informed by empirical data. In this connection, performance measures of various kinds and audit data are important and, to the extent that the primary justification for public services is that they should serve the public, it can be argued that the results of user surveys and public opinion data are especially important.

Conclusions

By adopting a relativistic approach to administrative justice, Mashaw's work and the developments it has inspired, challenges the view that there are any invariant principles of procedural fairness that apply in all contexts.[21] This may, at first, seem surprising but, on reflection, should not be since it is generally agreed that this is true of substantive justice. Procedural fairness is no less a contested concept than substantive justice in that, although it can be defined in a fairly uncontroversial way (as 'a proper balance between competing claims to procedural protection'), the terms in which it is defined (ie, what constitutes 'a proper balance' and even what are to count as 'claims') are the subject of considerable disagreement. Compared to the external approaches to administrative justice considered above, two of the advantages of an internal approach are that it focuses on the myriad of first-instance decisions rather than the much smaller number of decisions that are the subject of an appeal or complaint and that it focuses on them directly rather than at one remove and through a 'legal prism'. However, this is not to suggest that external mechanisms for achieving administrative justice can be ignored. Although they are not all-important, they are certainly not unimportant. The two approaches to the achievement of administrative justice need to be combined and one of the great strengths of the analytic framework outlined above is that, by embracing external as well as internal mechanisms for achieving administrative justice, it recognises this fact.

Recent Developments in the UK[22]

At the beginning of this chapter, it was argued that 'justice' is an 'essentially contested' concept, that is, a concept that can be defined in a fairly uncontroversial way (as 'a proper balance between competing claims') but the terms in which it is defined (ie, what constitutes 'a proper balance' and even what is to count as a 'claim') are the subject of considerable disagreement. If this is so for 'justice', it is doubly so for 'administrative justice'.

[21] Some followers of Mashaw, eg Sainsbury (1992), have attempted to develop a less relativistic conception of 'administrative justice'. Adopting the perspective of the individual citizen, he argues that administrative justice, defined as those 'qualities an administrative decision ought to exhibit, which provide arguments for the acceptability of its decisions', has two invariant components. These are, first, accuracy and, second, fairness, the latter comprising promptness, impartiality, participation and accountability. According to Habermas (1972), participation is a means of advancing rational discourse and, as such, plays an important role in legitimating the rule of law and the role of the state.

[22] The account that follows is based on that in Adler (2008b).

Three Approaches to Administrative Justice

A number of contrasting approaches to administrative justice can be identified. On the one hand, there is the approach that sees administrative justice in terms of the principles formulated by courts and other redress mechanisms that come into play when people who are unhappy with the outcome of an administrative decision, or with the process by which that decision was reached, challenge the decision and seek to achieve a determination in their favour. We can call this approach the *administrative law approach*. Although the decisions of the superior courts are of particular importance for the administrative law approach, those of other bodies, such as appeal tribunals and ombudsmen, are also important. Those who adopt the administrative law approach assume that the principles formulated by courts and other redress mechanisms are applied and put into effect by first-instance decision makers and that administrative justice is achieved in this way.

On the other hand, there is the approach that sees administrative justice in terms of the justice of routine administrative decisions. This approach does not accept that the formulation of principles by the courts and other redress mechanisms is sufficient and emphasises the importance of methods that are intended to improve first-instance decision making, such as recruitment procedures, training and appraisal procedures, standard setting and quality assurance systems. We can call this approach the *justice in administration approach*. While the administrative law approach focuses on the relatively small number of cases that come before the courts and other redress mechanisms and can be characterised as a 'top-down' approach, the justice in administration approach focuses on the huge number of first-instance decisions and can be characterised as a 'bottom-up' approach.

However, the choice is not simply between these two approaches. There is a third approach which sees the merits in both of the above approaches and seeks to combine them. It is thus more wide-ranging than either of these approaches because, although it recognises the importance of courts, tribunals, ombudsmen and other external redress mechanisms that the administrative law approach is pre-occupied with, it is also concerned with other (internal) means of enhancing the justice of administrative decisions that the justice in administration approach focuses on. We can call this approach the *administrative justice approach*.

The Swing of the Pendulum

The importance attached to these contrasting approaches to administrative justice has ebbed and flowed in recent years. Until recently, the administrative law approach was dominant—textbook discussions of administrative justice analysed the principles found in the judgments of the superior courts, particularly in actions of judicial review, and policy makers were relatively inactive. In parallel with this, socio-legal researchers undertook a number of studies of tribunals,[23] although there have been few studies of front-line decision making in recent years.[24] In addition, many government departments now conduct customer satisfaction surveys.[25] These two sets of developments embodied the justice and administration approach which constituted a challenge to the administrative law approach. However, the pendulum now appears to have swung towards the administrative justice approach. Thus, the Tribunals, Courts and Enforcement (TCE) Act 2007 defines the administrative justice system as:

> the overall system by which decisions of an administrative or executive nature are made in relation to particular persons, including—
>
> (a) the procedures for making such decisions,
> (b) the law under which such decisions are made, and
> (c) the systems for resolving disputes and airing grievances in relation to such decisions.[26]

In this definition, administrative justice embraces the concerns of the administrative law approach with the 'law in the books' and with the determinations of courts, tribunals and ombudsmen which resolve disputes and grievances, as well as those of the justice in administration approach with decision-making procedures.

The White Paper *Transforming Public Services: Complaints, Redress and Tribunals* (Secretary of State for Constitutional Affairs 2004) approaches administrative justice from the perspective of the normative expectations held by members of the public. Thus, it makes it clear (ibid: para 1.5) that:

> [w]e are all entitled to receive correct decisions on our personal circumstances; where a mistake occurs we are entitled to complain and to have the mistake put right with the minimum of difficulty; where there is uncertainty we are entitled to a quick resolution of the issue; and we are entitled to expect that, where things have gone wrong, the system will learn from the problem and will do better in the future.

The White Paper defines administrative justice in terms of these normative expectations, pointing out that they apply to the huge number of 'routine' administrative decisions that officials make every day. But, at the same time, it is largely concerned with reforming the procedures for dealing with disputes and complaints, and with improving the feedback from dispute and complaint-handling procedures to

[23] For a review of research on tribunal users' experiences, perceptions and expectations, see Adler and Gulland (2003).

[24] One major hurdle to conducting research of this kind is that it requires the approval of the government department or public body concerned, and they are distinctly unenthusiastic about this kind of research. One example is provided by Weber's research on the detention of asylum seekers at UK ports of entry. See Weber and Gelsthorpe (2000) and Weber and Landman (2002). The National Audit Office has carried out a number of enquiries, which have included appraisals front-line decision making. See, eg, National Audit Office (2003).

[25] For example, the Department for Work and Pensions (DWP) publishes an annual survey of Jobcentre Plus 'customers'. The most recent report is Johnson and Fidler (2008).

[26] TCE Act 2007 Pt 2 para 13(4).

first-instance decision makers, not because it believes that this is the only, or even the most important, means of ensuring that front-line decision makers 'get it right in the first place' but because it believes that this can contribute towards that end.

According to the White Paper (ibid: para 1.6), 'the sphere of administrative justice … embraces not just courts and tribunals but the millions of decisions taken by thousands of civil servants and other officials'. From the standpoint of this chapter, this is a most welcome change and points the way to a real enhancement of administrative justice for millions of people who are on the receiving end of administrative decisions. This will, however, call for a much more proactive approach on the part of policy makers and for the prioritising of administrative justice over competing pressures associated with lower units and efficiency savings. Fortunately, there are some hopeful signs—the recent formulation by the Parliamentary and Health Services Ombudsman (2008) of *Principles of Good Administration, Principles for Remedy and Principles of Good Complaint Handling* and the enhanced role in promoting administrative justice that has been given to the Administrative Justice and Tribunals Council (see Gulland's and Thompson's chapters in this volume) are a very good start. If such initiatives are taken seriously, they could go some way towards ensuring that everyone receives what is due to them, both in terms of how they are treated by administrative agencies and in terms what they receive from them. However, this will require a major commitment from those government departments and public bodies that make the decisions on which so many people depend.

References

Adler, M (2003) 'A Socio-Legal Approach to Administrative Justice' 25 *Law and Policy* 323.

—— (2006) 'Fairness in context' 33 *Journal of Law and Society* 615.

—— (2008a) 'The Idea of Proportionality in Dispute Resolution' 30 *Journal of Social Welfare and Family Law* 309.

—— (2008b) 'From Tribunal Reform to the Reform of Administrative Justice' in R Creyke (ed), *Tribunals in the Common Law World* (Annandale, NSW, The Federation Press) 153.

—— (2009) 'Tribunals ain't what they used to be', *Adjust Newsletter*, March, available at www.ajtc.gov.uk/adjust/09_03.htm.

Adler, M and Gulland, J (2003) *Tribunal Users' Experiences, Perceptions and Expectations: a Literature Review* (London, Council on Tribunals).

Adler, M and Henman, P (2008) 'Justice beyond the Courts: The Implications of Computerisation for Administrative Justice in Social Security' in A Cerillo and P Fabra (eds), *E-Justice: Information and Communication Technologies in the Court System* (Herschey, PA, IGI Global) 65.

Adler, M and Longhurst, B (1994) *Discourse, Power and Justice: Towards a New Sociology of Imprisonment* (London, Routledge).

Administrative Justice and Tribunals Council (2008) *Annual Report 2007/2008* (Norwich, The Stationery Office), available at www.ajtc.gov.uk/docs/Annual_Report_2007_8.pdf.

Baldwin, J, Wikeley, N and Young, R (1992) *Judging Social Security: The Adjudication of Claims for Benefit in Britain* (Oxford, Clarendon Press).
Barry, BM (1965) *Political Argument* (London, Routledge and Kegan Paul).
Bayles, M (1990) *Procedural Justice: Allocating to Individuals* (Dordrecht, Boston and London, Kluwer Academic Publishers).
Cabinet Office (2006) *The Judge over Your Shoulder: Judicial Review of Administrative Decisions*, 4th edn (London, The Stationery Office), available at www.tsol.gov.uk/Publications/judge.pdf.
Cane, P (2009) *Administrative Adjudication and Administrative Tribunals* (Oxford, Hart Publishing).
Council on Tribunals (2008) *Annual Report 2005/2006* HC 1210 (Norwich, The Stationery Office) available at www.council-on-tribunals.gov.uk/docs/ar_06.pdf.
Department for Constitutional Affairs (2004) *Transforming Public Services: Complaints, Redress and Tribunals* Cm 6243 (Norwich, The Stationery Office), available at www.dca.gov.uk/pubs/adminjust/transformfull.pdf.
Donoughmore Committee (1932) *Report of the Committee on Ministers' Powers* Cmd 4050 (London, HMSO).
Dworkin, RM (1986) *A Matter of Principle* (Oxford, Clarendon Press).
Franks Committee (1957) *Report of the Committee on Tribunals and Enquiries* Cmnd 218 (London, HMSO).
Fuller, L (1978) 'The Forms and Limits of Adjudication' 92 *Harvard Law Review* 353.
Galanter, M (1983) 'The Radiating Effects of Courts' in K Boyum and L Mather (eds), *Empirical Theories about Courts* (New York, Longmans) 117.
Gallie, WB (1964) 'Essentially Contested Concepts' in *Philosophy and Historical Understanding* (London, Chatto and Windus).
Galligan, D (1996) *Due Process and Fair Procedures* (Oxford, Clarendon Press).
Genn, H (1994) 'Tribunal review of Administrative Decision Making' in G Richardson and H Genn (eds), *Administrative Law and Government Action* (Oxford, Clarendon Press) 249.
Habermas, J (1992) *Between Facts and Norms* (Cambridge, Polity Press).
Halliday, S (2004) *Judicial Review and Compliance with Administrative Law* (Oxford, Hart Publishing).
Harlow, C and Rawlings, R (1997) *Law and Administration*, 2nd edn (London, Edinburgh and Dublin, Butterworths).
Honoré, AM (1970) 'Social Justice' in RS Summers (ed) *Essays in Legal Philosophy* (Oxford, Basil Blackwell) 61.
Hood, C (1991) 'A New Public Management for all Seasons' 69 *Public Administration* 3.
—— (1998) *The Art of the State: Culture, Rhetoric and Public Management* (Oxford, Clarendon Press).
House of Commons Library (2006) *Judicial Review: A short guide to claims in the Administrative Court*, Research Paper 06/44, available at www.parliament.uk/commons/lib/research/rp2006/rp06-044.pdf.
Johnson, S and Fidler, Y (2008) *Jobcentre Plus Customer Satisfaction Survey 2007* DWP Research Report No 480 (Norwich, The Stationery Office), available at http://research.dwp.gov.uk/asd/asd5/rports2007-2008/rrep480.pdf.
Leventhal, GS (1980) 'What Should be Done with Equity Theory? New Approaches to the Study of Fairness in Social Relationships' in KJ Gergen, MS Greenberg and RH Willis (eds), *Social Exchange: Advances in Theory and Research* (New York and London, Plenum Press) 27.

Lind, EA and Tyler, TR (1988) *The Social Psychology of Procedural Justice* (New York and London, Plenum Press).
Lipsky, M (1980) *Street Level Bureaucracy: Dilemmas of the Individual in Public Services* (New York, Russell Sage Foundation).
Local Government Ombudsman (2006) *Delivering Public Value: Annual Report for 2005/06* (London, The Commission for Local Administration in England).
Mannheim, K (1952) *Essays in the Sociology of Knowledge* (London, Routledge and Kegan Paul).
Mashaw, JL (1974) 'The Management Side of Due Process: Some Theoretical and Litigation Notes on the Assurance of Accuracy, Fairness and Timeliness in the Adjudication of Social Welfare Claims' 59 *Cornell Law Review* 772.
—— (1983) *Bureaucratic Justice: Managing Social Security Disability Claims* (New Haven and London, Yale University Press).
—— (2006) 'Accountability and Institutional Design: Some Thoughts on the Grammar of Governance' in M Dowdle (ed), *Public Accountability* (Cambridge, Cambridge University Press) 115.
Miller, D (1976) *Social Justice* (Oxford, Clarendon Press).
—— (1999) *Principles of Social Justice* (Cambridge, Harvard University Press).
Mullan, D (1975) 'Fairness: the New Natural Justice' 25 *University of Toronto Law Journal* 281.
National Audit Office (2003) *Getting it Right, Putting it Right—Improving decision-making and appeals in social security benefits*, HC 1142 (London, The Stationery Office), available at www.nao.org.uk/publications/0203/getting_it_right,_putting_it_r.aspx.
Parliamentary and Health Services Ombudsman (2006) *Making a Difference: Annual Report 2005–06* HC 1863 (London, The Stationery Office) available at www.ombudsman.org.uk/pdfs/ar_06.pdf.
—— (2008) *Principles of Good Administration, Principles for Remedy and Principles of Good Complaint Handling* (London, The Stationery Office), available at www.ombudsman.org.uk/improving_services/principles/index.html.
Rawls, J (1972) *A Theory of Justice* (Oxford, Clarendon Press).
Richardson, G (1984) 'The Legal Regulation of Process' in G Richardson and H Genn (eds), *Administrative Law and Government Action* (Oxford, Clarendon Press) 105.
Rothstein, B (1999) *Just Institutions* (Cambridge, Cambridge University Press).
Sainsbury, R (1992) 'Administrative Justice: Discretion and Procedure in Social Security Decision-Making' in K Hawkins (ed), *The Uses of Discretion* (Oxford, Clarendon Press) 295.
—— (2008) 'Administrative Justice, Discretion and the "Welfare to Work" Project' 30 *Journal of Social Welfare and Family Law* 323.
Scottish Civil Courts Review (2007) *A Consultation Paper* (Edinburgh) available at www.scotcourts.gov.uk/civilcourtsreview/SCCCompleteR.pdf.
Selznick, P (1980) *Law, Society and Industrial Justice* (New Brunswick and London, Transaction Books).
Thibaut, J and Walker, L (1975) *Procedural Justice: a Psychological Analysis* (Hillsdale, New Jersey, Laurence Erlbaum Associates).
Tribe, L (1988) *American Constitutional Law*, 2nd edn (New York, Foundation Press).
Tyler, T (1988) 'What is Procedural Justice? Criteria Used by Citizens to Assess the Fairness of Legal Procedures' 22 *Law and Society Review* 103.

—— (2000) 'Social Justice: Outcome and Procedure' 35 *International Journal of Psychology* 117.

Weber, L and Gelsthorpe, L (2000) *Deciding to Detain: How decisions to detain asylum seekers are made at ports of entry* (Cambridge, Institute of Criminology, University of Cambridge).

Weber, L and Landman, T (2002) *Deciding to Detain: The organisational context for decisions to detain asylum seekers at UK ports* (Cclchester, Human Rights Centre, University of Essex).

7

The Organisation of Administrative Justice Systems: The Role of Political Mistrust

ROBERT A KAGAN

Introduction

In *Total Justice* (1985), legal historian Lawrence M Friedman outlines a dramatic shift in the legal culture of economically advanced democracies over the last century and a quarter. He argues that in tandem with unparalleled increases in societal wealth, technological sophistication and governmental capacity, citizens have become less fatalistic about the hazards and injustices of life. They have developed a generalised expectation that modern societies now have the ability to reduce the risks and impact of impoverishment, disease, injury, environmental degradation, crime, discrimination, and economic instability. If these things *can* be done, people come to believe, governments should make sure they *are* done. In competitive democracies, political leaders respond to such expectations. So decade after decade, governments conduct studies, hold hearings, enact more laws, create more rights, regulate more risks, extend legal liability to more sources of harm, and spend more money on social benefit programmes.

One consequence has been the proliferation of specialised government agencies charged with implementing the policies of the administrative-regulatory state. Today, the bulk of official legal decisions are made not by judges but by 'eligibility workers' processing files in welfare and unemployment insurance offices, by regulatory inspectors and tax auditors, by licensing officials, immigration officers, and assorted other bureaucrats. At the same time, however, the agencies created to fulfill demands for total justice come under criticism for failing to do so, or for acting arbitrarily and unjustly themselves. Administrative officials are squeezed between public expectations for 'total justice' and, on the other side, by never-fully-adequate funding and the inevitable pathologies of bureaucracy. Hence administrative agencies are repeatedly investigated, studied, reorganised, expanded, downsized, reviewed by courts, and subjected to new legal mandates.

Many scholars of law and administration, not surprisingly, have turned their attention to issues of 'administrative justice'. A great deal of administrative law scholarship focuses on the legal procedures and standards that reviewing courts have imposed on administrative agencies. Other scholars have addressed the way administrative agencies organise their own internal decision processes. One strand of this intra-agency research has been normative: the effort to specify 'the principles that can be used to evaluate the justice inherent in administrative decision-making' (Adler 2003: 323–24) and to determine how administrative decision making should best be organised.

A related strand of intra-agency scholarship, to which this paper seeks to contribute, entails the *empirical study* of administrative decision making. Scholars in this tradition assume that issues of optimal institutional design can better be addressed if we had more systematic knowledge of how agencies actually conduct case-by-case decision making, why agencies differ in that regard, and what difference that makes. To conceptualise variation among the many species in the administrative rainforest, some empirically-oriented scholars have offered analytic typologies of administrative justice systems (Adler 2003; Mashaw 1983). This paper seeks to contribute to that conceptual agenda, as well as to offer some thoughts about the role of trust, or mistrust, in shaping the way administrative decision systems are organised and behave.[1]

The first part of the paper will suggest a typology of ways of organising administrative decision making authority, encompassing both (a) case-by-case decision making by 'front-line' officials—the 'street-level bureaucrats' (Lipsky 1980) who interact directly with members of the public, and make decisions that directly affect their fates, and (b) modes of structuring appeals from, or review of, front-line decisions. The second part deals with why a political system adopts one or another way of organising administrative decision systems, discussing especially the role of political mistrust in that regard. The third part addresses the decision-making behaviour of administrative officials in individual cases, presenting a typology of styles of administrative rule application. The fourth and final part returns to the challenge of explanation, identifying some of the factors that shape the style of rule application adopted by administrative bureaucracies, again paying special attention to the nature and intensity of political mistrust. Throughout, most of the illustrative examples I provide will be drawn from the empirical and legal literature on administrative agencies in the United States, partly because that is what I am most familiar with, partly because, especially when contrasted with accounts of administrative governance in Great Britain, Japan and Western Europe, it nicely highlights the significance of political mistrust.

[1] I present several typologies that I have found useful in my own efforts to describe and compare administrative decision-making systems. These typologies do not conflict with the conceptual schemes proposed by Adler and Mashaw, but seem to lie athwart them. My hope is that scholars in the field will find it illuminating to compare and discern the relationships among these related typologies.

Institutional Design for Administrative Decision Making

In contemporary democracies, administrative agencies are creatures of law. They are charged with the implementation of public policies embodied in legislation. Statutes (and implementing regulations) establish and delimit administrative authority, define the agency's mission, specify the benefits they may grant and the penalties they may impose, articulate (with widely-varying degrees of specificity) the principal norms and standards that should govern officials' decisions, and prescribe the procedures that decision makers must follow. Statutes set forth (again, with varying degrees of specificity) the rights of the citizens and organisations with whom the agency interacts, as well as the remedies those citizens and organisations can pursue when they feel their rights have been violated.

At the same time, the very act of entrusting the implementation of governmental policies to an administrative agency suggests the importance of a different, less legalistic set of values. As Philip Selznick (1969: 14–16) put it, one of social functions of administration, perhaps its primary function, is not to determine 'the legal co-ordinates of a situation' in light of pre-established legal rules, but 'to get the work of society done,' to refashion 'human or other resources so that a particular outcome will be achieved.' Administration, from that perspective, requires specialisation, the accumulation of experience, and the application of expertise to complex and changing social contexts—precisely because those contexts vary too much to be boxed in by the generalisations embedded in fixed legal rules, prescribed in advance. Administrative decision making, in this view, requires judgment. Administrative officials who exercise power over the agency's clients or regulated parties need discretion to adapt agency action to the individual case and the particular circumstance. And the administrators' specialised training and knowledge guides, limits, and legitimates their exercise of discretion.

But in societies dedicated to the rule of law, the exercise of discretion by the many different administrative decision makers in large agencies raises the spectre of inconsistency. Similar cases may be treated differently because some individual officials may be biased or lazy. Political conservatives worry that in benefit-providing agencies, naïve front-line officials will reward the undeserving and pay out more than the state and its taxpayers can afford. Activists on the political left, conversely, worry that bureaucrats in benefit-granting agencies will make moralistic, overly stingy judgments. Regulated businesses fear that enforcement officers will be indifferent or hostile to the legitimate arguments of business firms, while pro-regulation activists fear that such officials will be swayed toward undue leniency by the blandishments of regulated businesses. From these concerns, rooted in wide-spectrum distrust of administrative discretion, stem demands for more formal legal controls on decision makers, both substantive and procedural.

There are many ways of dealing with this 'dilemma of rule and discretion'. In his seminal work *Bureaucratic Justice* (1983), Jerry Mashaw identifies three. First, demands for administrative accuracy, efficiency, and consistency suggest that decision-making systems should be organised around principles of bureaucracy, emphasising uniform application of detailed legal rules. Secondly, and conversely, when policymakers think administrators should above all be responsive to the particular needs and circumstances of agency clients, officials should be granted discretion to decide on the basis of their professional expertise. Third, still other administrative constituencies demand the right to challenge both bureaucratic rigidities and the fixed assumptions of agency professionals on legal or moral grounds—which implies the right to adversarial procedures and judicial review.[2] Mashaw concludes that those who design administrative decision systems, facing all three sets of demands, often adopt procedures that incorporate some blend of that tri-fold set of values, although they typically put the primary emphasis on one: 'bureaucratic rationality', 'professional treatment', or 'legal/moral judgment'.

Building on the work of Mashaw and others, I have found it useful to conceive of the organisation of policy-implementing processes as varying along two distinct dimensions, as pictured in Figure 1: (a) legal formality versus informality, and (b) hierarchy versus participation.

With respect to the first dimension, administrative policy–implementation varies in the extent to which substantive decisions and decision-making procedures are structured by, and expected to conform to, written legal rules. The more detailed and specific those legal rules, the more 'formal' or 'legalistic' the decision-making system is. In contrast, in 'informal' processes, administrative decision makers are granted more discretion, guiding legal rules are more general, less constraining, both substantively and procedurally. Decision-making processes can in principle be located at various points along this formal-informal dimension. For example, an agency's decision-making procedures can be quite formal and legalistic, while the rules constraining officials' substantive decisions are more

Figure 1: The Organisation of Decision-making Authority in Administrative Agencies

DECISION MAKING PROCEDURE	**DEGREE OF LEGAL CONTROL** INFORMAL ⟵⟶ FORMAL	
HIERARCHY ↑	expert or political judgment	bureaucratic legalism
↓ **PARTICIPATION**	negotiation/ mediation	adversarial legalism

[2] Adler (2003) adds still other expectations that often shape systems of administrative decision making, such as demands for greater efficiency.

general, leaving more room for judgment; such an agency would be classified as somewhat less formal than a decision system whose procedural *and* substantive standards are prescribed by detailed legal rules.

With respect to the second dimension, in *hierarchically-organised* administrative systems, case-by-case decision-making procedures are dominated by an agency official who is relatively insulated from pressures by individual applicants or regulated entities. At the other end of this dimension are systems that employ *participatory* decision-making processes, in which the individuals or organisations who are subject to the agency's decisions have considerable opportunity to make arguments to each other and to officials, and hence to actually influence agency decisions. Again, real-world agency decision-processes can occupy various points along this hierarchy–participation dimension. Consequently many administrative decision systems to do not precisely resemble any of the 'ideal types' shown in the four quadrants of Figure 1; rather, they combine some elements of two or more types, or contain a sequence of decision-types, one for front-line decisions, another for appeals. In principle, however, both front-line agency decision making and second-phase (and subsequent) review or appeal processes can be characterised in terms of an approximate location within the spaces in Figure 1.[3]

Expert/Political Judgment

As suggested by the upper left quadrant in Figure 1, some administrative decision processes are *hierarchical*, in the sense that an official decision maker (as opposed to the individual or organisation subject to agency action) controls the process and the standards for decision, yet *informal*, in the sense that the decision's authoritativeness rests on the professional or political judgment of individual officials, not conformity with detailed legal rules. For example, in many Western European countries, decisions concerning eligibility for certain disability and workplace injury benefits are made by a panel of government-appointed physicians (or a mixed panel of physicians and social workers), based on their professional judgment. Or picture a social worker who, in evaluating a client's request for social assistance, is authorised to make discretionary judgments about need (and desert) under all the circumstances of the particular case. Or a land use planning agency which has discretion to grant or deny applications for 'variances' from zoning regulations based on its general—essentially political—judgment about whether the project's likely benefit to the community outweighs its potentially adverse neighborhood impact. The more purely expertise-driven such a system is, then the more restricted is the role for legal representation, argument, and influence by

[3] The typology in Figure 1 reflects the distinction between hierarchical and party-influenced modes of legal decision making and adjudication developed by Thibaut and Walker (1978) and Damaska (1975), as well as the typology of bureaucratic decision modes in Mashaw (1983), from which I derive the additional category 'expert judgment' (which I expand to include 'political judgment' as well). Figure 1 is adapted from the typology presented in Kagan (2001:10).

affected citizens and organisations, and the less likely the officials' decisions are to be reversed by appeals to higher officials or to courts.

Bureaucratic Legalism

An administrative decision-making process characterised by a high degree of hierarchical authority and legal formality (the upper right quadrant of Figure 1) resembles the ideal–typical bureaucratic process as analysed by Max Weber. Governance by means of bureaucratic legalism emphasises uniform implementation of centrally devised rules, vertical accountability, and official responsibility for fact finding. Here, too, the more hierarchical the system, the more restricted the role for legal representation and influence by affected citizens or contending interests. In contemporary democracies, the pure case of bureaucratic legalism is usually softened in some respects, but it is an ideal systematically pursued, for example, by tax-collection agencies.

Adversarial Legalism

Figure 1's lower right quadrant refers to policy-implementing and decision processes that are closely-constrained by formal procedural rules, but in which hierarchy is weak—private individuals and organisations have formal legal rights to present evidence and arguments, often with the aid of lawyers. The ideal-type is best exemplified by adjudication in American courts, where the introduction of evidence and invocation of legal rules is dominated not by the judge (as in European civil legal systems) but by contending parties' lawyers.[4] But adversarial legalism also creeps into administrative decision making. As described by Philippe Nonet (1969), California's workers' compensation administration was originally designed to provide insured benefits to injured workers without costly legal conflict, but gradually was transformed into an intensely adversarial and legalistic system as a result of persistent judicial appeals and advocacy by claimants' lawyers. Many American administrative agencies entrust front-line decisions to experts or to rule-guided bureaucrats, but allow appeals to quasi-independent intra-agency 'administrative law judges', who follow adversarial procedures, with active participation by conflicting lawyers.[5] In many agencies, decisions on pollution control permits or land use permits must be preceded by formally-scheduled hearings in which neighbours and advocacy groups can make objections and requests.[6]

[4] Even in comparison with the British 'adversarial system', hierarchical, authoritative imposition of legal rules is relatively weak in courts the United States, where judges defer more to lawyers in the conduct of trials and are more open to novel legal arguments by the parties' lawyers (Atiyah and Summers 1987: 109–34).

[5] See eg Mashaw (1983) for an analysis of the role of administrative law judges in deciding social security disability appeals.

[6] For accounts of such processes, see Dwyer et al (2000), Welles and Engel (2000) and Gunningham, Kagan and Thornton (2003).

Negotiation/Mediation

An administrative process in the lower left quadrant of Figure 1 allows the individuals or organisations who seek to invoke or resist the agency's authority to present and argue their cases in an informal manner. In this modality, regulatory officials charged with implementing anti-discrimination or consumer protection law, for example, often mediate disputes between a complainant and an employer or a merchant, fostering a negotiated settlement (Silbey 1980–81). The process is nonlegalistic, since neither procedures nor substantive dispositions are dictated by formal law.

Political and Legal Accountability and Sequential Decision Systems

In establishing and reforming administrative agencies, political authorities generally insist on a variety of *accountability mechanisms*, not only to structure front-line decision making but also to provide mechanisms of accountability or review, hoping thereby to legitimate administrative decision making in the eyes of a variety of potential critics. There are at least six commonly employed modes of review: (1) case-by-case appeal (by dissatisfied citizens or organisations) to higher officials in the agency; (2) appeals to administrative tribunals that are independent of the agency, in whole or in part;[7] (3) appeals to courts; (4) appeals to political officials who are either explicitly or implicitly authorised to reverse agency decisions;[8] (5) complaints to an ombudsman's office; and (6) systematic 'top-down' review of front-line decisions via an administrative *audit system*, designed to sample decisions, detect patterns and identify ostensibly deviant cases or decision makers.

In many agencies, as suggested earlier, these forms are mixed and sequenced. Thus in the US Social Security Disability programme, front-line decisions are based on the bureaucratic application of detailed rules to facts submitted in writing by applicants and their physicians. But they can be appealed to an intra-agency panel in which the applicant appears and speaks in person, often with the

[7] In the US, there are approximately three times as many intra-agency, quasi-independent 'administrative law judges' and 'hearing officers' in federal governmental agencies as there are judgeships in the federal courts. Whereas federal courts conduct approximately 100,000 evidentiary hearings per year, approximately 700,000 hearings per year are conducted by just four federal agencies: the Social Security Administration, the Immigration and Naturalisation Service, the Board of Veteran Appeals, and the Equal Employment Opportunity Commission (Resnick 2008: 126–27).

[8] Those dissatisfied with administrative case-by-case decisions sometimes appeal to their elected legislative representative, even though those officials have no legal or political authority to overrule agency; the hope is that the representative will nevertheless have informal political influence. In the US, most agencies will grant expedited consideration to 'inquiries' from elected legislative members on behalf of a dissatisfied constituent, even if agency officials feel secure in ultimately rejecting the politician's 'appeal'. Whenever, in the US or elsewhere, the agency feels considerable pressure to accede to the politician's views, one might classify that as approaching a system of appeals based on political judgment.

aid of legal counsel (Mashaw 1983). Some agencies combine case-by-case appeals with managerial quality-control audits. In some systems, parties simultaneously appeal to higher administrative levels and present their complaints to legislative representatives, seeking their intervention or pressure.

Political Mistrust and the Organisation of Administrative Justice

Why does administrative decision making in one program resemble the ideal-type of bureaucratic legalism, while another emphasises expert judgment, or a third adversarial legalism? It seems premature to offer any full-blown explanatory theory. Reviewing the socio-legal literature on regulatory enforcement style, for example, I concluded that numerous causal factors are important, including features of the agency's legal mandate and powers, the agency's task environment, its political environment, and the attitudes of agency leaders (Kagan 1993). As one step toward the development of an explanatory theory, however, this section offers some thoughts about political mistrust in shaping the political and legal accountability mechanisms for, and hence the structure of, administrative decision-making systems.

The creation of an administrative programme typically involves at least some faith in administrative expertise as the basis for policy-elaboration and implementation. Due to the complexity of legislative goals and the programme's social context, the legislature usually cannot formulate its goals in the form of specific legal rules. Hence implementation is assigned to an agency, whose officials specialise in the policy area, gather and analyse relevant data, and employ accumulating expertise to make context- and case-specific judgments about what decision will best fulfil the agency's principal purposes. If faith in expertise inclines legislators and agency leaders toward an 'expert judgment' model of case-by-case decision making, a decline in that faith should lead them—from the outset or after some negative experiences—to impose a more formal and legalistic decision system on the agency. Whether political mistrust of expert judgment results in a shift toward bureaucratic legalism or toward adversarial legalism depends on the source and particular nature of that mistrust.

Resort to 'bureaucratic legalism' often reflects national political leaders' concern that local administrative officials, influenced by local cultural, political, or economic pressures, will not remain faithful to the central government's policy goals. Sometimes bureaucratic legalism is instituted to allay mistrust of the even-handedness and probity of administrative officials on the part of the public at large or of particular constituencies. Advocacy groups for patients charge nursing home regulators with laxness in enforcing the regulations. Political conservatives may fear that a welfare agency will be staffed by soft-hearted social workers who are not sufficiently vigilant about welfare fraud. For politicians, therefore, employing bureaucratic legalism to structure the administrative decision system helps mollify such critics, while giving politicians a greater measure of control over policy outcomes. For the agency, bureaucratic legalism, with its display of decision making driven by detailed legal rules, provides the trappings (and, often, the reality) of impersonality and neutrality, helping to legitimate its day-to-day decisions to individuals and regulated organisations to whom the agency must say 'no.'

'Adversarial legalism' reflects political distrust of 'bureaucratic legalism' as well as distrust of expert judgment. In one scenario, adversarial legalism is institutionalised when political leaders, judges, interest groups, or advocacy organisations believe that an administrative bureaucracy is too legalistic, that its officials apply rules mechanically, without sufficient regard to the equity of the particular case. The remedy is to expand avenues for citizens or regulated enterprises to participate in the decision-making process, to have the opportunity to impress on officials alternative ways of looking at the facts and the merits of the case. When political and legal elites are concerned that an agency will not be truly *responsive* to such arguments, they are more likely to require the agency to adopt formal, adversarial procedures, including rights to representation by lawyers, along with rights to appeal to the courts.

The mistrust that is conducive to adversarial legalism is most prevalent when political authority is fragmented or uncertain, for example, in federal polities, or systems based on separation of powers, like the United States, where top administrative agency officials may be appointed by elected executives loyal to one political party while the legislature is controlled by a different political party. In such politically fragmented regimes, legislators worry that an agency, now or in the uncertain political future, will be headed by an official appointed by a president or governor who is hostile to the legislative majority's policy priorities and who will push front-line bureaucrats to subvert those policies in case-by-case decisions. The legislator's solution is to empower individuals, regulated entities, and advocacy groups to appeal wayward administrative decisions to an independent tribunal or to the courts. Lawyers and the judiciary thus are enlisted as enforcement agents for the legislature's enacted preferences. The prevalence of this scenario in the United States goes a long way toward explaining the relatively high levels of adversarial legalism that since the mid-1960s have been built into major federal social benefit and regulatory programs (Kagan 2001: chapter 3; Melnick 2004). This scenario is less likely, conversely, in the parliamentary governments of Western Europe, where, in contrast with the US, newly elected governments do not routinely replace the whole top level of agency officials with politically partisan appointees, and where the national bureaucracy is in general more highly respected than are governmental bureaucracies in the United States.

Front-line decision-making processes are often reshaped over time through interaction with appeal systems. The more often citizens and regulated entities mistrust and *contest* the exercise of authority by front-line decision makers, and the more often appeals result in reversals, the more one would expect front-line officials to add formal requirements to initially informal processes, hoping to reduce the incidence of appeal and reversal. For example, a 1974 Congressional statute requires local school districts to provide 'an appropriate public education' to students with physical and mental disabilities. The statute mandates, first of all, a negotiation-based decision process, in which parents meet annually with school officials and 'special education' experts to work out a contractual plan for their child's placement and assistance. (Neal and Kirp 1986). If no agreement is reached, the parents can appeal to a school district-level administrative review panel, and then, at least in some states, to a state-level review panel. Finally, a dissatisfied parent can appeal to a court. Each successive appeal is more formal, more adversarial. One consequence of this structure is that courts have made many of the crucial interpretations of the statute (Melnick 1994), thereby creating more formal substantive rules that constrain the initially informal negotiation process. Another consequence has been that in anticipation of judicial review, the first-level negotiated meetings often have become more procedurally formal and legalistic. According to Neal and Kirp (1986: 355):

> Adversariness and legalism seem to characterise the conduct of hearings. Rather than adopting an informal negotiating format, the due process hearings tend to provide a forum for culmination of long-term bad relations between the school and the parents involved. Involving lawyers aggravates the situation, rendering proceedings more legalistic. Emphasis on compliance with procedural matters such as notices, signatures, and time deadlines offers an easy substitute for harder substantive questions.[9]

Similarly, American welfare agencies have evolved from bodies staffed by trained social workers, exercising a degree of professional judgment, to bodies staffed largely by non-professional bureaucrats who legalistically follow detailed regulations, forms, and checklists (Simon 1983). This evolution was propelled in large part by the 'welfare rights movement' of the 1960s, which regularly challenged discretionary local administrative judgments and policies in court, winning decisions which, among other things, required agencies to establish 'due process' hearing procedures to which welfare rights lawyers could appeal front-line decisions (Melnick 1994). Conservative politicians, seeing this as a threat to fiscal control, enacted more detailed rules and mandated administrative audits that were designed to constrain front-line officials' discretion and encourage more stringent decisions (Brodkin and Lipsky 1983). The introduction of a review system based on adversarial legalism, in short, stimulated efforts to control front-line officials' judgment via tighter bureaucratic legalism. Social workers, with their capacity for expert judgment (and higher salaries), became unnecessary and were replaced by clerks.

[9] By way of contrast, the British administrative decision-system for 'special education', at least when first established, emphasised 'professional judgment' rather than formalised negotiation and adversarial legalism (Kirp 1982).

Styles of Administrative Decision Making

Agencies vary not only in the density and specificity of legal rules that are meant to govern case-by-case decisions, but also in what one might call the agency's 'culture of rule-application' (Kagan 1978: 88–90). The key point of variability is how officials in a particular agency or office deal with the inevitable shortcomings of administrative regulations, forms, and checklists. Rules are based on generalisations; they say that under circumstances a, b, and c, the appropriate decision is X, since X will best advance the agency's policy goals. The generalisation is that X will always be appropriate. But the social world, diverse and always changing, is too complex for rule-makers to imagine. Hence many rules will be over-inclusive in some situations. A particular case may involve not only circumstances a, b, and c, but also d and e (a combination not recognised in any existing rule). In such a case, decision X, a legally proper application of the rule, may produce a result that skews the policy that the rule was formulated to implement. Or decision X, while in some way advancing the agency's policy, will be perceived as extremely unfair or inhumane, or will have other adverse consequences. Agencies that mechanically apply rules in those kinds of cases can trigger a public or political backlash, or alienate regulated businesses whose co-operation is important to the fuller achievement of agency policy goals.[10]

This episodic mismatch between agency goals and the dictates of particular rules occurs not only with respect to substantive rules but also with respect to evidentiary rules. To use another stylised example, the regulations governing decisions in an agency that provides certain benefits (such as income maintenance grants for poor families, or border entry to would-be immigrants) might say, 'the benefit [or permit] shall not be granted unless the applicant presents convincing documentary proof of a, b, and c.' What if the applicant's situation does entail a, b, and c, but she cannot provide documentary proof of one or more of those factual circumstances? Can the agency official rely on the applicant's oral statements if they seem convincing? The issue is whether the official is allowed to treat the regulation as a presumptive rule, rebuttable by other kinds of evidence, or whether she is compelled by supervisors and agency heads to treat it as a hard-and-fast, unbendable, absolute rule.

In *The Nature of the Judicial Process*, New York Court of Appeals Judge Benjamin Cardozo (1921: 19–25) discussed one way in which common law judges deal with potential conflicts between existing rules and desired social consequences. Judicial decision making, he wrote, ideally is a two-step process: the judge, while assessing the facts of the case, first 'looks backwards' to pre-existing rules (precedents) to discern what they seem to require, but then 'looks forward' to assess the consequences of following an ostensibly applicable rule. When the results of literal rule application would be patently unjust or unwise, a judge 'worthy of his office' must

[10] See Bardach and Kagan (2002: 109–19) for an account of how legalistic enforcement of occupational safety and other regulatory programs in the late 1970s in the United States led to resistance by industry, to frequent litigation that diverted agency personnel from their primary tasks, and fuelled presidential candidate Ronald Reagan's anti-regulation rhetoric.

Figure 2: Modes of Rule Application in Administrative Bureaucracies

EMPHASIS ON ADHERENCE TO RULES	EMPHASIS ON REALISATION OF AGENCY POLICIES/SOCIAL VALUES STRONG ← → WEAK	
STRONG ↑	legal creativity	legalism
↓ WEAK	discretionary judgment	retreatism

consider reinterpreting the rule, or if so authorised, create a new rule for cases of the kind he is considering.

Some administrative agencies enable and encourage their officials, in deciding individual cases, to adopt Cardozo's model of judicial creativity. Some do not, fearing it would at best lead to too much inconsistency and at worst open the door to bias and corruption. The pattern of possible responses can be characterised in light of the ideal-types set out in Figure 2.[11]

In some agencies, the reigning culture of rule application pressures administrative officials to follow the dictates of the written regulations, even if they feel the rule-based decision would not 'make sense' in the particular case; at the extreme, officials might be socialised not to 'look forward' at consequences at all. I call that a 'legalistic' decision-making style, represented by the upper-right quadrant in Figure 2. At the opposite extreme, labeled 'discretionary judgment' in Figure 2, the agency's internal culture values achievement of official policy goals and responsiveness to the variety of individual situations more than it values strict rule-following. In cases in which the two goals appear to conflict, agency decision makers can make *ad hoc* exceptions to the rule.

The upper-left quadrant (labeled 'legal creativity') refers to agencies whose culture strongly emphasises both rule-based decision making and responsiveness to broader agency purposes. When the rule-based decision seems to frustrate policy goals, agency officials are authorised, alone or in consultation with colleagues and supervisors, to reinterpret existing rules, that is, to adopt innovative readings or to articulate principled exceptions (new sub-rules) which support the preferred outcome. Observing this practice in a US agency that administered a nationwide price and wage freeze in the early 1970s, I wrote (Kagan 1978: 91–92):

[11] Figure 2 is adapted from Kagan (1978: 95).

> That is not to say that a rule *must* be abandoned whenever the result in a single case seems unfair: the issue is whether a better, more specific rule can be devised, taking into the costs of ... carving out an exception to the old one. The key to this difficult process is a continuing effort within ... [the agency] to develop common conceptions of that institution's proper purposes.[12]

Not all agencies, not all such officials, are so dedicated. The lower right-hand quadrant of Figure 2 uses the label 'retreatism' to capture the response of agency officials who face hard cases—conflicts between rule and agency goals—and who seem to abandon both goals. This sometimes occurs when officials lack the time, resources or wit to cope with the problem. Sometimes it happens because officials are indifferent, weakly committed to either rule-following or the achievement of agency policy goals. In an agency whose internal culture fails to discourage retreatism, officials deal with difficult choices by temporising and accumulating backlogs of undecided cases, or by making endless demands for more information or proof, or by processing cases in a pro-forma, ritualistic fashion, with little attention to legal accuracy or consequences, or at the extreme, by deciding on the basis of bribes. Retreatism does not conform with any normative notion of administrative justice. But unfortunately, as Franz Kafka taught us decades ago, it captures people's experience with administrative bureaucracy in many places in the world. Hence retreatism deserves a place, I think, in the empirical study of administrative decision making, along with attention to the factors that engender and sustain it.

Factors Influencing Styles of Administrative Decision-Making

Variations in styles of rule application arise first of all from the personality, role-conceptions, and political commitments of individual decision makers, which can vary even within a single office. Second, officials can also be pushed away from legalism and toward legal creativity by the skill and persistence with which particular parties or their legal advocates present their arguments—a factor that varies from case to case. (Kagan 1978: 148, 154–57). Third, cases in which it is likely that the agency's decision will be reported in the news media tend to elicit more careful and thoughtful modes of rule application.[13]

[12] In *Regulatory Justice* (Kagan 1978: 91–92), I labeled the upper-left-hand quadrant, here labeled 'legal creativity', the 'judicial mode' of rule-application, because it reflects Cardozo's account of judging and because it is commonly observed in American courts, which combine an 'instrumentalist' approach to judicial decision making (Atiyah and Summers 1987: 404) with norms of legal craft that call for principled rather than ad hoc justifications for legal innovations (Wechsler 1959). My emphasis on institutional purpose as the key to coherent legal creativity in agencies reflects Philip Selznick's writings on 'responsive law' (Nonet and Selznick 2002: [1978]).

[13] By analogy, it has been shown that US Court of Appeals judges are less likely to decide cases on the basis of their own political values when they serve on panels with judges from another political party, who might file a dissenting opinion that calls attention to the majority's legal reasoning (Cross and Tiller 1998).

Fourth, and perhaps most important, beyond the *ad hoc* sources of variation just mentioned, administrative offices tend to develop distinctive internal cultures of rule application (Id at 88-90)enforced by on-the-job training, peer pressure and performance reviews—cultures that promote one of the modes of rule-application set forth in Figure 2. The critical question, therefore, is 'What shapes an office's dominant style of rule application and decision-making?' The socio-legal literature provides some clues, pointing to a series of influential factors.

Organisational Variables

A legalistic style is encouraged by burdensome caseloads, combined with organisational and external pressures for rapid decision making. Under such conditions, discretionary judgment and 'legal creativity' do not flourish, for they take time and mental effort, close attention to the likely human consequences of routine rule application. In a US inflation-control agency that in the early 1970s processed a flood of requests to raise prices or wages, officials in certain offices were under severe pressures to give prompt responses. I observed (and later wrote) that in those offices,

> officials tended to read inquiries more and more rapidly, through a set of lenses which picked out only the key words that enabled the official to place the case into a routine category, screening out information about the inquirer's financial situation and what it would mean for him [if his request were refused].' (Kagan 1978: 147–48).

Legalistic decision making also is more likely when decision making is based on paper dossiers or occurs in highly formal settings. Conversely, administrative officials are more likely to bend the rules when the organisation of decision-making places them in face-to-face interaction with individuals or regulated entities (Kagan 1978: 152). A retreatist style seems more likely in an agency that is so starved for resources and well-trained personnel that frustration and demoralisation set in.

Degree of Professionalism

Even in face-to-face settings, modes of decision making can and do vary. Christopher Jewell's (2007) study of welfare case-workers in California, Sweden, and Germany showed that in a welfare office in Malmo, Sweden, professionally-trained caseworkers were embedded in an office culture that emphasised mutual consultation; they had a nuanced decision-making style, responsive to the needs of particular clients. Their counterparts in the United States, conversely, had much less professional training and were embedded in an office culture that emphasised legalistic adherence to rules and regulations. A similar relationship between professionalism and more flexible rule application has been found in studies of regulatory inspectors (Bardach and Kagan 2002: 152–58). If the inspector has experience and knowledge, he or she can more confidently judge the merits of a regulated enterprise's arguments about the 'unreasonableness' of applying a regulation strictly in the particular case; without such knowledge, the inspector finds it 'safer' simply to enforce the rule legalistically. In Germany, regulatory officials concerned with bank safety and soundness are career employees, subjected to much more extensive education and training than their counterparts at the US Federal Reserve Board. The highly professional German officials, consequently, are trusted to make programmatically sensible judgments, whereas the American regulators are bound by an immensely voluminous, complex, and detailed body of legal rules, and are expected to apply them legalistically (Rubin 1997).

The Agency's 'Task Environment'

The missions and social functions of administrative agencies vary widely, as do the nature of the 'clienteles' officials deal with on a daily basis. Police officers in communities with high levels of violent drug-dealing, gun ownership, or hostility to the police face a markedly different 'task environment' than officers who work in middle-class suburbs. Hence one might expect differences in the way they interpret and enforce departmental regulations, criminal laws, and the rules of criminal procedure.

Shover et al (1984) studied two offices of the US Office of Surface Mining (OSM), which regulates the environmental impact of strip mining. Both were responsible for enforcing detailed regulations that required them to issue citations and cessation orders whenever they detected violations. The OSM office in West Virginia, in the Appalachian Mountains, had to deal with many small, privately owned, often recalcitrant mining companies. Officials in that office applied the regulations more legalistically than their counterparts in the OSM office in the Western plains of Montana. The western OSM officials interacted with many fewer, but much larger corporations. Those mining operations were owned by major petroleum companies; they were well funded, concerned with their corporate reputation, and environmentally sophisticated. With fewer sites to visit, the Western OSM officials came to know the regulated enterprises well, and the enterprises knew they would be subject to prompt repeat visits if the inspector found a violation. The Western OSM office, Shover et al found, emphasised 'discretionary judgment' in applying the rules. It issued few citations or cessation orders because the companies were generally co-operative in abating and preventing violations.[14]

One aspect of the difference in task environment between the Western and Eastern OSM offices, and hence in their decision-making style, was the extent to which officials felt they could trust the regulated company officials they dealt with

[14] For a more complete account and analysis of studies showing the influence of task environment and political environment (among other variables) on regulatory agencies' enforcement style, see Kagan (1993).

Figure 3: Error-Avoidance and Decision-Style in a Benefit-Granting Agency

AGENCY DECISION STYLE	APPLICANT IS REALLY ELIGIBLE ←→	INELIGIBLE
TRUSTING/DISCRETIONARY ↑	OK	Type I error: 'wasted' resources
↓ MISTRUSTFUL/LEGALISTIC	Type II error: injustice, hardship	OK

Figure 4: Error-Avoidance and Decision-Style in a Regulatory Agency

AGENCY DECISION STYLE	APPLICANT IS REALLY HONEST ←→ CO-OPERATIVE ←→	DISHONEST UNCO-OPERATIVE
TRUSTING/DISCRETIONARY ↑	OK	Type I error: risk to public
↓ MISTRUSTFUL/LEGALISTIC	Type II error: alienated, less co-operative entity	OK

when those officials offered arguments for a more flexible rule interpretation. How genuine was their asserted commitment to follow the law, or work toward the social goals it embodied? Almost every agency official who decides individual cases faces a version of this trust issue. The frequency and difficulty of making that judgment, which varies across task environments, is likely to be an important influence on an agency's decision-making behaviour.

What is more, there are risks for the administrative official, and hence for the agency, in being too untrusting (which we might call a Type II error) as well as too trusting (a Type I error). Figures 3 and 4 outline the choices that officials in a benefit-granting and a regulatory agency face in determining the honesty and co-operativeness of an applicant for benefits or a regulated businessman who makes a plea for an exception to the usual rule.

The OSM inspectors in Montana had more tools to detect whether the entities they regulated were honest and co-operative (more frequent visits) than their colleagues in West Virginia. They also had more reason to expect that the firms they regulated had rational reasons to be co-operative (frequent inspector visits, plus concern for public image). Hence a discretionary decision style generated less risk of error than would a legalistic style. But many task environments are more like that faced by the Eastern OSM inspectors, in which the risk of a Type I error (excessive leniency) is higher, and incentives to adopt a more legalistic style are correspondingly greater.

The Agency's 'Political Environment'

The agency's solution to the dilemmas posed in Figures 3 and 4 often is not solely a product of its rational analysis of the relative risks of Type I and Type II errors. Its solution often depends on which risk important actors in the agency's political environment—elected political leaders, interest groups, journalists and voters—regard as the risk to be avoided most. If a conservative government-in-power pushes hard for eliminating 'welfare cheating' and 'waste', agencies are likely adopt more rules aimed at that goal and apply them legalistically, even if administrative officials think it will result in many Type II errors.

Similarly, regulatory agencies tend to enforce rules legalistically when they are subject to public criticism for perceived laxity (Bardach and Kagan 1982). Conversely, they are more likely to adopt a retreatist style when potential advocates for strict enforcement remain silent or when violators enjoy the backing of political authorities (Gunningham 1987). Scholz and Wei (1986) found that state-level offices of the US Occupational Safety and Health Administration (OSHA) enforced federal regulations more legalistically in states with higher rates of labor union membership and higher frequencies of complaints about violations. In a separate study in New York state, Scholz et al (1991) found that OSHA officials enforced the same set of rules more legalistically in counties whose legislative representatives were liberal Democrats than in counties represented by more conservative Republicans.[15]

More subtly, administrative officials often are affected by the political attitudes of the communities in which they live and work. Mashaw (1971) found that social welfare officials in poorer, politically conservative rural counties in Virginia interpreted and applied eligibility rules very strictly, while officials in wealthier, urban counties did the opposite. Variations in local political culture produce different law-enforcement styles in municipal police departments (Wilson 1968). Hedge et al (1988) found that inspectors employed by a West Virginia state agency had a less legalistic, more accommodative way of applying strip mine control regulations than inspectors in the West Virginia office of the federal government's regulatory agency for strip mines.

[15] For a similar finding with respect to local political climate and environmental law enforcement in Great Britain, see Hutter (1988).

National Political Differences and Administrative Decision Style

The nature of the political environment also features prominently in explanations of why administrative agencies in the US often have a more legalistic decision-making style than administrative agencies in other Western democracies. In the United States, as suggested earlier, a political tradition characterised by mistrust of concentrated governmental power and bureaucracy has produced a significant level of adversarial legalism in the organisation of administrative decision-making systems. The same mistrust affects the behaviour, or rule-application style, of front-line administrative decision makers.

Christopher Jewell, mentioned earlier, conducted an observational and interview-based study of decision making by front-line officials in welfare offices in Malmo, Sweden, Bremen, Germany, and several California counties. Summarising his findings, Jewell (2003) wrote:

> One way to simplify how social assistance is administered is to offer set benefits based on the typical needs for a household of a given size. ... U.S. welfare policy has followed this approach, reflecting a fundamental distrust of front-line workers. ... The price of greater formal predictability, though, is less assurance that claimants receive sufficient support, as caseworkers lack the authority to tailor aid to individual circumstances.

On the other hand, Jewell noted, in Germany and especially in Sweden, caseworkers are trusted to exercise more individual judgment in adjusting the amount of aid in cases where applicants have special needs:

> The German approach involves considerable articulation [of rules] and continual regulatory development to define the parameters of basic need. The administration of this complex set of rules is delegated to senior level careerist public officials with extensive training in regulatory interpretation, an expertise ... I call "regulatory entitlement scholarship". By contrast, the Swedish approach is characterised by more limited regulatory codification. National regulations consist of a "frame law" of general principles while most program guidelines are developed by local government with comparatively limited operational details. This challenge of "rule scarcity" is addressed through a reliance on the social pedagogical training of a staff with a well-developed consultation culture, a ... constitution of program authority I call a "social work ethos". (Jewell 2007: 15, 384–85).

Behind these cross-national differences in administrative decision-making style, of course, lie significant differences in national political traditions and attitudes toward social welfare, as explicated in the 'three worlds of welfare' described by Esping-Anderson (1991) and in Harold Wilensky's magisterial *Rich Democracies* (2002). Similarly, comparative studies of enforcement decision making by nursing home inspectors in Australia, Great Britain, and the US (Braithwaite 1993, Day and Klein 1987) found that American regulations concerning quality of care are more detailed and prescriptive and are enforced more legalistically. Accompanying governmental inspectors on visits to American nursing homes, John Braithwaite was struck by 'the culture of distrust' generated by the more mechanical, document-checking style of the American inspectors, as compared with the more interactive, discussion-based style of British and Australian inspectors. Similar patterns were reported in Steven Kelman's (1981) comparative study of workplace safety regulation in US and Sweden and David Vogel's (1986) comparison of environmental regulatory enforcement in the US and the UK. Each of these studies locates the primary cause of these differences in national political structures and political cultures.

In the late 1990s, I led a team of researchers who carried out nine case studies of multinational corporations, each of which conducted similar operations in the US and in another economically advanced democracy (eg, the Netherlands, the UK, Canada or Japan). Each study examined in detail the corporation's parallel encounters with each country's administrative officials in dealing with similar regulatory and legal issues. In each case study, the corporation's officials in its American operations experienced state and federal administrative regulations and procedures as more detailed, more complex, more legalistically-enforced, and more costly to comply with than were similar regulations in the comparison country. Moreover, compliance costs were significantly higher for the corporation's US branch—even though substantive measures taken by the company's US and non-US operations were quite similar. Costs in the US were higher because the corporate facilities in the US routinely had to spend far more money on lawyers and on certifications, studies, tests, and reports needed to document its compliance with regulations (Kagan and Axelrad 2000). Corporate officials attributed the higher accountability costs to the 'culture of mistrust' that Braithwaite mentioned. Compared to their counterparts in other rich democracies, American administrative officials were perceived as more defensive, more afraid to use their own judgment, more afraid of criticism from their superiors or politicians. They acted more legalistically, in short, because the agency itself was the subject of mistrust by actors in its political environment—including pro-regulation advocacy groups and politicians ready to criticise the agency for leniency and ineffectiveness, and conservative politicians ready to criticise the agency for overzealousness.

In an atmosphere of mistrust of the agency's professionalism, adopting a legalistic style of rule application provides bureaucratic officials a somewhat safe haven. A vicious circle ensues. In an atmosphere of mistrust of the agency's professionalism, legislatures are less likely to fund the agency adequately and more likely to constrain its decision making with more detailed rules, which in turn makes it easier to challenge agency decisions in court. All this, of course, increases the likelihood that the agency officials will act legalistically rather than thoughtfully, which increases the likelihood that they will be viewed as unprofessional and untrustworthy.

Conclusions

When political parties, interest groups, legal experts or political leaders distrust the competence, political neutrality, and fairness of bureaucrats, they are inclined to demand stricter control of administrative discretion through detailed rules, rights to participate in administrative decision-making processes, more formal and adversarial legal procedures, and searching judicial review of administrative decisions. When that occurs, administrative systems are driven or at least nudged toward more formal, bureaucratic and adversarial modes of structuring the processes for deciding individual cases. In terms of the typology outlined in the discussion of Figure 1, the administrative process becomes more formal, less reliant on professional judgment in dealing with hard cases, and less reliant on political judgment in dealing with controversial ones.

Secondly, at the level of individual administrative decision making, under conditions of political distrust, individual officials are more likely to be pressured toward a legalistic style of applying rules and deciding cases. That is, in terms of the typology outlined in the discussion of Figure 1, political distrust and the tighter legal accountability that implies push individual decision makers away from both discretionary judgment and legal creativity in interpreting and applying legal rules and regulations.

When the political distrust had been 'deserved'—in the sense that the administrative agency had indeed accrued a track record of ineptitude, bias, sloppiness, dishonesty or unresponsiveness—then the move toward greater legal specificity, adversarial checks, and close fidelity to rules may well result in an increase in the incidence of administrative justice. When the opposite is the case—the agency and its personnel are reasonably competent, honest, and politically neutral—the intensification of legal controls may well have the opposite consequence, increasing rather than decreasing the incidence of administrative injustice.

Those relationships, it should be noted, are stated in highly contingent terms—'more likely' or 'might well have the opposite consequence.' That is because much careful scholarship and thinking need to be done in order to: (1) more carefully describe and classify the many varieties of administrative decision-making systems in the modern state; and (2) identify and explicate the political, cultural, and task-environment factors that influence the design and operation of administrative decision systems. This chapter, and this volume, will, it is hoped, help advance that agenda.

References

Adler, M (2003) 'A Socio-Legal Approach to Administrative Justice' 25 *Law and Policy* 323.

Atiyah, PS and Summers, RS (1987) *Form and Substance in Anglo-American Law: A Comparative Study of Legal Reasoning, Legal Theory, and Legal Institutions*. (Oxford, Clarendon Press).

Bardach, E and Kagan, RA (2002) *Going by the Book: The Problem of Regulatory Unreasonableness* (New Brunswick NJ, Transaction Books, first published by Temple University Press in 1982).

Braithwaite, J (1993) 'The Nursing Home Industry,' in M Tonry and AJ Reiss, Jr (eds), *Beyond the Law: Crime in Complex Organizations* (Chicago, University of Chicago Press).
Brodkin, E and Lipsky, M (1983) 'Quality Control in AFDC as an Administrative Strategy' 57 *Social Services Review* 1.
Cardozo, B (1921) *The Nature of the Judicial Process* (New Haven, Yale University Press).
Cross, F and Tiller, E (1998) 'Judicial Partisanship and Obedience to Legal Doctrine: Whistleblowing on the Federal Courts of Appeals' 107 *Yale Law Journal* 2155.
Damaska, M (1975) 'Structures of Authority and Comparative Criminal Procedure' 84 *Yale Law Journal* 480.
—— (1986) *The Faces of Justice and State Authority: A Comparative Approach to the Legal Process* (New Haven, Yale University Press).
Day, P and Klein, R (1987) 'The Regulation of Nursing Homes: A Comparative Perspective' 65 *The Milbank Quarterly* 303.
Dwyer, J, Brooks, R and Marco, A (2000) 'The Air Pollution Permit Process for US and German Automobile Assembly Plants' in R Kagan and L Axelrad (eds), *Regulatory Encounters: Multinational Corporations and American Adversarial Legalism* (Berkeley CA, University of California Press).
Esping-Andersen, G (1991) *The Three Worlds of Welfare Capitalism* (Cambridge, Polity Press).
Friedman, LM (1985) *Total Justice* (New York, Russell Sage Foundation).
Gunningham, N (1987) 'Negotiated Non-Compliance: A Case Study of Regulatory Failure' 9 *Law and Policy* 69.
Gunningham, N, Thornton, D and Kagan, RA (2003) *Shades of Green: Business, Regulation and Environment* (Stanford, CA, Stanford University Press).
Donald, D, Menzel, D and Williams, G (1988) 'Regulatory Attitudes and Behavior: The Case of Surface Mining Regulation' 41 *Western Political Quarterly* 323.
Hutter, B (1988) *The Reasonable Arm of the Law? The Law Enforcement Procedures of Environmental Health Officials* (Oxford, Clarendon Press).
Jewell, C (2003) *Responding to Need in the 'Three Worlds of Social Welfare': How Welfare State Traditions Impact the Role Caseworkers Play in Shaping Welfare Policy in the United States, Germany and Sweden* (PhD Dissertation, Jurisprudence and Social Policy Program, University of California, Berkeley).
—— (2007) *Agents of the Welfare State: How Caseworkers Respond to Need in the United States, Germany and Sweden* (New York and Houndmills, Palgrave Macmillan).
—— (2007) 'Assessing Needs in the United States, Germany, and Sweden: The Organisation of Welfare Casework' 29 *Law and Policy* 380.
Kagan, RA (1978) *Regulatory Justice: Implementing a Wage Price Freeze* (New York, Russell Sage Foundation).
—— (1993) 'Regulatory Enforcement' in D Rosenblum and R Schwartz (eds) *Handbook of Regulation and Administrative Law* (New York, Marcel Dekker).
—— (2001) *Adversarial Legalism: The American Way of Law* (Cambridge, Harvard University Press).
Kagan, R and Axelrad, L (eds) *Regulatory Encounters: Multinational Corporations and American Adversarial Legalism* (Berkeley, University of California Press).
Kelman, S (1981) *Regulating America, Regulating Sweden: A Comparative Study of Occupational Safety and Health Policy* (Cambridge, MIT Press).
Kirp, DL (1982) 'Professionalisation as a Policy Choice: British Special Education in Comparative Perspective' 34 *World Politics* 137.

Lipsky, M (1980) *Street Corner Bureaucracy* (New York, Russell Sage).
Mashaw, J (1971) 'Welfare Reform and Local Administration of Aid to Families with Dependent Children in Virginia' 57 *Virginia Law Review* 818.
—— (1983, *Bureaucratic Justice: Managing Social Security Disability Claims* (New Haven, Yale University Press).
Melnick, R Shep (1994) *Between the Lines: Interpreting Welfare Rights* (Washington, DC, Brookings Institution).
—— (2004) 'Courts and Agencies,' in MC Miller and J Barnes (eds), *Making Policy, Making Law: An Interbranch Perspective* (Washington, DC, Georgetown University Press).
Neal, D and Kirp, D (1986) 'The Allure of Legalisation Reconsidered: The Case of Special Education' in D Kirp and D Jensen (eds) *School Days, Rule Days: The Legalisation and Regulation of Education* (New York, Falmer Press).
Nonet, P (1969) *Administrative Justice* (New York, Russell Sage Foundation).
Nonet, P and Selznick, P (2002) *Law and Society in Transition: Toward Responsive Law*, 2nd edn (New Brunswick, NJ, Transaction Books, first published by Harper and Row in 1978).
Resnick, J (2008) 'Courts: In and Out of Sight, Site, and Cite' 53 *Villanova Law Review* 101.
Rubin, EL (1997) 'Discretion and Its Discontents' 72 *Chicago Kent Law Review* 1299.
Scholz, JT, Twombly, J and Headrick, B (1991) 'Street Level Political Controls Over Federal Bureaucracy' 85 *American Political Science Review* 829.
Scholz, JT and Wei, FH (1986) 'Regulatory Enforcement in a Federalist System' 80 *American Political Science Review* 1249.
Selznick, P (1969) *Law, Society and Industrial Justice* (New York NY, Russell Sage Foundation).
Shover, N et al (1984) 'Regional Variation in Regulatory Law Enforcement: The Surface Mining Control and Reclamation Act' in K Hawkins and J Thomas (eds), *Enforcing Regulation* (Boston, Kluwer-Nijhoff).
Silbey, SS (1984) 'The Consequences of Responsive Regulation' in K Hawkins and J Thomas (eds), *Enforcing Regulation* (Boston MA, Kluwer-Nijhoff).
Simon, WH (1983) 'Legality, Bureaucracy, and Class in the Welfare System' 92 *Yale Law Journal* 11.
Thibaut, J and Walker, L (1978) 'A Theory of Procedure' 66 *California Law Review* 541.
Vogel, D (1986) *National Styles of Regulation: Environmental Policy in Great Britain and the United States* (Ithaca, NY, Cornell University Press).
Wechsler, H (1959) 'Toward Neutral Principles of Constitutional Law' 73 *Harvard Law Review* 1.
Wilensky, H (2002) *Rich Democracies* (Berkeley, CA, University of California, Press).

8

A Cultural Analysis of Administrative Justice

SIMON HALLIDAY AND COLIN SCOTT

Introduction

In recent years we have seen rapid change in the organisation of public management (see the chapters by Gamble and Thomas and by Clarke, McDermont and Newman in this volume). Various developments and innovations, sometimes captured in the notion of the 'new public management', have significantly altered the character of public administration. This presents quite a challenge for theorists of administrative justice. The values and processes which infuse new public management sit in some tension with traditional conceptions of administrative justice, particularly within legal theory. To what extent should the concept be extended to embrace these real-world developments? Would it stretch the notion of administrative justice too far to include within it the values associated with the market and consumerism? Would this rob the concept of its analytical purchase? Or, if the notion of administrative justice is to be so extended, how should we understand the relationship between traditional conceptions and newer conceptions? Is there any kind of logic or shared foundation which connects the old and the new? Further, is there more to be said about administrative justice that is not captured by existing theory, even including a focus on new public management?

These are important questions for the field. They form the background to this chapter in which we develop a typology of administrative justice—an analytical framework which captures the variations in how 'administrative justice' might be conceived. In developing typologies, of course, it is wise to recognise previous significant works in the field. We seek to build on such and provide further insights into them. In this vein, we position the contributions of Jerry Mashaw and Michael Adler, who have similarly developed typologies, as important and helpful examples of, respectively, a traditional legal theory of administrative justice and more recent theorising in light of the new public management. We also consider the contribution of Robert Kagan (in this volume) and its implications for understanding Mashaw. We ultimately situate these administrative justice theories within a broader analytical framework which has been derived from anthropology and been used to great effect in political science. We use grid-group cultural theory, developed initially by Mary Douglas (1982b), as the foundation for our ideal typology. Grid-group cultural theory, we suggest, is a particularly useful analytical framework for this endeavour. It promises two significant advances to the theory of administrative justice. First, it offers a richer understanding of the relationships between existing conceptions. Second, it reveals new conceptions of administrative justice which has not hitherto been discussed in the field. We will set out this in much greater detail in due course. First, however, we must examine what is meant by 'administrative justice' for the purposes of this chapter.

What is Administrative Justice?

Following Mashaw, we define administrative justice as 'the qualities of a decision process that provide arguments for the acceptability of its decisions' (1983: 24). There are two related features of this deceptively simple definition worth stressing at the outset. First, Mashaw was not talking about any old decisions. His focus was on 'implementing decisions' (1983: 16) or 'administrative adjudication' (ibid: 23) by public bodies. His concern was with the organisation of decision-making systems within agencies which have been 'charged with implementing the policies of the administrative-regulatory state' as Kagan phrases it (in his chapter in this volume). To this end, Mashaw used the administration of social security disability law as his case study.

Second, Mashaw's primary focus was on processes which produce decisions. It might seem trite to repeat this. However, our point here is that there are many features of an administrative system which, although relating to decision making, do not actually constitute the decision-making process itself. Matters such as rights of redress or the regulation of public administration—broad issues of public accountability which precede, accompany and follow decision-making processes—are, of course, interesting, important and worthy of enquiry. They are matters which could be (and are) meaningfully discussed under the umbrella of 'administrative justice'. However they are not the direct concern of this chapter. Like Mashaw, our focus here is on the notion of justice as it relates to primary decision-making processes—what Kagan (in this volume) describes as 'intra-agency scholarship'. As we will explain further below, it is important to keep this distinction clear in order to maintain the clarity of the cultural typology of administrative justice we develop.

As noted above, our primary reference points are, first, the celebrated typology constructed by Mashaw (1983) and, second, its subsequent development by Michael Adler (2003, 2006) within the context of UK public service delivery. Although this work is now very well known, for the purposes of our analysis it is summarised briefly below.

Mashaw's Typology of Administrative Justice

From the critical literature about the administration of social security disability law, Mashaw (1983) detected three different perspectives on the appropriate goals of the administration. He believed that these diverse critiques reflected distinct conceptions or 'models' of administrative justice: (1) bureaucratic rationality, (2) professional treatment, and (3) moral judgment. These models of administrative justice, he suggested, were each attractive in their own right, but were highly competitive: 'the internal logic of any one of them tends to drive the characteristics of the others from the field as it works itself out in concrete situations' (ibid: 23). So, on the ground, we may expect to see evidence of each model in action, though one will generally be dominant.

The bureaucratic rationality model is concerned with efficiency—the values of accuracy (targeting benefits to those eligible under the programme) and cost-effectiveness. In devising the programme, legislators or policy makers have decided who is eligible and who is not—it has made the value judgments about deservingness. The task of the administrative system is to implement those preferences on a grand scale in as accurate and consistent a way as possible, and with a concern for economy:

> [t]he legitimating force of this conception flows both from its claim to correct implementation of otherwise legitimate social decisions and from its attempt to realize society's pre-established goals in some particular substantive domain while conserving social resources for the pursuit of other valuable ends. (ibid: 26)

Discretionary judgments by individual officers are antithetical to the goals of accuracy and consistency. Instead, the administrative system must operate on the basis of clear rules and guidance which tell low-level officers how to process claims and which promote consistency of decision making.

Professional treatment, by way of contrast, has at its heart the service of the client. Medicine is clearly the exemplar. The goal of the system is to meet the needs of the individual claimant. The administrative system is about matching available resources to claimants' needs through the medium of professional and clinical judgment. Information about the claimant must be obtained, but accuracy is not a normative concern.

> The professional combines the information of others with his or her own observations and experience to reach conclusions that are as much art as science. Moreover, judgment is always subject to revision as conditions change, as attempted therapy proves unsatisfactory or therapeutic successes emerge. The application of clinical judgment entails a relationship and may involve repeated instances of service-oriented decision making… Justice lies in having the appropriate professional judgment applied to one's particular situation *in the context of a service relationship*. (ibid: 28–29)

Mashaw's third model is that of moral judgment. This model derives from traditional notions of court-centred adjudication. The function of such adjudication is not just to resolve disputes about facts, but is also to decide between the competing interests of litigants—what Mashaw describes as 'value defining' (ibid: 29). Issues such as reasonableness, deservingness and responsibility are not questions of fact, but rather are matters of judgment. Accordingly, litigants must be afforded administrative protections in the dispute so that they can have an equal opportunity to present their case, rebut allegations against them, and argue for their interests to be privileged. The adversarial element often cannot be transposed over to the context of administrative adjudication,[1] but in certain respects the claimant is nevertheless treated *as if* he/she is in dispute over a rights claim. The administrative system views the claimant as someone who has come to claim a right, and revolves around giving the claimant a fair opportunity to fully participate in the process of adjudicating whether the right exists or is to be denied: '[t]he important point is that the "justice" of this model inheres in its promise of a full and equal opportunity to obtain one's entitlements' (ibid: 31).

Adler's Typology of Administrative Justice

Adler has been much influenced by the pluralistic approach of Mashaw—his recognition of the plurality of normative positions about the justice of decision processes and the fact that models of administrative justice have to compete with each other in the social reality of public administration (Adler 2006: 621). However, he saw the need to supplement and update Mashaw's typology (2003, 2006). Adler uses the language of 'ideal types' rather than models, and adds three new models of administrative justice (Adler 2003). They are: (1) managerialism; (2) consumerism; and (3) markets. Managerialism gives autonomy to public sector managers. Managers bear the responsibility for achieving prescribed standards of service in an efficient way and enjoy the freedom to manage their departments to this end. They are subject to systems of performance audit, and the administrative system revolves around publicly demonstrating the quality of administration according to defined performance indicators. Like Mashaw's bureaucratic rationality model, the focus of this ideal type is on the administrative system as a whole, and only indirectly on the plight of individual citizens (who are presumed to benefit from the attainment of an efficient and well-performing system).

By way of contrast, the plight of the citizen is at the heart of Adler's consumerism ideal type. Here, the administrative system revolves around producing consumer satisfaction. This involves an active engagement with the citizen as a consumer of public services, and a responsiveness by the administration to dissatisfaction on the part of its consumers. The levels of service to be enjoyed by consumers, the standards of good administration, are often defined in 'customer charters'. In contrast to managerialism, accountability comes from the ground up—from the consumers themselves—through complaints systems.

[1] By way of contrast, the stress Sainsbury (2008) places on 'moral judgment' envisions the situation where a public agency has to decide between completing claims of citizens such as planning decisions.

The final ideal type added by Adler is that of the market. Here the administrative system is driven by the goal of competitiveness. The citizen here is viewed as a rational customer choosing services from a range of providers. The administrative system revolves around making its services as attractive to the customer as possible. Whereas under consumerism the administrative system was accountable to citizens through complaints systems ('voice'), under the market ideal type, the administrative system is accountable to the market itself and subject to the ever present possibility that the citizen will choose another service provider ('exit').

Building on Mashaw and Adler

The typologies of Mashaw and Adler are important and insightful. Both have been influential within the field of administrative justice research. Their work also represents a formidable basis from which to begin the task of constructing a new typology. With this in mind, we should again state clearly the nature of our contribution in this chapter. In keeping with the intentions of Mary Douglas who developed the grid-group analytical framework, 'the object is not to come up with something original, but gently to push what is known into an explicit typology that captures [existing] wisdom' (1982a: 1).

Specifically, we aim to construct a typology of administrative justice along two dimensions derived from grid-group cultural theory. This, we believe, has at least two benefits. First, it permits us to understand better how different 'ideal types' relate to each other. A disadvantage of Mashaw's typology is that this relational quality is absent. It is not clear from his account how, if at all, the various ideal types are connected. Of course, this is simply an unavoidable limitation of the method he adopted to construct his typology. As noted above, Mashaw in large part derived his ideal types from the range of critical literature around US disability benefits administration. However, where typologies are created to match observation in this way there is a danger that categories are formed from different dimensions and that the resulting typology is uneven or lopsided—what Thompson et al describe as 'categorical ad hocracy' (1990: 14). By way of contrast, building a typology along two dimensions gives us basic criteria with which to compare existing administrative processes. Typologies should aid comparison and the use of these two dimensions is a key enabling feature towards this end. A typology using dimensions offers us a better method for understanding the ways in which, and the extent to which, various administrative processes differ from each other in terms of their values, qualities and underlying logic.

Indeed, the typology developed by Kagan (in this volume) is very helpful in this regard. He offers us dimensions which allow us to see how Mashaw's models of justice relate to each other. We may recall that Kagan sets out two dimensions: (1) participatory—hierarchy; and (2) legal formality—legal informality. If we impose these dimensions onto Mashaw's schema, we can see that *bureaucratic rationality* corresponds to Kagan's category of 'bureaucratic legalism' as a product of hierarchy and legal formality, *professional treatment* corresponds to Kagan's category of 'expert or political judgment' as a combination of hierarchy and legal informality, and *moral judgment* corresponds to 'adversarial legalism' as a combination of participation and legal formality. Further, a comparison between Kagan's typology and that of Mashaw reveals that Mashaw's typology was indeed lopsided. Kagan's addition of 'mediation/negotiation' as a combination of participation and informality balances out and completes Mashaw's contribution.

The second benefit to be gained from developing a cultural typology of administrative justice is that, given the scope and ambition of grid-group theory, we believe it is possible to build a typology which is exhaustive in the sense that it captures all observed and potential forms of administrative justice. One of the limitations of Mashaw's work is that it was a product of a particular method at a particular moment in time in US political history. By its nature, then, we should not expect his typology to be exhaustive. Indeed, Adler demonstrated precisely that in updating Mashaw's typology some years later in the context of contemporary UK public administration, taking account of the emergence of the new public management. However, our argument is that, even with the addition of Adler's work, there is more to be said about administrative justice. In fact, following on from our discussion above, Adler's contribution to Mashaw and Kagan renders the overall schema lopsided again. Our intention is to map the existing typologies onto a much larger analytical frame in a way that sheds light on the dimensional connections between Adler, Mashaw and Kagan, and reveals further conceptions of administrative justice not hitherto explored in the literature. First, however, we must explore grid-group cultural theory and its potential for distilling a broad typology of administrative justice.

Grid-Group Cultural Theory

As already noted, our starting point for constructing our typology is the cultural theory of Mary Douglas (1982a, 1982b), developed most notably by Thompson et al (1990). Although this theoretical framework is now well established within the social sciences, and has been used extensively by Christopher Hood in his analyses of public administration (Hood 1998; Hood et al 1999; Bevan and Hood 2006) and by Fiona Haines (2005) in her study of regulation, it is worth summarising again for the purposes of this chapter. As we will see, grid-group cultural theory shares the normative pluralism of Mashaw and Adler. However, it argues that this pluralism is limited by virtue of being structured around two basic dimensions: grid and group.

The epistemological starting point of grid-group cultural analysis is that human perception and consciousness are mediated by culture. But cultures vary, of course. Drawing on a wealth of anthropological studies from various parts of the world, Mary Douglas developed her analytical framework as a way of facilitating meaningful comparisons between cultures—a framework for showing the basic ways in which cultures differ from each other. Grid-group cultural theory reduces social variation to a 'few grand types' (Douglas 1982a: 2). The two dimensions of 'grid' and 'group' produce four ideal types of cultural bias—'four extreme visions of social life' (Douglas 1982a: 2). The dimensions reflect the answers to two basic questions: 'who am I?' (group) and 'how should I behave?' (grid) (Thompson and Wildavsky 1986). According to Thompson et al (1990),

> [t]he variability of an individual's involvement in social life can be adequately captured by two dimensions of sociality: grid and group. *Group* refers to the extent to which an individual is incorporated into bounded units. The greater the incorporation, the more individual choice is subject to group determination. *Grid* denotes the degree to which an individual's life is circumscribed by externally imposed prescriptions. The more binding and extensive the scope of the prescriptions, the less of life that is open to individual negotiation. (ibid: 5)

From this very general starting point, grid-group cultural theorists have developed an exhaustive typology of cultural biases corresponding to the four[2] possible combinations of the grid and group dimensions. A cultural bias is a way of seeing the world, a set of mutually supportive assumptions and values that make up a coherent approach to life. The claim is that cultural biases may colour everything, from the social construction of nature, to perceptions of risk and blame, to normative views about political culture. Hood (1998), for example, has applied the notion of cultural bias to develop a basic typology of approaches to public management. As he notes, the theory 'aims to capture the diversity of human preferences about "ways of life" and relate those preferences to different possible styles of organisation, each of which has its advantages and disadvantages but is in some sense "viable".' (1998: 7)

In the same way, we suggest, the analytical framework offered by grid-group cultural theory permits us to develop a pluralistic but exhaustive typology of 'the qualities of a decision process that provide arguments for the acceptability of its decisions' (Mashaw 1983: 24).

The four cultural biases can be summarised as follows:

Low-Group/Low-Grid—'Individualism'

For the individualist all boundaries are open to negotiation. The individual enjoys the capacity for mobility up and down without barriers of rank or status. S/he is free to operate unconstrained by the pressures of group membership

[2] Thompson et al (1990) include a fifth bias—that of the hermit who has withdrawn from coercive social relations and so is 'off the map'. For this reason we do not apply or operationalise this cultural bias.

or normative prescriptions about how and when s/he can relate to others and engage with society. In keeping with a perspective which stresses the pursuit of individual self-interest, the individualist seeks to replace authority with regulation of the self.

Low Group/High Grid—'Fatalism'

The fatalist feels constrained and controlled by societal norms and issues of rank, role and status. But at the same time the fatalist is isolated and excluded from group membership. The fatalist, then, is marked by a sense of powerlessness and resignation. Life seems unpredictable. Good times or bad times appear to come to him regardless of his skill, character or diligence.

High Group/High Grid—'Hierarchism'

The combination of high grid and high group means that hierarchism is marked by a respect for expertise and authority and a sense of the collective. Loyalty is rewarded and hierarchy respected. The exercise of authority and the existence of inequality are justified on the grounds that they enable people to live together harmoniously. All benefit from such authority and expertise as it is exercised for the common good. The individual knows his/her place in a world that is securely bounded and stratified.

High Group/Low Grid—'Egalitarianism'

By way of contrast to hierarchy, there is a suspicion of authority within egalitarianism. A sense of the collective exists, but the aims of the group, and the means of achieving them, must be decided by the group members on an equal basis. Although the boundary of the group is clear, producing insiders and outsiders, within the group all statuses are ambiguous. Equality and consensus are key themes within egalitarianism.

Figure 1: Grid Group Analytical Framework of Cultural Biases

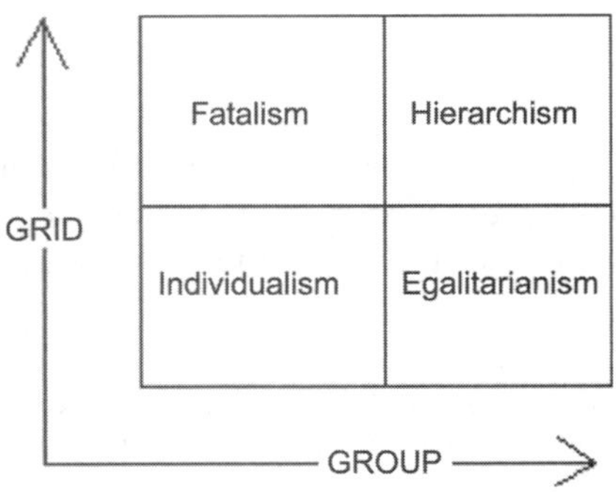

Grid Group Cultural Theory and Public Management

The above overview, by its nature, is cast in fairly broad terms. Its vantage point is high and its scope wide. Nevertheless, we suggest that grid-group cultural theory can be harnessed and applied to the concept of administrative justice to develop ideal types. Our first step in this process is to consider the work of Christopher Hood who has explored how cultural theory might be applied to ways of organising public administration. As Hood (1998: 8) points out, '[p]ut the "grid" and the "group" dimensions together, and they take us to the heart of much contemporary and historical discussion about how to do public management.'

According to Hood, each cultural bias described by cultural theory produces a distinct and basic logic of 'good administration'. For the individualist, good administration takes place within a market and is driven by competitive forces. For the hierarchist, good administration harnesses and relies on expertise and authority within government. For the egalitarian, it is marked by consensus between public officials and the citizens they serve. These three ideal types, of course, match widely recognised and basic modes of governance: hierarchy, market and community (Scott 2006; Mashaw 2006).

It is harder to derive an image of 'good' administration from fatalism. Fatalism, as its name suggests, is a negative view on life—a sense of powerlessness and exclusion. At the level of the individual, we may associate it with the classic 'lumpers' (Genn 1999) and 'sceptics' (Cowan and Halliday 2003) in relation to disputing, and with 'withdrawal' tendencies in relation to citizens' use of public services (Simmons et al 2007). More generally, as a cultural bias fatalism lacks the trust in government associated with hierarchism, and the sense of freedom in a market marked by individualism. The fatalist's observation of life is that it is random and unpredictable. Fatalism, then, entails an abandonment of a belief that outcomes can be achieved through positive action. Nevertheless, from this negative 'is' we may derive the positive 'ought' that public management should also (or, at least, might as well) reflect this unpredictability. As Thompson et al note, although analytically defensible, the fact/value distinction obscures the extensive interpenetration of facts and values in the real world: '[w]ays of life weave together beliefs about what is … with what ought to be … into a mutually supportive whole' (1990: 22).

In this vein, Hood introduces the notion of 'how-to-do-it ideas' (1998: 14) whereby fatalism can be linked to prescriptions for positively designing institutions. He links what he terms 'contrived randomness' as such a prescription with a fatalistic cultural bias. Hood refers here to situations where chance is used as a central aspect of organisational life. Random internal audits, for example, capture contrived randomness. Similarly, an organisation might make working conditions unpredictable. If officials are posted unpredictably, and so cannot know with whom they will be working, by whom they will be supervised, who will be their clients and so forth, they can be prevented from joining with colleagues or clients to organise 'scams' or anti-system conspiracies. 'Contrived randomness' Hood suggests, can be seen in parts of the civil service, the tax bureaucracy or the military where postings are of limited-term or where relative strangers are required to work together on projects.

A Cultural Typology of Administrative Justice

The final stage in constructing our typology is to consider the implications of these ways of organising public administration for administrative process. What characteristic decision-making processes emerge from these ideal types of public management, and what are the justifications for them which reflect the various cultural biases? These are set out below and summarised in Figure 2 below.

'Hierarchist' Administrative Justice

The combination of high grid and high group means that considerable value is placed on authority and expertise. Within the hierarchist bias, government is trusted to act on behalf of the collective. Citizens are not expected to participate in decision-making processes. Public officials, rather, are expected to exercise their skill and judgement for the public benefit, and citizens are content to be passive objects of this official discretion—such is their station. Decision-making processes within hierarchism should support the exercise of expert judgement and/or the accurate and efficient implementation of higher orders.

Figure 2: A Cultural Typology of Administrative Justice

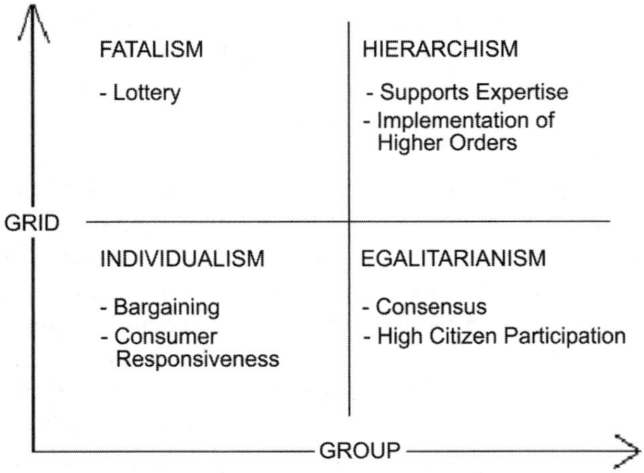

'Egalitarian' Administrative Justice

By way of contrast, the egalitarian bias with its combination of low grid and high group is sceptical and distrustful of governmental authority and expertise. It favours decision making by consensus and seeks to equalise the position of all those in the group. In the context of administrative justice, this translates into citizens and public officials being equal partners in decision-making processes. Decision-making processes within egalitarianism should be all about reaching consensus and so marked by very high citizen participation.

Administrative Law's Affinity With Hierarchism—Egalitarianism

We can note at this stage that Kagan's vertical dimension of 'participatory—hierarchy' set out in his chapter in this book corresponds to the vertical 'grid' dimension of cultural theory. However, the continuum running between a hierarchist conception of administrative justice and an egalitarian conception should also be familiar to administrative lawyers. It is reflected to a notable extent in administrative law doctrine. The flexibility of the doctrine of procedural fairness, for example, captures the shifting strength of administrative protections relating to citizen participation. Indeed, the connection between hierarchism's and egalitarianism's visions of administrative justice parallels the continuum drawn by Galligan between what he calls 'bureaucratic administration' and 'fair treatment' (1996: 237–40). The variability of the intensity of judicial review—the competition between judicial control and agency autonomy (Craig 2003: 510)—also reflects the extent to which the expertise and authority of government should be respected and supported. We might frame the extent of citizen participation in decision processes as capturing the core element of grid-group cultural theory's application to administrative justice.

We must stress, however, that there are further gradations of citizen participation which lie beyond these analyses and towards the ideal of decision making by consensus. Legal theories of administrative justice, including that of Mashaw, are somewhat narrower (or shorter) than our cultural analysis of administrative justice. Decision making by consensus between officials and citizens is a conception of administrative justice which has received insufficient attention in the field.

'Individualistic' Administrative Justice

As we noted above, individualism is marked by the ability of individuals to negotiate their own way through life, untrammelled by group mandates and social rules and prescriptions. This produces a cultural bias which revolves around self-interest and personal responsibility and sees the market as the appropriate model of social organisation. Hood (1998) applies this directly to public management and draws out an ideal type where public services are delivered in a competitive environment. But one might still legitimately wonder what the characteristic decision-making process is which reflects this image of good administration. Sainsbury, for example, reflecting on Adler's work, has questioned whether conceptions of administrative justice associated with new public management reveal any new and distinctive decision processes on a par with Mashaw's description of: (1) of implementation of rules (bureaucratic rationality); (2) the application of expertise (professional treatment); or (3) the judging between competing claims (moral judgment) (Sainsbury 2008). It is clear that individualism has influenced the organisation of public management (Hood 1998), including various features of public accountability. The rise of complaints systems are but one example (Simmons et al 2007). But, recalling our earlier distinction between decision processes and other features of public accountability, does this fail to alter the fact that the decision-process itself is non-individualist? For example, even although medical practitioners may be the subject of customer satisfaction surveys, their decision making as doctors may still comprise the application of expertise. Equally, although public agencies may have to provide services in a competitive environment and so be incentivised (perhaps financially) to improve the customer experience, alterations may not relate to the actual mode of decision making, but rather to additional aspect of service delivery such as waiting times, courtesy, clarity of communication, and so forth. To what extent, then, can we identify a distinctive decision process associated with an individualistic cultural bias?

The answer is that bargaining is the characteristic mode of decision making in market settings. This is a decision process about reaching consensus (just like egalitarianism) but not within the context of a group. Rather, the citizen-consumer is in the driving seat. It is about matching supply to individual demand. This permits us to suggest that in the context of administrative justice, an individualistic cultural bias would produce an ideal typical decision process which involves bargaining and consumer responsiveness. The market is a mode of social organisation which encourages suppliers to carve out some kind of competitive advantage for themselves. An individualist system of decision making would be organised to privilege agency competitiveness and customer satisfaction over other values. Accuracy and expertise are not important values in themselves in the context of individualism. Within individualism it is the customer who is always right and who always knows best. To the extent, then, that decision-making systems privilege customer care and satisfaction to the exclusion of accuracy and expertise, we are seeing the influence of an individualistic approach to administrative justice. Indeed, we might suggest that the extent of agency responsiveness to consumer needs and desires captures the core of the 'group' dimension of cultural theory when applied to administrative justice.

'Fatalistic' Administrative Justice

Fatalism represents terrain that has largely been unexplored in relation to administrative justice. The suggestion of a fatalistic conception of administrative justice, then, offers something quite distinctive to the field, albeit potentially controversial. Within fatalism life is unpredictable—sometimes good, sometimes bad.

A general sense of powerlessness and exclusion produces a cultural bias which permits no positive prescription for achieving outcomes. It is difficult to derive directly a notion of administrative justice from Hood's description of 'contrived randomness' as an ideal type of public management. However, we may follow Hood's example of developing a 'how-to-do-it' idea which reflects a fatalistic cultural bias. In this vein we can focus on the notion of a lottery as a characteristic decision-making process within fatalism. Although there may be a temptation to associate lotteries with egalitarianism or notions of equality—the idea that lotteries are fair because everyone has an equal chance of winning—this is to confuse ends with means. The point about fatalistic administrative justice is that the active use of randomness in decision-making processes marks the abandonment of any faith in our ability to positively design just processes of administration. Instead, we delegate responsibility to the Fates.

Ideal Types and Social Reality

We should stress, of course, that the above are ideal types. Ideal types are analytical mechanisms—combinations of dimensional extremes—designed to help us understand a much messier social reality. A typology offers us the tools with which we may compare and contrast varying visions of 'good administration.' Importantly, then, our ideal types are normative and not descriptive. We recognise that our typology can be used to help characterise real-world decision processes and, more significantly, to distinguish *between* processes. Equally, we recognise the intimate relationship between the normative and the descriptive in that real-world decision-making processes are designed with normative aims and values in mind. Nevertheless, the character of our typology is not primarily descriptive. Rather, we have constructed a broad framework which captures: (1) the variety of ways in which one might possibly design a decision-making process; and (2) the underlying justifications for such designs: to use Mashaw's phrase again, 'the qualities of a decision process that provide arguments for the acceptability of its decisions' (1983: 24). For these reasons, we should not expect to find such ideal types in pristine form in the real world. They operate on an analytical rather than empirical level. Moreover, as a framework of normative ideals, they will inevitably be broader than what we see in the real world with all its familiar compromises and imperfections. In other words, the cogency of this cultural typology of administrative justice should not be judged by testing it against empirical descriptions of real-world public administration. We should not approach the typology through the lens of empirical reality. Rather, we should observe, describe and compare empirical realities through the lens of this normative typology.

Notwithstanding the above, we recognise that our typology will fail to have any analytical purchase if it bears no relation whatsoever to what we can see in, or imagine about, administrative processes in the real world. Further, by pointing to familiar decision processes within public administration and divining their underlying rationales, it may help to bring our typology into focus a little more.

We suggest that it is not hard to identify elements of these ideal types at play within public administration.

Hierarchism

The familiar development and implementation of policy within many front-line public bureaucracies reflects a hierarchist bias. Of course, empirical research about street-level bureaucracy (Lipsky 1980) paints a complex picture of implementation where 'policy' is formed from the bottom-up as much as from the top-down. Nevertheless, it is still not hard to see in the design of policy programmes in domains such as social security, housing and social work the importance attached to the implementation of rules and the application of expertise.

Egalitarianism

Hood (1998: 62) notes that the egalitarian bias can be

> applied to the control of public-service provision by society at large. At that level, the formula implies maximum face-to-face interactions between public-service producers and clients, and indeed as far as possible a dissolution of the difference between 'producer' and 'client' altogether.

A good example of importance being attached 'group' decision making, one which takes us beyond the level of citizen participation usually envisaged by administrative law doctrine, lies in consensus-seeking in regulatory policy making (Coglianese 2001). To a lesser extent, the stress on community consultation in areas of policy such as planning and education also reflects an egalitarian bias.

Fatalism

In relation to fatalism, there are some clear contemporary examples of government making decisions through random processes. The selection of persons to serve on juries is an example (Duxbury 1999). Randomness rather than reason is judged to be fairest both to those selected to serve and to criminal defendants. Randomness is also seen in some allocation of school places (Turvey 2008) and, in some countries, in immigration visa lotteries. Randomness only features as the basis for the justice of an administrative decision where it is deliberate. Accordingly, other metaphorical lotteries, such as the 'postcode lottery' in provision of healthcare in different regions, are not included within this discussion.

Individualism

It is clear that public service delivery has in recent decades been significantly affected by individualist approaches to public management (though these ideas have a much longer pedigree—see Hood 1998: chapter 5). Managerialism, consumerism and marketisation in the public sector certainly reflect the individualist cultural bias particularly clearly. But is there any evidence of bargaining or the matching of supply to demand in contemporary administrative processes? In many policy domains, such as social security administration, it may be difficult to conceive of such a thing. However, bargaining is far from uncommon in other policy areas such as environmental regulation enforcement (Hawkins 1984) or telecommunications regulation (Hall et al 2000). As Hall et al (ibid: 111–12) note in relation to their observation of a 'diplomatic-bargaining' style of decision making within Oftel:

> [s]uch a style is commonly observable in institutional decision-making generally ... and in regulatory decision-making more particularly … and links in to a vast literature on negotiation and bargaining within organisations and policy communities. It is less programmed than the Cartesian-bureaucratic style, in that the final outcome depends on what the various participants will accept rather than on the pre-set objectives of any one organisation. (2000: 111–12)

Reflections on Mashaw, Adler and Kagan in Light of Cultural Theory

Having constructed a basic typology of administrative justice from grid-group cultural theory, we must now return to the typologies of Mashaw, Adler and Kagan. To what extent can we map their models or ideal types onto ours?

Mashaw

Starting with Mashaw, we can see that his 'moral judgment' model with its stress on 'preserv[ing] party equality and control', 'promot[ing] agreed allocations' and the 'application of common moral principles' (1983: 31), betrays an egalitarian stress on participative decision-making processes which aspire to consensus. Although, as we suggested above, the extent of participation may be stronger, 'moral judgment' represents a move 'down grid' from hierarchism and so may be associated with egalitarianism. We can also suggest that Mashaw's 'bureaucratic rationality' model with its focus on the 'correct implementation of otherwise legitimate social decisions' (1983: 26) fits well with the hierarchist stress on accurate and efficient implementation of higher orders. But what about Mashaw's 'professional treatment' model with its stress on the application of professional or clinical judgment? This too would seem to fit well with a hierarchist vision of administrative justice which additionally stresses the value of expertise and the importance of decision-making processes which support such expert judgments. We suggest that Mashaw's 'professional treatment' model and his 'bureaucratic rationality' model do, indeed, both fall within a hierarchist ideal type of administrative justice. As Hood notes, '[h]ierarchism is not a single organizational model but a family of related approaches, differing in the way that "groupness" and "gridness" are manifested' (1998: 97). Hood distinguishes (1998: 75) between types of rule (immanent and enacted) and types of groups (task or profession-specific and public-sector-specific). This produces different types of hierarchist organisation and can account for the difference between the 'bureaucratic rationality' and 'professional treatment' visions of administrative justice. 'Professional treatment' has a greater stress on professional expertise and the application of immanent rules, akin to a traditional professional organisation such as medicine. 'Bureaucratic rationality' has a greater stress on a more generic public-sector specific group, implementing enacted rules. Kagan's distinction (in this volume) between legal formality and legal informality is also helpful here, as noted earlier. But both models of administrative justice reflect a hierarchist bias with its focus on public officials fulfilling their authoritative and expert roles on behalf of the collective. The difference between professional treatment and bureaucratic rationality, then, reflects a second-order distinction, rather than a first-order distinction which accounts for the difference of them both from 'moral judgment'.[3] As a whole, Mashaw's typology would fit within the right-hand side of our cultural typology of administrative justice.

Adler

Turning to Adler, how should we interpret the ideal types he suggests: 'consumerism' 'markets' and 'managerialism'? To do this we must recall the important distinction we made earlier between decision-making processes and other features of public management and accountability. What are the actual decision-making processes inherent in Adler's ideal types? Consumerism, according to Adler (2003: 334).

> embodies a more active view of the service user, who is seen as an active participant rather than as a passive recipient of bureaucratic, professional, or managerial decisions. It can thus be characterised in terms of the active participation of consumers in decision-making, customer satisfaction, the introduction of 'consumer charters,' and the use of 'voice'...

The stress on consumer participation and agencies' pursuit of customer satisfaction suggests that 'consumerism' fits very well within our category of individualism. Similarly with 'markets': 'decision-making in the market involves the matching of demand and supply and is made with reference to the price mechanism' (2003: 334). Adler's category of 'markets' then, would also seem to fit squarely within our category of individualism. Indeed, we might question whether 'markets' and 'consumerism' betray any real difference in terms of decision-making processes per se. To what extent is the matching of demand

[3] This analysis makes some connection, then, with Galligan's view that 'professional treatment' falls within the continuum between his models of 'bureaucratic administration' and 'fair treatment' (1996: 237).

and supply different from the participation of consumers in decision making with a view to customer satisfaction? At most, we suggest, these would reflect only slight gradations within individualism. Managerialism, we suggest, is more problematic as an ideal type of administrative justice. Although Adler is correct to highlight changes in public management which reflect managerialism—the rise of managerial autonomy, performance audit and performance rewards—it is unclear to us that managerialism represents a distinctive decision-making process. Nevertheless, in 'consumerism' and 'markets' Adler has made an important contribution which would fall within the bottom left-hand quadrant of our cultural typology of administrative justice.

Kagan

We noted above that Kagan's typology outlined in his chapter in this book helps us reflect on Mashaw. We suggested that Kagan's categories of 'bureaucratic legalism,' 'expert or political judgment' and 'adversarial legalism' could be mapped onto Mashaw's categories of 'bureaucratic rationality' 'professional treatment' and 'moral judgment'. A question remains, however, about how to interpret Kagan's category of 'negotiation/mediation' a combination of participation and legal informality. Although Kagan uses the language of 'negotiation' it is not in the same sense, we suggest, as we have used it in relation to individualism. Rather, Kagan (in this volume) is referring to a decision-making process which

> allows the individuals or organizations subject to the agency's authority … considerable opportunity to present and argue their cases in an informal manner. In this modality, regulatory officials charged with implementing anti-discrimination or consumer protection law, for example, often mediate disputes between a complainant and an employer or a merchant, fostering a negotiated settlement. The process is non-legalistic, since neither procedures nor substantive dispositions are dictated by formal law.

We can see the parallel with 'moral judgment' whereby a decision must be reached in relation to competing interests. Further, the pursuit of a mediated solution agreeable to the parties, and participation of the parties in reaching that solution reflects something an egalitarian bias. Accordingly, we suggest that this is a helpful second-order distinction to be made in this regard and an important addition. Kagan's typology, then, like Mashaw's, fits within the right-hand quadrants within our wider cultural typology of administrative justice.

Conclusions

This chapter has offered an elaboration and theorisation of the variety of models of administrative justice found in the literature. If cultural theory is of value in abstracting from these different analyses of administrative justice, it is in offering a complete set of family of forms of administrative justice. This permits us to see better the connections between differing visions of administrative justice discussed in the existing literature. Cultural theory also significantly expands the scope of administrative justice theory. Indeed, the exercise of mapping existing typologies onto our cultural framework reveals that existing work on administrative justice is relatively narrowly framed. Traditional legal conceptions of administrative justice are restricted to the right-hand side of our framework and do not exhaust the full potential of the egalitarian vision of administrative justice with its stress on decision making by consensus. Adler has certainly offered an important complement to legal conceptions by focusing our attention on individualism. However, there has still been a general failure hitherto to engage with the existence and potential of fatalistic modes of administrative justice.

At the beginning of this chapter we noted that it is wise, in developing ideal typologies of this kind, to acknowledge previous significant works in the field. We might add here that it is also wise to stress the limitations of our work. The ambition of this chapter has been fairly modest: it was simply to construct a typology which we believe can be useful as an analytical tool in the field. As an analytical tool it could be put to many purposes, but we have not pursued them here. In particular, given that typologies aid comparison, it might be used as a foundation for characterising changes in the style of administrative justice within particular public agencies across time, or between various public agencies within a fixed time period. Equally, it might generate questions about why particular modes of administrative justice become dominant at particular moments in particular agencies. Important work in this regard has been carried out,[4] including by those we have discussed in this chapter.[5] More work in this regard would be beneficial for the field. Further still, if one approaches the issue of administrative justice through the lens of everyday legal consciousness, such as Marc Hertogh's chapter in this volume, cultural theory and a typology of administrative justice may help us understand the varieties of ways in which people, including public officials, engage with administrative legality and process (or it may act as a useful foil). However, despite the insights of existing work, and the importance of such research projects, we must stress that our contribution in this chapter is preliminary to this kind of scholarship.

Acknowledgements

The research on which this chapter draws was generously funded by the Nuffield Foundation and we are very grateful for its financial support. Additionally, the Nuffield Foundation hosted a seminar where a preliminary

[4] See eg Buck (1998), Sunkin and Pick (2001) and Sainsbury (2008).
[5] Adler and Longhurst (1994), Adler (2008) and Kagan (in this volume).

analysis was presented to a group of academic experts. This was a lively event from which we gained a great deal. We are very grateful to the following people who took part: Michael Adler, Varda Bondy, Trevor Buck, Sharon Gilad, Jackie Gulland, Jeff King, Richard Kirkham, Rick Rawlings, Genevra Richardson, Roy Sainsbury, Richard Simmons, Brian Thompson, and Sharon Witherspoon. We also benefited from written comments after the event from a number of those who attended.

References

Adler, M (2003) 'A Socio-Legal Approach to Administrative Justice' 25 *Law and Policy* 323.

—— (2006) 'Fairness in Context' 33 *Journal of Law and Society* 615.

Adler, M and Longhurst, B (1994), *Discourse Power and Justice* (London, Routledge).

Bevan, G and Hood, C (2006) 'What's Measured Is What Matters: Targets And Gaming In The English Public Health Care System' 84 *Public Administration* 517.

Buck, T (1998) 'Judicial Review and the discretionary Social Fund: The Impact on a Respondent Organization' in TG Buck (ed), *Judicial Review and Social Welfare* (London and Washington, Pinter).

Coglianese, C (2001) 'Is Consensus an Appropriate Basis for Regulatory Policy?' in E Orts and K Deketelaere (eds), *Environmental Contracts: Comparative Approaches to Regulatory Innovation in the United States and Europe* (The Hague, Kluwer Law International).

Cowan, D and Halliday, S (2003) *The Appeal of Internal Review* (Oxford, Hart Publishing).

Craig, P (2003) *Administrative Law* (Oxford, Oxford University Press).

Douglas, M (1982a) 'Introduction to Group-Grid Analysis' in M Douglas (ed), *Essays in the Sociology of Perception* (London, Routledge and Kegan Paul).

—— (1982b) 'Cultural Bias' in Douglas, M (ed), *In the Active Voice* (London, Routledge and Kegan Paul).

Duxbury, N (1999) *Random Justice* (Oxford, Oxford University Press).

Galligan, D (1996) *Due Process and Fair Procedures* (Oxford, Oxford University Press).

Genn, H (1999) *Paths to Justice* (Oxford, Hart Publishing).

Hall, C, Hood, C and Scott, C (2000) *Telecommunications regulation: culture, chaos and interdependence inside the regulatory process* (London, Routledge).

Haines, F (2005) *Globalization and Regulatory Character* (Farnham, Ashgate).

Hawkins, K (1984) *Environment and Enforcement* (Oxford, Oxford University Press).

Hood, C (1998) *The Art of the State: Culture, Rhetoric and Public Management* (Oxford, Oxford University Press).

Lipsky, M (1980) *Street-Level Bureaucracy: Dilemmas of the Individual in Public Services* (New York, Russell Sage).

Mashaw, J (1983) *Bureaucratic Justice: Managing Social Security Disability Claims* (New Haven, Yale University Press).

—— (2006) 'Accountability and Institutional Design: Some Thoughts on the Grammar of Governance' in M Dowdle (ed), *Public Accountability* (Cambridge, Cambridge University Press).

Sainsbury, R (2008) 'Administrative Justice, Discretion and the "Welfare to Work" Project' 30 *Journal of Social Welfare and Family Law* 323.

Scott, C (2006) 'Spontaneous Accountability' in M Dowdle (ed), *Public Accountability* (Cambridge, Cambridge University Press).
Simmons, R, Birchall, J, and Prout, A (2007) 'Hearing Voices: user involvement in public services' 17 *Consumer Policy Review* 234.
Sunkin, M and Pick, K (2001) 'The Changing Impact of Judicial Review: The Independent Review Service of the Social Fund' PL 736.
Thomson, M, Ellis, R and Wildavsky, A, (1990) *Cultural Theory* (Boulder, Westview Press).
Turvey, K (2008) 'The Loaded Die is Cast' *Guardian* 11 March, available at http://education.guardian.co.uk/admissions/story/0,,2264168,00.html.

9

Through the Eyes of Bureaucrats: How Front-line Officials Understand Administrative Justice

MARC HERTOGH

Introduction

With the rapid rise of the 'administrative state' (Waldo 1948), an increasing number of scholars have also turned their attention to issues of 'administrative justice'. One strand of scholarly endeavour has a strong *analytical* focus and seeks 'to build or dissect normative theories of administrative justice' (Halliday 2004: 115; see also Halliday and Scott, in this volume). This approach is aimed at specifying 'the principles that can be used to evaluate the justice inherent in administrative decision-making' (Adler 2003: 323). A second strand entails the *empirical* study of administrative decision making and uses conceptions of administrative justice 'as a starting point for enquiry, rather than as the end point of enquiry' (Halliday 2004: 115). Using several analytical models or typologies of administrative justice (Mashaw 1983, Adler 2003), this strand looks at 'how agencies actually conduct case-by-case decision making, why agencies differ in that regard, and what difference that makes' (Kagan, in this volume). It is this approach which is adopted in this chapter.

Since Michael Lipsky's (1980) pioneering work, students of public administration have recognised that public policy 'is not best understood as made in legislatures or top-floor suites of high-ranking administrators', but is, in important ways, actually made 'in the crowded offices and daily encounters of street-level workers' (Lipsky 1980: xii). Typical features of these 'street-level bureaucrats' or 'front-line officials' in welfare departments, lower courts, legal service offices, and other agencies is that they work directly with the public and that they have wide discretion over the dispensation of benefits or the allocation of public sanctions. As Maynard-Moody and Musheno (2003: 157) point out, street-level workers are the 'coal-miners of policy': they do the hard, dirty and sometimes dangerous work of the state.

Over the years, empirical studies have suggested that street-level bureaucrats' own perceptions of law and justice play a significant role in administrative decision making. Mashaw (1983: 15), for example, in his important book *Bureaucratic Justice*, wondered whether in bureaucratic operation there might be 'not merely the pure play of ambition, self-interest, or inertia that confounds our collective ideals but also a striving for normative goodness.' Following his general idea that 'organisations and the bureaucrats who inhabit them have their own goals, desires, [and] motivations' (ibid: 68), Mashaw found that the Social Security Administration had generated its own 'internal law of administration' (ibid: 213). Several years earlier, Kagan (1978) had reached a similar conclusion in his analysis of the implementation of a wage-price freeze. He found that the agencies involved had developed a strong preference for deciding cases speedily and efficiently as well as correctly and fairly. Yet, according to Kagan, this 'compulsion' was not the product of 'a bureaucratic love of efficiency for its own sake, or of the desire of officials to go home early' (ibid: 141), but 'it was rooted in the notion that prompt decision making is an important component of doing justice.' Officials themselves 'felt that citizens had a basic right to a prompt answer' (ibid: 127). Finally, in their more recent study *Cops, Teachers, Counselors*, Maynard-Moody and Musheno (2003) concluded that street-level decisions and actions are guided less by rules or procedures and more by officials' own beliefs and norms about what is fair. Or, in the words of a police officer who acted as one of their respondents: 'I can't say I follow the rules completely. I don't. But I interpret them in each situation and make the best call. Yeah, from my own value system, I suppose' (ibid: 3). Based on these and other examples, Maynard-Moody and Musheno conclude that cops, teachers, and counselors 'first make normative judgments about offenders, kids, and clients and then apply, bend, or ignore rules and procedures to support the moral reasoning.' (ibid: 155).

These studies underscore the idea that 'street-level beliefs are … essential to understanding the modern state' (Maynard-Moody and Musheno 2000: 333). Yet, thus far this idea has not been developed further in most of the administrative justice literature. This chapter attempts to fill this void and asks: How do front-line officials understand administrative justice? It aims to contribute to the development of a theoretical framework for analysing administrative justice. In particular, it seeks to study street-level beliefs by further developing the analytical concepts of 'legal consciousness' and 'legal alienation'.

First, the chapter introduces two different conceptions of legal consciousness. While the first conception asks 'How do public officials experience (legal principles of) administrative justice?', the second conception focuses on 'What do public officials themselves experience as (important principles of) administrative justice?' Next, both conceptions will be applied in an exploratory case study which focuses on the work of front-line officials in the Netherlands. Based on this case study, the chapter then focuses on the fact that front-line officials often appear to be alienated not only from their work and their clients, but also from the law. This section asks: how can we understand the concept of 'legal alienation' and how may it be employed in a study of administrative decision making? Using a typology of 'legal citizenship', it suggests that public officials can be characterised as 'legalists', 'loyalists', 'cynics', or 'outsiders'. Next, the chapter discusses three ways in which a focus on street-level beliefs can contribute to the study of administrative justice. In the final section, the chapter concludes that front-line officials not only play an important role in the formulation and implementation of public policy, but also in the realisation of normative ideals of administrative justice.

Exploring Front-Line Officials' Legal Consciousness

How do front-line officials understand administrative justice? Or, in more general terms, how do they relate to law? On a cold winter's day, anyone who takes a walk outside immediately realises the impact of the wind-chill factor. This is the temperature that a person feels because of the wind. For example, a thermometer may only read minus two degrees Centigrade outside. But when the wind is blowing at 45 kilometres per hour, the wind-chill factor causes it to feel as if it is minus 10 degrees Centigrade. For a good understanding of the local weather conditions we should therefore take into account both objective and subjective elements. The same holds true for law. If we want to understand the social significance of law, we should not only focus on the law in the books, but also on the way that people experience law. This 'legal wind-chill factor' plays a central role in legal consciousness studies (see, eg Engel 1998; Silbey 2005). This chapter aims to apply these considerations to the varieties of ways in which front-line officials understand administrative justice.

Legal Consciousness Studies

Using a popular definition, legal consciousness could simply refer to 'all the ideas about the nature, function and operation of law held by anyone in society at a given time' (Trubek 1984: 592). Yet, under this general heading, various researchers have applied the term in different ways. Legal consciousness can refer both to aptitude, competence or awareness of the law, and to perceptions or images of law. Most empirical studies in the first category date back to the 1970s. Using large statistical surveys, many of these so-called KOL (Knowledge and Opinion about Law) studies point to low levels of legal knowledge and considerable variations in attitudes to law and the legal system. More recent studies argue that legal systems are not simply 'social facts acting upon society' (law and society). Instead, law is the label given to a certain aspect of society (law in society). This has, more recently, led researchers of legal consciousness to focus more on 'images of laws and legal institutions that people carry around in their heads and occasionally act upon' (Engel 1998: 139). Unlike the early KOL studies, the fieldwork involved in these more recent examples is often detailed descriptive ethnography. As I have argued elsewhere, we can differentiate between an 'American' and a 'European' conception of legal consciousness (Hertogh 2004).

An 'American' Conception

Most of the contemporary literature on legal consciousness originated in the United States. Merry (1990), for example, studied litigation and mediation among working-class Americans in two New England towns. In her book *Getting Justice and Getting Even*, she looks at the ways people, who bring personal problems to the courts, think about and understand law and the ways in which people who work in the courts deal with their problems. Similarly, Nielsen (2000) examined the legal consciousness of ordinary citizens concerning offensive public speech. Drawing on observations in public spaces in three California communities and on in-depth interviews with subjects recruited from these places, she analysed variations across race and gender groups in attitudes about how offensive public speech should be dealt with by law. Finally, in their book, *The Common Place of Law*, Ewick and Silbey (1998) developed an empirically based theory of legal consciousness. In over 400 in-depth interviews they asked New Jersey residents general questions about their lives and the problems they faced in their schools, workplaces, and communities, allowing respondents to elaborate on whether and how they thought of law's role in these spheres. Based on their interviews, Ewick and Silbey identified three predominant types of legal consciousness. Subjects can be 'Before the Law', impressed by its majesty and convinced by its legitimacy, 'With the Law', utilising it instrumentally and generally understanding law as a game, and 'Against the Law', cynical about its legitimacy and distrustful of its implementation.

These studies by Merry, Nielsen, and Ewick and Silbey, are three representative examples of an 'American' conception of legal consciousness. The primary focus of this conception is: *How do people experience (what is officially recognised as) law?* In these three studies 'law' is considered an independent variable. The definition of 'law' is provided by the researcher and is not part of the empirical enquiry itself.

A 'European' Conception

In his review of the current literature, Engel (1998: 139) has argued that 'studies of legal consciousness have sometimes forgotten important lessons from the past'. A prominent example of this is that, although decades of law and society research have convincingly demonstrated that '[d]ifferent groups have different kinds of law', most studies still focus almost exclusively on 'official' law. Yet, law is not necessarily an instrument of state power and its connection with the state is 'a problem to be studied rather than a fact to be assumed'. Moreover, '[e]ven if one focuses on "official" law, one still finds a significant dependence on unofficial or customary rule structures to determine norms of reasonableness or fairness'

(Engel 1998: 139). Engel therefore calls for a view on legal consciousness 'from below'. The basis for such a view may be found in the European tradition of the sociology of law, most notably in the work of the Austrian legal theorist Eugen Ehrlich (see Hertogh 2009).

In 1912, Ehrlich presented a unique research project aimed at studying the 'living law' of the peoples of the Bukowina in southeastern Europe, where Armenians, Germans, Gipsies, Jews, Hungarians, Romanians, Russians, Ruthenians and Slovaks lived side by side. To study the legal consciousness of these people, Ehrlich wanted his project to register those ideas and personal histories that were typical for their own ideas of law (*Rechtsauffassung der Leute*) (Ehrlich 1967: 44). To Ehrlich, the law is a notion (*Gedankengebilde*) that lives in people's heads and which can be identified on the basis of people's attitudes. Legal consciousness in this sense essentially refers to people's own ideas about law, regardless of any 'official' laws. Law is considered a dependent variable, the definition of law is not provided by the researcher, but is part of the empirical enquiry itself. I will refer to this as a 'European' conception of legal consciousness. The primary focus of this conception is: *What do people experience as 'law'?*

Public Officials' Legal Consciousness

Thus far, most legal consciousness studies have focused on 'working-class Americans' (Merry 1990), the 'welfare poor' (Sarat 1990), and 'ordinary citizens' (Nielsen 2000). There are only a handful of studies in which the concept of legal consciousness has been applied to public officials. One notable exception is Cooper's (1995) paper on the legal consciousness of British local government actors during the late 1980s and early 1990s. Her paper shows how the process of juridification has produced a number of varied and contradictory legal images in local government. While some government actors depicted law as oppressive, powerful, and politically significant, for others, it functioned primarily as an environmental nuisance, resource or taken-for-granted condition of local government activity. Cooper concludes that the legal consciousness of local government officials is not principally that of powerful subjects. 'Despite their state location, many municipal actors depicted their relationship to law in ways that paralleled legal consciousness amongst the powerless.' (Cooper 1995: 521)

In the remaining part of this chapter, the two conceptions of legal consciousness that were discussed earlier will be applied to front-line officials' beliefs about administrative justice (see Figure 1). Treating law as an independent variable, our first research question is: 'How do public officials experience (legal principles of) administrative justice?' Then, taking law as a dependent variable, we also ask: 'What do public officials themselves experience as (important principles of) administrative justice?'

In the next section, both perspectives will be applied in an exploratory case study.

Figure 1: Legal Consciousness and Administrative Justice

An 'American' conception of legal consciousness: How do public officials experience (legal principles of) administrative justice? A 'European' conception of legal consciousness: What do public officials experience as (important principles of) administrative justice?

The Story of the Indonesian Quarter[1]

This case study considers the work of front-line officials in the Netherlands and how these officials understand the legal ideal of the *Rechtsstaat*. This ideal plays an important role in the Dutch system of administrative justice (see De Ridder and Tollenaar, in this volume). These officials were actively involved in the re-development of the 'Indonesian quarter', a run-down neighbourhood in the town of Zwolle. The case study is based on the empirical material of a six-month evaluation study (Hes 2001), supplemented with material from local and national newspapers.[2]

Background

The 'Indonesian quarter' is a small and predominantly blue-collar neighbourhood in Zwolle, a provincial town in the eastern part of the Netherlands.[3] Many consider this area, which is wedged between a busy motorway and a small industrial area, the seedy part of town. There are about 350 houses in this area, most of which form part of a number of social housing projects that provide accommodation for some 1,000 inhabitants. Unemployment rates in this area are extremely high. Many people depend on social security for their income and many of them have serious financial problems. Most children leave school early and social life in this community is very limited. The crime rate is the highest in Zwolle.

In the mid 1990s, after a series of smaller incidents, the Indonesian quarter was the scene of severe street violence. After a fight, the members of a black family, who had only just moved to Javastraat, were forced to leave their home by other people in the neighbourhood. A curfew and police in riot gear were needed to

[1] This case study has been adapted from Hertogh (2004).

[2] All interview fragments and other quotations in this section were translated from Dutch into English.

[3] The name of this quarter does not refer to the ethnic background of its inhabitants, but to the fact that the streets in this area are named after towns and islands in Indonesia (the former Dutch colony in the East Indies).

restore public order. In the aftermath of these events, many people left their houses and moved to other parts of town. In response to these developments, the mayor and other members of the municipal government decided it was time for a change. They approached three men who had previously worked in the neighbourhood—Joop (a social worker concerned primarily with homeless young people), Wessel (a local policeman) and Freddie (an official from the local housing association)—and asked them to set up the so-called 'Neighbourhood Intervention Team Zwolle' (NITZ) to help restore the sense of community and security. To this end, the local government (backed by the municipal council) transferred some of its authority to the NITZ team, especially with regard to the allocation of low-rental housing. The work of the NITZ team has been evaluated. The overall conclusion is that their approach was controversial but successful (Hes 2001: 121). The Indonesian quarter is no longer considered a 'no-go area', more people are involved in voluntary community work, less damage is done to the local houses, and the crime rate has dropped considerably.

How Do Public Officials Experience Administrative Justice?

Following its interpretation in legal doctrine, the ideal of the *Rechtsstaat* is usually understood to include the legal values of legality, equality, fundamental human rights, the separation of powers, and the right to an independent court (see De Ridder and Tollenaar, in this volume). Treating law as an independent variable, this 'official' interpretation of the *Rechtsstaat* is held constant and the first part of our case study focuses on the front-line officials' attitudes and reactions to two of its principles in particular: legality and equality.

Legality

According to Dutch law, the principle of legality requires that every administrative act that affects the rights and freedoms of an individual has a statutory basis. For the members of the NITZ team and some of their colleagues, however, this principle does not play an important role in their day-to-day decision making. Most decisions concerning the internal organisation of the NITZ team are, for instance, largely informal and are in no way based on official rules and regulations. As a result, those who are not closely connected to the team often have a hard time figuring out the responsibilities of each individual team member. The way in which front-line officials in the Indonesian quarter play down the importance of legality is also illustrated by the attitude of the local police towards privacy. During her fieldwork, the researcher had noticed that the police discussed and exchanged private information about tenants without much restraint. When she confronted them with some of the provisions of Dutch privacy law, their typical reaction was as follows: 'Privacy? That's something I infringe on every day … Privacy cannot be handled by legislation, but should be considered in each individual case instead.' (cited in Hes 2001: 40).

Perhaps the most telling example of the way in which the members of the NITZ team think about legality is reflected in their most controversial scheme in the Indonesian quarter: the allocation of low-rental housing. Their approach consisted of neglecting the general rules and regulations of official housing policy and replacing them their own rules. About these and other examples, the evaluation study concludes: 'To defend the good cause, official rules are often put aside' (ibid: 119). Moreover, '[t]he fact that something "works" is considered far more important than whether it is legally permissible' (ibid: 107). Although the way in which the NITZ team decides on the allocation of local houses goes against official (national) rules and regulations, the mayor of Zwolle openly defended this approach. In an interview with a national newspaper he claimed: 'Sometimes it is better to put the formal rules aside, provided that you have a clear concept and your policy is supported by the municipal council.' (cited in Groen 2001a: 1).

In their efforts to restore public order and security in the Indonesian quarter, the NITZ team is sponsored by an organisation called the *Stichting Maatschappij, Veiligheid en Politie* (the Society, Security and Police Foundation). With regard to the role of the police, the managing director of this organisation argues as follows:

> Murder, theft and violence—these are all things the police can never tolerate, in these cases strong police action is called for. In other cases, however, it might be beneficial to bend the rules somewhat or to be flexible in the implementation of the rules.' (cited in Groen 2001b: 1).

Whereas the legal ideal of the *Rechtsstaat* puts great emphasis on the 'rule of law, not of men', the members of the NITZ team and other local officials seem to have changed this principle into a 'rule of men, not of law'.

Equality

The principle of equality is anchored both in the Dutch Constitution and in statutory law. Article 1 of the Constitution guarantees equal treatment of all persons in the Netherlands in equal circumstances. In addition, the Equal Treatment Act seeks to ban discrimination on the grounds of religion, belief, political opinion, race, sex, hetero- or homosexual orientation, or marital status.

In the mid 1990s, police in riot gear were sent to the Indonesian quarter after local citizens had forced a black family to leave their newly rented house in Javastraat. To prevent similar incidents in the future, the NITZ team decided to develop a completely new, and highly controversial, policy. Previously, the distribution of low-rental housing in Zwolle (and in most other Dutch towns) had been subject to a detailed housing policy. This policy gave all citizens in Zwolle in similar circumstances the same opportunity to rent a house. All future tenants were awarded 'housing credits' based on the number of family members and the time they had been on the waiting list. On the basis of these credits, town officials then decided who was eligible for a house in Zwolle (including the Indonesian quarter). After several conflicts, however, the municipal government transferred most of its authority for the allocation of houses to the NITZ team. They effectively chose to put the official system aside, and made the NITZ team responsible for the allocation of low-rental housing in the Indonesian quarter. Consequently, town officials no longer decided on who was eligible for which house on the basis of their housing credits, but from then on the members of the NITZ team themselves decided who they thought would be the most suitable tenant of a particular house. Team member Freddie explained: 'We [the members of the NITZ team] conducted several interviews, and we considered whether a newcomer would fit into the neighbourhood and the neighbourhood would suit him.' (cited in Groen 2001b: 9).

In effect, this meant that tenants from ethnic minorities were excluded from social housing in the Indonesian quarter, because people in this neighbourhood felt that they did not fit in. This caused great controversy among many people in other parts of Zwolle, who not only objected to the discrimination against foreigners but also complained that those who happened to live in the Indonesian quarter did not have to comply with the general housing policy and were thus given preferential treatment.

Discussion

Looking through the lens of an 'American' conception of legal consciousness, this case study provides us with some important clues about the attitudes of front-line officials towards administrative justice. Two major elements of the *Rechtsstaat*—legality and equality—do not seem to play a significant role in their day-to-day decision making. Rules and regulations are put aside in favour of more informal solutions and the allocation of houses favours some tenants in the Indonesian quarter over others. In terms of Ewick and Silbey's (1998) typology, members of the NITZ team are predominantly 'with' and 'against the law'.

Yet, this perspective also leaves a number of important questions unanswered. We used a definition of the *Rechtsstaat* which can be derived from the Dutch Constitution, statute law, and from writings in constitutional and administrative law. Next, we compared this 'official' definition of legality and equality with the attitudes and opinions of street-level workers in the Indonesian quarter. But how do front-line officials themselves feel about this legal interpretation? What do they consider important principles? What is their ideal of the *Rechtsstaat*? In order to address these and similar issues, we now consider the concept of administrative justice as a dependent variable.

What Do Public Officials Experience as Administrative Justice?

The evaluation study of the NITZ team attributes much of the team's success to, what is referred to as, the 'personalistic value orientation' (Hes 2001: 96) of its members. This orientation is characterised by a strong emphasis on the special circumstances of each individual citizen. This is reflected in two values that will be referred to as responsiveness and material equality.

Responsiveness

Whereas in the 'official' definition of the *Rechtsstaat* the legitimacy of administrative action is its statutory basis (legality), local officials in the Indonesian quarter themselves feel that their legitimacy should instead be based on their close co-operation with the neighbourhood and its citizens (regardless of their legal status). The NITZ team is not oriented towards fitting their individual decisions into a system of general rules, but towards individual citizens and their unique circumstances (Hes 2001: 95).

Prior to the establishment of the NITZ team, people in the Indonesian quarter felt a deep sense of mistrust towards the town authorities. They felt abandoned by the authorities, who refused to listen to their complaints and did not even bother to send a police car when they reported a break-in. After the violent incidents in the mid 1990s, this was one of the first things that Joop, Wessel, and Freddie were keen to change. From that moment on, most of their actions were inspired by the central value of responsiveness. Or, as Freddie put it: 'Not a single stone from the pavement should be removed without consulting the local people first.' (cited in Groen 2001b: 9).

Public officials in Zwolle consider this one of the 'cultural pillars' of their approach. In a brochure for future employees, the town council summarises what they see as typical for the 'Zwolle perspective'(www.zwolle.nl):

> Town government should be at the heart of society, outward-looking and co-operative. Policy is not made from behind a desk, public officials know what's going on in Zwolle and their work is directed at the needs of the client. There is a very close co-operation with all partners in the city.

Town officials and politicians pay regular visits to all quarters of Zwolle. During such visits, either on foot or by bicycle, officials take note of problems in the Indonesian quarter that require further attention, and all members of the community are encouraged to walk or cycle with them. One official summarises their attitude as follows: 'Our golden rule is: listen to what the residents say. Our second rule: do not shy away from creative solutions.' (cited in Groen 2001b: 9).

This is also reflected in the interviews with local police officers. According to one policeman: 'The rules are made by the residents themselves, it is our job to help them enforce these rules.' (cited in Hes 2001: 43).

His position is illustrated by the following events. For a long time, many people in the Indonesian quarter had complained about heavy traffic from the nearby motorway that used the small streets in their neighbourhood to avoid traffic jams. At one point, several inhabitants of the Sumatrastraat decided to block their street with a concrete pole and a wire fence. Only two days after this incident, members of the community met with town officials. As a result of this meeting, the Sumatrastraat was formally closed by way of a removable fence, which allows only a limited number of cars to pass. Moreover, local inhabitants were made responsible for this fence. This solution goes against official traffic rules, and people in other parts of Zwolle objected to what they considered a bonus for anti-social behaviour.

Material Equality

The 'personalistic value orientation' of the NITZ team is also reflected in their attitude towards equality. In the Indonesian quarter, front-line officials are less inspired by the idea of 'general justice', which focuses on official rules and general norms (*Normgerechtigkeit*), and adhere more to the idea of 'individual justice' that emphasises individual solutions for specific problems (*Einzelfallgerechtigkeit*). In their opinion, one should not focus on treating all people equally, but consider ways that may help restore the equal position of individuals instead. It is, in other words, not the intent but the result of their actions that should promote equality. In some cases, this may require favouring some citizens over others.

This attitude is most clearly expressed in the way the NITZ team—and the local housing association in particular—use so-called 'special contracts' for the allocation of houses. In these contracts, each tenant is treated differently and each has to fulfil different requirements to be eligible for a house. In one of these contracts, Mrs A, who had been refused a house before, was offered a house on the specific understanding that she would *not* allow her two sons to move in with her. Moreover, she was obliged to arrange for other members of her family to take care of her. Both sons of Mrs. A, who had a rather notorious reputation in the locality, were also offered a house. Previously, they lived in a caravan. In their contracts, the men were explicitly prohibited from drinking more than one litre of beer a day. In his defence of these and other unusual contracts, the managing director of the local housing association claimed: 'You may argue, equal cases should be treated equally. But that simply doesn't hold for the Indonesian quarter. Here, there are no equal cases.' (ibid: 61).

With regard to these and other examples, the evaluation study concludes: 'Justice is done by recognising the importance of individual differences and by treating the neighbourhood favourably' (ibid: 117). While the legal definition of the *Rechtsstaat* adheres to a concept of 'formal equality', the members of the NITZ team and others acted upon the value of 'material equality'(ibid: 106).

Discussion

Following a 'European' conception of legal consciousness allows us to analyse administrative decision making in the Indonesian quarter 'from below'. This provides us with a completely different image of this neighbourhood. Unlike the previous rather grim picture, which focused on 'official' law and which led to the conclusion that front-line officials do not follow the legal principles of legality and equality, this alternative perspective suggests that local officials are motivated by two different values instead: responsiveness and material equality. To most front-line officials involved in the re-development of the Indonesian quarter, these values represent two important fragments of their own ideal of the *Rechtsstaat*. Both values do not constitute some degree of more or less *Rechtsstaat*, but a different type of *Rechtsstaat* altogether.

On a more general level, this case study illustrates that the role of front-line officials may be quite different from the role that is usually ascribed to them in the literature. This also has important consequences for our understanding of administrative justice. According to Maynard-Moody and Musheno (2000), the dominant scholarly narrative starts from the premise that street-level workers are 'state-agents'. They are basically government employees who are charged with carrying out the plans and policies of government agencies. Moreover, this view acknowledges the inevitability of discretion and emphasises that self-interest guides street-level choices, street-level workers use their discretion to make their life easier, safer and more rewarding. Based on extensive fieldwork in five agencies, however, Maynard-Moody and Musheno argue that street-level workers themselves tell quite a different story. Their decisions and judgments exist in the context of rules, procedures, and agencies but these are 'case specific and are guided by normative, rather than legal, ordering' (ibid: 347). Also, contrary to the dominant scholarly view, street-level workers define their work in terms of relationships, not rules (ibid: 352). Both elements are clearly illustrated by the events in the Indonesian quarter. The members of the NITZ team are not passive 'state agents' whose decisions are primarily driven by self-interest, but active 'citizen agents' who base their decisions on normative choices:

> Rather than discretionary state-agents who act in response to rules, procedures, and law—sometimes following the rules, [at] other times bending or ignoring them—street-level workers describe themselves as citizen agents who act in response to individual citizen clients in specific circumstances. (Maynard-Moody and Musheno 2000, 348)

As will be discussed in the next section, this has also important consequences for the role of law in administrative decision making.

Front-line Officials and Legal Alienation

According to Lipsky (1980: 75), 'street-level bureaucrats' work is alienated work'. First, Lipsky argues, the compromises required of street-level workers reduce the extent to which they are able to respond to clients in a fully human way. Second, street-level work is inauthentic. 'In defense of the myth of altruism, street-level bureaucracies devote a relatively high proportion of energies to concealing lack of service and generating appearances of responsiveness' (Lipsky 1980: 76). Finally, street-level bureaucrats are alienated from their clients. In addition to issues of job dissatisfaction, however, the perspective of 'alienation' may also be an important tool for understanding a different aspect of street-level work, which is more directly relevant for students of administrative justice. Street-level workers are often not only alienated from their work and their clients, but also from the law.

Although the classic ideal of a bureaucracy emphasises the strict application of law, rules, and administrative procedures, this 'expectation of law abidance' (Maynard-Moody and Musheno 2003: 4) is not reflected in our case study. Joop, Wessel, Freddie and other front-line officials in the Indonesian quarter regularly neglected the official rules and regulations and replaced them with their own rules. To them, the fact that something 'worked' was considered far more important than whether it was legally permissible. Other empirical studies suggest that this case of legal alienation is not unique to the Netherlands.

In the United States, Mashaw (1983: 11) has argued that '[t]he normative structures created by legislation and by judicial decision making are often, if not usually removed from the concrete experience of bureaucratic implementation.' Similarly, Maynard-Moody and Musheno (2003: 93) suggest that, for street-level workers, 'fairness has little to do with the bureaucratic norm of treating everyone the same or even fairly implementing laws and regulations.' Instead, 'fairness and justice mean responding to citizen-clients based on their perceived worth.' In the United Kingdom, Cooper (1996) has described several examples of non-compliance, 'institutional disobedience' and 'administrative illegality' by local governments in the late 1980s and early 1990s. Moreover, Halliday (2004: 60), in his study of the routine decision-making practices of local authority housing departments, concluded that 'decision-makers (…) reject the normative authority of law.' He describes this as 'a lack of faith in law's ability to provide the right decision outcome' (Halliday 2004: 60). As a result, 'Legality, as an external normative system, has failed in such instances to penetrate and take hold of the internal administrative value system.'(ibid).

The goal of this section is to further develop the idea of alienation from law. How can 'legal alienation' be understood and conceptualised, and how may it be included in studies of administrative justice?

What is Alienation?

The concept of alienation has a long and controversial history. Whereas some argue that it should be considered 'one of the great traditions in sociological thought' (Seeman 1959: 783), others claim that 'we shall always be reduced to confusion when we read about alienation' (Ludz 1976: 3). The concept was particularly popular during much of the 1960s and 1970s and has produced a small library of literature in many different fields, including sociology, philosophy, social psychology, and political science. According to Ludz (ibid: 7) the concept of alienation, as it is used in contemporary social science, can be traced back to two sources: the theory of alienation established by Karl Marx and the theory of anomie developed from Emile Durkheim's work. Empirical research on alienation has been concentrated on two main areas: work and politics. Whereas Marx focused on *objective* alienation, most contemporary studies look at *subjective* alienation. Here, the focus is no longer on the *circumstances*, but on different *sentiments* of alienation (Seeman 1975: 114).

What is Legal Alienation?

Whereas the general alienation literature could easily fill a small library, there are still only a few studies available on alienation from law. Gibson and Caldeira (1996), for example, refer to 'legal alienation' as one of the indicators for analysing the legal cultures of Europe. Moreover, Genn (1999: 247), in her study of the legal experiences of ordinary citizens in England and Wales, concludes that '[r]espondents' views of the legal system often conveyed a sense of alienation from the institutions and processes of the law.' Finally, Rattner and Yagil (2004) have included the idea of alienation in their study of the willingness of three groups of Israeli citizens to take the law into their own hands.

In this chapter, legal alienation will be defined using Friedman's influential dichotomy. Friedman (1975: 223) distinguishes between an internal and an external legal culture. While the 'internal' legal culture refers to the 'legal culture of those members of society who perform specialised legal tasks' such as a judge or a lawyer, the 'external' legal culture is the 'legal culture of the general population'. Following this distinction, a preliminary definition of legal alienation may now be formulated in the following terms: legal alienation refers to a perceived gap between an external and an internal conception of law. In this chapter, the 'external' approach also includes front-line officials' beliefs and ideas about law, which can be contrasted with the official ('internal') version of the law.

We can break down this preliminary idea of 'legal alienation' by applying four general types of alienation, which were first introduced by Seeman (1959), to the field of law. The first type of legal alienation is 'legal powerlessness'. This idea of alienation may be defined as the individual's expectation that his own behaviour cannot determine the occurrence of the outcome of legal processes. The second type is 'legal meaninglessness'. Whereas the previous type of legal alienation refers to the sensed ability to *control* outcomes, this second meaning essentially refers to the sensed ability to *predict* the outcome of legal processes. The third meaning of legal alienation is what Sampson and Jeglum-Bartusch (1998) refer to as 'legal cynicism'. This 'anomie about law' refers to a state of normlessness in which the rules of the dominant society (and hence the legal system) are no longer considered binding on a community or on a subgroup of the population (Sampson and Jeglum Bartusch 1998: 782). The final type of legal alienation is 'legal value isolation'. The alienated in this sense are those who assign low reward value to those legal goals or beliefs that are typically highly valued in a given society.

A Typology of Legal Citizenship

How can we apply these theoretical ideas about legal alienation to an empirical analysis of administrative decision making? Halliday (2004) has identified a number of conditions which maximise compliance with administrative law. These include both the level of legal knowledge of front-line officials and their level of 'legal conscientiousness', which he describes as their 'commitment to legality' or their 'faith in law to produce the right outcome' (ibid: 53–54). In a similar way, our analysis of legal alienation needs to address two basic questions. First: 'Are public officials aware of the law?' How much do they know about the legal system in general, about specific rules and regulations, or about a particular court case? Second: 'Do public officials identify with law?' To what extent does the law reflect their own personal values, their own sense of right or wrong, and their own ideas of justice? To consider these issues more systematically, we can transfer both questions to a simple two-by-two matrix (Figure 2). The first question, which may be referred to as the 'cognitive' dimension of legal alienation, has been put on the horizontal axis. The second question, which reflects the 'normative' dimension, is placed on the vertical axis. Each field then corresponds with a different mode of 'legal citizenship' (Hertogh 2006). Although this typology was originally designed to study the ideas and beliefs of the general population, it may also be applied to analyse the varieties of ways in which front-line officials relate to law.[4]

Figure 2: Four Modes of Legal Citizenship

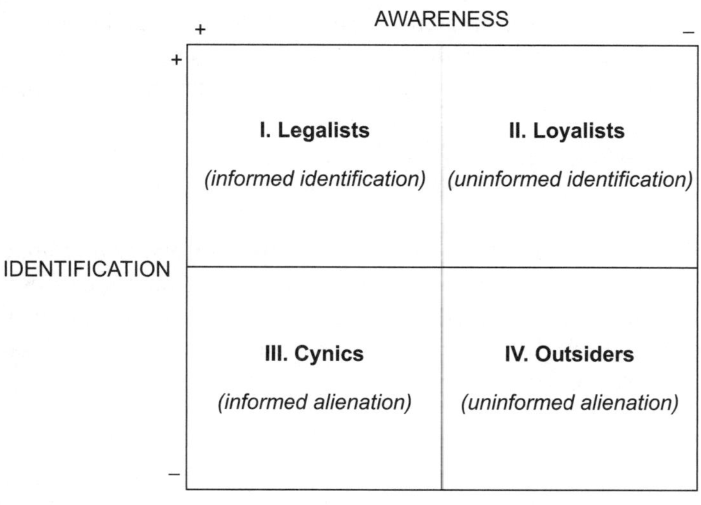

[4] These different types of legal citizenship are 'situationally specific'—depending on a concrete situation, officials act according to one particular mode of legal citizenship. Yet, if this situation changes, their mode of legal citizenship may change accordingly. It should be noted that Figure 2 does not consider how officials relate to 'the law in general'—instead, it refers to one particular field of law in a given situation.

Legalists

The first mode of legal citizenship is that of the 'legalists'. Here, public officials are well aware of the law. Also, these officials generally identify with law. This mode corresponds with the classic image of the bureaucrat, which is still reflected in some handbooks on public law and public administration.

However, from our case study of the Indonesian quarter and from many other studies, we know that this image is not always an accurate reflection of reality. First, although, in theory, it may seem self-evident that all public officials know the law, in practice things are often much more complicated. According to some officials, there are simply too many local, national and international rules. Moreover, sometimes the dissemination of legal knowledge is seriously limited by the organisational complexity of an agency. A caseworker in Halliday's study explains, for example, that in her organisation not all officials are equally informed about important court cases. 'The knowledge is not shared', according to this official. And she continues: 'You're only told if it's your case. And the rest of the unit don't really know what's gone on and what's happened' (Halliday 2004: 49). Second, our case study illustrates that not all public officials equally identify with law. A local policeman in Zwolle puts it like this: 'Criminal law is long out of date. ... It's much better to address people directly and to improve their personal living conditions, so that you enable them to live in accordance with the rules.' (cited in Hes 2001: 43). Members of the NITZ team also rejected Dutch privacy law and neglected the official rules for the allocation of low-rental housing.

The fact that a high level of legal awareness and a high level of legal identification are not self-evident among street-level bureaucrats, suggests that—besides the mode of the 'legalists'—there are at least three additional modes of legal citizenship.

Loyalists

The second mode of legal citizenship is the mode of the 'loyalists'. Here, public officials generally identify with law as well. Contrary to the previous mode, however, their level of legal awareness is rather limited. Yet, despite the fact that they only have a general idea of what the law is, they feel that the rules of the legal system should be respected.

Cynics

In the third mode of legal citizenship, and similar to the first mode, public officials are well aware of the law. However, the degree in which these officials identify with law is much lower. They know the law, but they are also highly critical about the law. This is the mode of the 'cynics'. They generally do not feel that their own values are sufficiently reflected in the law.

Outsiders

The fourth, and final, category are the 'outsiders'. In this mode of legal citizenship, public officials' awareness of the law is very limited. These officials do not identify with law either. This is the mirror-image of the first mode. While the 'legalists' almost automatically turn to law, the 'outsiders' have turned their backs to law.

Sliding Scale

Figure 2 may also be read as a sliding scale from 'legal identification' to 'legal alienation' in administrative decision making. At one end of the continuum are the 'legalists'. Here, there is no sign of legal alienation whatsoever. This mode is followed by the 'loyalists'. This mode of legal citizenship points towards 'uninformed identification' with the law, a first, weak sign of legal alienation. With the 'cynics', the level of alienation slowly increases. And at the other end of the continuum are the 'outsiders'.

This typology may be helpful for analysing how front-line officials relate to law and to administrative justice. In our case study, the opinions and decisions of the members of the NITZ team reflect important elements of legal alienation, in particular 'legal cynicism' and 'legal value-isolation'. In terms of our typology, most local officials in the Indonesian quarter may be characterised as 'cynics' and 'outsiders'.

Three Lessons for Administrative Justice

Having introduced the theoretical conceptions of 'legal consciousness' and 'legal alienation', we will now return to the models of Mashaw (1983), Kagan (2006, 1978), Adler (2003) and Halliday and Scott (in this volume). Using our case study of the Indonesian quarter as an illustration, how may a focus on 'street-level beliefs' contribute to our understanding of administrative justice?

Legal Consciousness and Administrative Justice

As Kagan (1978: 86) notes, 'the simplest and perhaps still the most prevalent conception of rule application parallels Max Weber's construct of formal-rational legal thought.' This idea 'approximates the ideal of formal justice, i.e., unbiased, universalistic, prompt, and predictable decision making' (Kagan 1978: 86). Following the ideal of the *Rechtsstaat,* it is exactly this approach which was taken as our point of departure for the case study of the Indonesian quarter. Dutch administrative law puts great emphasis on the principles of legality and equality. While according to the first principle every administrative act should have a statutory basis, the second principle states that equal cases should all be treated equally.

This approach to administrative justice fits well with Mashaw's (1983) first model of 'bureaucratic rationality'. The legitimating force of this conception flows from 'its claim to correct implementation of otherwise legitimate social decisions' (Mashaw 1983: 26) and it emphasises a hierarchical structure of organisation. Moreover, the Dutch official approach corresponds with what Halliday and Scott refer to as a 'hierarchist' model of administrative justice. 'Decision-making processes within hierarchism should support the exercise of expert judgment and/or the accurate and efficient implementation of higher orders.'(Halliday and Scott, in this volume).

However, as our case study has suggested, administrative justice 'in the books' does not always equal administrative justice 'in action'. This becomes particularly clear when we focus on front-line officials' legal consciousness. Contrary to the official model of administrative justice, the idea of 'general justice' does not play an important role in the day-to-day decision making of the front-line officials in the Indonesian quarter. Instead, their work is motivated by the idea of 'individual justice', which aims at promoting the principles of responsiveness and material equality.

With its emphasis on the individual client, this approach of the NITZ team corresponds with Mashaw's (1983) model of 'professional treatment'. According to Mashaw (ibid: 27), this conception of administrative justice recognises both the 'singularity of individual contexts' and the 'intuitive nature of judgment'. Rather than focusing on substantive and procedural rules or hierarchical controls, the public official is guided by his own professional norms and reaches decisions 'that are as much art as science' (ibid: 28). Likewise, in our case study the members of the NITZ team distributed the low-rental housing based on a number of unusual contracts. In their defence, they argued that there are simply no equal cases in this neighbourhood. Other aspects of the approach in the Indonesian quarter also seem to fit with Mashaw's model of 'moral judgment'. This conception of administrative justice is primarily aimed at 'preserving party equality and control' (ibid: 31). According to Mashaw, 'the "justice" of this model inheres in its promise of a full and equal opportunity to obtain one's entitlements.' Moreover, 'the decider is to a degree passive' (ibid: 30) and the parties themselves control how much of their lives is put at issue. This focus on participatory decision making is also reflected in the Indonesian quarter. Their golden rule is: listen to what the residents have to say. Also, according to some officials, the rules should be made by the residents themselves and they consider it their job to help them enforce these rules. Several examples in our case study also reflect a strong preference for a 'contextual interpretation' (ibid: 31).

Some of these characteristics also fit Adler's (2003) model of 'consumerism'. Similar to the approach of the NITZ team in Zwolle, this model emphasises the importance of administrative responsiveness. Moreover, it considers the citizen 'as an active participant rather than a passive recipient of bureaucratic, professional, or managerial directions' (Adler 2003: 334). Finally, the normative beliefs of the front-line officials in Zwolle seem to correspond with what Halliday and Scott refer to as an 'egalitarian' model of administrative justice. 'Decision-making … should be all about reaching consensus and so marked by very high citizen participation.' (Halliday and Scott, in this volume).

Legal Alienation and Administrative Justice

Based on both the 'emphasis on adherence to rules' and the 'emphasis on realisation of organisational ends' in a bureaucracy, Kagan (1978 and in this volume) has identified four modes of rule application, which he refers to as: 'legal creativity', 'legalism', 'discretionary judgment' and 'retreatism'. According to Kagan (in this volume), the key point of variability is how officials deal with 'the inevitable shortcomings of administrative rules and regulations' and 'the forms, checklists, and manuals that are used to get front-line officials to follow the rules.' Our case study suggests that an additional factor in creating a specific culture of rule application is the level of legal alienation in an agency. Are front-line officials aware of the law? And how much do they identify with law? The members of the NITZ team are critical and sometimes cynical about the law. This is also reflected in the way in which they apply, for instance, the rules for the allocation of low-rental housing.

In this way, Kagan's typology of rule application (loosely) fits our typology of legal citizenship (see Figure 2). Kagan's first mode of rule application, 'legal creativity', corresponds with the 'legalists' category. This particular type of rule application presupposes that officials both know and support the law, although sometimes they may also reinterpret the existing rules. The second mode, 'legalism', is most likely in an agency which is dominated by 'loyalists'. Although they do not know all the legal details (and their practical consequences), they strictly follow the rules. Moreover, the third mode, 'discretionary judgment', corresponds with the way in which most 'cynics' relate to law. They know the law fairly well, yet following their own rules is considered more important than following the law. Finally, clearly reflecting a substantial level of legal alienation, Kagan (in this volume) notes that front-line officials in a culture of 'retreatism' are often 'indifferent' and 'weakly committed to rule-following or to the achievement of agency policy goals'. These officials may be characterised as 'outsiders'.

In designing his typology, Kagan was inspired by Robert Merton's (1957) work. Following Merton, he also mentions a fifth type of rule application, which he calls: 'rebellion'. This refers to 'the affirmative rejection of officially prescribed ends and means and the substitution of a radically different set of goals and values' (Kagan 1978: 95, footnote 25). This also reflects a high level of legal alienation. Although Kagan (1978: 95) notes that '[b]ureaucrats can rarely get away with using their positions *consistently* to pursue public policies strikingly different from those prescribed by legislatures and their superiors', our case study suggests this is precisely what happened in the Indonesian quarter. Moreover, this type of rebellion is clearly demonstrated in Cooper's (1996) study of 'institutional disobedience' in British local government.

Different levels of legal alienation may also help to explain why some bureaucracies favour a vision of 'good administration' which Halliday and Scott (in this volume) refer to as a 'fatalistic' model of administrative justice. In their view, the point about fatalistic administrative justice is 'the abandonment of any faith in our ability to positively design just processes of administration' (Halliday and Scott, in this volume). Similar to feelings of alienation, this conception of administrative justice involves 'a general sense of powerless and exclusion'. As Halliday and Scott suggest, these attitudes may be associated with well-known categories of disputing individuals like 'lumpers' and 'sceptics'. Yet, as our case study suggests, sometimes these attitudes may also play a prominent role among public officials. A culture of 'fatalistic' administrative justice seems more likely to develop in an agency with 'cynics' and 'outsiders' then in an organisation which is completely dominated by 'legalists' and 'loyalists'.

External Mechanisms to Promote Administrative Justice

Courts, but also tribunals and ombudsmen, are generally recognised as important external mechanisms of achieving administrative justice. Yet, a growing number of empirical studies show that judicial review and other forms of external accountability are not always effective (see Hertogh and Halliday 2004). Or, as Horowitz (1980: 91) put it, 'judicial norms have generally only seeped into the cracks rather than, as courts might wish, flowed into the main channels of administrative life.' There are several ways to analyse this lack of compliance. Adler (2003: 328) argues that '[t]he more authoritative the judgments are ... and the stronger the enforcement procedures are, the greater the impact they are likely to have and the more effective they are likely to be in achieving administrative justice.' This is similar to what Tyler (2006) refers to as an 'instrumental' approach of legal compliance. '[P]eople are viewed as shaping their behaviour to respond to ... incentives and penalties associated with following the law' and to judgments about the personal gains and losses resulting from different kinds of behaviour (ibid: 3). When we look at administrative justice through the lens of legal consciousness, however, it becomes apparent that legal compliance is not all about authority and enforcement, but is also dependent of front-line officials' own beliefs and expectations. Tyler calls this a 'normative' approach, which focuses on 'people's internalised norms of justice and obligation' (ibid: 4). In this view, one obeys the law 'because one feels the law is just' (ibid: 4).

In the case of the Indonesian quarter, Dutch administrative courts usually emphasise the 'official' definition of the *Rechtsstaat*, including the legal principles of legality and equality. As previously argued, this approach corresponds both with the 'bureaucratic' (Mashaw) and the 'hierarchist' (Halliday and Scott) models of administrative justice. By contrast, the front-line officials themselves favour a mixture of different conceptions of administrative justice, which include elements of both the 'professional treatment' and 'moral judgment' model (Mashaw), the model of 'consumerism' (Adler) and the 'egalitarian' model (Halliday and Scott).

Following Tyler's 'normative' approach, it is likely that this tension between the official and the most preferred models of administrative justice must seriously limit the effectiveness of the courts. Moreover, it may increase the level of legal alienation.

As Loveland (1994) has noted, situations like these confront administrative lawyers with a pressing dilemma. Should they continue with, what he calls, 'efforts to force their square legal pegs into round administrative holes' or should they instead begin to fashion 'a dialectical relationship between a top-down value system rooted in legal principle and bottom-up rationality drawn from bureaucratic practice'? (ibid: 232). An empirical study of Dutch administrative courts and the National ombudsman suggests that one way to create such a 'dialectical relationship' may be working towards more 'co-operative' control (Hertogh 2001). In the Netherlands, in individual cases administrative agencies comply more with court rulings then with the ombudsman. Yet, in the long run, the ombudsman has a greater 'policy impact' then the courts. It turns out that the most decisive factor for their impact is the style of control used by administrative courts and the National ombudsman. 'Coercive' control used by the courts (based on the use of authority backed by sanctions) is less effective in promoting administrative justice then 'co-operative' control used by the ombudsman (based on communication and negotiations). Those who apply a co-operative style of control believe that external control can only be effective if it corresponds with the language of the government agency concerned and allows them to respond in terms of their own criteria of understanding. As a result, and contrary to Adler's (2003: 328) previous suggestion, the recipe for stepping up control may not be to strengthen official authority or sanctions, but rather to increase the responsiveness of the courts to front-line officials' own beliefs about administrative justice.

Conclusions

The quest for a 'magic formula' (Adler 2003: 336) of administrative justice requires both a normative and an empirical analysis. There are many competing views about the goals of the administrative process and about the best way of achieving those goals. Which of these views will serve the public interest best and which of these justice models will be the most desirable can only be decided in a normative discussion. However, this normative exercise can, and should be, informed by empirical data. This chapter has offered an alternative framework for the empirical study of administrative decision making.

While most previous studies of administrative justice have been primarily concerned with the views of judges, politicians and legal scholars, this chapter focuses on the beliefs and ideas of street-level bureaucrats. How do they understand administrative justice? After introducing the analytical concepts of 'legal consciousness' and 'legal alienation', and after applying these concepts in an exploratory case study, the main conclusion of this chapter is that front-line officials not only play an important role in the formulation and implementation of public policy, but also in the realisation of normative ideals of administrative justice. Or, to paraphrase Michael Lipsky, administrative justice is not best understood as made in legislatures or top-floor suites of high-ranking administrators, because in important ways it is actually made in the crowded offices and daily encounters of front-line officials.

References

Adler, M (2003) 'A Socio-Legal Approach to Administrative Justice' 25 *Law and Policy* 323.

Cooper, D (1995) 'Local Government Legal Consciousness in the Shadow of Juridification' 22 *Journal of Law and Society* 506.

—— (1996) 'Institutional Illegality and Disobedience: Local Government Narratives' 16 *Oxford Journal of Legal Studies* 255.

Ehrlich, E (1967) 'Die Erforschung des Lebendes Rechts' in M Rehbinder (ed), *Eugen Ehrlich. Recht und Leben. Gesammelte Schriften zur Rechtstatsachenforschung und zur Freirechtslehre* (Berlin, Duncker and Humblot, originally published in 1912).

Engel, D (1998) 'How Does Law Matter in the Constitution of Legal Consciousness?' in B Garth and A Sarat (eds), *How Does Law Matter?* (Evanston, IL, Northwestern University Press).

Ewick, P and Silbey, S (1998) *The Common Place of Law: Stories from Everyday Life* (Chicago, University of Chicago Press).

Friedman, LM (1975) *The Legal System: A Social Science Perspective* (New York, Russell Sage).

Genn, H (1999) *Paths to Justice. What People Do and Think about Going to Law* (Oxford, Hart Publishing)

Gibson, JL and Caldeira, GA (1996) 'The Legal Cultures of Europe' 30 *Law and Society Review* 55.

Groen, J (2001a) 'Zet soms regels opzij in achterstandswijk. Politici pleiten voor onorthodoxe aanpak gemeentebesturen na succes in voormalige Zwolse crisiswijk' *de Volkskrant*, 26 January, 1.

—— (2001b) 'Beetje soepel met de regels' *de Volkskrant*, 26 January, 9.

Halliday, S (2004) *Judicial Review and Compliance with Administrative Law* (Oxford, Hart Publishing).

Hertogh, M (2001) 'Coercion, Co-operation, and Control: Understanding the Policy Impact of Administrative Courts and the Ombudsman in the Netherlands' 23 *Law and Policy* 47.

—— (2004) 'A "European" Conception of Legal Consciousness: Rediscovering Eugen Ehrlich' 31 *Journal of Law and Society* 457.

—— (2006) *Rechtsvervreemding: tussen rechtsstaat en rechtsgevoel* (Den Haag, Boom Juridische uitgevers).

—— (ed) (2009) *Living Law: Reconsidering Eugen Ehrlich* (Oxford, Hart Publishing).

Hertogh, M and Halliday, S (eds) (2004) *Judicial Review and Bureaucratic Impact: International and Interdisciplinary Perspectives* (Cambridge, Cambridge University Press).

Hes, J (2001) *Recht doen aan de buurt* (Dordrecht, Stichting Maatschappij Maatschappij, Veiligheid en Politie).

Horowitz, DL (1980) 'The Courts as Monitors of the Bureaucracy' in CH Weiss and AH Barton (eds), *Making Bureaucracies Work* (Beverly Hills, CA, Sage Publications).

Kagan, RA (1978) *Regulatory Justice: Implementing a Wage-Price Freeze* (New York, Russell Sage).

Lipsky, M (1980) *Street-Level Bureaucracy: Dilemmas of the Individual in Public Services* (New York, Russell Sage).

Loveland, I (1994) 'Irrelevant Considerations? The Role of Administrative Law in Determining the Local Connection of Homeless Persons' in G Richardson and H Genn (eds), *Administrative Law and Government Action* (Oxford, Clarendon Press).

Ludz, PC (1976) 'Alienation as a Concept in the Social Sciences' in R Geyer and R Schweitzer (eds), *Theories of Alienation: Critical Perspectives in Philosophy and the Social Sciences* (Leiden, Martinus Nijhoff Social Sciences Division).

Mashaw, J (1983) *Bureaucratic Justice: Managing Social Security Disability Claims* (New Haven, Yale University Press).

Maynard-Moody, S and Musheno, M (2000) 'State Agent or Citizen Agent: Two Narratives of Discretion' 10 *Journal of Public Administration Research and Theory* 329.

—— (2003) *Cops, Teachers, Counselors. Stories from the Front-Lines of Public Service* (Ann Arbor, University of Michigan Press).

Merry, SE (1990) *Getting Justice and Getting Even: Legal Consciousness among Working-Class Americans* (Chicago, University of Chicago Press).

Merton, RK (1957) *Social Theory and Social Structure* (New York, The Free Press).

Nielsen, LB (2000) 'Situating Legal Consciousness: Experiences and Attitudes of Ordinary Citizens about Law and Street Harassment' 34 *Law and Society Review* 1055.

Rattner, A and Yagil, D (2004) 'Taking the Law into One's Own Hands on Ideological Grounds' 32 *International Journal of the Sociology of Law* 85.

Sampson, RJ and Jeglum-Bartush, D (1998) 'Legal Cynicism and (Subcultural?) Tolerance of Deviance: The Neighbourhood Context of Racial Differences' 32 *Law and Society Review* 777.

Sarat, A (1990) '"The Law is All Over": Power, Resistance, and the Legal Consciousness of the Welfare Poor' 2 *Yale Journal of Law and the Humanities* 343.

Seeman, M (1959) 'On the Meaning of Alienation' 24 *American Sociological Review* 783.

—— (1975) 'Alienation Studies' 1 *Annual Reviews of Sociology* 91.

Silbey, S (2005) 'After Legal Consciousness' 1 *Annual Review of Law and Social Science* 323.

Trubek, D (1984) 'Where the Action Is: Critical Legal Studies and Empiricism' 36 *Stanford Law Review* 575.

Tyler, TR (2006) *Why People Obey the Law* (New Haven, Yale University Press, originally published in 1990).

Waldo, D (1948) *The Administrative State: A Study of the Political Theory of American Public Administration* (New York, The Ronald Press Company).

Part 3

Public–Private Issues

10

Towards the Horizontal Effect of Administrative Justice Principles

DAWN OLIVER

Introduction

In this chapter I shall focus on the arguments surrounding the possible extension of principles of administrative justice to private decision making. In other words, to borrow a phrase from European law, I shall discuss the potential for developing the 'horizontal effect' of administrative justice. I shall consider the scope for extending both human rights protection and the substantive grounds for judicial review (irrationality, procedural impropriety and illegality) to purely private activity. My focus is on actions and decision making with no taint of 'publicness' about them. I shall not, therefore, say much about 'vertical effect' questions, such as: whether a decision maker is a standard or core 'public authority' under section 6 of the Human Rights Act 1998, or whether a function performed by a private body is 'public' under Part 54 of the Civil Procedure Rules 1998 (CPR)[1] or 'of a public nature' under section 6 of the HRA, although I do have views on these matters. These issues are discussed by Feldman in his chapter in this volume. It is, I think, clear that if a private body is exercising coercive powers or authority that would normally be unlawful under statutory or common law powers, then the exercise of those powers will be regarded as a 'function of a public nature' under section 6 of the Human Rights Act 1998 (HRA) and a 'public function' under Part 54 of the CPR and the case law on amenability to judicial review.[2] Thus decisions on matters such as the restraint or coercive medication of mental patients in private hospitals or of prisoners; the licensing and disciplining of professionals by, for instance, the Inns of Court, the Law Society or the General Medical Council, and interference with rights of access to common law markets (the issue in the *Hammer Trout Farm* case[3]) are undoubtedly 'public'.

[1] The Civil Procedure Rules are regularly updated. The latest version is available at www.justice.gov.uk/civil/procrules_fin/index.htm.

[2] See *Hammer Trout Farm* case [2003] EWCA Civ 1056 and Oliver (2004). See discussion of these issues in Feldman's chapter in this volume.

[3] [2003] EWCA Civ 1056.

There is debate, which I shall not go into here, as to whether or when activity by private bodies that does not involve coercion or the exercise of normally unlawful authority is or should be judicially reviewable or subject to section 6 of the HRA. Here questions include: how relevant is the relationship between private service providers and standard public authorities, public financing, regulation of the private service provider, and so on.[4] My main reason for arguing, as I have done, that decisions other than those in the categories noted above by private bodies should not be subject to the claim for judicial review or treated as 'functions of a public nature' under the HRA is that I would regard it as circular to label such decisions as 'public' *merely* to expose them to the standards associated with judicial review and the direct effect of the Human Rights Act *without being precise about what the elements of 'publicness' are.*

The problem is that there are no satisfactory criteria for deciding whether a decision is 'public'. I do not have any *principled* objections to requiring private decision makers to comply with duties of fairness and reasonableness and so on which might be imposed in public law, though there are commonly *pragmatic* objections to such an extension. One of these is that in public law respondents are protected under CPR Part 54 by very short time limits, requirements for claimants to obtain permission to apply, and discretion as to the award of remedies. I would object to private respondents benefiting from such quasi-immunities.

There are also separation of powers issues here—whether or when it is appropriate for the courts, rather than Parliament and the executive, to extend the substantive principles of judicial review and human rights protection to private relationships. These can raise rather polycentric issues. I do have objections to labelling bodies 'public' simply to impose such obligations on them, because of the risk it poses of undermining pluralism in society by co-opting civil society organisations into the state, in effect nationalising them, by labelling them public and thus possibly reducing the sphere of pluralism itself.

It is worth noting at this point a trend in many jurisdictions (the USA being a striking exception) to extend constitutional or international *human rights* protections—which are normally assumed to have primarily vertical effect—to the private sphere.[5] This has been done in a range of ways, one of which has been to develop the common law or, in non-common law systems, civil or private law so as to protect rights 'horizontally'. This protection may be:

— direct (though possibly only if there is a lacuna in the ordinary law), as in Greece, India, Ireland, Italy, Spain and South Africa (constitutional rights) and France (ECHR rights);
— indirect via *interpretation* of ordinary law as in Greece and Israel (constitutional rights), Denmark, England and Wales and Spain (ECHR rights); or
— indirect via *development* of private law, as in Canada, Israel and New Zealand (constitutional rights), England and Wales (ECHR rights).[6]

[4] See Craig (2002), Feldman (in this volume) and Seventh Report of the Joint Committee on Human Rights (2003–04).
[5] See Oliver and Fedtke (2007).
[6] See Oliver and Fedtke (2007).

The horizontal effect of human rights raises concerns in many jurisdictions about interference with the law of contract and legal uncertainty. If horizontal effect of Convention rights were to be widely extended in the UK, issues as to unintended consequences and economic implications could arise. These are discussed below.

If judicial review principles were to be extended to private sector decision making, this would be consistent with trends in other areas of the law, for instance human rights, in some other jurisdictions *towards an integrated and nuanced approach to public and private activity and decision making*, often based on public policy and awareness of the scope for abuse of private power. I welcome such trends.

At this stage, a number of basic points need to be clarified—the meanings of 'administrative justice' in this context and the substantive principles it entails; the distinctions between decision making and action or inaction in implementing decisions; and the relevance of privatisation to our topic.

The Meanings of Administrative Justice

There are both procedural and substantive elements to administrative justice. *Procedurally*, it is generally taken to include the possibility of recourse to courts (whether by way of statutory appeal or judicial review) or tribunals or ombudsmen to challenge decision makers. This is a central aspect of administrative justice and one to which I shall return shortly. *Substantively*, administrative justice includes the imposition of certain duties on decision makers beyond, naturally, the duty to act within the bounds of 'legality'. These include duties to act fairly, both procedurally and substantively, reasonably and/or proportionately, and to take into account the interests of those affected by decisions and public interests. They are often referred to as duties of good administration.[7] The Parliamentary Ombudsman published her 'Principles of Good Administration' in March 2007,[8] many of which reflect the principles associated with judicial review, although they also include others of a 'non-legal' nature. These standards are central to the ways in which the English courts have developed their common law jurisdiction in judicial review to control broadly 'public' decision making and they extend into the standards by which ombudsmen, including for instance the Financial Services Ombudsman, deal with complaints.

We need to remember that the imposition of decision making duties in public law is not limited to the exercise of the common law jurisdiction in judicial review and, to the extent that they are relevant to our topic, to the HRA requirements. Similar duties are in fact embodied in *legislation* regulating the

[7] This phrase was first used by Galligan (1982).

[8] At the same time, the Parliamentary Ombudsman published 'Principles for Remedy' and 'Principles of Good Complaints Handling'. They were all reprinted with minor amendments in February 2009.

decision-making practices of many public bodies. The Franks Report[9] laid down duties of 'fairness, openness and impartiality'. These were accepted and are put into effect in the Tribunals and Inquires Act 1992, which consolidates provisions that were in the Tribunals and Inquiries Act 1958. For instance, section 10 of the 1992 Act imposes a duty on tribunals to give reasons for their decisions. Public inquiries into planning and compulsory purchase decisions are required to meet these standards. Such standards may also be reflected in the requirements imposed by regulators on those they regulate. Thus, the Financial Services Authority requires banks and other financial service providers to 'treat customers fairly'. And the Financial Ombudsman Service determines questions about decision making in private matters, which are discussed by Merricks in this volume. So my concern is not only with the possible development of *common law* horizontal effect. It also embraces statutory provisions for horizontal effect of standards of good administration and the development of soft law standards by ombudsmen.

But nowadays administrative justice extends beyond these principles of good administration: under section 6 of the HRA it is unlawful for a public authority to act incompatibly with the Convention rights that are incorporated into UK law in various ways in that Act. It is significant that this provision imposes limits on the powers of public authorities—it is not concerned with decision making but with action that might breach a person's rights under the ECHR. Hence in this consideration of the horizontal effect of administrative justice we shall consider the application of both substantive principles of judicial review and human rights in the private sphere.

Decision Making

It follows that we need to separate *decision making* by private bodies, which may lead to action or inaction, from action or inaction itself. Action or inaction flowing from a decision may be unlawful and may therefore give rise to a remedy such as declaration, injunction, specific performance or damages. Such is the case, for example, if action taken on the basis of a private decision is in breach of contract, or if it is or would be tortious, or in breach of statutory requirements such as those of employment law, landlord and tenant law, or in breach of equitable requirements in relation to trusts or directors' duties and so on.

When discussing decision making, rather than action implementing a decision, I am concerned with requirements that certain procedures be followed or that certain mental processes take place before a decision is taken that affects another person negatively. I hope I may be excused for summarising these briefly so that we can have them in mind when considering their possible extension to horizontal

[9] *Report of the Committee on Administrative Tribunals and* Enquiries, Cmnd. 218 (1957).

decision making. These requirements include, in public law: (i) giving a person who may be adversely affected by a decision an opportunity to know what the case against him or her is and to make representations, possibly the giving of reasons for decisions and so on—generally duties of procedural propriety; and (ii) the taking into account of relevant matters and the exclusion of irrelevant matters, respecting the legitimate expectations of those affected by a decision—rationality and substantive fairness. These are obvious concerns of the Administrative Court in the exercise of its *common law* judicial review jurisdiction. They are intrinsic to that subject. But, as we shall see, similar standards apply *at common law* in some private decision making. My position, then, is that there is considerable potential for these principles to be extended further into private decision making. But, as indicated above, major issues arise as to whether, to what extent, and in what circumstances, their extension to private decision making should be done by statute or by the courts or via ombudsmen.

There are significant differences between public and private decision making.

In public decision making, issues may arise as to the need for the courts to defer to the decisions of public bodies on the grounds of their democratic accountability. In private decision making, there will be no case for deference to decision makers on that ground. There may, however, be a need for a version of deference based on the decision maker's expertise, managerial prerogatives and so on.

In public decision making, according to the orthodox view, public bodies do not have rights or interests of their own—they should not 'spin' information in order to exonerate themselves or protect themselves from political criticism, or indulge their own moral values without linking them to the public interest, for instance.[10] And public bodies do not count as 'victims' under Article 34 of the European Convention on Human Rights and so cannot claim human rights protection. The balance to be achieved in public decision making is between private rights and interests, on the one hand, and public interests, on the other. This is discussed by Mullen in this volume. In making the balance, a reasonableness or proportionality test is applied by the courts. In private decision making, by contrast, both parties have rights and interests. Conflicts between the rights and interests of decision makers and those affected by their decisions will arise and will have to be resolved by a court. This too may involve a proportionality test, but one that focuses on the extent to which one party's rights or interests may be restricted for the sake of the other party's rights or interests.

Challenges to public decisions must, since *O'Reilly v Mackman*, be brought under Part 54 of the CPR in the Administrative Court. Challenges to private decisions may be made in the Queens Bench or Chancery Division of the High Court, and possibly in the county court. So there will be no requirement for permission

[10] *Derbyshire CC v Times Newspapers* [1993] AC 534; *Griffiths v Smith* [1941] AC 170, 205–06 (Lord Porter); *Padfield v Minister of Agriculture* [1968] AC 997 (Lord Upjohn); *R v Somerset CC, ex p Fewings* [1995] 1 All ER 513 (Laws J); *Whalley v Watson*, The Times 21 March 2000. See also Oliver (2000a).

to be obtained to proceed against a private decision maker and the normal limitation period will apply.

In public decision cases, the remedies of the prerogative orders will be available, plus injunctions and declarations, but not damages. Where private decisions are challenged, the prerogative orders will not be available, but injunctions and declarations will be; if those remedies are not suitable, damages may even be awarded.

The Human Rights Act 1998

The HRA does not provide for direct horizontal effect: as we have noted, section 6 provides in effect that 'public authorities' must respect Convention rights. The Act does, however, require judges to take some steps to extend human rights protection to the private sphere. Under section 3, the courts are under a duty of rights-compatible statutory interpretation, a duty that applies in all cases and not only those where the respondent is a public authority—this is a form of indirect interpretive horizontal effect.[11] And, under section 6, the courts as public authorities are under a duty not to act unlawfully by acting incompatibly with Convention rights. This has been taken to mean that the courts may develop the common law so as to provide private sphere protection for Convention rights, for example in relation to privacy.[12] We may refer to this as a 'developmental indirect horizontal effect'. These provisions in the HRA give effect and statutory expression to a new and important public policy in favour of the protection of human rights across the legal system, in both public and private law, and in statute based law, common law and equity.

Clearly if a private body *acts* in breach of the Convention rights of another person, the courts will consider whether that breach constitutes a tort or another wrong for which a remedy may be awarded. In so doing, they may have to carry out a proportionality exercise in which they weigh up the interests of both parties and any public interest allowed for in the Convention. They will not be concerned with the decision-making process of the respondent. If a private *decision* to act in breach of Convention rights as they are protected under sections 3 and 6 of the HRA has been made and not yet implemented, a court would consider whether a preventative remedy by way of injunction or declaration should be made. Again, they will not be concerned with the decision-making process of the respondent—merely requiring private decision makers to *take into account the Convention rights of individuals when making decisions* would not, in itself, provide substantial or substantive protection to those rights. In human rights cases it is the *courts* which have to decide what protection Convention rights require and to balance conflicts between private parties' Convention rights, or the Convention rights of

[11] See eg *Ghaidan v Godin Mendoza* [2004] AC 557.

[12] See *Venables v News Group Newspapers* [2001] 1 All ER 908; *Campbell v Mirror Group Newspapers* [2004] 2 AC 457; *Douglas v Hello! (No 3)* [2006] QB 125 (CA).

one party as against the interests of another, and the public interests which many Convention rights refer to, such as protection of health and safety and the rights and freedoms of others, and to award remedies.

Remedies

It is central to the jurisdiction in public law judicial review cases that the courts will not substitute their own view of what decision the body should take, but will, rather, impose procedures and reasoning processes on the decision maker. This position is based on separation of powers: most decision-making powers are conferred on public bodies by statute and it would be flying in the face of the statute for the courts to usurp the statutory powers of the public body and substitute their own decisions.

There need not be the same inhibitions about usurping decision-making powers exercised by private bodies where the courts impose duties of fairness and rationality on their decision making. The powers of private decision makers are normally inherent and recognised at common law, or derived from contract, trust deeds, articles of association, etc, rather than from statute alone. Thus the considerations which preclude the courts from substituting their own view and awarding damages, for instance, or other remedies for a wrongly taken public decision do not normally apply to private decision making. By way of example, in employment cases, the court or tribunal will decide whether a dismissal was unfair, and award a remedy accordingly, and will not normally remit the decision to the employer to remake it. If a decision has been taken in breach of a fair procedure but it is not clear whether, had a fair procedure been followed, a different decision would have been made, the courts may award damages for the loss of a chance of a favourable decision.[13]

On the subject of remedies, we shall consider in due course whether remedies—and, if so, which remedies—may be granted against private decision makers in the absence of a normal cause of action, such as a claim for breach of express or implied contractual terms or restraint of trade.

In cases where the courts exercise their functions under section 6 of the Human Rights Act in developing the common law to extend human rights protection indirectly, the remedies available will depend upon the facts: if the action complained of is, for instance, tortious (as in some privacy cases) or in breach of an express or implied term of a contract, then damages may be awarded. Other private law remedies that may be suitable include declarations, injunctions, and specific performance. If the matter is resolved by a compatible interpretation of a statutory provision, the statute will govern the remedy. Thus, in landlord and tenant cases, this may involve granting a surviving same-sex partner security of tenure—as in *Godin v Ghaidan Mendoza*, discussed below.

[13] See *Chaplin v Hicks* [1911] 2 KB 786; for awards of damages for breach of duties of natural justice see the Scottish cases of *Tait v Central Radio Taxis (Tollcross) Ltd* 1989 SC4 (First Division), and *McMillan v Free Church of Scotland* 1861 SC 1314.

Privatisation: a Red Herring?

One of the issues considered in this book is the impact of *privatisation* on the scope of administrative justice (see chapter by Gamble and Thomas in this volume). My own view is that the history of an enterprise and its 'privatisation' in the context of the possible imposition of good administration and human rights standards on private decision making is rather a red herring. A very wide range of economic activities in the British economy were once in public ownership and have since been privatised. I do not see how that history itself should affect the extent to which duties of good administration and respect for human rights do or should extend to decision making in that enterprise once it is in the private sector. For instance, parcel delivery, coal mining, iron and steel and car manufacturing were all in public ownership many years ago, but no-one would suggest, I think, that for that reason the companies involved today should be subject to duties of good administration or respect for human rights which other, never-nationalised companies should not be subject to.

As we all know, there have been cases about whether formerly publicly-owned and run services, once privatised, are under the same duty to respect human rights and good administration standards as they were when those services were publicly owned, on the basis that they are performing functions of a public nature or public functions. I have already indicated that I do not propose to go over the case law or the academic commentary on it here. But this question as to whether *privatised* bodies or bodies contracting with public authorities to provide services are to be regarded as performing functions of a public nature is, it seems to me, largely a short-term, transitional problem. In a few years time we shall probably find that those depending on such bodies for their care, education, etc, were not involved with these bodies at the time of privatisation and it would be completely anomalous if residents in care homes that were once, perhaps twenty years previously, in public ownership, had greater rights to benefit from duties of good administration and respect for their rights on the part of the service providers than those in care homes that were in private ownership before the period of public sector provision, or that were established only recently. And given that core public bodies contract out functions such as cleaning, rubbish collection and so on which are 'acts' the nature of which is private under section 6 of the HRA,[14] the mere fact of contracting out or privatisation cannot be determinative of the duties of the private sector bodies providing those services. What is important is the impact of these decisions on individuals or on the public interest. It is much more fruitful, then, to focus on the possible development of duties of good administration and respect for human rights in purely private sector decision making, regardless of a history of privatisation.

[14] See discussion of this in *London and Quadrant Housing Trust v Weaver, Equality and Human Rights Commission intervening* [2009] EWCA Civ 587, [28], [39]–[41], [73]–[79] (Elias LJ).

Towards 'Direct Horizontal Effect' of Principles of Good Administration

Our principal concern then is whether private sector enterprises, charitable or commercial, that have power to make decisions, which can adversely affect individuals in their security or other interests,[15] or the general public interest, in important ways should be subject to duties of good administration in their decision making. The bodies that are in this position of power include most employers (and employment is already regulated so that these duties broadly apply to decision making by employers), landlords (and landlord and residential tenant relationships are also regulated by statute) and bodies that provide or withhold services of special importance to individuals, for instance low cost housing, private hospitals, care homes, schools for the disabled, rail and bus services, universities and so on. Anti-discrimination law applies to these so that some protection from substantively arbitrary decisions is built into the law already.

Characteristics of many of these services are: (a) that they cannot necessarily be afforded by those who require them; (b) there is strong competition for them, especially where quality is variable; and (c) there is a shortage of them—the market does not and cannot meet everyone's needs. They are not however monopolies, so the 'monopoly' case for imposing special decision-making duties on them does not apply.

My main concern from here on then is with whether, when and how good administration standards of the kinds applied in judicial review can or should be applied to purely private—horizontal—decision making.

Developing the Common Law

If no legislation has been passed on matters such as decision making by private bodies exercising powers which impact in important ways on individuals, then the question arises of whether or in what circumstances it is appropriate for the courts, in the exercise of their power to develop the common law, to impose good administration standards on private decision makers. There is, in my view, ample case law on this to lay the foundations for common law and equitable development in this direction in certain situations and relationships.

It will help at this point to review the case law on private sector decision making, and in particular the extension of duties of procedural fairness and reasonableness to these processes.

Much of the case law on decision making by *private* bodies goes back to the pre-*O'Reilly v Mackman*[16] period, and in particular to a line of cases in which

[15] Honoré (1982).
[16] [1983] 2 AC 237.

Lord Denning and others elaborated principles under which the Queen's Bench Division or county courts could, in effect, impose duties of good administration on decision making in the private sphere—what we would now call horizontal decision making. However, some of the cases go back to the late nineteenth century. There is not the space here to examine that case law in detail,[17] but briefly the position before *O'Reilly* was as follows.

Administrative law was not at that time a sub-species of public law. Lord Denning claimed, in 1971, that '[i]t may truly be said that we have developed a system of administrative law. These developments have been most marked in the review of decisions of statutory bodies: but they apply also to domestic bodies'.[18]

Principles of good administration, especially the duty to act fairly and reasonably,[19] apply (inter alia) to self-regulatory bodies set up by powerful associations such as the Stock Exchange, the Jockey Club, and the Football Association, but also to other bodies such as trade unions when exercising disciplinary powers or making decisions that would negatively affect their members or officials,[20] a pension fund making a decision about whether to deprive a person of a pension,[21] and a mutual insurance society deciding whether to expel a member.[22]

The courts' jurisdiction to impose these principles did (and does) not necessarily rest on express or implied contractual terms or restraint of trade.[23] The legal justification for the court's imposition of duties of good administration was the 'righting of wrongs',[24] for instance to prevent abuse of monopoly power,[25] to protect against restraints of trade[26] and to protect property rights,[27] a person's right or liberty[28] to work,[29] reputation, dignity and status.[30] It is difficult to avoid here a parallel with the development of the law of negligence, which reached the point where liability arises if it is fair, just and reasonable to impose it.

The thread that runs through the cases imposing these duties on private sector decision making is essentially public policy—these bodies exercise power[31] that can 'make or mar' a person.[32] It is the impact on the object of the decision that

[17] For fuller discussion see Oliver (1997, 1998, 1999, 2000b). For a summary of the position in relation to natural justice, see Jackson (1973).

[18] Per Lord Denning in *Breen v Amalgamated Engineering Union* [1971] 1 All ER 1148, 1153.

[19] Megarry V-C in *McInnes v Onslow Fane* [1978] 1 WLR 1520, 1530.

[20] Lord Denning in *Breen* at 1154; see also *Stevenson v United Road Transport Union* [1977] ICR 893.

[21] *L'Association de Bienfaisance et de Retraite de la Police de Montréal* [1906] AC 535, 538–40 (PC).

[22] *Wood v Woad* (1874) LR 9 Ex 190.

[23] *Nagle v Feilden; McInnes v Onslow Fane, Bradley v Jockey Club* and *Mullins v Jockey Club*, below.

[24] See *Bagg's case* (1615) Co Rep 936 and 77 ER 1273; *R v Barker* (1763) 3 Burr 1265.

[25] *Nagle v Feilden* [1966] 1 All ER 689.

[26] Ibid at 639; *Enderby Town FC* at 219; *Dickson v Pharmaceutical Society* [1970] AC 403.

[27] *Nagle v Feilden* at 694.

[28] See *McInnes v Onslow Fane* [1978] 1 WLR 1520, 1530 (Megarry V-C).

[29] *Nagle v Feilden* at 639. But *cf Mullins v Jockey Club* [2006] EWHC 986 (QB).

[30] *Breen* at 1156–57.

[31] *Lee v Showman's Guild* at 1181 (power to affect the livelihood); *Nagle v Feilden* at 694. *McInnes v Onslow Fane* at 1530; *Enderby Town FC v FA* [1971] 1 All ER 215, 219.

[32] *Breen*, above, at 1154. Compare the discussion of ombudsmen by Merricks in this volume.

gives rise to the decision making duties, based more generally on a developing specific public policy to protect individuals against the abuse of power.[33]

The line of cases on which the foregoing propositions are based came to an end—until recently—when *O'Reilly v Mackman* introduced a doctrine of *procedural* exclusivity requiring public law cases to be brought under the then RSC Order 77, now CPR Part 54. Quite illogically this case has been understood to change *substantive* private law. The point was made by Webster J in *Shearson Lehman Hutton Inc v Maclaine Watson and Co Ltd* that the difference between public and private law rights had to do with the procedures by which they might be protected rather than their substance.[34] The fact that proceedings by writ or originating summons could no longer be taken in public law cases after *O'Reilly* was somehow assumed to mean that complaints of breach of natural justice or unreasonableness could not be brought by writ or originating summons even in private law, and that, therefore, these principles only applied in public law. *O'Reilly* stifled what had, in my view, been healthy, incremental common law development of substantive decision-making principles, which was not limited to what we now call public law and did not entail a substantive as opposed to procedural and remedial public–private divide. A simple example will illustrate this: Jackson's *Natural Justice*, published in 1973, made no distinction between public law and private law and identified duties of natural justice in trade union decision making, decisions on the appointment of a vicar by a bishop, and decisions by the National Association for Mental Health, Universities, the Greyhound Racing Association, the Football Association, and the Jockey Club. Not all of these rested on contract or were exercises of coercive power or special authority or decisions we would now regard as public or of a public nature.

In fact the principles being elaborated in pre-*O'Reilly* case law have plenty of potential for development and could go some way towards resolving some of the problems arising from the fact that important services are increasingly provided by private bodies which do not, as, noted above, comfortably meet either the public function or the function of a public nature tests in the CPR and in section 6 of the HRA. Whether they should be so developed is a matter we shall come to shortly.

Recent Common Law Developments: Bradley v Jockey Club *and* Mullins v Jockey Club

In the last five years or so, there has been a flurry of case law in this area, especially in relation to the Jockey Club.[35] In *Bradley v Jockey Club*,[36] a jockey complained of

[33] *Nagle v Feilden* at 694; *McInnes v Onslow Fane* [1978] 1 WLR 1520, 1530; *Enderby Town FC v FA* [1971] 1 All ER 215, 219. See also Sedley (2000).

[34] [1989] 2 Lloyds Rep 570, 625.

[35] There has also been a body of case law on the powers of independent schools to exclude pupils and the way in which statutory provisions and/or public law notions of fairness may be read across to the contract between the school and the parent: see *Russell Gray v Marlborough College* [2006] EWCA Civ 1262.

[36] [2005] EWCA Civ 1056.

his disqualification by a Disciplinary Committee of the Jockey Club, upheld by an Appeal Board, as a result of findings that he had been guilty of corrupt conduct in the sport for some years. He claimed an injunction and damages for breach of contract against the Jockey Club. Bradley lost the case on the merits, but the Court of Appeal agreed with Stephen Richards J, who had heard the case at first instance, that the court had a supervisory jurisdiction in the matter, meaning that the court could impose principles of good administration on the decision maker in question. Bradley based his claim in part on terms and implied terms in the Jockey Club rules, and in part, relying on *Nagle v Feilden*, on his 'fundamental right to work in his business'. The Court of Appeal and Richards J rejected this latter basis for the exercise of jurisdiction.

Richards J found that the Appeal Board was a separate body from the Jockey Club; its decisions were reviewable, but on a non-contractual basis. The normal judicial review principles applied. This is an important point since the Appeal Board was not exercising a public function in this private law action. The contractual obligation of the Jockey Club, Richards J found, was to give effect to the Appeal Board's decisions so far as they were lawful. He stated:

> 37. That brings me to the nature of the courts' supervisory jurisdiction over such a decision. The most important point, it seems to me, is that it is *supervisory*. The function of the court is not to take the primary decision but to ensure that the primary decision-maker has operated within lawful limits. It is a review function, very similar to that of the court on judicial review. Indeed, given the difficulties that sometimes arise in drawing the precise boundary between the two, I would consider it surprising and unsatisfactory if a private law claim in relation to the decision of a domestic body required the court to adopt a materially different approach from a judicial review claim in relation to the decision of a public body. In each case the essential concern should be with the lawfulness of the decision taken: whether the procedure was fair, whether there was any error of law, whether any exercise of judgement or discretion fell within the limits open to the decision maker and so forth. …
>
> 40. …[T]he supervisory role of the courts should not involve any higher or more intensive standard of review when dealing with a non-contractual than a contractual claim.

The Court of Appeal approved of Richards J's approach, and also agreed with Richards J that, given the facts of the appellant's conduct, a penalty which deprived him of his right to work was the only appropriate one.

Lord Phillips MR gave the main judgment in this case, and Scott Baker and Buxton LJJ agreed. Buxton LJ added, briefly, that *Nagle v Feilden* went no further than to say that the court could intervene when there was a general and discriminatory rule preventing a certain category of people practising a profession irrespective of their behaviour, their competence, or their disciplinary record. It did not establish a general 'right to work'. By implication the justifications for the decision in *Nagle* were restraint of trade and/or general public policy.

In a more recent case, *Mullins v The Jockey Club,*[37] the disqualification of a horse after a urine test disclosed drugs was challenged. The case was brought by a claim for judicial review. Stanley Burnton J held that the Jockey Club and its Appeal Board were not public authorities for the purposes of proceedings under CPR Part 54 and transferred the proceedings to the Queen's Bench Division.[38] Burnton J accepted the submission for the claimant that the court would interfere with a decision of a body such as the Appeal Board of the Jockey Club if that decision was arbitrary or capricious or was based on a misinterpretation of the applicable rules of the sporting body in question. Significantly, counsel for the Jockey Club accepted that the QBD had a supervisory jurisdiction over tribunals such as the Appeal Board, *irrespective of the existence of a contract* between the claimant and the tribunal or the body appointing it. This is in line with the approach of Richards J in *Bradley.*

Burnton J expressed the provisional view that 'there is no jurisdictional (in the narrow sense of the word) boundary to the power of the Court to grant declaratory relief in this context'.[39] 'The importance of the challenged decision to the parties is an important factor, and I do not think that the extent or the exercise of the jurisdiction [to award declaratory relief] is to be determined ... by the correct interpretation of [the rules]'.[40] This decision opens up considerable scope for the extension of good administration standards to horizontal decision making and for providing remedies in case of a breach, especially where a body is exercising disciplinary powers that will have a serious impact on an individual, for instance on the ability to earn a living.

On this basis, the jurisdiction to grant declaratory relief does not depend upon the existence of a contract but rather on the *impact of the decision on those affected.* That factor justifies the jurisdiction to grant a remedy.

We move here into the rather technical area of the jurisdiction of the courts to grant remedies such as declarations, interlocutory injunctions, and the prerogative orders in the absence of a cause of action in contract or tort or for equitable wrongs. We do not have the time to explore these issues here, though I have done so elsewhere.[41] In summary, there is authority for the view that declarations may be granted in the absence of a cause of action, and that interlocutory injunctions may be granted in support of claims for declarations. This approach was adopted by Carnwath J in *Stevenage Borough FC Ltd v Football League Ltd*[42] for instance. Damages however will not be awarded in the absence of an action in contract or tort.

[37] [2006] EWHC 986 (QB).

[38] Ibid at [34]–[35].

[39] Ibid at [39].

[40] For a summary of the position, see Oliver (1998: 218–23).

[41] See ibid.

[42] The Times 1 August 1996 (not otherwise reported, but discussed in Oliver *Common Values and the Public-Private Divide* (1999) at 211–12 and 221–22; and see Court of Appeal Report (1997) 9 *Administrative Law* 907.

Some Comparative Points

It is worth noting at this point that in Scotland the jurisdiction going by the name of 'judicial review' imposes roughly the same substantive good administration standards as apply in England and Wales, but it extends to the private sphere and does not attach the label 'public' to the decisions and functions that are subjected to these standards.[43] A judicial review or contractual jurisdiction could be available in relation to a decision of an arbiter not to proceed,[44] decisions of the Roman Catholic Church,[45] the Scottish Football Association,[46] a taxi service membership association,[47] the Free Church of Scotland,[48] the Scottish Women's Amateur Athletic Association,[49] a local Labour Party branch[50] and the Scottish branch of the British Show Jumping Association.[51] In only some of these cases has the court's jurisdiction been based in membership contracts.[52]

In New Zealand, too, much of what we regard as substantive judicial review applies to private, horizontal decision making. For instance trade unions, the kennel club, a public company, an underwriters' association, and a working men's club.[53]

We in England and Wales could go down that road too, though cautiously. In other words we—through the courts' development of the common law and, where appropriate, Parliamentary legislation (as has already been put in place in relation to employment and residential tenancies) should develop private law, not public law, so as to extend these duties to much private decision making.

Issues for the Public–Private Divide

In even suggesting that principles of good administration normally associated with public law might be extended to—or, more accurately, might apply to and be further developed in respect of—private sector decision making I am raising issues about the public–private divide and whether it would be appropriate in principle to cross it. My view, as I guess many may know, is that there is no public–private *divide*. Since that view has been criticised on various grounds, I would like to take this opportunity to clarify my position. Briefly, in suggesting

43 See Oliver (1998: Annex); *West v Secretary of State for Scotland* 1992 SC 385. And see Lords Hope and Rodger in *Davidson v Scottish Ministers* [2005] UKHL 74.

44 *Forbes v Underwood* (1886) 13 R 465.

45 *McDonald v Burns* 1940 SC 325.

46 *St Johnstone FC v Scottish FA* 1965 SLT 171.

47 *Tait v Central Radio Taxi (Tollcross) Ltd* 1989 SC 4 (First Division).

48 *McMillan v Free Church of Scotland* 1861 SC 1314 (Court of Session).

49 *Gunstone v Scottish Women's Amateur Athletic Association* 1987 SLT 611.

50 *Brown v Executive Committee of the Edinburgh District Labour Party* 1995 SLT 985.

51 *Lennox v Scottish Branch of the British Show Jumping Assocn* 1996 SLT 353.

52 See *Breen*, above, comments in the decision in *Lennox*, above, and *McMillan v Free Church of Scotland*, above.

53 See A Beck and others (2010) *McGechan on Procedure* (looseleaf), para JA3.06.07 and cases cited there; Oliver (2002: 91), Rishworth (2007).

that there is no public–private divide I am not saying that something called public law and something called private law do not exist. Nor am I saying that they are the same. Let me illustrate the point by analogy: it is clear that the law of marriage and child law both exist and that they are not the same. They overlap. And it would be hard and pointless to seek to separate them into watertight categories. I am saying, then, that public and private law cannot be *divided* from one another in any categorical, significant or meaningful way and thus that an integrated approach to the substantive law of decision making is wise.

For instance, while it might be possible to separate purely 'public' institutions, such as ministers and statutory regulators, from others, the implications of such an institutional distinction do not separate these institutions in other ways from private ones. In our constitutional theory, purely public bodies do not have their own selfish interests—they are supposed to be acting altruistically and promoting public interests. But what we call public law is not limited to the observation that public bodies have no interests. The principles of altruism and selflessness are not the essence of public law. Nor are those principles confined in their application to 'public law' cases. The law relating to fiduciaries and charities also imposes duties of altruism and selflessness on private decision makers.

Public bodies are under duties of fairness and rationality when making decisions that affect others adversely; but equity imposes similar duties on fiduciaries, trustees and company directors. And, of course, public bodies are subject to much of the same private law of contract, tort, property law, etc, as binds private bodies.

Public bodies are expected to operate in a non-partisan way. But that is not the essence of public law: so are many private bodies—charities, non-governmental organisations and so on.

Public bodies enjoy some quasi-immunities, for instance under CPR Part 54, but it does not follow that that is a good thing, or that private bodies may not enjoy somewhat similar privileges, for example where discretionary equitable remedies are sought.

Cane (2003) identifies some peculiarly public law values—openness etc. But the fact that these values are important, special and central in public law does not, surely, prevent their being extended in varying degrees to private law?

Towards the Horizontal Effect of Human Rights

In a number of cases the courts have developed a private law right to privacy,[54] despite the fact that in principle the rights under the European Convention on Human Rights have only vertical effect in the UK. The courts have taken into account the facts that Article 8 of the ECHR provides that 'Everyone has the right to respect for his private and family life, his home and his correspondence' and that by section 6 of the Human Rights Act they, as public authorities, act unlawfully

[54] See *Venables v NGN*, *Godin v Ghaidan Mendoza* and *Campbell v MGN* in n 11 above.

if they act incompatibly with Convention rights. Without actually developing a right to privacy in so many words, the courts have interpreted legislation compatibly with Article 8 (as in *Godin v Ghaidan Mendoza*, where the surviving partner of a same sex couple was held to be entitled not to be discriminated against on grounds of sexual orientation when claiming the right to remain in the rented home of his deceased partner), and developed the law relating to confidentiality (an equitable right) so as to protect the rights of individuals against press intrusions, as in the *Venables* and *Campbell* cases. In the latter class of case the courts have had to balance the rights of the press against those of individuals.

The Care Home Cases

The above have been cases where the rights and interests of the parties have had to be weighed up so as to produce proportionate results, but broader 'polycentric' issues have not arisen. There are other situations, also involving Article 8 of the ECHR, in which complex public interests issues do arise. One area in which this causes problems is the provision of care homes. In a number of cases residents of private care homes have claimed that their removal from their homes would constitute an interference with their Article 8 rights.[55] To succeed they have had to claim that the provider of the accommodation is performing a function of a public nature under section 6 of the HRA. This issue is discussed at length in Feldman's chapter in this volume. The case law had developed so that commercial and independent charitable care homes were not considered to be performing functions of a public nature when housing residents, whether those residents were self-paying or paid for by their local authorities under duties under the National Assistance Act 1948. As a result of the controversy caused by these decisions section 145 was inserted into the Health and Social Care Act 2008 at a late stage of the legislative process, to the effect that care homes are to be taken to be exercising a function of a public nature in providing for residents who are paid for under the 1948 Act. Thus when such a care home wishes to remove a resident the resident may apply to the court alleging a breach of Article 8. That of course is not the end of the story as it does not follow that the resident will be entitled to remain in the home. The court will have to balance the claims of the resident against a range of other considerations. On the face of it section 145 provides desirable protection for publicly paid-for residents. But let us consider the implications. My point is that the issues here are complex and a more tailor made, well considered response to problems which are, essentially, about security of tenure in care homes, ought to have been devised.

First, section 145 produces a highly anomalous position in that self-paying residents in a care home will not receive the same protection as paid-for ones, despite the fact that the self-paying residents may be just as vulnerable, for instance if they are disabled or lacking in family support or friends to help them.

[55] See *YL v Birmingham CC* [2008] UKHL 27; *R (Heather) v Leonard Cheshire Foundation* [2002] EWCA Civ 366.

But quite apart from that, the questions whether residents of care homes should have security of tenure, and if so, how it should be provided for, raise a large number of issues of public policy. Slotting a section into a bill at a late stage is not necessarily the right way to go about giving horizontal effect to a human right to respect for one's home.

If a government were minded to introduce legislation regulating the ability of private care homes to move residents to other homes, or to evict them, there would normally be consultation leading to a White Paper dealing with the issues prior to the introduction of a bill into Parliament. Care homes and their representative bodies, care home 'customers'—the elderly, disabled and so on and organisations representing their interests such as Age Concern—and their representatives and family members, local authorities and others who would be affected in the discharge of their social service commitments and their expenditure by a change in the law, would all contribute to the consultation.

This is, essentially, a polycentric issue. The interests and rights of residents under Article 8 ECHR to respect for their homes and private lives have to be balanced against a whole range of other considerations:

— the privacy, property and management rights of the owners;
— the impact of residential security of tenure on the economic viability of a care home;
— whether and when it would be appropriate to expect owners of care homes to provide services, eg full nursing care, which they have not contracted to provide or are not in a position to provide;
— the effect of security of tenure and regulation on the supply of care home places;
— the wider public interest in encouraging or not encouraging the provision of private care homes;
— the interests of local authorities in being able to find places they can afford to pay for in private care homes;
— public interests in the modernisation of care home provision, which may require that the owners obtain vacant possession of rooms.

If after due consultation the government were to introduce legislation on the matter and it were passed—after the airing of such issues again in Parliament—the Act would have to give jurisdiction to the county courts or establish a tribunal to deal with disputes. It would no doubt provide decision makers and courts or tribunals with guidance as to the circumstances in which residents could or could not be moved or evicted; it would set up appeal procedures and so on. It would specify procedures for bringing cases before the courts, and the remedies available both to residents and to care home owners—possession orders, compensation and so on.

As long as such requirements for consultation and careful consideration are met, I would have no principled objection to legislation providing for residents of care homes to enjoy security of tenure. There are, however, arguments both ways about how such problems should be dealt with, and they should be carefully considered before the law is developed so as to extend human rights into the private sphere, whether by statute or common law.

Summary and Conclusions

The principles of good administration normally associated with public law have only recently, and mistakenly, been considered to be exclusively applicable in public law. Before the *O'Reilly* decision, these principles applied to a range of private decision making, especially in relation to disciplinary and restraint of trade decisions by domestic bodies. But the imposition of duties of fair and rational decision making has not been the sole creation of the common law. Parliament has also imposed statutory, non-contractual duties of fairness and rationality on some powerful private bodies. Employment statutes impose such duties on employers in many situations, especially relating to discipline and dismissal. The Housing Acts impose duties of fairness and reasonableness on certain landlords, for instance requiring notice to quit and in effect reasonable grounds for seeking possession, which would include rent arrears and nuisance to adjoining neighbours caused by tenants.

In recent years the case law has developed further, especially in relation to sporting bodies. Thus duties of fairness and rationality need not be consensual: they may be non-contractual and *imposed*, for instance in equity or as a matter of public policy.

In relation to rights of privacy and respect for one's home under Article 8 the courts have developed horizontal effect cautiously by statutory interpretation and incremental change to the common law principles. But since horizontally effective human rights enable the courts to substitute their own views for those of private decision makers, the extension of the horizontal effect of human rights is far more complex than the extension of principles of good administration to private decision making.

In extending the horizontal effect of good administration standards and human rights into the private sphere, the courts should be sensitive to the rather complex legal, political, social and economic issues that such developments can involve. The relationships that are at stake in the sporting cases and those involving the press are bipartite, not polycentric. But extension of horizontal effect, without proper legislative provision, into many other areas should be done with caution.

References

Cane, P (2003) 'Accountability and the Public/Private Distinction' in N Bamforth and P Leyland (eds), *Public Law in a Multi-layered Constitution* (Oxford, Hart Publishing).

Craig, P (2002) 'Contracting Out, the Human Rights Act and the Scope of Judicial Review' 118 LQR 551.

Honoré, T (1982) *The Quest for Security* (London, Stevens).

Jackson, P (1973) *Natural Justice* (London, Sweet & Maxwell).

Galligan, D (1982) 'Judicial review and the Textbook Writers' 2 *Oxford Journal of Legal Studies* 257.

Beck, A, Broadmore, TG, Dobson, R, Finlayson, C, Radich, P and Wild, J (2010) *McGechan on Procedure* (Wellington, Thomson Reuters New Zealand).

Oliver, D (1997) 'The underlying values of public and private law' in M Taggart (ed), *The Province of Administrative Law* (Oxford: Hart Publishing).

—— (1998) *Common Values and the Public-Private Divide* (London, Butterworths).

—— (1999) 'Lord Denning and the Public/Private Divide', *Denning Law Journal* 71.

—— (2000a) 'The Frontiers of the State: Public Authorities and Public Functions under the Human Rights Act' PL 476.

—— (2000b) 'Review of Non-statutory Discretions' in C Forsyth (ed), *Judicial Review and the Constitution* (Oxford, Hart Publishing) 307.

—— (2002) 'Public Law Procedures and Remedies: Do we need them?' PL 91.

—— (2004) 'Functions of a Public Nature under the Human Rights Act' PL 329.

Oliver, D and Fedtke, J (eds) (2007) *Human Rights and the Private Sphere: A Comparative Study* (London, Routledge-Cavendish).

Rishworth, P (2007) 'New Zealand: Taking Human Rights into the Private Sphere' in D Oliver and J Fedtke (eds), *Human Rights and the Private Sphere: A Comparative Study* (London, Routledge-Cavendish).

Sedley, S (2000) 'Public and Private Power' in C Forsyth (ed), *Judicial Review and the Constitution* (Oxford, Hart Publishing).

11

Where and How Should the Private Sector Ombudsman Be Seen in the Administrative Justice Landscape?

WALTER MERRICKS

Introduction

In this paper I seek to explore the place of private sector ombudsman schemes (and in particular the Financial Ombudsman Service) in the world of administrative justice; their particular features and their contribution, together with those of public sector ombudsmen, to administrative justice; and the extent to which private ombudsman decision making contributes to the notion, explored in Dawn Oliver's paper, of a horizontal effect of administrative justice principles.

The Administrative Justice System

It was in the White Paper *Transforming Public Services: Complaints, Redress, and Tribunals* (Department for Constitutional Affairs 2004) that the first connection was made in the official policy literature between the dispute resolution model of private sector ombudsmen and the world of tribunals and administrative justice. The White Paper contained a description of the operating model of the Financial Ombudsman Service, and drew attention to some of its key features (ibid, paras 4.13–4.21). These it saw as the inquisitorial style, the graded tiers of intervention from conciliation to final ombudsman decision, the paper and telephone interaction, and the absence of hearings. It contrasted these with the adversarial, hearing-based model operated by tribunals. The White Paper called for a new approach to resolving disputes, and promised that the Department would take the lead on coordinating redress policy across Government. It committed the Government to taking 'a systemic view across the various means of tackling disputes, and the roles of the different organisations that provide them (courts, ombudsmen, tribunals, independent complaint handlers etc)' (para 6.3).

The legislation that followed, the Tribunals, Courts and Enforcement Act 2007, established the Administrative Justice and Tribunals Council (AJTC) to carry forward this work, and gave the new council a remit that requires it to keep under review the administrative justice system, by which is meant 'the overall system by which decisions of an administrative or executive nature are made, including the systems for resolving disputes and airing grievances in relation to such decisions'.[1] So the remit of the AJTC is not only to look at how disputes about primary decision making are resolved, but also to examine primary decision making itself.

Public Sector, Public Services, Public Nature, Public Law

It is early days for the AJTC which has a large remit inherited from the former Council on Tribunals, together with the additional duty to examine this broadly defined administrative justice system beyond the tribunal world. It is by no means clear—perhaps deliberately so—how wide the statutory definition is intended to be. The reference to decisions of an administrative or executive nature could be said to be either tautological, or so wide as to encompass almost anyone making any decision anywhere about anything. To counter this, it may be tempting for some to see the administrative justice system as confined to what is generally known as the public sector, enormous as even that undoubtedly is. After all the title of the White Paper was 'transforming public services', whatever they are. There are clearly government departments and agencies, and local government bodies; there are public authorities of the kind that must comply with the Human Rights Act (because they perform 'functions of a public nature'), and bodies that are subject to judicial review (because they 'exercise a public function') in the Civil Procedure Rules Part 54; and the Law Commission (2008: paras 4.99–4.100) has proposed a new definition of 'truly public activities' in private law so that, where it is satisfied, 'duty of care' would no longer be used to determine liability.[2] And Oliver (see her chapter in this volume) would extend the horizon of administrative justice to bodies that exercise power that can 'make or mar' a person, even if they have 'no taint of publicness' about them, with a view to requiring them to adhere to principles of good administration.

[1] Tribunals, Courts and Enforcement Act 2007 Sch 7, para 13(4).

[2] Instead, liability would only exist where the same three tests are met as would be used in public law cases to determine the availability of damages: conferral of benefit, serious fault and causation of loss. This means that no liability would exist for failures in 'truly public' activities which fall short of being 'serious faults'.

Private Sector, Private Law

But my focus of concern is even wider, since it includes bodies that not only have no taint of publicness but are not, in Oliver's terms, exercising powers that can make or mar people. The 'truly private' sector is composed of commercial (and some not-for-profit) entities providing goods or services, whose relations with those to whom they are provided are principally based on the law of contract, sometimes on the law of tort, and also on the law of trusts—all classed by lawyers as fields of private law. In my field, I can easily instance banks, insurance companies and building societies, the latter being mutual organisations, and providers of occupational pensions who are mostly trustees serving beneficiaries. These bodies may irritate people by their primary decision making resulting in poor service, or wrongly damage people by causing them actual financial loss. The traditional view is that their capacity to inflict damage is limited and normally not long lasting, and at any rate this damage can be remedied through private law claims. However ombudsmen are invading this commercial territory at some pace.

Private Sector Ombudsman Schemes

First up was the Insurance Ombudsman, started as a voluntary scheme in 1981, and followed by schemes in banking, building societies and investment firms, before all these were merged into the Financial Ombudsman Service by the Financial Services and Markets Act 2000. Then there is the Pensions Ombudsman, whose remit mainly covers work-based pension schemes, which was provided for by legislation in 1991. More recently, legislation has provided for ombudsman-style dispute resolution schemes in the fields of social housing,[3] legal services,[4] telecommunications providers,[5] energy services companies, estate agents, providers of postal services[6] and higher education institutions.[7] And I am deliberately ignoring the developments in the public sector ombudsman schemes that are indubitably part of the administrative justice system.

[3] The Housing Ombudsman Service was set up under the Housing Act 1996.

[4] The Office for Legal Complaints was established under the Legal Services Act 2007; the Scottish Legal Complaints Commission was established under the Legal Profession and Legal Aid (Scotland) Act 2007.

[5] Otelo (the Telecommunications Ombudsman) established under the Telecommunications Act 2003.

[6] Energy Ombudsman, Estate Agents Ombudsman, Postal Services Redress Scheme were set up under the Consumers, Estate Agents and Redress Act 2007.

[7] The Office of the Independent Adjudicator for Higher Education established under the Higher Education Act 2004; in Scotland, complaints against higher education institutions are investigated by the Scottish Public Services Ombudsman.

There is clearly a common appetite for offering consumers (note that our language used here refers to consumers, customers or even clients rather than citizens) an alternative to the much-criticised civil courts through an accessible free service for resolving disputes arising from primary decision making. A common thread that characterises the fields in which ombudsman schemes have been established is the imbalance of power and resources between the consumer and businesses. In conception this is no different to the imbalance of power between the citizen and the government department, which was recognised as justifying the establishment of the Parliamentary Ombudsman in 1967. In addition the promoters of private sector ombudsman schemes have been conscious of the deficiencies of the civil courts as mechanisms for providing effective dispute resolution. Even with advances in accessibility and reductions in 'cost risk' in small claims courts, no one seems to regard the private ombudsman model as redundant.

But we can ask what it is that brings together the customers of banks, estate agents, universities, phone companies, housing associations, solicitors, and electricity providers, yet excludes those of rail companies, airlines, vets, accountants, used car traders and members of sporting bodies. Given that the entire former group are the subject of statutory schemes, we need look no further than the attention and interest that particular government departments have given, or in some areas been required to give. Pension schemes fall within the remit of the Department for Work and Pensions; banks and financial companies that of HM Treasury; estate agents, telephone and electricity companies that of the Department for Business Enterprise and Regulatory Reform (dBERR);[8] housing associations that of Communities and Local Government; universities that of the Department for Innovation Universities and Skills (DIUS); lawyers that of the Ministry of Justice (MoJ). Each of the government departments has, either enthusiastically or grudgingly, sponsored schemes that they can see provide a worthwhile role in their respective sector—but it is painfully clear that none of these departments sees beyond its own departmental interest or has much understanding of the administrative justice context of which its scheme is now a part. Even the above analysis is simplistically confined to departments and ministries in England and Wales. Some of the schemes referred to have a UK wide remit, while others are confined to England and Wales. The AJTC, with its UK-wide remit, can be expected to have its work cut out.

Cross departmental coherence and joined-up government are often seen by students of public administration and connoisseurs of Whitehall as the graveyard of public policy, and this area of consumer redress provides a classic example. Developments have proceeded in a blinkered and haphazard way. The British and Irish Ombudsman Association, largely on the receiving end of these unstructured developments, has sought to engage government, with—it must be admitted—limited success, with the aim of finding a home for

[8] In relation to telecommunications companies, this was a result of an EU Directive.

more joined-up thinking through dialogue with the Cabinet Office, the MoJ and dBERR.

Do Private Sector Ombudsmen Belong in the Administrative Justice System?

Against this somewhat unpromising background, what is the case for private sector ombudsman schemes to be seen as within the realm of the administrative justice system? The first approach might be a pragmatic one. The AJTC is the only statutory body with a public policy remit that could cover the role of private sector ombudsman schemes, and as it is clear that no one else is looking across departmental boundaries, it would at least be an advance if the AJTC were to see these schemes as falling within the administrative justice system. And while the definition of administrative justice is so elastic, it is unlikely that anyone would object. Against this, it could be argued that the amount of attention that AJTC would give to private sector ombudsman schemes is likely to be very limited, and its influence on departments as weighty as the Treasury or the dBERR is likely to be rather small.

A stronger and more principled argument would emphasise the common function of ombudsmen and tribunals, that is, dealing with complaints about and appeals from disputed primary decision making. Neither ombudsmen nor tribunals are primary decision makers. Both are reactive rather than proactive institutions—although there is a lively debate among public sector ombudsmen as to whether they should also have a power to launch 'own initiative investigations'. More important perhaps is the common approach of both public and private ombudsman schemes to dispute resolution—little reliance on hearings, a graduated and flexible approach that includes early evaluation, an inquisitorial rather than an adversarial approach and a deliberate policy of feeding back lessons learned from the complaints they see and the decisions they make to the institutions within their remit. The White Paper deliberately sought to encourage tribunals to see whether aspects of this model could profitably be adopted as part of their decision making—the 'new approach to resolving disputes'. 'We believe that government has much to learn from the success of ombudsman schemes,' the White Paper declared, 'our purpose is to reclaim the idea of flexible dispute resolution for a new era' (Department for Constitutional Affairs 2004: para 4.20). Section 2(3) of the Tribunals, Courts and Enforcement Act 2007 now requires the head of the Tribunals Service to develop 'innovative methods of resolving disputes' of the type that come before tribunals. The high-volume Appeals Service, which dealt with social security appeals and is now part of the Tribunals Service, has been running a pilot scheme to test whether early neutral evaluation of cases is worthwhile (Tribunals Service 2007: paras 95–96). So it would hardly be logical to exclude either private or public sector or ombudsman schemes from the administrative justice system if policy-makers are looking to make a comparison of and mutual learning between the different decision making styles of tribunals and ombudsmen.

The Financial Ombudsman Service: Some Background

Background

I first set out some background about the Financial Ombudsman Service. We are a good example of what can be described as 'structured institutional arrangements'. We have a clear and limited remit to deal with unresolved disputes between consumers and financial firms as an alternative to the civil courts. The Financial Services and Markets Act 2000 created a compulsory jurisdiction over financial firms to provide for a 'scheme under which certain disputes may be resolved quickly and with minimum formality by an independent person' (ibid: s 225). It requires us to determine the outcome of complaints on the basis of what 'in the opinion of the ombudsman, is fair and reasonable in all the circumstances' (ibid: s 228). We are required to take into account the law, regulatory rules, and good industry practice (Financial Services Authority 2009: DISP 3.6.4), but are expected ultimately to rely on our own instinct for fairness. And we are empowered not only to make monetary awards (of up to £100,000) against a respondent firm, but also to make directions requiring a firm to take such steps as we consider fair—and the Act specifically states that such a direction may include steps that a court could not order (Financial Services and Markets Act 2000: section 229). Final decisions made by an ombudsman, if accepted by the complainant, are binding on the respondent business (ibid: section 228), a provision which leaves a disappointed complainant free to reject a decision, and thus leaves their legal rights against the business unaffected.

Since 2001, we have dealt with over 750,000 disputes between consumers and financial firms. In the financial year 2009–10 we forecast the need to resolve 165,000 disputes (Financial Ombudsman Service 2009). One particularly significant area of our work over the last few years has been the resolution of complaints about endowment policies intended to repay mortgage loans—relied on by some 5 million UK households—where we dealt with some 300,000 complaints. As a result of our operation and that of the Financial Services Authority, financial firms have paid approximately £2.3 billion to consumers in compensation. One can be forgiven for wondering how the courts would have coped had there been no ombudsman. As it is the courts have not been troubled at all by this, perhaps one of the most extensive civil redress exercises ever to have been undertaken in the UK.

We are a statutory body (undoubtedly a public body) but we deal with private disputes. Essentially most of these disputes between individuals and financial firms relate to contractual, or tortious liability. They involve insurance contract law, alleged breaches of contract by banks (or by customers), and breaches of duties of care by professional advisers towards their clients. Many of the principles involved are set out in detailed rules made by the Financial Services Authority, which are themselves part of the law since a breach of the rules that causes loss is actionable by virtue of the Act (Financial Services and Markets Act 2000 s 150). For instance, firms are required by rules only to sell to customers investments that are 'suitable' for their circumstances—but on one view that is merely a regulatory restatement of the duty of care of professional advisers not to sell inappropriate products to investors. And we assert that there is no difference in the standard to be applied to advisers before or after the coming into force of that particular rule.

So the FOS is a real alternative to the courts for consumers with what are essentially civil claims. And with few exceptions consumer claims that would be within our remit are simply not litigated. Apart from debt or enforcement proceedings, the courts rarely see claims about bank accounts, mortgages, credit cards, insurance policies, investment advice, or pension policies. The FOS has effectively cornered the market. This is hardly surprising, since the service is free to consumers and financial firms are obliged to tell complaining customers about the FOS. We provide the parties with a reasoned, merits-based outcome in every case, something that occurs in only a tiny proportion of civil cases where the fear of incurring costs drives litigants to settle most claims. The fact that dissatisfied consumers can refer their complaints to us cost- and risk-free influences financial firms in the way they handle complaints. Without the ombudsman service, it is questionable whether the myriad of day to day disputes between financial businesses and their customers would be as fairly resolved.

Procedures

We provide procedural fairness before making decisions—not normally by holding hearings, but by providing provisional assessments and inviting the parties in dispute to make representations on them. We make extensive use of 'early evaluation'. While only those individuals who have been appointed to our ombudsman panel may make final binding decisions, our adjudicators (that is, our caseworkers, who examine and investigate complaints in the first instance) resolve a high percentage of disputes themselves. They do this by expressing to the party likely to be disappointed an initial, non binding, reasoned opinion about the merits of the complaint and by inviting comments; perhaps after some discussion or correspondence, resulting, in over 90 per cent of our cases, in a resolution. It is only when an adjudicator's view is not accepted that the case is passed to an ombudsman for a final decision. And if the ombudsman proposes to reach a different outcome to that proposed by the adjudicator, the ombudsman issues a provisional decision and invites representations from the parties. Thus any party who is likely to be disappointed receive a reasoned assessment of the likely outcome with an opportunity to respond to it before the final decision is made.

Any party wanting a hearing can ask for one, but not until the case has reached the stage where it is being considered by an ombudsman. Where the ombudsman is of the opinion that the case cannot be fairly decided without convening a hearing—perhaps because the case turns on a dispute about what was said at a meeting of which there is no record—he will arrange a hearing. But this is extremely rare. The vast majority of the 9,000 cases a year determined by ombudsmen did not require hearings. The number of hearings each year is under 50.

Structure and Accountability

As an independent statutory body with a board, a chief executive/chief ombudsman and a senior management team, we are similar to a non-departmental public body. So, we produce an annual report, report on our budget, accounts, unit costs and productivity, have our own website, run our own user satisfaction surveys and quality assurance schemes, and commission occasional external reporters to review our operations. We make a substantial investment of resources contacting our major stakeholders—industry sectors, regulators, consumer bodies, specialist journalists—consulting them about corporate plans and policy issues. We see these two-way interactions and feedback to our user community as vital. These aspects of governance and accountability are not unusual in self-standing public bodies, and other ombudsman schemes operate similarly. Although the Financial Ombudsman Service is large, compared to the civil courts or to tribunals, it is small. But these larger courts and tribunals have less well established and less visible forms of business improvement and accountability.

Judicial Review

It is interesting to recall that, before we became a statutory body, at least one of our predecessor schemes, indeed the scheme for which I was formerly responsible (the Insurance Ombudsman Bureau), had been ruled a private body, and therefore immune from judicial review.[9] Frankly, I do not think we were behaving any differently under the IOB scheme than we are now.

But now as a public body we are clearly judicially reviewable. There is no doubt that we determine the civil rights and obligations of respondent firms.[10] While disappointed complainants can pursue other remedies and the courts may be reluctant, on this ground, to grant permission for judicial review, it is by no means

[9] *R v Insurance Ombudsman, ex p Aegon Life* [1994] COD 426.

[10] See European Convention on Human Rights Art 6: 'In the determination of his civil rights and obligations, ... everyone is entitled to a fair and public hearing within a reasonable time by an independent and impartial tribunal established by law'.

excluded. Since the establishment of the Financial Ombudsman Service a small number of decisions of ours have been challenged by way of judicial review.[11] In only one have we been found wanting so far.[12] The most significant decision has been in a Court of Appeal case[13] in which the Court rejected a series of attacks on the structure and powers of the ombudsman. It confirmed that the words of the Act did not confine the ombudsman to reach results that a court would reach, and decided that despite the absence of a hearing before an ombudsman decision, the scheme was fully human rights compliant. Stanley Burnton LJ, giving the leading judgment, reviewed in some depth the principle of the rule of law and its applicability to our scheme, together with the interpretation of Article 6 of the European Convention on Human Rights. Neither the Convention, nor section 3 of the Human Rights Act 1998, nor the principle of the Rule of Law, required the court to depart from the natural and ordinary meaning of the words of section 228(2) of the Financial Services and Markets Act, he asserted,[14] that complaints are to be determined by reference to what is fair in the opinion of the ombudsman.

In his judgment, Rix LJ made some wider observations.

> FOS's case-load, as indicated above, is a heavy one, indicating a need for the alternative dispute resolution service that it provides. That service is the dominant purpose of the statutory scheme: as section 225(1) states—"This Part provides for a scheme under which certain disputes may be resolved quickly and with minimum formality by an independent person". It is a special feature of that scheme that it is voluntary so far as consumers are concerned and only compulsory (within the limit of £100,000) on the part of the financial firms which provide services to such consumers. Those financial firms, however, are operating within a regulatory and commercial environment whose rules, guidance, standards and codes of practice should be well-known to them. Those matters are not equally well-known to consumers, however, who rather approach the relevant transactions with general notions of what they might reasonably expect. ...
>
> Nowadays, however, huge numbers of consumers have pensions, make investments, and enter into insurance contracts of all kinds. Our insurance law, for instance, has been based on a statute, the Marine Insurance Act 1906, designed for marine insurance but given a dominant status over insurance contracts in general, which encapsulates the common law of over a century ago. For some years the insurance ombudsman (now within the FOS scheme) has been developing a new common law of insurance for consumer contracts, without which the courts would have been constrained to find, or alternatively to reject, solutions to problems from which they have been in the main shielded. This new ombudsman-developed law is in turn being considered by the Law Commission as part of its current review of certain areas of our insurance law. ... However, it is possible

[11] Eg *R (Norwich and Peterborough Building Society) v Financial Ombudsman Service* [2002] EWHC 2379 (Admin); *R (Green t/a Green Denman & Co) v FOS* [2003] EWHC 338; *R (Young Ridgway and Associates) v FOS* [2004] EWHC 3371; *R (IFG Financial Services Ltd) v Financial Ombudsman Service* [2005] EWHC 1153.

[12] *R (Garrison Investment Analysis) v Financial Ombudsman Service* [2006] EWHC 2466.

[13] *R (Heather Moore and Edgcomb Ltd) v Financial Ombudsman Service* [2008] EWCA Civ 642.

[14] Ibid [51] (Stanley Burnton LJ).

to see in the "fair and reasonable" jurisdiction of the ombudsman the source not merely of an alternative dispute resolution service but of an important new source of law.

That "fair and reasonable" jurisdiction may be flexible and (subject to judicial review) for the ombudsman and not for the courts to discern: nevertheless, these are concepts long familiar to English law, and, given the legal and industry background to which the scheme rules bid the ombudsman to have regard, it is hard to think that the parties to complaints submitted to the ombudsman's jurisdiction will find themselves in unrecognised country ... In my judgment, the following values are all to be appreciated and brought into a pragmatic balance: that an efficient and cost-effective and relatively informal type of alternative dispute resolution should not to be stifled by the imposition of legal doctrine; that the opportunity for the development of new ideas fitting to financial service industries operating in consumer markets should be appreciated for the benefits they can bring; that on the other hand transparency, consistency and accessibility as to the principles which inform the ombudsman's determinations remain virtues in this new setting; and that publicity as to those principles and those determinations can assist in that regard.'[15]

Private Sector Decision Making

How far does our role impose on financial firms duties that are significantly different from those that private law casts on them? Private law gives private bodies a wide measure of freedom of contract,[16] and we respect firms' right to make decisions that are within what we call a sphere of 'legitimate commercial judgement'. Provided that their contract terms contain valid terms entitling them to do so, firms can decide to increase or reduce interest rates for the products they offer or adjust insurance premiums for different sectors of what is a competitive market without being required to have any particular process for making these decisions. They can decide not to contract at all with an individual, provided their decision is not unlawfully discriminatory. If you have certain criminal convictions, many insurance companies will decline to insure you at any price, and we will not interfere.

There are at least two areas where standards of primary decision making (as opposed to contractually fair outcomes) are being imposed on financial firms by the FSA. The first, and most controversial, is the principle on which the FSA is placing increasing emphasis as part of its shift to more principles-based regulation, namely that of treating customers fairly—or TCF as we know it (Financial Services Authority 2006). TCF includes a requirement on senior management of a firm to ensure that any new products that it launches are designed to meet the needs of identified customer groups, and targeted accordingly, and

[15] Ibid [86]–[89].

[16] Subject of course to some significant limitations such as those in the Unfair Terms in Consumer Contracts Regulations 1999 SI 1999/2083.

that records are kept of how these decisions are reached. The FSA is stressing the need for firms to consider TCF throughout the product life-cycle, from initial design to after-sales service, including its handling of complaints. It is possible therefore that a firm may escape regulatory sanction, even if an adverse incident has occurred, if it can show that it was following TCF procedures. On the other hand, if poor outcomes for customers do occur following a failure to follow TCF procedures, the regulator is likely to take a harsher view.

The second area is the requirement on firms, when considering complaints, to investigate them, and in responding to them, adequately address the subject matter of the complaint in a formal response, giving reasons if they reject it (Financial Services Authority 2009: DISP 1.4.1). So even if firms are not accountable for the procedure by which their decisions are made, they cannot (or should not) reply to the question 'why isn't my claim justified?' with the answer 'because we say so'. This *final response* is also the gateway to accessing the ombudsman, since the firm must, in its final response, inform the customer of the right to refer the matter to us. So in theory we should not see an inadequately reasoned response.

Good Administration in the Private Sector

Nevertheless, these requirements fall short of the full 'good administration' principles as formulated recently by the Parliamentary and Health Services Ombudsman (2008b). An insurance company is not obliged to give a policy-holder an opportunity to make representations before rejecting a claim, nor is a mortgage lender required to do so before deciding to seek repossession of a home. These decisions, are ones that can have a very substantial impact—that can 'make or mar' a person's life. We would investigate the substantive fairness of such decisions (and order them to be reversed if appropriate), but we would not necessarily concern ourselves with the internal procedure that had been followed to arrive at the decision. There may of course be cases where following a proper procedure will be relevant. For instance, if a health insurer decides that it will no longer cover claims for the costs of important treatment without consulting the company's chief medical officer, we might criticise that, and even require the decision to be made again properly. But we are unlikely to do that unless there was at least some doubt about whether a different outcome ought to be reached.

In private law, as opposed to public law, we are more concerned with outcomes and less with the process of decision making. In determining disputes, whether a firm intended, to use the FSA's phrase, to treat its customers fairly is unlikely to be our focus. In reaching a determination about a fair remedy, the question of whether unfair treatment resulted from deliberate, reckless or negligent behaviour or merely from a well-intentioned error of judgment is of less importance than the impact of the treatment on the claimant. Except when there appears to be systemic misconduct, we do not normally require to see the plans a firm made or the precautions it took to ensure that fair outcomes were reached. We look at the result of the unfair treatment and remedy it. This follows the common law approach. Absent fraudulent conduct, an individual injured by a tortfeasor will generally recover the same financial compensation for his or her injury whether this was caused by a deliberate, reckless or negligent act.

When I say that we care nothing as to whether the firm behaved deliberately, recklessly or negligently, that is only true to the extent that we are assessing loss and redress. But of course when we observe misconduct by financial firms we draw this to the attention of the regulator who has appropriate disciplinary powers—in much the same way that a civil court judge might expect to do. In our wider role of drawing lessons from our cases and feeding back our observations to firms, the general public, regulators and policy-makers, we are, of course, concerned with standards of conduct in decision making and complaint handling. We draw attention to concerns and trends, and publish them.

We have the right to arrive at decisions based on what is fair and reasonable and to award compensation going beyond that which the law would offer. We have developed this in the area of non-financial loss—that is what we know as payments for distress and inconvenience for maladministration (Financial Ombudsman Service 2008). The courts have recognised this head of damages in contracts providing for pleasure or peace-of-mind, first in the 'holiday' cases,[17] but later in a wider range of circumstances.[18] We look at the question of payments for distress and inconvenience on a broader basis than the courts do. Bingham LJ (as he then was) put it starkly: 'A contract-breaker is not in general liable for any distress, frustration, anxiety, displeasure, vexation, tension or aggravation which his breach of contract has caused.'[19] He, of course, did add that this general rule did not apply to contracts where the object is to provide pleasure, relaxation or peace-of-mind. In any event, whatever the state of the law the courts would apply, the ombudsman certainly does regard it as important that financial service providers who cause people distress or inconvenience through errors or contract breaches should compensate them and we routinely make them do it. The financial industry itself frequently pays compensation to customers to whom they admit they have provided poor service that has obviously led to inconvenience or distress.

This poor service, or maladministration frequently consists of procedural errors, failures to adhere to process that are contrary to reasonable expectations, or failure to remedy errors promptly. These, as we shall see, are not far away from the principles of administrative justice that emerge from public law.

Do Public Law Remedies Help?

One could argue that attempts to extend public law principles into the private sphere are going to be of little benefit unless the substantive outcomes can be

[17] *Jarvis v Swans Tours Ltd* [1973] 1 All ER 71.
[18] *Farley v Skinner* [2001] UKHL 49.
[19] *Watts v Morrow* [1991] 4 All ER 937.

addressed, as well as procedural formalities. It is little comfort to be able to have quashed, for example, an objectionable decision of a planning committee, or of a bank's repossession decision, on the grounds that the committee had been improperly constituted or the bank's decision had been made by a manager whose promotion to the role had not been confirmed, if the same decision would inevitably have been reached if it had been properly made. The administrative courts, for all their famed judicial interventionism, are still confined to the polite, but unrealistic, fiction that the claimant is interested only in the process and not in the outcome. In the Jockey Club cases to which Oliver refers,[20] Messrs Bradley and Mullins were not interested in ensuring that the procedures of the Club were kept within lawful bounds. Mr Bradley wanted to carry on riding, and Mr Mullins to have his horse run.

None of this is to ignore the potential intrusiveness of private law (and public enquiry) into decisions that look on the surface to have little taint of 'publicness' (to use Oliver's phrase) about them. There can hardly be a more ghastly example of such scrutiny than that given to the decision of the board of directors of Equitable Life to pay differential bonuses to certain groups of its policyholders. This was a purely private, mutual-insurance society. The directors' actions led to an adverse House of Lords decision, the near collapse of the society, cuts in the value of millions of pensions and investments, an enquiry by a senior judge, a High Court action by their successor directors against them individually that would undoubtedly have bankrupted them had it succeeded, an enquiry by the Parliamentary Ombudsman, and admissions and apologies by the government for maladministration by regulators. Or we could also cite the scrutiny given by the civil courts to decisions admittedly of a public body, the Bank of England, in relation to its supervision of BCCI. Not quite the most encouraging examples of the exercise of private law principles by the civil courts.

Horizontal Extension

Oliver identifies private sector enterprises that 'have the power to make decisions that can adversely affect individuals in their security or their interests, or the general public interest in important ways; bodies that provide or withhold services of special importance to individuals', as potential candidates for the horizontal imposition of public administration principles. I might put the criteria slightly differently, and point to significant imbalances of power or knowledge, particularly when it comes to redress. Interestingly most of the candidates she identifies, low cost housing, hospitals, universities, and most forms of social care, are subject to some forms of regulation and are covered by ombudsman schemes (although air, rail and bus services are not).

[20] *Bradley v Jockey Club* [2005] EWCA Civ 1056; *Mullins v Jockey Club* [2006] EWHC 986.

Should procedural maladministration be the most important object of scrutiny (either by the courts or the ombudsman), or should we be more concerned when it leads to detrimental outcomes? It is important to note that it is the procedural processes preceding decision making—giving affected persons a right to make representations, taking into account relevant and excluding irrelevant considerations, and respecting legitimate expectations—that Oliver puts forward as principles for extension into private sector decision making. Of course we can take it as self-evident that better decision making ought to flow from adherence to these principles. But in some areas they will come at the cost of speed, economy and efficiency of delivery. In relation to many simple financial products for example, decisions on whether customers are eligible are generated by automated systems that are designed to take account of what the offering company sees as considerations relevant to its business but which may not be the considerations a potential customer would regard as relevant. Offering those refused the product a right to make representations is not practical. And commercial entities cannot always be held to deliver on expectations (to their staff, shareholders or customers) in quite the same way that public institutions can and should.

But, as we have seen in the Financial Ombudsman Service, we do hold service providers to account for failure to adhere to good administration practice where this has resulted in distress or inconvenience. This is perhaps a part of the process of horizontal imposition of public law principles that Oliver identifies.

The Parliamentary Ombudsman

The Parliamentary Ombudsman is empowered to consider claims that a person has sustained injustice as a consequence of maladministration by public bodies. Here public bodies are defined in a list to which bodies are added after conscious thought at the time they are created. If we are going to have a separate procedure for claims to judicial review under Part 54 of the Civil Procedure Rules 1998, might it not be preferable to have a list of bodies whose decisions are judicially reviewable rather than relying on attempts by the courts to define their 'publicness'? We may also note what private lawyers would call the 'causation aspect'. The Ombudsman does not investigate claims of mere maladministration unless they lead to injustice. This question has been essentially at the heart of two disputes between the Government and the ombudsman following two reports: first, her report on collapsed occupational pension schemes (Parliamentary and Health Service Ombudsman 2006); and then on Equitable Life (Parliamentary and Health Service Ombudsman 2008a). In the former, did employees rely on the government's allegedly misleading leaflets in deciding to contribute to pension schemes, or would they have done that anyway? The government may have had the most perfect machinery for arriving at decisions about how these leaflets should be drafted, but maybe in breach of these the task was delegated to a junior official to complete on a Friday afternoon. And in Equitable Life, how far were the losses sustained by investors caused by the admitted regulatory maladministration, and how far by the mismanagement by Equitable Life?

In commending the role of the public ombudsman I should also draw attention to the publication by the ombudsman of *Principles of Good Administration* (Parliamentary and Health Service Ombudsman 2008b). Students of administrative justice will find that her principles mirror very largely many of the themes of public law principles. Rightly, of course, she hopes that better administration will lead to fewer complaints and fewer injustices. Her Principles are targeted and designed with the practicality of administering public bodies in mind, and derived from her office's long experience of dealing with complaints about how things can go wrong. So while, for example, her principle of 'acting fairly and proportionately' could come straight out of a public law textbook, her principle of 'being customer focused' is of a different order,[21] and includes admonitions about service standards, timescales for action, and coordination with other service providers.

Care Home Rights

Oliver's paper spends some time examining the rights of residents in care homes to respect for their homes, and whether and if so how they might be extended. The Parliamentary Ombudsman has also been at the heart of another important issue concerning the rights of care home residents, namely whether their care should be properly and lawfully paid for by the NHS. This issue was first highlighted in a 1999 Court of Appeal decision.[22] But since then the Ombudsman has received over 5,000 complaints and issued a number of reports that have had the effect of requiring the Department of Health to carry out hundreds of thousands of individual re-assessments of residents, and to provide restitution involving many millions of pounds to those who have paid for care but should have received free treatment. Despite the Court of Appeal's judgment, it is clear that, without the intervention of the Parliamentary Ombudsman, the unlawful treatment of these care home residents would have continued unabated and that little restitution would have been paid. The Scottish Public Services Ombudsman has taken a similar interest in long term care issues, as has the Ombudsman of Ireland.

Now the government has, in the Health and Social Care Act 2008, taken the step of declaring that statutory provision of care home accommodation is to be regarded as a function of a public nature for the purposes of the Human Rights Act. It is open to question as to what effect this will have in practice on care home residents, providers, or indeed on the handling of disputes about care home provision. Would it not have been better, or at least as good, to consider an

[21] A point also recognised by the Government in its discussion of whether good administration principles could or should be made justiciable. See Ministry of Justice (2009: para 3.46).

[22] *R v North and East Devon Health Authority, ex p Coughlan* [2000] 3 All ER 850.

ombudsman scheme? We need look no further for a model than the USA, where the State Long-term Care Ombudsman Program, authorised by the federal Older Americans Act, now requires every State to create an Ombudsman Program to 'investigate and resolve complaints made by or on behalf of older individuals who are residents of long-term care facilities'. Something similar was of course recommended here by the ill-fated Royal Commission on Long Term Care (Sutherland 1999). And there are ombudsmen for the elderly in Sweden, Finland and Norway. An ombudsman would have the flexibility to be able to balance the many considerations Oliver identifies as needing to be taken into account, in a way that I fear the courts or tribunals would find difficult. In appropriate cases an ombudsman could protect a resident from an improper decision to evict him or her from a home: if the best the courts could do was to award damages for the loss of a chance of a reasonable decision or a declaration that the eviction was a breach of her rights, which sounds distinctly under-whelming.

It is ironic that the recent decision of the House of Lords on the liability in negligence of public bodies should have concerned a care home wrongly closed as a result of local authority action, where the focus was not that of the residents whose stay in the home was summarily disrupted, but that of its proprietors who suffered financial loss as a result.[23] The decision broke no new ground. Despite the injustice, while there might have been a duty of care to the residents, there was none owed to the proprietors. The action complained of took place before the coming into force of the Human Rights Act, and their Lordships gave the strongest indication that the outcome would have been different had human rights duties played a part. It is not recorded whether the residents received any redress.

The Law Commission's Consultation Paper on Administrative Redress

It is in this very field—the liability of public bodies either in negligence or for monetary remedies in public law—that the Law Commission (2008) has put forward proposals for financial redress where a public body in exercising its powers has been guilty of 'serious fault' causing loss to those for whom its powers were designed to provide benefit. Although this proposal has been subject to considerable criticism (see, for example, Cornford 2009 and Fordham 2009), the present situation where a claimant can recover damages for breach by a public body of a rule of EU law intended to confer rights on individuals, whereas if the breach was of English law no action would lie, is clearly unsatisfactory. Alongside this proposal, the Commission also suggests that there should be greater flexibility between the public sector ombudsman schemes and the courts, and a suitable

[23] *Trent Strategic Health Authority v Jain* [2009] UKHL 4.

mechanism to enable the movement of cases between them. It has proposed that an ombudsman should be able to refer points of law to be determined by the courts. However, for understandable reasons, this power is only recommended for the public sector ombudsman schemes. It is for consideration whether the Financial Ombudsman Service should have a similar power to refer issues to the courts, an issue on which the AJTC might have a view.

In the rules of the Financial Ombudsman Service, we do have power to cease consideration of a complaint if the respondent firm alleges that a novel or important point of law is involved and undertakes to start proceedings and to pay the legal costs of the complainant (Financial Services Authority 2009: DISP 3.3.5). So far this test case procedure has not been used,[24] although a not dissimilar process has been used to bring to court the lawfulness of certain charges by banks relating to unauthorised overdrafts in current accounts.[25] Before the court action started we had received 40,000 complaints on this issue.

During the life of the Financial Ombudsman Service, there have been a number of occasions when a legal issue has arisen, mostly having been raised by a financial firm suggesting that the approach we were proposing to take was wrong and challengeable in law. Apart from inviting the firm to bring a test case, our only option, having considered the legal submissions, was to proceed with whatever decision seemed fair to the ombudsman, and to see whether the matter was challenged by way of judicial review. An instance would have been the long and bitterly contested issue of how former members of the Equitable Life Assurance Society should be compensated out of the funds of the remaining members for the mis-selling by the society to them of pension policies. This was an issue on which the ombudsman eventually issued an 80-page decision largely devoted to issues of law (Financial Services Ombudsman 2005).

Conclusions

I have advocated a broad view of the administrative justice system and argued that private sector ombudsman schemes should be seen squarely within it. They have dispute resolution procedures which have attracted the interest of others within the administrative justice field. The Financial Ombudsman Service was seen by the draftsmen of the Government's White Paper *Complaints, Redress and Tribunals* (Department for Constitutional Affairs 2004) as of particular interest. As such it has since been subject to substantial scrutiny, and, more recently, approval by the

[24] There was a similar test case provision in the rules of the Personal Investment Authority Ombudsman scheme (a predecessor of the Financial Ombudsman Service). Two cases resulted: *Equitable Life v Hyman* [2000] 3 All ER 961, the House of Lords decision on the lawfulness of Equitable Life's bonus allocation scheme; and *Needler Financial Services v Taber* [2002] 3 All ER 501, on whether payments on demutualisation should be set off against pension mis-selling redress claims.

[25] *Office of Fair Trading v Abbey National plc and ors* [2009] EWHC 36 (Comm).

higher courts. The advent of the Administrative Justice and Tribunals Council (AJTC) creates an opportunity for private sector ombudsman schemes to be seen in a new light. Most tend to be seen as part of the regulatory structure of the sector or industry concerned. The Financial Ombudsman Service is inevitably seen by most observers as part of the financial services consumer protection regime and the same is true of the energy, the telecommunications and estate agency ombudsmen. But an equally valid perspective is to see them as non-court justice dispensers—a function now given the broad title of administrative justice.

I have also argued that the particular features of private sector ombudsman schemes have an innovative contribution to offer to the administrative justice system. This was first identified in the White Paper *Complaints, Redress and Tribunals* (ibid). Whilst the emphasis in the tribunal field will for the immediate future be on the development of the Tribunals Service, it would be surprising, indeed disappointing, if the predominantly hearing-based model of tribunal operation remained wholly unchanged. But private sector ombudsman schemes are effectively an alternative to the civil courts, and it is here that one would naturally expect the greater exploration of mutual learning. How far could the civil courts successfully adopt hearing-free resolution of disputes? Is there scope for sharing our experience on business improvement, user satisfaction and quality assurance with local courts and tribunals?

Finally how far do private ombudsman schemes contribute to the horizontal effect of administrative justice principles? Oliver starts by identifying the kind of bodies or sectors in which it would be right for the law to impose administrative justice procedural principles. For her, this means going beyond the territory of bodies obviously recognisable as public—where we know that public sector ombudsmen are to be found. She wishes to extend to principles of good administration to bodies that exercise substantial powers.

Most private sector ombudsmen have been established in sectors characterised by imbalances of power in relation to access to justice which are seen to justify the creation of an out-of-court dispute resolution scheme in the first place. But it is in the area of remedies that we find a distinctive difference. For courts administering public law, breaches of good administration will normally result in the quashing of a decision with no financial redress and sometimes no more than a requirement to take the decision again applying the correct legal procedures. Ombudsmen have a wider range of proactive remedies, including financial compensation where appropriate. We are already applying some of the remedies that the Law Commission wishes to provide.

In conclusion, I admit my scepticism about the effectiveness of the courts and the law in delivering substantive, let alone procedural, justice to the mass of our citizens. As someone who is fascinated by the conundrums thrown up by administrative justice and the law, I find myself continually asking: 'so what?' So what, if private bodies have new duties cast on them by a developing indirect horizontal side-swipe? So what, if public bodies are exposed to quasi-tortious responsibilities? They will happily ignore them so long as there is no mechanism that makes the corresponding rights for consumers and citizens come alive. Private sector ombudsman schemes are already major contributors to that endeavour and have much to offer to the development of administrative justice.

Disclaimer

In October 2009, Walter Merricks stepped down as Chief Ombudsman of the Financial Ombudsman Service after 10 years in the post. He wrote this chapter while chief ombudsman in his personal capacity and his views should not be taken to be those of the Financial Ombudsman Service.

References

Cornford, T (2009) 'Administrative Redress: the Law Commission's Consultation Paper' PL 70.

Department for Constitutional Affairs (2004) *Transforming Public Services: Complaints, Redress and Tribunals* Cm 6443 (London, The Stationery Office), available at www.dca.gov.uk/pubs/adminjust/transformfull.pdf.

Financial Ombudsman Service (2005) *Mrs E (lead case) v Equitable Life Assurance Society*, available at www.financial-ombudsman.org.uk/faq/pdf/Equitable_GAR_final_decision.pdf.

—— (2008) *Technical note compensation for distress, inconvenience or other non-financial loss*, available at www.financial-ombudsman.org.uk/publications/technical_notes/distress-and-inconvenience.htm#1.

—— (2009) *Corporate Plan and Budget 2009–10*, available at www.financial-ombudsman.org.uk/publications/pb09/index.html.

Financial Services Authority (2006) *Treating Customers Fairly—Towards Fair outcomes for Consumers*, available at www.fsa.gov.uk/pubs/other/tcf_towards.pdf.

—— (2009) *Handbook: Dispute Resolution: Complaints (DISP)*, updated on a daily basis and available at www.fsa.gov.uk/Pages/handbook/.

Fordham, M (2009) 'Monetary awards in judicial review' PL 1.

Law Commission (2008) *Administrative Redress: Public Bodies and the Citizen* (Consultation Paper No 187) available at www.lawcom.gov.uk/docs/cp187_web.pdf.

—— (2009) *Rights and Responsibilities: developing our constitutional framework* Cm 7577 (Norwich, The Stationery Office), available at www.official-documents.gov.uk/document/cm75/7577/7577.pdf.

Parliamentary and Health Services Ombudsman (2006) *Trusting in the Pensions Promise: Government bodies and the security of final salary occupational pensions* HC 984, available at www.ombudsman.org.uk/pdfs/pensions_report_06.pdf.

—— (2008a) *Equitable Life: a decade of regulatory failure* HC 815, available at www.ombudsman.org.uk/pdfs/equitable_life_part_205_guide_and_summary.pdf.

—— (2008b) *Principles of Good Administration*, available at www.ombudsman.org.uk/improving_services/principles/index.html.

Sutherland, Sir Stewart (1999) *With Respect to Old Age: Long Term Care—Rights and Responsibilities* (Report of the Royal Commission on Long Term Care) Cm 4192 (London, The Stationery Office).

Tribunals Service (2007) *Transforming Tribunals: Implementing Part 1 of the Tribunals, Courts and Enforcement Act 2007*, Consultation Paper Code Number CP 30/07 (London: Ministry of Justice) available at www.justice.gov.uk/docs/tt_consultation_281107.pdf.

Part 4

Comparative Perspectives on Administrative Justice

12

Administrative Justice in Australia

ROBIN CREYKE*

Introduction

The concept of 'administrative justice' is a relatively new one. Although the early practitioners in Australia's administrative law system used the term, it went into abeyance in the late 1980s and did not re-emerge until the turn of this century. With its reappearance, however, it is timely to explore what it entails. Although there appears to be no agreement in Australian discourse as to its meaning, its importance has been widely appreciated. As Sir Anthony Mason, put it: '[a]dministrative justice is now as important to the citizen as traditional justice at the hands of the orthodox court system' (Mason 1989: 130). The observation underlines another justification for exploring what is administrative justice. A heightened consciousness of human rights in Australia has led administrative lawyers to extol the value of administrative law—the principal area of law associated with administrative justice—as a protector of rights (Bradley 1995: 347; Creyke 2006: 257; McMillan 2006). At the same time, the element of 'administrative' in the expression encapsulates a competing goal, namely, 'to maximise the common good' (Galligan 1996: 237). The tension between the protection of individual rights and the need to take account of the interests of the wider community is inherent in the concept of administrative justice.

Administrative law institutions and principles are the principal means by which administrative justice is provided. Independent and impartial review, investigations into maladministration or individual complaints, access to and protection of information held by government, all based on principles of lawfulness and good administration, are integral to the just outcomes which are the focus of administrative law (Commonwealth of Australia 1976: 350). It is, therefore, within the precincts of administrative law that an examination of this topic occurs.

This chapter considers first how the expression 'administrative justice' has been used in Australian writing, including the ways in which it has been shaped by judges and tribunal members. Next, certain questions are explored to see whether the answers assist with an understanding of the meaning that administrative law

* This chapter is based on Creyke 2007, and author wishes to acknowledge the considerable assistance of Tom Galvin in revising it for publication in this book.

bodies are most likely to give to administrative justice. In particular, how should we assess whether administrative justice has been achieved, and how embedded in administrative culture is the administrative justice concept in Australia?

The Current System of Australian Administrative Law

The 1970s and 1980s saw a remarkable transformation of administrative law in Australia. Under the enlightened guidance of a report by the Commonwealth Administrative Review Committee (Kerr Committee),[1] supplemented by reports of two other committees (Committee on Administrative Discretions 1973a, 1973b; Committee of Review 1973), a comprehensive new approach to administrative law was adopted.

At the federal level, a codified form of judicial review was introduced,[2] the Federal Court was set up as a second-tier judicial body below the High Court—the body at the apex of Australia's judicial system—to administer nationally the judicial review jurisdiction; and a multi-purpose merit review body, the Administrative Appeals Tribunal (AAT), was established.[3] There was to be a statutory right to reasons,[4] an Ombudsman,[5] and later a Freedom of Information Act 1982 (Cth) (FOI Act), and a Privacy Act 1988 (Cth). The package allowed for specialist tribunals, generally where the demands for review are high, and the new structure was monitored by an Administrative Review Council (ARC). This structure was set up alongside existing common law rights of judicial review offered by courts, including the entrenched jurisdiction of the High Court to grant the prerogative remedies of mandamus, prohibition and injunction.[6] In brief, this period in the 1970s and 1980s revolutionised the opportunities for the citizen to challenge decisions made by government and opened the way for an enhanced measure of administrative justice. The success of the system has seen it progressively being adopted by the states and territories (Creyke and Groves 2010: 5–7).

Subsequently, it became common practice for agencies to offer internal review as a precursor to external review. Moreover, other administrative law standards have been imposed through codes of conduct and service charters, and consultation with stakeholders has been introduced, especially in developing statutory rules.

[1] The committee was set up to examine whether there should be a further avenue of judicial review by a Commonwealth superior court, and whether Australia should introduce legislation akin to the Tribunals and Inquiries Act 1958 (UK): Administrative Review Committee, Commonwealth Government, *Commonwealth Administrative Review Committee Report* (1971) [1] (Kerr Committee Report).

[2] Administrative Decisions (Judicial Review) Act 1977 (Cth) (ADJR Act).

[3] Administrative Appeals Tribunal Act 1975 (Cth) (AAT Act).

[4] ADJR Act s 13; AAT Act s 28.

[5] Ombudsman Act 1976 (Cth).

[6] Australian Constitution s 75(v).

In addition, the use of alternative dispute resolution (ADR) as a means of responding to people's complaints is being strongly fostered by government (Faulkner 2008; McClelland 2008). The system can be said to provide a comprehensive and integrated package of institutions and principles, each component designed to provide 'justice to the individual' (Commonwealth Administrative Review Committee 1971: para 12). Collectively these moves have resulted in the development of standards for good administration that are now widely accepted and applied (Creyke and McMillan 2002: 163). How well the system provides administrative justice is a focus of the following discussion.

The Concept of 'Administrative Justice' in Australia

'Administrative Justice' in the Australian Literature

Early Writings

Although the expression 'administrative justice' does not appear in the reports that led to modern Australian administrative law, an embryonic form of that concept underpinned the proposals. Certainly, what has been accepted as a feature distinguishing 'justice', as provided by the courts, from 'administrative justice'—that is, that justice to the individual must be tempered by the needs of public administration and the collective good—was clearly understood and was a key principle underpinning the proposals (Kerr Committee 1971: para 12). As the Kerr Committee Report pointed out, its recommendations were designed to 'ensure the establishment and encouragement of modern administrative institutions able to reconcile the requirements of efficiency of administration and justice to the citizen' (Kerr Committee 1971: para 389).

Despite the prominence of these key objectives, the Kerr Committee Report did not attempt specifically to define 'administrative justice'. Nor did it address issues such as how to balance 'efficiency' with 'justice to the individual', whether these notions should apply across the spectrum of administrative law bodies and rights, by what criteria or standards should the balance between justice to the individual and efficient public administration and the public good be measured, and how to assess whether administrative justice was being achieved. These elements were left to subsequent commentators on the topic.

Later Developments

The first attempt to provide a systematic analysis of administrative justice in Australia occurred in 1999 at the annual conference of the Australian Institute of Administrative Law (AIAL) on the theme of 'Administrative Justice—The Core and the Fringe' (Creyke and McMillan 2000). Surprisingly, while the papers explored multiple facets of administrative justice from its application by tribunals (O'Connor 2000: 68) and the Ombudsman (McLeod 2000: 58), constitutional issues (J Kirk 2000: 78; L Kirk 2000: 106), how administrative justice can be measured (Neave 2000: 124; McDonald 2000: 138), what consumers expect of administrative justice (Koller 2000: 150; Cronin, 2000: 163), and administrative justice in the corporate world (Cameron 2000: 178; Bennett 2000: 192), none of the commentators attempted to define the notion. That may have been because, in the words of Craig, 'there are differing conceptions of administrative justice' (Craig 2000: 28), and, as the editors of the publication noted, the notion is an elusive one and '[t]hose seeking a definition of "administrative justice" will … need to recognise that the essence of the concept is tempered by conflicting (and legitimate) interests' (Creyke and McMillan 2000: 3). As a minimum, 'administrative justice is a philosophy that, in administrative decision-making, the rights and interests of individuals should be properly safeguarded' (Creyke and McMillan 2000: 3–4). However, even that description is insufficient because, as McMillan later reflected[7] 'administrative justice' includes the need for government agencies to balance justice in the individual case with other imperatives, such as government policy, consistency, and the need for efficient operation within budgetary constraints (McMillan 2000b: 71–72).

This description of the concept has generally been accepted in Australia; namely, that the juxtaposition of 'administrative' and 'justice' requires attention to both distributive justice as well as the protection of individual interests. So it has been these two facets of administrative justice, rather than the triumvirate of interests, to which Mashaw refers—'bureaucratic rationality', 'professional treatment' and 'moral judgment' (Mashaw 1983: 21–43; Craig 2000: 29–30)—that has been the focus of discussion by Australian writers and adjudicators. A consequence is that, in Australia, the issue has become which of the competing elements should predominate.

Proponents of the view that the collective good should take precedence over individual interests are not plentiful. A notable exception—although not recent—was found in the Interim and Final Reports of the Committee on Administrative Discretions (Bland Committee). Bland recommended:

- a narrow definition of discretionary powers;
- limitations of the Ombudsman's jurisdiction;
- the exclusion, at least initially, of appeals to a tribunal in social security and welfare matters;
- a brake on the proliferation of specialist tribunals;
- some tribunals should only have recommendatory functions; and
- denial of the need for a body to monitor the administrative law system, and for judicial review of the failure to make a decision

(Committee on Administrative Discretions 1973a: 30–32; Committee on Administrative Discretions 1973b: 44–49).

[7] Albeit in the context of the place of tribunals in the system of administrative review.

Had it occurred, acceptance of these recommendations would have severely limited access to administrative bodies within Australia and produced an unduly pared-down notion of administrative justice.

The alternative and more generally accepted view is that since 'justice' focuses on the recipient, it is the recipient's interests that should take precedence. This view equates 'administrative justice' with 'social justice' or 'justice for individuals' (Free 2000: 2) and clearly supports the emphasis on safeguarding the rights and interests of individuals (Creyke and McMillan 2005: 13ff). Those adopting this approach argue that administrative justice can be achieved by giving preference to just administrative outcomes and fairness in administrative law processes. This goal is most likely to be achieved in administrative law institutions within the investigative and human rights arms of administrative law with their strong focus, for example, on disadvantaged groups such as prisoners, those in remand centres (Groves 2002: 181) or in migration detention (Crock 2002, 2006). Another practical reason for this outcome, as seen in relation to the Office of Ombudsman, is:

> [b]ecause it is free of charge, non-adversarial and because the office shoulders the burden of investigating complaints rather than requiring complainants to prove any kind of formal 'case', the Ombudsman's role has been emphasised as an important or potentially important tool in achieving social justice. (Brown 1993: 21)

On balance, Australian writers fall into one or the other of these two camps.

'Administrative Justice' in Adjudicative Bodies

The case law supports these contrasting meanings of administrative justice, while generally favouring protection of individual, rather than collective interests. Until the 1980s, the expression 'administrative justice' was used regularly[8] by members of the AAT. References then ceased but have reappeared in the last three to five years,[9] probably due to the growing use of 'administrative justice' elsewhere in common law jurisdictions. The early cases, not surprisingly, are mostly about decisions by welfare and income support agencies[10] and refer frequently to 'principles of consistency, fairness and *administrative justice*' (emphasis added).[11]

[8] See, eg, *Re Buhagiar and Director-General of Social Services* (1981) 4 ALD 113, 113, 121 (Hall SM, Oxby and McLelland MM). See also *Re Emery and Director-General of Social Security* (1983) 5 ALN No 102; *Re Farah and Director-General of Social Security* (1984) S137/83; *Re Kaiser and Director-General of Social Security* (1983) 5 ALN No 176; *Re Roe and Director-General of Social Security* (1983) S82/108; *Re Keuker and Director-General of Social Security* (1984) 5 ALD 626.

[9] *Re Logan and Chief Executive Officer of Customs* (2005) 40 AAR 377; *Theo v Secretary, Department of Family and Community Cervices* [2005] AATA 699 (Unreported, Fisher M, 25 July 2005); *Jatan v Secretary, Department of Families, Community Services and Indigenous Affairs* [2006] AATA 229 (Unreported, Fisher M, 13 March 2006); *Francis v Secretary, Department of Education Science and Training* [2006] AATA 336 (Unreported, Fisher M, 10 April 2006).

[10] These cases to 2009 contain over 35 references to the expression, three-quarters of which appear in the decisions made to the mid-1980s.

[11] See eg *Re Buhagiar and Director-General of Social Services* (1981) 4 ALD 113, 121 (Hall SM, Oxby and McLelland MM) (emphasis added). See also *Re Drake and Minister for Immigration and Ethnic*

Although, this suggests that the AAT saw 'administrative justice' as distinct from fair process, it is clear that it also regarded a just outcome for the applicant as a measure of whether administrative justice has been achieved.

Within the court system, it is clear that the judges accept that the legal standards associated with judicial process must be modified in relation to decisions made by the executive, including tribunals, to reflect executive priorities and pressures. As the Full Federal Court noted in *NAAV v Minister for Immigration and Multicultural Affairs*:[12]

> Procedural fairness lies at the heart of administrative justice as a longstanding requirement of the common law and is reflective in Australia, as in other common law countries, of ordinary concepts of justice. Properly applied it does not lay upon decision-makers burdensome procedural requirements of the kind that would be expected of a court of law. What Lord Shaw said in *Local Government Board v Arlidge* [1915] AC 120 at 138 is still valid: 'that the judiciary should presume to impose its own methods on administrative or executive officers is a usurpation. And the assumption that the methods of natural justice are *ex necessitate* those of Courts of justice is wholly unfounded.'

At the same time, in a frequently cited passage, Brennan J—in *Attorney-General (NSW) v Quin* (*Quin*)—warned that courts are not well equipped to advance the competing priorities within administrative justice. As he put it:[13]

> [T]he judicature is but one of the three co-ordinate branches of government and ... the authority of the judicature is not derived from a superior capacity to balance the interests of the community against the interests of an individual. The repository of administrative power must often balance the interests of the public at large and the interests of minority groups or individuals. The courts are not equipped to evaluate the policy considerations which properly bear on such decisions, nor is the adversary system ideally suited to the doing of administrative justice: interests which are not represented as well as interests which are represented must often be considered.

Some judges clearly adopt a focus on social justice. Kirby J, until 2009 a justice of the High Court of Australia, was a strong proponent of this tendency. As he put it:

> It has been said that the attainment of administrative justice is not the object of judicial review. At the same time, this Court should not shut its eyes and compound the potential for serious administrative injustice demonstrated by the appellant. It should always take into account the potential impact of the decision upon the life, liberty and means of the person affected.[14]

Courts and tribunals in Australia are, therefore, alive to the central conundrum within 'administrative justice.' At the same time, there is a dearth of judicial

Affairs [No 2] (1979 2 ALD 634, 639 (Brennan J); *Nevistic v Minister for Immigration and Ethnic Affairs* (1981) 34 ALR 639, 647 (Deane J).

[12] (2002) 123 FCR 298, 447 (French J).

[13] (1990) 170 CLR 1, 37 (Brennan J). See also Blackwell (2003: 182).

[14] *Re Minister for Immigration and Multicultural Affairs, ex p Applicant S20/2002* (2003) 198 ALR 59, 98 (citations omitted). Note that Kirby J dissented in that case. Kirby J was commenting on Brennan J's remarks in *Quin* (1990) 170 CLR 1, 35–36.

guidance on the circumstances in which to give primacy to either the fair treatment view of administrative justice, or to the Weberian model of bureaucratic administration (Allars 1997a: 411).

Administrative Law Institutions in which Administrative Justice Applies

The following discussion illustrates the views of Australian writers and adjudicative bodies about which administrative law bodies are most likely to be focused on administrative justice. The predominant support appears to be for an expansive view of the relevant institutions.

Early Writing

Early writers were equivocal about the appropriate institutions from which to expect administrative justice. Lindsay Curtis, a senior Commonwealth government official with responsibility for implementing the 1970s administrative law reforms, refers to 'administrative justice' in the context of discussions of the Ombudsman, the tribunal system and internal review (Curtis 1989: 55, 65, 67–68). Since at that time, the 'trinitarian' view of power within the state prevailed strongly among Australian writers, and each mechanism he nominated was in the executive branch, it may be inferred that he saw administrative justice as applying within the executive, not the judicial arm of government.

The recommendations of the Kerr Committee report were not so confined. The report makes it clear that its proposed reforms were intended to cover the spectrum of administrative law institutions. The reform package that emerged was a comprehensive scheme with interrelated elements including courts, tribunals, a 'right to reasons' procedure, an ombudsman-type body, access to information rights, and a body to monitor the arrangements (Kerr Committee 1971: chapter 21). Hence, the report's recommendations were that the principles underpinning the reforms, including the notion of administrative justice, were to infuse all elements of the proposed administrative law structure.

Textbook Writers

An index search for 'administrative justice' in Australian and United Kingdom administrative texts is illuminating. There is generally no entry (Allars 1990, 1997b; Aronson, Dyer and Groves 2009; Craig, 2008; Creyke and McMillan 2005; cf 2nd, 2009; De Smith et al 2007; Douglas, 2009; Sykes 1997; Tomasic and Fleming 1991) and, in the few texts where 'administrative justice' does appear (eg Wade and Forsyth 2009), the index makes no reference to the bodies that should provide administrative justice.

Other Writings

Presenters at the 1999 AIAL conference took an inclusive view of the field. The core institutions they listed were courts, tribunals, anti-discrimination and other investigative agencies, Royal Commissions, parliamentary inquiries, advisory bodies that assist government in its policy-making function, and decision makers within agencies. Their list extended, however, to the fringe dwellers of administrative law—public utilities, regulatory bodies that supervise commercial conduct, private sector decision makers such as industry ombudsman, and commercial and community bodies that have embraced administrative law standards.[15]

This broad view is also found in other writings (Harris 2000: 222; Mason 1989: 130; McMillan 2001: 217). French J, then a judge of the Federal Court, now the Chief Justice of the High Court of Australia, in a paper on administrative justice, listed the following institutions:

— internal and external review bodies (including both tribunals and courts);
— the Ombudsman;
— Members of Parliament and Ministers;
— non-government organisations;
— the media; and
— Auditors-General

(French 2001: 30. See also Barker and Simmonds 2004: 23; French 2003: 1; Groves 2002: 181).

Law reform commissions have taken opposing views. The Discussion Paper *The Accessibility of Administrative Justice* by the Queensland Parliament's Legal, Constitutional and Administrative Review Committee supports the broader view of the 'footprint' of administrative justice to encompass:

— courts exercising judicial review;
— tribunals;
— the Ombudsman;
— the bodies which regulate access to and protection by government of personal information; and
— bodies which monitor subordinate law-making

(Legal, Constitutional and Administrative Review Committee 2005: para 3.1).

By contrast, the Australian Law Reform Commission, in its four-year survey of the Australian civil litigation system, appears to have used 'administrative justice' to refer solely to decision makers within the executive branch. As the Commission noted in its final report 'the administrative justice system … [includes] federal and state tribunal members, registrars, case officers and federal and state agency decision makers' (Australian Law Reform Commission 2000: para 2.222).

These writings reflect the spectrum of views about the province of administrative justice. At the same time, the survey indicates that the majority of writers conclude

[15] The broader view is found explicitly or by implication in a number of the papers collected in Creyke and McMillan (2000b); Bennett (2000: 192); Cameron (2000: 174); Cronin (2000: 164, 167); L Kirk (2000: 106); Koller (2000: 150); McLeod (2000: 60–61); Malone (2000: 209); Neave (2000: 132–37); and O'Connor (2000: 68–69).

that administrative justice is required of all segments of the administrative law community.

Courts

A passage by Brennan J in the High Court's decision in *Quin* is indicative of the view of the courts:

> [T]he duty and jurisdiction of the courts to review administrative action do not go beyond the declaration and enforcing of the law which determines the limits and governs the exercise of the repository's power. If, in so doing, the court avoids administrative injustice or error, so be it; but the court has no jurisdiction simply to cure administrative injustice or error.[16]

This classic passage, in describing the boundaries of judicial review in Australia, also indicates the subtle interplay between courts and tribunals in the field of administrative justice. Although the quotation suggests that administrative justice is more strongly associated with primary decision makers, internal reviewers and tribunals, the courts, when exercising judicial review, also engage in 'administrative justice' as a by-product of judicial review. As the High Court also noted: 'judicial review often remedies administrative injustice or error but that … is an occasional consequence rather than its rationale'[17]. On these readings it is principally tribunals and agencies which must abide by standards of administrative justice. At the same time, if administrative action involves egregious error, that error may properly be found to breach the administrative law standards set by the courts. Common examples of such failures are a breach of natural justice[18] and excessive delay in a tribunal's decision making.[19] If errors of these kinds are corrected on remission to the tribunal or decision maker, the court can be said to have been involved in ameliorating administrative injustice.

However, it is the core bodies within the executive arm which are principally involved in offering administrative justice in Australia—tribunals, investigative bodies such as Ombudsman and human rights institutions—to which the discussion now turns.

Tribunals

The centrepiece of the Kerr Committee report was the recommendation to establish a multi-purpose merit review tribunal. As the report noted: 'it has been universally accepted that judicial review by the courts … cannot provide

[16] (1990) 170 CLR 1, 35–36.

[17] *NAIS v Minister for Immigration and Multicultural Affairs* (2005) 228 CRL 470. See especially: at 200–01 (Kirby J).

[18] See eg *NAIS v Minister for Immigration and Multicultural and Indigenous Affairs* (2005) 228 CLR 470, 507 (Kirby J), although the majority also found that delay constituted a breach of natural justice; *Griffith University v Tang* (2005) 221 CLR 99, 137 (Kirby J); *Re Minister for Immigration and Multicultural Affairs, ex p S20/2002* 198 ALR 59, 98 (Kirby J).

[19] *NAIS v Minister for Immigration and Multicultural and Indigenous Affairs* (2005) 228 CLR 470, 502 (Kirby J); *Jago v District Court of New South Wales* (1989) 168 CLR 23, 26 (Brennan J).

for an adequate review of administrative decisions' (Kerr Committee 1971: para 5). So the report recommended 'review by tribunals other than the courts as one of its essential elements' (Kerr Committee 1971: para 7), because review on the merits 'is usually what the aggrieved citizen is seeking' (Kerr Committee 1971: para 58). Merit review enables people to obtain, generally at modest cost, a pension, benefit or licence, the reduction in amount owing, waiver of a fine, the right to see a document, the reduction in charges, or the permission to import goods at a concessionary rate of tariff.[20] Tribunal review is, as a consequence, usually a more effective response to an individual complaint than is review by the courts.

This recommendation was accepted and, following the passage of the Administrative Appeals Tribunal Act 1975 (Cth), the AAT commenced operating in 1976. The AAT was the first tribunal within a common law country to offer merit review for decisions across government, a model now replicated in the states and territories (Fleming 2008: 91–92). However, as can be expected in a federal system there are local differences. Amalgamation of merit review tribunals has not occurred everywhere, and South Australia and Tasmania have located their administrative review jurisdiction in their court systems.[21] New South Wales has in effect two amalgamated multi-purpose tribunals in the Consumer Trader and Tenancy Tribunal, and the Administrative Decisions Tribunal.[22] The Northern Territory has not yet adopted a multi-purposes tribunal. The most significant difference, however, between the AAT and these state and territory bodies is that their jurisdiction covers civil as well as administrative matters.[23]

Aside from the bold experiment of a multi-purpose tribunal, specialist tribunals have also been set up to handle reviews in high volume areas of public administration. Federally, these include student assistance, income support, migration and refugee matters, while throughout Australia, tribunals make decisions or undertake reviews in professional disciplinary matters, guardianship and property management for incompetent adults, conflict of interest issues for local governments, consumer and tenancy, and other matters (Forbes 2006: chapters 2–5). Figures showing usage of the major tribunals indicate that for some considerable time, Australians have been resorting to tribunals to handle the settlement of even their more serious disputes (Maher 1994: 84).

[20] Although it is conceded that the average gross costs of a hearing before the Administrative Appeals Tribunal in 1997–98 of $3,594 as compared with Family Court costs of $1,693 or the costs of an Australian Industrial Relations Commission hearing of $2,242, are high (Australian Law Reform Commission 1999: 84, Table 4.7).

[21] SA: District Court Act 1991 (SA); Tas: Magistrates Court (Administrative Appeals Division) Act 2001 (Tas).

[22] Consumer, Trader and Tenancy Tribunal Act 2001 (NSW) and the Administrative Decisions Tribunal Act 1997 (NSW).

[23] ACT: ACT Civil and Administrative Tribunal Act 2008; NSW; Administrative Decisions Tribunal Act 1997; Qld; Queensland Civil and Administrative Tribunal Act 2009; Vic: Victorian *Civil and* Administrative Tribunal Act 1998; WA: State Administrative Tribunal Act 2004.

There are many reasons. The choice of tribunal members with expertise to match the subject matter covered by the tribunal leads to confidence by applicants and agencies that the tribunal understands the issues and will bring an informed judgment to the decision-making task. There is also now a peak coordinating body—the Council of Australasian Tribunals, set up in 2002—for tribunal training, conferences, and for developing benchmarks for tribunal operations and these steps are contributing to the professionalism of tribunal members.

Tribunals also have advantages in accessibility and expertise. Hearings are generally required to be informal, rules of evidence are not required, assistance is provided with completion of application forms, interpreters are available, often free of charge, and alternative dispute resolution processes are used where mediated outcomes are possible. Tribunal members are generally chosen for their mix of skills, so the dominance of the legally-trained member is minimised and emphasis is given to possession of expertise in the matters being litigated. The agency whose decision is being reviewed is also often not represented, particularly before the specialist, intermediate tribunals at the federal level, such as the Veterans' Review Board, the Refugee Review Tribunal, the Migration Review Tribunal, or the Social Security Appeals Tribunal. The absence of agency representation, too, reduces the level of formality of the hearing, and minimises stress for applicants appearing before an adjudicative body, often for the first time. These features of tribunals contribute to their deserved reputation for accessibility (Australian Law Reform Commission 2000: chapter 9).

The growth in tribunals, whether specialist in nature or with a broad jurisdiction, has been a general phenomenon in Australia. Not surprisingly, therefore, by contrast with the workload of the courts,[24] tribunal output has been spectacular. Since 1976 the major federal tribunals alone have handled over 500,000 decisions and reviews.[25] The federal tribunal system has the highest figures for individual tribunals. For example, the AAT finalised over 6,000 cases in 2008–09 (AAT Annual Report 2009: 21), and collectively, in 2008–09, the Migration Review Tribunal, the Refugee Review Tribunal (MRT and RRT Annual Reports 2009: 32), the Social Security Appeals Tribunal (SSAT Annual Report 2009: 23) and the Veterans' Review Board (VRB Annual Report 2008: 17) completed in the region of 26,000 cases, making the combined caseload of these major federal tribunals

[24] The figures for administrative law decisions in the Australian federal court system have been either stagnant or declining over the last three years: figures supplied by the High Court of Australia, the Federal Court of the Australia, and the Federal Magistrates Court for 2004–05 to 2008–09.

[25] *Annual Reports* of the Commonwealth Administrative Appeals Tribunal, the two migration tribunals (currently known as the Refugee Review Tribunal and the Migration Review Tribunal), the Social Security Appeals Tribunal and the Veterans' Review Board.

in excess of 32,000 claims.[26] Nor do these figures include the output of a host of smaller Commonwealth tribunals.[27]

When to these numbers are added the work of state and territory tribunals, it is apparent that tribunals are operating at the busier end of the adjudicative spectrum. In Victoria alone, the Victorian Civil and Administrative Tribunal hears between 80,000 and 90,000 matters a year, about one-tenth of which are administrative law matters, mostly in relation to guardianship and management of property, and complaints of discrimination (Victorian Civil and Administrative Tribunal Annual Report 2007: 7).

These features have indicated a high degree of satisfaction within Australia for tribunal review as an adjudicative option and have led to a deserved international reputation.[28] Commenting on the AAT and its steady accretion of jurisdiction over its lifetime,[29] Mendelsohn and Maher (Mendelsohn and Maher 1994: 84) notes:

> As a matter of everyday political reality, it is hard to accept that if, on balance, the external merits review system has been detrimental to the overall public good, this would have escaped the scrutiny either of politicians with a keen eye to satisfying their constituents, or of the organised groups which represent the interests of tribunal users especially those individual who, in terms of the struggles of everyday life, are most at risk in their dealings with Commonwealth administrators.

That degree of satisfaction is apparent not only among users of the system, but also within government. Research by the author and a colleague involving over 40 Commonwealth agencies has indicated that there is strong support for external review, including by tribunals. The close-to-400 individual respondents involved in this research reported positively that tribunals met administrative law objectives by focusing decision makers' attention on their task, and by enhancing accountability and compliance with the law. Approval was also expressed for the quality of the tribunals' reasons, and the respondents substantially agreed that there were no untoward drawbacks on agencies from either the philosophy or approaches of members of tribunals, nor did the review impact too heavily on agency resources, procedures or processes (Creyke and McMillan 2002: 166–81, 185–90). It is notable, too, that it is tribunal review, not court review, which has played the greatest part in interpreting agencies' legislation (Curtis 1998: 47).

[26] *Annual Reports* for 2008–09 for the Commonwealth Administrative Appeals Tribunal, the Social Security Appeals Tribunal, the Veterans' Review Board, the Migration Review Tribunal and the Refugee Review Tribunal.

[27] These include the Australian Competition Tribunal, the Classification Review Board, the Copyright Tribunal, the Defence Force Discipline Appeal Tribunal, the National Native Title Tribunal, the Professional Services Review Tribunal, and the Superannuation Complaints Tribunal.

[28] For example, the Foreword to the Leggatt Review (Leggatt 2001: 3) noted that '[t]he visit to Australia was valuable … because it afforded an opportunity to inspect at first-hand the only tribunal system in any common law jurisdiction that is in important respects well in advance of our own'.

[29] The AAT now has jurisdiction under over 400 separate Commonwealth Acts or regulations: Commonwealth Administrative Appeals Tribunal, *Annual Report 2008–09* (2009) 11.

Partly for this reason, the survey found that it was the AAT which was regarded as the external review body that had the most beneficial impact on administrative decision makers (Creyke and McMillan 2002: 172–73, 186–87).

From these findings it may be concluded that tribunals have met the challenge to find 'a sensible balance … between the need for tribunal familiarity with the operations of the executive branch and the need for tribunal fairness and autonomy' (Mendalsohn and Maher 1994: 94). In particular, as Maher (ibid: 84) noted that:

> [i]n terms of public impact, the AAT has had a dramatic influence. Especially in the area of disputed social welfare benefit entitlement … the AAT has provided a review mechanism where previously there was a void. … For those members of the Australian community at the most disadvantaged end of the socio-economic spectrum, the provision of an effective system of external merits review has proved to be a major advance in the securing of individual rights.

In summary, tribunals have managed satisfactorily to balance the competing elements of administrative justice so as to provide a measure of justice to Australians that, prior to the 1970s, was virtually unknown.

Ombudsman

The Ombudsman offices were among the earlier of the administrative law bodies to be established throughout Australia. The justification for setting up ombudsman offices was to provide public accountability and ensure administrative justice for the individual (Creyke and McMillan 1998: 2). If the right to complain against government is one of the most significant of one's civic rights and freedoms, then the Ombudsman offices are a pre-eminent source of protection of these rights.

There are state and territory Ombudsman operating alongside the Commonwealth Ombudsman.[30] The Commonwealth office has been described as 'one of the main instruments of administrative review at the federal level' (Administrative Review Council 1983: 24). Moreover the principal Ombudsman offices have been supplemented by specialist Ombudsman offices with jurisdiction over particular subject areas such as tax, defence, community services, and health complaints,[31] and a measure of the success of the office has been its replication in a host of private-sector bodies.

The role of the Ombudsman is to investigate maladministration by government, a term which covers a wide spectrum of matters. An investigation may

[30] Principal Legislation: Cth: Ombudsman Act 1982; ACT: Ombudsman Act 1989; NT: Ombudsman (Northern Territory) Act 1980; NSW: Ombudsman Act 1974; Qld: Ombudsman Act 2001; SA: Ombudsman Act 1972; Tas: Ombudsman Act 1978; Vic: Ombudsman Act 1973; WA: Parliamentary Commissioner Act 1971.

[31] The Commonwealth Ombudsman is also the Defence Force Ombudsman, the ACT Ombudsman, the Taxation Ombudsman, the Postal Industry Ombudsman, Immigration Ombudsman and the Law Enforcement Ombudsman. However, complementary specialist bodies have been established: the Commonwealth Inspector-General of Tax (to handle systemic complaints about the operation of the taxation system); and the Inspector-General of the Australian Defence Force.

follow a complaint or result from an own motion inquiry by the office.[32] Typically, the Commonwealth Ombudsman resolves some 35,000 complaints a year, and, since the office was established in 1976, it has handled over 650,000 complaints (Commonwealth Ombudsman Annual Reports 1977–78 to 2008–09). At the state and territory level, the combined Ombudsman offices typically finalise over 35,000 complaints a year.[33] That is, the major Ombudsman offices are dealing with some 70,000 complaints annually in Australia.

Two-thirds of individual complaints 'are resolved in favour of the complainant, substantially or in part' (Senate Standing Committee on Finance and Public Administration 1991: para 5.8). Surprisingly, 'by far the most common remedial action in cases where complaints are found to be justified ... is an adequate explanation by the agency' and '[t]he most common concrete outcome obtained is expedited action by the agency' (ibid: para 5.9; Commonwealth Ombudsman 2003: 15–16). The Commonwealth Ombudsman noted that in only half the complaints finalised was a substantive issue involved (Commonwealth Ombudsman 2003: 12–13). The significance of these findings is that it is often not civil or political rights, or even economic or social rights that are at the forefront of people's concerns when they complain to government. This is a reminder that administrative justice is about protection of interests and is not necessarily a synonym for rights protection.

Features of the Ombudsman schemes that are popular are the independence of the office—the Ombudsman offices report either to the Prime Minister or Premier, or to the Parliament—as well as their inexpensive and informal mode of operations.[34] Specific areas in which the offices have had particular success are complaints about police operations, an area of particular sensitivity for civil liberties, and in the effective handling of *ex gratia* payments. *Ex gratia* payments provide for compensation in circumstances in which, although government action has met the letter of the law, the outcome in an individual case has been inequitable or unjust.

The value of the Ombudsman is illustrated by the recent history of the office in Victoria, which culminated in the constitutional entrenchment of the office in that State.[35] The purpose of the entrenchment was, as the Premier noted in his second reading speech to the Constitution (Parliamentary Reform) Bill 2003, to ensure 'that Victoria has the strongest possible democratic safeguards' (Victorian Hansard 2003: 1).

It is not only its primary, complaint-handling role which makes the Ombudsman so successful. The production of whole-of-government reports is another

[32] Ombudsman Act 1976 (Cth) ss 5, 10, 15. Each State and Territory has legislation containing standards in substantially similar terms.

[33] *Annual Reports* 2008–09 for the States and Territories showed complaints finalised for the year of over 35,000.

[34] The Ombudsman Office takes over a complaint it agrees to investigate and conducts the inquiry.

[35] Constitution Act 1975 (Vic) s 94E.

feature of the Ombudsman role that demonstrates admirably the dual focus of administrative law—providing appropriate avenues for individual complaints, while encouraging systemic reform within public administration. Ombudsman offices have developed manuals of 'best practice' standards for the public service, and fact sheets designed to provide easy 'how-to' guides to officials and citizens, and have produced reports that are influential in developing benchmarks for administrative action and decision making. At the Commonwealth level, these include reports into the dangers of relying on oral advice by government, and on complaint handling by agencies.[36] The implementation of reports such as these has the capacity to enhance fair and equitable treatment of individuals in their interaction with government.

The effectiveness of Ombudsmen processes in meeting administrative justice goals is illustrated by the following extract:

> First, the investigation of individual decisions ensures that they will be examined to determine whether they have been made according to law, by reference to guidelines that are fair, lawful and applied in a reasonable manner. Secondly, the role of Ombudsmen in identifying systemic flaws in administrative practices and policies or, in some cases, the problems that are caused by the absence of an appropriate policy, increases the likelihood that the sources of unfair and arbitrary decisions will be detected and corrected. Thirdly, Ombudsmen are often directly involved in the formation or revision of administrative practices, to ensure that agencies adopt fair and lawful procedures. It should also be noted that the informal negotiations used by Ombudsmen often convince administrative officials to acknowledge and correct errors. A mechanism that enables administrative officials to detect and voluntarily correct errors is a useful supplementary means of ensuring rationality in decision making. (Groves 2002: 204)

Other advantages are the possession by Ombudsman offices of coercive or investigative powers (Craig 2000: 28). These can provide protection for witnesses and bestow on these institutions functions akin to those of a Royal Commission without its attendant costs. This facility was graphically demonstrated in contrasting the Palmer (Palmer 2005) and Alvarez (Commonwealth Ombudsman 2005) inquiries into the immigration department's wrongful detention of two Australian citizens, Cornelia Rau and Vivian Alvarez (or Solon). The first was an executive inquiry with no legislative backing, and the report noted that 'a small number of people declined to be interviewed' (Palmer 2005: para 1.5). By contrast, when the Ombudsman took on the related Alvarez inquiry, the report pointed out that 'the authority provided by the Ombudsman Act 1976 (Cth) meant that all relevant witnesses could be interviewed' and the inquiry could examine a wide range of relevant files including those held by the private contractor responsible for the detention centre (Commonwealth Ombudsman 2005: 6). Following these events, the Commonwealth Ombudsman was asked to examine 247 other immigration

[36] *Issues Relating to Oral Advice: Clients Beware* (1997); *A Good Practice Guide for Effective Complaint Handling* (1997); *Balancing the Risks—Own motion investigation into the role of agencies in providing adequate information to customers in a complex income support system* (1999).

detention cases. The resulting reports which identified flawed decision making and wrongful detention in the majority of cases have contributed significantly to reform in this sensitive area of public administration (McMillan 2007: 1).

The private sector ombudsman offices are also proactive. This is illustrated by an electronic Complaint Line for Australian consumers with links to private sector ombudsman offices, statutory ombudsman offices and government consumer affairs agencies, as well as ADR schemes, the benchmarks for industry-based customer dispute resolution schemes,[37] and a step-by-step guide to access their services.[38]

These examples illustrate that Ombudsman provide an admirable level of both protection for complainants and accessibility. These advantages led Sir Anthony Mason (2007: 15), a former Chief Justice of the High Court and a member of the Kerr Committee, to note of the Commonwealth Office that:

> [o]f the major [Kerr Committee] reforms, the Ombudsman has been perhaps the most successful. … Ombudsmen have succeeded in dealing expeditiously and effectively with a very large number of complaints at very low cost. … [T]he influence of the Ombudsman's activities on the performance of the public service and of government agencies has been most beneficial. It has resulted in a growing understanding that public power is to be exercised for the benefit of the people, that decisions must take account of the interests of stakeholders in accordance with the requirements of due process, and that they must be adequately explained.

In that respect the Ombudsman's office has a distinct advantage because it is not cast in the role of an adversary of government. It works with government departments in investigating complaints, although it may ultimately find fault with what a department has done. Ombudsmen have shown that it is possible to maintain good working relations with government departments without compromising independent decision making.

That commendation has been due in no small part to the fact, that, in the absence of determinative powers, the ombudsman's offices have successfully trod that difficult line between the opposing elements of administrative justice—protecting individuals, while not impeding to too great an extent the efficient and effective management of government for the benefit of the public as a whole. The achievement of that balance was explained by Biganovsky, the former South Australian Ombudsman and the longest serving of any such officer in Australia, to observe that:

> Agencies do listen to the Ombudsman as (a) an authoritative body which has amassed a wealth of experience in its dealings with the public sector; (b) as a body that may provide useful recommendations based on a pattern of complaints; [and] (c) as a body that commands a credible degree of respect and moral authority with most agencies, especially those with whom there have been common dealings. (Biganovsky 1994: 285)

[37] The benchmarks are familiar to administrative lawyers, being accessibility, independence, fairness, accountability, efficiency and effectiveness.

[38] See Complaint Line: www.complaintline.com.au.

Human Rights Institutions

It is often asserted that Australia is one of the few western nations not to have a Bill of Rights. What is not said is that the Commonwealth, the States and the Territories do have anti-discrimination laws and human rights laws,[39] there is a common law code of rights developed by the judiciary (Pearce and Geddes 2006: 165), and the courts are able to resort to international instruments.[40] Specifically named human rights statutes have also been introduced in the Australian Capital Territory[41] and in Victoria,[42] and a federal statute is under consideration. However, the reach of these statutes is limited. Breaches of the legislative rights standards[43] result only in a declaration of incompatibility by the courts, to which a response must be provided by the parliament and the executive.[44] International law may be considered in interpreting the human rights standards. However, the introduction of such material must be weighed against the desirability of relying on the ordinary meaning of the legislation, of not prolonging proceedings, and whether the international material interpreting the international norms is readily accessible.[45] An effective element of the schemes is that legislation requires there to be scrutiny of bills and subordinate legislation against the human rights standards in the Acts.[46] However, a failure of a Bill to comply with the standards does not invalidate the operation of any law.[47]

It is speculative to identify why Australia has been slow to embrace specific human rights legislation and why the reach of those Acts which have been introduced is so limited. It may have been natural caution on the part of the governments, or executive resistance. One hypothesis, however, is that a developed, well-known, and effective system of administrative law obviates the need for such legislation (Allan 2003: 176; Creyke 2003; Gearty 1993: 89; McMillan and Williams 1998: 63). In other words, the level of administrative justice in

[39] The main state and territory anti-discrimination and human rights statutes are: ACT: Discrimination Act 1991, Disability Services Act 1991, Human Rights Act 2004, Human Rights Commission Act 2005; NSW: Anti-Discrimination Act 1977; Community Services (Complaints, Review and Monitoring) Act 1993; Disability Services Act 1993; NT: Anti-Discrimination Act; Disability Services Act; Health and Community Service Complaints Act; Qld: Anti-Discrimination Act 1991; Disability Services Act 2006; SA: Disability Services Act 1993; Equal Opportunity Act 1984; Health and Community Services Complaints Act 2004; Racial Vilification Act 1996; Tas: Disability Services Act 1992; Health Complaints Act 1995; Sex Discrimination Act 1994; Vic: Disability Act 2006; Equal Opportunity Act 1995; Charter of Human Rights and Responsibilities Act 2006; Racial and Religious Tolerance Act 2001; WA; Criminal Code Chap XI—Racist Harassment and Incitement to Racial Hatred; Disability Services Act 1993; Equal Opportunity Act 1984; Health Services (Conciliation and Review) Act 1995; Spent Convictions Act 1988 (WA) Pt 3 Div 3.

[40] *Minister for Immigration v Teoh* (1995) 183 CLR 273.

[41] Human Rights Act 2004 (ACT).

[42] Charter of Human Rights and Responsibilities Act 2006 (Vic).

[43] Largely based on standards drawn from the International Covenant on Civil and Political Rights: Human Rights Act 2004 (ACT) Pt 3.

[44] The limitations replicate in part those applying under the UK Human Rights Act 1998.

[45] Human Rights Act 2004 (ACT) s 31.

[46] Eg Human Rights Act 2004 (ACT) s 38.

[47] Ibid s 39.

Australia has been an adequate substitute for rights-specific jurisprudence.[48] As an early report on whether Australia should have a Bill of Rights noted: 'there is already in place in Australia a complex of laws, institutions and traditions operating to protect fundamental rights and freedoms' (Senate Standing Committee on Constitutional and Legal Affairs 1985: para 2.1). To paraphrase a sentiment initially focused solely on judicial review:

> The fundamental contribution of [administrative law] to individual rights is to give reality to those rights by means of access to a forum where the lawfulness [and merits] of decisions and actions may be tested. (Robertson 1992: 43)

Supporting this hypothesis is the level of usage of existing anti-discrimination and rights-protection legislation. The Australian Human Rights Commission (AHRC)—the national body—has been operating since 1981.[49] In the nearly 30 years of its existence, the Commission has formally dealt with over 37,000 claims (Human Rights and Equal Opportunity Commission Annual Reports 1981–82 to 2008–09). In addition, the Commission receives about 9,000 queries a year that are not included in these figures. To the 2,500 federal claims handled annually by AHRC must be added the roughly 10,000 complaints a year dealt with by State and Territory human rights and equal opportunity bodies, bringing the annual total collectively to some 21,500 complaints.

The Commission's functions are discharged by means of public education, investigation and conciliation of complaints, as well as reports to the federal Attorney-General on breaches of standards in the legislation.[50] For constitutional reasons, AHRC, unlike its State and Territory counterparts, does not have power to make conclusive determinations,[51] and the remedial powers of the Commission are limited to making recommendations for redress.[52] Nonetheless, given the sensitivity of Ministers and government agencies to adverse publicity, this reporting function is an effective way to encourage compliance with the principles to which the legislation gives effect.[53] Nor do the numbers of applications to the human rights and anti-discrimination bodies suggest that the absence of determinative powers at the federal level has been a deterrent to usage.

[48] The argument is the reverse of the view expressed by Lord Hoffman in *Wainwright v Home Office* [2003] UK HL 53, in a decision in which the House of Lords decided there was no common law right to privacy, that '[T]he coming into force of the Human Rights Act 1998 weakens the argument for saying that a general tort of invasion of privacy is needed to fill gaps in the existing remedies'.

[49] The initial legislation which set up the Commission was passed in 1981.

[50] Human Rights and Equal Opportunity Commission Act 1986 (Cth) ss 11, 20, 31.

[51] *Brandy v Human Rights and Equal Opportunity Commission* (1995) 183 CLR 245.

[52] Human Rights and Equal Opportunity Act 1986 (Cth) ss 11(1)(f), 28, 29, 31(b), 34, 35. See too *Brandy v Human Rights and Equal Opportunity Commission* (1995) 183 CLR 245.

[53] These rights and principles include not only those anti-discrimination rules in the Act but also the rights which are annexed as schedules to the Act or which have subsequently been declared. The Human Rights and Equal Opportunity Act 1986 (Cth) s 3 defines 'human rights' to mean 'the rights and freedoms recognised in the Covenant, declared by the Declarations *or recognised or declared by any relevant international instrument*'. Instruments recognised subsequently have included the *UN Convention on the rights of the child*.

The effectiveness of existing legislation is enhanced because it applies not only to the public sector, but also to the private sector. In other words, the human rights and equality standards apply to all Australians. Another beneficial feature of the human rights and anti-discrimination bodies is that, like the Ombudsman offices, the institutions take over the inquiry and undertake the investigation. Accordingly, there is no cost or litigation burden on the applicant, a significant fillip to the achievement of administrative justice.

Measuring Administrative Justice

There is little point in requiring that bodies provide administrative justice if there is no way of assessing whether administrative justice has been achieved. Indeed, the development of standards by which that assessment can occur gives meaning to the expression 'administrative justice'. As one writer put it: 'administrative justice cannot be measured without defining what it is' (Neave 2000: 124). Meaning and measurement are symbiotic.

This continues to be an area which has been under-explored. The rhetoric that administrative justice means fairness is insufficiently precise to be helpful. Nonetheless, it is common to see the test for administrative justice stated in these terms. Indeed, until the late 1990s, Australian authors frequently referred simply to administrative justice as 'code' for a just outcome (Chaaya 1997: 547; Crock 2004: 51; Crock and Gibian 1998: 463),[54] or fair process (Crock 2004: 51; Finn 2002: 239). To do so fails to take account of the alternative, collective good, element of the definition.

They were not alone. Galligan (1996: 237) suggested that the principal concern of administrative justice means:

> [t]o treat each person fairly by upholding the standards of fair treatment expressed in the statutory scheme, together with standards derived from other sources. The primary object is still an accurate and proper application of authoritative standards but the emphasis is now on accuracy and propriety in each case, not just in the aggregate.

Although this passage refers to 'standards derived from other sources' and 'authoritative standards', it is not clear what these standards entail. Do they include judicial review standards, or broader administrative law standards such as equality, effectiveness, efficiency, independence, integrity, accountability and human rights principles?[55]

[54] See eg Transcript of Proceedings, *Re Minister for Immigration and Multicultural Affairs, ex p Epeabaka* (High Court of Australia, I R L Freckelton, 10 October 2000).

[55] See, eg, the *Legislative Standards Act 1992* (Qld) s 4, which requires that drafters of legislation strive not to breach common law principles enshrining rights such as the right not to be self-incriminated, the principle that legislation not be retrospective, and that natural justice be accorded.

There is no dearth of statements of principles for an effective administrative justice system. Returning to an Australian context, French J derived administrative justice standards of 'lawfulness, fairness, rationality and intelligibility' from what he described as the 'basic and well-established grounds of judicial review' (French 2001: 30; French 2003: 1).[56] At the same time, he acknowledged that the attributes of accessibility, affordability, and timeliness were desirable features of administrative justice imposed on decision makers and tribunals (French 2001: 30). Even with these additions, the list is not sufficiently concrete. Performance measures need to be prescriptive to be helpful and indicators for effective and efficient administration should be separately itemised.

In 1994, the Access to Justice Advisory Committee attempted to categorise what was required for an effective administrative justice system. The report (Access to Justice Advisory Committee 1994: para 13.9) concluded:

> [A]n administrative justice system fails if it does not provide:
>
> a comprehensive, principled and accessible system of merit review;
> a requirement that government decision makers inform persons affected by government decisions of their rights of review;
> a simplified judicial review procedure by comparison to judicial review under the common law;
> a right for persons who are affected by decisions to obtain reasons for those decisions;
> broad rights of access to information held by government; and
> an adequately resourced ombudsman or commissioner of complaints with a general power to review government action.

While prescriptive as to institutions and access rights, the list provides little guidance as to how these institutions should operate or how rights are to be provided in order that the outcome and the process can be seen to be administratively just. Nor does it acknowledge the alternative imperatives of public administration.

In 1995, the Commonwealth Ombudsman's office identified independence, jurisdictional certainty, investigative and coercive powers, accountability, an ability to make statements in the public interest, accessibility, impartiality and fairness as essential features of an effective ombudsman's office (quoted by Barbour 2002: 58). Other commentators have listed: flexibility and informality; confidentiality; externality; discretion to refuse to investigate; accountability to the Parliament rather than the executive; and having the ability to undertake 'own motion' inquiries and to possess determinative not just recommendatory powers (Barbour 2002: 59). Again, these are a valuable collection of principles but they require translation into more concrete indicators to be effective.

The ARC's report on the federal tribunal system (Administrative Review Council 1995: para 2.10) identified as objectives of the tribunal system: fairness,

[56] In 2003, his Honour had truncated the list to 'lawfulness, fairness and rationality in the exercise of public power'. See French (2003).

accessibility, timeliness, informality and having effective mechanisms to ensure that agencies become aware of and comply with tribunal decisions. It noted (ibid: para 5.88), however, that there was a lack of reliable and comparable statistical information on evaluating tribunal performance against these measures.

These lists of principles are deficient on two counts: they give no indication of how achievement of the principles is to be measured. In other words they have not attempted to translate principle into performance measures; nor do they give equal listing to the principles (and indicators) which should underpin realisation of the competing priorities of government.

The first attempt to identify methods of measuring administrative justice arose at the 1999 AIAL conference. Although what follows does scant justice to the relevant papers, in summary their conclusions were that:

> what is needed is a suite of indicators, particularly when there are multiple and competing objectives, as for example, with the measurement of 'administrative justice'; (McDonald 2000: 142)
>
> external factors which can adversely affect measurements, such as barriers to review, the absence of legal aid, or the quality of representation, must be allowed for; (Neave 2000: 128–29)
>
> indicators must be expressed in terms of desired outcomes or outputs, that is, performance measures or benchmarks; (McDonald 2000: 142) and
>
> performance measures should be used to produce genuine improvement and accountability, not symbolic ends (McDonald 2000: 147; Neave 2000: 128, 137).

This list establishes a framework for the development of performance measures but goes no further. However, at the 1999 conference, despite the difficulty of assessing 'complex and contested objectives' (Neave 2000: 127), some attempt was made at least to set principles to guide the balancing process (McDonald 2000: 142–43; Neave 2000: 127, 140):

> the costs of performance measurement should not outweigh the benefits; (McDonald 2000: 139–40; Neave 2000: 126)
>
> 'efficiency' should not be privileged over 'effectiveness'; (Neave 2000: 128–29)
>
> prescriptive performance measures should not lead to 'goal displacement', such as emphasising 'output targets over accuracy'; (McDonald 2000: 150; Neave 2000: 126)
>
> when competing objectives such as 'administrative efficiency' or 'justice' are being measured, the indicators are likely to produce different answers; (Creyke and McMillan 2000: 6–7) and
>
> the indicators will vary with the perspective of the views being measured, be they official, citizen, court or tribunal. Social security recipients are likely to have a different view of whether they have been offered administrative justice to that of the public official who is subject to government fiscal and other policies and efficiency and effectiveness constraints. To take a more controversial example, a person seeking refugee status is likely to have a view of administrative justice which differs from that of an immigration

> department, which is alert to preventing unlawful entrants coming into the country. Similarly, a lawyer, court or tribunal is likely to consider independence, compliance with procedural protections and legal standards, and the availability of broad grounds for challenge as more likely to meet the standard, whereas timeliness or courteous treatment may be the paramount interests of an applicant. (Neave 2000: 132–35)

These are still early days in performance measurement. It is relatively common to find quantitative measurements, for example, of costs and delays,[57] but relatively uncommon to find figures on qualitative aspects of administrative justice, including whether decisions have been 'fair and just'. This recognises the difficulty of devising standards for measuring complex notions such as 'justice' (Neave 2000: 125–26, 130–32). In addition, little attempt has been made to reconcile the measures devised for the competing elements of administrative justice. However, measurement, if conducted appropriately, has the advantage that it encourages government to consult user groups. Such practices reflect the values of participatory democracy, and are capable of resolving some of the tensions inherent in the dichotomy between administrative and justice values.

Consultation identifies what priorities different players in the system would give to aspects of administrative justice, with some unexpected results (Koller 2000: 150; Malone 2000: 209). This is illustrated by two Australian studies. A Senate inquiry into the Commonwealth Ombudsman's office concluded that 'complaints predominantly are about delays, errors and misunderstandings' rather than correct outcomes, and that 'financial implications, where they exist, are typically small' (Senate Standing Committee on Finance and Public Administration 1991: 57). Equally unexpected were the findings of the 1996 federal *Administrative Appeals Tribunal Client Satisfaction Survey*. The respondents indicated they valued speedy resolution of disputes, client-centred premises and speedy responses to telephone calls and letters over independence of the Tribunal, and 'clear reasons for decision' (Australian Law Reform Commission 1998: para 11.41). In other words, administrative justice varies according to the individual's interests and needs and is often focussed solely on matters of process, not substance.

This analysis has indicated that, although a start has been made on the measurement of administrative justice, much remains to be done. The methods by which benchmarks or indicators of performance are identified are an important part of the process, not least when objectives or principles, such as 'administrative' and 'justice', may conflict.

[57] For example, such statistics were provided for courts and tribunals in the 1990s: Australian Law Reform Commission (1998: para 11.4); Australian Law Reform Commission (2000: para 2.222). However, there is less information on comparable figures for primary decision makers. In addition, the Productivity Commission provides in its annual *Report on Government Services* a snapshot of court administration for courts throughout Australia. Figures in the Report, however, relate only to numbers of cases, finalisation and clearance rates, and costs: see Productivity Commission (2006, para 6.7).

A Culture of Administrative Justice

Having appropriate rules, standards and institutions is not enough.[58] Unless the ethos of administrative justice is embedded, the system will be ineffective. As French J (French 2000: 20–21) put it:

> [W]hat administrative justice means in practice depends upon the culture reflected in the practices and attitudes of ministers, departments, authorities, statutory office holders and individual departmental officers, administrative review tribunals and the courts. The vast majority of official decisions which affect people will not go to review and their compliance with standards of administrative justice will depend on the attitudes of the people who make them.

There is a dearth of empirical work on such issues (Australian Law Reform Commission 1998: paras 1.27–1.46). However, there have been two major studies in Australia on executive perceptions of administrative law. The studies provided insights into how well officials, at least at the federal level, have embraced the underlying principles of administrative justice, and how agencies have reacted to findings by courts in favour of applicants for judicial review (Creyke and McMillan 2002: 163; Creyke and McMillan 2004a: 82; Creyke and McMillan 2004b: 161).

The first study involved 40 government agencies and over 360 federal government official decision makers. Questions referred principally to the impact of external review by courts and tribunals. The overall picture was gauged best by the question 'does administrative law achieve its core objectives?' That question was designed to test, for example, whether:

decision makers give consideration to the impact of their decisions on those who are affected, a key aspect of 'administrative justice';

the executive explains and justifies its exercise of power (executive accountability); and

administrative law review has a normative impact on the way in which decision making is carried out (good administration).

As the study notes, these objectives were too broad for a single question, but the responses to the question gave an indication of attitudes towards administrative law and its aims, including the provision of administrative justice.

There was a surprisingly high level of agreement that external review met its core objectives. Some 93.7 per cent of officers concluded that external review was an important mechanism for ensuring that decision makers were accountable (Creyke and McMillan 2002: 167). Individual comments to the effect that: external review is 'crucial to honest and sound decision-making'; that it is a 'safety valve';

[58] It is for this reason that codes of conduct and service charters such as the *Australian Public Service Code of Conduct* and *Australian Public Service Values* are imposing new standards of professionalism on officials: see eg Public Service Act 1999 (Cth) ss 10, 13. See also *Hot Holdings Pty Ltd v Creasy* (2002) 210 CLR 438, 465–67 (Kirby J).

that it 'keeps us honest'; and that 'without it consistency across the agency would be abysmal' are indicative of this support (ibid: 167). 85 per cent of officers perceived external review as an important mechanism for ensuring that officers complied with the law, and 79.7 per cent agreed that administrative law beneficially directs the attention of decision makers to the impact of their decisions on individuals (ibid: 167).

Other relevant responses were that external review does not undermine government policy (81.7 per cent of respondents) and that external review bodies do not give too much emphasis to individual rights when making decisions (62.7 per cent) (ibid: 169). Nonetheless, only 51.1 per cent agreed that external review bodies adequately understand the context for and pressures on government decision making. However, in relation to whether administrative law has drawbacks in its impact on agency resources, procedures and procedures, 67.3 per cent of officers rejected the proposition that external review redirects resources unacceptably to the resolution of individual complaints. At the same time, only 45 per cent of respondents agreed that the benefits of external review justified the costs to the agency, a statistic generally at odds with the previous replies. It was noteworthy that the answers to this question were more positive from service-delivery agencies than from policy departments (ibid: 168–71). On the whole, the responses indicated a high degree of approval for, and hence acceptance of, the benefits of review by courts and tribunals.

Even more striking was the parallel 10-year study into the outcomes of judicial review before the Federal Court and the High Court. The judicial review study measured the final outcome in cases where an applicant had been successful before the court, and was verified by both the applicant, or their legal representative, and the agency. The findings are a testament to a culture of compliance. Since success in a judicial review hearing results only in an order remitting the application to be decided afresh in accordance with law, the ultimate finding may in fact be the same as the original decision. There is no requirement to find in favour of an applicant. Indeed, the authors expected that in most cases the final decision would confirm the original result. Contrary to that expectation, the results showed that in most cases (80.1 per cent for agencies; 74.8 per cent for applicants) not only did the agency reconsider the application in accordance with the court order, but that, in possibly as high as 78 per cent of cases, the outcome for the applicant was favourable (Creyke and McMillan 2004a: 86–87). This indicates that not only was a win in a judicial review hearing likely to lead to a favourable outcome for the litigant, but findings adverse to an agency were often a precursor of wider systemic benefits. As the study noted (ibid: 98):

> Individual rulings are frequently followed by other governmental action to amend legislation, change policy, rewrite manuals or alter decision-making procedures and practices.

Overall, the studies reflect an understanding of the competing imperatives underpinning administrative justice within Australian public administration, and a level of comfort that the tribunals, ombudsman, and courts in Australia have achieved a balance that is acceptable to public administration.

Conclusion

The Kerr Committee identified the central elements of administrative justice—efficiency and justice to the individual—but failed to spell out how the two would co-exist. The subsequent attempts to explore the notion suggest that it is unlikely that any conclusive test for administrative justice can be identified. Rather, reliance must be placed on the wisdom of officials, tribunal members and courts to judge which of the competing elements identified are to be advantaged in particular circumstances. There must also be an acceptance that both elements are relevant, as chameleon-like 'administrative justice' takes its meaning from its context.

To do this requires the executive, the courts and the tribunals to be clear about their understanding of 'administrative justice'. That in turn requires attention to two other considerations: (i) since administrative justice can only be effected through institutions, the impact of the powers and functions of each institution must be considered; and (ii) in addition, the values which that concept embodies must also be identified (Creyke and McMillan 2000: 3–4).

Those values will need to encompass both the 'administrative' and the 'justice' elements of 'administrative justice'. It is not possible in the abstract to decide on the balance between the two. Which element takes precedence will depend on the circumstances, and providing guidance on those circumstances requires the development of benchmarks. In turn, these benchmarks must be mapped, for example, by performance indicators. Those measures, developed for each administrative law institution, will provide the blueprint for administrative justice in Australian administrative law. It is this task that now faces Australian administrative law practitioners and researchers.

References

Access to Justice Advisory Committee (1994) *Access to Justice—an Action Plan* (Canberra, Commonwealth Parliament).

Administrative Appeals Tribunal Annual Reports 2003–04 to 2008–09.

—— (2009) *Annual Report 2008–09.*

Administrative Review Council (1983) *Annual Report 1982–83.*

—— (1995) *Better Decisions: Review of Commonwealth Merits Review Tribunals,* Report No 39.

Allan, J (2003) 'A Defence of the Status Quo' in T Campbell, J Goldsworthy and A Stone (eds), *Protecting Human Rights—Instruments and Institutions* (Oxford, Oxford University Press).

Allars, M (1990) *Introduction to Australian Administrative Law* (Sydney, Butterworths).

—— (1997a) 'Review of DJ Galligan, *Due Process and Fair Procedures: A Study of Administrative Procedures* and JM Evans et al, *Administrative Law: Cases, Text and Materials*' 19 *Sydney Law Review* 411.

—— (1997b) *Australian Administrative Law: Cases and Materials* (Sydney, Butterworths).

Aronson, M, Dyer, B and Groves, M (2009) *Judicial Review of Administrative Action*, 4th edn (Sydney, Law Book Co).

Australian Law Reform Commission (1998) *Review of the Adversarial System of Litigation: Federal Tribunal Proceedings*, Issues Paper No 24 (Canberra, Commonwealth of Australia).

—— (2000) *Managing Justice: A Review of the Federal Civil Justice System*, Report No 89 (Canberra, Commonwealth of Australia).

Barbour, B (2002) 'What are the Essential Features of an Ombudsman?' in R Creyke and J McMillan (eds), *Administrative Law: The Essentials* (Canberra, AIAL).

Barker, M and Simmonds, R (2004) 'Delivering Administrative Justice in WA' 84 *Reform* 23.

Bennett, A (2000) 'Aspects of Private Sector Regulation' in R Creyke and J McMillan (eds), *Administrative Justice—The Core and the Fringe* (Canberra, AIAL).

Biganovsky, E (1994) 'New values for old? Is the review genie trapped inside the lamp of scrutiny?' in S Argument (ed), *Administrative Law and Public Administration: Happily Married or Living Apart under the Same Roof?* (Canberra, AIAL).

Blackwell, J (2003) 'A Discussion of the Duty and Jurisdiction of the Courts to Review Administrative Decisions' 3 *Queensland University of Technology Law and Justice Journal* 182.

Bradley, AW (1995) 'Administrative Justice: A Developing Human Right?' 1 *European Public Law* 347.

Brown, AJ (1993) 'Administrative Justice for Aboriginal People—Can it be Done?' 3 (61) *Aboriginal Law Bulletin* 21.

Cameron, A (2000) 'Administrative Justice at the Fringe of Government—Corporate Regulation' in R Creyke and J McMillan (eds), *Administrative Justice—The Core and the Fringe* (Canberra, AIAL).

Chaaya, M (1997) 'Proposed Changes to the Review of Migration Decisions: Sensible Reform Agenda or Political Expediency?' 19 *Sydney Law Review* 547.

Committee of Review (1973) *Prerogative Writ Procedures: Report of Committee of Review*, Parliamentary Paper 56 (Canberra, Commonwealth Parliament).

Committee on Administrative Discretions (1973a) *Report of the Committee on Administrative Discretions*, Parliamentary Paper No 53 (Commonwealth Parliament).

—— (1973b) *Report of the Committee on Administrative Discretions*, Parliamentary Paper No 316 (Commonwealth Parliament).

Commonwealth of Australia (1976) *Royal Commission on Australian Government Administration*, Report.

Commonwealth Ombudsman (1997a) *A Good Practice Guide for Effective Complaint Handling.*

—— (1997b) *Issues Relating to Oral Advice: Clients Beware.*

—— (2003) Annual Report 2002–03.

—— (2005) *Inquiry into the Circumstances of the Vivian Alvarez Matter*, Report No 3.

—— Annual Reports 1977–78 to 2008–09.

Craig, P (2000) 'Three Perspectives on the Relationship between Administrative Justice and Administrative Law' in R Creyke and J McMillan (eds), *Administrative Justice—The Core and the Fringe* (Canberra, AIAL).

—— (2008) *Administrative Law*, 6th edn (London, Sweet & Maxwell).

Creyke, R (2003) 'The Performance of Administrative Law in Protecting Rights' (paper presented at a Conference on Human Rights, Melbourne, December).

—— (2006) 'Administrative Justice: Beyond the Courtroom Door' *Acta Juridica* (University of Cape Town Law Journal) 233.

—— (2007) 'Administrative Justice—Towards Integrity in Government' 31 *Melbourne University Law Review* 705.

'Creyke, R and Groves, M (2010) 'The Continuing Evolution of Administrative Law: An Academic Perspective' 59 *Admin Review.*

Creyke, R and McMillan, J (1998) 'Introduction: Administrative Law Assumptions ... Then and Now' in R Creyke and J McMillan (eds), *The Kerr Vision of Australian Administrative Law—At the Twenty-Five Year Mark* (Canberra, ANU Centre for International and Public Law).

—— (2000) 'Administrative Justice—The Concept Emerges' in R Creyke and J McMillan (eds), *Administrative Justice—The Core and the Fringe* (Canberra, AIAL).

—— (2002) 'Executive Perceptions of Administrative Law—An Empirical Study' 9 *Australian Journal of Administrative Law* 163.

—— (2004a) 'Judicial Review Outcomes—An Empirical Study' 11 *Australian Journal of Administrative Law* 82.

—— (2004b) 'The Operation of Judicial Review in Australia' in M Hertogh and S Halliday (eds), *Judicial Review and Bureaucratic Impact: International and Interdisciplinary Perspectives* (Cambridge, Cambridge University Press).

—— (2005) *Control of Government Action* (Sydney, LexisNexis Butterworths)

Crock, M (2004) 'Judging Refugees: The Clash of Power and Institutions in the Development of Australian Refugee Law' 26 *Sydney Law Review* 51.

—— (2006) *Seeking Asylum Alone: A Study of Australian Law, Policy and Practice Regarding Unaccompanied and Separated Children* (Sydney, Themis Press).

Crock, M and Gibian, M (1998) 'Before the High Court: *Minister for Immigration and Ethnic Affairs v Eshetu*' 20 *Sydney Law Review* 457.

Crock, M and Saul, B (2002) *Future Seekers: Refugees and the Law in Australia* (The Federation Press: Sydney).

Cronin, K (2000) 'The Role of Legal Education in Achieving Administrative Justice' in R Creyke and J McMillan (eds), *Administrative Justice—The Core and the Fringe* (Canberra, AIAL).

Curtis, L (1989) 'Crossing the Frontier Between Law and Administration' 58 *Canberra Bulletin of Public Administration* 55.

—— (1998) 'The Vision Splendid: A Time for Re-Appraisal' in R Creyke and J McMillan (eds), *The Kerr Vision of Australian Administrative Law—At the Twenty-Five Year Mark* (Canberra, ANU Centre for International and Public Law).

De Smith, SA, Woolf, H, Jowell, JL and Le Sueur, A (2007) *De Smith's Judicial Review*, 6th edn (London, Sweet & Maxwell).

Douglas, R (2009) *Douglas and Jones's Administrative Law*, 6th edn (Sydney, The Federation Press).

Faulkner, Senator J (2008) 'Transparency and Accountability: Our Agenda', *11th Annual Australian Institute of Judicial Administration Tribunals Conference*, Queensland, 30 October.

Finn, C (2002) 'The Justiciability of Administrative Decisions: A Redundant Concept' 30 *Federal Law Review* 239.

Fleming, G (2008) 'Tribunals in Australia: How to achieve independence' in R Creyke (ed), *Tribunals in the Common Law World* (Sydney, The Federation Press).

Forbes, JRS (2006) *Justice in Tribunals*, 2nd edn (Sydney, The Federation Press).

Free, S (2000) 'Across the Public/Private Divide: Accountability and Administrative Justice in the Telecommunications Industry' in R Creyke and J McMillan (eds), *Administrative Justice—The Core and the Fringe* (Canberra, AIAL).

French, Justice RS (2000) 'Administrative Justice in Australian Administrative Law' in R Creyke and J McMillan (eds), *Administrative Justice—The Core and the Fringe* (Canberra, AIAL).

—— (2001) 'Judicial Review Rights' 28 *AIAL Forum* 30.

—— (2003) 'The Equitable Geist in the Machinery of Administrative Justice' 39 *AIAL Forum* 1.

Galligan, DJ (1996) *Due Process and Fair Procedures: A Study of Administrative Procedures* (Oxford, Clarendon Press).

Gearty, CA (1993) 'The European Court of Human Rights and the Protection of Civil Liberties: An Overview' 52 CLJ 89.

Groves, M (2002) 'Ombudsman's Jurisdiction in Prisons' 28 *Monash University Law Review* 181.

Harris, S (2000) 'Another Salvo Across the Bow: Migration Legislation Amendment Bill (No 2) 2000 (Cth)' 23 *University of New South Wales Law Journal* 208.

Human Rights and Equal Opportunities Commission, Annual Reports 1981–82 to 2007–08.

Kerr Committee (1971) *Commonwealth Administrative Review Committee Report*, Parliamentary Paper No 144 (Canberra, Commonwealth Parliament).

Kirk, J (2000) 'The Constitution and Administrative Justice' in R Creyke and J McMillan (eds), *Administrative Justice—The Core and the Fringe* (Canberra, AIAL).

Kirk, L (2000) 'The Constitutionalisation of Administrative Justice' in R Creyke and J McMillan (eds), *Administrative Justice—The Core and the Fringe* (Canberra, AIAL).

Koller, S (2000) 'Back from the Fringe—What Consumers Expect from Administrative Justice' in R Creyke and J McMillan (eds), *Administrative Justice—The Core and the Fringe* (Canberra, AIAL).

Legal, Constitutional and Administrative Review Committee, Queensland Parliament (2005) *Accessibility of Administrative Justice: Discussion Paper.*

Mendelsohn, O and Maher, L (1994) 'The Australian Experience in Merits Review Tribunals' in O Mendelsohn and L Maher (eds), *Courts, Tribunals and New Approaches to Justice* (Melbourne, La Trobe University Press).

Malone, A (2000) 'Digital Television Regulation—Administrative Justice and the Public Interest' in R Creyke and J McMillan (eds), *Administrative Justice—The Core and the Fringe* (Canberra, AIAL).

Mashaw, JL (1983) *Bureaucratic Justice* (New Haven, Yale University Press).

Mason, Sir A (1989) 'Administrative Review: The Experience of the First Twelve Years' 18 *Federal Law Review* 122.

—— (2007) 'The 30th Anniversary: A Judicial Perspective' 58 *Admin Review* 15.

McClelland, The Hon R MP (2008) 'Keynote address' *11th Annual Australian Institute of Judicial Administration Tribunals Conference*, Queensland, 30 October.

McDonald, L (2000) 'Measuring Administrative Justice—Lessons from the Report on Government Services' in R Creyke and J McMillan (eds), *Administrative Justice—The Core and the Fringe* (Canberra, AIAL).

McLeod, R (2000) 'Administrative Justice—An Ombudsman's Perspective on Dealing with the Exceptional' in R Creyke and J McMillan (eds), *Administrative Justice—The Core and the Fringe* (Canberra, AIAL).

McMillan, J (2000a) 'Administrative Justice—An Ombudsman's Perspective on Dealing with the Exceptional' in R Creyke and J McMillan (eds), *Administrative Justice—The Core and the Fringe* (Canberra, AIAL).

—— (2000b) 'Administrative Tribunals' 76 *Reform* 71.
—— (2001) 'An Academic Contribution to Australian Administrative Law' 8 *Australian Journal of Administrative Law* 214.
—— (2006) 'The Role of the Ombudsman in Protecting Human Rights (Paper presented at the Conference on Legislatures and the Protection of Human Rights, The University of Melbourne, 21 July).
—— (2007) 'Lessons for Public Administration: the Ombudsman Investigation of Referred Immigration Cases' (Paper presented at an Institute of Public Administration Australia seminar, Canberra, 6 August).
McMillan, J and Williams, N (1998) 'Administrative Law and Human Rights' in D Kinley (ed), *Human Rights in Australian Law* (Sydney, The Federation Press).
Migration Review Tribunal (2009) *Annual Report 2008–09.*
Neave, M (2000) 'In the Eye of the Beholder—Measuring Administrative Justice' in R Creyke and J McMillan (eds), *Administrative Justice—The Core and the Fringe* (Canberra, AIAL).
O'Connor, Judge K (2000) 'Defining Administrative Justice—Perspectives from a New Tribunal' in R Creyke and J McMillan (eds), *Administrative Justice—The Core and the Fringe* (Canberra, AIAL).
Palmer, M (2005) *Inquiry into the Circumstances of the Immigration Detention of Cornelia Rau: Report.*
Pearce, D, and Geddes, R (2006) *Statutory Interpretation in Australia*, 5th edn (Sydney, Butterworths).
Productivity Commission (2006) *Report on Government Services.*
Refugee Review Tribunal (2009) *Annual Report 2008–09.*
Robertson, A (1992) 'Judicial Review and the Protection of Individual Rights' in J McMillan (ed), *Administrative Law: Does the Public Benefit?'* (Canberra, AIAL).
Senate Standing Committee on Constitutional and Legal Affairs (1985) *A Bill of Rights for Australia?* (Canberra, Commonwealth of Australia).
Senate Standing Committee on Finance and Public Administration (1991) *Review of the Office of the Commonwealth Ombudsman* (Canberra, Commonwealth of Australia).
Social Security Appeals Tribunal (2009) *Annual Report 2008–09.*
Sykes, EI et al (1997) *General Principles of Administrative Law*, 4th edn (Sydney, Butterworths, 1997).
Tomasic, R and Fleming, D (1991) *Australian Administrative Law* (Sydney, Law Book Co).
Veterans' Review Board (2009) *Annual Report 2008–09.*
Victorian Civil and Administrative Tribunal (2008) *Annual Report 2008–09.*
Victorian Hansard (2003) *Constitution (Parliamentary Reform) Bill, Second Reading*, 1 (30 July).
Wade, Sir W and Forsyth, C (2004) *Administrative Law*, 10th edn (Oxford University Press, 2004).

13

Administrative Justice from a Continental European Perspective

ALBERTJAN TOLLENAAR AND KO DE RIDDER

Introduction

The Story of Ahmet

Ahmet Okci is a barkeeper in Almelo, a town in the eastern part of the Netherlands. In the last months of 2008 he is awaiting the start of the criminal proceedings. A conviction is inevitable, as it is perfectly clear that he took one of the aldermen of Almelo and five of his civil servants hostage, using a gun. This crime caused a major turmoil as crimes like this don't often take place: not in the Netherlands and certainly not in a quiet town like Almelo.

A few months later, the peace in Almelo seems to be restored. Meanwhile, journalists have been doing research into the circumstances and the causes of this crime. What was it that pushed Ahmet, known as a calm and law-abiding person, to commit this crime? This research uncovered some curious facts. Ahmet wanted to do some renovations to his café. He was under the impression that a building permit would not be necessary and, after signing the tenancy contract, immediately started work on his café. After a few weeks hard work, he received a letter from the municipal authority notifying him that he would need permits for his activities. He immediately applied for a building permit and simultaneously applied for the other permits that he needed to develop his café. He was optimistic about his chances since there were no obvious obstacles that would require the local authority to reject his applications. In any case, his café was situated in an area in which there were several other cafés, all of which were running without encountering any bureaucratic problems. Because he had taken out several loans and needed income as soon as possible to pay the interest, he continued with his renovations.

After a few weeks it became clear that the local authority was not willing to co-operate. First, the building permit was rejected because the authority planned to develop the area in which Ahmet's café was situated. As a part of this plan, the area in which his café was situated would be rebuilt over a ten year period. There was no obvious reason why Ahmet could not open his café before this activity began. But the alderman responsible for the development project demanded that he amend the duration of his tenancy contract. Unless he signed a limited-duration tenancy contract for a period of five years, the building permit would be rejected. After a lot of pleading Ahmet decided to give in and reduced the duration of his tenancy contract to five years.

The other permits, amongst which the licence required for a catering establishment and a permit for an outdoor terrace on the pavement, were still under investigation. The decision-making procedure took more time than Ahmet had expected. Since he needed the income, he started work on renovating his café and, when he had finished the renovations, he opened his café. Only a few weeks later he received two letters from the local authority. The first was a rejection of the terrace permit. The argument used by the local authority was that the square situated in front of the café was occupied by a stand. In fact the square was large enough for the stand to be moved to somewhere else in the square, without bothering Ahmet or the stand. But when Ahmet suggested this reasonable solution, his arguments were waved aside. Ahmet was furious as the local authority seemed to be more co-operative with other cafés that had opened terraces without even having a terrace permit.

The second letter contained a penalty demanding that Ahmet close his café, as he still didn't have the necessary licence under the Licensing and Catering Act. Ahmet went to court and the administrative judge annulled this decision, considering that it was too early to impose a penalty, as the investigation regarding the permit had not been concluded. It might still be possible to legalise the café. Soon after this decision, the local authority formally rejected Ahmet's application for a licence, referring to some vague suspicions concerning Ahmet's wife and one of his employees. With reference to the Public Administration Probity Screening Act, these suspicions provided an opportunity for the authority to reject the application. Now the legalisation of the café was impossible and Ahmet would have to close it. After receiving the letter with this last message, Ahmet became furious, burned down his café and took the alderman and a few public servants hostage.

This dispassionate description of the facts of the story makes it clear that the interaction of a citizen with an administrative authority can be complex and sometimes bewildering. From Ahmet's perspective, he only encountered sabotage from the municipal officials. He could not make sense of the local authority's decision making. As far as he could see, in his case the municipal officials went by the book whereas, in cases involving neighbouring cafés, they were lenient. Ahmet felt that he was treated as an outsider, an alien, and that he lacked direct access to the decision makers inside the local authority—an advantage that other café owners had. Furthermore, as far as he could see, he had won his case in court: the administrative judge had found the local authority's decision making wanting. This made it even harder for him to understand the final decision, which had made it impossible for him to open the café. From the point of view of the municipal government, however, the decision was entirely consistent with the law and with municipal policies. A weighing of all the interests at stake resulted in the conclusion that Ahmed's interest had to give way. So was justice achieved in this case?

What about Administrative Justice?

Administrative justice is an elusive concept. As a normative ideal, it involves general notions about how government bodies and public agencies should deal with their citizens. The core idea is probably that of *fairness*. A public authority should use its powers in a fair, efficient and effective way, showing due appreciation for the interests of the citizens that are involved in a decision or action of that agency. Even though it is relatively easy to agree on the general idea, there is a lot of ambiguity in this concept once it is put into practice.

Often, what administrative justice should be in real life administrative situations becomes clearer when it is contrasted with its counterpart, administrative injustice. Thus, for most people, it is simply unacceptable that powers that have been conferred on a public authority are used differently in situations that do not really differ. Equal treatment is a universal human ideal. With reference to Ahmet's case, there is at least a suspicion that the municipal authority violated this principle of equal treatment. Furthermore, for most people in Western societies, it is unacceptable if obtaining a permit depends on whether or not the applicant has privileged access to the staff of a public agency. String pulling, favouritism, preferential treatment and nepotism are all anathema in the administrative state. In Ahmet's case, there is a lingering doubt that, unlike Ahmet, other entrepreneurs enjoyed the benefit of inside connections. To counter any such unfair administration, authorities are usually required to offer clear and transparent reasons to support their decisions, such as why a permit was granted or rejected. In this case, the explanation that was offered was limited, to say the least.

At the same time, fair treatment is not always as clear cut as it may seem at first glance. Public authorities are called upon to promote the general interest as much as they are required to respect the interests of individual citizens. *Effectiveness* therefore is an additional requirement of administrative decision making. Beyond that, public agencies are expected to be parsimonious with public resources. In that sense administrative justice also consists of efficient provision of public services. What seems unfair from the perspective of one specific private interest could turn out to be perfectly reasonable when the wider interests of the effective and efficient conduct of public affairs are taken into account.

When it comes to an outline of administrative justice, it is important to include these overlapping prerequisites of administrative behaviour. Thus the core of administrative justice is the absence of administrative arbitrariness.[1] If there is a choice between alternatives that do not imply arbitrary use of administrative

[1] *Cf* Herweijer (2007).

powers, administrative justice can be realised by assessing the *efficiency* of an administrative act in giving the citizen what he needs without causing any unnecessary nuisance. Furthermore justice has to do with the *effectiveness* of the measures involved.

In this chapter we try to present the concept of administrative justice from a Continental point of view. One important preliminary remark has to be made. It is not our ambition to give an overview of the different Continental systems as such, as the differences between these systems are immense. For our purposes, it is sufficient to highlight some variations and factors that safeguard or endanger administrative justice. The factors that were chosen are those that can be found in all Continental legal systems. One could say that these factors form a 'typical' Continental view on administrative justice.

In Part I of this chapter, we elaborate on the concept of administrative justice. This leads us to a definition of the concept that is inviolable regardless of the variations in national systems and in national views of 'justice'. In Part II, we express the central aim of administrative justice in terms of a more concrete set of principles that are recognised by all national systems. It is the *order* or the *prioritisation* of these principles and the methods that are used to *safeguard* these principles, which differ. In Part III, we describe some variations that are used on the Continent to safeguard the principles that form the basis of the abstract notion of administrative justice.

I. The Genesis of Administrative Justice

The Rise of the *Rechtsstaat*

Once upon a time there was a *Rechtsstaat* in Continental Europe without democracy and without courts. The rule of law in government affairs was ensured by something called 'bureaucracy'. Administrative decisions were the product of public bureaucracy, without the involvement of politicians or judges. It was decision making by bureaucrats, professionals whose expertise was in applying general rules to individual cases. Where did bureaucratic administration come from? Some have suggested that bureaucracy is a by-product of the *Rechtsstaat*, the rule-of-law state.[2] Administrative justice would have required such a specialised decision machine. From this perspective, bureaucratic administration is the, perhaps disagreeable yet unavoidable, companion of public administration based on the rule of law. From an historical point of view, however, there is more reason to argue the opposite: the bureaucracy introduced and elaborated the rule of law[3] and in doing so created the *Rechtsstaat*.

[2] Donner (1984).

[3] Strictly speaking, the 'rule of law' is an Anglo-American concept, while bureaucracy and *Rechtsstaat* are Continental inventions. *Rechtsstaat* literally means 'law-based state'.

From the end of the eighteenth century, in most Continental countries, an organisation of professional civil servants carved out a position for itself between the government (the ruler) and the citizenry, which became the principal institution for the dispensation of public justice. Bureaucracy was a great success: the miracle of the nineteenth century. Not only in the German and Austrian empires—the two outstanding examples—but in most parts of the continent the bureaucratic law-based state became the core of public administration. The pre-Weberian German literature glorified this administrative invention. Bureaucracy shaped the principles of legal certainty and equality before the law. It constrained the arbitrary exercise of authority and it purged particularistic ways of dealing with public affairs. In so doing, a body of administrative law was created that made governmental decisions more predictable and fair. Administrative procedure legislation codified bureaucratic practice and the legal arsenal of the bureaucracy became more and more refined. Elsewhere in Europe comparable developments took place. The victorious march of bureaucracy found its ultimate triumph in Sweden, where the monopoly of the state bureaucracy over administrative decision making was laid down in the constitution.

What explains the immense success of this administrative device? For one thing, bureaucracy offered many more advantages than disadvantages for both the parties in an administrative relationship, that is for the sovereign and the citizen. Citizens indeed were charged with some fixed obligations that they could no longer escape, but these obligations were equally distributed and predictable and no longer the result of the arbitrary decisions of a ruler. The citizens now knew what their obligations were, and public authority was exercised within the confines of the law. As for the other party, while the ruler lost some of his power to the bureaucracy, in exchange he gained the certainty that individual citizens would fulfil their obligations under the law and that he would be able to count on a constant source of revenue. These trade-offs are what can be characterised as the political economy of the bureaucratic *Rechtsstaat*: an exchange that for all parties involved produced a more advantageous allocation of rights and obligations.

The bureaucratic state administration had a number of specific features that explain why it was so capable of fulfilling its mediating role between the ruler and the citizenry. We know the characteristics of bureaucracy primarily from the account of it that Max Weber gave at the beginning of the twentieth century. The bureaucratic *Rechtsstaat* by that time was already past its prime: Weber himself took an active part in the reforms that led to a democratic *Rechtsstaat* that would eventually break up the bureaucracy's monopoly on public decision making.[4]

One set of features primarily concerns us here: classical bureaucracy comprised a corps of civil servants with a very specific set of attitudes. Their stated interest was to do justice, *sine ira et studio*, without prejudice, unequal treatment or other forms of arbitrary rule. Their oath of office led them to the correct execution of the law. Unlike in previous times, these civil servants did not, in any sense, own

[4] Beetham (1974).

the tools of their trade: public powers. Thus, they could not use those powers for personal gain. The culture of these administrators had more similarity with that of the present-day judiciary than that of the modern public employee. Administrative decision making was the creation of law. While nowadays bureaucracy is associated with too many rules, classic bureaucracy operated with far more discretionary authority than one would expect. Discretion was applied on the basis of bureaucratic judgement, in two or three instances if so required. If a citizen felt slighted by a primary decision, he could find recourse in an administrative appeal—with all its advantages such as adjudication *ex officio*, integral assessment and substitutive decisions. The bureaucratic ideal in many ways comes close to what Kagan calls the *judicial mode* of rule application.[5]

The Dutch Exception

Unlike most of the continent, the Netherlands were slow to develop anything that came close to bureaucracy. The reason is that, for a long time, the country lacked a strong central government.[6] Napoleonic rule established some bureaucratised agencies, notably the Internal Revenue Service and the Public Prosecutor's Office. But, because public affairs in the Netherlands always took place in a negotiated environment, political dominance was strong, long before politics were democratised. Even today, political control of the administration prevails.[7] Nowhere else in Europe is the primacy of the political realm as overriding as it is in the Netherlands. For a long time the established belief was that high-quality public decision making requires a high-quality public administration. Struycken, a leading scholar in public law at the beginning of the twentieth century, emphasised the necessity of a good administrative apparatus for good administrative decision making to such an extent that he denounced legal protection of the administration as superfluous and possibly harmful. The right administration of justice should instead be founded on the careful selection and training of public servants—an approach totally in line with the bureaucratic model.[8] Struycken's views undoubtedly helped to prevent the creation of an administrative court system for most of the twentieth century.

In 1976, the *Wet administratieve rechtspraak overheidsbeschikkingen* established a general legal remedy against decisions of administrative authorities. The

[5] Kagan (1978) distinguishes three other, less attractive ways of administrative justice. The *legalistic mode* ignores the purpose of the rules that are applied; the *unauthorised discretion* ignores formal compliance to those rules, while *retreatism* does both.

[6] Daalder (1985).

[7] To be sure, in the 1980s and 1990s, autonomous agencies became popular for a while. Yet the reason for this popularity was primarily economic; it was considered to be a way for introducing market oriented management in the civil service.

[8] Struycken (1910: 46): 'Through a better organisation of the administration and through redesigning and improving legal-administrative procedures, the already present public spirit of the administration can be unfolded in full'.

legislature took its clues primarily from other Continental (from German and French) examples. This law for legal protection was basic and unrefined, and required further improvement. It lasted until 1994 when a more sophisticated statute for administrative procedures and administrative courts (the *Algemene wet bestuursrecht*) was enacted. From then on, administrative relations have undergone a change of perspective. The *Algemene wet bestuursrecht* and its predecessors shifted the emphasis on securing administrative justice from the input side to the output side of the administrative system. The quality of the bureaucrats, and the quality of administrative procedures that *produce* administrative decisions, were no longer considered crucial for administrative justice; rather recourse to the courts *after* the fact became all important. To an increasing extent, administrative agencies and citizens became two autonomous parties, each pursuing its own interests, while administrative procedure became more and more adversarial. The Netherlands at last joined the ranks of those Continental countries that secure administrative justice by regulating bureaucracies. In two respects however, there is still a difference with mainstream bureaucratic governance. First, Dutch public agencies cannot, for the most part, rely on a strong and enduring bureaucratic tradition. Secondly, the primacy of politics in many agencies, and certainly in municipal administration, poses the threat of arbitrary decision making. We now turn to the specifics of administrative justice in this somewhat uncharacteristic example of neo-Weberian administration.[9]

II. Principles Related to Administrative Justice

An Attempt to Concretise Abstraction

There are two ways of approaching the elusive concept of administrative justice. One way is to consider administrative systems and examine the extent to which they have the properties and capabilities to produce administrative justice. A prime example of this inductive line of reasoning can be found in the research of Adler.[10] The question whether or not a *system* is able to provide justice can be answered using the notions of the different models of justice that Adler presents.

A second way to get a handle on the concept of administrative justice is to assess whether justice was administered in a specific case. For example, to what extent did Ahmet meet justice? Was the way he was treated by the local authorities 'fair'? It is clear, in that case, that the local authority brought the suspicion of arbitrariness onto themselves by being more lenient towards the other cafés in the area.

[9] In their study of the effects of 25 years of New Public Management, Pollitt and Bouckaert (2005) conclude that what they call Neo-Weberian States (mainly Continental European States) largely resisted the pull of flexible efficient market-like public governance in favour of traditional law-based administration.

[10] Eg Adler (2003).

The municipal government seemed not to care whether or not these cafés had the necessary permits, while in Ahmet's case the rules were applied strictly. From the perspective of third parties who were involved the strict application of rules in Ahmet's case might be justifiable: the rules are meant to protect their individual rights. But what about the non-application of these same rules with regard to the other cafés?

Another problem lies in the condition imposed by the municipal authority that the terms of the lease should be limited. One could justify this requirement using *efficiency* as the relevant normative framework. The time-limited lease provided more certainty that the café would be closed once the area was redeveloped. At that point, this requirement would save the municipal government, and thus the taxpayer, the money that would have to be paid as compensation for loss resulting from administrative shortcomings. Although it might be considered efficient administration, it is difficult to accept this type of requirement from a legal point of view. Acts by an administrative body have to be founded on an explicit legal authority. From a Continental legal point of view, the administrative discretion to weigh different interests is limited by the legislature. If the act that is applied does not provide the administrative body with the authority to make a requirement regarding the duration of the lease, the administrative body is not allowed to impose it. As it happens, with regard to building permits, Dutch legislation is very strict and does not allow an administrative authority any discretion whatsoever to weigh interests or to demand additional requirements that are not directly related to the public interests involved.

This example shows that notions of administrative justice can collide. On the one hand, there are the legal principles of equal treatment and of legitimate expectations derived from the more general prohibition of arbitrariness. On the other hand, there are the practical notions of effective use of powers with regard to a general interest and of efficiency in providing public services, both to Ahmet and to interested third parties.

Where the Continental View Differs

Many of the more specific norms that are couched in the ideal of administrative justice are generally recognised, regardless of the specific national environment. Everywhere in developed jurisdictions, one may find such legal requirements as fair treatment, transparency of decision making, effectiveness, equal treatment, legal certainty, honouring legitimate expectations and the proportionality of administrative measures. Many of these principles coincide with general notions of sound administration or principles of good governance.[11] Thus the ideal of administrative justice is a common property of administrative systems the world over.

[11] See eg Commission of the European Communities (2001).

If one wants to identify one distinguishing feature of the Continental view on administrative justice, the *principle of legality* immediately comes to mind. In the Continental tradition, any use of public power has to be based on legislation. 'Fair' treatment is in many ways the treatment the legislature has in mind when conferring a specific power on an administrative body. The use of administrative powers without a legitimate foundation in the law is usually regarded as 'unfair'. Only on rare occasions, associated with a state of emergency, can an administrative act without a legal basis be justified. The interventions by the Dutch Minister of Finance during the take-over of Fortis Bank were a violation of the Dutch Government Accounts Act. This act requires the approval of parliament before the government can take an interest in a private company. The turbulent market situation has made it impossible to follow the formal approval procedure as any public debate about a possible transaction would have affected the stock market.

Another example is administrative action on a smaller scale. Hes uncovered the way municipalities tried to support persons through the provision of social assistance.[12] Entitlement to social assistance is based on the Social Assistance Act and persons receiving social assistance have a number of obligations, under which the obligation to search for paid employment. Many of the clients of the social services are socially unable to work, due, for example, to alcoholism or other types of addiction. Hes discovered that civil servants sometimes made a contract with clients, limiting the amount of beer the client could drink during the day, on penalty of lowering their social assistance. As there is no legal foundation for these contracts, enforcement of the terms before a court would be impossible. One could even argue that the municipal officials abused the lack of knowledge of their clients with regard to their legal rights. Nevertheless these kinds of agreements may be very effective as the 'contract' binds the clients at least morally and may help to reduce their consumption of alcohol.

These examples illustrate the difference that appears in comparing administrative justice from a Continental point of view with administrative justice in common law jurisdictions. A strong belief in the principle of legality can be found across the French, German and Dutch administrative systems. In these systems, there is considerable unease when administrative bodies conduct their actions without a clear legal basis.[13]

III. Safeguarding Administrative Justice

On the Continent, administrative justice is first of all a characteristic of the *individual* relationship between the government and its citizens. The continental systems regard the relationship between an administrative body and a citizen

[12] Hes (1981).
[13] Seerden (2007). See for France p 77, for Germany p 120 and for the Netherlands p 167.

as a *special* relationship, subject to special rules and special courts. Thus, many of the continental administrative systems have some set of uniform procedural standards that regulate the way in which administrative authorities have to use their administrative powers. Procedural elements such as inquiry into the facts of the case when an application has been filed, time limits within which an authority has to respond and the format for the decision itself, have been regulated in administrative procedure acts. Together, these rules regulate entire administrative decision-making systems. The traditional assumption is that governmental authorities comply with the law and that actual administrative behaviour will be a mirror image of the procedures in the statutes. In reality, these procedural rules leave a lot of leeway, even if authorities do not take the opportunity to deviate. The latitude an administrative authority enjoys within the boundaries of the law, or administrative *contra legem* behaviour beyond those boundaries, only becomes evident when a conflict arises and is taken to court. Then a judge is called upon to interpret the law and determine what administrative justice is in that particular case. The function of the court is not to solve a dispute between two litigating parties, but to determine whether the administrative agency followed the rules of decision making. In other words, an important characterisation of the way administrative justice is safeguarded in Continental systems is the emphasis on formal legal protection. This gives rise to a number of thorny issues. We now discuss three of these issues: the never ending quest for a clear *definition* of the administrative relationship between an administrative authority and a citizen; the unattainable aspiration for *clear legal standards in legislation* and the *limited control* of administrative authorities legal protection has to offer.

Defining an Administrative Relationship

The first issue that arises with the principle of legality is the problem of defining an administrative relationship. An administrative relationship, that is, a relationship between a public authority and a citizen, is always partly a legal relationship. Even though relationships between public agencies and citizens may involve far more than just legal aspects, there will always be one or more legal rules governing an administrative relationship. In the Netherlands, the focus of regulating administrative decision making is the 'administrative relationship', the legal part of the relationship between a public authority and a citizen. Within the framework of the Dutch Administrative Law Act, this legal relationship is anchored in what is called a *decision*, ie in a legal act by an administrative authority.[14] It follows from this strict definition that other acts, which are not necessary *legal* acts, such as providing information or declaring a legal position, are not decisions and are therefore not subject to administrative regulation. As a consequence, administrative justice as upheld by the courts is limited to decisions and decisions only.

[14] The French and German systems have the same approach. See Seerden (2007).

In order to establish whether the administration has been 'fair' a 'decision' has to be evaluated against the legal norms laid down in administrative law.

A second major defining attribute of an administrative relationship, next to the decision being made, is the *parties involved*. The Dutch General Administrative Law Act only provides rights for *interested parties*. It is therefore especially relevant to establish what citizen-parties are involved in the emerging administrative relationship. Who for instance is allowed to enter into public consultation before the decision is made and whose interests should be taken into account when the authority is weighing the relevant interests?

The meaning of these delineating attributes is not as clear as one could expect and thus the demarcation of an 'administrative relationship' tends to be somewhat fluid. In the Netherlands, what is called 'subjectivisation' is discernable: the objectively defined administrative relationship is transformed, in part, into a horizontal relationship, which has some similarities with a contractual relationship. In particular, the question of which parties should be allowed into the administrative relationship is in a constant state of flux. A topical question is whether it is appropriate to apply some form of relativity to the concept of 'the interested party' as is the case in German administrative law.[15] Since the boundaries of the concept of 'the interested party' are ultimately determined by law and legal policy, without legislative intervention such changes can be effected only gradually and in relatively marginal ways. Introducing the relativity requirement would require legislative intervention. In a recent court case, an environmental group was deemed not to be an interested party in a decision about an environmental permit, because, according to the ruling judge, the objectives of this group, as formulated in its charter, were too vague.[16] Here a consequence of the emphasis placed on legal protection as the method of safeguarding administrative justice has come to light. Initially it resulted in large numbers of appeals against individual administrative decisions. Among other things, it meant frustrating major projects. After (political) complaints from administrative agencies, we can now see a backlash in the form of court decisions limiting the persons and organisations who are allowed to influence the decision-making process.

Clear Legal Standards

A *second* issue, related to the founding of administrative justice on the principle of legality, is the need for *adequate legislation*: legislation which avoids vague legal standards that require further interpretation by administrative bodies. In the ideal world, administrative bodies and administrative courts are supposed to be '*la bouche de loi*'. Nevertheless it is clear that at least some interpretation is inevitable, as the legislature cannot possibly anticipate all the consequences of

[15] de Poorter (2004).
[16] Tolsma, de Graaf and Jans (2009).

general rules. Rapid technological developments, and the growing complexity of a global society, make it even more necessary to react quickly with new rules and legal standards. The legislative process is not tuned to fast retorts and tailor-made problem solving. The gap between the theory of 'complete legislation' and the practice of incomplete and open norms has two different types of consequences.

Administrative Rule making

First of all, vague legislation provides administrative bodies with an incentive to formulate their own rules and regulations, in order to bridge that gap. Sometimes such administrative rules originate from a hierarchical relationship between two administrative bodies. In Germany, for example, the Chancellor is allowed to lay down guidelines for her Ministers. This is more or less logical as the Chancellor is the '*primus inter pares*' and derives this regulatory power directly from the German Constitution.[17] Similar administrative rules can be found in hierarchical guidelines laid down by a central authority for local government.[18] Yet, without a hierarchical relationship, administrative bodies develop their own rules and standard operating procedures for interpreting legal standards. However, this category of rules is denied existence in many Continental administrative systems as it conflicts with the principle of legality. It is argued that the administrative power to make individual decisions does not imply a regulatory authority as the legislature has demanded that administrative bodies should weigh individual interests and should not hide behind a general rule that has no legal basis.[19]

In the Netherlands, administrative rule making that standardises the application of a specific power has acquired legal status in the form of so called 'policy rules'. An administrative body is legally authorised to formulate policy rules as long as they refer to matters within its competence. An administrative body may also be specifically authorised by law to lay down policy rules pertaining to the administrative competence of another administrative body. If the authority to lay down policy rules is absent, the rules laid down are referred to as guidelines or 'pseudo policy rules'.[20] It is precisely because of the legal basis for the establishment of policy rules that some observers see major similarities between policy rules and universally binding regulations.[21] The importance of policy rules increases as legislation becomes increasingly vague. Sometimes the tasks assigned by administrative rules are so complex that administrative bodies cannot carry

[17] § 65 Grundgesetz.

[18] Bröring (1993); Lust (2007: 23).

[19] See Tollenaar (2008) for the debate on the legal effect of these rules.

[20] *CR v B* (Central Appeals Tribunal) 19 November 2003, *AB* 2004, 119 with note by Bröring.

[21] Bröring (1993). In legal practice it has also proved difficult to make a distinction between the two. See *ABR v S* (Administrative Law Division of the Council of State) 1 February 2006, *AB* 2006, 152 and *ABR v S* 9 August 2006, both with notes by Tollenaar.

them out lawfully without detailed guidance.[22] As a result, the total amount of regulation in a certain area appears to be somewhat invariable—when the legislature withdraws, the gap left behind is filled by administrative rule making. Thus the result is not a reduction in the quantity of law but a change in the way in which regulation is formalised. Ultimately, in administrative bureaucracy, people are looking for a digital answer to the question: is it allowed or not? An interesting phenomenon in this context is the ongoing digitalisation of administrative decision making: by its very nature it produces such digital answers. Whether this matches the classic approach to administrative decision making, which demands that every decision must take account of the specific circumstances that have a bearing on the case, can be questioned.[23]

Political Decision Making

Vague legislation not only leads to administrative rule making. A second consequence of vague legal standards is, that individual administrative decision making has been exposed to political interference—at least in the Netherlands. Where decision making is related to general rules or policy rules, political interference is defensible. Where it requires a weighing of general and specific interests, there is need for officials who are elected or who can be held responsible in a political forum to legitimate the final decision. Decision making in individual cases, however, for example, the issuing of a permit or licence, should be undertaken without political interference. Any political interference will affect such highly regarded principles as equality and legal certainty, whether it advantages or disadvantages the individual citizen. The example of Ahmet shows that political interference may lead to unequal and arbitrary decisions: the surrounding cafés were allowed to open and to exploit the terrace, even without a permit, on the strength of support from politicians. Ahmet, being an alien, lacked access to the aldermen and other municipal officials.

The exclusion of political interference is relatively rare in the Netherlands. For example, with regard to the decisions based on tax law, the relevant Minister has the authority to issue a designation order in individual cases. This means that, although the Tax and Customs Administration is authorized to make tax assessments, the Minister may instruct the agency to change any individual assessment. The decision to use this power is inevitably a political one. A few years ago, the Tax and Customs Administration decided to waive the collection of taxes in a certain neighbourhood because it was clear that the costs involved in the collection of the taxes (for example the costs of police deployment) would exceed the revenue. Once the media exposed this decision, the issue was addressed in parliament. The members of parliament thought it was unacceptable to reward non-co-operative

22 Tollenaar (2006).
23 Bovens and Zouridis (2002).

persons by what amounted to a tax exemption and required the Minister to intervene to ensure that the taxes were collected at any price.

Many permits, licences and subsidies, especially at the local level, are issued by administrative bodies made up of politicians. The local alderman for example, is a politician who is quite often the leader of his political party. His or her decisions are therefore not always based on a technical weighing of interests, but are more often based on a political assessment of their consequences. It is obvious that this threatens the legal quality of the decision. Political decision making has arbitrariness as one of its defining characteristics.

The Void Caused by the Emphasis on Legal Protection

Next to the problems of defining 'administrative relation' and attaining clear legal standards, a third issue connected with the founding principle of legality in continental systems is the emphasis on *judicial review*. Easy accessible legal protection against alleged administrative transgressions is a cornerstone of the continental efforts to preserve administrative justice. Increasingly, this legal protection has to be provided by independent administrative courts. This was not always the case. During the first half of the twentieth century, the safeguarding of administrative decision making in the Netherlands developed mainly within the administrative hierarchy. Administrative justice was preserved using the instrument of administrative supervision: a citizen could challenge administrative decisions by appealing to an administrative body higher up in the hierarchy (administrative appeal).[24] The higher administrative body had the power to completely reconsider the challenged decision. European case law put an end to this system.[25] Administrative appeal has been replaced—or supplemented—by legal protection in administrative courts.

The change from administrative appeal to legal protection in the administrative court has meant that the safeguarding of administrative justice became focussed more and more on the output side, on the decisions themselves, instead of the administrative system that produces those decisions. The administrative court is only interested in the decision at hand and in the litigation it generated. The administrative court's aim is not to assess whether the decision is in accordance with objective law. Rather, it responds to the grievances brought forward by the interested party who has appealed against the decision. One consequence is that, in the dispensation of administrative justice, the question that is addressed is not whether, in view of the legislation and the general principles of proper administration, the citizen has received what he or she is entitled to, but whether the citizen's objections justify changing the decision.

[24] There are exceptions: the Dutch Central Appeals Tribunal has existed for over 100 years.
[25] *Benthem v the Netherlands* (App no 8848/80) (1985) Series A no 97, 1.

The administrative court seems to be less and less inclined to focus on the substantive correctness of a decision, focusing instead on formal standards, for example, on how the decision was prepared and conveyed. In assessing the decision, the administrative court takes administrative discretion into account and is therefore more likely to reverse a decision on the grounds that it does not understand the decision in question (lack of motivation) than on the grounds that the decision in question is substantively incorrect.[26] This is an important consequence, as in the system of administrative legal protection the conflict does not end with the decision of the administrative court. The conflict only ends if the court decides in favour of the administrative body and declares the appeal unfounded. If the court rules that the decision has some shortcomings, the decision will be annulled. After a formal reversal, it is up to the administrative authority to make a better decision, because no judgment has been made as to the substantive quality of the decision.[27]

Consequence: a Scale of Administrative Justice?

In the previous sections we discussed devices for safeguarding administrative justice that can be found in continental administrative law systems. The strong emphasis on the principle of legality results in the regulation of not only the substantial aspects of decision making, but of the procedural aspects, too. Furthermore, the principle of legality calls for easy accessible legal protection and for a clear definition of the administrative relationship. This pattern can be found not only in the Netherlands, but also in Germany, France and Belgium.[28] What now is the kind of administrative justice that this set of safeguards is producing?

Intuitively, one would regard administrative justice as a dichotomous variable: an administrative decision or act is either just or unjust. Yet, the administrative justice being generated by continental administrative law systems is better understood as an *ordinal* variable: to be measured on a scale from low justice to high justice, or from minimum quality to maximum quality.[29] On this scale, minimum quality can be regarded as the quality of decision making that satisfies the administrative judge, or in other words: the quality that would prevent the judge from annulling an individual decision.

A decision is 'judge-proof' if the administrative body making that decision did not exceed the limits of its administrative powers. If the statute allows the administrative body a degree of discretion, the administrative body has to take into account the principles of equality, legal certainty and proportionality when

[26] *ABR v S* (Administrative Law Division of the Council of State) 11 April 2003, AB 2003, 281 with note by AT Marseille.

[27] It is conceivable that a decision of poor substantive quality is repeatedly annulled on formal grounds, replaced by a decision which is substantively identical, and then again annulled on formal grounds. For an example of this, see Zwart (1999: 90 ff).

[28] Seerden (2008).

[29] Herweijer (2007).

making a decision. In accordance with the *trias politica* (separation of powers), the judge is expected to be lenient when it comes to weighing the competing interests within this discretion: if the legislature gives the administrative body a discretionary power, this power should be executed after a weighing of interests by the (politically accountable) administrative body. As a result, administrative courts deal primarily with *procedural* quality, and an annulment of an administrative decision is usually based on formal deficiencies: the administrative body wrongly ignored certain facts, or the reasoning on which the decision was based is not valid.

Thus 'judge-proof 'decisions do meet a minimum standard of administrative justice, Yet, it is clear that 'judge-proof' is a poor representation of the ideal of administrative justice. For instance, an administrative body can fulfil the procedural requirement of due care by offering interested parties the opportunity to file opinions or reservations on a draft of the decision, while disregarding the content of those opinions and reservations. After all, the legal standard of 'hearing' does not require 'listening'.

On the upper end of the scale, there is a different notion of administrative justice. Not the acceptable decision, but the *right* decision, is the norm. Instead of applying the test whether the grounds for an appeal against a decision are strong enough for a nullification, as a judge does, the question that has to be answered is whether the decision is intrinsically correct. This requires a full assessment of the administrative decision of and the way the administrative body made it. This is typically the question that supervisors and inspectors tend to answer when they assess administrative decision making. Moreover, such an assessment is not restricted to legal norms but embraces standards like client friendliness, transparency, effectiveness and efficiency as well. Although these standards can supplement legal norms, lawfulness remains the basis of administrative justice. Many administrative bodies cut the corners of the legal quality of their decision making in order to be efficient and save money or in order to increase the supposed effectiveness of their decisions. Client friendliness towards one citizen can imply client unfriendliness or, even, unlawful behaviour towards other citizens. The intensive interpretation of legal norms, together with non-legal norms such as transparency and client friendliness, forms the maximum level of administrative justice.

Concluding Remarks

The main goal of this paper was to describe the concept of administrative justice from a Continental European point of view. The origin of the Continental approach lies in the attempt to limit arbitrary decision making by authoritarian rulers. The French revolution can be regarded as a revolution against the abuse of power by an elite, which bought or inherited powers to take decisions unilaterally that affected the interests of individual citizens. It led to the separation of administrative positions from persons with that position, which coincides with the German-based idea of the anonymous bureaucracy: public competences have to be executed by professionals, who aim to promote the general interest.

In a further development, it became necessary to devise mechanisms to control and correct administrative actions and decisions. As a result, on the continent, the administrative relationship became more and more codified: written down in general rules and acts, based on the 'will of the legislature'. Nevertheless, writing 'complete' legislation turned out to be an unattainable aspiration. Public authorities always exercise a residual kind of discretion; either because the legislature considers an individual weighing of interests necessary or because the practical application of the rules leaves the public authority with room for choice, for example, with regard to the prioritising of the decisions it has to make.[30]

The way public authorities use their administrative discretion while executing a statutory task can be regarded as the main 'object' of regulation in administrative law.[31] Administrative law is in essence the legal reaction to the fear of an arbitrary use of these powers, violating general principles of legal certainty and equality. There are two possible solutions to filling this gap and to protecting the citizen against the arbitrary use of discretionary powers. These solutions can be derived from the 'separation of powers' between the legislature, the executive and the judiciary. Where the executive has discretion, fear of the arbitrary use of powers can be removed by giving the judiciary the power to intervene by applying principles and defining standards of proper conduct. As a result, in individual cases, decisions can be struck down if the judge finds that a general principle has been violated. This approach has the disadvantage that it can be hard to transpose norms and standards from one case to another.

The other solution is for the legislature to set procedural standards. The Legislature can specify norms of due care, norms about legal reasoning and standards concerning the involvement of interested parties in decision making. It is clear that the Continental approach to administrative justice relies more on the legislature than on the judiciary. In many Continental legal systems the legislature has defined the administrative relationship between government and citizen and has specified norms that governmental bodies have to take into account in their dealings with citizens. Furthermore, the legislature has delineated precisely what competences public authorities can bring to bear, and who can be addressed by the decisions or acts of those public authorities. In many countries these norms are laid down in a general administrative procedures act that is applicable in all situations in which a public authority makes a decision or constitutes an act that addresses a citizen.[32]

30 Lipsky (1980).
31 Caranta (2008).
32 Eg Seerden (2007).

The Continental tendency of uniform codification leads to three conclusions. First of all, the codification of administrative norms drives out the professional attitude of the public servant. The original goal of the public servant, which was to provide fair, reasonable and effective decisions, is increasingly replaced by an attitude of following written rules and norms and acquiring 'judge-proof' decisions. After all, the rules determine whether or not the court will accept a decision as lawful. As a result, administrative justice from a Continental perspective is, to a large extent, equivalent to whatever conforms to the rules and statutes. This leads to an attitude of 'going by the book' even when the legislature actually wished for an attitude of professional judgment. For example, the duty to give reasons for a decision is, for all practical purposes, merely a formal standard. The decision has to address the relevant facts and statutory provisions but whether or not the citizen concerned actually understands the reasons is of lesser importance.

The second conclusion has to do with the *review* of the decisions and acts of public authorities. Within the Continental framework, the codification of norms and standards brings up the question of the extent to which judicial review can improve overall administrative justice. Although one might expect that the administrative courts would be able to actively seek justice, to help citizens obtain their rights and to balance the unequal relationship between the almighty government and the dependent citizen, reality is different. In accordance with the principle of the separation of powers, the court has to respect the decisions being made by a public authority whenever the legislature provided the public authority with discretion. And although the object of the procedure is a specific decision, the court's assessment is mainly limited to the formal aspects of the decision, assessing whether or not the public authority used the right procedure, rather than assessing whether the decision itself is fair? The judge is neither entitled nor equipped to assess the substantive quality of the decision. He is not—to give an example—a medical professional who is able to evaluate the medical examination on which the public authority based its decision.[33]

As a result, judicial review does not provide administrative justice, at least not in the sense that the citizen receives what he is entitled to. As compensation for this shortcoming, the Dutch system of administrative law has a less formal complaints procedure, a pre-judicial objections procedure and intervening supervisory bodies. None of these devices fully reflects the British approach of administrative justice, where tribunals play an important role as an easy accessible institution using experts to bring justice to the citizen. In the Netherlands, neither the objections-procedure nor the supervisory bodies can really provide justice as these tribunals might do. The pre-judicial 'informal' objections procedure is more and more formalised and reflects the way in which the court assesses decisions.

[33] *Cf* Tollenaar, Marseille and de Graaf (2008).

It does not guarantee an expert review. Supervisory bodies lack the incentives and the tools to correct public authorities in individual cases. Thus there appears to be a gap between the Continental approach to administrative justice and administrative justice in the common-law tradition.

The third and final conclusion elaborates on these non-judicial mechanisms for guaranteeing administrative justice. Recently, in the wake of New Public Management (NPM) initiatives, more and more managerial instruments for improving administrative quality, such as benchmarking and certification, have been deployed. These are mainly voluntary instruments with 'no strings attached'. Nevertheless they appear to be more crucial for administrative justice than judicial review. Norms are internalised by the organisation, without the pitfalls of the administrative law system as described above. Interestingly, these mechanisms appeal to professional standards as the norms and standards in both benchmarking and certification procedures are set by 'peers'. Codification of administrative norms and an administrative system that relies on reviewing compliance with these norms, will always need a supplementary system that focuses on the administrative professional—the neo-Weberian bureaucrat.

References

Adler, M (2003) 'Socio-Legal Approach to Administrative Justice' 25 *Law and Policy* 323.

Beetham, D (1974) *Max Weber and the Theory of Modern Politics* (London, Allen and Unwin).

Bovens, MAP and Zouridis, S (2002) 'From Street-Level to System-Level Bureaucracies: How Information and Communication Technology is Transforming Administrative Discretion and Constitutional Control' 2 *Public Administration Review* 174–84.

Bröring, HE (1993a) *Richtlijnen* (Deventer, Kluwer).

—— (1993b) 'Beleidsregels. Een beknopte biografie' in JL Boxum et al (eds), *Aantrekkelijke gedachten* (Deventer, Kluwer).

Caranta, R (2008) 'On Discretion' in S Prechal and B van Roermund (eds), *The Coherence of EU Law: The Search for Unity in Divergent Concepts* (Oxford, Oxford University Press).

Commission of the European Communities (2001) *European Governance, a White Paper* (Brussels).

Daalder, H (1985) 'Sturing, het primaat van de politiek en de bureaucratische cultuur' in MAP Bovens and WJ Witteveen (eds), *Het schip van staat. Beschouwingen over recht, staat en sturing* (Zwolle, WEJ Tjeenk Willink).

de Poorter, JCA (2004) 'Het belangvereiste in bestuursrechtelijke procedures' in EC Pietermaat and JCA de Poorter (eds), *Toegang tot de rechter: processuele openbaarheid en belang* (Jonge VAR-reeks 2) (The Hague, Bju).

Donner, AM (1984) *Werkt de rechtsstaatsidee bureaucratie in de hand?* (Amsterdam, Noord-Hollandsche Uitgevers Mij).

Herweijer, M (2007) 'Inquiries into the quality of administrative decision-making' in KJ de Graaf, AT Marseille and J de Ridder (eds), *Quality of Decision-Making in Public Law* (Groningen, Europe Law Publishing).

Hes, J (1981) *Tussen wal en schip, tussen recht en hulpverlening: een empirisch-theoretische verkenning in de eerstelijns (rechts)hulpverlening* (Deventer, Van Loghum Slaterus).
Kagan, RA (1978) *Regulatory Justice: Implementing a wage-price freeze* (New York, Russell Sage Foundation).
Lipsky, M (1980) *Street-level Bureaucracy: Dilemmas of the individual in public services* (New York, Russell Sage Foundation).
Lust, S (2007) 'Administrative law in Belgium' in RJGH Seerden (ed), *Administrative Law of the European Union, its Member States and the United States* (Antwerp, Intersentia).
Pollitt, C and Bouckaert, G (2005) *Public Management Reform—A comparative analysis* (Oxford, Oxford University Press).
Seerden, RJGH (ed) (2007) *Administrative Law of the European Union, its Member States and the United States* (Antwerp, Intersentia).
Struycken, AAH (1910) *Administratie of Rechter. Beschouwingen over de moderne rechtsstaatsgedachte naar aanleiding van de aanhangige ontwerpen tot regeling der administratieve rechtspraak* (Arnhem, Gouda Quint).
Tollenaar, A (2006) 'Beleidsregels' in KJ de Graaf and AT Marseille (eds), *Algemeen bestuursrecht/Bestuursprocesrecht* (loose-leaf) supplement 5, March.
—— (2008) 'Soft Law, Policy Rules and the Quality of Administrative Decision-Making' March, available at SSRN: http://ssrn.com/abstract=1113349.
Tollenaar, A, Marseille, B and de Graaf, K (2008) 'Establishing Facts by the Administrative Judge', November, available at SSRN: http://ssrn.com/abstract=1294303.
Tolsma, HD, de Graaf, KJ and Jans, JH (2009) 'The Rise and Fall of Access to Justice in the Netherlands' April, available at SSRN: http://ssrn.com/abstract=1383478.
Zwart, T (1999) 'De republiek der rechters?' in HRBM Kummeling (ed), *Het bestuursrecht als agenda voor het staatsrecht* (Deventer, WEJ Tjeenk Willink).

14

Administrative Justice in a Scandinavian Legal Context: From a Liberal and a Social State to a Market State or a Milieu State

CARSTEN HENRICHSEN*

Introduction

In Scandinavian legal theory there has been a growing interest in recent years in the fundamental values of public administration, such as administrative justice. The development of public administration has raised some crucial questions about how to ensure what has been called the *public ethos* in contrast to the increasingly urgent demand for efficiency. The growth of public expenditure has forced the political authorities to balance administrative justice with efficiency, and jurists—working theoretically as well as in practical ways—on such matters have had to re-think their positions concerning the fundamental values of public administration.

However, this development is certainly not the only reason for being concerned with administrative justice. In Denmark, and in other Scandinavian countries, the pressure on the public ethos has increased in the present period in which the public sector has been subject to massive and very rapid changes. In particular, the idea of applying market mechanisms—in the form of privatisation, public procurement and contract management—has attracted attention from a legal point of view, since these mechanisms seem capable of challenging the traditional notions of value associated with government and the public sphere.

When describing the public ethos, jurists often refer to those special values that are associated with democracy and the constitutional state, concepts derived from a tradition that dates back more than 150 years. However if the description of the democratic and constitutional elements of the state is limited to its historical basis, it will risk losing some important nuances in the set of values that characterise the contemporary public ethos. The public ethos is not an invariant concept: it is, on the contrary, subject to the ravages of time.

* This chapter is an elaborated—and translated—version of an article published in a report for the Danish Research Project on 'Power in Denmark' (Jørgensen 2003: 81–104).

The aim of this chapter is to show how certain parts of the public universe of values, specifically those that are affiliated with the constitutional state and with democracy, gradually change over time. A movement can cause old values to be forced out by new ones, but a change of circumstances and a change in the conception of values, can also necessitate a new interpretation of the old values. The study of these conditions embraces the whole of the period from the middle of the nineteenth century to the present day, and the changing notions of value will be analysed in light of legal developments in the Scandinavian countries, primarily using concrete examples from Danish legislation.

In the first section, I make some comments on the concept of administrative justice since—in spite of its relevance—it is not really familiar in a Scandinavian context. The analysis of administrative justice from a Scandinavian point of view starts, in the next section, with an account of the historical basis of this phenomenon, which argues that, since the middle of nineteenth century, society has been a community based on the rule of law and that the state has been governed by law. From this analytical starting point, things begin to get more complicated. The development from 'a liberal state' to 'a social state'—both governed by law—is well known in most civilised countries of a 'Western' type. Its consequences for public values in general, and for administrative justice in particular, are however less well understood—and are discussed in the following section.

Developments in the present period make things even more complicated and describing what has been happening in society in recent times is certainly difficult. This applies particularly to a situation, like the present one, where society is highly complex and constantly changing. The question of which direction the development will take in the future can be analysed on the basis of present trends in public policy and public administration. To a certain degree however, future possibilities entail a choice of values. This becomes clear when some contradictory tendencies in present-day society are analysed. Two principal possibilities, referred to as 'the market state' and 'the milieu state', are identified. My thesis is that these models of public policy and public administration are both possible heirs to the present welfare state, at least in the Scandinavian countries.

Since this account needs to be put into an international perspective, I refer to some modern Anglo-American theories in order to identify some similarities and differences between the four models of administrative justice for which I argue, and similar models that can be found in the socio-legal literature. Finally, I make some concluding remarks on the practical implications of the theoretical approach adopted in this chapter.

The Concept of Administrative Justice

From a Scandinavian point of view, the introduction of the term 'administrative justice' marks an essential simplification of the linguistic possibilities of communication in relation to Anglo-American legal thinking. While Scandinavian legal theory—which is grounded in the Continental European law tradition—has, for a long time, had a more or less precise, but well-established, term for administrative justice, this has not been the case in Anglo-American theories of public law. The Danish concept '*retssikkerhed*' originates from the German idea of '*rechtsicherheit*' and the French idea of '*securité public*'. Since Dicey, the dogmatic (British) theory of public administration has been concerned with different facets of administrative justice, such as 'law and order', 'the rule of law', 'process of law', 'due process' and 'due process of law'. This approach lacks a unifying term that encompasses all these facets. Administrative justice is such a term, even if it has been developed for empirical—socio-legal—purposes, for example, for referring to 'the principles that can be used to evaluate the justice inherent in administrative decision-making' (Adler 2003: 323). Using the term merely as encompassing these principles is, in effect, synonymous with the German/Scandinavian concept '*rechtsicherheit*'.

Still it must be acknowledged that the concept of 'justice' has, long ago, been brought into disrepute in Scandinavian positivistic legal thinking. It has been argued that justice is a political value without a precise meaning—at least as far the substantive meaning of the term is concerned—and that, as such, it is not a term that can be used for scientific purposes (Ross 1959). However, this should not present an obstacle to using the term 'administrative justice', a concept that encompasses all the above-mentioned principles. Furthermore, there is a strong tradition in the British theory of administrative law of using the term 'natural justice' to refer to some specific elements of the broader concept of administrative justice (for example, the duty to act fairly, the rule against bias, the right to be heard, etc). From a legal positivistic point of view, this term could be considered even more provocative, since legal positivism has arisen in opposition to natural law of every kind, purporting to give an empirical answer to the question of applicable law. The theoretical position of positivistic legal thinking however, has been subjected to considerable criticism in recent decades, and—without going into details—it can be concluded that, from a Scandinavian point of view, using a term like administrative justice to characterise one of the most crucial values in public administration is not a problem.

Accepting that the concept of administrative justice is broadly synonymous with the German/Scandinavian term 'rechtsicherheit' creates opportunities for comparative analyses of this phenomenon in different countries. Of course, this presupposes that the concept is given the same meaning everywhere. However, the precise meaning of the term 'administrative justice' is not absolutely clear. On the contrary, a closer look at the use of this term in Scandinavian legal thinking reveals many varying interpretations, amongst which the most common refers to the possibility that citizens (applicants or claimants) have their entitlements fulfilled in administrative decision making. This interpretation, however, leaves us with some problems: if the law does not give a precise description of these entitlements or of the circumstances in which they are to be delivered or, even worse, if the law delegates the power to the administration to make its own rules (regulations or enactments), this leaves the authorities with some discretion to make their own decisions. It is not clear what the meaning of administrative justice should be in such situations.

One may, of course, insist on the demand for precise rules as a necessary precondition for talking about administrative justice. However, a normative position like that is objectionable, simply because it is not realistic in a complex and changeable world where the legislature has been forced to delegate considerable power to the administrative authorities. In a previous study (Henrichsen 1997), I have attempted to determine in what reasonable sense one can speak about administrative justice in such circumstances, instead of insisting on demanding the impossible. To do so, however, creates—at least by implication—different concepts of administrative justice. So, from that point of view, it is less important to define the term administrative justice in general than to describe the circumstances and the conditions under which one can speak about administrative justice. As the analytical basis for such an approach, I have chosen the ideal type, and the theoretical basis for this sort of model-building is a historical conception of public administration.

It follows from the above that administrative justice can be seen as part of a public universe of values that is associated with two fundamental elements of the state, democracy and the constitutional state. The purpose of this chapter is to show how certain parts of the public universe of values have changed since they were established, with particular reference to those values that are associated with democracy and the constitutional state, ie administrative justice and other fundamental legal values, which constitute the basis of what has been called the 'public ethos'. As already mentioned, I use the analytic technique of model-building based on ideal types.

Construing the ideal types, I use a simple model consisting of four dimensions: two concerning the (changing) fundamental values of democracy and constitutionalism, and two concerning the (changing) values of administrative justice, characterised in terms of goals and means, referred to here as 'considerations' and 'guarantees' of administrative justice. The whole model encompasses four types of state government, each of which is characterised by a distinct form of administrative justice, that are either sequential or competitive. Although that is what the model tells us, in practice all sorts of administrative justice can be found in present-day public administration. However, my empirical thesis is that there is a certain minimum of correspondence between the actual form of administrative justice in public administration and the democratic and constitutional values that are dominant in a particular part of the legislation.

Democracy, the State Governed by Law and the Community Founded on the Rule of Law

Fundamental Democratic Values

The starting point of any analysis of public values in the community of today concerns the character of the community as a political democracy. The decisive factor that determines which values the public should respect and encourage is democracy as a form of government. The community develops the laws that are necessary for promoting these values through the democratic process. Thus the law and the democracy are closely connected. Democracy—the democratic form of government—can in reality only be implemented on the basis of a set of legal norms that determines how the community is to be governed—usually expressed in a constitution that is binding on governmental agencies. It is characteristic of these norms that power originates from the will of all and that it is exercised to serve the general will in the broadest sense.

However democracy is more than a certain form of government. It also has a substantive component by virtue of the values on which the democratic ideal is founded. These values are connected with the conception of the individual as an independent being with the ability to recognise his or her legal obligations ('the individual as subject to the law'). It follows that the individual assumes a central position in a democratic system. The individual has a value of his or her own, a value that must have the opportunity to maintain and develop itself in the community. This opportunity entails respect for values such as freedom and equality—values that can be seen as manifestations of one fundamental value, namely respect for the dignity of the individual. In order to protect these values, laws in the form of human or fundamental rights are required. This is normally ensured by guaranteeing these rights in the constitution.

The protection of fundamental rights may clash with the handling of other concerns of the community. For example, the right to own private property can damage or hinder other legitimate interests of the community. The protection of fundamental rights is not absolute; limitations are made in order to address the general concerns of the community. The protection of the rights of the individual is based on the fundamental idea that the individual, as a part of the community, must tolerate such limitations in his or her freedom of action that are considered necessary, in order to make the community work—on the assumption that the independence of the individual is preserved. This fundamental idea is still valid today, even if the balance between the individual and the community is not fixed and varies over time due to changes in the notion of value. The classic example is the right to expropriate private property for compensation.

Legal Protection and Administrative Justice

The law also defines society and the state as organisational units of a certain type, as a community founded on the rule of law and as a set of institutions governed by law. The community founded on the rule of law is characterised by a set of legal norms that define the legal status of the individuals under the various conditions of life in a society. In this legal system the individual is ensured a certain measure of freedom—everything is allowed unless it is explicitly prohibited or commanded. The essential fundamental value in this is the legal protection of the citizens, which constitutes administrative justice in a broader sense. In practice this protection is guaranteed by the courts and other legal institutions.

The existence of a legal system and a set of law-enforcement institutions, are the essential characteristics of the community founded on the rule of law. This defining characteristic of the community founded on the rule of law is consistent with both the concentration of power in an absolute monarchy and with the dispersion of power in a constitutional democracy. By means of the state governed by law, the community founded on the rule of law is supplied with those special qualities that characterise the contemporary governance of a state. These special qualities have made possible the growth in the legal protection of citizens through the provision of procedural guarantees of 'fair process', which constitutes administrative justice in a narrow sense (comparable with 'natural justice' in British law). The state governed by law is ideologically rooted in the 'age of enlightenment' and is a leading element in liberal democracy. The radical innovation in the liberal concept of the state governed by law is that official public regulatory interventions are subject to legal control, and the grant of fundamental rights to citizens through the use of procedural rules limits the power of the state.

In this context, administrative justice refers to the stability and security of the social community that legal standards also aim to achieve. Stability and security are important, first and foremost, in the relationship between the state and its citizens. In this sense, administrative justice means 'distinct rules that can be trusted' (Axberger 1988: 165), that is, rules that promote the use of uniform solutions to diverse problems. The crucial element in this context is the possibility for the individual of predicting the legal consequences of governmental actions and, in that sense, predetermine the decisions of public authorities. The predictability of public interference in private matters—sometimes referred to as 'regulatory intervention'—becomes the essential criterion for establishing administrative justice for citizens—at least according to the classical understanding of the ideal of administrative justice that originates from the establishment of the state governed by law in the middle of the nineteenth century.[1]

Constitutional Guarantees for Administrative Justice

The state governed by law has never had explicit roots in the Danish constitution—in contrast, for example, to the German constitution where the state is explicitly described as a 'democratic and social state governed by law' (*Grundgesetz* Art 20). The concept of a 'state governed by law' has—in a Danish and Scandinavian context—been imported from German jurisprudence, and has traditionally been used as a collective term for the fundamental guarantees of administrative justice that are established in the legal system in order to protect the life, freedom and property of citizens. In spite of this, the Danish constitution and the legal system in general still contain many essential elements of these constitutional guarantees.

[1] From a historical perspective, this ideal of administrative justice replaces the consideration of equity—which originates from Roman Law—that former used to play a very prominent role.

Thus, the Danish state can undoubtedly be characterised as 'a state governed by law'.

The guarantees for a state governed by law are linked to the existence of a constitution that lays down specific rules for the governance of the state. These rules ensure that the principle of the separation of state powers provides an organisational guarantee against the abuse of power. Finally the rules must protect the independence of citizens against legislative interference by granting certain material guarantees. These guarantees ensure that the constitution provides a degree of stability in the governance of the state. This is achieved, in part, through the written form of the constitution and, in part, through the special procedure by which constitutional amendments can be made. The reality in these guarantees is illustrated by the fact that the Danish constitution has only been changed four times since its passage in 1849, most recently in 1953. However, this claim must not be exaggerated. Other countries, which can also be characterised as democratic states governed by law, function very well without a written constitution because their constitutional rules are based on legal tradition.[2] On the other hand the complicated procedures for moving amendments can be an argument for either adopting a liberal interpretation of the constitution or for taking a broad view of those parts of the constitution that are outdated, leaving the constitution as a historical document without any real significance. From an ideal point of view, the specific rules for the governance of the state ensure that the state governed by law is 'a constitutional state'.

The guarantees for a state governed by law are also linked to a number of—partly derived—fundamental principles for governing the state. These refer to the legality of the government, the fact that public interference in civil matters demands the authority of a legal act as well as a need for coherence with present legal standards. With this so-called principle of legality, which can be derived from the principle of the separation of powers mentioned above, limits on the power of the state are achieved, since the state—due to the general character of the laws—is bound by its own laws. This also applies to the organisational presumption that the state can always be held responsible for the legality of its governance, whether it be the highest political organ, the government, or—as in Denmark—the minister, the so-called rule of ministers. This also applies to a number of material demands that supplement the principle of legality and guarantee a generally impartial application of the law, for example, non-statutory legal doctrines concerning the misuse of power, equality and the principle of proportionality. Combined with these principles the constitutional state appears as a state based on law (in a narrow sense), a 'law state' so to say.

The guarantees for a state governed by law are not completely realised in this manner. At a procedural level, a number of fundamental principles are involved. These are relevant to the role of the courts—and to the Parliamentary

[2] For example, the United Kingdom, which does not have a written constitution but was one of the first European nations to introduce a parliamentary system of government in the late 17th century.

Commissioner for Administration (the Ombudsman)—as independent organs for regulating the activities of the government. With legal authority as a leading element, specialisation of the regulatory framework to cover different areas of law and a hierarchic structure with inferior and superior levels of decision making, these principles can be applied to the bureaucratic structure of the state. This bureaucracy is staffed by a neutral corps of officials (civil servants) who, in the Scandinavian countries, typically have a law degree. This results in an extensive formalisation of administrative procedures that guarantee 'fair' treatment for the citizen. Because of this, it also helps to guarantee the legality and correctness of decision making by the administration. In this sense the state governed by law can be characterised as 'a procedural state'.

It follows from the above that a state governed by law can be characterised as 'a law state', 'a constitutional state' and 'a procedural state'. These elements are all realised in the present legal order in Denmark, and in other Scandinavian countries, although the transformation has not taken place concurrently since a great deal of relevant legislation has only been passed recently.[3] Because of this, it is almost as if the characterisation represents an idealistic picture, unrelated to the actual administration of the state. This is apparent in organisational relations where the principles of the separation of state powers and of ministers' responsibility have lost some of their importance. This has happened as a consequence of the recognition of the principle of Cabinet responsibility and the establishment of a number of tribunals and other commissions for administrative purposes. In a similar way, the rise of the social or welfare state has resulted in a development of administrative structures that have gradually moved the administrational apparatus away from the bureaucratic ideal type.

Because possible deviations from the principles of the state governed by law are usually conceived of as errors, the classical formulation still gives a reasonably correct picture of what jurists traditionally associate with the construction, despite the statements above.

From the Liberal State Governed by Law to the Social State Governing by Law

Changed Perspectives on the State and the Administration

Following the evolution of the classical liberal state governed by law into the social state governed by law, with its emphasis on the formal aspects of state activities,

[3] Examples of recent legislation in Denmark are the Ombudsman Act (1954), the Act of Ministers' Responsibility (1964) and the Administrative Fairness Act (1964). More recently, the latter has been replaced and supplemented by the Administrative Procedure Act (1985) and the Administrative Publicity Act (1985).

which took place during the twentieth century, there has been a radical change among Danish and Scandinavian jurists in their understanding of the state as a regulatory body in society. The classical conception of a state governed by law involved protecting citizens *from* the state. However, with the rise of the welfare state, this conception changed to the protection of the citizens *by* the state, brought about by regulation and public institutions that protect the welfare of the citizens in every possible way (Dalberg-Larsen 1984).

This change from one conception of the state to another resulted from changes that the state governed by law and the community founded on law have undergone in the past century. The central element in the present development of the community founded on law has been the designation of formal legal norms that ensure private property, freedom of contract, freedom of trade as well as the conventional freedom rights. These rights have characterised the community founded on law in the past: the purpose of these rights was to put citizens in a position where they could take care of themselves.

While the self-liability of citizens was dominant in the original form of the community founded on law, the right to self-determination has become the core of the modern form of the community founded on law due to the increasing public assumption of welfare functions. In order to ensure the welfare of the citizens, they are put into a position where they can make decisions concerning their own circumstances, which should not be limited by unemployment, sickness, accidents, age or a lack of basic necessities.

A change in the conception of equality that underlies this approach is taking place. Equality was originally a formal question, concerned with whether everyone had 'equal rights' in the sense of rights and duties that were determined by general rules that applied to everyone. These rules should have been synonymous with the prohibition of subjective discrimination and arbitrary treatment. However, with the coming of the welfare state, the ideal of equality gradually acquired a substantive meaning. This became a question of 'equal access' to all the public (free/tax financed) benefits and services. In practice this was ensured by granting citizens a legal entitlement to the benefits in question, instead of treating benefits as charity or allocating them on the basis of more or less random judgments.

The historical background for this evolution is the emergence of industrialism at the end of the nineteenth century. During this period, those parts of the population who were employed in the new industries suffered from social problems and from widespread poverty because of their exposed social positions. However the gradual democratisation of the state created a political basis for giving higher priority to social welfare objectives. This task was initiated privately but, as its span increased, it gradually came under public control. The rights of the individual were then accompanied by a set of (material) social rights, of which some were guaranteed by the constitution. These constitutional rights found expression in provisions to undertake public initiatives that were not politically binding, or, at least, were not conceived as such in former (Danish) jurisprudence. Instead the improvements consisted in the implementation of these policies—the right to education, to work and to unemployment relief—which enabled individuals to control their own lives. These improvements were enacted through a number of public regulations and institutional measures (such as social security benefits and transfer income).

Fundamental Values in the Social State Governing by Law

In a similar manner, this approach can be applied to the superstructure of the state, in historiography described as the evolution of 'a liberal state governed by law' into 'a social state governing by law'. It should be noted that this account can lead to the view that administrative justice—as a leading value in the classic state governed by law—is a concept that belongs to the past and that is has been replaced by a concern with efficiency, which is of increased importance because of the expansion of public activities throughout the post-war period.

This development has left its mark on the theory of administrative law in the twentieth century. Administrative justice and efficiency are increasingly seen as opposites that inaugurated a demand around which should be given priority: they are the basic values that characterise debates on politico-legal issues in Denmark, and in other Scandinavian countries, today.[4] These debates highlight the defensive position, into which jurists are put by groups of growing influence, such as economists and political scientists, as defenders of an ideal of administrative justice that is considered to be obsolete, or, at least, to slow down the rational improvement of public administration.

At first the growing clash of interests between administrative justice and efficiency leads to a concretisation of the ideal of a state governed by law and its implications for administrative justice. In this concretisation, importance is attached to the formal demands of public activities (by a formalisation of the procedural rules) and to procedural controls (by rules that grant rights of access to documents, and established a Parliamentary Commissioner for Administration and numerous administrative tribunals). From a traditional politico-legal perspective, these arrangements have provided a (necessary) compensation for the loss of guarantees of administrative justice that the increasing use of framework laws, causing extensive delegations to the administration, has led to recently (especially in the area of public services).[5]

A considerable number of problems are, however, resolved by finding solutions to definite, individual problems. These solutions are based on standards regarding the amount of professional assistance required and the sought after objectives. Appropriateness and, in a wider sense, thoughtfulness—meaning consideration for

[4] The classic in this 'genre' is Christensen (1972).

[5] Using traditional terminology, this phenomenon can be described as a way of replacing the material ideal of administrative justice, which is lost when the authority to regulate and assess is given to public administration by law, with formal procedural guarantees. For a critique of this notion, see Henrichsen (1997: 223 ff).

the special conditions of a particular case—become key-elements in the assessment of administrative justice in these particular areas. They contrast with the traditional concern for lawfulness and predictability in exercising public authority. Formalised ways of making decisions and extensive control mechanisms are not necessarily the best guarantees for appropriate administration. The degree of precision in the description of public objectives on the other hand has considerable practical relevance. The same applies to the professional standards of frontline civil servants and the possibility of holding officials and/or authorities to account for mistakes and negligence, whether through disciplinary measures or through compensation.

The designation of the objectives of public activities has been on the agenda as a—legally inspired—instrument for managing public activities. These objectives tend to be of growing importance due to the increased application of object clauses in legislation. Today the professionalisation of public activities is relevant in a number of service areas, implying the need for educational and in-service training courses and for upgrading the professional qualifications of public employees. The possibility of holding public officials or authorities to account for mistakes and negligence corresponds with this, because of the tendency to let the special liability of professionals extend to groups of public employees, for example, in the implementation of complaints and compensation arrangements in the health services sector.

In politico-legal thinking about public administration, the fundamental clash between administrative justice and efficiency as rival benchmarks for public activities is reflected in the object clauses of the legislation, the norms and ethics of the professions and the possibility of holding someone to account for mistakes and negligence. Efficiency—in a wide sense—is therefore just a matter of fulfilling given objectives. In practice this requires the contribution of economic, personnel and organisational resources, together with the establishment of mechanisms that prevent mistakes and negligence.

On the other hand it is obvious that objectives as well as resources must be modified to take account of the circumstances at any given time. Seen from the perspective of administrative justice, limitations of certain activities are not problematic, as long as there is a reasonable correlation between the desirable (as stated in the objectives) and what is attainable (with the given resources). On the other hand problems can arise if, for example, cutbacks force through the abandonment of objectives that, formally, remain unaltered. In that case, both administrative justice and efficiency would be damaged. However it should not prevent savings—due to restructuring and technological improvements—from being achieved without compromising administrative justice. The possibility of increasing productivity in public administration through a more effective exploitation of resources should always be considered in activities that demand substantial resources.

The paradigm of administrative justice in the social state that has been suggested as an alternative to the traditional conception of administrative justice in the liberal state is particularly aimed at public service activities. It follows that the paradigm of administrative justice in the liberal state still dominates in the classical area of public regulatory intervention. In practice however, the lines between the two paradigms cannot be drawn this sharply. The boundaries between regulatory intervention and service activities fluctuate—some service activities contain elements of regulatory intervention, in which the legal status of the citizen is determined by the authorities and where traditional considerations regarding administrative justice have continuing importance.[6] On the other hand, it must be expected that the values reflected by the paradigm of the social state will influence the demands of administrative justice that apply to traditional regulatory intervention. So, for example, the Danish Administrative Procedure Act contains elements that only can be explained using a standard of administrative justice that also attaches importance to the considerate treatment of citizens (see the discussion of thoughtfulness above).[7]

The Technocratisation of Public Activities

The organisational contrast to the bureaucracy of the liberal state can be characterised as 'a technocracy' that evolves on all levels of the public sector—first, in connection with the public benefits and services delivered by various professions and, secondly, in connection with enhanced management, which is transferred to 'generalists' with specialist education (in economics and the social sciences) in a way that increasingly drives out the earlier monopoly of the legal profession.

At the same time this development is connected to a shift in the norms and values of civil servants, whose neutrality is replaced by professional involvement, to ensure that frontline employees get through their work. This professional involvement gives rise to a distance between the individual as an employee and as a professional. Loyalty towards the politicians in power has been turned into loyalty towards the values and ethical standards of 'good conduct' associated with the profession. Likewise, the claims of loyalty towards the politicians in power that are addressed to top-level administrational staff tend to intensify the demand for personal identification with the values of management.

Despite the fact that conditions regarding staff and organisation rarely result in statutory initiatives, these tendencies are to some degree reflected in legal realities. The vigorous limitations on the establishment of civil servant status that have been introduced recently reflect this development. Rules that enable public employees to participate in administrative activities ensure that they are more than obedient instruments of management decisions. The ethical norms of the professions limit the obligation to comply with the (subjective) political dictates

[6] Eg, access to the use of constraint in psychiatric treatments and the removal of children from their homes because of neglect.

[7] Eg, the demands of justification simultaneously with a decision from the administration under the authority of the Administration Procedure Act. The traditional benchmark for administrative justice would only demand a subsequent justification.

that loyalty would require. Furthermore, although a change of political leadership rarely leads to a change in administrational leadership, the expansion of administrative activities requires guidance on political-tactical matters, the employment of personal advisors for ministers, and a growing 'consumption' of leading civil servants in both central and local government.

The public ethos has been influenced by these changes in governmental institutions. The technocratisation and professionalisation of public (service) activities are synonymous with the accession of new sets of values in the public sector. These new values promote a picture of public authorities as institutions of 'good will'. They certainly possess great power—by virtue of the wide scope given to their activities in the legislation and the monopoly of knowledge of the professions regarding appropriate solutions to practical social problems—but, according to their self-conception, that power is always exercised in the interests of citizens. However this model has been opposed by more conventionally thinking jurists, who have stressed the classic ideals of a state governed by law. Good intentions are met with doubts and it is suggested that the interests of citizens should be promoted through a conversion of framework laws into more definite laws that grant specific rights and real legal claims to social benefits.[8]

This backlash however must be seen in the light of the underlying development of government during the twentieth century, a development that has gradually raised doubts regarding the legitimacy of the entire project of the social state, as described in the following section.

From the Social State to the Market State

The Closed Organisational Society

The development of the modern welfare state can—according to Jürgen Habermas (1981)—be characterised as a repression or 'colonisation' of civil society because the public gradually takes over the functions of civil society. The members of society are tied into a legal net of social rights and obligations, while local networks (family and institutions in the local community) lose their importance for social cohesion. It is also possible—following Niklas Luhmann (1981)—to detect a corresponding development of the superstructure of the state governed by law, in which regulation changes character from distinguishing between the legal and the illegal into becoming a tool that can solve all sorts of social problems in society.

The analyses of these two German sociologists uncover new problems and conflicts of value in the development of the modern welfare society. They include the accentuation of the increased difficulties that arise with the justification of public

[8] For a more detailed description see Henrichsen (1997: 141 ff) with examples from Danish and Norwegian politico-legal thinking.

efforts in areas where citizens increasingly feel they are being treated as legally incompetent and are alienated from public institutions (Habermas). It also applies to the accentuation of the growing problems concerning the management of the societal relations in situations where the legal system becomes more complex and open to exterior political, economic and other non-legal influences (Luhmann). Both these sociologists agree that this combination of problems regarding legitimacy and management inevitably leads to democratic problems at the governmental level. In this way, fundamental democratic values are at stake in a way that resonates with common understandings of political systems in the 1970s and 1980s.

The fact that citizens experienced a loss of influence over the development of society—at a time where political democracy was strengthened by rules of eligibility and suffrage that allowed citizens to influence the government more than ever—is a paradox. This paradox must however be seen in the light of the immense expansion that public activities underwent during this period. This expansion exempted a number of matters from the close embrace of civil society: matters in which the individual could usually make his own decisions.[9] At the same time, the expansion created a complex and highly specialised network of public regulation and public institutions that are often closed to individual influence.

The complications that arise in governing society have been intensified by the tendency to involve local authorities and organised groups in political-administrative decision making. As a consequence, policies are the outcome of a number of different interests and considerations that lead to opaque compromise solutions. Likewise the increasing use of framework and enabling Acts has made administrative organisations and their employees into active planners in the political decision-making processes, enabling them to pursue their own administrative interests.

The overall result of this development can be characterised as a very specialised organisational society. The problems regarding management created by this development do not only affect the individual as a citizen but also the representatives who are elected by the people, who are gradually put into the position of spectators of developments they can hardly influence. The development leads to the 'self-isolation' of the political-administrative system as a whole as well as of the inter-connected sub-systems (public authorities and institutions), which become impenetrable to outside influences.

The Modernisation of the Public Sector

It is in this light that the increasing demand for citizen-influence at the end of the twentieth century must be seen. It currently affects a number of areas, including, in particular, the municipal area, with rules about democratic planning,

[9] Eg, (official) child care instead of (private) caring for children, formal education for increasingly long periods, old peoples' home instead of nursing at home, etc.

neighborhood council democracy and institutional user democracy. Attempts are being made to make public activities more transparent and more responsive to demands from citizens regarding rules for evaluating public involvement, information for users and the possibility of choosing the form of benefits themselves. The aim is to promote administrative and institutional openness and greater responsiveness to the changing wishes and demands of citizens. However these considerations are not in any way new. It has been traditional to involve organised interest groups (and local organisations) in political-administrative management. The novelty is the intensification of the direct involvement of citizens, on the assumption that the interests of citizens not always are looked after by interest groups (and municipal home rule organs) that supposedly represent the citizen.

The stated purpose is furthered by a number of initiatives that ought to (re-)create the political possibility of managing a public sector that has become increasingly unmanageable. This applies to the struggle against an 'overregulated' society and the corresponding tendency to promote 'over scrupulous justice' at any cost, for example, by the simplification of rules, deregulation and decentralisation. It applies to challenges to free public benefits and the underlying demand for guaranteeing the 'total welfare' of the individual, for example, through acquiescence to private pensions, the introduction of user charges and the division of the public benefits into 'core benefits' and 'supplementing benefits'. It applies to the efforts to contain the influence of organised groups as well as their ability to block the 'necessary' policies, for example, by reducing and phasing out arrangements for consultation and representation. And it finally applies to the confrontation of the narrow administrative self-interest, for example, by the intensifying economic management, introducing salary systems that promote productivity, adopting 'payment by results' contracts and making the leading values in the management of the public institutions more visible.

These initiatives all aim at what can be characterised as a revitalisation of the traditional parliamentary chain of command. A central idea is the incorporation of incentive structures into the administrative and institutional sectors with the aim of promoting adaptation and the development of public benefits. The introduction of incentive structures combined with so-called 'value based management' must be seen in this perspective. Other more 'system enhancing' elements of the continuing effort to modernise public administration concern the formation of public companies, public procurement and the privatisation of areas of public efforts, perhaps supplemented by governmental or municipal participation in private companies and public support for 'self-supporting networks'.

These initiatives herald a new form of modernisation, a course that tendentiously leads the development away from a traditional—politically determined—regulation of public activities to a system based on a market determined self-regulation. This self-regulation is not intended to be subject to politically detailed regulation, but it will of course be politically controlled. On the contrary, the development leads towards the de-politicisation of the public grant of benefits, in which political management is replaced by a direct—market determined—relationship between the (public and private) producers and the recipients of the benefits. The intention is to reshape the public sector into being the supplier of the social benefits that the citizens need at the price the citizens are willing to pay. The character of the individual changes from being a citizen, who makes demands (of increased welfare) on the political rulers, into a consumer or a customer, who exerts influence on a market for social benefits.

Towards a Market or Minimal State

The entire philosophy of management that the above-mentioned initiative reflects is founded on the fundamental liberal idea that individuals can identify their preferences and make rational decisions in order to satisfy their own wants. In the international—economic and political—theoretical world, this idea finds expression as 'Public Choice' and 'New Public Management'. This philosophy of management is apparently also supported by the fact that social rights are increasingly conceived as natural rights. Additional space for the satisfaction of individual wants and needs has been created. In this way, the possibility of self-realisation or self-development is regarded as the fundamental value that characterises the operation of present-day post industrial society. At the same time, it leads to an expansion of the concept of liberty that is opposed to the concepts of autonomy and self-liability.

The prospects of this development could be the market or minimal state—inspired by some modern (Anglo-American) political philosophy, eg Nozick (1974)—which has been formulated as a vision for the future in political debate.[10] In the discussion below, I deal very briefly with the market state. According to its proponents, the responsibility of the state for the welfare of the citizens is limited to securing a minimal supply of welfare benefits under a private—or mixed public–private—administration, and otherwise securing the most basic functions of society. The consequence of such a reduction in government activity would—in the last resort—involve a relinquishment of the fellowship of values that the state and society represent (Lundquist 1998). With the production of more or less individualised welfare benefits based on the market mechanism, that would enable individuals to choose freely between benefits according to their resources and their needs, there would be no need to require that social problems are solved on a collective basis. Such problems would instead be solved through the market, perhaps supported by a legal system that determines the specific ground rules for the production and exchange of welfare benefits.

In the absence of clear rules that confer rights on members of the public, citizens would be forced to look after themselves by raising legal actions against the producers of the benefits; and would have to argue their case with reference to market principles and basic fundamental rights. In this way, the law and the

[10] For some Nordic jurists, eg Graver (2002: 147 ff), the market state is already a reality.

legal system would become instruments for solving the conflicts caused by the development of society, a development that has been seen in other countries, where the market economy has greater presence, for example in the USA, where there is a tendency to deal with all sorts of problems in terms of rights that are subject to legal proceedings, a phenomenon that is frequently referred to as 'rights talk' (Porsdam 2002). Such a development would rely on an increased amount of judicial activism, a phenomenon that has traditionally been very limited in Denmark and the other Scandinavian countries, where the courts normally refuse to deal with 'political' issues. However this tradition has been put under pressure by the law enforcement system of the European Community (The European Court)—a system that stands for an active integration of the legal systems of the member states (Graver 2000).

From the Social State to the Milieu State

The Problems of the Risk Society

The evolution of a social state into a market state is one possible consequence of modernisation. Another possibility is that the social state evolves into what has been characterised as a network or milieu state (Sand 1996; Henrichsen 1997) and, in this discussion, I use the latter expression.[11] This development is related to that aspect of modernisation that aims at democratising the public structures of decision making by strengthening the political possibilities of managing and increasing the influence of citizens.

Both the market state and the milieu state reflect reactions against the organised social state and against organisational society in a whole. However there are other perspectives on the milieu state in so far as the idea of it is connected to another feature of the development of society that has attracted increasing political attention for a generation. It is what has been characterised as the risk society (Beck 1986). The expression refers to the increasing difficulties that are connected with managing and controlling a development of society that is characterised by an industrial over-exploitation of natural resources. The development also generates material wealth and, as a result, production as well as the products and the total social effects of production cause a number of specific risks for the individual. At the same time the problems are increased by tendencies towards

[11] The two expressions relate to each other as form and content: The expression 'network state' refers to changing—non-hierarchic—forms of interaction between the authority and the citizen in connection with solving definite social problems; whereas the expression 'milieu state' reflects an administrative practice with an emphasis on solving social problems where they arise, namely 'in the milieu'. See the text below concerning prevention as an alternative to the remedial efforts that characterise large numbers of public activities.

the internationalisation and globalisation of production, trade and the economy that characterise contemporary society.

The idea of a milieu state came into existence as a reaction to these problems, but it increasingly appears as a counterpart of the liberal market state (Leyland and Woods 1997: 446). This new approach questions the case for self-development of the individual as a fundamental value, legitimising the liberal project of phasing out or 'marketising' public efforts of any kind. By contrast, it recognises that real societal circumstances constitute limits or barriers to the realisation of this consideration, and that collective efforts will be necessary to prevent risks regarding health and well-being resulting from the production of material goods. At the same time it should be noted that public efforts still are required in order to equalise social, cultural and ethnical differences that can affect the possibility of individual development. Finally, it is important to emphasise that the premises of the market economy concerning fair competition and complete information limit the complexity of the benefits that can be supplied by the market.

The evolution towards a market state would imply a reactive solution to societal conflicts by means of a more or less political legal system. The alternative to this is the regulation of the conditions of society, which implies that problems are handled proactively through interaction with the affected interests. The point of such an interaction is to create a balance between short-term economic (commercial) interests and long-term considerations for health, environment and society (Henrichsen 1997: 397). The challenge for management consists of creating equal possibilities of development for the individual, including insuring against the unintended consequences of societal production, meaning that the traditional symptom-treating 'reparative' activities of the welfare state must be expanded in order to engage—and thereby prevent—problems where they arise, namely 'in the milieu'—hence the term 'milieu state'. If political attempts at management are expanded into an effort that seeks to unite short-term considerations for production with long-term societal considerations, it implies that the authorities will assume an active role as mediators between conflicting considerations and interests. The idea of the milieu state is developed for such purposes.

The Milieu State as Problem Solver

The milieu state is not a pure 'model of thought', but represents ideas that are rooted in a development of legal regulation that began years ago in the fields of planning and environmental protection. This regulation has increasingly been based on the idea of preventing societal problems by using sustainability as a normative pivotal point for managerial initiatives. A characteristic of this is that it attempts to unite conflicting societal interests in a dialogue emphasising the concrete possibilities of achieving solutions through the establishment of special procedures for public decisions. In Denmark, this kind of governance has existed for a long time in two areas: in the working environment, and in practical planning. Practical planning has been carried out within the area of protecting the environment by means of special procedures known as milieu assessment (for evaluating the impact of certain projects).

With dialogue as the pivotal point for solving societal problems, the stage is set for a politicisation of public activities that tend to oppose the professionalisation of the public activities of the welfare state—as well as the judicialisation of the administrative routines of decision making in the liberal state governed by law. The model is inspired by the reflexive—procedurally determined—legal forms that have been debated in continental and Nordic jurisprudence since the 1980s and can be seen as the counterpart of the material legal form of the social state and the formal legal form of the liberal state governed by law (Teubner 1988). The perspective in such a procedurally determined arrangement of the relations between state and citizen is a revival of the state with separated powers in a new sense—namely, a division of power at the local level where the interests of the citizens are particularly affected by societal developments.[12]

An administrative equivalent of reflexive theory is the adhocracy model of organisation. It has flat multi-disciplinary organisational structures that are especially suitable for promoting creativity and innovation in employment and decision-making processes (Mintsberg 1979). The 'adhocratic' model is securing a foothold in parts of the public administration. In this context the placement of the individual employee is—expressed simplistically—determined by a loyalty towards the task, towards the project that the authority or institution currently works on, since neither political-administrative management nor the acquired professional norms can be expected to solve the problems that new and changing tasks present. Officials are supposed to confront reality openly by acknowledging the differences in the cases they encounter.

The perspective characterised by prevention, dialogue and project organisation can be expanded to include other sectors of the society in addition to public planning and environmental protection. For a long time there have been efforts to ensure a higher degree of prevention within the health sector, and the numerous problems connected with 'social inheritance' are also receiving an increasing amount of attention. The dialogue procedures have gained a footing in institutional work with societal problems. Examples of this are the demands for differentiation in school legislation (where the goals and means of the education are determined in collaboration with the individual pupil), the demands of informed consent in health legislation (where the goals and means of the treatment are determined in agreement with the patient) and the insertion of a principle of dialogue in social legislation (which has given the citizen the possibility of participating in the treatment of his or her case).

[12] *Cf* the concept of 'governance', which has been used in modern political theory as an expression for a structure of management with participation of private agents and as a counterpart of the organs of the state and the municipality that are elected by the people ('governments').

Fundamental Values in the Milieu State

The prevention of societal problems, institutional arrangements characterised by dialogue and the politicisation of public decision making reflect a number of fundamental values that differ from those that characterise a market state. Although the benchmark of values, namely securing the self-development of individuals in accordance with their wishes and their needs, remains the same, the concretisation of this ideal of liberty differs in the two types of state. The market state gives the individual options for choosing welfare benefits, the range of the options is limited by the market, and the benefits are only available as long as there is a market for them. On the other hand, the milieu state aims to increase the liberty of the individual when it comes to choosing possible ways of self-development.

Partly as a consequence of this, the ideal of equality is differently utilised in the two models. The market state uses rules that ensure equal rights to the benefits that the individual can and will pay for so that the rights are connected to concrete welfare benefits. As for the milieu state, the ideal of equality is concretised as a matter of securing 'equal possibilities' for individuals to develop accordance with their personal abilities and wishes. Rights and obligations are connected to the possibilities of influencing the (social and health related) conditions of life that might appear to hinder these possibilities.[13] In this connection, the concretisation of the ideal of equality must be seen as an expansion of the standards of equality that have been predominant in the liberal state ('equal rights') and the social state ('equal access').

From a perspective that emphasises legal protection, the model of the market state emphasises the security of a transparent market for the production and distribution of welfare benefits—benefits that, as far as possible, comply with the citizen's needs and wishes. In the context of the milieu state, the ideal of legal protection must be defined as a demand for equal treatment when solving societal problems for the citizen (Henrichsen 1997: 339). This consideration is connected to the dialogue-based organisation of the relationship between authorities and citizens mentioned above. It refers to an expansion of the ideal of legal protection in relation to predictability and thoughtfulness that has already been mentioned as core elements of the concept of administrative justice.

The notions of value of the milieu state are not clearly articulated in the current work of changing and renewing the public sector, even though they are, in some respects, a continuation of the modernisation trail concerned with the democratisation of the public decision making. On the other hand they are rooted in the

[13] In 1992 a provision (§ 110b) of a 'right to environmental and social milieu' was inserted into the Norwegian constitution. This provision states that certain normative principles for legislation, including the principle of a right to a certain environmental quality, solidarity with future generations and the civil right to information regarding environmental matters. Likewise, the Finnish constitution of 1999 (§ 20) states that the commonalty must promote a healthy environment, and that everyone can influence decisions regarding matters that concern their personal environment.

long-term development of certain parts of the legal order, especially in public planning and environmental protection but also in other areas. As far as the notions of value in the market state are concerned, the opposite seems to be the case. These notions do not have a long history but they have had a considerable effect on the political debate concerning future possibilities for the government.

Confrontation with Model Building in International Socio-Legal Theory

Recapitulation of the Central Theses

The preceding analysis covers a number of elements of public administration that situate it in its historical context, as a state governed by law and as an essential aspect of solidarity associated with the modern legal community. For this reason, it is particularly relevant to speak of a 'public ethos' in referring to those special values that the public must take responsibility for. However, the characteristics of a state governed by law are not unchangeable, and likewise the public contribution to the maintenance of the legal community is not static. The question is not so much whether the new values will gain a footing in the development of the organisation and in the management of the state, but rather whether established values gradually will attain new and wider meanings that reflect the general development of the values in the society. The public ethos in the four models of the state is set out in Table 1 below.

From a legal theory perspective, the public ethos in the Scandinavian countries is historically associated with the values of the law state. These values have

Table 1: The public ethos in a historical and futuristic perspective

	Law state	**Social state**	**Milieu state**	**Market state**
Fundamental democratic values	Self-responsibility/ equal rights	Self-determination/ equal access	Self-development/ equal possibilities	Self-development/ own possibilities
Fundamental constitutional values	Protection against abuse of power	Protection by use of power	Protection by separation of power	Protection by renounciation of power
Considerations of administrative justice	Formal law/ predictability	Material law/ thoughtfulness	Reflexive law/ equality	Responsive law/ dissimilarity
Guarantees of administrative justice	Rule management/ judicialisation	Goal management/ professionalisation	Value management/ politicisation	Market management/ de-politicisation

changed in relation to the growth of the social state, and further changes are coming up—caused by the general development of values in society—with the market state and the milieu state as actual possibilities for further developments of the public sector.

As far as the idea of administrative justice is concerned, it was originally—in the law state—characterised by the citizens' ability to predict their own legal position. However, it expanded in the social state to include the demands for thoughtful treatment, emphasising the resolution of individual problems. Further development of the public sector in the direction of a market state or a milieu state will bring new values into focus, respectively dissimilarity (the different preferences of individual citizens) and equality (the possibility of citizens influencing their own way of life).

These different ways of concretisating the ideal of administrative justice are connected with different areas of public activities, with a differentiation between the classical exercise of authority (emphasising predictability), public service (emphasising thoughtfulness), public regulation (emphasising equality) and market-based activities (emphasising dissimilarity). However the different types of administrative justice should not be exclusively connected to these activities, since more recent developments form a supplement to the established order in every sort of public activity.

So the overall assessment is that the public ethos is a much more diversified concept today than it was at the time of the establishment of the law state in the mid-eighteenth century. It is, nevertheless, a fact that many jurists still conceive the values of the law state as the most central of values. If reality—the development of law and society—does not correspond to the ideal of the law state, it is perceived as a threat to the values of the law state which ought to be handled by further regulation of public activities. Conversely the differentiation of the ideal of administrative justice can be stretched out so far that it will become difficult to maintain a distinction between a public and a private ethos. This could happen if the public sector is subjected to the logic of market in significant ways. For some jurists, this constitutes a reason for considering other ways of developing and renewing the public sector, for example in the direction of the milieu state.

Comparative Perspectives on the Legal and the Social State

From a historical point of view, it should be clear that the first two models of administrative justice—based on respectively the law state and the social state—are sequential, since they represent the different stages of the historical development of public administration from the middle of the eighteenth century until 1980s. And from the same point of view the two last models—based on what I have called the milieu state and the market state—are highly competitive, since they are influenced by, and are responses to, contradictory tendencies in the contemporary development of public administration.

From an empirical point of view, however, elements of all sorts of administrative justice can be found in present-day public administration. Thus both the values of the law state and those of the social state will be repeatedly encountered across the public sector. Detailed legal regulations ensure predictability, which is still a crucial value, and (professional) thoughtfulness remains essential in public service activities. And in the course of historical development there has also been strong competition between these elements of administrative justice, with jurists advocating a formalisation and judicialisation of public service activities.

Though it is new—at least from a Scandinavian perspective—to see thoughtfulness and professionalisation as distinct values of administrative justice opposing traditional values like predictability and bureaucratisation, this was not unfamiliar in an international theoretical context. These two models of administrative justice are similar to two of Mashaw's 'justice models' (1984: 31), that is, to the models he characterises as 'bureaucratic rationality' and 'professional treatment', although I was not aware of this at the time when I was developing my own theory of administrative justice back in the 1980s (Henrichsen 1982).

The similarity between the models becomes even greater if one compares Table 1 above with the reshaping of Mashaw's models that has been undertaken by Adler (see Adler 2006: 620 and his chapter in this volume). Adler's models of the bureaucratic and professional conceptions of administrative justice are almost completely identical with my own models of justice in a law state and in a social state described above. In order to emphasise the comparison between my own models and Adler's models, I have revised these two models of classical administrative justice in Table 2 below, describing legal values and guarantees for their realisation in three systematic dimensions: functions, structures and processes.

The first dimension concerning the *functions* of the state is described in terms of a fundamental distinction between public administration and public service, between what can be seen as the administration of general rules concerned with citizens' rights and duties on the one hand and the provision of services like health, education and social welfare on the other hand. This distinction too appears in Adler's model in that he point out that rule application is a characteristic of bureaucratic

Table 2: Revised models of administrative justice in the legal and social state

Model	Functions	Structures	Processes
Law state	Public administration	Bureaucratic	Applying rules
legal values	equal rights	impersonal treatment	predictability
legal guarantees	precise rules	centralised/hierarchical	judicialisation
Social state	Public service	Technocratic	Applying knowledge
legal values	equal access	personal treatment	thoughtfulness
legal guarantees	precise goals	decentralised/interpersonal	professionalisation

organisations, while (social) service is a legitimating value or goal in professional activities. Focusing more explicitly on these two functions provides an opportunity to stress what should be considered to be the fundamental legal values and guarantees of these functions, as shown in Table 2: Administrative justice in public administration is seen as a question of ensuring equal rights and duties based on a system of precise rules, leaving no space for discretion, while administrative justice in public service is seen as a question of ensuring equal access to services defined (in law or elsewhere) by precise goals about what to be done in every single case.

Concerning the *structure* of the state, it should be clear too that both models are based on a fundamental assumption that there is a difference in the structuring of public administration and public service which Adler—following Mashaw—expresses in terms of respectively bureaucratic and professional organisation. Using general organisational theory this distinction could also be expressed in terms of classical and professional bureaucracy (Mintsberg 1979) or, as in my own model, in terms of a distinction between 'bureaucracy' and 'technocracy'. In characterising these structures, Mashaw and Adler do so in terms of hierarchical (in the first case) and interpersonal (in the second) relationships. In Table 2, these relationships have been supplemented with some further characteristics, since impersonal treatment is seen as a legal value in bureaucratic administrative decision making while the opposite is the case in technocratic decision making, and since the centralised and decentralised structuring of activities are assumed to be means for realising these values.

With regard to state *processes*, I adopt Adler's terminology to describe the differences between decision making in bureaucratic and professional organisations in terms of applying rules and applying knowledge. However, I have tried to clarify these processes in Table 2 by specifying predictability and judicialisation as central legal values and guarantees of bureaucratic, rule-based decision making, and thoughtfulness and professionalisation as fundamental values and preconditions for the technocratic, goal-orientated treatment of individual problems. So thoughtfulness, corresponding to Mashaw's use of the term of 'client satisfaction', and predictability, as an obvious equivalent to 'accuracy' in Adler's model of bureaucratic justice, express the core of administrative justice in former and in current forms of public administration. And though the judicialisation of administrative decision-making processes in recent years has been seen to compensate for a lack of administrative justice in a material sense in public service activities, I find this more relevant in relation to traditional rule application, while professionalisation should be considered as a guarantee of administrative justice in decision-making processes based on the application of knowledge.

Partly for the same reason, I do not consider Adler's 'legal' model of administrative justice—or Mashaw's 'moral judgement' model—as a model that is distinct from my own law state and social state models. It apparently describes features of decision making in courts, tribunals and ombudsmen dealing with complaints and grievances in relation to first instance administrative decision making. However, from an analytical point of view—describing normative features of a law state and a social state as a whole—this aspect must be considered to be a part of the concept of administrative justice. This does not prevent it from being useful to make this distinction in empirical—socio-legal—studies of administrative justice, but this is not the aim of my own model-building.[14]

Comparative Perspectives on the Milieu State and Market State

In the continuing development of public administration, other values have come into focus. Analysing the development Adler suggests some further models—the managerial, consumerist and market models—all clearly refer to administrative reforms from the mid-1980s onwards. These models can be seen as representing alternative possibilities for the future development of administrative justice, analogous to the models of the market state and the milieu state mentioned above. To make these models comparable with Adler's, I have indicated in Table 3 below some further characteristics of administrative justice in a market state and in a milieu state. However it is not easy to compare the models since they are based on different conceptions of the competing characteristics of administrative justice.

The three models that Adler has identified to describe current developments of public administration might all be considered as different aspects of the same trend based on the ideas of New Public Management (NPM). As such they represent different aspects of the market state model in the figure above, whereas the milieu state model apparently has no equivalents in Adler's model-building. This fact needs some supplementary comments in order to clarify the differences between the market state and milieu state models.

As mentioned above, the milieu state and the market state can both be seen as ongoing developments of the social state. They have the same goal of securing the self-development of the individual in accordance with his or her own wishes and needs. The concretisation of this ideal of liberty however is fundamentally different in these two models of the state. While the market state aims to give the citizens a choice between various sorts of social benefits and the production of

Table 3: Revised models of administrative justice in the market and milieu state

Model	Functions	Structures	Processes
Market state	Public assignments	Private enterprise	Applying contracts
legal values	own possibilities	responsive	dissimilarity
legal guarantees	precise standards	independent	de-politicisation
Milieu state	Public regulations	Adhocratic	Applying mediation
legal values	equal possibilities	reflexive	equality
legal guarantees	precise values	self-regulatory	politicisation

[14] See the discussion of this model in Adler's chapter above.

these benefits is determined by the matching of supply and demand, the milieu state aims to increase the liberty of the individual to chose his own form of self-development and the degree of liberty in this model is determined by political decisions made in the course of a dialogue-based interaction between citizens and those in charge of delivering public benefits.

As far as administrative justice in a market state is concerned, it is important to ensure that there is sufficient freedom of choice between various (public and) private services. Instead of insisting on certain services, and complaining about faults and shortcomings in them, the citizen can simply choose another producer of the service in question. In this way, administrative justice is a question of dissimilarity and the guarantee for obtaining this value is the de-politicisation of service production by leaving (public and) private enterprises to respond to consumers' demands and wishes. This model is very much like Adler's market model.

In contrast, administrative justice in the milieu state is focused on equality, that is, on equal treatment of citizens in a dialogue-based process in which the public authorities act like mediators. This is very often the situation in environmental law, where long-term interests focused on milieu or ecological values have to be weighed against the short-term interests of business and efficiency. Dialogue techniques have also been used in public service activities to ensure the equal treatment of all citizens, although full equality in contacts between authorities and citizens is clearly an illusion. In this regard however, the model of the milieu state is more relevant to public service activities with preventive purposes, since such activities leave a space for authorities and citizens to try out new ideas about how to prevent social problems from arising.

The milieu state implies a high degree of citizen participation in public activities. In this sense, it seems very much alike Adler's consumerist model, which is one aspect of NPM. In contrast to this model, it is not the citizen as a consumer of public services as much as the citizen as such who is pivotal in the milieu state model.[15] Instead of talking about consumer satisfaction and participation, it would—from this point of view—be more precise to characterise this model in terms of citizens' rights to participate in public decision making in order to influence decisions relevant to their own way of life. As such, the milieu state is actually a response to the costumer-thinking of the market model, which emphasises citizens' rights and responsibilities to respect other peoples' interests in collective affairs in contrast to the market model, which considers people to be customers who act solely in terms of their own interests.

However the milieu state is also a response to Adler's managerial model, which is another aspect of NPM that emphasises the importance of internal incentives for greater efficiency in the public sector. Since these incentives are usually based on an element of competition, this model should be seen as a variant of the market state rather than an original model with its own implications for administrative

[15] *Cf* the discussion of Adler's consumerist model in Halliday and Scott's chapter above.

justice. However this fact does not deprive the model its worth as an analytically distinct model with its own characteristics.[16] Adler stresses internal characteristics like managerial autonomy and performance indicators and audit. The external counterpart of these characteristics—elaborated standards of service—should put the individual in a different—and potentially stronger—position than the client in the social state.

There is no doubt that consumerist and managerial thinking have been dominant in public reforms in the Scandinavian countries in recent years, transforming the public sector in the image of the management logic of private enterprise. On the other hand, it has often been pointed out in political debate that the market model, involving public procurement and other forms of privatisation, should be the real successor to the social (welfare) state. This model has likewise received a great deal of support from EC legislation. However, it has had less of an impact in practice, at least in Denmark and Norway, although it seems to have been more successful in Sweden.

By comparison, the milieu state—in Denmark—had its rise back in the 1970s and 1980s in connection with some grand environmental law reforms, which stressed the necessity of involving citizens in public planning and regulation. At this time, there was a strong desire for preventive measures for dealing with social problems. In addition, municipal reforms in the '70s brought the idea of citizens' participation in public affairs to the fore as compensation for the reduction of local democracy when many small municipalities were joined to form fewer and larger units. However attempts to realise these ideas in public law were met with heavy resistance from local authorities and other organised interests, who felt that their power was under threat from non-governmental forces.

More recently, since the beginning of the new millennium, the Danish Government has downgraded environmental and other preventive measures. However, the current climate change and financial crises could result in the milieu state moving up to the top of the agenda again, acknowledging that collective efforts are necessary to solve such problems and that our long-term agenda requires the involvement of citizens in public decision making. At any rate, it is too early to discard the model since it clearly constitutes a realistic response to future problem solving in public affairs.

In addition to the shifting circumstances for administrative reform, it is notable that many years experiences with NPM techniques have revealed some problematic aspects of these efforts to renew the public sector. The managerial regime has generated a flow of standard programmes that have enmeshed public institutions in a net of more or less inflexible rules. Standard programming, which is often a result of public procurement, implies specification of the public functions that will be consigned to private enterprise on basis of contract. Programmes can be altered in line with new public procurements but the privatisation of

[16] *Cf* Halliday and Scott (in this volume), arguing that 'it is unclear to us that managerialism represents a distinctive decision-making process'.

public services involves public authorities no longer being able to use their own experience to develop new forms of problem solving. In any case, the gains from such techniques have turned out to be less than expected.

There is still much ideology connected with the choice of market strategies and very little research on their real effect. So the debate about market—as well as consumerist and managerial—techniques is far from over, and has, in reality, only just begun.

Conclusions

This chapter has highlighted a set of elements in the public sector that, from a historical point of view, place it in an administrative justice context and as a fundamental force of solidarity in the modern 'law society'. So it is clearly reasonable to speak about the 'public ethos' that expresses those special values that are associated with the public sector. However, the elements of administrative justice are far from unchangeable. It is not so much a question of brand new values that are needed but rather of established values that are acquiring new, and expanded, meanings.

The historical legacy stems from the law state of the nineteenth century and the social state of the twentieth century. However, from the end of last century, two tendencies have emerged that, each in their own ways, have broken with the historical legacy. As a result, four different stages in the legal development of the public sector can be identified: in addition to the law state and the social state, a milieu state and a market state were identified. It is clear that the values of the law state and those of the social state will both be essential in some parts of the public sector, probably within the areas of public administration and public service activity. However it is characteristic that the values of the social state also convey a number of (new) demands for classical public administration.

The market state and the milieu state both aim for the same goal: personal self-development. Whereas the market state emphasises individualistic values, the milieu state maintains a number of collectivistic values, which serve as guides for the governance of society. In practice, the difference appears in the emphasis placed by the former on current welfare services for meeting individual wants and needs and, by the latter, on more long-term needs for securing the individual's quality of life. In terms of administrative justice, this difference can be expressed as a difference between dissimilarity (in relation to public services) and equality (in relation to public regulation). These possibilities for developments in the public sector are not fundamentally changed by managerial strategies, since this should be seen as a variant of the market strategy that emphasises the internal aspects of public activities. It is a fact, however, that the managerial strategy has been dominant in administrative reform in the Scandinavian countries for a number of years.

However it is also a fact that experience with all sorts of market regulation, internal and external, has turned out to be less convincing than expected. A trend towards overregulation and a lack of flexibility are problematic aspects of these strategies. Moreover, the political and administrative authorities have recently been challenged by climate change problems and financial crises, which seem to call for collectivistic efforts that could bring the milieu state back onto the political agenda again. If so, this would clearly have implications for administrative justice as a fundamental part of the public ethos. However it is difficult to predict the future development of the public administration. There is no way of forecasting the future, since it is basically a question of political choice. The only thing one can be sure of is that there are certain alternatives in the present situation and that some of these alternatives could be said to offer a better choice than others. The milieu state is one such alternative.

References

Adler, Michael (2003) 'A Socio-Legal Approach to Administrative Justice' 25 *Law and Policy* 323–52.

—— (2006) 'Fairness in Context' 33 *Journal of Law and Society* 615–38.

Axberger, Hans-Gunnar (1988) *Eko-brott, Eko-lagar och Eko-domstolar* [*Ecology Crime, Law and Courts*] (Stockholm, Allmänna förlag).

Beck, Ulrich (1986) *Risikogesellschaft* [*The Risk Society*] (Berlin, Duncker and Humblot).

Christensen, Bent (1972) 'Effektivitets- og retssikkerhedshensyn i forvaltningen' ['Considerations of Effeciency and Administrative Justice in Public Administration'] 26 *Nordiske Juristmøde* 333–55.

Dalberg-Larsen, Jørgen (1984) *Retsstaten, velfærdsstaten og hvad så? Sammenhænge mellem retsudvikling og samfundsudvikling* [*Law State, Welfare State and so what? Relationships between Development of Law and Society*] (København, Akademisk Forlag).

Graver, Hans Petter (2002) *Forvaltningsrett i markedsstaten Studier i europæisering af forvaltningsretten* [*Administrative Law in the Market State*] (Oslo, Fagbokforlaget).

Habermas, Jürgen (1981) *Theorie des Kommunikativen Handelns* [*Theory of Communicative Action*] (Frankfurt am Main, Suhrkamp).

Henrichsen, Carsten (1982) 'Retssikkerhed og effektivitet i den offentlige forvaltning' [*Administrative Justice and Effeciency in Public Administration*] *Orientering om fremtidsforskning* 6–23.

—— (1997) *Retssikkerhed og moderne forvaltning. En retspolitisk studie i samspillet mellem stat, forvaltning og borger*, Disputats [*Administrative Justice and Modern Public Administration. A Politico-Legal Study of the Relationship between State, Public Administration and Citizen*] LLD Thesis (København, Akademisk Forlag).

—— (2003) 'Offentlige værdier i retlig belysning. Fra retsstat og socialstat til markedsstat eller miljøstat' ['Public Values from a Legal Perspective. From Law State and Social State to Market State and Milieu State'] in TB Jørgensen (ed), *På sporet af en offentlig identitet—Værdier i stat, amt og kommuner* (Aarhus, Aarhus Universitetsforlag) 81–104.

Jørgensen, Torben Beck (ed) (2003) *På sporet af en offentlig identitet—Værdier i stat, amt og kommuner* [*On the Track of a Public Identity—Values in State, Regional and Municipal Government*] (Aarhus, Aarhus Universitetsforlag).

Leyland, P and Woods, T (1997) *Administrative Law Facing the Future: Old Constraints and New Horizons* (London, Blackstone Press).

Luhmann, Niklas (1981) *Politische Theorie im Wohlfartsstaat* [*Political Theory in the Welfare State*] (München, Olsog-Aktuell GmbH).

Lundquist, Lennart (1998) *Demokratins väktar. Ämbetsmännen och vårt offentliga etos* [*Guardian of Democracy. The Public Servants and our Public Ethos*] (Lund, Studentlitteratur).

Mashaw, Jerry (1983) *Bureaucratic Justice: Managing Social Security Disability Claims.* (New Haven, Yale University Press).

Mintsberg, Henry (1979) *The Structuring of Organisations* (Englewood Cliffs, NJ, Prentice Hall).

Nozick, Robert (1974) *Anarchy, State and Utopia* (New York, Basic Books).

Porsdam, Helle (2002) *Fra pax americana til lex americana: En diskussion af dansk retliggørelse som en påvirkning fra USA* [*From Pax Americana to Lex Americana: A Discussion of Danish Legalisation as an Influence from the United States*] (Århus: Magtudredningen).

Ross, Alf (1959) *On Law and Justice* (Berkeley and Los Angeles, CA, University of California Press).

Sand, Inger-Johanne (1996) *Styring av kompleksitet: rettslige former for statlig rammestyring og desentralisert statsforvaltning* [*Regulating Complexity: Legal Forms of centralised and decentralised State Government*] (Bergen-Sandviken, Fagbokforlaget).

Teubner, Gunther (1983) 'Substantive and Reflexive Elements in Modern Law' 17 *Law and Social Review* 239–86.

Part 5

Current Developments in Administrative Justice in the UK

15

Grievances, Remedies and the State—Revisited and Re-appraised

PATRICK BIRKINSHAW

Introduction

This chapter surveys the development of redress of grievances over a period of more than 30 years. In the 1970s, there was little work on the redress of grievance by lawyers that did not involve courts or ombudsmen. Today, internal methods for resolving complaints and grievances are *de rigueur*. The chapter examines developments in administrative justice in the courts, the new tribunal structure, ombudsmen, and includes an analysis of the EU dimension and alternative dispute resolution. The author uses his experience in Freedom of Information legislation and related work to examine some problems concerning redress of grievance in the provision of public services, or services for the public, by private contractors. The author notes that, in the 1970s, complaints were excluded on procedural grounds and concludes by arguing that other forms of exclusion and technological developments pose serious threats to human integrity today.

Background

In retrospect, the attraction of grievance redress to me as a young academic came from disquiet over an attitude expressed by Benjamin Disraeli: 'Never complain and never explain'. If you're on the receiving end, lump it. If you are giving it out, say nothing, or as little as possible, by way of justification.

Grievances, Remedies and the State[1] emerged from a series of concerns. First, there was unmet legal need. People with problems resolvable by legal processes, legal techniques and/or legal assistance were not getting the help they needed. Secondly, public lawyers concentrated on judicial remedies and, in public law,

[1] Birkinshaw (1985).

academics concentrated on judicial review. Looking back over 30 years, the position in judicial review then, both in terms of numbers of applications and the unsophisticated nature of judicial review, was in stark contrast with the position today. There was still the legacy of Lord Shaw's dictum in *Local Government Board v Arlidge*: 'If administration is to be beneficial it must be master of its own procedure'.[2] This was an academic preoccupation because judges had made numerous suggestions, judicial and extra-judicial, that non-judicial remedies would be appropriate in many cases where people had a grievance against public bodies. Matters were often best dealt with relatively informally and judicialisation of the administrative process would lead to a paradise for lawyers and a waste of resources. As expressed by Lord Hoffmann in *Runa Begum*:[3]

> On the other hand, efficient administration and the sovereignty of Parliament are very relevant. Parliament is entitled to take the view that it is not in the public interest that an excessive proportion of the funds available for a welfare scheme should be consumed in administration and legal disputes.

More to the point, many people with grievances were not going to the newly created ombudsmen—in those days the Parliamentary, Health Services and Local Government Ombudsmen. The representative 'filter' operated in the Parliamentary and Local Government schemes. They dealt with the tip of the iceberg and some subject areas were notably missing.

Thirdly, there was a concern with how authorities actually dealt with and responded to complaints or grievances where no formal or articulated channels were publicised. This concern emerged from work experience in free representation and grievance handling. How do bodies deal with complaints and grievances when the processes are unannounced and largely subterranean? This formed the basis of an article with Norman Douglas Lewis based on our work in local government[4]—Douglas was the inspiration for much of this subject area. In the absence of any data, we sent questionnaires to all local authorities in England and Wales seeking information on dispute handling. The responses varied—as one would expect—from authorities where processes were non-existent to those that gave detailed accounts of their complaints procedures. I vividly recall comments like 'I suppose the rate-payer should have a right to complain about spilled refuse from dustbins or non collection'—now, of course, a major cause for complaint as we move to introducing two-weekly collections in England. I carried out empirical research beyond local government to assess how departments, agencies and other public bodies managed the handling and resolution of complaints—internally, as well as a result of intervention, for example by an MP. Mrs Thatcher's Private Office assured me it was a subject the Prime Minister took most seriously.

[2] [1915] AC 120.

[3] [2003] UKHL 5 para 44.

[4] Lewis and Birkinshaw (1979). A valuable review of the literature was undertaken by Rawlings for the ESRC. See Rawlings (1986).

Although my primary concern was with the redress of grievances, I also focused on participation in decision making and policy making. Again and again, procedures that existed were not available for complaints of a policy nature or for those that questioned the 'merits' of policy. A theme I was interested in was participation in decision making to avoid disputes arising. Although the rule-making procedures in the USA might afford participation rights, they were not widely seen as an answer in an English, or a British, context. By the time the second edition of *Grievances, Remedies and the State* came out in 1994, 'reg neg',[5] as it was called in the USA, and the opportunities it provided for participation by affected interests in the regulatory process, was becoming more evident. By the mid 1990s, the area of regulation after privatisation in England was witnessing exercises in policy making that bore some resemblance to US practices, albeit without the Administrative Procedure Act framework. Our most developed system of participation was in the planning process. The 'Big Inquiries' of the 1970s–1990s brought home to government the increased delays that resulted from more effective participation and the fact that the agenda was being opened up to include questions that had previously been off-bounds. Government plans to remove public inquiries into major projects have been announced, restricting public inquiries to local, site-specific subjects.[6] The policy aspect of major infrastructure projects, including the need for such projects, will be assessed and determined centrally by an Infrastructure Planning Commission. The Commission will give permission for development in accordance with National Policy statements made by government. The statements will be considered by Parliament and will undergo consultation.[7] I develop this below. The absence of an opportunity to participate through adequate consultation in the policy of nuclear new-build was a major reason for the judicial declaration that the Blair government's decision on nuclear policy was unlawful.[8]

For tribunals, the evidence revealed poor standards and a number of serious problems concerning, for example, their independence and the lack of representation. The term 'tribunal' covered very different types of bodies, ranging from those with narrow adjudicatory functions to multi purpose agencies or policy applying and/or making bodies.

The picture was one of muddle if not chaos. Good practices were not publicised and were often unannounced accompaniments to statutory avenues for making representations or complaint. There was a tendency for the obstreperous and the pushy to engage with what practices there were.

When my work commenced, the model of the 'state' was one that had been set in the mould of the 1970s—hegemonic, corporatist and pre-privatised—although all that was soon subjected to dramatic change. The state never goes

[5] Regulatory negotiation. See also Pritzker and Dalton (eds) (1990).

[6] HM Government (2007).

[7] Planning Act 2008.

[8] See *Greenpeace* n 16 below.

away, it merely reforms. Any analysis today would have to address the privatised, globalised, Europeanised, devolved, performance-targeted, packaged, off-loaded and contractualised state. Today, nationalisation is back on the agenda. There was very little concern with Europe in the first edition of *Grievances, Remedies and the State*, although this had changed by the time the second edition came out in 1994. This was also before the period of New Public Management (NPM), joined-up government, e-government, and so on—all of which have had a significant influence on grievance redress procedures. The advent of the Internet, and of opportunities for citizen participation that were not foreseen at the time, have created other problems that will be examined briefly later in the chapter.

The state in the period 1976–83 was very much in the role of provider and protector with heavy corporatist overtones. The terms are those of Wolfgang Friedmann in *The State and the Rule of Law in a Mixed Economy* (1971). The state was also an umpire through numerous administrative channels, sometimes charted, more often not. In the period 1984–97, these roles remained dominant as the state moved into privatising and off-loading mode, becoming a regulator and an entrepreneur/contractor, and getting best value for money (VFM) for the taxpayer through competition and introducing private sector techniques. In the period 1997–2007, the contractual role became more important in the provision of services. As the Private Finance Initiative and Public Private Partnerships (PPSs) assumed greater prominence, the state became more of a facilitator and policy maker, while policies were implemented, and sometimes formulated, by private actors. The state was still an umpire, but the pressures of ECHR Art 6 forced the judicialisation of more and more roles that, in the mid 1980s, the executive assumed without challenge. But today, the big issue is whether the executive is finding ways of bypassing judicial controls and techniques. I address this point in my conclusion. More recently, in the period from 2007–09, financial collapse has led to nationalisation and to massive government intervention on both sides of the Atlantic.

Developments

Today, proportionate dispute resolution is the order of the day. After Leggatt's review of tribunals,[9] the Government published its proposals 'to improve the whole end to end dispute resolution process'.[10] The emphasis was on getting things right in the first place so as to avoid disputes and, where there were disputes, resolving them before resort to tribunals or ombudsmen. The subject of citizen-based, proactive complaints management has even been reported

[9] Leggatt Report (2001). See also Partington (2001).
[10] Department for Constitutional Affairs (2004).

on by the National Audit Office, which has produced figures on costs and numbers.[11]

The House of Commons Public Administration Committee has also published a report entitled *When Citizens Complain*, to which the Government has responded.[12] The Committee reported on some enduring themes that result in the articulate and persistent getting better treatment. Insisting on complaints in writing, and not by phone or e-mail, does not appear to be consistent with the Disability Discrimination Act. Better use should be made of *Directgov*[13] to coordinate best practice as government websites converge. Government should explore the scope for a nationwide, common access point for all non-emergency public services, a recommendation that the Government is exploring. The Committee was disturbed that a 'poor standard of complaint handling is raised by so many complaint reviewers', suggesting that there is 'a systemic problem with first-tier complaint handling by government organisations'. Complainants should be fully informed of the progress of their complaint; public bodies should learn more from complaints, monitor them carefully and use the information to improve the service they provide; and the Cabinet Office should have a central role in overseeing this monitoring. Use of independent intermediate complaints handlers as a second tier stage where there are large numbers of complaints should be considered. Public bodies should publish details of complaints received and those upheld by independent reviewers such as ombudsmen. The Committee recommended that there should be a 'champion' across government, preferably in the Cabinet Office, to publicise best practice. The Cross-Government Complaints Handlers Network was set up in 2006 and, the Committee suggested, this self-organised body could be developed into a more formal body.

Judicial Remedies

I remain a firm believer in effective internal procedures for complaint resolution, as I explain below. So I start at a strange place: judicial remedies and their growing sophistication. I have written about the European influence on our judicial remedies, particularly on judicial review. This includes not only matters of substance, such as civil rights, the ECHR and the Human Rights Act, but also constitutional matters such as Parliamentary sovereignty, exemplified by *Factortame*[14] and *Jackson v Attorney-General*[15]—the latter concerning the review of the Act abolishing hunting

[11] National Audit Office (2005). See also Law Commission (2008a).

[12] House of Commons Select Committee on Public Administration (2008a and 2008b), without acknowledging lifting the title from Lewis and Birkinshaw *When Citizens Complain: Reforming Justice and Administration* (1993). The National Audit Office (2008) has reported critically on complaints processes in the NHS and social care. See nn 100 and 101 and text below.

[13] The official website of the UK Government for its citizens, providing information and online services for the public all in one place. See now: www.data.gov.uk.

[14] [1991] 1 All ER 70 (HL).

[15] [2005] 4 All ER 1253 (HL).

with dogs enacted under the Parliament Acts. The maturity of judicial review also covers such matters as policy development, none of which is more sensitive than nuclear new-build. *R (Greenpeace) v Secretary of State for Trade*[16] is a remarkable decision in which the government's new-build programme was ruled unlawful because of breaches of our obligations under *Aarhus*[17] and the denial of legitimate expectations. The growing maturity of judicial review also involves questions of procedure (so often the hand-maiden to substance). The important decision in *Tweed v Parades Commission for NI*[18] has widened the possibilities for disclosure of documents under judicial review procedure where the context requires a more detailed scrutiny of the factual circumstances of a challenge. I say more about the influence of ECHR Article 6 later on. The 'never explain' syndrome has been whittled away but not completely dissipated for there is still no general statutory duty to give reasons for decisions in England and Wales. Among the newly named remedies we can now add the possibility of an interim declaration in England and the power of a court to substitute its decision for that of a tribunal or inferior court.[19]

The high profile given to human rights protection is a welcome development. I was sceptical about human rights' advocates in the 1970s and early 1980s, although I was impressed by Leslie Scarman's book[20]—the proponents were, I felt, often devotees of elitist politics, propelling civil and political rights but saying little about social and economic rights. The state was often seen as the problem and my belief was that the disengaged needed effective procedures and assistance on the ground. In my view, the effective protection of human rights and effective procedures are not incompatible. There is now a Commission for Equality and Human Rights. Northern Ireland had a commission on human rights before England and Wales, and Scotland established a Commission on Human Rights, which lacks the power to assist in proceedings but is empowered to promote human rights, identify best practice within public authorities, conduct inquiries, intervene in legal proceedings and, where appropriate, recommend changes.

The Human Rights Act makes the protection of human rights a responsibility of all three branches of government, and a Joint Committee on Human Rights has been established to ensure a more focused Parliamentary oversight of human rights protection. The role of the judiciary has been well described by others and I will say more about the judges when I look at European influences.[21] The ultimate judicial sanction is a declaration of incompatibility of legislation with a Convention right. By July 2006 there had been 20 such declarations, five of which

[16] [2007] EWHC 311 (Admin). See, however, *R (Edwards) v Environment Agency* [2008] UKHL 22.

[17] Convention on Access to Information, Public Participation in Decision-Making and Justice in Environmental Matters (1998).

[18] [2006] UKHL 53.

[19] Tribunals, Courts and Enforcement Act 2007 s 141. The power is subject to limitations.

[20] Scarman (1974).

[21] Judges themselves have been vigorous advocates of human rights protection especially Steyn, Sedley and Laws. Judicial decisions under the Human Rights Act have sometimes been disappointing but the impact of the Act has been a force for the good.

were overturned on appeal.[22] Special procedures exist to fast track the amendment of legislation by regulations. The Government's role when presenting a Bill is to declare compatibility—that a Bill is in conformity with the Convention, or if it is not, that it intends to proceed with the Bill in any event, and I know of only one occasion where incompatibility has been declared.[23] Obviously the Government has missed some. The Ministerial Legislation Committee of the Cabinet receives memoranda from departments on how draft bills impact on the Convention and whether such an impact is necessary, proportionate and non discriminatory. Where the Government is mistaken, they should heed the rulings and advice of the courts and Parliament respectively and the Prevention of Terrorism Bill (2004–05) showed that process in a favourable light when government plans to extend periods of executive detention were rejected. Devolution legislation has its built-in safeguards protecting Convention and Community rights.

Tribunals Service

The development of a system of administrative tribunals based on the proposals in the White Paper referred to above[24] and the creation of the Tribunals Service as an executive agency of the Ministry of Justice (a Ministry which Douglas Lewis and I recommended in *When Citizens Complain* (1993)) which has responsibility for 16 tribunals originally under the Department for Constitutional Affairs and to which several others have been added, and may be added in the future, has introduced a pervasive, but not universal, system of first- and second-tier administrative adjudication. Appeals go to the Court of Appeal. The *Tribunals, Courts and Enforcement Act 2007* provides the legal basis for these changes. The scheme aims to make tribunals manifestly independent from those upon whose decisions they are hearing appeals and to provide a properly national network of hearing centres providing greater accessibility and to provide better information advice and support. The 'flexible', two-tier structure under a Senior President and comprising Tribunal Judges and Tribunal Appellate Judges came into full effect in November 2008. A Rules Committee will be established. The White Paper said nothing about increased legal aid suggesting that increased accessibility and simplicity and efforts at compromise will reduce the need for lawyers. The reforms coincide with Government plans for legal services reform in the Legal Services Act 2007, and proposals for changes to legal aid that, many lawyers argued, would seriously undermine, if not bring an end to, legal aid practice.[25]

The advent of the Administrative Justice and Tribunals Council to replace the Council on Tribunals is potentially a very important development—it revived

[22] Department for Constitutional Affairs (2006). See also Joint Committee on Human Rights (2008) and Ministry of Justice (2009: 41).

[23] Communications Bill (2002–03).

[24] See n 10 above.

[25] See the evidence given to the Select Committee on Constitutional Affairs Committee (2007).

memories of the Administrative Conference of the United States which performed a sterling service in the USA advising government on administrative law but which fell victim to Newt Gingritch's contract with America, as well as the Australian Administrative Review Council.[26] The Council will keep the administrative justice system as a whole under review, asking how it can be made more accessible, fair and efficient and advising the Minister of Justice, Scottish Ministers, Welsh Ministers and the Senior President. It will seek to ensure that the relationship between courts, tribunals, ombudsmen and ADR reflects the needs of users.[27] Members will be appointed by the Minister of Justice, Scottish and Welsh Ministers—the chairman by the Minster for Justice.

Notable exclusions from the two tier tribunal structure and transfer of jurisdiction include the Special Immigration Appeals Commission (SIAC), the Investigatory Powers Tribunal, and the Competition Appeals Tribunal, the Employment Tribunal (ET)[28] as well as many local government tribunals. The Foreign Compensation Commission and Financial Services and Markets Tribunal may have powers transferred although originally they were not to be included. The present position of the Asylum and Immigration Tribunal (AIT) is similar to that of the Employment Tribunal but it has been the subject of consultation and is likely to be incorporated into the Tribunals Service in the near future. For a fuller account, see Thompson's chapter in this volume. SIAC deals with highly charged terrorist cases and may operate in secret by way of special counsel. The concern expressed by the House of Lords in *MB v Secretary of State for the Home Department*[29] highlights that tendency towards secret justice brought about by the war on terrorism and serious crime. In the 1970s, the context was the Diplock courts and the informal procedure for deportation on grounds of national security—famously absolved by Lord Denning.[30]

The Tribunals Service is an illustration of that movement towards greater independence and judicialisation of administrative appeals. To take one example, following litigation,[31] since 2 July 2001, Housing Benefit Review Boards have been replaced by tribunals set up under the Child Support, Pensions and Social Security Act 2000. Some areas are resistant. Education appeal panels no longer contain members of the authority but the panel members are appointed by the LEA and a powerful case has been made for their complete independence as tribunals.[32]

[26] Buck (2005).

[27] Explanatory Memorandum to the Bill, paras 29–31.

[28] Although the Employment Tribunal was not brought into the first-tier Tribunal, the administration of employment tribunals will be incorporated into the Tribunals Service and its judiciary will be subject to the Senior President of Tribunals.

[29] [2007] UKHL 46 and *Roberts v Parole Board* [2005] UKHL 45. See, however, *RB (Algeria) etc v Secretary of State for the Home Department* [2009] UKHL 10 and *Secretary of State v AF* [2009] UKHL 28.

[30] *R v Secretary of State for Defence ex parte Hosenball* [1977] 3 All ER 472 (CA). SIAC was created to meet the criticism of the European Court of Human Rights in *Chahal v UK* (1996) 23 EHRR 413.

[31] *Tsfayo v UK* [2007] HLR 19.

[32] Sturgeon (2006).

Ombudsmen

Ombudsmen are seen in some quarters as poor cousins to the courts—'a useful adjunct to any system of administrative law'—and they have been given some searching and hostile scrutiny by the courts, particularly by two leading public lawyers, Lord Woolf and Sedley LJ. Statutory ombudsmen are, naturally enough, subject to judicial review but that review has sometimes been invasive. In the *Croydon* case,[33] the courts showed how difficult life under judicial review could be when the Court of Appeal ruled that the ombudsman must continually have regard to the appropriateness of advising the complainant to seek a judicial remedy and, in determining whether or not to take up a complaint, likelihood of success for the complainant in litigation should not be a factor that enters into the reckoning. Public authorities do not have the procedural protection from ombudsmen in England that they had from the courts. *Balchin*[34] illustrated a court that was determined to get its target. It reminded me of Lord Diplock's assertion that there was no question that could not be turned into a question of jurisdictional fact where the courts wished to intervene. The question in *Balchin No 1* was failure by the Parliamentary Ombudsman (PO) to give any weight to the impact of new legislative powers on the behaviour of a local authority that refused to purchase blighted property, and whether or not the Secretary of State might have been influenced by those new powers to act more persuasively and successfully vis-a-vis the reluctant authority. After three successful judicial reviews quashing three PO reports and findings of inadequate reasons by the PO, and almost 20 years, the Balchins were recommended payments of £100,000 by both the department and council. It was an invasive review but the Balchins obtained their relief. An editorial in *The Ombudsmen*[35] noted that the Cabinet Office was consulting on the reform of public sector ombudsmen by means of a Regulatory Reform Order with the aim of providing a more streamlined service (see below).

Faced by judicial setbacks, Julian Farrand, the Pensions Ombudsman, issued a *cri de coeur*, arguing that the courts did not understand the role and techniques of the ombudsman, who was doing justice on the substance and not according to strict rules. Legal validity was for the courts: legitimating power's empire by the provision of independent recommendations on maladministration was a part of the ombudsman function. For administrators, their task was delivery of an efficient service in an equitable manner. Over time the boundaries of legality and maladministration have shifted and overlapped so I am not entirely convinced by

[33] [1989] 1 All ER 1033. The then local commissioner felt nonetheless vindicated by the ruling insofar as: his investigation was not ruled unlawful, only his conclusion; he had properly entered into an investigation of a decision which the authority claimed was not 'administrative' but 'judicial'; and the court ruled that, had the ombudsman exercised discretion to investigate, the court would not be minded to review him on that account alone.

[34] *No 1* [1997] JPL 917; *No 2* (2000) 2 LGLR 87; *No 3* [2002] EWHC 1876 (Admin).

[35] Issue 27, November 2005.

confident statements of their distinctiveness.[36] There may be good reasons to opt for one process rather than the other but there should be flexibility in allowing movement between courts and ombudsmen.[37]

Lord Woolf was in a more positive frame of mind in *Anufrijeva*.[38] He favoured a much closer relationship between the courts and ombudsmen and suggested that courts in human rights cases should take a steer from ombudsmen decisions on compensation for maladministration. There are reminders to the ombudsmen that there is a judge over their shoulder—the NHS case which found fault in the Health Ombudsman investigations but more importantly confirmed that the HO had no powers of investigation at large.[39] But the public sector ombudsmen were given a powerful vindication by the courts in the *Liverpool* case when the benefits of an ombudsman investigation were seen both in terms of access to information and the adoption of a more relaxed and more embracing test for bias in a planning decision than the courts would have adopted.[40] Despite an overlap in jurisdiction the Court of Appeal emphasised the investigatory and fact-finding tools of the ombudsmen that they do not possess—even post-*Tweed*. In local government, their findings of fact are binding on the authorities investigated subject to review.[41] The Court of Appeal has found that the Secretary of State acted irrationally in rejecting a finding of maladministration by the PO.[42] A finding of maladministration by the PO may not in itself be binding, but a Minister must have cogent reasons for rejecting it (para 72). The Law Commission has published a detailed report on *Administrative Redress: Public Bodies and the Citizen*,[43] Part 5 of which is a very helpful account of the relationship between courts and the ombudsmen.

The European Union Ombudsman published a speech on the relationship between legality and good administration in 2007.[44] European ombudsmen often have a brief to take on board human rights and, in Eastern Europe, ombudsmen are often major champions of human rights. The Irish, Scottish and Welsh ombudsmen are increasingly thinking of the human rights' aspects in their work. The PO has produced *Principles of Good Administration* (March 2007) number one of which,

[36] See Carnworth LJ in *Secretary of State for the Home Department v R (S)* [2007] EWCA Civ 546. There are situations where the courts have refused a remedy and the ombudsman has provided one, or vice versa: *Reeman v Department for Transport* [1997] 2 Lloyd's Rep 648 and Case No C557/98 HC 20 (1999–2000).

[37] Law Commission (2008b: Pt 5).

[38] [2004] 1 All ER 833.

[39] *Cavanagh et al v HSC* [2005] EWCA Civ 1578.

[40] In *R v Local Commissioner for Administration, ex parte Liverpool City Council* [1999] 3 All ER 85 the High Court interpreted the powers of the local ombudsman benevolently. The defendants claimed there was a remedy by judicial review but that process would not have uncovered the information that the complainants to the Commissioner required to sustain a successful challenge. The Commissioner's decision to proceed and also her decision to apply a more relaxed test of 'bias' in a planning decision were lawful, a decision upheld by the Court of Appeal: [2001] 1 All ER 462.

[41] *R v Local Commissioner for Administration, ex p Eastleigh BC* [1988] 1 QB 855.

[42] *R (Bradley) v Secretary of State for Work and Pensions* [2008] EWCA Civ 36. See Kirkham et al (2008). See also, *R (EMAG) HM Treasury* [2009] EWHC 2495 (Admin).

[43] Law Commission (2008b).

[44] European Union Ombudsman (2007).

'Getting it Right', includes 'Acting in accordance with the law and with due regard for the rights of those concerned'. Those rights would include human rights.

The arrival of the Administrative Justice and Tribunals Council, described above, with a brief to scrutinise administrative justice in the round, will hopefully produce a more co-operative relationship. The real danger in recent years has come from central government refusal to accept the ombudsman's findings and recommendations in the Department for Work and Pensions[45] and the 'Debt of Honour' cases,[46] following the Government's refusal to accept the ombudsman's recommendations under the Code of Practice on Open Government. The Government's refusal to accept the decision of the PO has weakened a system that was supposed to operate on compromise and acceptance. If it does not work that way, what is the point of it? Censure and findings of illegality have come from the courts in three cases where the PO has been rebuffed by government.[47]

A further point relates to the absence in England of a joined up ombudsmen system such as those that exist in Scotland and Wales and to some extent Northern Ireland. A Select Committee has been examining this question for over eight years[48] but without movement until a regulatory reform order in 2007 (SI 2007/1889) facilitated collaboration in investigations by the Parliamentary, Health Services and Local Government Ombudsmen and the sharing of information. The reform will enable the Ombudsmen to appoint and pay a mediator or other appropriate person to assist them in relation to any complaint they are investigating and obviate the necessity of requiring previous notification to a local authority of a complaint where no purpose would be served.

The same Select Committee report also recommended an end to the MP filter reference for the PO—this has not occurred. Nor in public sector ombudsmen in the UK is there an own initiative power of investigation, which is a feature of overseas models.

Europe

Given my low profile on EC law in the first edition (changed by the second edition) it is ironic that much of my work over the last 15 years has concentrated on

[45] House of Commons Select Committee on Public Administration (2006b). The Select Committee points out that the PO's intervention has resulted in considerable improvement to the Financial Assistance Scheme under the Pensions Bill, but not so as to meet her recommendations. See House of Commons Select Committee on Public Administration (2007).

[46] House of Commons Select Committee on Public Administration (2006a): 'The Debt of Honour' investigation into *ex gratia* compensation schemes for those interned by the Japanese in World War II. See Kirkham (2006: 792). The PO found maladministration after an unsuccessful judicial review application but the PO had the benefit of additional documentation. The Court of Appeal found no fault on the Ministry's part in the non-disclosure. Delay has been criticised in the *Equitable Life* affair. See House of Commons Select Committee on Public Administration (2008) and HM Government (2009).

[47] *R (Elias) v Secretary of State for Defence* [2006] EWCA Civ 1293; *R (Bradley) v Secretary of State for Work and Pensions* [2008] EWCA Civ 36 (above) and *R (EMAG)* note 42 above.

[48] House of Commons Select Committee on Public Administration (2003).

European Public Law. I am not alone in noting how British public lawyers looked to the USA in particular for influence in the 1970s and 1980s. Since the 1990s, Europe has offered greater potential despite our very different traditions. Indeed, recent developments have shown the American judiciary to appear positively anaemic even under a written constitution compared with their British counterparts. In recent case law concerning the President's war on terror, the Supreme Court and the Federal Court of Appeal have spent a good deal of time hearing arguments about the scope of English *habeas corpus*.[49] How refreshing to see cases like *A v Secretary of State* robustly rejecting and condemning executive detention and the admissibility of evidence extracted by torture.[50] My preoccupation has been with the European influence on English public law. But influence has operated in both directions—we have given as well as received. The Citizen's Charter has been influential in continental countries and, as I show below, has fostered some non-judicial internal complaints procedures. The European Union Ombudsman (EUO) has added his voice and actions to the protection of citizens' rights. Indeed, Jacob Soderman, the previous EUO, was dismissive of the Parliamentary Ombudsman's approach and powers. The EUO has championed access to information (and human rights, and one should note that the UK ombudsmen are not required to take account of ECHR jurisprudence and decisions as courts and tribunals are) and has encouraged a union of ombudsman services throughout the European Union—the European Network of Ombudsmen. This comprises almost 90 offices in 30 countries with representatives from national and regional levels both within and outside the EU. Not all continental countries have adopted the ombudsman—Germany is a leading example of a country that has not dome so, although Parliamentary Petitioner Committees provide an ombudsman-like role. The EUO claims that there is an effective mechanism for co-operation on case handling.[51] National and regional ombudsmen may ask for written advice on EU law relevant to a complaint. Best practice is shared via seminars, meetings, newsletters, an electronic discussion forum and a daily electronic news service. In 2005, 945 complainants were advised to turn to their national ombudsman and 91 complaints were transferred directly to the competent ombudsman. The topic of a 2005 seminar—'The role of ombudsmen … in the application of EU law'—must have been an ill-chosen subject for ombudsmen from the UK because of their limited powers to deal with complaints for which there is a legal remedy. The themes dealt with in the newsletter have included the Fundamental Rights Agency of the EU, access to documents and data protection, discrimination and obstacles to free movement, prison-related problems, healthcare and difficulties for immigrants.

[49] *Hamdi v Rumsfeld* 542 US 507 (2004); *Rasul et al v Bush* 542 US 466 (2004). *Hamdan v Rumsfeld* 126 S Ct 2749 (2006) and *Boumediene et al v Bush et al* No 06-1195 12 June (2008) have improved the reputation of the Supreme Court.

[50] [2004] UKHL 56 and [2005] UKHL 71.

[51] European Union Ombudsman (2005: 31).

One of the most significant initiatives from the EUO was the publication of a Code on Good Administration. The Code sets out in detail what the fundamental 'right to good administration' in the Charter of Fundamental Rights of the European Union entails.[52] The Charter is not present directly in the EU Reform Treaty (Lisbon) but it is referred to as legally binding, and therefore enforceable by the European courts. A legally binding Protocol sets out the UK qualifications.[53]

I was asked by the EU Ombudsman to produce a paper on the benefits of internal complaints mechanisms within a European framework. This was part of an initial research effort that led to the Code, although the final product bore very little resemblance to my contribution. Much of my paper was influenced by British and Irish approaches and, in the British case, by the Citizen's Charter and its successors. But the Irish have also developed sensitivity towards internal procedures. There is no doubt that the common law systems have caused some difficulty for our continental colleagues—the emphasis upon informality, approachability, the confusion of review, appeal and second decision were all invariably alien to their legal and bureaucratic cultures. The Code achieved a compromise which did not jar with civil law thinking so that it provides in Article 16(2) a right for a hearing for every member of the public before a decision affecting his rights or interests is taken and in Article 16(1) officials must respect 'rights of defence'.

Despite the resistance to informality there has nevertheless been a significant drift towards non-adjudicatory procedures—even in French, German and Italian cultures—and to which they have had to adapt. A greater emphasis on regulatory commissions in France, for instance, has seen some of them, for example the *Commission Nationale Informatique et Libertés* and the *Commission de Régulation de l'Energie*, develop grievance remedial roles. Periodically, there are calls for the development of '*règlements non juridictionnels des litiges administratifs*', but the outcome so far has been rather disappointing. Although ADR is not in a period of strong development in French administrative law, a reform that would enlarge the possibility of using arbitration in administrative matters has been recently proposed by the *Conseil d'Etat*, and will probably emerge in the near future.[54] Since 1986, mediation accompanying litigation in the administrative courts in France has been possible but is quite rare.

My book *European Public Law*, published in 2003, stated that, in many European countries, there were internal procedures that were sometimes mandated as a matter of law under administrative procedure acts. These tend to be formal and bureaucratic. In Sweden, challenge must take place quickly so as not to interfere with the rights of others and it is built into German and Dutch administrative law.[55] More recently, Boyron has argued that, in France, Germany and the UK

[52] See Art 41 of the EU Charter.

[53] The Charter has been referred to for the first time by the ECJ: *Parliament v Council* [2007] ECR I-5769, para 38.

[54] I am grateful to Professor Jean Bernard Auby for this information.

[55] Birkinshaw (2003: 504–09).

(she refers to England), the movement to new forms of governance, new public sector management techniques, regulation and off-loading have brought about new convergences in movements towards ADR: '[I]t is possible to detect a feeling of unease as regards the evolution of public administration and the law relating to it.'[56] EU policies that are implemented within national and regional administrations and agencies make it difficult to trace lines of accountability in multi-tiered arrangements—consider the EUO comments above, and the differences between the FOI and Data Protection regimes. Furthermore, cross fertilisation of influences means that administrative law has to show flexibility in adapting to new influences as the division between the public and the private becomes ever more blurred. Boyron speaks of a crisis in administrative law and among administrative lawyers. In this crisis, new forms of dispute resolution are resorted to: first because others have done so; secondly, because they avoid lengthy and expensive judicial processes and are part of cost cutting. One thinks here of legal aid reforms in England and Wales, which have as their objective the reduction of the legal aid bill—who needs lawyers in the new processes of mediation? Mediation is common in public law claims in England, it may be used in France and there are signs of it emerging in Germany, albeit as an adjunct to litigation. Germany has not developed the ombudsman technique to the same extent that the UK and France have. Boyron addresses the European Commission draft directive[57] on mediation in civil and commercial disputes—again as adjuncts to litigation. My own experience on cross-border enforcement of traffic penalties supports her conclusion: one must be cautious in pointing to similarities in comparative development.

Joined-up ombudsmen have now been joined by joined-up competition authorities in Europe and a competition law, very much based on EU models, in the form of the UK Competition Act 1998. Much of the ammunition for investigations comes from complaints from undertakings and individuals, inevitably for self-interested reasons. There is joined up thinking in relation to competition where there is a European Network of Competition Authorities. In order to assist with applying the rules on co-operation contained in Regulation (EC) 1/2003, the Commission has published a *Notice on Co-operation with the Network of Competition Authorities*,[58] which explains the operation of the European Competition Network. This comprises all the national competition authorities and the Commission.

A network also exists for consumer redress, as seen in Regulation (EC) 2006/2004, which came into force at the end of December 2006.[59] Its purpose is to ensure that so-called intra-Community infringements of consumer law can be

[56] Boyron (2007: 263) and see also Boyron (2006: 320).

[57] COM (04) 718 final.

[58] Commission Decision 2004/C 101/03, (2004) OJ C 101/43.

[59] Regulation 2006/2004 of the European Parliament and of the Council of 27 October 2004 on cooperation between national authorities responsible for the enforcement of consumer protection laws (the Regulation on consumer protection cooperation) [2004] OJ L364/1. I am grateful to my colleague Christian Twigg-Flesner drawing my attention to this provision.

combated. These are infringements of legislation implementing various consumer protection directives that have a cross-border element to them, usually because a trader based in one Member State harms consumers in another. The Regulation puts into place measures for mutual assistance and information sharing to create a pan-European enforcement network. Each Member State is required to designate competent authorities and a single liaison office that will be responsible for the application of the regulation.[60] Such authorities must be given the necessary investigation and enforcement powers, and a non-exhaustive list of these is given in Article 4(6) of the Regulation. They also need to be adequately resourced.[61]

One area that features poorly concerns air carriers and consumer redress and I lean here on work by my colleagues.[62] According to Jacques Barrot, European Commission Vice President for Transport, Regulation (EC) 261/2004 provided 'proper protection of consumers' rights' and was given aggressive publicity by the Commission. The regulation, which replaced an earlier regulation and codes of practice, sought to protect consumers' rights where they were denied boarding by scheduled and low-fare airlines, and by charter flights where the flights were cancelled or delayed. It was opposed by the industry, which challenged its legality before the ECJ.[63] There is certainly a problem—in 2002 over 250,000 passengers in the EU were denied boarding rights, but, despite all the rhetoric from the Commission, the regulation is not clearly drafted and allows 'let outs' for the airlines in vague terms, for example, where cancellation is due to 'extraordinary circumstances'. A frequent suspicion is over booking but the airline claims there was a problem with a larger plane and the replacement was too small for the number of passengers. Although regulations are directly applicable and thereby usually directly effective, a body had to be designated by the Member State to ensure the regulation was enforced. In the UK, the Air Transport Users Council, to which passengers may complain, is a powerless body: understaffed and under resourced. In my own experience, carriers treat the Council with contempt. It reminded me of one of the classic reasons for establishing a quango in a problematic area: set up a cipher devoid of power to give the appearance of doing something. The Civil Aviation Authority is the enforcer of the regulation but the relationship between the two public bodies is unclear. There is a longer story here that colleagues of mine have taken up elsewhere. They contrast the European emphasis on protecting rights (with toothless procedures) with the US approach, which is based on giving consumers information about service standards and what is offered and letting them make a choice.[64] At the end of the day, in the UK one has to sue and go to court.

In terms of regulatory activity what a spider's web we have weaved in relation to our domestic avenues for appeals from, or reviews of, the decisions of regulators

[60] Art 4(1).
[61] Art 4(7).
[62] Varney and Varney (2008).
[63] Case C-344/04 *R (IATA and ELFAA) v Department of Transport*.
[64] See n 62 above. For a consumer-friendly interpretation of the EC regulation, see Case C-549/07 *F Wallentin-Hermann v Alitalia LAI SpA* (ECJ 22 December 2008).

in the utilities. The position of grievance redress in the nationalised utilities and services of general interest was pitiful. The Competition and Services (Utilities) Act 1992 began the process of introducing Citizens Charter-type redress mechanisms into the utility arena. Although it was assumed that competition would enhance service provision and thereby improve standards of service and reduce gripes, the complaints industry has grown and grown. Furthermore, the legislation covering utilities and communications (now the Utilities Act 2000, Postal Services Act 2000, Water Act 2003, Communications Act 2003) has fashioned a three-tier structure for redress of grievances, but the relationship between the various avenues is not clear and the Enterprise Act 2002 gives regulators concurrent powers with the Office of Fair Trading (OFT) to investigate 'super complaints'.[65] How many foresaw that social objectives would assume greater prominence in regulation, guidance and then legislation under a continental influence of *service public*?[66] The promotion of services of general economic interest in the EU Treaty at Amsterdam[67] suggested core European values. Their elevation to the Charter of Fundamental Rights under Part II of the aborted EU Constitutional Treaty,[68] together with a right to health care, afforded them full legal status as part of the Treaty. They were initially bitterly opposed by Blair's government and then watered down at British insistence.[69] A protocol qualifies the UK position.

Finally on the European scale, on 15 February 2007, the EU Council adopted Regulation (EC) 168/2007 establishing a European Union Agency for Fundamental Rights (FRA). Like most agencies in the EU, it does not possess executive powers. The Fundamental Rights Agency replaces and builds on the work of the European Monitoring Centre on Racism and Xenophobia (EUMC). Going beyond the work of the Monitoring Centre, FRA will have three key functions: collecting information and data, providing advice to the European Union and its Member States, and promoting dialogue with civil society to raise public awareness of fundamental rights. The FRA is an advisory and information gathering/disseminating body. It will neither examine individual complaints, possess regulatory decision-making powers, monitor the situation of Fundamental Rights in the Member States for the purposes of Article 7 of the Treaty of the EU nor deal with the legality of legislative acts within the meaning of Article 230 of the Treaty (which refers to the

[65] Ss 204–05, Sch 9 Pt 2 and SI 2003/1368. See Consumers, Estate Agents and Redress Act 2007 Pt 2 on complaints handling and redress schemes against regulated providers in energy, water and postal markets.

[66] Prosser (2005).

[67] TEU Art 16 EC. Under the Lisbon Treaty on the Functioning of the EU, Treaty Art 14, the European Parliament and Council are to make regulations setting out the principles and conditions of such services and a Protocol exists. The Charter of Fundamental Rights was to have the same legal effect as the Lisbon Treaties: Art 6 EU. The Treaty was rejected by Ireland in June 2008 but has now been ratified by all member states.

[68] The wording in Article 96 of EUCT Pt II states that the Union 'recognises and respects access to services of general economic interest' and the British commentary says it 'does not create any new right' (Foreign and Commonwealth Office 2005: 71).

[69] Goldsmith (2004).

Court of Justice's power to review the legality of Community acts), nor question whether a Member State has failed to fulfil an obligation under the Treaty within the meaning of Article 226.

ADR developments

ADR covers a broad spectrum of procedures. The Citizen's Charter and Better Governance programmes all promoted non-judicial grievance redress to the fore of activity and guidance was issued by the Cabinet Office on complaints procedures.[70] Internal grievance procedures are now a universal requirement and a pervasive practice in the public sector. ADR procedures using mediation and conciliation were a focal point of the Woolf reforms in civil justice procedure[71] and found their way into the aborted EU Constitution.[72] Woolf sought to encourage their use in public law litigation[73] but with only limited success.[74] Arbitration is of long standing but other processes did not exist, or if they did, did so only in a subterranean world. Every senior civil servant has stories of those seeking an amendment of a decision ending up in the Minister's office, being patted on the back and emerging successfully. Human—but fair, one asks? Now complaints, conciliation and mediation procedures are universally practised and, in some cases, are even mandated by law. The Department for Constitutional Affairs (now the Ministry of Justice) has published an ADR pledge[75] under which all departments and agencies have made the following commitments:

- ADR will be considered and used in *all* suitable cases wherever the other party accepts it.
- Government Departments will provide appropriate clauses in their standard procurement contracts on the use of ADR techniques to settle their disputes, the precise method of settlement being tailored to the details of individual cases.
- Central Government will produce procurement guidance on the different options available for ADR in Government disputes and how they might be best deployed in different circumstances. This will spread best practice and ensure consistency across Government.
- Government Departments will improve flexibility in reaching agreement on financial compensation, including using an independent assessment of a possible settlement figure.
- Government Departments will put in place performance measures to monitor the effectiveness of this undertaking.

[70] Cabinet Office (1998).
[71] CPR 1.4(2)(e).
[72] Art III-269(g).
[73] *R (Cowl) v Plymouth* [2002] 1 WLR 202 (CA); *Anufrijeva*1[2003] EWCA Civ 1406.
[74] *Halsey v Milton Keynes General NHS Trust* [2004] EWCA Civ 576; *Burchell v Bullard* [2005] EWCA Civ 358.
[75] This can be accessed at www.dca.gov.uk/civil/adr/adrrep_0102.htm#part2.

Civil servants are being trained as mediators but we do not know a great deal about these practices. Furthermore, such proceedings are often accompanied by confidentiality for the parties involved—how do we know that they are working in the general interest as opposed to individual interests of the parties involved?

Amongst other things, publication schemes under the UK Freedom of Information legislation should identify procedures, doing a similar job to the US FOIA, under which all formal and informal procedures in US agencies have to be publicised. It was, and in some cases is, not clear whether internal procedures deal with complaints or grievances, whether they are a precursor to external challenge, and whether the primary reason for having them is for internal management or customer service. The Cabinet Office realised in the 1990s, when it described complaints as jewels from which to learn and improve service, that the two objectives of good management and customer service may be conflated. Effective and accessible internal procedures have many benefits, but they have to exist alongside other independent procedures where fairness requires adjudicatory techniques. Careful thought must then be given to their relationship.

Although the impact of the HRA may have led to an increasing judicialisation of our public service, the courts have shown that they will not require public service providers or state agents to set up procedures satisfying the strict tests of ECHR Article 6 for internal review of rights protected by Article 6 where somewhere in the process there is an opportunity for appropriate judicial challenge of primary facts and the decision is made by parties who are independent—this is not strictly interpreted—of the initial authority. Where a decision complained against ultimately rests on broad discretionary determinations of policy or expediency, a full review on the merits is neither necessary nor appropriate. Where internal review procedures do exist and where they establish questions of primary fact and determine civil rights protected by Art 6, there would have to be an appeal capable of reviewing facts to an independent body acting judicially. The principles have been developed in the following case law.

In *Tsfayo*[76] (App No 60860/00) the case involved a Housing Benefit and Council Tax Benefit Review Board (HBRB) comprising five councillors from the council. Housing Benefit is a form of means-tested assistance for tenants in rented accommodation. It was an Article 6-protected human right. Not only was the HBRB not independent from the executive, it was directly connected to one of the parties to the dispute. The High Court held that no procedural safeguards would be adequate to 'overcome this fundamental lack of objective impartiality' (para 46). Since the Court

> did not have jurisdiction to rehear the evidence or substitute its own views as to the applicant's credibility, there was never any possibility that, in this case, the central issue would be determined by a tribunal that was independent of one of the parties to the dispute. (ibid)

[76] See n 31 above.

The procedure therefore constituted a breach of Article 6. *Tsfayo* was decided in England before the Human Rights Act came into effect. The limited nature of judicial review over the procedures in question at the relevant date had already been established.[77] Review cannot upset findings on the weight of evidence (though *Tweed* should be recalled). The lack of independence and its effect may not be sufficiently scrutinised by the court. Would bias in the composition of a board itself not be subject to review?

There have been several high profile cases in which the House of Lords has sought to limit the encroachment of Article 6 in public administration. In *Alconbury*,[78] a case dealing with the application of planning policy by the Secretary of State, and in *Runa Begum (FC) v London Borough of Tower Hamlets*,[79] the extent and limits of judicial review of administrative decisions were set out.

The House of Lords in *Runa Begum*, a case concerning a homeless application, stressed that although the housing officer in a homeless case had been called upon to resolve some disputed factual issues, these findings of fact were, per Lord Bingham, 'only staging posts on the way to the much broader judgments' concerning local conditions and the availability of alternative accommodation, which the housing officer had the specialist knowledge and experience to make. Although the housing officer could not be regarded as independent, since she was employed by the local authority that had made the offer of accommodation which *Runa Begum* had rejected, statutory regulations provided substantial safeguards to ensure that the review would be independently and fairly conducted, free from improper external influences. Any significant departure from the procedural rules would have afforded a ground of appeal.

The Court of Human Rights held that the decision-making process in *Tsfayo* was significantly different. In contrast to *Alconbury* and *Rena Began*, in *Tsfayo*, the HBRB was deciding a simple question of fact: was there 'good cause' for the applicant's delay in making a claim. The HBRB found her explanation to be 'unconvincing' and rejected her claim for back-payment of benefit. No specialist expertise was required to determine this issue. The factual findings in *Tsfayo* cannot 'be said to be merely incidental to the reaching of broader judgments of policy or expediency which it was for the democratically accountable authority to take' (para 45) as in *Alconbury*.

The British and Irish Ombudsmen Association (BIOA) has produced a *Guide to Principles of Good Complaint Handling*.[80] The Commission for Local Administration (CLA) and numerous other ombudsmen have produced guidance documents for their subject areas. The Parliamentary and Health Service Ombudsman has produced guidance on several subjects and has produced *Principles of Good Complaint*

[77] *R (Bewry) v Norwich City Council* [2001] EWHC Admin 657 (Moses J).

[78] *R v Secretary of State for the Environment, ex p Holding and Barnes, Alconbury Developments Ltd and Legal and General Assurance Society Ltd* [2001] UKHL 23.

[79] [2003] UKHL 5, [7]–[8]. On rights of hearings before Parole Boards, see *Smith v Parole Board* [2005] UKHL 1.

[80] British and Irish Ombudsmen Association (2007).

Handling[81] with six core features. BIOA is a representative body of ombudsmen, including statutory and voluntary ombudsmen, and public and private ombudsmen. It refers to ombudsmen as commissioners—bucking the trend—and complaints reviewers as office holders. Their organisations are referred to as schemes. The *Guide* is a distillation of best practice and its agreed principles in complaint handling are: clarity of purpose of the scheme's role, intent and scope, flexibility and responsiveness to individual needs, openness and transparency to demystify 'our service', proportionality, efficiency—meeting challenging standards of good service, quality outcomes—and resolution leading to positive change. As well as language, literacy and disability factors, complaints reviewers must be alive to socio-economic differences. Although ombudsmen schemes are a second stage after the internal complaints procedures, the CLA guidance is for primary complaints handlers. Ombudsmen usually have to ensure that the complainant has directed his or her complaint to the body complained against and that resolution has been attempted locally. The body complained against is called an 'organisation' and due emphasis is placed on that body learning from complaints as well as on close liaison between such bodies and 'schemes' and commissioners. The PO has emphasised the need for close co-operation with public services, for example, health bodies, Customs and Excise, the Home Office and the Ministry of Justice, to produce more effective public services as well as more efficient procedures for handling complaints. In other words, the PO wishes to make the ombudsman's long experience of complaint resolution available to public service organisations in order to enhance service delivery and thereby reduce the number of complaints.

Despite the enormous emphasis on the operation of internal complaints procedures, we still have a great deal to discover about them. However, we know a great deal more then we did. But is this concentration on complaints procedures encouraging captiousness and querulousness? Is it sidelining real complaints? For instance, the re-use of public sector information regulations are accompanied by the provision of detailed complaints procedures.[82] These procedures deal with complaints from those who wish to publish public sector information for commercial or other use but whose requests are not successful. But the real issues—pricing of documents and what can be re-used—are not on the agenda and cannot be complained against. Furthermore, many people criticise internal procedures for constituting an unnecessary delay. I now turn to the UK Freedom of Information Act complaints procedures, where an influential campaigning group has made this accusation.

Freedom of Information

Under the Freedom of Information Act (FOIA) 2000, the Information Commissioner (IC) has to be satisfied that the applicant for information has

[81] Parliamentary and Health Service Ombudsman (2009).
[82] SI 2005/1515.

asked for a review by the public authority that has received a request for information. Public authorities have to provide internal procedures for second review. Up to 115,000 bodies are covered as public authorities from mighty departments of state to small medical practices, and the requirement that a different person to the one who made the initial decision should conduct a review may cause real problems in small bodies. Notable exclusions from FOIA are the security and intelligence services and the Serious and Organised Crime Agency—and the Queen and Royal Family. The former have complaints schemes but not access rights set up under statute, namely the Regulation of Investigatory Powers Act 2000 and the Serious Organised Crime and Police Act 2005.

After a request for a second opinion is made, a complainant who is not subsequently given access to the information he or she has requested may then approach the Information Commissioner. From the Commissioner there is a right of appeal to the Information Tribunal that possesses very broad powers of appeal. Further appeal on a point of law may be made to the High Court. The FOIA for Scotland avoided the tribunal and followed the original model of judicial review put forward in the 1997 White Paper. The arguments of the Campaign for Freedom of Information against internal processes included the fact that it would cause unnecessary delay and that it would simply amount to a further barrier to effective redress. But there would be serious implications for the workload of the Information Commissioner if there were no internal review since it provides opportunities for quick correction, opportunities to change system failure by learning from experience by those delivering programmes and so on. The ultimate say of Government is maintained by a veto, which ensures that government has the last say by virtue of FOIA section 53. To date, the veto has been exercised on two occasions. There are several interesting de facto practices accompanying the legislation: the veto takes place after consultation with the whole Cabinet, sensitive information has to be examined in the Cabinet Office by the IC, and a Clearing House is established in the Cabinet Office for more difficult requests.

On openness, I gained invaluable experience and insight while working for NIREX (N) Ltd and subsequently the body that absorbed N, the Nuclear Decommissioning Authority, between 2001 and 2008. N advised the nuclear industry on the safety of nuclear waste disposal. N was advised to become more transparent in its operations after it lost a planning appeal in the late 1990s to build a deep-based repository for intermediate level nuclear waste. N's record, along with that of the nuclear industry generally, had been poor in terms of secrecy and unresponsiveness. To attempt to win over public support and to build up confidence, N developed a programme of transparency, which included a voluntary code on access to information held by N, the appointment of a transparency panel that advised on the content of the code, its operation and its review and which also acted as an ombudsman for those dissatisfied with refusals by N to disclose information under the terms of the code. This was several years before the FOIA and the Environment Information Regulations (EIR) 2004 came into effect. In addition to the usual exemptions in FOI regimes, the code contained an additional exemption: N could not disclose where this would contravene government policy on non-disclosure. N received many requests for information with very few refusals: but one request was persistently refused. This concerned the 'historical' site list for possible suitable deep deposit repositories. Although it was generally assumed that there were 12 sites, there were in fact several hundred. The reason for not disclosing the list was because the government had decided that it should not be released and disclosure was exempt under the terms of the N code on access: disclosure would contravene government policy. We consistently recommended disclosure. Our decision was recommendatory only. Matters changed when FOIA and the EIR became operational and the information was disclosed.

By this time, Nirex had come under government ownership and was taken away from the ownership of the nuclear industry. The role of the Transparency Panel had also been expanded and its membership increased by two to provide advice on transparency in all N's operations: safety approval, research, ownership, internet protocols, personnel and management relations, and customer relations, as well as the ombudsman role (for three members). N came top from a survey of public and private bodies engaged in energy or utilities in terms of their transparency conducted by Global Partners. In 2007, the government announced that Nirex was to be dissolved and taken over by the Nuclear Decommissioning Authority (NDA). The point of this is that NDA had never been subjected to anything like N's transparency policy—nor had any public authority. It will be contracting an estimated value of £65 billion (2007 levels) with private companies to manage nuclear de-commissioning—mainly giant American corporations who are likely to expect maximum commercial confidentiality in their relationships with NDA and in its operations. And then the government announced a change in policy on nuclear new-build that led to the *Greenpeace* litigation outlined above. Nirex has gone but its successor operates as a division of NDA. The functions of the Independent Transparency Panel have gone 'in-house'.

Nirex was the most developed body within the public and private sector in terms of its approach to transparency, dealing with complaints about FOIA (the panel continued under FOIA and EIR in its recommendatory capacity and, as far as I know, was the only public body to have such an independent panel for FOIA requests) and opening up its operations to external scrutiny. Its publications scheme and its approach to transparency were applauded as models for benchmarking by the Information Commissioner. I hope the lessons are not lost.

The wider question of participation in major projects, including nuclear re-build, was addressed by the Government in May 2007 in *Planning for a Sustainable Future,* published contemporaneously with *Meeting the Energy Challenge.*[83] This has attracted criticism of centralisation in the planning process and removal of

[83] HM Government (2007) and Department of Energy and Climate Change (2007) respectively.

tried and tested legal procedures at big public inquiries. The relevant provisions are now set out in the Planning Act 2008. The Government wishes to expedite the process and has brought forward an Infrastructure Planning Commission as an 'independent quasi judicial' body to determine major planning applications in accordance with policy determined nationally and, for example in energy, that means at Whitehall in respect of devolved administration. It recalls to some extent the Planning Inquiry Commission from the 1968 Town and Country Planning Act that was never used. Nine months is seen as an appropriate period for the Commission to examine and determine applications. The Secretary of State may determine some applications. It is intended that, in examining applications, greater use will be made of written representations and that there will be less reliance on oral representations. There will be restrictions on the use of cross-examination by interested parties at a hearing. Legal challenge to a decision will be made by judicial review within six weeks.

Contracting by Government

This topic was touched on in the previous section. It will become a matter of increasing importance in terms of grievance redress. The Department for Constitutional Affairs (now the Ministry of Justice) addressed the question of the scope of ADR in this area. Public authorities have been advised by lawyers acting for private contractors that they should not hand over information given by contractors that is protected by contractual terms, or by the law of confidentiality, even in furtherance of FOIA requests. This, it is claimed, would be a breach of contract. This seems to me to cross the threshold of legality. Firms should identify in schedules what information should not be published. The courts have observed that contractual clauses protecting confidentiality may be stronger than non-contractual confidentiality.[84] But the information must still be 'confidential' by law. There is a public interest override to contractual confidentiality—a point that was emphasised in the PPP litigation over the London underground.[85] The Office of Government Commerce lost an appeal before the Information Tribunal on disclosure of information concerning 'gateway reviews' on procurement contracts concerning ID schemes and has appealed to the High Court even though the reviews were written with FOIA in mind.[86]

All of these points refer to sensitivity about transparency—how much will be protected by commercial confidentiality? But wider problems attend the following: Where is the locus for a complaint by the affected citizen? How much will be unchallengeable and on what issues may the public complain? Compare the cases

[84] *Associated Newspapers Ltd v HRH Prince of Wales* [2006] EWCA Civ 1776.

[85] *LRT v Mayor of London* [2003] EMLR 4.

[86] FS50070196 and FS50111129. See EA/2006/0068 and EA/2006/0080 and *Office of Government Commerce v Information Commissioner* [2008] EWHC 737 (Admin). The High Court found fault with the manner in which the Information Tribunal reached its conclusion and ordered a re-hearing.

of *Kathro*[87] and *Smith v NE Derbyshire PCT*.[88] In the former, third parties—local residents—were held to have no interest in challenging a PPP arrangement between a local authority and a contractor concerning major redevelopment even though the wrong procedure was chosen for the procurement. It was *res inter alios acta* and the Contracts (Rights of Third Parties) Act 1999 did not offer assistance. In the latter third parties, again local residents should have been consulted about new arrangements on provision of medical care under specific duties on consultation in section 11 of the Health and Social Care Act 2001. Sometimes Parliament is alerted, sometimes not. We need a new law of public contract addressing the inadequacy of third party redress and the whole question of public involvement in the formation of 'public contracts'—I hasten to add that this is not a known legal concept.[89]

Reports emerge that prison discipline is to be taken over in some prisons by the private contractors running the prisons[90] and private escorts are to determine whether young prisoners may be safely confined within adult prisons.[91] These seem to me to be 'public functions' for the purposes of the HRA. What is the scope of the HRA in the private sphere? What is a 'public function' under the HRA has been argued before the House of Lords. The answer given was that a private care home was not performing public functions in taking in residents who were partly or wholly paid for by a local authority, even though such homes work closely with local authorities.[92] Privatising the state and constitutionalising the private contractors. In an era of public–private partnerships, we need to be far clearer about the details and lines of accountability of state surrogates, who can complain and how.

Conclusions

The period in which I began working on grievance redress focused upon unmet need, entitlement and fairness in treatment. Effective means of ventilating complaints and grievances were often lacking. There was procedural exclusion. Since then, as I have indicated, we have moved along considerably and constructively in the wide area of grievance redress.

87 *R (Kathro) v Rhondda Cynon Taff County BC* [2001] EWHC Admin 527.

88 *Smith v NE Derbyshire PCT* [2006] EWCA Civ 1291. See also *R (Menai Collect Ltd) v DCA* [2006] EWHC 727 (Admin); *R v Wear Valley DC* [1985] 2 All ER 699; *Bradley v Jockey Club* [2005] EWCA Civ 1056 and *Mullins v Jockey Club* [2006] EWHC 986 (QBD) and supervision of private arrangements.

89 Birkinshaw (2006).

90 *The Guardian* (London 17 April 2007).

91 *The Guardian* (London 30 April 2007).

92 *YL v Birmingham City Council and Others* [2007] UKHL 27. Health and Social Care Act 2008 s 145 reversed the decision in *YL*. Under the Act, regulation is to be carried out by the Care Quality Commission. See Joint Committee on Human Rights (2007).

Today, I believe there are different forms of exclusion, possibly in some cases procedural, but in many cases the result of governmental decision making: a good term might be 'executive and substantive exclusion'. We do not have the calamity of *Guantanamo* and the excesses of executive justice, not yet, but we have whole areas where decisions and their impact are secreted from public scrutiny and complaint—except, and this is not an answer—through the ballot box. This seems true in the following areas in the UK:

Surveillance[93]

Surveillance has been investigated by the Constitution Committee of the House of Lords and is a subject of widespread concern. We are among the most widely surveyed people in the world: one CCTV camera per every 14 individuals, the Identity Card fiasco, the database for the NHS, and a Communications Data Bill for storage and retention of all electronic and mobile communications. What safeguards are there? Much of what happens is beyond the pale of the Data Protection Act. While the Information Commissioner *may* conduct certain assessments under section 42 of that Act, he is not an ombudsman as under FOIA.

Foreign policy

Foreign policy is still very much the preserve of prerogative, although the courts have made an incursion into the use of prerogative powers in overseas governance and human rights.[94] The Government's White Paper *Governance of Britain*[95] recommends that, with some exceptions, treaty powers should be subject to Parliamentary approval. The Human Rights Act has been held to have extraterritorial effect[96] and Security Council resolutions for Iraq should be applied taking precedence over but respecting ECHR rights.[97] But the decision on war in Iraq was approved by a misinformed Parliament. Is it still appropriate for virtually all foreign policy to be outside the range of approval and challenge by Parliament even if the changes in the White Paper come into effect? The sensitivity of diplomatic and international relations as well as national security have left indelible stains on the face of justice.[98]

[93] Surveillance Studies Network (2006). House of Lords Select Committee on the Constitution (2009).

[94] *R (Bancoult) v Secretary of State for Foreign Affairs* [2006] EWHC 1038 (Admin), affirmed [2007] EWCA Civ 498, reversed [2008] UKHL 61.

[95] Ministry of Justice (2008).

[96] *Al Skeini* [2007] UKHL 26; *cf R (Quark Fishing Ltd) v Secretary of State for Foreign Affairs* [2006] 1 AC 529.

[97] *Al Jeddah* [2007] UKHL 58; see *HM Treasury v M al Ghabra* [2010] UKSC 2.

[98] See: *RB (Algeria) v Secretary of State for the Home Department* [2009] UKHL 10; *R (Corner House Research) v Director of the Serious Fraud Office* [2008] UKHL 60; *R (Bancoult) v Secretary of State for Foreign Affairs* [2008] UKHL 61; *R (Binyam Mohamed) v SoS FA* [2009] EWHC 152 (Admin).

Policy Formulation

Policy formulation is given exemption under the Freedom of Information Act—the merits of policy are usually tucked away from challenge or complaint. Take, as one example, prison overcrowding. That is beyond effective challenge although subject to extra-judicial complaint by senior judges. Yet look at the changes in prison complaints and disciplinary hearings brought about by judicial decisions both in domestic courts and in the Court of Human Rights. This appears an enormous improvement since the 1970s. But the prison estate and conditions may in some respects actually be worse.

Social Exclusion

As well as executive exclusion there is social exclusion. This seems particularly acute in the following areas.

— E-government and e-services, and different levels of service depending on security clearance and access to IT—in effect, different people get different levels of service relating to their status.[99] The National Audit Office in its Report on Citizen Redress made the point forcefully.[100]

— Privacy in modern society becomes a luxury for those who can afford it—secluded protected estates for the wealthy and so on.

— Privileging access to precious commodities like education and health. These are universal services but privilege gives easier access to elite institutions or better forms of treatment. In health we have seen a reformulation of grievance procedures, as well as new procedures for resolution of tort claims and no end of statutory consultation and participation schemes, but the chances of being killed in hospital have increased since the 1980s. Despite all the attention, a survey conducted by the Patients Association in 2008 revealed an NHS complaints system that is 'cumbersome, variable and takes too long'.[101] A National Audit Office report found serious problems with NHS and social care complaints processes and listed a detailed set of recommendations.[102]

Is the result a new form of social stratification, or an old one with a different exterior but the same essence. My belief is that it is new and more insidious. What, if this is the case, are the consequences for those with complaints and grievances but no voice?

One final point: I adverted in the second edition of *Grievances, Remedies and the State* to the consideration of a Director of Civil Proceedings—an idea which

[99] Taylor, Lips and Organ (2006). See also Cabinet Office (2009) and Equality Bill 2009.

[100] See n 11 above.

[101] www.patients-association.org.uk/News/228.

[102] National Audit Office (2008).

came from Lord Woolf's pen. I believe that idea still has currency. The Director would assist litigants and survey litigation in the public law civil side. Given the reforms taking place in legal services in England and Wales under the Legal Services Act 2007, and market-based strategies for awarding legal aid that have been vehemently criticised by professional bodies, the call for such an office may now be greater. The proposals on legal services were set out in the White Paper on *The Future of Legal Services: Putting Consumers First*,[103] which was published in October 2005. These include setting up a Legal Services Board and an Office for Legal Complaints and new ombudsmen, and enabling legal services to be provided under new business models. Some of these proposals are an improvement on existing professional domination. A Director, however, would not be constrained by market considerations. An ideal place for the Director to occupy would be in a reformed and institutionally independent Attorney-General's office.

Acknowledgments

I am grateful to Jean Bernard Auby, Mike Varney and Christian Twigg-Flesner for their advice on comparative and EU aspects of complaining.

References

Birkinshaw, P (1985) *Grievances, Remedies and the State* (London, Sweet & Maxwell).

—— (2003) *European Public Law* (London, Butterworths).

—— (2006) 'Contrats publics et contractualisation de l'action publique: un point de vue anglais' 5 *Revue Francaise de Droit Administratif* 1015.

Boyron, S (2006) 'The rise of mediation in administrative law disputes: experiences from England, France and Germany' *Public Law* 320.

—— (2007) 'Mediation in Administrative Law: The Identification of Conflicting Paradigms' *European Public Law* 263.

Buck, T (2005) *Administrative Justice and Alternative Dispute Resolution: the Australian Experience* (London, Department for Constitutional Affairs).

British and Irish Ombudsmen Association (2007) *Guide to Principles of Good Complaint Handling*, available at www.bioa.org.uk/docs/BIOAGoodComplaintHandling.pdf.

Cabinet Office (1998) *How to Deal with Complaints*, June, available at archive.cabinetoffice.gov.uk/servicefirst/1998/complaint/b5intro.htm.

—— (2009) *New Opportunities: Fair Chances for the Future* (White Paper) Cm 7533, available at www.hmg.gov.uk/media/9102/NewOpportunities.pdf.

Clementi, Sir David (2004) *Review of the Regulatory Framework for Legal Services in England and Wales: Final Report* (London, Department for Constitutional Affairs).

[103] Department for Constitutional Affairs (2005). This followed a Review of the Regulatory framework for Legal Services in England and Wales carried out by Sir David Clementi. See Clementi (2004).

Convention on Access to Information, Public Participation in Decision-Making and Justice in Environmental Matters (1998) Denmark, 29 June, available at www.unece.org/env/pp/documents/cep43e.pdf.

Department for Constitutional Affairs (2004) *Transforming Public Services: Complaints, Redress and Tribunals* (Cm 6243).

—— (2005) *The Future of Legal Services: Putting Consumers First* (Cm 6679).

—— (2006) *Review of the Implementation of the Human Rights Act* (London).

Department of Energy and Climate Change (2007) *Meeting the Energy Challenge*, White Paper (Cm 7124).

European Union Ombudsman (2006) *Annual Report 2005*, available at www.europarl.europa.eu/ombudsman/report05/pdf/en/rap05_en.pdf.

—— (2007) *Legality and Good Administration: Is there a difference?* available at www.ombudsman.europa.eu/speeches/en/2007-10-15.htm.

Foreign and Commonwealth Office (2005) *Treaty establishing a Constitution for Europe: Commentary* (Cm 6459).

Goldsmith, Lord (2004) 'The Charter of Rights—a Brake not an Accelerator' *European Human Rights Law Review* 473.

HM Government (2007) *Planning for a Sustainable Future*, White Paper (Cm 7120).

HM Treasury (2007) *The prudential regulation of the Equitable Life Assurance Society: the Government's response to the report of the Parliamentary Ombudsman's investigation* (Cm 7538).

House of Commons Select Committee on Constitutional Affairs (2007) *Implementation of the Carter Review of Legal Aid* (Third Report of Session 2006–07) HC 223 1 and 2.

House of Commons Select Committee on Public Administration (2003) *Review of Public Sector Ombudsmen in England* (Third Report of Session 2002–03) HC 612.

—— (2006a) *A Debt of Honour* (First Report of Session 2005–06) HC 735.

—— (2006b) *The Ombudsman in Question: the Ombudsman's report on pensions and its constitutional implications* (Sixth Report of Session 2005–06) HC 1081.

—— (2007) *Pensions Bill: Government Undertakings relating to the Financial Assistance* (Fifth Report of Session 2006–07) HC 523.

—— (2008a) *When Citizens Complain* (Fifth Report of Session 2007–08) HC 409.

—— (2008b) *When Citizens Complain: Government Response to the Committee's Fifth Report of Session 2007–08*, HC 997.

House of Lords Select Committee on the Constitution (2009) *Surveillance: Citizens and the State* (Second Report of Session 2008–09) HL 18-1 and 18-2.

Joint Committee on Human Rights (2007) *The Meaning of Public Authority under the Human Rights Act* (Ninth Report of Session 2006–07) HL 77/HC 410.

—— (2008) *Monitoring the Government's Response to Human Rights Judgments* (Thirty-first Report of Session 2007–08) HL 173/HC 1078.

Kirkham, R (2006) 'Challenging the authority of the Ombudsman: The Parliamentary Ombudsman's special report on wartime detainees' 69 MLR 792.

Kirkham, R, Thompson, B and Buck, T (2008) 'When putting things right goes wrong: enforcing the recommendations of the ombudsman' PL 510.

Law Commission (2008a) *Housing: Proportionate Dispute Resolution* (Cm 7377).

—— (2008b) *Administrative Redress: Public Bodies and the Citizen*, Consultation Paper 187 (London).

Leggatt Report (2001) *Tribunals for Users—One System One Service*, available at http://www.tribunals-review.org.uk/leggatthtm/leg-00.htm.

Lewis, ND and Birkinshaw, P (1979) 'Taking Complaints Seriously, A study in Local Governement Practice' in Partington M and Jowell J (eds), *Welfare Law and Policy* (London, Francis Pinter).
—— (1993) *When Citizens Complain: Reforming Justice and Administration* (Buckingham, Open University Press).
Ministry of Justice (2008) *The Governance of Britain—Constitutional Renewal* (Cm 7342-I/II/III).
—— (2009) *Responding to Human Rights Judgments. The Government's Response to the Joint Committee on Human Rights' Thirty-first Report of Session 2007–08* (Cm 7524).
National Audit Office (2005) *Citizen Redress: What can do if things go wrong with public services*, HC 21 (2004–05).
—— (2008) *Feeding back?: Learning from complaints handling in health and social care*, HC 853 (2007–08).
Parliamentary and Health Service Ombudsman (2008) *Equitable Life: A Decade of Regulatory Failure* (Fourth Report Session 2007–08) HC 815.
—— (2009) Principles of Good Complaint Handling, available at www.ombudsman.org.uk/pdfs/Principles_of_Good_Complaint_Handling.pdf.
Partington, M (ed) (2001) *The Leggatt Review of Tribunals: Academic Seminar Papers* (Bristol: Centre for the Study of Administrative Justice).
Pritzker, D and Dalton, D (eds) (1990) *Negotiated Rulemaking Source Book* (Washington DC, Administrative Conference of the United States).
Prosser, T (2005) *The Limits of Competition Law: Markets and Public Services* (Oxford, Oxford University Press).
Rawlings, R (1986) *The Complaints Industry: A Review of the Socio-legal Research on Aspects of Administrative Justice* (London, ESRC).
Scarman, Sir Leslie (1974) *English Law—The New Dimension* (London, Stevens and Sons).
Sturgeon, S (2006) 'The Case for an Education Appeals Tribunal in the Tribunals Service' 10 *Education, Public Law and the Individual* Issue 2 (2006) www.council-on-tribunals.gov.uk/adjust/item/eatts.htm.
Surveillance Studies Network (2006) *A Report on the Surveillance Society* for the Information Commissioner, available at www.ico.gov.uk/upload/documents/library/data_protection/practical_application/surveillance_society_full_report_2006.pdf.
Taylor, J, Lips, M and Organ, J (2006) 'Freedom with Information: Electronic Government, Information Intensity and Challenges to Citizenship' in Chapmanand RA and Hunt M (eds), *Open Government in a Theoretical and Practical Context* (Farnham, Ashgate).
Varney, M and Varney, E (2007) 'Grounded? Air Passenger Rights in the European Union' in Howells G, Nordhausen A, Parry D and Twigg-Flesner C (eds), *Yearbook of Consumer Law 2008* 171.

16

A Holistic Approach to Administrative Justice?

TOM MULLEN

Introduction

This chapter deals with two questions. The first concerns the boundaries of the subject of administrative justice. The second concerns the similarities and differences, and the relationships, between the characteristic institutions of administrative justice in the United Kingdom, and how they might be combined so as to improve administrative justice.

The Scope of Administrative Justice

The term 'administrative justice' may be used either prescriptively or descriptively. Used prescriptively, it refers to the principles that may be used to evaluate the justice inherent in administrative decision making, that is, the principles to which administrative justice ought to conform (Adler 2003). In his chapter in this volume, Adler argues that the core of justice is that 'everyone should receive what is due to them' and that, as such, administrative justice has both procedural and substantive aspects with the former focusing on correct outcomes (persons get what they are entitled to both in terms of benefits and burdens) and the latter on procedural fairness (persons get what they are entitled in terms of the manner in which they are treated). Used descriptively, the term 'administrative justice' denotes a field of inquiry. We need to be clear what we mean by *administrative* decision making, that is, which social processes are grouped together for analysis under the rubric of administrative justice. In this chapter, I use the term to refer essentially to decisions made and actions taken by government bodies of all kind so the justice in question is that due to the citizen[1] from the state.

Given that the starting point is the concern to ensure that individuals receive what is due to them, it is important to consider both initial decision making about

[1] I use the term 'citizen' loosely to cover all persons who have dealings with public bodies and not just those who are citizens in a strictly legal sense.

benefits and burdens and mechanisms for appeal or review of decisions which fail to distribute benefits and burdens appropriately. As to the former, however effective redress mechanisms are, it is surely better for public bodies to get it right first time when making decisions affecting citizens. As to the latter, there are a number of processes and institutions which enable citizens to pursue grievances against, or resolve disputes with, the state, for example, courts, tribunals, ombudsmen and inquiries.

What is most obviously excluded from the field of administrative justice as defined above is decision making and mechanisms for redress in the private sector, that is, where decisions are made and action taken by private individuals and corporations affecting other private parties and disputes arise concerning those decisions and actions. The concept of justice is not, of course, peculiar to the public sector. However, there are important distinctions between citizen–state relations and relations between private persons. There are expectations that apply to public bodies that do not apply to citizens generally, for example relations between state and citizen are based on authority rather than consent, and public bodies pursue the public interest in their actions. These differences are likely to have consequences for the design of decision-making systems and mechanisms for redress that result in different approaches being taken to delivering justice in the public as opposed to private sector. The chapters by Oliver and Merricks in this volume discuss the applicability of administrative justice to private sector disputes in more detail.

Of course, in contrast to some other countries, there is no tradition of a formal separation of public and private law in the UK, and some mechanisms for the redress of grievances and of dispute resolution are used in both the public and private sectors. The ordinary courts are available for claims against both public bodies and private persons alike, and both the tribunal and the ombudsman model have been applied to private sector disputes. Accordingly, while our concern is with justice in the public sector, there may be lessons to be learned from private sector procedures that can be applied in the public sector (and *vice versa*), provided due account is taken of the contextual differences.

A second possible limitation concerns the nature of the decisions being taken by public bodies. If the governing principle is that citizens should receive what is due to them, that might be thought to suggest that the field of inquiry should be limited to questions of entitlement or obligation and to exclude situations where the decisions are made about matters in respect of which the citizen has no entitlement, for example, where there is a discretionary power to confer some benefit. However, what citizens are due in such cases is proper consideration of their personal situation. Such decisions merit a degree of scrutiny even if that scrutiny is carried out in a different way from the scrutiny of decisions involving entitlements. The requirements of administrative justice and the appropriate scope of inquiry extend, therefore, to all decisions affecting significant *interests* of citizens.

The field of inquiry might be extended even further by including consideration of how complaints against public bodies are dealt with. While some complaints are essentially appeals against decisions, other complaints concern, not the content of decisions, but other administrative failings such as delay, rudeness, insensitivity, obstructiveness and poor advice. It might be argued that these do not come within the field of administrative justice because the correctness of decisions is not in question. However, there are both principled and pragmatic reasons for considering the arrangements for handling complaints as part of administrative justice. The principled reason is that persons are entitled to be shown respect by public bodies and so are due not just correct (or at any rate, defensible) decisions about substantive entitlements, but also considerate treatment by public bodies. One pragmatic reason is that existing institutions are not all structured around the distinction between appeals and other challenges on the one hand, and complaints of administrative failings on the other. Ombudsmen, in particular consider both complaints about decisions and complaints relating to service failure. A second reason is that citizens with grievances may not, in invoking a complaints procedure, be making a clear cut distinction between challenges to decisions and complaints of service failure, either because they do not make this distinction in their own minds, or because their grievances may contain elements of both, and may find a rigid distinction between complaints and appeals confusing (National Audit Office 2005). For a fuller discussion, see Dunleavy's chapter in this volume.[2]

The Institutions of Administrative Justice and Relationships between Them

Although perfecting initial decision making is an important, perhaps the most important, goal that a system of administrative justice might have, I want to concentrate in this chapter on institutions and processes for the redress of grievances against the state, that is, those concerned with putting things right when bad decisions are made. The United Kingdom has evolved a complex set of institutions and processes for redress of grievances, which have evolved at different times and in response to different pressures. They include courts, tribunals, ombudsmen, inquiries, and various forms of review and complaints procedure both internal and external to the body whose decisions or actions give rise to the dispute. I wish to take an overview of these institutions, consider the extent to which the distinctions between them continue to make sense and consider what combination of institutions and processes provides the best answer to the question of how best to resolve disputes between citizen and state.

The current system evolved in an ad-hoc and piecemeal fashion. This is recognised in the most recent government review of administrative justice, the 2004

[2] It may be interesting to note that the definition of the field of inquiry suggested here is broadly compatible with that in para 13 of Sch 7 to the Tribunals, Courts and Enforcement Act 2007, which defines the remit of the Administrative Justice and Tribunals Council.

White Paper *Transforming Public Services: Complaints, Redress and Tribunals* (Secretary of State for Constitutional Affairs 2004), hereafter referred to as the 'White Paper'. This was the first comprehensive review of the whole field of administrative justice undertaken by a government department[3] in the UK, and might fairly be described as taking an overview of administrative justice. It suggested that the existing approach to administrative justice was unsatisfactory. Among the general criticisms were that there was insufficient focus on the needs and desires of citizens, existing systems of redress did not consider people's problems as a whole, the system of remedies was 'a patchwork' to which no coherent design or design principle had ever been applied systematically, existing systems of redress were not as successful as they might be, and there was too much emphasis on courts, lawyers and legal aid. The White Paper stated that citizens were entitled to expect: (a) correct decisions in the first place; (b) where a mistake occurs, the opportunity to have it put right with the minimum of difficulty; and (c) where things go wrong, that the system will learn from the problem and do better in the future. In short, the aims of a system of administrative justice ought to be getting it right first time, putting mistakes right, and learning from mistakes.

Although stressing the importance of getting it right first time, most of the analysis in the White Paper concentrated on the second aim—putting it right—and, therefore, on arrangements for redress of grievances. Early resolution of disputes, cheapness and informality were particularly strong themes. The White Paper (para 2.3) stated that the Department would

> promote the development of a range of tailored dispute resolution services, so that different types of disputes can be resolved fairly, quickly, efficiently and effectively, without recourse to the expense and formality of courts and tribunals where this is not necessary.

Reference was made to a wide range of alternative dispute resolution processes including adjudication, arbitration, conciliation, early neutral evaluation, mediation, negotiation, and ombudsmen. However, the most significant concrete proposal was the creation of a unified tribunals system which, in addition to providing formal hearings and authoritative rulings would have a mission to resolve disputes fairly and informally either by itself or in partnership with others. This proposal was given legislative effect by the Tribunals, Courts and Enforcement Act 2007 and, at the time of writing, implementation is well underway (see the chapter by Thompson in this volume).

The White Paper, therefore, raised the question of how to create a rational system for the redress of grievances that is not necessarily tied to the existing mix of institutions and processes. In order to pursue this question, we need to compare institutions and processes, establish their key differences and similarities, and evaluate their performance against the goals of administrative justice. In the next part of this chapter, I compare existing institutions in terms of five characteristics: the

[3] The White Paper was prepared by the Department for Constitutional Affairs. Following re-organisation in 2005, responsibility for administrative justice passed to the Ministry of Justice.

criteria they employ in deciding whether to uphold challenges to administrative decisions (decision criteria), whether they are independent and impartial, whether they make binding decisions, their methods of inquiry and the degree of formality of their proceedings. At the risk of some oversimplification, it may be said that the UK has evolved at least five different models of decision making for redress of grievances, each of which is associated with a particular set of institutions although the correspondence between institutions and processes is not perfect. These are the formal/adversarial model of adjudication traditionally associated with courts, the informal/enabling model of adjudication associated with tribunals, the two different inquisitorial models one adjudicative and the other non-adjudicative associated with external review (the former) and ombudsmen (the latter), and a hybrid form of decision making associated with public inquiries.[4]

Having distinguished between adjudicative and non-adjudicative processes, I need to define what I mean by adjudication. I am using it to refer to a process in which a dispute between identifiable parties is referred to a third party for decision and in which the parties are entitled to present proofs and reasoned argument for a decision in their favour. This is broadly consistent with Fuller's definition (Fuller 1978) but some would add additional requirements.[5] Certain specifics flow from this definition including that the parties should have certain procedural rights and that the adjudicator should be impartial. While this definition excludes a wide range of decision-making procedures operating in society, it still has a broad reach and is capable of accommodating a wide spectrum of existing decision-making processes. It should be noted that it is not part of the definition that adjudicative processes for making decisions need be wholly adversarial as opposed to inquisitorial to some degree, nor that that procedure entails oral hearings. An inquisitorial and written process would count as adjudication provided the adjudicator was impartial and the parties affected had sufficient opportunity to put their case to him or her.

Dispute Resolution Procedures and Institutions Compared

The Courts

The courts are the traditional forum for resolving disputes about legal rights and obligations, and play a significant role in securing redress of grievances against the state. Cases involving such grievances fall broadly into three types: applications

[4] For reasons of space and because they are used to perform a variety of functions of which redress of grievances is only one, inquiries will not be further discussed in this chapter.

[5] Some would add the additional requirement that the adjudicator's decision should be reached by applying pre-existing rules to the evidence received. See Richardson (1994).

for judicial review; appeals under statutes; and 'private law' actions such as claims based on breach of contract or negligence. Whatever the form of action, the jurisdiction of the courts is based primarily on the commission of legal wrongs, that is, a person can only expect a remedy from a court when the person or body being sued has done them some legal wrong which may be an act or a decision or a failure to act or decide.

One of the key characteristics of courts, therefore, is that their criteria for questioning administrative decisions are essentially criteria of legality. In analysing this concept, I shall concentrate on judicial review and appeals since these both involve direct challenges to decisions, whereas private law actions will often not do so. The concept of legality is an extended one which gives the courts power to correct errors of law and at least some errors of fact, and allows a degree of supervision of the discretionary element in decision making and of the procedures followed by the initial decision maker. In judicial review, administrative decisions may be challenged in court: (i) on the basis that they are based on a misunderstanding of the relevant law or a failure to apply it properly; (ii) that there is no adequate factual basis for the decision (although the extent of inquiry into the facts permitted is relatively limited in judicial review); (iii) that any discretion has not properly been exercised; or (iv) that the procedure followed was not fair.[6] Although the general principles of judicial review give the courts some control of the discretionary element in decision making, they fall far short of full scale review of the merits of decision. So, a decision cannot normally be challenged on the ground that it is 'unwise' or 'unfair' if no specific legal defect can be demonstrated. Where there is a right of appeal, the grounds of appeal depend upon the relevant statute. Some statutory rights of appeal are expressed in terms which appear to be broad enough to permit consideration of the merits of the original decision. However, courts tend to be reluctant to overturn decisions purely on the merits and so there may not in practice be a great difference between the approach of the courts in cases of judicial review or appeals, although there may be more scope for inquiry into the facts in appeals. Given the decision criteria are criteria of legality, some citizens' grievances are excluded from consideration by the courts. If the grievance relates to the substantive fairness of a lawful decision or administrative failings such as rudeness or delay (unless there is a specific legal obligation to decide within a time limit), the courts will not entertain it.

A second characteristic of the courts is that they are expected to be impartial and enjoy a high degree of independence from the executive bodies that take decisions which affect citizens. The difference between these two characteristics is that impartiality is the desired state of mind for adjudication, whereas independence refers to structural factors, such as security of tenure, that are designed to encourage judges to be independent (Robson 1951). A third characteristic of courts is that their decisions are typically binding on the parties to the action. Thus, if the

[6] See Craig (2008) for a detailed account of the grounds of judicial review including the scope for review of fact.

court decides that a public body has wrongly withheld a benefit from a person, then that public body is obliged to make the benefit available to that person. There are some technical limitations on the remedies available in certain contexts, but the general principle that decisions are binding on all parties to an action, including any public bodies, is clear.

The fourth characteristic of courts relates to the methods that are employed to reach decisions. Courts in the United Kingdom have traditionally adopted an adversarial form of process, with substantial oral and written elements. The standard forms of procedure in civil cases have required extensive written pleadings and, where cases were not settled, oral hearings (sometimes very lengthy) to lead and test evidence as to the facts and debate questions of law. The process was governed by detailed procedural rules and the way in which the parties could seek to establish facts restricted by laws of evidence. Rights of audience were restricted so that individuals had to be represented by lawyers or represent themselves.[7] Judges tended to act as umpires, their job being to see fair play rather than to 'get at the truth'. Thus the initiative in progressing the case and the way in which it was pleaded was left largely to the parties. The whole tone and style of proceedings tended to be very formal particularly in the higher courts. However, it is important to note some qualifications. What has just been described is the traditional approach. Since 1978 in England and Wales, and since 1985 in Scotland, simplified forms of process have been available for judicial review cases, which have speeded up judicial review litigation, and since the early 1970s simpler, less formal procedures have been introduced for a wide range of civil cases that are of low financial value or deemed otherwise suitable for such procedures. The significance of these changes is discussed below.

Tribunals

Over the last century or so, tribunals have offered an alternative model of adjudication to the courts. Although there are much earlier examples of specialised jurisdictions separate from the ordinary courts, tribunals as we understand them today developed along with the welfare state. The growth of the functions of the state created a need for additional capacity for resolving disputes between the citizen and the state. Tribunals were deliberately adopted as an alternative to the courts. The option of having disputes in relation to many administrative functions resolved by the ordinary courts was never seriously considered. Government Ministers and civil servants perceived courts to be slow and expensive. They thought that the cost of using them would be disproportionate given the amounts

[7] In addition, parties can be accompanied by a 'McKenzie Friend'. A 'McKenzie Friend' is not technically a representative but is a non-legally qualified person who sits with one of the parties during a hearing to offer advice and assistance. The 'McKenzie Friend' is not allowed to address the court. The term comes from a divorce case, *McKenzie v McKenzie* [1970] 3 All ER 1034, where the husband was representing himself and wished to have the assistance of a non-legally qualified person at court.

likely to be in dispute in many cases, and that the courts would be unable to cope with the volume of cases generated. In addition, there were concerns, based on the experience of nineteenth century social legislation, that courts might be unsympathetic to social welfare legislation and interpret it contrary to its intent (Arthurs 1985). Moreover, the trade unions, whose views carried considerable weight in this context, perceived the courts as unsympathetic to the interests of their members. Although mainly used, therefore, to resolve citizen v state disputes, the rationales offered for avoiding courts (cost, delay and possible antipathy to social legislation) could also be applied to some disputes between private parties and the tribunal model was also in time applied to, among other areas, rent control in private sector housing and employment disputes.

Tribunals do, however, have many similarities to courts. The Franks Committee famously settled the argument about the nature of tribunals. It rejected the assumption behind much of the official evidence submitted to it, which was to the effect that tribunals were machinery for administration, stating instead, that they were properly to be regarded as machinery for adjudication and that their key characteristics should be 'openness, fairness and impartiality' (Franks 1957). Franks also suggested that tribunals were different from courts in important respects, and that this often gives them advantages over courts, namely cheapness, accessibility, freedom from technicality, expedition and expert knowledge of their particular subject.

The criteria tribunals apply in questioning administrative decisions are, as with the courts, essentially criteria of legality. In most cases, the rights of appeal to tribunals have been unrestricted rather than being confined to a point of law. Citizens have, therefore, been able (at least in theory) to appeal decisions on questions of fact, questions of law and questions of discretion. There is generally more scope than there is in judicial review proceedings to question the factual conclusions of the initial decision makers. Where there is an unrestricted appeal from a decision, the tribunal can in theory differ from the initial decision maker on the merits of the case even where there is no clear mistake of fact or law. It is not clear how frequently in practice tribunals second-guess initial decision makers in this way. So, as a matter of law, tribunals enjoy somewhat greater scope to question initial decisions than do courts in the exercise of their judicial review jurisdiction, but the difference in practice may not be great, justifying the conclusion that both apply criteria of legality in considering challenges to administrative decisions.

A second shared characteristic is impartiality and independence. While expected to be impartial, tribunals have not traditionally enjoyed such firm guarantees of independence as the ordinary courts; but recent reforms, including those under the Tribunals, Courts and Enforcement Act 2007, have tended to strengthen that independence. A third point of similarity is that tribunals make binding decisions. The parties, including the relevant government departments, are obliged, subject to any further rights of appeal, to accept the decisions of tribunals on appeals and applications made to them.

The distinction between courts and tribunals is to be found primarily in their methods of inquiry and the degree of formality attaching to proceedings. In tribunals the parties have the essential procedural rights associated with court procedures, including the right to appear at an oral hearing at which proofs and arguments may be presented. Procedures are generally simpler. In particular, there are not complex written pleadings. The rules of evidence do not apply although this difference may be less significant than it was formerly. Proceedings tend to have a less formal style and tone because of the venues in which they are held, the absence of court dress (wigs, gowns, etc) and attempts by tribunal chairs and members to create an informal atmosphere. There are no restrictions on rights of audience.

In addition, it is often said that tribunals are, or at least ought to be, inquisitorial.[8] However, it is important to note that tribunals have not wholly rejected the adversarial approach. Rather, they have applied an inquisitorial gloss to a basically adversarial process. If the process were thoroughly inquisitorial, the adjudicator would take charge of the case, decide what evidence was required and so forth. This is not how tribunals operate. The conduct of the case remains to a large degree in the hands of the parties. It is primarily their responsibility to decide what evidence to present and what arguments to raise. However, procedures have tended to assume that an oral hearing will take place and that the hearing itself will not be wholly adversarial. Tribunal chairs and members are expected to play an enabling role, putting the appellant at ease and assisting him/her to bring out facts and arguments that may assist his or her case, particularly where the appellant is unrepresented (Leggatt 2001: paras 7.1–7.5).

A further difference between tribunals and courts relates to the expertise of adjudicators. This has two dimensions. When Franks referred to expert knowledge of their particular subject area as being an advantage of tribunals over courts, he meant technical expertise in the functional area concerned, as opposed to expertise in law. This technical expertise was supplied by the 'wing members', who would have qualifications and/or experience appropriate to the subject area; for example, a tribunal which had to consider medical evidence might include a doctor, and a tribunal dealing with rent controls might include a surveyor or a valuer. The difference from the ordinary courts is that, where courts require expert opinion, they have traditionally relied on the evidence of expert witnesses or court-appointed assessors. With tribunals, although expert evidence may be led, the membership of the tribunal itself may include persons with the relevant expertise.

Franks did not identify the opportunity to specialise in one area of law as an advantage of tribunals but one of the things that the existence of specialised tribunals permits is the opportunity for chairs and members to develop expertise in defined areas of law and perhaps also in the general principles of administrative law,

[8] See Carnwath (2009) for a recent discussion.

although this has since been recognised by the Leggatt Review (Leggatt 2001: para 1.13). By contrast, even though there is a substantial degree of specialisation within the ordinary courts—for example, High Court judges generally work within only one division[9]—judges in the ordinary civil courts tend to have a broader jurisdiction than do chairs and members of tribunals.

Ombudsmen

Ombudsmen present a third model of decision making. As indicated above, ombudsmen display some important similarities to courts and tribunals. They are expected to be impartial, and the principal public sector ombudsmen have strong statutory guarantees of independence. Where they most obviously differ from courts and tribunals is in lacking the power to make binding decisions and in their decision criteria. The statutes setting up the principal public sector ombudsmen did not impose on public bodies a legal obligation to implement ombudsmen's decisions and did not give ombudsmen powers of direct enforcement. This lack of the power to make binding decisions means that they cannot be classified as a form of adjudication.

Ombudsmen's criteria for making decisions are significantly different from those of courts and tribunals. The statutory ombudsmen may uphold complaints only where the complainant has sustained injustice or hardship in consequence of maladministration[10] or (except in the case of the Parliamentary Ombudsman) where there has been a service failure.[11] 'Maladministration' is not defined, and the legislation also provides that ombudsmen are not entitled to question the merits of a decision taken without maladministration. Ombudsmen are, therefore, entitled to question decisions which are perfectly lawful but are deemed defective in some other way which amounts to maladministration. Their remit also extends beyond the 'correction' of bad decisions to encompass passing judgment on, and providing remedies, for administrative failings which do not call into question the appropriateness of a decision on the complainants rights or interests—for example, delay in making a decision, rudeness or giving poor advice. The difference in decision criteria is reinforced by statutory provisions which state that ombudsmen will not normally investigate matters in respect of which the person aggrieved has a right of appeal to a tribunal or remedy in court.[12]

[9] In Scotland, a more generalist approach prevails. The Court of Session is not split into divisions, and judges have a very wide civil jurisdiction and, as they also sit in the High Court of Justiciary, a wide criminal jurisdiction. The sheriff court also has both a broad civil and a broad criminal jurisdiction.

[10] See eg Parliamentary Commissioner Act 1967 s 5.

[11] The other ombudsmen all have jurisdiction to investigate service failures and, in the context of complaints against the NHS, the exercise of clinical judgment. See eg Scottish Public Services Ombudsman Act 2002 s 5.

[12] See eg Parliamentary Commissioner Act 1967 s 5(2). However, there is a discretion to investigate where it is not reasonable to expect the person to have resort to the remedy.

So, ombudsmen's decision criteria are substantially different from those of courts and tribunals. There is also a marked difference in methods and procedure. The methods used by ombudsmen are thoroughly inquisitorial. Once a complaint is accepted, ombudsmen take the initiative in investigating it, rather than relying on the complainer or the body complained about to determine the course of the investigation. In general, ombudsmen do not hold hearings, proceeding instead by interviewing relevant persons and gathering in all relevant correspondence and other written records. They are not restricted in gathering information, or the conclusions which they may reach, by detailed procedural rules or rules of evidence. Importantly, the statutory ombudsmen have coercive powers so that the body complained about is obliged to supply all the information relevant to the decision on request. A consequence of the investigative approach is that both the complainer and the body complained against lack the sort of procedural rights associated with court or tribunal process. From the complainant's perspective, the process is relatively informal.

External Reviews

The term 'review' has no fixed meaning in administrative law, so it is important to clarify what I mean by it and whether it represents a distinct model for resolving grievances. As indicated above, a number of statutes impose a legal requirement on public bodies to review their own decisions. However, although these are statutory procedures, they do not in other respects appear to represent a distinct model from the standard public authority complaints procedure. An 'independent' element may be injected into the review by the requirement that it be conducted by a different person, but this feature is common to many non-statutory internal complaints and review procedures.

The particular type or review I wish to examine is that provided by the Independent Review Service (IRS) for the Social Fund. The Social Fund, which was established in 1988 under the Social Security Act 1986, replaced provision previously made under the Supplementary Benefit Scheme. It provides a range of grants and loans, which may be paid to meet needs additional to normal weekly requirements for those on means-tested benefits. There is a structural division within the fund between the regulated Social Fund and the discretionary part of the fund. The former covers maternity, funeral and cold weather payments. Payments are entitlements paid in accordance with regulations, and claimants have a right of appeal to a tribunal. Payments out of the discretionary part of the fund, such as community care grants and crisis loans, are made at the discretion of officials constrained by local office cash limits, and are subject to internal review within the local office and external review by the IRS (Buck 2009).

Both the Social Fund itself and the replacement of rights of appeal to tribunals by reviews were controversial. The latter was the subject of a highly critical report from the Council on Tribunals (1986). As indicated, although there is no right to appeal an adverse decision to a tribunal, the claimant has the right to seek a review. There are two stages of review. The first takes place in the local office. The second is carried out by Social Fund Inspectors employed by the Independent Review Service for the Social Fund (IRS). The principal function of the IRS is to provide independent reviews of discretionary Social Fund decisions. Its other functions include helping the responsible agency (currently called Jobcentre Plus) to improve the standard of its decision making and customer service through regular feedback, training and advice, and providing advice and information to the relevant government department (Department for Work and Pensions) on Social Fund policy and the need for reform.

A Social Fund Inspector's review of a decision is conducted in two stages (IRS 2008; Buck 2009: ch 5). At the first stage, the Inspector considers whether the decision maker has: (i) interpreted and applied the law correctly, including whether he has had regard to all the relevant considerations and excluded irrelevant considerations; (ii) acted fairly and exercised his discretion reasonably; and (iii) observed the principles of natural justice. If the decision has been reached correctly, applying these tests, then the Inspector conducts the second stage review, during which he or she considers the merits of the case, decides whether the decision was a right one in the circumstances; and takes account of any relevant changes in circumstances and new evidence. The Inspector has the power to confirm the decision by Jobcentre Plus, refer the application back to Jobcentre Plus to make a fresh decision, or make any decision which the agency could have made (substituted decisions). It is clear, therefore, that the Social Fund Inspectors have a remit to consider both questions of the legality and the merits of decisions.

Although lacking the statutory guarantees of independence which courts and tribunals have, the IRS is intended to operate independently of, and has a clear structural separation from, the initial decision makers in Jobcentre Plus, and has acquired a reputation for impartial decision making. The decisions made by the IRS are binding on officials in local offices. The methods and procedures used resemble those of ombudsmen more than those of courts or tribunals, being investigative and paper-based, and relatively informal from the claimant's perspective.

Compared to courts, therefore, there are similarities in relation to independence, and to the binding nature of decisions and decision criteria, although the latter are somewhat broader than those of the courts. The differences are the truly inquisitorial process, and the lack of technicality in terms of procedure and evidence, and the informality of proceedings. However, the IRS process can be properly be considered a form of adjudication, given that it has the power to make binding decisions, and the parties have some (albeit limited) opportunity to present proof and argument.

Compared to ombudsmen, the similarities are independence, methods and procedures for inquiry and informality. However, unlike ombudsmen, the IRS has the power to set aside decisions, and seems to have greater freedom to question the merits of decisions. It does, therefore, appear to represent a distinct model of grievance redress, which is significantly different from both courts and tribunals on the one hand and from ombudsmen on the other.

The similarities and differences between the institutions discussed in this section are summarised in Table 1 below. The comparison is based on 'ideal' types and, therefore, does not take account of the convergence between them in recent years which is discussed in a later section of this chapter.

While the UK has evolved this complex and varied set of arrangements for redress, it cannot be said that it represents the evolution of a coherent plan. The various institutions and processes have evolved at different times and in response to different political and other pressures. It is not, therefore, surprising that, as both the Franks Committee and the White Paper have noted, there have not been any clear principles for the allocation of jurisdiction to different grievance redress mechanisms that have been consistently applied. Consider, for example, the allocation of jurisdiction between tribunals and courts. Possible grounds for allocating disputes to one or other include the value of the amounts in dispute relative to the cost of litigation, the importance of the interests at stake to the litigant, the public or private character of the dispute, and the complexity of the legal and/or factual issues likely to be encountered. Although many low value claims have been allocated to tribunals, tribunals also deal with some high value claims, and claims of a very modest value have continued to be processed through the ordinary courts, although simplified procedures have been introduced for low value claims in the courts. Of course, many legal claims are not about money. These may be considered in terms of their importance to the parties. Judgments of what is more or less important will often be contentious, but some of the disputes that are litigated in the ordinary courts are of minor import by any standard. Equally, it is clear that matters of very great importance in both financial and non-financial terms are dealt with by tribunals. Examples include claims for political asylum and, more generally, the right to enter and remain in the UK, claims to remain at liberty in the community rather than be detained in an institution under the Mental Health Acts, and claims for unfair dismissal and unlawful discrimination. As these examples illustrate, allocation of jurisdiction does not, as in the French legal system, follow a public–private divide. Tribunals deal with some disputes between private parties while courts still deal with many citizen v state disputes. As for complexity, it would be misleading to state that courts deal with cases which

Table 1: Characteristics of main grievance-redress mechanisms in the UK

	Courts	Tribunals	Ombudsmen	External Reviews
Independent	yes	yes	yes	yes
Binding decisions	yes	yes	no	yes
Decision criteria	legality	legality	maladministration/ injustice	legality and merits
Method	adversarial	modified adversarial	inquisitorial	inquisitorial
Formality	high	Low	low	low

are legally and/or factually more complex than the cases that tribunals deal with. In many of the areas dealt with by tribunals, there are voluminous, complex and frequently changing bodies of statute law, amplified by precedent. Sometimes, in addition, tribunals will need to appreciate the effect of European Union Law, the European Convention on Human Rights and/or other international instruments. Social security, immigration and employment law are three such areas.

The allocation of jurisdiction between judicial institutions and ombudsmen has more to commend it. Whereas courts and tribunals consider questions of legal rights and obligations, ombudsmen consider complaints by citizens and assess whether they are justified against standards of good administration, and this original division of labour has been largely maintained at least as far as public sector ombudsmen are concerned.

The creation of a fresh model of review for the Social Fund was not the result of the application of accepted design principles but the product of more short-term political considerations. It is likely that the decision to substitute reviews for the right of appeal to an independent tribunal was motivated by concerns over the strains put on the system by surges in the number of appeals in the 1980s and by a concern that rights of appeal to tribunals might undermine the cash limits on payments that had become an integral feature of the benefits scheme (Mullen 1989).

The discussion so far has largely been of the current set of institutions as originally designed. However, there has in recent decades been a degree of apparent convergence between the different institutions. But, before considering that, I shall attempt to evaluate the performance of the existing institutions.

Evaluation of Dispute Resolution Procedures and Institutions

The performance of existing institutions will be evaluated against the following criteria, all of which relate to the general aim of providing effective redress for defective decisions and actions:

- the probability of producing appropriate outcomes (ie, detecting and correcting errors while not overruling sound decisions);
- impartiality and independence;
- fairness of procedures;
- speed;
- cost; and
- accessibility.

Some of these criteria may be viewed differently from different perspectives, for example, the person with a grievance is probably most interested in the cost to him or her of using the remedy, whereas the government and citizens generally have an interest in the cost of running the system. Similarly, the citizen may have a different view from the government of what is a reasonable time to wait for a decision. It should also be understood that there may be conflict between different criteria, for example, between the speed and the thoroughness of a redress mechanism, and this may lead to trade-offs being made.

The Courts

While courts certainly enjoy a high reputation for impartiality and independence, for the fairness of their procedures and for their ability to produce appropriate outcomes to disputes (ie, by accepting the good claims and rejecting the bad ones), they are generally perceived to perform less well against the other criteria (speed, cost, accessibility). That is, of course, a generalisation since the extent to which these strengths and weaknesses are evident varies according to context. It is also important to note that this evaluation refers to the traditional approach to civil litigation and does not cover the performance of courts operating under the simplified forms of procedure that have been introduced in recent decades. These will be discussed below.

The comparative slowness of court procedures is largely a product of their working methods and the approaches lawyers take to litigation. It is fair to say that this negative perception is derived largely from the standard operating procedures of the courts in cases that largely comprise private sector disputes. The introduction of simplified procedures for judicial review has reduced those elements of delay in processing cases that were attributable to the to traditional court procedures and methods of pleading, although the enormous growth in the caseload has been a countervailing force, with applications for leave to seek judicial review increasing from 533 in 1981 to 6,458 in 2006.[13] Of course, not all disputes between citizen and state that go to court use the judicial review procedure. Homelessness appeals in England and Wales, for example, are dealt with in the county court.

The questions of cost and accessibility are closely linked because the cost of litigation affects the ability of ordinary people to pursue or defend cases in the courts. Courts are undoubtedly relatively costly mechanisms for resolving disputes, both from the perspective of the person pursing a grievance, and from the perspective of the government and taxpayer. From the government/taxpayer perspective, the high cost as compared to other procedures arises mainly from the high salaries paid to judges, the high fees charged by lawyers, and the length of time taken to process cases. From the litigant's perspective, it is the high cost of legal representation (except where 'no win, no fee' or conditional fee arrangements are available)

[13] Judicial Statistics for England and Wales. The steadily growing caseload has been a matter of concern to judges and officials for some years. It appears that, even after the reforms which followed the Bowman Committee Report (Bowman 2000), the pressure has continued to grow and that waiting times at all stages of the procedure had deteriorated significantly. See discussion in Bondy and Sunkin (2009).

again generated by the high earnings that lawyers expect and the amount of time devoted to preparing and presenting cases. The policy in recent years of increasing court fees with a view to recovering from litigants a higher proportion of the costs of running the courts has also raised the cost barrier to potential litigants other than those who qualify for an exemption on income grounds, but this effect is likely to be modest in relation to the cost of legal representation. Legal aid provides only a very partial solution, given that a large proportion of the population falls outside the financial eligibility limits. There may also be other non-cost based problems of accessibility arising from the non-availability of expert advice and the failure of citizens to perceive their grievance as one that it is worth seeking advice on (Genn 1999).

In saying that the courts are generally thought to produce appropriate outcomes, it should be appreciated how limited is the meaning to be attached to the idea of appropriate outcomes in this context. In an adversarial system of justice, courts decide cases on the basis of the evidence and arguments put before them. A judgment that courts in general produce appropriate outcomes, therefore, means that their decisions as to the disposal of cases are appropriate in the light of the evidence and arguments actually presented. It is, of course, possible that erroneous administrative decisions will go uncorrected when they are challenged in court because the parties fail to present the information or the arguments that the court needs in order to justify overturning the decision. This is more likely to happen when persons do not have adequate advice or representation. To the extent that it happens, it is a limitation on the effectiveness of courts as grievance-redress mechanisms.

Tribunals

Tribunals are generally thought to score highly in terms of appropriate outcomes, impartiality and independence, and fairness of procedures and are also thought to have advantages, at least in comparison to courts, in terms of speed, cost and accessibility. There is no evidence that there is any general problem of inappropriate outcomes, at least in the narrow sense mentioned above (ie, that decisions are justified on the basis of the evidence and arguments put before the tribunal) not being reached. As regards the broader sense (the likelihood that erroneous initial decisions are in fact corrected), tribunals are, in theory, better placed to get at the 'truth' of the matter by adopting an inquisitorial approach. They may assist the unrepresented litigant to bring out his case. Whether they are truly more likely than the ordinary courts to detect and correct erroneous official decisions is not something that can be proved on the basis of the available research evidence. No such systematic comparison has ever been conducted. and such a comparison would be very hard to make, not only because courts and tribunals deal with different kinds of dispute but also because of the difficulty of assessing whether the decisions of the courts and tribunals are correct or not. However, research suggesting the tribunals perform their enabling role well (discussed below) may be treated as indirect evidence that they are more likely than courts to pick up official errors.

Whatever difficulties may have been experienced in particular tribunals in the past, there has been no serious concern over the impartiality of tribunals in recent years. However, Leggatt did express concerns about the independence of tribunals from sponsoring departments. These have been addressed by the Tribunals, Courts and Enforcement Act 2007 which has strengthened the institutional guarantees of independence in several ways, including breaking the link with sponsoring departments by creating a new unified tribunal service, which is an executive agency of the Ministry of Justice, and extending to tribunals the duties to safeguard the independence of the Judiciary imposed on the Executive by the Constitutional Reform Act 2005.[14]

Tribunal procedures tend to be simpler than those of the ordinary courts, but they are generally perceived to satisfy the essential requirements of fair adjudication (ie, notice of the case to be met, opportunity to present one's own case, etc). It is also accepted that, in practice, tribunals generally dispose of cases more speedily than courts, at least as compared to standard court procedures rather than the simplified procedures used for low value cases. This is due to procedures being less complex than the standard procedures of the ordinary courts, and the absence of complex pleadings.

As to cost, tribunals are usually substantially cheaper to operate for the government than are courts. This greater cheapness flows from, among other things, proportionally greater use of fee-paid chairs/judges as opposed to salaried judges, and greater throughput of cases. These factors combine to produce lower unit costs per case. The lowest costs were achieved by the Appeals Service in dealing with social security appeals.[15] These were estimated in the White Paper at just under £200 per case. Legal aid costs are also lower than for courts because availability is more restricted than it is for court proceedings.

However, there may be a cost barrier for the citizen. Although there is no equivalent of court fees, and no danger of having expenses awarded against the appellant or applicant for most tribunals, the cost of legal representation may be high.[16] Without going into detail, legal aid for tribunals, particularly for representation at hearings, has been available on a much more limited basis than it has for the ordinary courts. This has been because, in the twentieth century, policy on tribunals was developed on the assumption that it was not necessary to provide legal aid for representation at tribunals because citizens ought to be able to present their own case. If this assumption is incorrect, then unless adequate

[14] See Tribunals, Courts and Enforcement Act 2007 s 1.

[15] Now absorbed into the Tribunals Service.

[16] In a recent study (Adler 2009) only about one in five (19%) of those who were represented at tribunals paid anything for it (including those represented on a 'no-win, no-fee' basis). Of those who were not represented, about one in four (26%) said that they did so because they could not afford representation.

representation, including where necessary legal representation, is funded in other ways, there is a significant accessibility problem.

The restrictions on legal aid, and variations in the coverage of other sources of advice and representation, make it essential to test the proposition that the different model of adjudication offered by tribunals makes it possible for the citizen effectively without legal, or perhaps any, representation. Academic commentators have often been highly critical of this characterisation of tribunals, arguing that it does not fit the facts for many tribunals. There are a number of reasons why it might be thought that unrepresented citizens would have difficulty representing themselves effectively before tribunals. It is certainly true that in most tribunals the procedure is straightforward, there are no technical rules of evidence, and the tone of the proceedings is less formal than in the ordinary courts. However, the approach in at least some tribunals may be adversarial and legalistic. Moreover, the substantive law may be exceedingly complex, as discussed above. It can also be argued that advocacy is a skill in its own right, and one which requires practice to develop, and that citizens vary widely in relevant personal characteristics such as intellectual capacity, educational attainment, oral and/or written communication skills and psychological and emotional attributes such as confidence and emotional fortitude.

A body of empirical research over the years (eg, Genn and Genn 1989; Genn 1994) has tended to support this critique and to suggest that unrepresented appellants are at a disadvantage, that they are less likely to achieve successful outcomes than those who are represented, that the inquisitorial approach does not in practice make up for the absence of representation, and that in any event some tribunals, notably immigration tribunals and employment tribunals, remain highly adversarial.

Until recently, this sceptical view of the claims traditionally made for tribunals has been the academic orthodoxy. However, more recent research suggests that the performance of tribunals in this regard may be improving. Thus, a study to compare the experiences of white, black and ethnic minority users of three tribunals (Genn et al 2006) found a generally high level of professionalism among the tribunal judiciary, that tribunals used a wide range of techniques to enable users to participate effectively in hearings, and that most users were able to present their cases reasonably well. However, it also found that there were differences in language, literacy, culture, education, confidence and fluency which transcended ethnic boundaries and which significantly affected users' ability to present their case, and concluded that there were limits to the ability of tribunals to compensate for users' difficulties in presenting cases. It also found that, in one of the three tribunals, unrepresented users were less likely to succeed, and ethnic minority users slightly less likely to succeed than white users.

The most recent research (Adler 2009) also questions the negative view of the enabling capacity of tribunals. Adler's research examined appeals and applications to five different tribunals: Criminal Injury Compensation Appeal Panels, Employment Tribunals, Social Security Appeals Tribunals, Special Educational

Needs and Disability Tribunals (England), and Additional Support Needs Tribunals (Scotland). It found that success rates varied according to both whether the appellant or applicant was represented and, if not, whether he or she had received pre-hearing advice, and also found considerably lower representation 'premiums' than earlier research such as that by Genn and Genn (1989). The research distinguished between the success rates of unrepresented appellants who had received pre-hearing advice and those who had not. Those who had received pre-hearing advice did significantly better: pre-hearing advice appeared to reduce the 'representation premium' substantially. The research included observations of tribunal hearings and from these were calculated an activism indicator, an interventionism measure and an enabling score. The findings of this aspect of the research may be summarised by saying that tribunals appear to have become more active, interventionist and enabling since earlier studies. Adler, therefore, argued that the decline in representation premiums is likely to be due to two factors: first, that pre-hearing advice is important and helpful to applicants/appellants (and this dimension may have been neglected in previous studies); and second, that tribunals have, in the intervening years, become much better at living up to one of their supposed aims, namely adopting a genuinely enabling approach.

Accordingly, there are grounds for believing that tribunals may be better than courts at enabling the unrepresented user to present his or her case, and that they have become better in recent years at performing the enabling role, but there also appear to be grounds for concluding that there remain significant access to justice problems for citizens, and that the enabling approach is not the complete answer to these.

Ombudsmen

Ombudsmen are generally perceived to perform well in achieving appropriate outcomes (although the measure of what is an appropriate outcome is different from courts and tribunals) and have a high reputation for impartiality and independence, fairness and the thoroughness of their procedures.[17] As regards speed, the picture is less clear cut. Examination of the targets that ombudsmen set themselves for clearing cases suggest that this is not a particularly speedy remedy, and the Parliamentary Ombudsman has in the past been criticised for applying Rolls Royce investigatory techniques regardless of whether they are necessary for achieving a remedy in the particular case, thus causing delay in processing complaints. However, many complaints are no longer subject to the full investigative process because of changes in practice. In addition, all ombudsmen now encourage 'local' resolution of disputes, most public authorities have established complaints procedures and there are now a number of 'mini-ombudsmen' such as the Adjudicator for Complaints about HM Revenue and Customs and the

[17] For a recent review, see Kirkham (2007).

Valuation Office. As a result, the statutory ombudsmen today operate very much as second- or third-tier complaints mechanisms for complaints that have not been resolved through first- or second-tier procedures. This is likely to mean that such complaints as are subject to full investigation are such as to merit detailed and thorough inquiry and to take longer. Accordingly, evaluation of speed as a dimension of performance is difficult.

As far as the citizen is concerned, ombudsmen clearly provide a low cost model of grievance redress. There is no fee for complaining, and, once a complaint is accepted, the ombudsman and the body complained against bear the cost of investigation. There is no evidence that citizens are put off complaining by worries about cost. As for cost to the government and the taxpayer, in general public sector ombudsmen publish accounts. However, they tend not to publish information on the unit costs of investigations. This makes systematic comparisons with other grievance procedures difficult, but it is generally assumed that costs per investigation are higher than they are for the more economical tribunals (White Paper: para 5.19). Having said that, it is important to compare like with like. Comparing unit costs per investigation makes most sense when comparing 'routine' complaints and 'routine' appeals. As noted above, ombudsmen have increasingly become second- or third-tier complaints handlers and so may be dealing with more complex or difficult cases. Also, an ombudsman investigation may lead to the resolution of a large number of similar disputes. Where this occurs, the costs incurred may be seen as low in relation to the value of the investigation.

Technicality of procedure and formality of tone do not appear to be major issues. As to other dimensions of accessibility, there may be issues around the extent to which the general public and/or various types of adviser are aware of the existence and role of the various ombudsmen. It has been suggested that the Parliamentary Ombudsman, in particular, does not have a sufficiently high profile (Seneviratne 1994; Kirkham 2007).

External Reviews

As indicated above, this grievance-redress mechanism was introduced amidst considerable controversy. However, an early evaluation of the review procedure was relatively positive (Dalley and Berthoud 1992) including its ability to produce appropriate outcomes, while pointing out the difficulties entailed in reaching a judgment about whether outcomes are appropriate in terms of meeting persons' needs in the context of a cash-limited social security benefit. We can also note that, in recent years, a high proportion of the decisions reviewed were changed, for example in 2007–08, 50.9 per cent of decisions were changed and this resulted in total spending of over £5.5 million from the Social Fund budgets (IRS 2008). It is clear that it is a procedure that regularly overturns official decisions.

While lacking the strong legal guarantees of independence typical of courts, tribunals and the statutory ombudsmen, the IRS has clear functional independence from the agencies whose actions it reviews and, in practice, it appears to operate in an impartial manner. As with ombudsmen, there is no evidence that the use of investigative procedures gives rise to perceptions that the procedure is unfair. Although there is no oral hearing, applicants have a significant input as, after receiving the paperwork from the local office, the inspector writes to the applicant setting out the facts relating to the relevant issues and any questions that the inspector has. The applicant then has the opportunity to comment on the case and answer any questions raised, and is invited to give the inspector any extra information that he or she thinks is important.

The process is relatively speedy compared to tribunals and ombudsmen if the normal timetable is adhered to. IRS staff have consistently met the 12-day target in more than 95 per cent of cases for budgeting loans, crisis loans and community care grants (IRS 2008). To this may be added the time taken for the papers to reach the IRS for which the average time nationally was eight days in 2007–08. Taking these facts together, the average case was disposed of within 20 days in 2007–08. The target for urgent cases is to complete the review within 24 hours. This was achieved in between 75 per cent and 94 per cent of cases depending on the month in 2007–08.

As to cost, the IRS service, like that of the statutory ombudsmen is entirely free to the applicant. The cost to the government and the taxpayer compares favourably with that for tribunals at approximately £200 per case and extremely favourably with courts (IRS 2008). From the information available, it is not clear whether there might be other problems relating to accessibility, for example, lack of visibility.

Overall, an evaluation of the effectiveness of external review by the IRS as a mechanism of redress for the citizen in dispute with public authority reveals a mainly positive picture across all criteria, although there is the possibility that there may be an issue of visibility.

Convergence Among Redress Mechanisms

The preceding sections have compared existing grievance-redress institutions and procedures for redressing grievances and evaluated their performance. Each of these alternatives was originally conceived of as offering a distinct approach to dispute resolution. In this section, I want to consider the extent to which there has already been convergence among them.

Changes in Courts

It can be argued that, in recent decades, courts have to some extent become more like tribunals as a result of the introduction of simplified forms of procedure. These have been used for resolving claims of low financial value and certain other categories of disputes. The special procedures for judicial review have already been discussed, but there are other procedures of broader scope which have been introduced with, among other aims, enabling ordinary citizens to present their own cases without the need for legal representation. The small claims procedure was introduced in England and Wales in 1973. The summary cause procedure was introduced in Scotland in 1976 and a separate small claims procedure was introduced in 1989. Reforms of a similar nature have been introduced in many other jurisdictions. The scope of the small claims procedure has been extended following the Woolf reforms (Woolf 1995, 1996) and now covers all claims with a value below £5,000. It was intended to provide a cheap and simple mechanism for resolving consumer disputes, and there are many differences between it and the traditional model of litigation. The procedure is relatively simple, there is no provision for disclosure, hearings are relatively informal with few rules restricting the availability or presentation of evidence, and experts may not be used without leave. Although legal representation is permitted, the legal costs that may be awarded are limited, and legal aid is not available to cover the cost of legal representation.

Changes in Tribunals

As noted above, the Franks Committee confirmed that tribunals were to be regarded as machinery for adjudication—a judgement that implied a degree of judicialisation—but were also expected to offer a simpler, less formal model of litigation. However, since Franks, the degree of judicialisation has been greater than Franks would have envisaged. Some of the changes pre-date the recent reorganisation of tribunals, but the reorganisation has added further twists to the judicialisation process. The former category includes extending the requirement for chairs to be legally legal qualified to tribunals in which non-lawyer chairs had previously sat, reducing the use of wing members, and increasing the use of 'paper' hearings. In the latter, may be included the 2007 Act's extension of the guarantee of judicial independence in section 3 of the Constitutional Reform Act 2005 to tribunals, applying the title 'judge' to all legally qualified members of the First-tier and Upper Tribunals,[18] and all recruitment of chairs and members being carried out by the Judicial Appointments Commission.[19]

Non-lawyer chairs had been widely used in social security appeals. Whereas tribunals dealing with national insurance benefits were chaired by lawyers, most chairs of supplementary benefit appeal tribunals (SBATs) were not legally qualified. However, the 1984 reforms which unified the formerly separate national insurance local tribunals (NILTs) and the SBATs finally eliminated non-lawyer chairs.[20] Another area in which lay chairs were widely used was taxation. Before

[18] 2007 Act s 4.

[19] Set up under the Constitutional Reform Act 2005 in order to 'select the best candidates, from a wide range of backgrounds, for appointment to the judiciary'.

[20] Health and Social Services and Socials Security Adjudication Act 1983.

the recent reorganisation, the General Commissioners of Income Tax were an exclusively lay tribunal hearing the more straightforward appeals and handling more than 25,000 cases per year. The more complex cases were left to the Special Commissioners. These and other separate tax tribunals have been rationalised into a single tax chamber within the new unified tribunal structure with effect from 1 April 2009. Although lay members transferred into the new structure, the loss of the separate jurisdiction is significant and likely to lead to a reduction in the extent to which non-lawyers chair tribunals.

Perhaps of even greater significance is the trend to reduce the role of lay members. As we have seen, the inclusion of lay members alongside lawyers was an essential feature of tribunal design. Franks justified this in terms of their expertise. In some tribunals, members had a specific technical expertise, but the requirement for technical expertise never accounted for all cases. However, it is clear that the role of lay members has long been thought by many to be an important and valuable aspect of tribunal adjudication in a variety of contexts and Leggatt's review received many representations in favour of wide use of non-lawyers (Leggatt 2001: para 7.19). The role of lay members seems to have been particularly valued in the context of social security (Wikeley 2000). Perhaps ironically this is the area in which the reduction in the role of lay members has proceeded furthest. Reforms introduced under the Social Security Act 1998 removed the need for lay members. Henceforth, tribunals required a legally qualified chair but could sit with one or two other members depending on the nature of the case. Most tribunals hearing social security appeals now consist of a legally qualified person sitting alone. The involvement of lay members in tax appeals may be further reduced as a consequence of their absorption into the new unified tribunal structure.

In fact, the whole question of the role of lay members in tribunals is under review. Both Leggatt and the White Paper raised the question of what the role of lay members in the future ought to be, and this led to a government review which reported in 2007.[21] In November 2007, the Government issued a consultation (Ministry of Justice/Tribunals Service 2007) which suggested principles for the use of non-legal members. The core principle is that 'Non-legal members are there to provide expertise. They should therefore be deployed selectively on the basis of the needs of the case'. Since then an order specifying the qualifications of non-legal members has been made.[22] Under the order, persons may be eligible by virtue of a qualification or on grounds of experience. Eligibility is broadly defined, and it remains to be seen whether, in practice, there will be a narrowing of the circumstances in which lay members are used.

I treat greater use of paper hearings as a form of convergence because one of the distinctions in practice between tribunals and courts has traditionally been that, in

[21] Summarised in Ministry of Justice/Tribunals Service (2007) *Transforming Tribunals: Implementing Part 1 of the Tribunals, Courts and Enforcement Act 2007*.

[22] The Qualifications for Appointment of Members to the First-tier Tribunal and Upper Tribunal Order 2008 SI 2008/2692.

tribunals, the normal approach has been to fix an oral hearing when the appeal is lodged, whereas in courts most cases do not result in an oral hearing on the merits, because they are settled or abandoned before that stage or are undefended. Here again, changes in the approach taken in social security appeals were introduced by the Social Security Act 1998. Since then, the appellant has had to 'opt-in' to an oral hearing and, if he or she does not do so, the case proceeds to a 'paper hearing'. This approach has continued in the social entitlement chamber of the first-tier tribunal which covers social security, child support and asylum support cases. The procedural rules state[23] that the tribunal must hold a hearing before making a decision which disposes of proceedings unless: (a) each party has consented to, or has not objected to, the matter being decided without a hearing; and (b) the tribunal considers that it is able to decide the matter without a hearing. It is also intended that the use of paper hearings will increase in tax cases and that the new consolidated procedure rules divide cases into four categories: 'default paper, basic, standard and complex'. The tribunal procedure rules[24] state that 'default paper' cases will usually be disposed of without a hearing. Whether judicialisation is the right word for this is open to question, but the move away from automatic oral hearings can be seen as a form of convergence with the ordinary courts.

Other forms of judicialisation have included the increasing complexity of procedural rules, the borrowing from the courts of procedural concepts, such as striking out, and empowering tribunals to administer the oath.

Another area in which the possibility of convergence has been created by the 2007 Act reforms is specialisation. As noted above, tribunals have tended to be more specialised than courts. Under the 2007 Act, most of the former function-specific tribunals with jurisdiction throughout Great Britain have lost their separate identity and have been replaced by a generic First-tier Tribunal and a generic Upper Tribunal. At first sight, it might appear as if tribunals are thereby becoming less specialised and thus more like the ordinary courts. But it is important to note that the new First-tier Tribunal is not a generic first instance administrative tribunal and the new Upper Tribunal is not a generic appellate administrative tribunal. How significant the change will be in terms of judicial specialisation remains to be seen. The First-tier Tribunal will, when fully operational, be divided into six chambers by subject matter and the Upper tribunal into four chambers (see Thompson's chapter in this volume).[25] But it is unlikely that judges and members will sit in all classes of cases within a chamber.

The jurisdiction of judges and members and, hence, their degree of specialisation is determined by the application of the processes of 'ticketing' and assignment. Ticketing is the process whereby judges are authorised to sit in particular classes of cases *within* a chamber. Assignment is the process whereby a judge already

[23] The Tribunal Procedure (First-tier Tribunal) (Social Entitlement Chamber) Rules 2008 SI 2008/2685.

[24] The Tribunal Procedure (First-tier Tribunal) (Tax Chamber) Rules 2009 SI 2009/273.

[25] See also Carnwath (2009).

authorised to sit in one chamber is authorised to sit in a different chamber (Ministry of Justice/Tribunals Service 2007). These processes are intended to deliver the benefits to be expected from rationalisation (for example, greater consistency, and more flexibility in the deployment of judges and members) while retaining an appropriate degree of specialisation to ensure a high level of expertise on the part of judges and members. However, it is understood that, at the time of writing, the great majority of tribunal judges continue to sit exclusively in their former jurisdictions, and that certain practical difficulties are being encountered which may limit the extent to which tribunal judges are ticketed for, or assigned to, new areas. Accordingly, it is not yet clear whether the way judges are deployed under the new system will be substantially different from the way in which they were deployed under the former system. If there is to be no great difference in the way judges are deployed, then we will in practice continue to have (at least as regards judges and members) a specialised and differentiated tribunal system operating under the guise of a rationalised system.

A slightly different form of convergence arises from the push towards alternative dispute resolution (ADR). Encouraging parties and courts to consider ADR was an important aspect of the Woolf reforms and the Civil Procedure Rules positively encourage the use of ADR, for example, mediation, although as yet it appears that only a small proportion of potential litigants consider or use ADR.[26] Encouragement of ADR has also been built into the new unified tribunal service. The White Paper stated that the new unified tribunal system would have a broad remit to improve administrative justice under the rubric of proportionate dispute resolution. This aim has been carried forward into the 2007 Act. The Senior President of Tribunals has a duty in carrying out his functions to have regard to, among other things, 'the need to develop innovative methods of resolving disputes that are of a type that may be brought before tribunals'[27] and it is recognised that procedural rules for tribunals may make provision for mediation, although only with the consent of the parties.[28]

It does appear, therefore, that there has been significant convergence between courts and tribunals in recent years by virtue of changes to tribunals. It is important to note that these changes have been unevenly distributed and have not applied to all tribunals. Before the 2007 Act, policy on tribunals was developed separately for each tribunal or group of tribunals by the sponsoring department. As yet, the changes in courts and tribunals fall a long way short of eliminating the difference between them and the way they perform their task of adjudication. However, we can see certain trends occurring in both and the contrasts between them are less substantial than they were.

[26] This is true both of civil litigation generally (Genn 1998, 2007; MacDonald 2004) and of judicial review cases (Bondy and Mulcahy 2009).

[27] 2007 Act s 2(3).

[28] Ibid s 24.

Changes in Ombudsmen and External Reviews

The main point of convergence between ombudsmen on the one hand and courts and tribunals on the other relates to the status of ombudsmen's reports. As noted above, it was regarded as an essential feature of the principal statutory ombudsman schemes that they had no power to impose a remedy or enforce their decisions. However, the Court of Appeal's recent ruling in *R (Bradley and Others) v Secretary of State for Work and Pensions*[29] has enhanced the status of ombudsmen's reports. This was one of those rare cases in which a public body refused to accept an ombudsman's report: the Department for Work and Pensions had disputed both the findings and the recommendations of the Parliamentary Ombudsman's report into the Occupational Pensions Affair. The Court of Appeal held that public bodies are not entitled to dismiss ombudsmen's findings without good reason, and found the departmental response to the report to be, in part, illegal. This decision suggests that even if public bodies are inclined to dispute an ombudsman's decision, they will in future find it hard to do so. This is not the same as making ombudsmen's decisions binding either as to whether there has been injustice caused by maladministration or as to remedies but it is a significant change.

We have also seen that inquisitorial methods (one of the defining features of ombudsmen) can be combined with the authority to make binding decisions both in the case of some private sector ombudsmen and the IRS for the Social Fund. However, both Ombudsmen and the IRS remain substantially different from courts and tribunals by virtue of their methods and the public sector ombudsmen's lack of power to make binding decisions.

Convergence: Summary

This section has considered convergence between the various redress mechanisms in the UK in recent years. In the next section, I consider the implications of that convergence for the future development of redress mechanisms in the light of the aims of administrative justice.

The Implications of Convergence: The Way Forward for Administrative Justice

The set of grievance-handling institutions and procedures in the UK is relatively complex by comparison to those in some other jurisdictions. In France, for example, there is a system of general-purpose administrative courts[30] and, as a result,

[29] [2007] EWCA 242 (Admin).

[30] The Tribunaux Administrative, Cours Administrative d'Appel and the Conseil D'Etat.

there has not been a proliferation of *ad hoc* tribunals.[31] The balance of work as between institutions also differs from some overseas comparators, for example, in Norway, tribunals are not well developed, there is little resort to litigation in matters of public administration and ombudsmen play a larger role than in the UK (Buck 2004). In fact, reviewing other jurisdictions reveals a wide variety of ways of structuring mechanisms for redressing grievances against the state. We have also seen that the UK has neither evolved nor applied consistently clear principles for the allocation of jurisdiction to different grievance redress mechanisms, and that there has been significant convergence among the various institutions in certain respects. The UK experience also provides a wealth of evidence on the advantages and disadvantages of different forms of grievance-redress procedures. Taken together, these points raise the question of whether existing arrangements make sense and whether the current institutional boundaries and differences of approach are sustainable. Do we, for example, need such a variety of grievance redress mechanisms? Is there scope for rationalisation either within types of redress mechanisms as is already happening with tribunals or across them? Are some better at resolving citizen's grievances than others? What is the way forward in the UK context?

Accordingly, in this section of this chapter, I address a few over-arching issues relating to redress of grievances. I will not attempt to present a detailed blueprint for the future structure of redress mechanisms, but instead sketch out some possible ways forward which do not take existing institutions for granted. Before doing that, I shall make a number of preliminary points. First, in looking for the way forward, it is important to start from the right place. I shall treat it as being a matter of consensus that the aims of a system of administrative justice ought to be as stated in the White Paper, that is: getting it right first time; putting mistakes right; and learning from mistakes. This chapter has been mainly about the second of these but, if the aims are to be pursued in a coherent manner, mechanisms for the redress of grievances should be designed so as to encourage learning from mistakes in order to enhance the prospects of getting it right first time so far as so doing is consistent with their primary aim of correcting mistakes.

Second, it is important that proposals for the redress of grievances should be sensitive to context. There are no invariant procedures of administrative justice. One cannot apply a uniform set of procedural principles across the board (a point also made by Adler in his chapter in this volume). The application of a highly specific set of principles (eg, that appeals must always involve oral hearings)[32] to all areas of public administration would be a backward step because it would fail to take account of the features peculiar to each context in public

[31] However, some matters are considered by specialist tribunals (social security, taxation, professional discipline), although these are often regarded as 'private law' matters and are, therefore, supervised by the civil courts. See Brown and Bell (1998).

[32] Richardson and Genn (2007) provide a valuable analysis of the advantages and disadvantages of oral hearings, and discussion of when oral hearings are appropriate.

administration (Ison 1999) and thus risk failing to provide an effective means of redressing grievances. Ison suggests that the significance of any particular principle of administrative justice cannot be seen in isolation from factors such as the structure and nature of policy making and rule making in that area, budgeting and finance, appointments, organisational culture, political and economic pressures, and methods of decision making. The likely effect of applying a particular principle cannot, therefore, be assessed without detailed knowledge of the specific administrative context. Therefore, he argues (ibid: 33) that administrative justice should be seen 'not as a subject on its own, and not as a rationale for some controlling overlordship, but as a body of thought that can be drawn upon in the design of a particular system, such as income tax, social security, the regulation of road transport, or occupational health.'

In deciding what the appropriate initial decision-making methods are, regard must be had to the goals of that area of public policy, the roles of the agencies charged with implementing them, and the environment in which they operate. In deciding on the appropriate redress mechanisms, regard must be had to the prior decisions about policies and initial decision making. Thus, for example, an administrative system which relies heavily on professional judgment and experience may require a different approach to redress from one in which decisions are made according to detailed rules. This does not mean that we cannot adopt general principles of administrative justice or attempt to generalise structures and processes (for example, creating a unified tribunal service), but we must ensure that general principles are not applied regardless of context resulting in a rigid 'one-size-fits-all' approach to the redress of grievances.

Third, there is the broader contextual question of what can be made to work in the UK. We have to consider our political and legal traditions, and whether any proposals for departures from them would produce strains and tensions that might undermine the goal of improving the redress of grievances. Arrangements that have worked in other jurisdictions may not be easy to transplant because the cultural presuppositions in the UK are different (Alison 1996).

Fourth, having emphasised the difference between expert representation and enabling models for the redress of grievances, I suggest that there are strong considerations of principle that favour the latter model. Citizens have positive entitlements to certain benefits and services from public bodies and negative entitlements not to suffer impositions and penalties other than those prescribed by law. Where benefits or services are wrongly denied or penalties or burdens wrongly imposed, then the public bodies concerned have failed in their primary mission. When such errors occur, matters should be put right with as little inconvenience to the citizen as possible. It should not be necessary to hire expensive lawyers or to endure long delays in order to gain redress. If arrangements can be developed which do not rely on expert representation but are at least as effective as the traditional adversarial approach of the courts in providing redress of grievances, then those should be preferred. Of course, the enabling approach has not always worked well in the past, either because it has been employed in the wrong contexts, or because it has not been adequately implemented, but there should be scope for more effective deployment of the enabling approach in future.

Fifth, any proposals for reform will have to take account of legal constraints. The courts have long applied the principles of natural justice to impose procedural requirements additional to those expressly mentioned in legislation. The requirements of natural justice could always be excluded by clearly drafted legislation. However, Article 6 of the ECHR imposes obligations of procedural fairness which are broadly similar to the requirements of natural justice.[33] It provides that in the determination of their civil rights and obligations persons are entitled to a fair and public hearing within a reasonable time by an independent and impartial tribunal established by law. These obligations are more difficult to exclude because of the terms of the Human Rights Act 1998 and because failure to observe them would be a breach of international obligations. It is neither appropriate nor necessary to engage in a full analysis of the jurisprudence under Article 6. It suffices to say that it does place significant constraints on the design of remedial systems in cases in which entitlements are conferred or burdens imposed by law. However, it is clear that the Article 6 requirements need not be satisfied by all grievance redress procedures, and that the initial remedy need not be article 6 compliant provided that somewhere in the system, there is the opportunity for the citizen to test the decision in a judicial forum, that is, one that is independent and impartial and makes binding decisions. Accordingly, even if a review procedure is not itself compliant, if there is a clear right of appeal to a court or tribunal then that is sufficient for the purposes of Article 6. Article 6, therefore, constrains but does not prevent experimentation with grievance redress procedures.

Inquisitorial and Adversarial Techniques

Given the approach I have taken to analysing redress of grievances, it makes sense to consider procedures before institutions. As indicated above, a number of different models for the redress of grievance have been deployed in the UK. The evidence we have as to how existing procedures operate suggests that more use should be made of inquisitorial techniques, which have proved quite successful in correcting errors by public bodies. Tribunals seem to have become better at enabling unrepresented appellants to present their cases effectively. More significantly, both ombudsmen and the IRS, using more thoroughly inquisitorial approaches, uphold a high proportion of complaints and requests for review. Among the advantages of the inquisitorial approach of ombudsmen and the IRS are that it eliminates the cost barrier to the citizen of obtaining a remedy and that its fact-finding advantages. One reason for this is that they are entitled to demand production of all the relevant information in the hands of the public body whose decision is being investigated.

[33] For a comparative analysis, see Craig (2003).

Looking to the future, there would also be more scope for using informal and speedy approaches to information gathering such as the telephone, a technique which has been used to good effect by the Financial Ombudsman Service. This might assist with early resolution of many disputes. However, in a system with an adversarial ethic such innovations in gathering evidence may be difficult to implement if they are thought not to satisfy the requirements of procedural fairness.

One possible approach to operationalising the greater use of investigative techniques would be to combine the external review of decisions with an appeal to a tribunal. This has been suggested by both Berthoud and Bryson (1997), in the context of social security disputes, and Ison (1999) as a more general technique in high volume administrative systems. Drawing on the experience of the Social Fund, a possible structure that might be applied in a range of administrative contexts in which legal rights are determined is, therefore, as follows:

Stage 1 The claimant lodges an appeal with a tribunal and, at the same time, the appeal is passed to an external/independent inspector; the tribunal sets a date for the hearing.

Stage 2 The inspector obtains the file, contacts the claimant and carries out a review; the inspector has the power to change the decision and will do so if he or she thinks it is appropriate.

Stage 3 If the inspector decides in favour of appellant, the hearing is cancelled. If he or she decides in favour of the agency, the inspector writes to the appellant, giving the decision and the reasons for it; the appellant may then withdraw the appeal but is not obliged to do so.

Stage 4 Assuming that the claimant wishes to proceed, the hearing will take place and the tribunal will deliver its decision.

Among the advantages of this way of proceeding are that the procedure is more likely to uncover relevant information than one which is reliant solely on an oral hearing, that it will not delay appeals, and that it should reduce the number of tribunal hearings overall by filtering out appeals which are bound to succeed or likely to fail. Grievance chasers who employ investigative techniques should also be better placed to provide useful feedback to first-instance decision makers. Given their greater access, as compared to courts or tribunals, to the files and the possibility of entering into dialogue with first-instance decision makers they should be better able to identify the reasons why bad decisions are made and the measures that are required to improve the quality of decision making. A further advantage of such arrangements is that they would comply with Article 6 of the ECHR, because the right of appeal to an independent judicial body is preserved.

Clearly, there is room for discussion concerning the precise details of any such proposal, and there may be practical difficulties in realising the suggested benefits. Among other things, it will be important to guard against 'claimant fatigue'. It is probably an approach that would only work well in certain contexts. However, trying to combine inquisitorial and adversarial techniques does seem a promising avenue to explore.

Alternative Dispute Resolution

The term 'alternative dispute resolution' has always referred to alternatives to the courts. Since tribunals, ombudsmen and inquiries have all been developed as alternatives to the courts, it could be said that ADR has always been central to administrative justice. However, the development of ADR as a mode of dispute resolution has been carried out primarily against the backdrop of private law disputes. Most public lawyers and other members of the administrative justice community have not, until recently, engaged in the ADR debate or considered the application of certain ADR techniques, notably mediation, to public law disputes.[34] However, the White Paper was careful to list the full menu of possible dispute resolution techniques and to suggest that there is room for greater use of these techniques in the public sector. Do they have anything to offer to administrative justice?

Of the list of techniques in the White Paper, adjudication and ombudsmen have already been discussed. Arbitration usually implies that the parties consent to take part. Apart from that it does not seem offer anything distinct from the formal/adversarial and informal/enabling models of adjudication offered by courts and tribunals.

Mediation involves an independent third party helping the parties in dispute to reach a voluntary and mutually-agreed resolution. It is the parties and not the mediator who determine the outcome. Mediation is usually interest-based, in the sense that it focuses on the needs and interests of the parties rather than on questions of rights or legal entitlements. Conciliation is similar to mediation, except that the conciliator offers an opinion on the settlement of the dispute (White Paper: para 2.11). There are limitations on the appropriate use of these techniques. Given the possibility of compromise, they are not appropriate in that class of citizen v state disputes in which disputes arise over legal entitlements and obligations. Citizens should not be encouraged to settle for less that they are entitled to. There are also concerns over the imbalances of power between citizen and state likely to exist in many contexts (Adler 2006). However, there may be contexts in which such concerns do not apply with the same force, and in which mediation or conciliation would be appropriate. For example, a three-way mediation might be of assistance in a neighbour dispute in which one or both neighbours was dissatisfied with the actions of a public sector landlord in responding to the dispute as well as being in dispute with each other. A second might be certain situations in which a public body has a high degree of discretion as to the provision it makes to meet a need, for example, for special educational needs (Harris and Smith 2009).

[34] For an exception, see the research by Bondy and Mulcahy (2009) into mediation in judicial review cases.

There also appear to be significant opportunities for effective use of mediation in the planning context (Scottish Government 2009b).[35]

In early neutral evaluation (ENE), an independent person assesses the claims made by each side, and gives an opinion on the strengths and weaknesses of each side's case and the likely outcome if the case proceeds to formal adjudication. Participation is voluntary and the parties are free to ignore the evaluator's opinion and to proceed with their claim. The benefits claimed for ENE include earlier resolution of disputes and cost savings through having fewer tribunal hearings. The Tribunals Service has established an Early Dispute Resolution Project designed to examine whether such alternative forms of dispute resolution 'can provide more efficient and effective remedies at lower cost and with less pressure on users' (Ministry of Justice/Tribunals Service 2007) and has funded two pilots. One involved voluntary judicial mediation in employment tribunals and the other examined whether a form or early neutral evaluation could be effective as a means of dealing with some Disability Living Allowance and Attendance Allowance appeals that would otherwise be resolved by an appeal to a tribunal. The results of evaluation of both projects are awaited. While it would be prudent to await the outcome of research, it is arguable that the aims of ENE, at least in the context of high volume administrative systems, could be better met by the kind of hybrid review/appeal system described above. That system has the advantages of producing a definite decision at the review stage and may well be better at fact-finding because of the nature of the investigative process. Also, as indicated above, it may be better adapted to providing feedback to initial decision makers.

In negotiation, the parties deal directly with each other and attempt to reach an agreed solution. They negotiate either in person or via a representative. It is a voluntary process and the outcome is not binding unless a formal agreement has been concluded. While negotiation takes place in certain regulatory contexts, outside those contexts, negotiation between citizen and state has not been systematically studied, and so it is difficult to evaluate its possible contribution to administrative justice. Concerns about citizens settling for less than they are entitled to and about imbalances of power apply here too. In addition, the ultra vires principle places significant constraints on the use of negotiation. Public bodies may not negotiate outcomes which conflict with their statutory mandates. Accordingly, while we must be open to all the possibilities for redressing grievances, it does not seem likely that ADR techniques will contribute to administrative justice except in a rather limited range of contexts.

Institutional Boundaries: Sustaining the Distinctions

Despite its apparent complexity, I suggest that the institutional structure could be broadly as in Table 1, with four main institutions and styles of decision making. These would be: (a) courts mainly offering formal/adversarial adjudication;

[35] Available at www.scotland.gov.uk/Publications/2009/03/10154116/0.

(b) tribunals offering informal/enabling adjudication; (c) ombudsman operating thoroughly inquisitorial methods leading to recommendations; and (d) external review operating thoroughly inquisitorial methods leading binding decisions. This would not be radically different from current arrangements but there could still be significant change within this broad framework, for example, the rationalisation of tribunals that is currently taking place.

Courts and Tribunals

Despite the convergence mentioned above, the distinction between courts and tribunals continues to be sustainable. This is, first, because there is an important role for the informal/enabling style of adjudication within the system of administrative justice. There is a principled case to be made for having remedies that the citizen can operate without having to rely on representation by lawyers. This requires the existence of an informal, enabling model of adjudication, but this has been imperfectly delivered in the past for a variety of reasons. It should be made a clear goal of policy to develop that approach. This means that the training of judges and tribunal members should include training on how to enable users of courts and tribunals to present their cases. It also means ensuring that there is adequate provision of advice (not necessarily by lawyers) as the research evidence on the success of tribunals in their enabling role suggests that pre-hearing advice makes a substantial difference to success rates for appellants.

However, picking up on the point made above about the importance of context, even with improved provision of advice, the enabling approach to adjudication will not always guarantee justice. Sometimes, representation will be necessary, and sometimes that will have to be specifically legal representation. Immigration control provides a good example. Appeals are dealt with by tribunals, the procedure is relatively straightforward as compared to the courts operating in Rolls Royce mode, but immigration tribunals in practice operate very differently from many other tribunals. The whole tone of proceedings is highly adversarial with witnesses frequently being subject to hostile cross-examination and credibility often being an issue (Genn and Genn 1989). It is also important to note that the stakes for appellants can be very high (removal from the UK, separation from family and sometimes risk to life). In such an environment, expert representation for the appellant is very necessary. The case for this was accepted a number of years ago, public funds are available and appellants are routinely represented.

However, in addition to providing public funding for certain forms of proceeding in which it is deemed generally appropriate, there needs to be provision for representation even in contexts in which representation is not required as a matter of routine, for particular individuals who might have particular difficulties coping with the demands of presenting their own cases, for example, because of learning difficulties.[36]

[36] A point recognised both by Leggatt (2001: para 4.22) and the White Paper (para 10.1).

That of course is to make the case for having an informal/enabling model of adjudication as well as a formal/adversarial model. Whether we require separate institutions to offer them is another question. In theory, the current distinction between courts and tribunals could be abolished and the jurisdiction currently exercised by tribunals transferred to the ordinary courts. The courts could then be structured so as to employ either formal adversarial adjudication or informal enabling adjudication in different contexts, as appropriate. However, there are a number of arguments in favour of maintaining the present distinction. First, relying exclusively on the ordinary courts to hear all appeals against official decisions would be likely to be disproportionately costly. Secondly, there is the question of how specialisation of the judiciary is handled. Modern legal systems require a substantial degree of specialisation if judges' claims to expertise in the law are to be credible.[37] It would not be reasonable to add social security cases, immigration cases and tax cases to the existing remits of the average county court judge or sheriff and for them to have appropriate levels of legal expertise in all these areas on top of the areas they are currently familiar with. The need for expertise in the relevant law is even more important where the adjudicator is expected to perform an enabling role to assist unrepresented appellants as opposed to being adversarial.

Thirdly, it may be easier for a separate system of tribunals to play a significant role in giving feedback to decision makers as compared to the ordinary courts. Courts have traditionally paid little attention either to the implementation of specific decisions or to the broader impact of their decisions. In most cases, once a case has been decided, the court can forget about it. If a decision has not been put into effect it is generally up to the 'injured' party to decide whether to take the matter further, for example by taking steps to enforce a decree for payment, but courts do not take the initiative in following up their decisions. Far less are they concerned that a specific decision which has been quashed is only one of many in which the same error has been made. It is not the function of the court to ensure that the agency concerned changes its approach in all similar cases. The functions of examining the whole case load for patterns, and providing feedback for decision makers are perhaps more easily incorporated within a separate tribunal system, particularly in view of the fact that specialisation ought to enhance the ability of tribunal judges to perform this role. However, ensuring that feedback actually improves initial decision making may prove to be a difficult task. Existing mechanisms have not been particularly successful.

There remains the question of how to allocate jurisdiction between courts and tribunals. Space does not permit this to be considered at length here. However, there is almost certainly some room for the reallocation of disputes as between courts and tribunals and perhaps also for re-organisation within the court system. One appreciates the historical reasons why judicial review has been

[37] Small jurisdictions may find operating specialised systems more onerous.

restricted to the superior courts,[38] but there may be a case for creating a similar broad jurisdiction in the lower courts to deal with grievances for which no statutory rights of appeal exist.

Ombudsmen

There are good reasons for maintaining the existence of ombudsmen and their separation from courts and tribunals, which reflect the important distinction between those grievances that refer to questions of legal right and legal obligations and those which refer to complaints about other administrative defects. A key part of the rationale for creation of public sector ombudsmen in the UK was that they could deal with complaints of the latter sort. That meant that they could employ different decision criteria from the courts (maladministration/injustice rather than illegality). Courts have no expertise which fits them to apply these criteria and questions of legitimacy would arise if they intervened on that basis. Moreover, the investigative methods employed by ombudsmen are very different from those traditionally employed by the courts. It was also deemed to be crucial that ombudsmen should not have the same powers of enforcement as courts and tribunals so that the relationship between them and administrative agencies could remain co-operative rather than adversarial. If the functions of ombudsmen were transferred to courts that can make binding decisions, they might not receive the same level of co-operation.

Equally, and for similar reasons, ombudsmen, as currently organised, could not replace courts or tribunals as the primary remedy for administrative injustice including claims based on entitlement. Courts and tribunals have the necessary expertise and are Article 6 compliant. However, as suggested above, there is scope for making more use of ombudsman-type inquisitorial procedures along the lines of the IRS for the Social Fund but the key thing is that the institutions operating these procedures should be separate from both the courts and the principal statutory ombudsmen. As subject-specific remedies they would be able to develop considerable expertise in their subject matter that would enhance their ability to identify systemic problems and provide feedback.

However, that does not mean that the relationship between ombudsmen, on the one hand, and judicial remedies, on the other, should not change at all. While the primary remedy in relation to matters of legal right should probably continue to be an appeal to an independent adjudicator, the existing presumption against ombudsmen investigating complaints in respect of which the complainer has a legal remedy should be relaxed to leave it more up to the judgement of ombudsmen whether to begin an investigation, especially where the remedy might lie in a court rather than a tribunal. There are a number of reasons why this might be a

[38] As a result of the Tribunals, Courts and Enforcement Act 2007 Act, a significant number of judicial review cases are in future likely to be heard in the Upper Tribunal.

useful development. First, a citizen's complaint about the way he or she has been treated may well raise questions both of legality and of administrative shortcomings. All elements of such complaints could then be dealt with in a single process. Second, the citizen may not be aware of whether his complaint has a legal remedy, particularly where the only potential remedy is judicial review. Third, assuming the effect of the relaxation of the presumption is to divert some cases away from the courts, the resolution of the case may be less costly to the public purse, taking all costs into account, than if it went to court, though much will depend on the circumstances of each case. Under this system, ombudsmen would have to work out criteria for deciding when to invoke the broader discretion that they would be given to investigate complaints notwithstanding that the complainer has a right of appeal or a right to seek judicial review, but this should not pose insuperable problems for the existing statutory ombudsmen who have built up great experience of public administration that could inform this judgment.

Conclusion

In conclusion, what I have argued in this chapter is that the UK has developed a number of different approaches to redress of grievances, each of which has contrasting features and each of which has certain advantages and disadvantages. The existing allocation of jurisdiction is neither wholly rational nor wholly irrational. The distinctions between the main forms of grievance redress remain tenable and each has a significant role to play in the future of administrative justice in the UK.

References

Adler, M (2003) 'A Socio-Legal Approach to Administrative Justice' 25 *Law and Policy* 323.
—— (2006) 'Tribunal Reform: Proportionate Dispute Resolution and the Pursuit of Administrative Justice' 69 MLR 958.
—— (2009) 'Tribunals Ain't What They Used To Be' in ADJUST Newsletter (March), available at www.ajtc.gov.uk/publications/publications.htm.
Allison, JWF (1996) *A Continental Distinction in the Common Law* (Oxford, Oxford University Press).
Arthurs, HW (1985) *'Without the Law': Administrative Justice and Legal Pluralism in Nineteenth Century England* (Toronto, University of Toronto Press).
Berthoud, R and Bryson, A (1997) 'Social Security Appeals: What do the claimants want?' 4 *Journal of Social Security Law* 17.
Bondy, V and Mulcahy, L (2009) *Mediation and Judicial Review: An empirical research study* (London, Public Law Project).
Bondy, V and Sunkin, M (2009) *The Dynamics of Judicial Review Litigation* (London, Public Law Project).

Bowman, Sir Jeffery (2000) *Review of the Crown Office List* (London, Lord Chancellor's Department).

Brown, N and Bell, J (1998) *French Administrative Law*, 5th edn (Oxford, Clarendon Press).

Buck, T (2004) *European Methods of Administrative Law Redress: Netherlands, Norway and Germany* (London, Department for Constitutional Affairs).

—— (2009, Third Edition) *The Social Fund: Law and Practice* (London, Sweet & Maxwell).

Carnwath, Sir Robert, 'Tribunal Justice—a New Start' 2009 PL 48.

Council on Tribunals (1986) *Social Security: Abolition of Independent Appeals under the Proposed Social Fund* (Special Report) Cmnd 9722 (London, HMSO).

Craig, P (2008) *Administrative Law*, 6th edn (London, Sweet & Maxwell).

—— (2003) 'The Human Rights Act, Article 6 and Procedural Rights' 2003 PL 753.

Dalley, G and Berthoud, R (1992) *Challenging Discretion: the Social Fund Review Procedure* (London, Policy Studies Institute).

Department for Constitutional Affairs (2004) *Transforming Public Services: Complaints, Redress and Tribunals* Cm 264 (London: HMSO), available at www.dca.gov.uk/pubs/adminjust/transformfull.pdf.

Franks Committee (1957) *Report of the Committee on Administrative Tribunals and Inquiries* Cmnd 218 (London: HMSO).

Fuller, L (1978) 'The Forms and Limits of Adjudication' 92 *Harvard Law Review* 353.

Genn, H (1994) 'Tribunal Review of Administrative Decision-Making' in G Richardson and H Genn (eds), *Administrative Law and Government Action* (Oxford, Clarendon Press).

—— (1998) *Central London County Court Mediation Scheme: Evaluation Report* (London, Lord Chancellor's Department).

—— (1999) *Paths To Justice: What People Do and Think about Going to Law* (Oxford, Hart Publishing).

Genn, H and Genn, Y (1989) *Representation at Tribunals* (London, Lord Chancellor's Department).

Genn, H, Lever, B and Gray, L (2006) *Tribunals for Diverse Users* (London, Department for Constitutional Affairs).

Genn, H, Fenn, P, Mason, M, Lane, A, Bechai, N, Gray, L and Vencappa, D (2007) *Twisting arms: court referred and court linked mediation under judicial pressure* Research Series 1/07 (London, Ministry of Justice).

Harris, N and Smith, E (2009) 'Resolving Disputes about Special Educational Needs and Provision in England' *Education Law Journal* 113.

Independent Review Service (2008) *The Social Fund Commissioner's Annual Report 2007/2008* (Leeds, Corporate Development Services), available at www.irs-review.org.uk/infocent/reports/ar0708/irsrep0708.pdf.

Ison, T (1999) 'Administrative Justice: Is it Such a Good Idea?' in M Harris and M Partington (eds), *Administrative Justice in the 21st Century* (Oxford, Hart Publishing).

Kirkham, R/Parliamentary and Health Service Ombudsman (2007) *Withstanding the Test of Time* 4th Report, 2006–2007, HC 421 (London, The Stationery Office).

Leggatt, Sir Andrew (2001) *Tribunals for Users—One System, One Service* (London, Lord Chancellor's Department).

MacDonald, F (2004) *The Use of Mediation to Settle Civil Justice Disputes: A Review of Evidence* (Edinburgh, Scottish Executive).

Ministry of Justice/Tribunals Service (2007) *Transforming Tribunals: Implementing Part 1 of the Tribunals, Courts and Enforcement Act 2007*, available at www.justice.gov.uk/consultations/cp3007.htm.

Mullen, T (1989) 'The Social Fund—Cash Limiting Social Security' 52 MLR 64.

National Audit Office (2005) *Citizen Redress: What citizens can do if things go wrong with public services* 2004–05, HC 21 (London, The Stationery Office), available at www.nao.org.uk/publications/0405/citizen_redress.aspx.

Partington, M and Kirton-Darling, E (2007) *Research Issues Paper (1): Feedback* (London: Tribunals Service).

Richardson, G (1994) *Law, Process and Custody* (London, Weidenfeld and Nicolson).

Richardson, G and Genn, H (2007) 'Tribunals in Transition: Resolution or Adjudication' PL 116.

Robson, WA (1951) *Justice and Administrative Law: A Study of the British Constitution* (London, Stevens).

Seneviratne, M (1994) *The Public Sector Ombudsmen* (Buckingham, Open University Press).

Wikeley, N (2000) 'Burying Bell: Managing the Judicialisation of Social Security Tribunals' 63 MLR 475.

Woolf, Rt Hon Lord (1995) *Access to Justice: Interim Report* (London, Lord Chancellor's Department), available at www.dca.gov.uk/civil/interim/woolf.htm.

—— (1996) *Access to Justice: Final Report* (London, Lord Chancellor's Department), available at www.dca.gov.uk/civil/final/index.htm.

17

Joining Up Citizen Redress in UK Central Government

PATRICK DUNLEAVY, SIMON BASTOW,
JANE TINKLER, SOFIA GOLDCHLUK AND ED TOWERS

Introduction

The concept of 'citizen redress' is a complex one. Starting from a mistake or error in delivering a public service to someone, redress implies:

— *providing a remedy*, so that a reversible harm done to a citizen is removed; or
— *reparation* is provided for a harm that cannot now be reversed (and for any extra costs incurred by the citizen in securing a remedy or reparation);
— in such a way that *justice* is visibly provided to the citizen.

But in addition, effective redress must provide:

— *correction* of the factors that led to the initial mistake, including;
— *reform* of any administrative processes forming part of the root causes of the initial failure, plus;
— a clear public *apology* for the error, as an outward sign of the organisation having learned appropriate lessons to prevent future repetitions.

Five of the terms italicised above are offered as synonyms in dictionary definitions of redress (the exception being 'apology'). From the evidence of focus groups with UK citizens conducted in 2003–04,[1] we know that the same is true about how ordinary citizens understand the concept of 'putting things right' in their dealings with government and other public sector agencies (Bartholomeou et al 2005; Dunleavy et al 2005). If something goes wrong (as people see it) in one of their dealings with government, their primary concern is to get it recognised and corrected as quickly, effectively and as cheaply as possible (in terms of the time, costs and effort involved in securing rectification).

[1] Four focus groups with citizens were undertaken by the research team as part of fieldwork for the *Citizen Redress* undertaken for the National Audit Office (NAO 2005). We used three scenarios to work through practical examples of how participants had complained or might complain.

Yet although citizens have a 'joined-up' view of redress, this is not how UK administrative law or culture currently sees things. In their contacts with government, citizens must instead quickly learn that there are multiple types and channels of redress, each of which is run by a different body or section, according to different rules and definitions and using different procedures. It often seems to require the equivalent of a PhD in (old-fashioned) public administration to understand and activate successfully the processes put in place. Worse still, redress processes are generally slow-moving, paper-bound and pretty ineffective in getting things put right. At the same time, the proliferation of bodies providing some form of rectification service has now built up into a substantial 'redress sector', or perhaps more bluntly put a 'redress industry', whose costs to taxpayers now comfortably exceed £1.5 billion a year across the public sector. Beset by signs that the redress industry is providing a lousy service at high cost, the government has constantly reorganised it, with some redress arrangements (notably those in the NHS and in the information arena) in a near-constant state of flux in recent years. Constant reorganisations have further compounded citizens' difficulties in understanding what rights and entitlements they may have to receive a decent standard of service. In the NHS and the information/privacy sphere, no sooner have new procedures been put in place than they have been replaced, supplemented or cross-cut by new ones.

In this chapter we focus chiefly on central government services, drawing especially on the information in the National Audit Office study of *Citizen Redress* (Dunleavy et al 2005). We have updated the data in that study to refer to more recent years from publicly available sources and so can comment briefly on the trends and patterns that have become evident since that report was published, at which time its recommendations were largely left un-acted upon. Although a wider study of all redress processes in the UK is ongoing, we retain a focus here on redress in UK and English national government, the issues covered in the NAO report. We consider chiefly:

- — the scale and chronic nature of large-scale redress problems in the UK;
- — the mismatch between what citizens expect to get and actually do get from redress experiences; and
- — some joined-up remedies that might offer opportunities to make quantum improvements in citizen redress processes in the future.

But first we begin by stressing the intellectual and conceptual need to break out of highly siloed official views of redress, which are also promoted (for understandable but nonetheless self-interested reasons) by the 'redress industry' itself.

Joining Up How We Think About 'Citizen Redress'

As defined above, the concept of 'citizen redress' was used in the NAO report to cover all the ways in which people may try to rectify what they regard as mistakes made by government agencies or public services. In 2005 we regarded this as covering:

— complaints;
— appeals against decisions;
— cases handled by ombudsmen (and some mediators and independent case-reviewers), which usually comprise a tiny sub-set of complaints; and
— legal cases before the courts questioning or seeking review of administrative decisions.

It is important to note that the *Citizen Redress* report did not cover the following large areas of complaints and appeals activities:

— the National Health Service (outside the national level agencies);
— the armed forces (outside the Ministry of Defence);
— devolved governments in Scotland, Wales and Northern Ireland;
— local government;
— sub-national police complaints and appeals;
— legal aid costs attaching to these areas.

We cannot yet hazard a guess as to what the overall scale and costs of redress services including those in sub-national government may be. But we can suggest that the numbers of redress cases involved and the level of costs to taxpayers are certain to be very substantial.

However, we now recognise that even our would-be comprehensive view of redress was itself too institutionally limited. The *Independent Review of Regulation, Audit, Inspection and Complaints Handling of Public Services in Scotland* (Crerar 2007) was the first analysis to go wider than *Citizen Redress,* because it included all the bodies above but pointed out that citizens now extensively turn also to regulators in order to try and get complaints acted upon. For instance, suppose that my child is studying German 'A' level and the school sixth form loses its main German teacher through illness, leaving the students to be looked after poorly by a succession of temporary teachers or teachers with insufficient qualifications. After I have complained to the school unavailingly to correct the situation, I hit on the idea of complaining about teaching standards at the school to Ofsted, thereby seeking to swing a regulator into action behind my complaint. Some critics in government and the redress sector speak disdainfully of this phenomenon as 'forum shopping' by dissatisfied customers of public services. But from most citizens' point of view, where the primary motive is to get a poor situation corrected, it is only common sense to try and involve a regulator if it seems more effective than other routes, or if other routes have already failed. Disparaging characterisations of forum shopping disguise from view the fact that citizens have not built the current complex and fragmented redress systems, and most would like to see a more integrated and effective system operating.

Figure 1 shows how the redress sector as a whole can now be defined, covering complaints mechanisms (including the two tiers common in the public sector, plus

Figure 1: A typology of the main citizen redress modes in UK central government

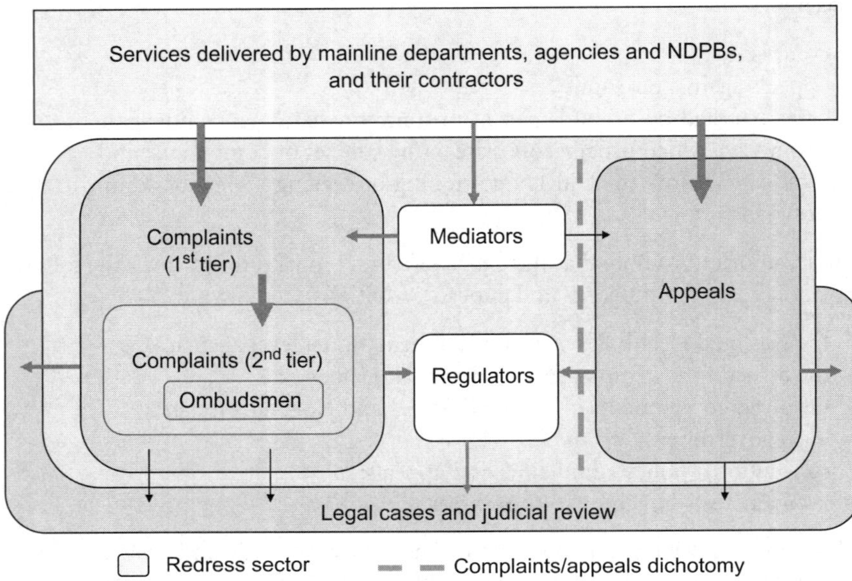

ombudsmen), appeals systems, mediators and case reviewers, and regulators being used to progress individual complaints. Finally, a tiny fraction of complaints, appeals and regulatory cases will progress into the law courts for different forms of judicial review process. This is an especially expensive progression when the complainant or appellant is entitled to receive legal aid both at earlier levels and for the court case.

Figure 1 also shows that our approach cuts across one of the most pervasive, important and counter-productive concepts in British official and administrative law culture—namely, the complaints/appeals dichotomy. According to this conventional view (perhaps even embraced by some of the contributors to this volume), a complaint focuses upon *defects in the process* that someone has undergone, usually a neglect or infringement of their rights to be accurately informed, or some form of wilful ignoring of due process or poor treatment of a citizen by officials (such as rudeness or prejudice of various kinds). This particular view of complaints means that civil servants and departments are often very sensitive about complaints, because they are closely and directly associated with administrative or legal processes for distributing blame, and so they may conceivably have adverse individual consequences for the officials involved. Most complaints processes are handled by internal administrative operations within departments and agencies themselves, usually involving a review by more senior officials of the paperwork in the case and sometimes of the conduct of the staff who were first involved. There may be more extensive interaction with the complainant at this stage, although this is often not done.

The data on complaints numbers that we have are minimal estimates of levels of dissatisfaction, because people in the civil service see complaints as impugning the organisation in some way. Although the Cabinet Office has issued guidance on how to define and recognise complaints, in practice government bodies have sharply varying procedures for beginning (allowing) the registration of a complaint, and hence how they are counted. Some public sector bodies are proactive in following up and registering complaints, an attitude that occurs mainly in smaller agencies and those without very frequent or regular problems with the public. Other organisations overtly and unashamedly endeavour to repel complaints. For instance, HM Revenue and Customs clearly breach Cabinet Office guidelines by consistently and absolutely refusing to accept complaints made over the phone or by e-mail and by insisting that complainants write a letter to them (the equivalent of demanding to be paid only by a paper cheque). Still other organisations have effectively created buffer zones in which a complaint is received but not registered as a complaint until the person involved has been talked to. This practice has been taken furthest in the NHS hospitals, where a key part of the role of Patient Advice and Liaison Service staff is to contact people (who in many cases think that they already have complained) with a view to heading them off by offering them a solution (for instance, a new date for their cancelled operation) so that a complaint does not have to be formally registered.

A very small proportion of all complaints, primarily those that are more serious or remain unresolved over very long periods, may also progress up to an independent complaints-handling agency, usually an ombudsman. The Parliamentary Ombudsmen holds the record for the fewest number of enquiries received (partly because of the so-called 'MP filter', which is administratively and functionally pointless) and for the diminutive number of cases handled. Some cases are also handled by case reviewers or mediators, notably in HMRC, where a highly expensive adjudication process often comes out in favour of the agency.

By contrast to this whole set of complaint mechanisms, appeals in the conventional view are seen as requests *for a substantive decision to be looked at again* in the light of (often further or more detailed) evidence, by a second body or an actor not involved in the original decision. In British government, citizens whose material situations are affected by state decisions in many fields, ranging from social security payments and taxation through to planning applications and applications to get children into schools, have been assigned a statutory right of appeal. Very large numbers of cases are regularly referred onwards or upwards to separate appeal bodies, which means that the problems of recognising an officially defined appeal are usually less severe than is the case with complaints. Even so we found in 2005 that many departments reported many fewer appeals to NAO than the numbers of appeals registered for the same time period by the parallel appeals body. In a few cases agencies may get back to citizens who appeal, in order to discuss their case in more detail. But in areas with bulk appeals this often does not happen—instead there is a relatively cursory internal case review, carried out by a more senior official looking only at already-held agency paperwork.

On a small scale Figure 1 also shows that mediation is beginning to be used as an alternative to appeals in some specialised contexts, for example, in special educational needs disputes (see Harris and Smith 2009). In 2007, the Tribunals Service launched a pilot scheme to test the use of 'alternative dispute resolution' procedures for those appealing against decisions on disability living allowance and attendance allowance (see Fitzpatrick 2008). The involvement of mediation primarily reflects good experience with it in other areas of law, plus a push to minimise the substantial legal aid costs of appeals.

Compared to complaints, appeals are seen by both administrators and politicians (but not by the public) as in a different ballpark from complaints. Many decisions, especially in social security, go on to be overturned on appeal, without any implication of failure attaching to the officials involved in these cases. Perhaps a degree of collective institutional embarrassment (and additional expense) may accrue for a government department or agency where appeals tribunals very frequently overturn their decisions. But the consequences for any given official or set of officials are generally remote and minor, a big difference from complaints.

The complaints versus appeals dichotomy has traditionally been treated in the administrative justice world and the associated academic literature as an unproblematic and self-evident one (indeed almost as self-evident and certainly as sacrosanct). Yet from our research, we are not convinced that this apparently foundational distinction has any relevance for most people. In our focus groups for the *Citizen Redress* study, we could find only one or two people amongst 60 participants who said that they really understood the distinction and no one who really valued it (Bartholomeou et al 2005). Most of our focus group respondents saw it as an official 'trap', designed to help partition a complex original cause for concern into small parts about which citizens could more easily be fobbed off. When the official distinction was explained, only a tiny handful of people saw it as valuable. A large majority argued instead that what they wanted in any complaint or appeal was for something to be put right, and that they would try any route open to them to attempt to achieve that.

Some complaints, a small proportion, are point of service issues that arise during administrative interactions, when someone is handled rudely, or carelessly or treated less well than others, or when their needs and interests are seemingly counted as being of little worth by officials. Such events may conceivably occur unlinked from people being unhappy about the substantive decision arrived at. But they rarely do: most people who complain do so because they are unhappy about the substantive decision or treatment in their case and they are looking for a second opinion, someone else more senior to check the decision or reverse it. Citizens typically only identify or recall things that annoyed them where they feel the lapses complained of have contributed to the 'wrong' decision being made from their point of view. Most people when they appeal are doing the same thing. And in appeal hearings, much of the evidence that citizens put forward also has a bearing upon the quality of the original process that was followed in their case, especially the reasonableness of the procedures, the quality of information given to them, the accuracy and adequacy of the information that officials collected or considered in reaching a decision, and the reasonableness and legality of what was decided.

From our extensive interviews with a range of officials we also formed the view that the complaints/appeals dichotomy is often destructive of administrative responsiveness in central government departments and agencies. In organisations that generate bulk appeals and complaints, the two systems are often operated in a completely separate ways, in different hierarchies or parts of the organisation—sometimes, in the very largest bodies, with a third specialist unit handling compensation payments. Complaint and appeals numbers are never apparently considered together—it is rare to find an official who even handles or is aware of both sets of numbers at once. The common messages that trends in complaints and appeals from citizens to administrative agencies offer up are almost never considered as a whole, even in a case like the design and implementation of tax credits, which gave rise to a huge volume of discontent. Government organisations have internalised the dichotomy to such an extent, and regard it as so fundamental or axiomatic, that they do not find it necessary to communicate to citizens their rights to complain and appeal in the same leaflet. Instead these closely- and inherently-linked processes are typically explained in separate leaflets or on quite distinct and often distant parts of the organisation's website, making no reference one to another.

The complaints and appeals dichotomy has been greatly undermined by the way that citizens can often now 'appeal' a refusal to act on a complaint by bidding it up to a regulator. Nor is this solely a product of unofficial behaviours, for in many different areas legal provisions have recognised that: (i) regulatory controls often require to be activated by complaints; and (ii) effective regulatory action against mistakes and bad policies can only be secured by deploying regulators' enforcement powers to secure changes. Partly in consequence, there has been a growing trend for regulatory bodies to be assigned the job of investigating complaints. From its creation in 2003 until 2009, the Healthcare Commission handled 'second tier' complaints against NHS trusts and authorities, although it badly under-estimated the workload that it would have to deal with and spent several years re-scaling its complaints functions to cope (NAO 2008). Since Spring 2009, the Commission's successor body as regulator has been the Care Quality Commission (CQC): it does not handle 'upper tier' complaints, all of which now have to go the Health Service Ombudsman. But the CQC does at least still overview the complaint processes and procedures being operated by NHS trusts and local authorities in health and adult social care.

Another important area where regulators have also been vested with complaints-handling roles that still operate is the safeguarding of information and privacy. The Information Commissioner, the Surveillance Commissioner and the Commissioner for the National Identity Card Scheme are different kinds of regulators who also handle complaints, indeed whose regulatory activities are largely initiated by complaints. (Admittedly the last two are 'strangely empowered' regulators without any enforcement capacity beyond publishing their reports, via the Home Secretary.)

A final basis for scepticism about the distinction between complaints and appeals is that some other modern redress systems run the two together from the outset, and some integrated redress systems also add in the compensation function and the ombudsman role. The multiple roles that the public sector treats as distinct (such as complaints handler, appeals mechanism, consumer regulator, compensation adjudicator, ombudsman and mediator) can all be addressed by one body designed on modern lines to act in a much more responsive way. The Financial Ombudsman Service opts for an inclusive approach to looking at whatever it is that makes a customer of a bank, insurance company or other financial institution unhappy or convinced that they have been unfairly treated or mislead in some way (FOS 2007, 2008; Merricks 2007). By adopting an inclusive approach, FOS can consider the totality of cases. And, in its initial investigation 'discovery' stage and its second interim judgement stage, FOS can build in a great deal of de facto mediation that helps with straightforward problem-solving.

Civil servants in the UK often suggest that the rights being protected by the redress system in the public sector are somehow uniquely extensive or distinctive to it. Yet the leading textbooks on service management in the commercial sector in fact focus on equally ambitious and far-reaching concepts. For instance, Tax and Brown (2000: 271) argue for a concept of 'service recovery' defined as 'a process that identifies service failures, effectively resolves customer problems, classifies their root cause(s), and yields data that can be integrated with other measures of performance to assess and improve the service system'. Similarly a leading figure in the field, Christian Gronross (2007: 127), points out that the customers of firms will be centrally concerned with three kinds of fairness:

Distributive fairness: the degree to which the outcome of the service recovery process equals what the customer thinks he or she deserved or needed, and the level of compensation and apology;

Procedural fairness: the degree to which customers feel that they could influence the recovery process, and the convenience and timeliness of the process; and

Interactional fairness: the degree to which customers consider interpersonal interactions during the process to be fair, honest and empathetic, including fair communication and behaviour.

This is indeed an extensive conception of service recovery, and one that many public bodies are still struggling to dimly perceive.

Of course, it might be argued that, in the private sector, there are only a few firms like Marks and Spencer or John Lewis who consistently attain a reputation for excellence in service delivery that would meet these criteria. And there are many firms, like some budget airlines or mobile phone companies, who manage to thrive despite acquiring reputations for ruthless behaviour and despite providing only minimal service standards for customers. Yet while public sector agencies perhaps more uniformly profess to adhere to good service standards, including responsiveness to complaints, in practice their performance can be as patchy as those of private firms. At the other extreme from the public sector's charters of good practice, there have been many recent incidents of 'service delivery disasters' where repeated complaints or requests for changes of policies or practices have been serially ignored by busy public service managers and workers. Recent cases include the Maidstone and Tunbridge Wells NHS Trust's failure to recognise or counter two successive outbreaks of the hospital-acquired infection *C. difficile* (causing over 90 deaths in 2007) (Healthcare Commission 2007a); or the Mid-Staffordshire NHS Foundation Trust's poor accident and emergency care over many years, leading to at least 400 preventable deaths (Healthcare Commission 2009); or the successive failures of social services and NHS staff to provide protection in the Baby Peter case in 2008 (Laming Review 2009). Each of these failings grew to be serious through public managers and staff serially ignoring or brushing off complaints and refusing to adjust policies or practices in the face of criticism. The first two of these cases also exposes the hollowness of the complaints/appeals dichotomy, since they were eventually resolved by a regulator following up a mass of complaints from many different citizens, while the third tragic case triggered both political and regulatory interventions to change practices.

The Large-scale and Chronic Nature of Redress Problems

The UK has a substantial problem with bulk redress volumes, whose areas of origins stay largely the same from year to year. We cannot cover the full range of redress processes in this short chapter, but we look at two chronic and large-scale problems where some numbers updating the *Citizen Redress* report can be gathered. We also cover the much smaller volume of Parliamentary Ombudsman cases.

In 2003–04, the *Citizen Redress* report estimated that within the central government sphere alone there were almost 1.4 million new redress cases annually at an annual cost of £510 million and involving nearly 9,400 staff (Dunleavy et al 2005: 44). Table 1 gives more details:

Table 1: UK central government redress cases, staffing and cost figures, 2003–04

	Appeals	Complaints	Ombudsmen and mediators	Total
New cases	803,000	543,000	42,000	1,385,000
Staff	6,200	2,200	990	9,390
Costs in £ million	66	59	73	510

It is clear that ombudsmen and mediators are much more expensive than the complaints system—indeed some redress mechanisms, notably the Parliamentary Ombusdman and the HMRC Adjudicator, both of which cost around £5,500 per case in 2003–04, appear to be particularly expensive on a crude cost per case basis. In addition to the direct expenditures charted above, there were estimated costs of nearly £200 million for central government cases alone, incurred by the Legal Services Commission, primarily in providing legal aid to appellants against central government decisions and certain kinds of complaints (especially in cases alleging poor treatment by the NHS or the police). This whole range of interventions produces total redress costs in 2003–04 of at least £710 million annually for central government. However, the LSC-funded Community Legal Aid service also supports a wide range of complaints and interventions—for example, its website advertises (in mid 2009) that in schooling alone it may help parents progress problems of bullying, secure more support for their child's learning needs, or contest exclusion decisions.

How have the costs for redress as a whole moved in the period since 2003–04? They are certain to have increased quite appreciably, for three reasons:

1. Conventional redress processes are very labour intensive, and hence their relative costs tend to climb over time (following the well-known 'relative price effect' set out by Baumol: see Mueller 2003: 510–11).
2. There are scant reasons for believing that labour productivity in the redress area has markedly improved, despite recent e-government advances elsewhere. The redress industry remains something of a laggard area in e-government and few of its bodies have enthusiastically adapted their websites to recognize or exploit the advantages of 'digital era governance' (Dunleavy et al 2008). In addition the channel diversification outlined in Figure 1 above suggests that economies of scale and scope will be hard to demonstrate—although the unification of the Tribunals Service is one significant potential counterweight (see below).
3. There is no reason to suppose that the overall levels of redress cases have fallen. We have undertaken some probes (discussed in the sections below) to track how the volumes of appeals, complaints and ombudsmen cases have changed in more recent years. While some areas show signs of reduced volume, others show substantial increases. We conclude that the overall numbers of people seeking redress are unlikely to have decreased.

Trends in Appeals

The *Citizen Redress* report showed that about two thirds of the overall costs arising from appeals at £245 million occur in appeals-handling agencies—the remaining third being incurred by the departments or agencies being appealed against. Subsequently most major appeals-handling bodies were reorganised into the now more integrated Tribunals Service, an executive agency of the Ministry of Justice (originally set up in April 2006 under the Department for Constitutional Affairs (DCA)). In a move described by Carnwath (2008) as a 'quiet revolution', it brought together the administrative functions for 16 Tribunals which the DCA had previously had responsibility for, plus five tribunals transferring from other government departments (see Ministry of Justice 2007). The Tribunals Service now has 3,000 staff, up from the 2,730 staff originally transferred in from six different government departments and over 170 locations. The total number of tribunal cases dealt with in 2007–08 was 548,600.

Although it is not possible to easily get a comprehensive picture of its costs, the Tribunals Service's initial Business Plan from 2006 put its running costs at £285 million per year—an increase of at least 16 per cent in three years since 2003–04. By 2007–08 the resource cost had risen further to £305 million, made up of £85 million staff costs; £140 million judicial costs; and £40 million accommodation. (This gives a low average cost per staff member of about £27,000.) The Tribunals Service's 2009–10 Business Plan put total expenditure at £307 million per year in 2008–09. However, it plans to reduce real operating costs by £12 million in 2009–10 under the Ministry of Justice's performance and efficiency programme. Table 2 below lists the most up-to-date information available for the tribunals (taken from the 2009–10 Business Plan). When looking at these figures, it should be remembered that the costs of appeals bodies themselves are only a part of the picture. Substantial costs are also incurred by departments and agencies in preparing cases for appeal and in attending tribunals: from the *Citizen Redress* data, we would expect these costs to be at least half of the Tribunals Service's own costs.

Clearly the new consolidated structure has potential benefits for citizens trying to locate and get information about the correct tribunal to use. And over time, as the previously very separate tribunals with their often distinctive terminologies and processes grow together, we may hope that the overall professionalism of tribunals will improve, their procedures will become more standardised and accessible, and citizens may find that information synergies can be realised. A genuinely integrated service should offer citizens a 'learn once' opportunity and reduce the very extensive uncertainties and confusions about what appeals are and how they operate, which we found amongst our focus group respondents and in the national survey conducted for *Citizen Redress*. Then, most respondents viewed appeals processes as complex, and felt that they seemed to operate very differently, each having their own distinctive concepts and items that were or were not allowable. At this time respondents saw this variation as part of officials trying to confuse the public, hoping to wear down their resilience to appeal and encourage them to forget about whatever it was they were objecting to.

Perhaps the most commented-on aspect of appeals procedures in our focus groups was the expectation amongst some (but not all) members of the public

Table 2: Caseload and expenditure data for appeals bodies under the responsibility of the Tribunals Service

Tribunal	Current caseload	Current expenditure estimate (£000)
Social Security and Child Support (formerly the Appeals Service *and* the Social Security and Child Support Commissioners)*	249,000	68,000
Asylum and Immigration Tribunal	152,000	80,000
Employment Tribunals Service	89,000	54,000
General Commissioners of Income Tax	*28,000*	*3,590*
Mental Health Review Tribunal	22,000	21,000
Tribunals Group **	20,000	12,000
Criminal Injuries and Compensation Appeals Panel	3,700	4,000
Special Educational Needs and Disability Tribunal (SENDIST)	3,300	4,000
VAT and Duties Tribunal	2,700	*2,370*
Pensions Appeal Tribunal	2,850	*2,050*
Adjudicator to HM Land Registry	1,820	Not found
Lands Tribunal	600	Not found
Special Commissioner of Income Tax	440	*180*
Transport Tribunal	460	*230*
Immigration Services Tribunal	20	Not found
The Commissioners Office	Not found	Not found
Financial Services and Markets Tribunal	Not found	Not found
Gender Recognition Panel	Not found	Not found
Information Tribunal	Not found	Not found
Pathogens Access Appeal Commission (PAAC)	Not found	Not found
Pensions Regulator Tribunal	Not found	Not found
Proscribed Organisations Appeal Commission (POAC)	Not found	Not found

* Includes about 5,960 cases from the Social Security and Child Support Commissioners.
** 'Other' tribunals.
Numbers in italics above indicate data that we have not been able to update and for which we have used numbers taken from Citizen Redress (2005).

that any procedure *should* take a very brief time but *could* also take a considerable length of time. Especially if they had personal experience of making appeals, citizens stressed the very long and daunting timescales that frequently attached to them. Nor were they wrong to do so. We came across cases of small appeals bodies that in 2004 were taking up to 2.5 years to investigate and adjudicate on cases arising from historic claims many years in the past, even though the sums of money at stake were relatively small or even trivial. It was well known that the Valuation Office Agency (part of HMRC) at that time always took the maximum six months it was allowed by law to consider council tax appeals cases. The Agency at that time usually concluded an agreement with the vast majority of appellants the week before their cases were due to be heard—so that while up to 140 cases would be listed for a single morning's hearing, in practice only one or two would actually be discussed. The Valuation Office Agency appears to have made significant progress since 2004 in reducing its timelines: by 2009 87 per cent of cases were being dealt with within a new two-month target. The Agency also introduced a new online tool to help customers determine whether or not they may have a case for an appeal. Yet despite this rectification of one conspicuous previous anomaly, there is still some significant stacking-up of appeals in buffer zones across government, which inhibits timely redress to citizens. Departments and agencies still seem to be hoping that citizens will get bored and discontinue their cases.

In other areas, where this is unlikely to happen because people have a strong pecuniary interest in the outcome of their appeals, disturbing evidence has emerged that DWP agencies in particular have increasingly stopped sending officials to attend appeals hearings in person. No doubt reflecting financial and staffing pressures, DWP has increasingly left their case to be construed from the written documentation by the tribunal chair and member(s) unaided. In research for the Citizens Redress report we estimated that the DWP was present in some tribunals in only around two-fifths of cases. Despite repeated stress by the appeals service on the importance of the government being represented in these cases, the attendance of DWP 'presenting officers' fell to 23 per cent during 2007–08 (President's Report 2008). This means that in three-quarters of cases the tribunal members got an asymmetric picture of the two sides of the case.

Trends in Complaints

One aspect of undertaking the original *Citizen Redress* report that gave us cause for concern was the fact that all the data involved had to be especially (and hence expensively) assembled, with a great deal of explanation to departments and agencies about why we wanted to collate complaints, appeals and ombudsman case information at the same time. We surveyed 281 central government organisations in total and received a response from just over 200 (73 per cent). Seven out of the 77 organisations not returning surveys were either ministerial departments or non-ministerial departments. Around one in four departments did not return the survey either due to having insufficient resources to fill in the questionnaire by the deadline (despite numerous extensions) or for other reasons. Table 3 below shows the full details for response rates. Two departments of state, both regularly in the news about serious problems involving abuses within different 'total institution' settings for which they were responsible, expressed the view that this survey was not relevant to their work. The information supplied also contained many omissions because departments and agencies could not supply data on the incidence and costs of redress issues.

Nowhere was this more of a problem than in collating basic data on complaints, with strong variations in the quality of available information on the number of complaints at department and agency level. Of the 204 organisations completing the survey, just under half (44 per cent) were able to provide a full response for the total number of complaints received in each year for 2001–02, 2002–03 and 2003–04 (see Table 4 below). However, just under one-third were not able to provide any data on the number of complaints they received. Again, a comparatively high proportion of ministerial and non-ministerial departments (around two fifths) were unable to provide any data, compared to one fifth of executive agencies and one third of other types of bodies. Around a quarter of all the different

Table 3: Response rate to the NAO *Citizen Redress* survey in 2003

	Departments	Executive Agencies	Other	Total
Survey completed	27	64	113	204
Survey not returned	7	8	62	77
Total	34	72	175	281

Source: Dunleavy et al (2005: 73–81).

Table 4: Summary table showing the quality of data on complaints in the *Citizen Redress* survey of central government organisations

	Departments	Executive Agencies	Other	Number	% of total
No data	11	13	35	59	29
At least one year but not the most recent year	2	3	7	12	6
At least the most recent year	4	11	24	39	19
All three years	10	37	47	94	44
Total	27	64	113	204	100

Source: Dunleavy et al (2005: 73–81).

bodies completing the survey were able only to provide partial data going back to two previous years.

Using public sources of information to try to update the *Citizen Redress* data, Table 5 below shows our best estimate of complaints at 30 prominent departments or agencies in UK central government in 2006. Where we have been able to identify current correct information, this appears in the first two columns. The sources for all remaining columns, including the cost information, are data already published in the *Citizen Redress* report. The Healthcare Commission has produced improved data on NHS complaints.

What trends are discernable in the period from 2001–02 to 2007–08? Some large increases are apparent. The annual complaints count for the HM Revenue and Customs in 2006–07 appears to have increased by two-fifths on its combined total in 2003, before dropping back in the following year. Complaints to the Child Support Agency also rose quite significantly in the period up to 2006–07, but declined strongly thereafter. Complaints to the IPCC about the police have grown more continuously, and the raw numbers for the Courts Service complaints are a lot higher, although numbers may be collected differently. The Passport Service and Jobcentre Plus generate quite large and buoyant complaints loads.

By contrast, some services and organisations show a declining trend in the number of complaints. Complaints to the Pension Service dropped by more than half between 2003–04 and 2007–08 as the substantial initial teething troubles of administering Pension Credits were overcome and the agency's policies became much more customer-focused. Complaints to the Legal Services Commission decreased by a third, and the smaller number of complaints about NHS Direct was halved during the relevant period. Overall five large agencies experienced increases, three experienced decreases and one changed in both directions at different times.

We broadened this analysis to include the top 100 organisations in terms of the number of complaints recorded in our 2003 survey. For each of these organisations, we searched through departmental or annual report covering the year 2006 for any data on the number of complaints received. It is worth keeping in mind that the top 10 complaints-generating organisations account for around three-quarters of complaints, and so there is a long tail of organisations receiving hundreds and tens of complaints (the organisation placed 100th in our survey received just 15 complaints in 2003–04). There were 13 departments in the top 100 complaints-generating organisations, only six of which provided specific figures in their 2005–06 departmental report on the number of complaints received. Executive agencies tended to exhibit a more pronounced 'all or nothing' attitude. So considerable detail was provided in cases where any information at all was given: more than half of agencies reported specific data on numbers of complaints in their annual reports. We found much more variation in other types of organisation, and the clear majority of bodies made no reference whatsoever to complaints in their main annual report.

Table 5: Data on total numbers of complaints for central government bodies, 2001–02 to 2007–08

	Complaints					Costs 2003/04 (£)
	2007/08	2006/07	2003/04	2002/03	2001/02	
NHS Complaints	131,020	138,400	133,870	133,870	.	.
Inland Revenue (now HMRC)	81,380	106,780	69,000	42,000	37,000	16,100,3000
Child Support Agency	37,600	63,680	49,220	29,540	27,740	10,526,000
Pensions Service (now PDCS)	18,570	29,140	41,030	13,590	.	4,364,000
Jobcentre Plus	45,790	.	40,020	.	.	3,580,000
Postwatch	8,450	.	25,000	15,000	4,500	1,300,000
NS&I	.	.	21,150	17,800	13,800	530,000
IPCC	28,960	26,270	16,000	.	.	.
Royal Mint	.	.	14,080	72,650	.	26,000
Driving Standards Agency	.	6,450	12,820	5,690	3,530	1,140,000
National Blood Service	.	7,490	11,660	6,960	2,030	342,000
HM Customs and Excise	na	na	9,470	9,470	11,890	2,409,000
DCS (now in PDCS above)	.	.	8,890	12,810	.	755,000
HM Court Service	26,280	.	5,820	7,390	.	.
UK Passport Service	.	8,550	5,420	3,890	1,390	1,216,000
Crown Prosecution Service	.	.	5,200	4,500	4,000	1,100,000
DVLA	4,390	3,620	4,580	3,390	3,590	568,000
Criminal Records Bureau	.	.	4,220	4,320	.	395,000

(continued)

Table 5: (Continued)

Legal Services Commission	1,870	2,540	2,990	3,550	.	175,000
Land Registry	3,040	2,480	2,850	3,020	3,590	.
Defra	.	.	2,630	3,310	3,550	800,000
Planning Inspectorate	.	1,740	2,100	2,100	2,060	.
CITB	.	.	2,000	.	.	375,000
Independent Review Service for Social	1,260	1,580	1,970	1,910	1,870	167,000
Valuation Office Agency	.	1,820	1,690	1,380	1,810	796,000
Office for Standards in Education	.	.	1,380	260	270	610,000
Student Loans Company	.	.	1,370	1,780	2,470	245,000
Highways Agency	.	.	1,330	1,510	2,190	305,000
NHS Direct	550	880	1,310	.	.	86,000
Coal Authority	.	.	1,220	1,170	820	20,000

Note: The abbreviations used are as follows: HMRC: Her Majesty's Revenue and Customs; PDCS: Pensions, Disability and Carers' Service; NS&I: National Savings and Investments; IPCC: Independent Police Complaints Commission; DVLA: Driver Vehicle Licensing Agency; DCS: Disability and Carers' Service; DEFRA: Department for Environment, Food and Rural Affair; CITB: Construction Industry Training Board.

The continued patchiness of published information on the number of complaints is very disturbing because issues on which departments do not record data are almost invariably the issues that are not being actively managed by anyone. Between February and March 2007 Mr David Laws MP asked a series of parliamentary questions to Ministers. He asked:

how many complaints were received by the Department and its executive agencies in (a) 1997–98, (b) 2001–02, (c) 2005–06 and (d) 2006–07 to date? *and*
how many staff worked in dedicated complaints units in the Department and its executive agencies for the equivalent period?

Table 6 provides a summary of these written questions and answers relating to complaints handling in key departments and their executive agencies that we have compiled. It clearly demonstrates that major citizen-facing government departments still do not collect data centrally on the number of complaints received by organisations for which they are responsible.

These data provide the most recent picture since our NAO survey of the number of complaints and the administrative arrangements that are in place across departments. They suggest that there is still much variation across major citizen and business-facing departments in terms of the quality of management information on complaints. Three departments, the Department for Work and Pensions (DWP), Communities and Local Government (CLG) and Department for Environment, Food and Rural Affairs (DEFRA), appear to be able to provide basic management data relatively speedily and without undue cost. Other major departments however do not have access to this information and hold to the view that to obtain it would incur disproportionate costs.

Turning to other indications of how complaints are being treated, Figure 2 presents evidence that the provision of information about the number of complaints on central government department and agency websites remained patchy in mid-2006. These data come from a comprehensive web census carried out for a subsequent NAO study. A majority of other organisations (mainly non-departmental public bodies) at this time made no mention of complaints procedures on their websites, while a substantial minority of executive agencies followed suit. However, amongst central departments themselves the largest group not only had findable complaints pages but also gave data on how many complaints had been made against them. A more common and restrictive form of feedback to citizens was (and still is) for agencies to report how long they are taking to process complaints against their target levels, but without actually saying how many complaints had been received.

One of the key areas that the *Citizen Redress* report was not able to cover, because it lay outside the National Audit Office's brief, concerned complaints within the National Health Service, where information collection recently improved during the period when the Healthcare Commission took top-level responsibility for complaints systems. Figure 3 shows that complaints seemed to increase quite noticeably in 2000–01, but then declined before peaking

Table 6: Summary of 2007 House of Commons Written Answers relating to complaints

Question relating to …	**Departmental response on questions relating to …**	
	Number of complaints	**Handling procedure and staff resources**
Chancellor of the Exchequer	Data not held centrally.	Data not held centrally.
Child Support Agency (CSA)	Detailed monthly data provided.	
Department for Constitutional Affairs (DCA)	Data not held centrally.	Data not held centrally.
Department for Culture, Media and Sport (DCMS)	Data not held centrally. Could not be provided without incurring disproportionate cost.	
Department for Education and Skills (DFES)	Data not held centrally. To gather this data would incur disproportionate cost.	No data provided—complaint handling is delegated where appropriate.
Department for Environment, Food and Rural Affairs (DEFRA)	Data provided for DEFRA agencies only.	Data provided for DEFRA and relevant agencies.
Department for International Development (DFID)		No data provided—public inquiry points cover complaints from the public.
Communities and Local Government (CLG)	Data provided on complaints for CLG and relevant agencies.	Data provided for CLG and for relevant agencies.
Department of Trade and Industry (DTI)		Data provided for DTI Response Unit only.
Foreign and Commonwealth Office (FCO)	Data not held centrally and would be disproportionately costly to compile.	
HM Revenue and Customs (HMR&C) on tax credits	No plans to publish management information on complaints.	
Home Office (Probation Service)	Data is not held centrally and may be available at disproportionate costs.	
Home Office Immigration and Nationality Directorate (IND)		IND is being overhauled through Complaints Change Programme.

Note: The data in this table are taken solely from written transcripts of the House of Commons Written Answers between 25 January 2006 and 6 March 2007. The exact dates are as follows relating to the rows in the table: Chancellor of the Exchequer: 26 February 2007; CSA: 25 January 2006; DCA: 26 February 2007; CLG: 5 March 2007; DCMS: 6 March 2007; DEFRA: 28 February 2007; DFID: 23 February 2007; DTI: 22 February 2007; FCO: 2 March 2007; HMR&C: 19 December 2006; Home Office (IND): 5 February 2007; Home Office (Probation Service): 18 February 2007.

Figure 2: The availability of data on complaints in annual reports found on central government organisations' websites in mid-2006

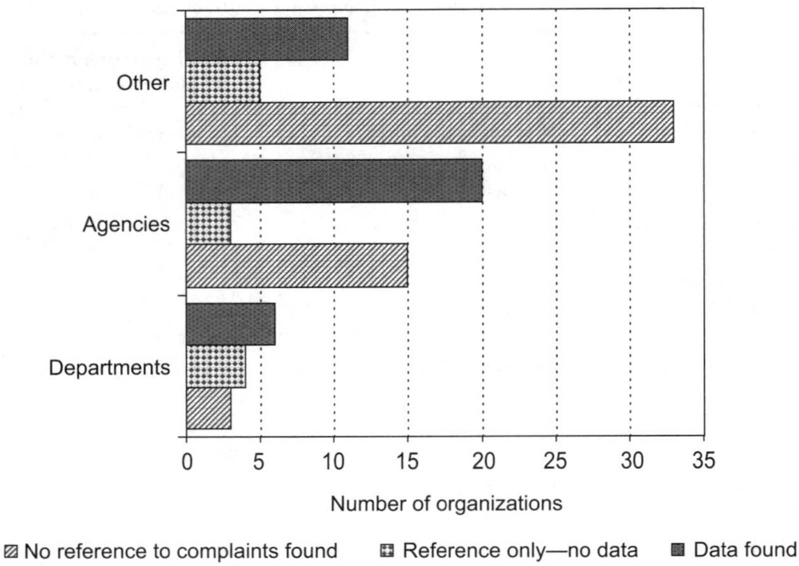

Source: Dunleavy et al (2007).

again in 2005–06. Overall the level of NHS complaints in aggregate has stayed broadly the same in recent years. But this actually implies that complaints per patient treated have declined appreciably—reflecting the fact that there has recently been a good deal more NHS activity than in the past, as Figure 4 demonstrates. Spending on the NHS also grew substantially across this period, so that perhaps we should have looked to see an improving effect on these lines. The incidence of NHS complaints across regions is quite consistent at about one complaint for every 8 NHS staff members across almost all areas—the exception being Yorkshire and Humberside, where the number is appreciably better at one in 12. In our current research we are looking at a detailed analysis of the incidence of complaints across hospital trusts. One interesting early result is that the rate of complaints per 1,000 treatment events is appreciably lower in larger hospital trusts compared with smaller hospital trusts—an effect that may reflect better-resourced PALS (Patient Advice and Liaison Services) in large trusts.

Trends in References to Ombudsmen

Since its establishment 40 years ago, the UK's office of the Parliamentary Ombudsman has been rather distinctive in handling a very small proportion

Figure 3: Complaints in the National Health Service, 1998–2007

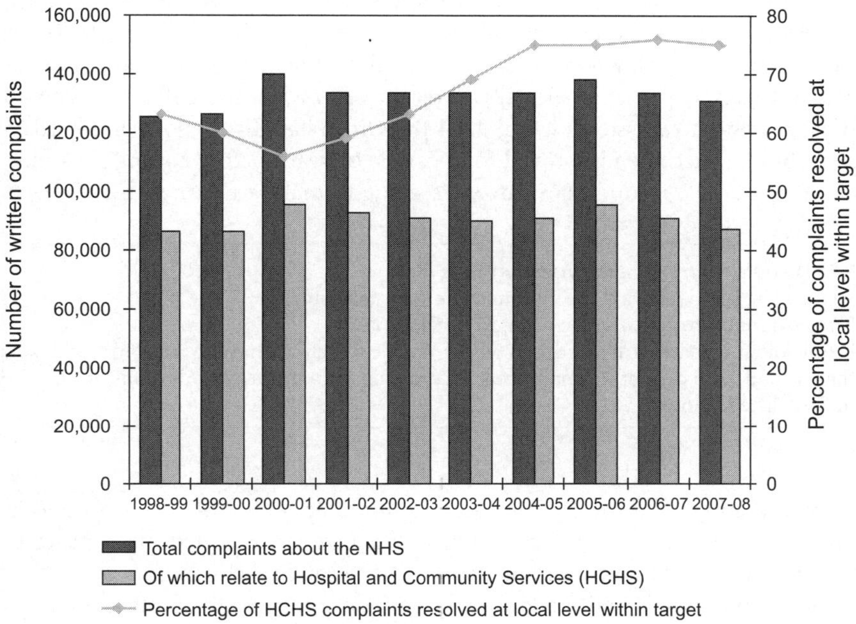

Figure 4: Trends in NHS expenditure and activities and in complaints since 2001

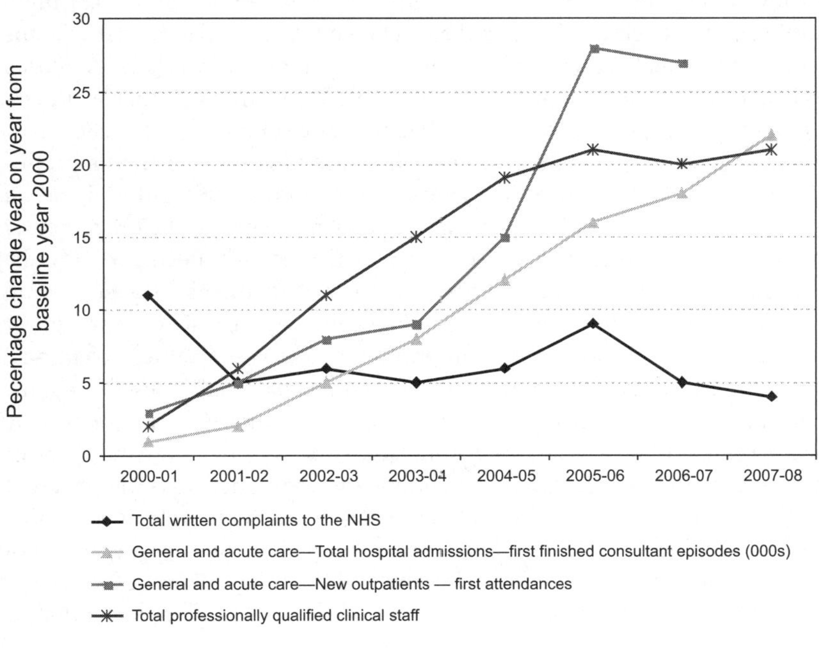

of complaints cases. Table 7 below shows that it continues the past pattern of completing investigations into a remarkably small overall caseload. Historically, the Office of the Parliamentary and Health Service Ombudsman (OPHSO) has operated in a rather low-key fashion, with little public contact, and little publicity about its role, perhaps especially in recent years when the Office was slow to adapt to web-based systems. Until 2004 the Office had a very poor and hard to use website, which then improved for a couple of years, before lapsing back after that. For example in mid-2009 anyone seeking to make a non-health complaint is greeted as follows:

> ***The Parliamentary Ombudsman may look at...***
> Please view list to see what the Ombudsman may look into.
> ***The Parliamentary Ombudsman CANNOT look at...***
> People often contact us about things we are unable to help with. With a few exceptions, the Ombudsman cannot normally look at complaints about the organisations or matters listed below.

Sources: OPHSO, 2009.

The many things that the Ombudsman cannot help you with are then listed in detail on the same page, but users must click through repeated other pages to eventually find what non-health issues the Office can in fact handle.

The Ombudsman's staff are located in London in one national office, and it is especially noticeable that the health staff are located far away from the trusts they are supposed to supervise. Most staff work on big test cases, where the outcome of one particular complaint can (and often must) be read across by the department or agency involved to apply to a whole class of cases. This type of work is very time-consuming and difficult and it requires a careful handling of relations between the Ombudsman personally and senior civil servants and ministers, which have not been happy in cases like compensation for those who lost savings in the Equitable Life collapse (Giddings 2001; Parliamentary and Health Service Ombudsman 2008b).

The prestige of the Ombudsman's role, her reporting to an increasing influential Parliamentary committee (the House of Commons Public Administration Select Committee) and, often, the strong personal influence of the office-holder are all powerful resources. The Office is also relatively well-funded and immune from Treasury cutbacks, because of its status as a Parliamentary agency. Yet in 2004 we found, in our interviews across Whitehall, that OPHSO did not appear to have very wide reach or a very high profile. In a very few, rather exceptional test cases, interviewees recognised that the Ombudsman had focused on some difficult and highly specialised issues of balance and interpretation, especially under the present Ombudsman, Ann Abraham. However, as a consequence of its institutional setting, its organisational culture and the leadership style of recent post-holders, OPHSO does not seem to have played much of a role in informing civil service thinking on the bulk handling of complaints. In every organisation in which we conducted interviews, complaints managers and senior officials told us that OPHSO sees such a small and exceptional fraction of complaints that its

Table 7: Complaints progressing to the Ombudsman from central government bodies

	PCA Complaints		
	2005/06	2004/05	2003/04
NHS Complaints	1,310	1,940	4,700
Inland Revenue (now HMRC)	560	380	470
Child Support Agency	210	.	.
Pensions Service (now PDCS)	100	.	.
Jobcentre Plus	260	.	.
Postwatch	.	.	.
NS&I	.	.	.
IPCC	.	.	.
Royal Mint	.	.	.
Driving Standards Agency	.	.	.
National Blood Service	.	.	.
HM Customs and Excise	.	30	50
DCS (now PDCS)	70	.	.
HM Court Service	50	.	.
UK Passport Service	10	.	.
Crown Prosecution Service	.	.	.
DVLA	30	.	.
Criminal Records Bureau	20	.	.
Legal Services Commission	60	50	70
Land Registry	20	20	20
Defra	20	30	50
Planning Inspectorate	40	.	.
CITB (Construction Industry Training)	.	.	.
Independent Review Service for Social	.	.	.
Valuation Office Agency	20	.	.
Office for Standards in Education	.	.	10
Student Loans Company	.	.	.
Highways Agency	10	.	.
NHS Direct	.	.	.
Coal Authority	.	.	.

Source: PCA Annual Reports.
Note: The abbreviations used are as follows: HMRC: Her Majesty's Revenue and Customs; PDCS: Pensions, Disability and Carers' Service; NS&I: National Savings and Investments; IPCC: Independent Police Complaints Commission; DVLA: Driver Vehicle Licensing Agency; DCS: Disability and Carers' Service; DEFRA: Department for Environment, Food and Rural Affair; CITB: Construction Industry Training Board.

ideas on what goes wrong and why were just not helpful. This limitation seems to severely reduce the impact that it can have as a source of influence for improving the bulk handling of complaints. And of course, like other public sector ombudsmen, OPSHO does not play any part in appeals processes so that it cannot give helpful advice on 'getting it right first time' either.

Given its historical set up and institutional trajectory, this limitation seems to be specific to OPHSO. We found that other ombudsmen, especially the Local Government Ombudsman and the Housing Ombudsmen, were viewed quite differently within their constituencies. They were seen as useful sources for public managers learning lessons—perhaps because they handle a much large number of complaints and maintain much closer links to the bodies that they supervise. This more modern pattern for operating an ombudsman service is also well developed by the unified public service ombudsmen operating in Scotland and Wales. They have the great advantage of dealing closely with specific groups of local authorities, NHS bodies and devolved governments, with all of which they are in constant contact and therefore have a good chance of getting to know. The Scottish and Welsh Offices have also been far more open in monitoring their own performance than OPHSO (see, for example, ORC International, 2008). Yet the greater prominence of an integrated office also has had some downsides for the postholder themselves, including some strong pubic criticisms over delays in processing cases (see www.scottishombudsmanwatch.org).

In focus groups and in a national survey conducted in 2003–04, we found very little public awareness of the UK Ombudsman's role, partly because of the confusion about titles which then prevailed. Respondents commented that having several 'aliases' for one person (with different titles for the parliamentary role and the health services role, both of them in turn differing from the popular label of 'Ombudsman') seemed confusing. In particular, we did not find anyone under 40 in our focus groups who knew what the Ombudsman did, although people in their 60s were a little better informed (Bartholomeou et al 2005). Subsequently some changes were made to the OPHSO website, now at the much better titled www.ombudsman.org.uk, yet as we noted above it remains strongly offputting for potential complainants.

What Citizens Expect and What They Get from Redress Services

For the NAO report we carried out extensive focus group work with citizens and customers of government agencies, and a very clear picture of what they were looking for from redress processes emerged. Citizens' first priority is to have clearly understandable redress processes that can be simply found and activated. Citizens are deeply confused by the official distinction between a complaint and an appeal, which has little meaning for them, and by the separation of information into distinct leaflets and parts of websites, instead of these being handled as a group of linked activities.

Many people who have problems with a service at an early stage want to discuss whether they have grounds for a complaint or appeal. Starting a complaint (or, to a lesser degree, an appeal) is often a daunting and difficult task for citizens, especially where they do not have (or have lost) a piece of paper that tells them whom to contact about complaining or appealing, or when phone calls are rarely answered (as was the case with contacting the organisations responsible for tax credits and child support in recent years). Of course, the vast majority of citizens go on the web to discover their rights and 70 per cent of British households now have internet access, a level that has risen sharply as the price of broadband has fallen (Dutton et al 2009: 7). Recent DWP research has shown that 51 per cent of its customers are internet-connected (see Dunleavy et al 2009). This still leaves 30 per cent of British households without internet access (although six per cent have had access in the past). The quarter of all households who have never had access are particularly concentrated in groups who are vulnerable or in some way disadvantaged, among people on low-incomes, people on benefits and amongst the elderly.

In our work in 2004, it was clear that ordinary citizens, especially, those who are disadvantaged or suffering from 'digital exclusion', often find it extremely difficult just to kick off a complaint or a request for an appeal. Many people ring up numbers that they get from the telephone book, a Citizens' Advice Bureau or some other type of advice line, and then find that they get referred from pillar to post being told: 'That's not us, we don't do that. We do complaints and you want an appeal' or something similar. In 2004 we did some mystery shopping with 20 government departments for the *Citizen Redress* report. One had to be confident and persistent to get from a general enquiry point to the relevant telephone number for making a complaint. When we discussed that experience with focus groups, there was considerable evidence that this was quite generally applicable, with many respondents mentioning that they had tried to initiate a complaint (or appeal) but then abandoned it because of the high transaction costs of proceeding to first base. Respondents said that unless you had a piece of paper with a specifically named official's telephone number on it (rather a rare commodity nowadays), it was very difficult to initiate a complaint. People without internet access found it particularly frustrating that they had to scavenge around to discover who to contact or what to do to find out more. The lack of a central information point on the Internet or a single phone number is thus a considerable problem. There have been local experiments launched by the Home Office with a 101 phone number for people to report non-urgent crime-related or vandalism-related matters and concerns. But the UK government has not yet experimented with the 311 public enquiry numbers pioneered successfully by some major US cities and states.

Complaints and appeals systems are also very poorly set up to give out information to the informal intermediaries who play a very important role in helping many of the least well-connected citizens consider making a complaint or an appeal. A recent Department for Work and Pensions study suggested that around two-fifths of their clients rely on intermediaries of various kinds (family, friends, people with internet access, care workers and Citizen Advice staff) to progress their cases when they have problems (DWP 2008). DWP found that their internal systems interacted poorly with people other than the client; their systems for allowing clients to authorise other people to assist them were still in development; and hence intermediaries' perceptions of DWP services were worse than those of clients themselves. While DWP has recently changed its stance in this area, other government departments and agencies more generally are still often not set up to handle intermediaries' frequent roles in redress processes.

Once citizens have got past first base and lodged a complaint or appeal, their second priority is to obtain a speedy recognition of where things have gone wrong (for whatever reason), a rectification of mistakes and an apology where this is appropriate. Many citizens who have had a bad experience of administrative processes also want an assurance that other people will not encounter the same problem, systems have been changed and lessons for the future have been learned by the organisation concerned.

Finally, most citizens support some modest compensation for those who have suffered a demonstrable loss, sufficient to put them back to where they would have been had correct decision been made or had appropriate processes been used initially. Both in our 2004 national survey and in most of our focus groups, respondents did not generally believe that large amounts of compensation should be paid from public funds—on the ground that this would encourage people to complain or appeal and detract from current service levels. However, a minority of people do feel strongly that public agencies should pay proper levels of compensation, including recompensing them realistically for the time and energy they have expended in securing rectification of an incorrect decision. For instance, this group suggest that compensation should be paid for having to take time off work to attend a tribunal hearing.

These citizen expectations are not unreasonable, especially for an administrative system such as that in the UK, which has an international reputation for being dynamic, customer-orientated and responsive. There have been more than two decades of strongly managed public sector reform efforts in Great Britain supposedly directed to enhancing administrative responsiveness and improving administrative justice. Despite the very substantial costs incurred by government in providing redress, we believe that citizens are generally receiving a poor level of service in the following ways:

The separation of complaints, appeals and regulatory systems creates difficulties for citizens from the outset in most government departments and many agencies. The overall redress system is highly fragmented and specific, especially in England where there are diverse ombudsmen. The rules covering complaints and appeals vary sharply from one policy area to another, and even the nomenclature used by government bodies (for instance, how they define and count complaints) is not standardised. Citizens usually have to begin again from scratch in learning how to complain or appeal, or even who to talk to about complaining or appealing, in each policy area. The Tribunals Service has begun moving along a path towards greater commonality in the rules for appeals-handling, but this will be a long process, not least because the costs and workloads of its different component tribunals still vary considerably. The relationship between regulatory and complaints systems is also inconsistent, with some regulators also handling complaints (indeed depending on complaints for their operation), other regulators supervising or over-viewing complaints systems but not handling individual complaints, and still others steering well away from complaints altogether.

Redress activities are not assigned high levels of priority in terms of the development of expertise and professionalism. These areas are often service backwaters with poorly qualified staff and managers, located on the periphery of organisations and not attracting much top management attention. We found evidence that, in some smaller executive agencies across central government, the agency head personally still took an interest in reviewing all complaints, using them in a traditional way as a sounding board to generate insights into how his or her organisation was performing on the ground. But this is very much an 'old fashioned' mode of operation now, and most of the senior officials who head departments and agencies no longer follow it. At best, data on trends in complaints and appeals may be considered in an aggregate way once a year by senior management teams, department or agency boards, and even here there was little evidence from our interviews that much serious attention was given to learning lessons from citizen' experiences. Ombudsman reports on complaints that were found to be well-founded would be followed up, but normally in a restrictive 'damage limitation' way only, because the cases were normally too exceptional to have implications for the broader conduct of departmental or agency business.

Current redress systems provide a poor standard of service for citizens in terms of two key areas. First, there is a difficult hiatus surrounding 'kicking off' a complaint or appeal where the citizen does not have high quality, agency-specific information available to them. Second, most redress processes still impose quite long delays before citizens get a response—although some very long delays have been reduced. When complaints or appeals are triggered, most organisations still create buffer zones into which files enter until a response or an appeal date is imminent. So citizens find it stressful and difficult to complain or appeal in the first place. And when they do, finally, manage to initiate a complaint or an appeal, they do not get a timely response and instead feel that departments and agencies are trying to exhaust their patience or bore them into dropping complaints or appeals through inaction.

Redress procedures also encourage counter-productive practices, especially in the big complaints- and appeals-generating department and agencies. Here there has historically been almost no effort at mediation and sometimes only weak following-up of complaints. Almost all appeal cases go straight into queues for hearings, with only brief checks by departments on whether a mistake has been made. Government organisations and complainants or appellants often then spend a great deal of time in acquiring large amounts of evidence that may not be relevant just in case it comes in useful at later stages, instead of sharp, focused and timely attention being given to the central point at issue. Add to this the point above that there is poor organisational learning by those government departments and agencies that are the largest generators of complaints and appeals, and it is not surprising that the same patterns of chronic malfunctioning persist over long periods, with little improvement or even focused management attention over time.

At the same time, the expectations applyied to small agencies or departments that do not interact much with the public, or whose interactions with the public rarely spark conflicts, are somewhat too weak at present. Some managers in such bodies proactively seek to resolve complaints arising on their patch in a speedy and efficient manner. And in other agencies or departments with somewhat more complaints, a central unit may also intervene speedily and effectively, contacting people to find out what the problem is and trying to use the extra information generated to get the original decision maker to rectify matters and to issue an apology. In fact, across most central government agencies it would now be perfectly feasible to move towards a 'low complaints' target. This might specify that almost no complaints should be generated and any that are should be very speedily and proactively resolved—say within the 15–20 days currently allowed for a first response. Yet in fact no changes have been taken to tighten up the effectiveness of the non-troublesome agencies' redress operations, or to set them further improvement goals. Instead, the dated Cabinet Office guidelines designed to let off the worst offenders create a non-taxing regimen for ordinary agencies.

To this can be added the perverse incentives created by the apparatus of 'Chartermarks' and similar procedures, which give out unwarranted prizes or recognition to 'lucky' agencies with few redress problems, while, in the 'unlucky' agencies that are big complaints generators, the efforts of many sincere and professional staff to deal with difficult redress issues go unrecognised. This *status quo* is counter-productive for staff morale in those key organisations with serious redress problems.

The organisation of the top-level ombudsman services seems problematic in the UK. A report published by the House of Commons Public Administration Select Committee during the 2002–03 Session called for the government to:

> move speedily to legislate to reform the wider public sector ombudsman system, including the establishment of a single gateway for complaints. … The Ombudsman exercises much-needed quality control and strengthens the hand of the citizen in dealing with the state. (House of Commons Public Administration Select Committee 2003)

Unfortunately, no such action has been taken. There is no integrated system of ombudsman services in England, such as is found in Scotland and Wales. Most really serious problems—such as abuse of children by their parents, or neglect of elderly persons' medical and social care—are inherently multi-agency problems. Equally the proportion of decisions being made in partnership working and joined-up-governance arrangements has grown very sharply in recent years. But, in such cases, ombudsmen can only investigate complaints in fragmented and non-joined-up ways. The Office of the Parliamentary and Health Service Ombudsman (OPHSO) does not fulfil the role of being a clear and well-known focus for citizen complaints that is carried out by (for instance) the Netherland National Ombudsman.

Conclusions: Improving Citizen Redress Services

Putting together the data on appeals, complaints and ombudsmen activities, we think that it is a conservative estimate to suggest that overall redress costs are likely to have increased since 2004 by the same amount as the increased spending on the appeals that are now run through the Tribunals Service, where spending has risen 23 per cent. There are areas where evidence of central departments holding down, or even reducing considerably, the costs of their redress activities has emerged. For instance, a more recent NAO study of complaints-handling in the Department for Work and Pensions suggests that complaints costs in 2006–07 had risen to only £19 million, compared with the *Citizen Redress* figure of £17.3 million (NAO 2008). However, there are special reasons why the pensions credit category of DWP complaints has fallen off, as new benefit systems have become routinised. So we should not confuse this one-off reduction with the overall patterns discussed above. Overall, we estimate that citizen redress costs (for UK central government alone, excluding the many other public sector bodies) are now in the region of at least £830 to £870 million a year. Across the whole of the public sector, citizen redress costs will be much more than this, perhaps double this amount. We should therefore see citizen redress as being at least a £1.6 billion 'industry'. And one central question this must prompt for citizens and taxpayers is: 'Are we getting good value for money?' Given the list of problems with which we ended section 3, we take it that the likely answer to this 'value for money' question is 'no'.

Moving towards better systems of redress clearly needs to tackle this problem in a careful way, preserving what works well in current systems, and what is still valued by citizens, especially the right to appeal and to get a second look by someone independent. There are a great many useful suggestions of an incremental kind in the recommendations of the NAO's *Citizen Redress* report. Table 8 below shows that there have been some encouraging signs of progress on some of them. For instance, between 2004 and 2006 the proportion of government websites where people can find out how to complain went up from 70 to 82 per cent.

Table 8: A summary of main recommendations from *Citizen Redress*, indications of progress, and some examples of change

Citizen Redress recommendation	Examples of recent progress
Some signs of progress	
Point 4, addressed to government. Keep under review web-based information about redress.	Slightly more organisations are now posting specific information about redress processes on their websites.
Point 2, addressed to government. Aim to improve quality of service and reduce costs of providing this service.	Some major agencies have run major overhaul of their complaints systems (eg the Child Support Agency (as was).
Point 12, government-wide. Develop a single point of contact for impartial information on redress options.	No central contract point exists. However, some local authorities have experimented successfully with integrated public service helplines (but only for their own services and issues).
Signs of mixed progress	
Point 2, addressed to government. Report on redress procedures both for complaints and appeals … as part of the annual report.	Just under half (49 per cent) of annual reports now contain at least some performance information about complaints. Just 37 per cent contain data on the number of complaints received. (see Figure 2 above).
Point 8, addressed to government. Collect information on appeals and complaints in a systematic way.	Major Whitehall departments still do not collect data centrally on complaints across their policy area.
Point 10, addressed to government. Learn lessons from successful appeals processes.	The new Tribunals Service provides a shared platform for standardising and improving appeals services.
Point 11, government-wide. Innovate with methods of mediation to reduce the chances that complaints or appeals escalate or move up the 'ladder of redress'.	Some changes may move in this direction, such as the DWP decision to involve an independent case reviewer across all their agencies.
More research required	
Point 1, addressed to government. Review how it defines a complaint against the widely used Cabinet Office definition. [HMRC, for instance, seems not to follow guidelines by requiring complaints only by letter.]	
Point 3, addressed to government. Review potential for handling of complaints and appeals in one common and unified process. [We would now suggest broadening this to look also at regulators' roles.]	
Point 5, addressed to government. Keep under review issues of access to information about redress *(ie minimizing the exclusion of certain groups)*.	

(*continued*)

Table 8: (Continued)

Point 6, addressed to government.
Take into account individual needs of different social groups vis-à-vis redress.
Point 7, addressed to government.
Canvas views of citizens or users of redress systems on how things could be improved. [Changes in DWP policies towards older people are a good example here.]

However, notwithstanding these improvements, we believe that the redress services that are available for UK citizens are still poor in avoidable ways, especially considering their substantial annual costs. Looking at the possibilities of more radical reforms, we identify a number of proposals that hold out the prospect of moving towards a much improved set of redress mechanisms. These might include:

Across the vast majority of departments and agencies, the government should commit itself to achieving and maintaining a 'low complaints' regime, a goal that is clearly feasible in a large number of departments and agencies that generate only a minimal number of complaints. In the remaining departments and agencies, which generate very large numbers of complaints and appeals, a different and more tailored approach is needed, involving phasing down the numbers of complaints and appeals by building in a greater measure of customer responsiveness from the outset. The processes needed to achieve improvements here would need to set demanding targets for reducing complaint and appeals, but spread over a realistic timescale.

The civil service and other public sector bodies need to do more to develop further the professionalism and expertise of staff within the citizen redress area, especially in those areas where complaints and appeals are most numerous. For example, departments and agencies with chronic and recognised complaints/appeals problems should be asked to appoint Chief Redress Officers (analogous to the role of Chief Information Officers in IT), whose job would be to try to get closer to the low or very low complaints regime that many of the best medium-sized agencies now operate at. All departments and agencies with large-scale and recurring caseloads of complaints or appeals should also be asked to co-locate their complaints and appeals functions and to link them closely with units that deal with customer satisfaction.

Citizen redress functions in high caseload areas might also be developed as a shared service area, where a small number of professionally-run and specialised units would proactively seek to deliver timely responses and to reduce the stacking up of complaints and appeals. Each such unit could handle a reasonably large number of client departments and agencies. By concentrating the management of complaints and appeals into fewer and more expert bodies within the civil service (or in outsourced providers), with a clear mission to provide improved redress, it might be possible to reduce the chronic sources of complaints and appeals and help organisations to learn lessons that would cut the incidence of mistakes or wrong decisions in the future. Stronger and more proactive telephone-based and internet-based methods of working could be introduced at the same time.

Instead of the current legalistic and detached appeals-handling processes that characterise government, there might be positive returns in moving towards the kind of solution offered by the Financial Ombudsman Service (FOS) in the financial services sector. The FOS delivers informal first-stage mediation in around 51 per cent of cases (Financial Ombudsman Service 2009: 56) and recharges the costs of continuing actions to companies, creating strong incentives for them to settle cases speedily. Compared with current appeals-handling in government, this is an effective service, it has high productivity and is effective in cost terms at £508 per case in 2009 (Financial Ombudsman Service 2009: 65).

The recommendations of the Crerar Report in Scotland (Crerar 2007) pointed the way to a strategy of reducing the many different complaints-handling regulators, ombudsmen and mediators in the long term, by considering whether roles and responsibilities could not be pooled and progressively taken over by fewer bodies. This approach needs to be extended in the UK as a whole in much the same way as the Tribunals Service is attempting to streamline and unify appeals. Adopting an overall redress perspective would allow for a more strategic review in the future, in place of the topsy-turvy response to particular administrative problems that has characterised the field in the past.

Whatever happens on the points above, we can see no rationale for continuing with the current strongly fragmented ombudsman arrangements in England. We would like to see a move towards a single regional-level ombudsman based in each government region, handling all the cases across central government, the NHS, regional bodies and local authorities that arise within their region. Regional ombudsmen would be able to get to know their patch in detail, to serve as very visible routes into complaining for the public, and to deal directly with their manageable sub-sets of public sector organisations on a recurring basis, so as to improve lesson-drawing and to spread good practice in more effective ways. They would be closer to customers, able to publicise their services locally and offer a joined-up service to complainants (ideally also covering also the police service). There should be competition amongst regional ombudsmen to improve services in their patch. The regional ombudsman offices could be supported by a small national ombudsman's office that would run a national call centre to publicise complaints procedures, and provide specialist back-up and legal advice to regional colleagues. There would still be a small need for a national ombudsman, whose workload would be small and would focus chiefly on major test cases, those with implications spanning across many complainants or many different government departments. The national ombudsman could also play a role in fostering the development of good practice by reporting on behalf of the body of ombudsmen to Parliament, spreading lessons from different regions and running a national contact and advice service (such as a UK equivalent of a 311 phone number or the Dutch ombudsman's communication function).

With the onset of the most severe recession for more than 60 years, the next few years will undoubtedly bring about major changes in how the UK's public administration is organised, and these changes are certain to spill over to some considerable degree into the redress sector. Yet proposals for reorganisation and greater efficiency measures are often vociferously opposed by the redress sector, and represented as attacks on vitally important civil liberties. It is indeed hard to contemplate some of the extensive changes that have been implemented recently (and are still being implemented) in the health sector without concluding that government has often moved on efficiency grounds to make changes that encroach on citizens' rights and their capabilities for seeking redress and to find independent support in doing so. However, we have sketched here an agenda that has a very different motivation, while holding out the prospect of achieving radically improved services to citizens and faster and more robust organisational learning by government departments, agencies and public bodies. It would be shame if the self-interested defensiveness of those in the current highly siloed redress sector is allowed to frustrate a push towards giving citizens a redress system that is simultaneously simpler, cheaper, more effective in 'putting things right' and more transparent about its own performance. All these four elements are needed to create a redress system that is more sustainable in the long-run, and hence can begin to build greater public understanding of how redress processes work.

Acknowledgements

This chapter draws heavily upon joint work with Professor Martin Loughlin (Law Department, LSE) and Professor Helen Margetts (Oxford Internet Institute, Oxford University) who, together with the authors of this chapter, undertook the research for, and wrote, the NAO report on *Citizen Redress: What citizens can do if things go wrong with public services* (National Audit Office 2005). This chapter reflects entirely the views and opinions of the authors, derived from their recent research and the public literature. It does not in any way represent the views of the National Audit Office.

References

Appeals Service (2008) *Report by the President of Appeal Tribunals on the standards of decision-making by the Secretary of State* (London, The Tribunal Service) available at www.appeals-service.gov.uk/Documents/SSCSA_PresRep07_08FINAL.pdf.

Bartholomeou, P, Campbell, R, Dunleavy, P, Margetts, H and Tinkler, J (2005) *Report on Four Focus Groups conducted for the Citizen Redress NAO report*, available at www.nao.org.uk/publications/0405/citizen_redress.aspx.

Brewer, B (2007) 'Citizen or customer? Complaints handling in the public sector' 73 *International Review of Administrative Sciences* 549–56.

British and Irish Ombudsman Association (2007) *Guide to principles of good complaint handling: Firm on principles, flexible on process* (London, BIOA) available at www.bioa.org.uk/docs/BIOAGoodComplaintHandling.pdf.

Carnwath, LJ (2008) 'Administrative justice–a quiet revolution' 30 *Journal of Social Welfare and Family Law* 283–86.

Community Legal Aid Service (2009) Education pages, available at www.communitylegaladvice.org.uk/gateway/education.jsp.

Crerar, L (2007) *Independent Review of Regulation, Audit, Inspection and Complaints Handling of Public Services in Scotland* (Edinburgh, Scottish Government) available at www.scotland.gov.uk/Publications/2007/09/25120506/0.

Dean, H (2004) 'Losing appeal? The Changing Face of Redress' 12 *Benefits* 3.

Department for Constitutional Affairs (DCA) (2004) *Transforming Public Services: Complaints, Redress and Tribunals* Cm 6243 (London, HMSO).

Department for Health (2004) *Learning from Complaints: Consultation on Changes to the Social Services Complaints Procedure for Adults* (Leeds, DoH) available at www.dh.gov.uk/en/Consultations/Closedconsultations/DH_4102052.

Department for Work and Pensions (2007) *Departmental Report 2007* (London, DWP).

—— (2008) *Performance from the Customer's View* (London, DWP Customer Insight).

Dunleavy, P, Margetts, H, Bastow, S and Boucek, F (2005) *Citizen Redress: What citizens can do if things go wrong with public services*, National Audit Office 'Value for Money' report, HC 21 (London, The Stationery Office) also available at www.nao.org.uk/publications and at www.GovernmentOnTheWeb.org.

Dunleavy, P, Margetts, H, Bastow, S, Escher, T and Tinkler, J (2007) *Government on the internet: progress in delivering information and services online*, National Audit Office 'Value for Money' Report, HC 529 (London, The Stationery Office), also available at www.nao.org.uk/publications and at www.GovernmentOnTheWeb.org.

Dunleavy, P, Margetts, H, Bastow, S and Tinkler, J (2008) *Digital Era Governance: IT Corporations, the State and e-Government*, revised edn (Oxford, Oxford University Press).

Dunleavy, P, Margetts, H, Raraty, D, Tinkler, J (and with Dorrell, D, Escher, T, Goldchluk, S, Hinds, L, Khan, MK and Reissfelder, S) (2009) *Department for Work and Pensions: communicating with customers* HC 421, National Audit Office 'Value for Money' report, also available at www.nao.org.uk/publications and at www.GovernmentOnTheWeb.org.

Dutton, WH, Helsper, E and Gerber, MM (2009) *The Internet in Britain* (Oxford, Oxford Internet Institute).

Financial Ombudsman Service (2007) *Annual Review 2006–07* (London, FOS).

—— (2008) *Annual Review 2007–08* (London, FOS).

—— (2009) *Annual Review 2008–09* (London, FOS).

Fitzpatrick, P (2008) 'Alternative Dispute Resolution in DLA and AA appeals' *Welfare Rights Bulletin* 203.

Giddings, P (2001) 'Whither the Ombudsman?' 16 *Public Policy and Administration* 1.

Gronross, C (2007) *Service Management and Marketing: Customer Management in Service* (Chichester, Wiley).

Gulland, J (2006) 'Second-tier reviews of complaints in health and social care' 14 *Health and Social Care in the Community* 206.

Harris, N and Smith, E (2009) 'Resolving Disputes about Special Educational Needs and Provision in England' *Education Law Journal* 113.

Healthcare Commission (2007a) *Investigation into outbreaks of Clostridium difficile at Maidstone and Tunbridge Wells NHS Trust* (London, Commission for Healthcare Audit and Inspection) available at news.bbc.co.uk/1/shared/bsp/hi/pdfs/11_10_07maidstone_and_tunbridge_wells_investigation_report_oct_2007.pdf.

—— (2007b) *Is Anyone Listening? A report on complaints handling in the NHS* (London, Commission for Healthcare Audit and Inspection).

—— (2008) *Spotlight on complaints: a report on second-stage complaints about the NHS in England* (London, Commission for Healthcare Audit and Inspection) available at www.nationalschool.gov.uk/policyhub/news_item/complaints_nhs_england09.asp.

—— (2009) *Investigation into Mid Staffordshire NHS Foundation Trust* (London, Commission for Healthcare Audit and Inspection), available at www.cqc.org.uk/_db/_documents/Investigation_into_Mid_Staffordshire_NHS_Foundation_Trust.pdf.

House of Commons Public Administration Select Committee (2003) 'PASC attacks "disturbing" evidence of government administrative failure', Press Notice No 8, available at www.parliament.uk/parliamentary_committees/public_administration_select_committee/pasc_pn_8.cfm.

—— (2008) *When Citizens Complain. Fifth Report of Session 2007–08* (London, The Stationery Office).

Laming Review (2009) *The Protection of Children in England: A Progress Report* (London, The Stationery Office), available at http://publications.everychildmatters.gov.uk/eOrderingDownload/HC-330.pdf.

Merricks, W (2007) 'The Financial Ombudsman Service: not just an alternative to court' 15 *Journal of Financial Regulation and Compliance* 135.

Ministry of Justice (2007) *Transforming tribunals: Implementing Part 1 of the Tribunals, Courts and Enforcement Act* (London, MoJ).

Mueller, D (2003) *Public Choice III* (Cambridge, Cambridge University Press).

Mulcahy, L (2003) *Disputing Doctors: the socio-legal dynamics of complaints about medical care* (Maidenhead, Open University Press).

National Audit Office (2005) *Citizen Redress: What citizens can do if things go wrong with public services* HC 21 (London, The Stationery Office) available at www.nao.org.uk/publications/0405/citizen_redress.aspx.

—— (2008) *Department for Work and Pensions: Handling Customer Complaints* HC 995 (London, The Stationery Office) available at www.nao.org.uk/publications/0708/handling_customer_complaints.aspx.

National Consumer Council (2008) *The Hunt Review: Response to the call for evidence to the independent review of the Financial Ombudsman Service* (London, NCC).

National Ombudsman of the Netherlands (2008) *Annual Report* (The Hague, de Nationale ombudsman).

ORC International (2008) *Scottish Public Service Ombudsman: Complainant Satisfaction Survey 2007* (Edinburgh, ORC International) available at www.scottishombudsmanwatch.org/files/SPSO_07_satisfaction_survey__21_February_2008.pdf.

Parliamentary and Health Service Ombudsman (2007a) *Annual Report 2006–07: Putting principles into practice* (London, The Stationery Office).

—— (2007b) *Principles of Good Administration* (London, The Stationery Office), available at www.ombudsman.org.uk/improving_services/principles/good_administration/index.html.

—— (2007c) *Principles for Remedy* (London, The Stationery Office) available at www.ombudsman.org.uk/improving_services/principles/remedy/index.html.

—— (2008a) *Annual Report 2007–08: Bringing wider public benefit from individual complaints* (London, The Stationery Office).

—— (2008b) *Equitable Life: a decade of regulatory failure* (London, The Stationery Office).

Sampson, F and de Silva, N (2001) *Police Conduct, Complaints and Efficiency* (London, Blackstone Press).

Scottish Public Services Ombudsman (2007) *Annual Report 2006–07* (Edinburgh, SPSO).

—— (2008) *Annual Report 2007–08* (Edinburgh, SPSO).

Tax, SS and Brown, SW (2000) 'Service recovery, research insights and practices' in TA Swartz and D Iacobucci (eds), *Handbook of Services Marketing and Management* (Thousand Oaks, CA, Sage Publications).

The Tribunal Service (2006) *Framework Document* (London, Department for Constitutional Affairs).

Varney, D (2006) *Service transformation: A better service for citizens and businesses, a better deal for the taxpayer* (London, The Stationery Office).

18

Current Developments in the UK—Complaints Procedures and Ombudsmen

JACKIE GULLAND

Introduction

Stephen Lawrence, Jean Charles de Menezes, a woman distressed at the scars left after a mastectomy, two disabled boys, unable to attend school because of a breakdown in transport arrangements.[1] These people all share one thing in common: their experiences of public services in the UK have been investigated by internal complaints procedures and ombudsmen.

Internal complaints procedures and ombudsmen, in many ways the poor relations of tribunals and courts, have often been neglected in discussions of administrative justice. Mulcahy (1999: 70) has argued that 'legal scholars have paid little serious attention to complaints procedures'. However, we know that far more people use internal complaints procedures than use tribunals and courts. The issues they deal with may range from the petty to the tragic, but, to the people who make complaints, these issues are important and they may raise matters of fundamental significance to public services and the way they are run.

In setting out to write this chapter, I considered a number of different ways of attempting to describe recent developments in complaints procedures and ombudsmen in the UK. Each attempt left me with more confusion than the previous one. Partly this is because there is considerable complexity in these developments and partly it is because social policy is a moving target: each time I thought I had made sense of the latest development, something else changed or I discovered something that I hadn't previously known about. This illustrates the point that there is no single 'system' of complaints procedures or ombudsmen in the UK. Complaints procedures and ombudsmen have developed in a haphazard fashion

[1] Respectively, the police complaints procedure (reported in MacPherson 1999 and Independent Police Complaints Commission 2008), the health services complaints procedure (reported in Parliamentary and Health Services Ombudsman 2008) and a local authority complaints procedure (reported in Scottish Public Services Ombudsman 2007a).

over the last 40 years or so. This is the result of the way in which public services are organised and delivered: some public services are the responsibility of central government, others of local government and, within these, as Lewis and Birkinshaw (1993) have recognised, public service agencies are all different and have 'different cultures, sensitivities and political pressure points', thus suggesting that 'it will be difficult, if not impossible to recommend similar procedures' for them (ibid: 142). Devolution has also added to the difficulty of describing the 'system'. Although aspects of complaints procedures have always varied across England, Wales, Scotland and Northern Ireland, devolution has brought about greater variation. Although this is potentially confusing, for the purposes of this chapter it offers us the opportunity to compare different approaches to similar problems and to consider the advantages and disadvantages that each of these brings.

Over the last 20 years, policies promoting privatisation and contracting out have further complicated the landscape. Many services that were once public are now private or are organised at arms length from government and it is not always clear to whom a complaint should be made if a problem arises. Other chapters discuss the increasingly blurred boundaries between public and private services and the difficulties this creates for making sense of 'administrative justice'. For the sake of clarity, this chapter will focus primarily on complaints procedures and ombudsmen relating to public services but will also refer to developments in the private sector where these are particularly relevant.

Instead of attempting to describe this complexity, in all its glorious detail, this chapter sets out to show how recent policy developments reflect some of the inherent tensions in complaints procedures and ombudsmen schemes. Although there are considerable areas of overlap in the issues concerning the two mechanisms, it is useful to consider them separately, in traditional procedural terms, with internal complaints mechanisms at the bottom of a 'pyramid' and ombudsmen at the top. The final section will consider the relationship between the two mechanisms.

Internal Complaints Procedures

Recent History of Internal Complaints Procedures

Since there is no 'system' of internal complaints procedures, the policy focus in the UK has been on the provision of guidance to public services on the operation of complaints procedures. The Citizen's Charter initiatives from 1991 established the expectation that all government services would have complaints procedures:

> At the very least, the citizen is entitled to a good explanation, or an apology. He or she should be told *why* the train is late, or *why* the doctor could not keep the appointment. There should be a well-publicised and readily available complaints procedure. If there is a serious problem, it should be put right. And lessons must be learnt so that mistakes are not repeated. (Cabinet Office 1991: 5)

The Cabinet Office reinforced this expectation with the publication of guides to good practice in implementing complaints procedures (eg, Cabinet Office 1998; Citizen's Charter Complaints Task Force 1993). Most of this guidance concerns fairly common-sense issues such as making procedures accessible, dealing with complaints quickly, ensuring confidentiality, keeping complainants informed and using complaints information to improve services. Despite this, most research on the effectiveness of public services complaints procedures has found that they do not work well (see below for some examples of this research).

Apart from the principle that public services should have complaints procedures and the provision of advice on how to run them, there has been no statutory requirement for public bodies to have complaints procedures or consistency in advice about how they should operate, except in relation to certain specific services: the NHS, local authority social care services and some education services.

While there has been continuing interest in complaints procedures in these difficult areas (see below for further details), policy interest in complaints procedures across public services was reignited by the Department for Constitutional Affairs White Paper (DCA 2004), which included 'complaints' in its title and, to an extent, in its discussion of redress mechanisms, although its primary focus was on tribunals. Around the same time the National Audit Office report on citizen redress (NAO 2005) took seriously the issue of complaints procedures as part of the administrative justice landscape. Complaints had arrived. Although the Tribunals, Courts and Enforcement Act 2007 has little to say about internal complaints procedures, the Administrative Justice and Tribunals Council has within its remit to 'keep the administrative justice system under review' (Schedule 7, paragraph 13(1)(a)) and, although internal complaints procedures are perhaps not the highest priority on the AJTC's agenda, in the first year of publishing its *Adjust* newsletter, the AJTC has included news about internal complaints in a variety of fields (AJTC 2008).

The most recent policy document coming from Westminster on complaints procedures as a whole is the House of Commons Public Administration Select Committee Report (House of Commons 2008). This report reiterates much of the Citizen's Charter's commitment to 'putting the user first' and to 'learning from complaints', while recognising that the complaints procedures set up under the Citizen's Charter initiatives have not always achieved these goals. The Report acknowledges some of the difficulties in complaints handling that were perhaps missing from the earlier optimistic statements about complaints, for example that complaints are not always easy to identify, that there is confusion between the notions of complaining and appealing and that people frequently need help to negotiate complaints procedures.

In an attempt to resolve some of these problems, the Select Committee Report recommends that there should be a 'single access point for all public services' (ibid: 15), which would enable people to get information and advice about complaining. It says that this should be 'nationwide' but, since it is concerned with the responsibilities of the UK Government, it does not address the complexities of devolution. The Report provides advice on good practice in complaints handling but stops short of proposing a single complaints mechanism for all public services, on the ground that organisations vary too much to make this possible. Finally the Report recognises that complainants will often seek an independent review of their complaint and that this is an essential part of a complaints procedure. (For a discussion of the role of independence in complaints procedures, see below.) The Report's general conclusion is that complaints procedures are not working effectively and that central government has a role in that it must 'champion good practice in complaints handling (ibid: 32), without prescribing how complaints procedures should operate in detail. Its recommendation is that this role should be taken by the Cabinet Office (ibid: 32). Perhaps because the Report starts from the notion of complaints as essentially consumerist, it makes no reference to the role of the Administrative Justice and Tribunals Council. Where it does refer to the role of the (Parliamentary and Health Services) Ombudsman, it does not portray the Ombudsman as the top of a complaints pyramid but more as a source of information on problems in public services, arguing that the number of complaints upheld by the Ombudsman should be a measure of quality control in public services (ibid*:* 28).

The Select Committee Report is concerned only with public services administered by the UK Government. It makes no reference to local authority services or to services administered by devolved administrations. Except in the case of specific local authority services (see the discussion below on social care and education), there has been no recent policy on local authority complaints handling in England. In Scotland, on the other hand, there has been an overall review of complaints handling in relation to all services within the Scottish administration's remit, including local authorities. Under the general task of reviewing 'regulation audit and inspection', the Crerar Review (Crerar 2007) considered the adequacy of complaints handling mechanisms in Scotland. This review, which acknowledged that complaints procedures were complicated and inconsistent across Scotland, was followed by the establishment of an action group by the Scottish Government that was asked to look at possible solutions to these problems. While standing back from recommending a common complaints procedure across all Scottish public authorities, the Action Group recommended a common procedure across particular service areas, such as local authorities. It also recommended minimising the number of specialist independent complaints handlers, suggesting instead that the Scottish Public Services Ombudsman should take on this role wherever possible, and that, in particular, it should take over responsibility for prison complaints (Scottish Government 2008: para 74). This approach, while concerning a much smaller administration and, consequently, a much smaller number of organisations and complaints, does look more like a 'complaints system' than that proposed by the House of Commons Select Committee. However, it also fails to take account of the complications resulting from the fact that Scottish citizens also have to deal with bodies which are not within the remit of the Scottish Government. So that, even if a more or less standardised complaints system was established in Scotland, people would still have to negotiate a multiplicity of different procedures when it came to dealing with their tax, social security or other issues reserved to Westminster. Similar difficulties would be encountered by the Welsh and Northern Irish administrations if they attempted to standardise complaints procedures within their borders.

Research on Complaints Procedures

Where there have been statutory complaints procedures, there has been somewhat more interest in ensuring their effective implementation and consequently, there has been more research on how they operate. Complaints procedures for health care have attracted particular interest, leading to reform of the procedure in 1996 and again, after continued criticism (eg, Department of Health 2003; Posnett et al 2001, Wallace and Mulcahy 1999) in 2004–05. By then, devolution of responsibility for health services meant that different procedures were developed at different dates in England, Scotland, Wales and Northern Ireland. Despite these reforms, recent research continues to highlight problems with health complaints (Commission for Health Care Audit and Inspection 2007; Health Service Ombudsman for England 2005, National Audit Office 2008). In England further reforms are planned for introduction in 2009 (Department of Health 2007 and 2008).

The other main statutory complaints procedure: that relating to local authority-provided social care services was also subject to a series of revisions during this period. Statutory procedures were introduced under the community care reforms of 1990. In England there has been a series of consultation papers on changes to the procedure, with reforms introduced in 2006 and more under discussion (Department of Health 2007). The Welsh Assembly Government amended the procedures for Wales in 2006, Northern Ireland included social care complaints in its 2006 consultation paper (Department of Health Social Services and Public Safety 2006), while in Scotland the procedure is likely to be included under the proposals coming out of the Crerar review (Scottish Government 2008).

What these reviews reveal is that complaints procedures in relation to social welfare are not simple and that the operation of them cannot simply follow common-sense guidance on accessibility and clarity. In the field of public services there is a constant tension between the need to provide quality services and the constraints of limited resources. However 'customer focused' public service providers might be, they will often be unwilling to devote scarce funds to what is often seen as time-consuming procedures that only attract 'difficult' people and that take resources away from people who need them more. Policy reviews of complaints procedures rarely address head on the issue of power relations between public services and 'service users'. For example, Linda Mulcahy's work on health complaints (Mulcahy 2003) shows that there are inherent conflicts between the concerns of patients and health professionals, and between those of doctors, managers and other health service staff. Similarly, in the field of social care, the power relationships and expectations of both service users and staff are not simple. Many users of social care services are not willing 'customers' (Clarke et al 2007). Some potential service users may be unwilling to use community care services for fear of being 'put in a home', or losing what independence they have. Users of mental health services may reject the 'services' that they are offered or forced to accept. Social services relating to children are particularly problematic from this point of view, since social services staff have considerable power. In relation to social security, Dean (2002) has argued that 'service users' are constructed in particularly powerless positions as 'welfare subjects'. Understanding the complexity of such relationships and their competing demands shows that the common sense approach to complaints procedures is not sufficient.

In a quite different field of public services—policing and prisons—there has been a long and bitter debate about complaints procedures. Here the debate is rather different and focuses less on 'service quality' and more on civil liberties and public safety. In relation to the police, the question of whether (potential) complainants are 'consumers' is even more in doubt (Clarke et al 2007), since complainants can include both victims and alleged perpetrators of crime, while it is difficult to imagine that those who might complain about prison conditions could be considered consumers at all. Even if, as has been argued—particularly in relation to the police (ibid)—these services have moved towards a more 'consumer focussed' approach, it is difficult to imagine that, in the context of recent developments in policing and on prison overcrowding, the voices of these 'consumers' are likely to be heard. Cavadino and Dignan (2007: 236) argue that the lack of transparency of what goes on in prisons makes it very difficult for complaints to be seen to be taken seriously. In these public services, given the complexity of the power relationships, there is often a call for complaints to be handled by independent bodies, rather than relying on internal procedures.

Independence in Complaints Procedures

Although the Citizen's Charter initiatives on complaints procedures emphasised the importance of internal procedures, there has been a growth in external or quasi-independent reviewers of complaints in many areas of public services. The debate on independent review in the field of health complaints has been heated and research has consistently shown that complainants are suspicious of internal review mechanisms. The current arrangements for review of health complaints are different in each of the devolved administrations: in Scotland and Northern Ireland the internal complaints procedure is followed immediately by the option of complaining to the Scottish Public Services Ombudsman or the Northern Ireland Ombudsman, while in Wales there is a separate independent complaints review body. In England the current arrangement is that the internal complaints procedure is followed by the option of complaining to the Health Care Commission, but it is proposed to replace this with a 'straight to the Ombudsman' procedure (Department of Health 2007). When a more independent element review was introduced in health complaints, the numbers of cases increased dramatically: from 3,993 to 8,000 per year in England (Commission for Health Care Audit and Inspection 2007) and from 321 to 732 in Scotland (Scottish Public Services Ombudsman 2006). This suggests that complainants prefer to send their complaints to an independent body, although the reviewing organisations themselves are concerned that many of these complaints could have been dealt with more effectively by the internal procedure (Commission for Health Care Audit and Inspection 2007).

Complaints in higher education provide another good example of the need for independence. In England, Wales and Northern Ireland, concern about the lack of an independent element in complaints procedures led to the creation of the Office of the Independent Adjudicator for Higher Education (for a discussion of its role, see Harris 2007) while, in Scotland, complaints about higher education are dealt with by the Scottish Public Services Ombudsman.

In relation to school education, a recent consultation document in England proposes the setting up of an independent complaints reviewer to deal with second tier complaints about schools (Department for Children Schools and Families 2008). The current arrangements are complex, with complaints about most types of schools having to go to the Secretary of State, while complaints relating to local authority policies and provision can be handled by the Local Government Ombudsman. The consultation paper considers two options: locating the new independent complaints body within the offices of the Local Government Ombudsman or within the offices of the Schools Adjudicators (which deal with a range of policy issues including schools admissions). Although a decision has not been reached, the proposals recognise that an independent element is necessary but show that there are a number of different ways in which it can be organised. The proposals also illustrate the way in which complaints procedures overlap with other mechanisms such as tribunals and courts. Parents who have grievances about special educational needs, school exclusions and school admissions are entitled to make appeals under a variety of pieces of legislation, which the proposals do not intend to change. Complaints can also be made to Ofsted if the problem relates to educational standards. The proposals do not attempt to resolve this complexity by changing the other mechanisms but by suggesting a 'portal which routes people dissatisfied with a service to the appropriate body' (Department for Children Schools and Families 2008: para 79).

Arrangements in Northern Ireland and Wales are similar to those in England, with some complaints being reviewable by the Secretary of State, some by the Ombudsman and others being appealable to a range of tribunal or court processes. The DCSF consultation paper applies to England only.

Complaints about schools in Scotland are also complicated, in that there are a number of separate statutory appeal and review procedures available for grievances relating to special educational needs (known in Scotland as additional support needs), admissions and exclusions. All other complaints are dealt with by internal complaints mechanisms, followed by the option of a complaint to the Scottish Public Services Ombudsman. In a recent review of schools complaints, the Scottish Consumer Council (2006: 2) called for 'a single, coherent system for external review'.

These examples illustrate the move towards having some form of independent element in complaints about education, while showing that there is a continuing distinction between grievances that have been given the status of 'appeals' and that can be heard by a variety of tribunals and courts, and 'all other grievances' that tend to be subsumed by complaints procedures.

In areas of public service reserved to Westminster, the Independent Case Examiner reviews complaints which have already been dealt with internally in relation to child support and social security benefits.[2] In other areas of public services, the Adjudicator's Office[3] deals with complaints about HM Revenue and Customs and Tax Credits, but also has responsibility for complaints about bodies that operate only in England and Wales (ie, the Valuation Office Agency, the Public Guardianship Office and the Insolvency Service). Meanwhile, the Independent Complaints Reviewer[4] also has a mixed remit, dealing with complaints about the Audit Commission, the Charity Commission, the National Archives and the Land Registry. Where these have devolved equivalents in Scotland, responsibility for reviewing internal complaints lies with the Scottish Public Services Ombudsman. Somewhat bizarrely, the Independent Complaints Reviewer also deals with complaints about the Northern Ireland Youth Justice Agency, without having an equivalent responsibility for similar services in England and Wales.

Despite the complexity of these arrangements for the independent review of complaints, these examples show that, in some fields at least, it has been recognised that internal complaints procedures are not sufficient. However the independent elements have been built up in a piecemeal fashion and it is not clear why they have been considered necessary in some areas but not others. The recent report by the Select Committee on Public Administration has argued that these bodies 'tend to be appropriate … where there are large numbers of individuals that would otherwise take cases all the way to the Ombudsman service' and that, in other areas, 'having a separate complaint review body would not be proportionate'(House of Commons 2008: 19). While it is understandable that this argument might apply to benefits and tax complaints—the Independent Case Examiner received around 5,000 complaints in 2007–08 (ICE 2008) while the Adjudicator's Office received 1,690 complaints relating to tax and tax credits (AO 2008)—it is hard to imagine that the National Archives generate sufficient complaints that would otherwise go to the Ombudsman and indeed the Annual Report for 2008 claims that no complaints about the National Archives were subject to a full investigation by the Independent Complaints Reviewer.

Apart from proportionality, there is an additional argument that including this intermediate layer of review between the internal complaints procedure

[2] Available at www.ind-case-exam.org.uk/index.asp.

[3] Available at www.adjudicatorsoffice.gov.uk.

[4] Available at www.icrev.org.uk.

and the relevant Ombudsman only creates further hurdles for complainants, leading to what has been described in other fields of administrative justice as 'appellant fatigue' (Cowan and Halliday 2003). The Select Committee on Public Administration has argued that this can be resolved by ensuring 'clear information and guidance' (House of Commons 2008: 21).

Whether it is necessary to have an intermediate layer of independent review like this and in such an incoherent fashion is not entirely clear. The solution in Scotland which has been, in most cases, to dispense with intermediate layers of review and have all complaints about public services go straight from the internal procedure to the Ombudsman, seems much more sensible.

Another area which has seen an upsurge in independent complaints handlers is the prison service. Confusingly these bodies use the name 'ombudsman' in England, Wales and Northern Ireland, although there is a debate as to whether they qualify as 'ombudsmen'. In England and Wales the Prisons and Probation Ombudsman handles complaints from prisoners and people on probation relating to their conditions but excluding issues such as conviction and sentencing. Although the ombudsman cannot investigate disputes about these matters, he can investigate disputes relating to disciplinary issues that can have a direct effect on the actual release dates of particular prisoners (Cavadino and Dignan 2007; Prisons and Probation Ombudsman for England and Wales 2008). As well as handling complaints from individuals, these ombudsmen have the additional remit of investigating deaths in prison and have been asked to take on special investigations of particular incidents (Cavadino and Dignan 2007). There is also a Prisoner Ombudsman in Northern Ireland, with a similar remit. The Prisons and Probation Ombudsman has also recently taken on responsibility for investigating complaints about immigration removal centres (Prisons and Probation Ombudsman for England and Wales 2008). In Scotland there is a Scottish Prisons Complaints Commission, with a similar (although more restricted) remit.

Although these ombudsmen are 'independent' of the prison service, there are still concerns around whether the posts are sufficiently independent and none of these posts has been accepted as meeting the full conditions for independence required for membership of the British and Irish Ombudsmen Association. All three prisons ombudsmen continue to regret their lack of statutory status (Prisoner Ombudsman for Northern Ireland 2008; Prisons and Probation Ombudsman for England and Wales 2008; Scottish Prisons Complaints Commission 2008).

Despite this debate regarding their status (and titles) as ombudsmen, the prisons ombudsmen also reflect the acceptance of a need for more visible independence than an internal complaints procedure can provide, in an area where complainants are likely to be highly cynical about the value of making complaints to those in charge.

The important point to note here is that, while internal complaints procedures are suitable for most complaints and will deal with most issues 'proportionately', many complainants also seek the opportunity to have their complaints heard by a body which is demonstrably independent of the body complained about. This has been shown clearly in relation to complaints about health services (Mulcahy 2003), police (Waters and Brown 2000), prisons (Cavadino and Dignan), social care (Gulland 2009), schools (Scottish Consumer Council 2008) and higher education (Harris 2007). Although very diverse in terms of what they do, these services have two things in common: professional power and the fact that they make significant differences to the lives of those they affect, in terms of their income, their health, their ability to cope with daily living, their educational opportunities, their safety or their civil liberties. In all of these areas, where there has been a serious incident or breakdown of service provision, it is difficult to think of people's experiences as 'consumer' issues where an informal 'sorting it out' approach will be sufficient. At this point people demand and should be entitled to an independent review of their complaint.

What we can see from recent developments in complaints procedures in relation to independence is, on the one hand, a resistance to setting up fully independent bodies: in health, social care and policing there has been a strong pull towards maintaining professional control over complaints, based on the idea that independent reviewers would not understand the issues. On the other hand, in recent years, policy in all of these areas has moved towards the provision of independent elements, with an acceptance that complainants do not trust 'insider only' approaches. This is not to say that complainants will necessarily be any happier with the decisions of independent reviewers. Complaints in higher education provide a good example here. Harris (2007) has shown that independent reviewers of higher education complaints tend to reject complaints because they are usually able to look only at procedural matters and not at matters of academic decision making. Most complaints are in effect challenges to academic decisions (course grades, discontinuation of studies) and, although complaints may be upheld in relation to the way in which these decisions are made, they are rarely able to achieve what the complainant wanted, that is, for their studies to be resumed or a pass mark to be awarded.

This leads to the question of the purpose of complaints procedures and the extent to which they are appropriate mechanisms for challenging substantive decisions.

Purposes of complaints procedures

As other chapters in this volume show, grievance mechanisms have a number of different purposes, including providing redress to individuals, providing information to management and maintaining professional standards in service provision. These different purposes are not always compatible, and so complaints procedures are sometimes better at achieving one purpose rather than another, or sometimes fail in all purposes.

Complaints procedures are usually seen as being primarily 'consumerist', casting the complainant in the role of 'consumer', for whom the procedure provides a 'voice' in the running of public services (Adler 2006; Mulcahy and Allsop 1997).

The following statement from the new body, Consumer Focus (which replaced the National Consumer Council) is representative of this view:

> Anyone who buys or uses goods or services, whether in the public or the private sector, is a consumer. This recognises that people are in a particular kind of relationship with providers whether they pay for goods and services directly (e.g. energy or groceries) or indirectly through taxation (e.g. health or local authority services). (Consumer Focus 2008: 40)

However, as the discussion above shows, people do not always see themselves as consumers of public services and, even when they do so, they may seek something rather different from a complaints procedure compared to their position as a consumer taking back faulty goods.

There are times when people seek more than this: to have a decision overturned (for example, where there is no formal appeal procedure or where appeal procedures appear inaccessible) or where they want a statement by an independent body that their complaint is valid, whether or not that includes individual redress of some kind. To this extent, evidence from research on complaints procedures supports Patrick Dunleavy's argument that it is unhelpful to distinguish between 'complaints' and 'appeals' (see Dunleavy's chapter in this volume). Many complaints may, in effect, be appeals. Evidence from social care, where there is no formal appeal procedure against local authority decisions, shows that people may use the complaints procedure in this way (Gulland 2007). In this particular area there has been consideration of introducing an appeal procedure to deal with disputes which are about substantive elements (Law Commission 2008b). Even in areas where there are separate appeals and complaints procedures, people may use complaints procedures to challenge substantive decisions. However, complainants are often seeking something that is different from an appeal about substantive matters. Research on health complaints has been particularly illuminating in this respect. Health complaints are often made after the fact and so are not 'instrumental' in the sense that complainants do not seek a specific action as a result. Lloyd Bostock and Mulcahy (1994) have described complainants' actions as 'calling the authority to account'. Where this is what a complainant seeks, he or she will look for a statement from the authority concerned that the problem has been noticed and that something will be done to prevent it occurring again. A simple apology may not be enough.

However, complaints have also been seen as a source of management information, an additional tool, along with audit and inspection, to enable managers to identify and resolve problems with public services and drive up quality. A procedure which is focussed on sorting out problems with a minimum of fuss may not provide the kind of formal recording mechanisms that are needed to provide management information. Reviews of complaints procedures have consistently told us that they have not been good at providing this information (National Audit Office 2005; National Audit Office 2008).

There are also complaints procedures that are intended to deal with a rather different range of problems: those concerned with the maintenance of professional standards and, in most cases these are set up separately from 'ordinary' complaints procedures, with quite different mechanisms, investigation processes and resolution options. The rationale behind these procedures is concerned with maintaining professional standards and, in extreme cases, protecting the public from harm. These types of procedures do not clearly fall within the term 'administrative justice', since their focus is on investigating alleged wrongdoing by professionals rather than on the meeting the needs of the complainant. Typical examples of procedures relating to public services include those relating to the health professions, for example procedures run by the Health Professions Council, the General Medical Council and the Nursing and Midwifery Council. Although these bodies deal with complaints that are rather different from those dealt with by, for example, the NHS complaints procedures, this will not always be clear to potential complainants. The General Medical Council's website provides case studies, advising potential complainants about when it is appropriate to use the GMC procedure and when the local health provider's complaints procedure is more suitable.[5]

In the field of complaints against the police, Smith (2004) has shown that complaints have a number of different dimensions (differentiating 'unprofessional behaviour, criminal conduct, tortious actions and unacceptable policy' (ibid: 28) and arguing that each of these has different implications for how complaints should be dealt with and that there should be separate procedures for complaints relating to the actions of individual police officers (including alleged criminal conduct) and those relating to issues of policy (ibid: 29).

Most discussions of complaints procedures tend to assume that their main purpose is consumerist, although recognising that they may also be useful for management purposes. The consumerist focus of most policy documents on complaints procedures stresses that complaints handlers should find out 'what complainants want'. The recent Select Committee Report says: 'Public services should seek to discover what complainants hope to achieve from making their views known' (House of Commons 2008: 18).

It is widely believed that most complainants want a 'simple apology' or an explanation for what has gone wrong (eg, Department for Constitutional Affairs 2004: 6; House of Commons 2008: 18). However, there has been very little research on what complainants do want, but such as there is, it suggests that things are a little more complicated than this.

Recognising that complaints procedures have a number of purposes is a first step in making them effective. As discussions of different models of justice have shown (Adler 2006), different mechanisms of dispute resolution reflect different values and may be more or less suitable for different purposes. Unless policy makers are clear about the purpose of complaints procedures, these procedures will continue to frustrate both the complainants and those who manage

[5] Available at www.gmc-uk.org/concerns/index.asp.

public services. The problem is that conflicting purposes lead to different styles of procedure, and procedures that are appropriate for some service areas may not be so for others. This takes us back to the inherent problem of complexity in complaints procedures and the impossibility of trying to establish standardised complaints systems for public services in the UK.

Complexity

Commentaries on complaints procedures usually start by describing their complexity and by showing that this makes it particularly difficult for citizens to know what to do when they are dissatisfied with public services. For example, in relation to public services in Scotland, the Crerar Report said:

> It is difficult for a complainant to navigate the present regime because of the number of complaints bodies, because providers have different ways of dealing with complaints and because it is not always clear which body should be responsible for dealing with the issue. (Crerar 2007, p88)

While the Public Administration Committee's Report on complaints about central government said:

> As the state commissions services from a wider array of organisations, it becomes more difficult to understand complaints systems. It can be a challenge simply to discover where first to complain, and who to contact if matters cannot be resolved. (House of Commons 2008: 11)

While these reports recognise complexity within a particular territory (eg, central government or a devolved administration), other reports recognise that people's problems do not fall neatly into these administrative categories. So a complaint about care services on discharge from hospital can concern central (or devolved) government responsibilities (social security and hospital services), local government responsibilities (social work services) and private or third sector provision such as housing or care services. Similarly a parent's concern about support for a child's special educational needs could involve the local authority, the health authority and social security.

Research shows that 'legal' problems often come in 'clusters', for example, family problems, employment problems and problems concerning money (Moorhead et al 2006). If we understand the problems that may be resolved by complaints procedures as 'legal' in their widest sense, we should not be surprised to find that the problems that people complain about (or could or should complain about) may also come in such clusters. The Law Commission's recent report on housing disputes is a good example of how people's problems may concern more than just one agency. The problems that lead to a housing dispute usually affect other aspects of a person's life as well, potentially leading to further disputes in different arenas, for example, money or employment problems (Law Commission 2008a: 18).

If the purpose of a complaints procedure or an ombudsman service is to provide information to government or to service managers, the fact that the complaints landscape is cluttered only matters because it makes it difficult for the complainant to navigate. The solution is fairly clear: simplification of complaints procedures.

If on the other hand we turn our focus on the potential complainant, it may be that the problem concerns a one-off problem with a particular service, perhaps similar to the 'consumer' problems that many existing complaints procedures are set up to deal with. However, it is equally likely that, if it is not a one-off problem, it could be one relating to a long term relationship between the complainant and the service provider, or it could be part of a much wider range of problems where complaining is only one option amongst many. With services involving long term relationships between providers and 'service users', complaints often have 'a history', in other words, they are not usually about one-off events but about a series of incidents or a long-running background of difficulties that culminate in a formal complaint (Simons 1995: 46). Once a complaint has been registered, a particular problem may be resolved, its focus may change, it may be intensified or something new and unrelated may crop up. This is when the complexity matters much more. Making the complaints procedure easier to navigate will not be sufficient, since the potential complaint may involve more than just one agency. It may also involve making more formal legal challenges to decisions, taking some other action entirely, or recognising that the problem cannot be resolved through 'legal' challenge at all.

The key to all of this is advice for complainants. Some of the more recent discussions of complaints recognise this (Adler 2008; House of Commons 2008). This brings us back again to the purpose of complaints procedures and what it is that complainants seek. The point is that people do not always just want an apology or to have a simple problem 'sorted out'. They make seek a rather more complicated outcome or they may not be sure what they want, other than to ensure that somebody pays attention to their problem and does something to prevent it happening again.

Some commentators have argued that, although complaints procedures may not be able to achieve these multiple purposes, ombudsmen are well placed to act both as the final adjudicators of complaints and as sources of information on problems with public services.

Ombudsmen

Recent History of Ombudsmen in the UK

Ombudsmen are sometimes seen as the appropriate independent bodies for dealing with complaints that cannot be resolved by internal procedures, although this is not their only role. Defining an ombudsman is difficult, as the name means different things in different countries and, even within the UK, there is a variety of different definitions (Seneviratne 2002). Generally speaking, however, public sector ombudsmen are independent bodies that investigate complaints about 'maladministration', usually only after the complainant has already exhausted any internal complaints procedure. The British and Irish Ombudsman Association (BIOA), although recognising that there is considerably variety in the way ombudsmen operate, requires applicants to satisfy four criteria:

> An Ombudsman scheme has to meet four key conditions to be recognised by the Association. Those conditions are independence of the Ombudsman from the organisations the Ombudsman has the power to investigate; effectiveness; fairness and public accountability. It is independence which, above all, distinguishes recognised Ombudsman schemes from other complaints procedures. Those who head the internal complaints procedures of their own organisations, even if described as Ombudsmen, are not wholly independent. (BIOA 2008)

BIOA provides detailed explanation of the meaning of 'independence' in its criteria for membership. On its website, it describes the ombudsmen as 'the last resort'.

As with internal complaints procedures, there is no ombudsman 'system' in the UK, although Ann Abraham (the current Parliamentary and Health Services Ombudsman) has argued that there is, at least in so far as ombudsmen are distinctively different from courts and tribunals (Abraham 2008). In this chapter I will not discuss the early history of Ombudsmen in the UK, since this has been done well by others (eg, Harlow and Rawlings 1997; Kirkham 2007b; Seneviratne 2002; Thompson 2006). Instead, I will look at recent developments and at the relationship between ombudsmen and internal complaints procedures.

There are several different public sector ombudsmen, dealing with different aspects of public services: the main ones are the Parliamentary and Health Services Ombudsman (PHSO), with responsibility for investigating complaints about central government services and about health services in England and the Local Government Ombudsman (LGO) covering local government in England. In the devolved administrations there are ombudsmen covering most public services: the Scottish Public Services Ombudsman (SPSO) and the Public Services Ombudsman for Wales (PSOW). In Northern Ireland, although there are two positions of ombudsmen: the Assembly Ombudsman for Northern Ireland and the Northern Ireland Commissioner for Complaints, these two offices are currently held by one person, known informally as the Northern Ireland Ombudsman (NIO).

Perhaps it is devolution that has been responsible for the biggest change in ombudsmen in recent years. The decision by the Welsh and Scottish administrations to set up 'umbrella' ombudsmen, covering most public services within their remit, is a break from the tradition of specialisation, established by the original Parliamentary Ombudsman in 1967, followed by Health Services and Local Government Ombudsmen in the 1970s. Although there has been consideration of merging the different ombudsmen in England (Colcutt and Hourihan 2000), this has been rejected in favour of encouraging co-operation between the Parliamentary and Health Services Ombudsman and the Local Government Ombudsmen through the Regulatory Reform (Collaboration etc between Ombudsmen) Order 2007 (SI 2007/1889).

As well as these core public services ombudsmen, in recent years there has been a proliferation of specialist ombudsmen, dealing with other public services (such as the Independent Police Complaints Commission and the various prisons ombudsmen), private services (eg, the Energy Ombudsman, the Financial Services Ombudsman, the Legal Services Ombudsman and the Pensions Ombudsman), and quasi public services (eg, the Housing Ombudsman Service, which investigates complaints about registered social landlords and, in some cases, private landlords).

Access to Ombudsmen

Almost all the public sector ombudsmen can be contacted directly by complainants, although they usually expect people to have exhausted any internal complaints procedure first. Although this seems straightforward, many people take their complaints straight to the ombudsmen without exhausting internal complaints procedures. These are sometimes described as 'premature complaints'. Recent figures suggest that they range between 20 and 40 per cent of complaints made to the public sector ombudsmen (PHSO: 19 per cent; SPSO: 40 per cent; LGO: 27 per cent) and that they are particularly problematic in certain areas. For example, in Scotland the SPSO has much a higher rate of premature complaints relating to housing associations (around 69 per cent of complaints) compared to those relating to health (around 29 per cent) (SPSO 2008: 17). The SPSO conducted a small piece of research relating to these premature complaints in 2007 and found that, most 'premature' complainants *had* approached the relevant authority before contacting the ombudsman, although they had not used the internal complaints procedure (SPSO 2007). This suggests that complainants are not contacting the ombudsman prematurely because of ignorance of the proper procedure but due to an absence of trust that the internal mechanism will meet their expectations. This research also found that the 'premature' complainants did not pursue their grievance further once it had been 'rejected' by the ombudsman. Premature complaints create problems, both for the ombudsmen, for whom they create extra work, and for the complainants, who are no doubt frustrated that the ombudsmen cannot deal with these complaints. The Cabinet Office's review of ombudsmen in England recommended that further research should be carried out into premature complaints (Colcutt and Hourihan 2000) but, other than the small piece of research carried out for the SPSO, no further work has been done on this.

In the case of the Parliamentary Ombudsman there is an additional barrier: the so-called 'MP filter'. This means complaints must be submitted by the complainant's Member of Parliament. This procedure dates back to the original legislation establishing the 'Parliamentary Commissioner for Administration' in

1967, when the role was seen primarily as one of assisting members of parliament in monitoring the activities of Government departments. This appears to be something of an anachronism today. Most commentators have advocated the abolition of the MP filter, including the Cabinet Office's review of public sector ombudsmen (Colcutt and Hourihan 2000) and the recent Law Commission Consultation Paper, which noted that: 'It can be seen as a product of its time, and the criticisms of it see it as no longer relevant to a mature ombudsman's service' (Law Commission 2008c: 28).

Although there is general agreement that the disadvantages of the MP filter outweigh the advantages (see eg Kirkham 2007a; Seneviratne 2002), the filter remains. The main hurdle appears to be that removing the MP filter would require an Act of Parliament, while other reforms have been achieved through subordinate legislation (Cabinet Office 2005).

Generally speaking, although access to the ombudsmen is straightforward, does not require legal advice and does not incur fees, ombudsmen are concerned that people do not know enough about their services and have been taking steps to increase their profile, through publicity and improved information on their websites.

Although much has been written from a legal perspective on ombudsmen and their activities (Kirkham 2007a and 2007b; Kirkham et al 2008; Seneviratne 2002, 2006 and 2008; Thompson 2001 and 2006) and there has been empirical research on the work of ombudsmen in the public sector (eg, ongoing work by Thompson et al 2008) and the private sector (Gilad 2008), there has been very little research on the experience of people who make complaints. Various ombudsmen have carried out satisfaction surveys (eg, Ipsos MORI 2007; MORI 1999) but, beyond this, the small piece of research carried out on behalf of the Scottish Public Services Ombudsman (SPSO 2007b) and the collective impressions gained by the ombudsmen offices (for example, Abraham (2008) argues that 'most customers are satisfied' with the service her office provides), we know very little about the experiences of people who make complaints to ombudsmen. As we have seen, a high proportion of complaints to the ombudsmen are rejected at an early stage and few of them are finally 'upheld' after a full investigation. It would be encouraging if we knew that recent efforts by the various ombudsmen to make their services more accessible and flexible were appreciated by complainants.

Patterns of Complaints to Ombudsmen

The main source of information on the activities of the ombudsmen is their own annual reports, which provide detailed statistics on a range of matters. Recent figures for complaints to the main public sector ombudsmen show that a small range of areas of public sector activity attract the majority of complaints. In relation to central government, the Parliamentary Ombudsman received 7,341 complaints during 2007/08—over a third of cases concerned complaints about the Department for Work and Pensions (2,574), followed by 2,342 concerning

HM Revenue and Customs (most of these concerning tax credits). Meanwhile the Health Services Ombudsman received 4,257 complaints relating to health services (PHSO 2008). The Local Government Ombudsman (England) received 17,628 complaints during 2007–08, of which 23 per cent concerned planning and building control and 21 per cent concerned housing (Commission for Local Administration in England 2008).

Similar patterns of complaints can be found with the devolved ombudsmen—according to the Scottish Public Services Ombudsman's most recent annual report, 23 per cent complaints handled by the SPSO concerned housing (either local authority or registered social landlords), 20 per cent concerned health, and complaints about planning, although a smaller proportion of the total, was the second largest category of complaints about local government (SPSO 2008). Housing (23 per cent), planning (21 per cent) and health (16 per cent) complaints also make up the largest categories of complaint to the Public Services Ombudsman for Wales (PSOW 2008).

In Northern Ireland complaints statistics are rather more complicated, because of the split between the Assembly Ombudsman for Northern Ireland and the Northern Ireland Commissioner for Complaints, and because the range of responsibilities is rather different from Scotland and Wales (for example, the Northern Ireland ombudsman deals with complaints about social security benefits and child support, areas which are covered by the Parliamentary Ombudsman in relation to Scotland and Wales). However, as with other parts of the UK, planning, housing and health are the most common areas of complaint (Northern Ireland Ombudsman 2008).

One of the difficulties in assessing the meaning of this pattern of complaints concerns the problem of how to count complaints. The figures discussed above are based on 'complaints received' by the respective ombudsmen, but many of these were not investigated, either because they were outside the ombudsman's jurisdiction, were 'premature' (ie, the complainant had not already used the relevant internal complaints procedure), the complaint was deficient in some way (for example insufficient information was provided for the ombudsman to pursue it) or, in the case of the Parliamentary Ombudsman, the complaint had not been properly made (ie, it had not gone through the MP). These categories of complaint make up a significant proportion of the complaints these ombudsmen receive. For example, 42 per cent of complaints to the Parliamentary Ombudsman in 2007/08 were considered to be 'not properly made' (PHSO 2008)—in other words, the MP filter had deterred complainants from making their complaint effectively. This problem applies only to the Parliamentary Ombudsman while the problem of 'premature complaints', which was discussed above, appears to be significant for all the ombudsmen.

Once a complaint has been accepted as relevant to the ombudsman's work it may still not lead to a formal investigation. The Parliamentary Ombudsman, for example, differentiates between 'interventions' where the ombudsman intervenes to resolve a problem and 'investigations' where a full investigation is carried out. The number of investigations carried out on complaints relating to the Department for Work and Pensions was only 78 and, on complaints relating to HM Revenue and Customs, it was only 160 (PHSO 2008).

It is only when a formal investigation is carried out and completed, that ombudsmen make a finding of whether or not the complaint was 'upheld'. This means that figures in an ombudsman's annual report describing the proportion of complaints upheld, or not, only provide part of the picture in relation to problems with public services. The ombudsmen are aware of this problem and do regard it as part of their duty to report on general patterns of complaints, including those which are considered premature, out of jurisdiction, or dealt with at an earlier stage.

This more flexible approach to dealing with complaints is no doubt better for both complainants and public bodies as well as being cheaper and more 'proportionate' than a full-blown investigation, but it does make it more difficult to make sense of ombudsman statistics.

The Role of Public Sector Ombudsmen

Most of the public sector ombudsmen in the UK have the task of investigating complaints relating to 'maladminstration' and are restricted from investigating complaints that relate purely to the merits of administrative decisions. However, commentators have argued that the concept of maladministration has been interpreted flexibly (Seneviratne 2002), suggesting that this restriction does not create too much of a problem. Having said that, the powers of some public sector ombudsmen have been expanded to include other issues. For example, in relation to health services, the Parliamentary and Health Services Ombudsman, is able to investigate 'service failure'. The devolved Scottish and Welsh Ombudsmen have also taken on this remit and, since 2008, so has the Local Government Ombudsman for England. In Wales the remit has been extended to include 'professional judgment' in relation to social care cases (Seneviratne 2006), on the basis that it did not make sense to allow doctors' 'clinical judgement' to be investigated while not making it possible to investigate the professional judgement of other professionals. Seneviratne (2008: 631) argues that, although 'maladministration' has always been interpreted very flexibly, it is helpful to have the inclusion of service failure formalised by legislation. This means that ombudsmen are able to investigate a wide range of complaints, although there are still some restrictions on what they can do.

One restriction is that ombudsmen cannot investigate complaints that deal with issues of law, or where there is an alternative legal remedy, although it has been established that failure to follow the law is maladministration (Kirkham 2004: 188; Seneviratne 2002: 42). This prohibition on investigating 'legal' complaints, and the parallel inability of courts to refer cases to ombudsmen, has been reconsidered recently, since it has been argued that it is too inflexible and not supportive of a 'proportionate' approach to resolving disputes (Kirkham 2007a;

Law Commission 2008c). See also Thompson's chapter in this volume for a discussion of the relationship between ombudsmen and courts.

The general trend amongst public services ombudsmen, recognising the importance of 'proportionate dispute resolution', has been away from formal investigation and towards earlier resolution of disputes (Abraham 2008; Seneviratne 2008). In England, the recent re-organisation of the Local Government Ombudsmen has included the provision of an advice service, accessible by telephone or online, as its first point of contact (Commission for Local Administration in England 2008). While this new approach to receiving enquiries has yet to be evaluated, it has a clearer focus on making sure that complaints are made appropriately and on advising complainants. Other public services ombudsmen are also changing their approach from formal investigation to informal approaches.

As well as dealing with individual complaints, as 'fire fighters', ombudsmen also have a role as 'fire watchers', providing an overview of problems with public services and alerting policy makers to these problems (Harlow and Rawlings 1997). The current Parliamentary and Health Services Ombudsman is confident that her office is effective in this role, citing the example of funding rivalries between the NHS and social care as one where the activities of her office were more effective than the courts could have been at bringing about changes in policy (Abraham 2008). The public sector ombudsmen report regularly in their Annual Reports on their achievements in bringing systemic problems to light. The Parliamentary Ombudsman notes the impact of her report on tax credits (PHSO 2007 and 2008). The Scottish Public Services Ombudsman points to the impact on Scottish Government policy of the ombudsman's investigations into problems with free personal care (SPSO 2008). However, the ombudsman schemes have been criticised in the past for the fact that they lack the power to conduct their 'own investigations', in other words to investigate potential problem areas without the lever of an individual complaint (Harlow and Rawlings 1997; Seneviratne 2002). Recent changes to the powers of the local government ombudsmen in England, however, enable the LGO to investigate matters that come to light as the result of a complaint, even if they are not the subject of the original complaint (Seneviratne 2008: 632). Seneviratne argues that this is a 'useful addition to the ombudsmen's powers'. The Select Committee Report on dealing with complaints suggests that patterns of complaints to the ombudsman should be used as evidence of problems in service provision, arguing that:

> The most reliable indicator of an organisation's ability to handle complaints effectively is likely to be the proportion of complaints upheld by the Ombudsman. … We recommend that government organisations should use as a performance indicator the proportion of complaints upheld by independent bodies such as the Ombudsman's office. (House of Commons 2008: 25)

This role is somewhat in conflict with one which promotes proportionate dispute resolution, informal working practices and minimising the number of complaints that are carried through to a full investigation and report, which seems to be the model adopted by the main public services ombudsmen in the UK.

A remaining point to consider is what happens when the public services concerned do not like the decisions of the ombudsmen. Ombudsmen systems have usually been praised for being effective in having their recommendations accepted, despite the lack of legal powers to enforce them (Seneviratne 2002) and it has been argued that, in the case of another administration, ombudsmen are more effective than courts in bringing about change (Hertogh 2001). However, others have argued that this perception has been challenged by recent cases (Kirkham et al 2008).

This brings us back to the question of the role of ombudsmen in the field of administrative justice. As with internal complaints procedures, strength in one role, for example, resolving disputes proportionately, may conflict with an ombudsman's ability to perform another role, for example, providing information to policy makers on wider problems, or challenging policy makers on matters with widespread legal implications.

The Relationship between Internal Complaints Procedures and Ombudsmen

Although very diverse, ombudsmen in the UK seem to be moving towards a common vision of their role as complaints handlers rather than as adjuncts to parliament, as envisaged by the original Parliamentary Commissioner for Administration. They are becoming more accessible, more flexible and less formal in their approach to complaints. With the exception of the MP filter (an anachronism which seems to be doomed), ombudsmen are attempting to make their procedures more accessible and easier to understand by the public. They appear to be taking on a role as advisers to potential complainants, including encouraging people to make better use of internal complaints procedures. The Parliamentary and Health Services Ombudsman, the Local Government Ombudsman and the Scottish Public Services Ombudsman all include advice on their websites on 'how to complain' to first-tier service providers.

In relation to the operation of complaints procedures, there seems to be a general move to have the ombudsmen as the main independent reviewers of individual complaints, especially in Scotland and Northern Ireland, although this is not consistent across the different administrations and, as described above, separate independent reviewers are cropping up in particular areas of public services. This is working against a shared understanding of the role of ombudsmen across the administrations.

While seeming, in most cases, to move towards this position at the top of the complaints pyramid, ombudsmen are also increasingly seeing their responsibilities as including the provision of advice to lower level complaints handlers. Again, all the main ombudsmen have recently published guidance on complaint handling (see, for example, Parliamentary and Health Services Ombudsman 2009a;

Public Services Ombudsman for Wales 2006) and some run courses on how to handle complaints (Commissioner for Local Administration 2008). The ombudsmen are consolidating their role as supervisors of internal complaints procedures as well as giving advice on avoiding complaints in the first place by promoting 'good administration' (Parliamentary and Health Services Ombudsman 2009b).

Public sector ombudsmen in the UK are confident in portraying their roles as 'people's champions' and as the experts in complaints handling. It is nearly 20 years since the Citizen's Charter initiatives encouraged public services to set up internal complaints procedures, to operate them competently and to value complaints as sources of information. Although increasing numbers of people use these procedures, there is still much dissatisfaction with the way that they operate and little evidence that complaints are being used to improve services. We can only hope that the ombudsmen's confidence in their role, up to a point, supported by policy makers, will have an impact on the effectiveness of first tier complaints in public services.

However, taking into account the variety of the services concerned, the complexities of modern governance and the fact that complaining means different things to different people, this is quite a challenge.

References

Abraham, A (2008) 'The Ombudsman and "Paths to Justice": a just alternative or just an alternative' PL 1.

Adler, M (2006) 'Fairness in Context' 33 *Journal of Law and Society* 615.

—— (2008) 'The Idea of Proportionality in Dispute Resolution' 30 *Journal of Social Welfare and Family Law* 309.

Adjudicator's Office (2008) *Annual Report 2008*, available at www.adjudicatorsoffice.gov.uk/pdf/report2008.pdf.

Administrative Justice and Tribunals Council (2008) *Adjust Newsletter*, available at www.ajtc.gov.uk/adjust/adjust_latest.htm.

British and Irish Ombudsman Association (2008) *Annual Report 2007–2008*, available at www.bioa.org.uk/docs/BIOA-AnnualReport2007-8.pdf.

Cabinet Office (1991) *The Citizen's Charter: Raising the Standard* Cm 1599 (London, HMSO).

—— (1998) *How to Deal with Complaints* (London, The Stationery Office).

—— (2005) *Reform of Public Sector Ombudsmen Services in England: a Consultation Paper* (London, Cabinet Office).

Cavadino, M and Dignan, J (2007) *The Penal System*, 4th edn (London, Sage).

Citizen's Charter Complaints Task Force (1993) *Effective Complaints Systems: Principles and Checklist* (London, Cabinet Office).

Clarke, J, Newman, J, Smith, N, Vidler, E and Westmarland, L (2007) *Creating Citizen-consumers: Changing Publics and Changing Public Services* (London, Sage).

Colcutt, P and Hourihan, M (2000) *Review of the Public Sector Ombudsmen in England* (London, Cabinet Office).

Commission for Healthcare Audit and Inspection (2007) *Is Anyone Listening? A Report on Complaints Handling in the NHS* (London, Commission for Healthcare Audit and Inspection).

Commission for Local Administration in England (2008) *Local Government Ombudsman Annual Report 07/08 Delivering Public Value* (London, Commission for Local Administration in England).

Consumer Focus (2008) *Consumer Focus: Work Programme to March 2010* (London, Consumer Focus).

Cowan, D and Halliday, S (2003) *The Appeal of Internal Review: Law, Administrative Justice and the (non-) emergence of disputes* (Oxford, Hart Publishing).

Crerar, L (2007) *Report of the Independent Review of Regulation, Audit, Inspection and Complaints Handling of Public Services in Scotland* (Edinburgh, Scottish Government).

Dean, H (2002) *Welfare Rights and Social Policy* (Harlow, Pearson Education).

Department for Children Schools and Families (2008) *A New Way of Handling Parents' Complaints About School Issues: Consultation Paper*, available at www.dcsf.gov.uk/consultations/downloadableDocs/Document.pdf.

Department for Constitutional Affairs (2004) *Transforming Public Services: Complaints, Redress and Tribunals* Cm 6243 (London, The Stationery Office).

Department of Health (2003) *NHS Complaints—Making Things Right* (London, Department of Health).

—— (2007) *Making Experiences Count: The Proposed New Arrangements for Handling Health and Social Care Complaints Detailed policy background* (Leeds, Department of Health).

—— (2008) *Reform of Health and Social Care Complaints Proposed Changes to the Legislative Framework*, available at www.dh.gov.uk/en/Consultations/Liveconsultations/DH_091505.

Department of Health Social Services and Public Safety (2006) *Complaints in the Health and Personal Social Services: A Consultation Paper* (Belfast, Department of Health, Social Services and Public Safety).

Gilad, S (2008) 'Accountability or Expectations Management? The Role of the Ombudsman in Financial Regulation' 30 *Law and Policy* 227.

Gulland, J (2007) *Complaining, Appealing or Just Getting it Sorted Out: Complaints Procedures for Community Care Service Users*, PhD Thesis, University of Edinburgh.

—— (2009) 'Independence in Complaints Procedures: Lessons from Community Care' 31 *Journal of Social Welfare and Family Law* 59, 59–72.

Harlow, C and Rawlings, R (1997) *Law and Administration*, 2nd edn (London, Butterworths).

Harris, N (2007) 'Resolution of Student Complaints in Higher Education Institutions' 27 *Legal Studies* 566.

Health Service Ombudsman for England (2005) *Making Things Better? A Report on Reform of the NHS Complaints Procedure in England* (London, The Stationery Office).

Hertogh, M (2001) 'Coercion, Cooperation and Control: Understanding the Policy Impact of Administrative Courts and the Ombudsman in the Netherlands' 23 *Law and Policy* 47.

House of Commons Select Committee on Public Administration (2008) *When Citizens Complain: Fifth Report of Session 2007–08* HC 409 (London: The Stationery Office).

Independent Case Examiner (2008) *Annual Report for Department for Work and Pensions, 2007–2008*, available at www.ind-case-exam.org.uk/en/pdf/reports/2007-2008/DWP_Annual_Report_200708.pdf.

Independent Police Complaints Commission (2008) *IPCC Annual Report* HC 898 (London, The Stationery Office).

Ipsos MORI (2007) *Customer Satisfaction Survey for the Local Government Ombudsman*, available at www.lgo.org.uk/about-us/surveys/customer-satisfaction-survey-2007/.

Kirkham, R (2004) 'When is it Appropriate to use the Ombudsman?' 26 *Journal of Social Welfare and Family Law* 181.

—— (2007a) 'New Legislation, Court Cases, Parliamentary Reports and an Anniversary: A Review of the Public Sector Ombudsmen in 2006–07' 29 *Journal of Social Welfare and Family Law* 3.

—— (2007b) *The Parliamentary Ombudsman: withstanding the test of time: 4th Report Session 2006–2007* HC 421 (London, Parliamentary and Health Service Ombudsman).

Kirkham, R, Thompson, B and Buck, T (2008) 'When Putting Things Right Goes Wrong: Enforcing the Recommendations of the Ombudsman' PL 510.

Law Commission (2008a) *Housing: Proportionate Dispute Resolution* Cm 7377 (London, Law Commission).

—— (2008b) *Adult Social Care Scoping Report*, available at www.lawcom.gov.uk/docs/adult_social_care_scoping_report_2008.pdf.

—— (2008c) *Administrative Redress: Public Bodies and the Citizen Consultation Paper* (London, Law Commission).

Lewis, N and Birkinshaw, P (1993) *When Citizens Complain* (Buckingham, Open University Press).

Lloyd-Bostock, S and Mulcahy, L (1994) 'The Social Psychology of Making and Responding to Hospital Complaints. An Account Model of Complaint Processes' *Law and Policy* 16, 123–47.

MacPherson, Sir William (1999) *The Stephen Lawrence Inquiry* Cm 4262-I (London, The Stationery Office).

Moorhead, R, Robinson, M and Matrix Research and Consultancy (2006) *A Trouble Shared: Legal Problems Clusters in Solicitors' and Advice Agencies* (DCA Research Series 8/06) (London, Department for Constitutional Affairs).

MORI (1999) *Complainants Survey 1999: Research Study Conducted for the Local Government Ombudsman* (London, Commission for Local Administration in England).

Mulcahy, L (1999) 'Sliding Scales of Justice at the end of the Century—a Cause for Complaints' in M Harris and M Partington (eds), *Administrative Justice in the 21st Century* (Oxford, Hart Publishing).

—— (2003) *Disputing Doctors: the Socio-legal Dynamics of Complaints about Medical Care* (Maidenhead, Open University Press).

Mulcahy, L and Allsop, J (1997) 'A Woolf in Sheep's Clothing? Shifts towards Informal Resolution of Complaints in the Health Service' in P Leyland and T Woods (eds), *Administrative Law: Facing the Future: Old Constraints and New Horizons* (London, Blackstone).

Mulcahy, L, Lickiss, R, Allsop, J and Karn, V (1996) *Small Voices: Big Issues an Annotated Bibliography of Literature on Public Sector Complaints* (London, University of North London).

National Audit Office (2005) *Citizen Redress: What Citizens Can Do if Things Go Wrong with Public Services* (London, The Stationery Office).

—— (2008) *Feeding Back? Learning from Complaints Handling in Health and Social Care* (London, The Stationery Office).

Northern Ireland Ombudsman (2008) *Annual Report of the Assembly Ombudsman for Northern Ireland and the Northern Ireland Commissioner for Complaints* NIA 182/07-08 (Belfast, Northern Ireland Ombudsman).

Parliamentary and Health Services Ombudsman (2007) *Tax Credits: Getting it Wrong? 5th Report, Session 2006–2007* HC 1010 (London, The Stationery Office).
—— (2009a) *Principles of Good Complaint Handling*, available at www.ombudsman.org.uk/improving_services/principles/complaint_handling/.
—— (2009b) *Principles of Good Administration*, available at www.ombudsman.org.uk/improving_services/principles/good_administration/index.html.
—— (2008) *Annual Report 5th Report Session 2007–2008* HC 1040 (London, The Stationery Office).
Posnett, J, Jowett, S, Barnett, P and Land, T (2001) *NHS Complaints Procedure National Evaluation* (York, Health Economics Consortium/NFO System Three Social Research).
Prisoner Ombudsman for Northern Ireland (2008) *Annual Report 2007/08* (Belfast, Prisoner Ombudsman for Northern Ireland).
Prisons and Probation Ombudsman for England and Wales (2008) *Annual Report 2007–2008* CM7434 (Norwich, HMSO).
Public Services Ombudsman for Wales (2006) *Guidance to Local Authorities on Complaints Handling*, available at www.ombudsman-wales.org.uk/uploads/publications/196.pdf.
—— (2008) *Annual Report 2007/08 of The Public Services Ombudsman for Wales* (Pencoed, Public Services Ombudsman for Wales).
Scottish Consumer Council (2006) *Complaints in Education* (Glasgow, Scottish Consumer Council).
Scottish Government (2008) *Fit for Purpose Complaints System Action Group Report to Ministers*, available at www.scotland.gov.uk/Topics/Government/PublicServiceReform/IndependentReviewofReg/ActionGroups/ReporttoMinisters.
Scottish Prisons Complaints Commission (2008) *Annual Report 2007–08* (Edinburgh, Scottish Prisons Complaints Commission).
Scottish Public Services Ombudsman (2006) *Annual Report 2005–06* (Edinburgh, Scottish Public Services Ombudsman).
—— (2007a) *Annual Report 2006–07* (Edinburgh, Scottish Public Services Ombudsman).
—— (2007b) *Summary of Research into Premature Complaints*, available at www.spso.org.uk/media-centre/research/research-premature-complaints.
—— (2008) *Annual Report 2007–08* (Edinburgh, Scottish Public Services Ombudsman).
Seneviratne, M (2002) *Ombudsmen: Public Services and Administrative Justice* (London, Butterworths/LexisNexis).
—— (2006) 'A new ombudsman for Wales' PL 6.
—— (2008) 'Updating the Local Government Ombudsman' PL 627.
Simons, K (1995), *I'm not complaining but … Complaints procedures in social services departments* (York, Joseph Rowntree Foundation).
Smith, G (2004) 'Rethinking Police Complaints' 44 *British Journal of Criminology* 15.
Thompson, B (2001) 'Integrated Ombudsmanry: Joined-up to a Point' 64 MLR 459.
—— (2006) 'The Scottish Public Services Ombudsman: Revolution or Evolution?' in A McHarg and T Mullen (eds), *Public Law in Scotland* (Edinburgh, Avisandum).
Thompson, B, Buck, T and Kirkham, R (2007) 'Researching Public Services Ombudsmen and Administrative Justice' 31 *The Ombudsman* 6.
Wallace, H and Mulcahy, L (1999) *Cause for Complaint* (London, Public Law Project).
Waters, I and Brown, K (2000) 'Police Complaints and the Complainants' Experience' 40 *British Journal of Criminology* 617.

19

Current Developments in the UK: System Building—From Tribunals to Administrative Justice

BRIAN THOMPSON

Introduction

Administrative justice in the UK used to be thought of as referring, wholly or primarily, to the arrangements for administrative tribunals which, acting as court-substitutes[1] determined disputes, particularly in statutory governmental schemes such as social security benefits. It was thought that, compared to courts, tribunals had the advantages of 'cheapness, accessibility, freedom from technicality, expedition and expert knowledge of their particular subject'.[2] The usual allocation of expertise in these tribunals was that the person who chaired the tribunal was legally qualified and the other, or 'wing', members had technical expertise or knowledge, as in disability appeal cases where one member was medically qualified and the other had knowledge of disability. This model was thought to be appropriate for some areas of private law, the largest example was employment disputes, where the 'wing' members were selected from panels of people representative of employers and employees as was done in National Insurance Local Tribunals.

Tribunals were cheaper than courts because the wing-members and the great majority of those who chaired them were part-time and, if paid a fee, this was an amount indicating that the post was one of public service rather than profit. They were accessible in that their proceedings were supposed to be such that legal representation would not be required, which their freedom from technicality fostered. All these factors contributed to the speed with which they conducted their business.

Where tribunals were used in governmental schemes (citizen versus state tribunals), they were generally managed by the sponsoring department and indeed

[1] See the distinction between court-substitute and policy-oriented tribunals in Abel-Smith and Stevens (1968: 220).

[2] Franks (1957: para 38).

this was also true of the tribunals resolving employment and property disputes (party versus party tribunals).

The number of tribunals increased during the twentieth century with the rise of the welfare state and, subsequently, the regulatory state has also fostered their establishment.[3] The proliferation of tribunals and the anticipated impact of the Human Rights Act 1998, once it was in force, led the then Lord Chancellor, Lord Irvine of Lairg to appoint a retired Court of Appeal judge, Sir Andrew Leggatt, to chair a Review of Tribunals. This was established with fairly prescriptive terms of reference which clearly indicated the expected features of the final report.[4] The remit sought to ensure that the arrangements for the delivery of justice, including the resolution of disputes between citizen and state, and party and party were:

timely, proportionate and part of an effective legal framework which developed the law systematically and was coherent with the courts;
compliant with the independence and impartiality requirements of Article 6 of the European Convention on Human Rights;
adequate for improving citizens' knowledge and understanding of their rights and responsibilities in relation to such disputes;
efficiently, effectively and economically managed, with respect for judicial independence and ministerial responsibility for the administration of public funds;

and that:

performance standards were coherent, consistent and public and effectively monitored and enforced;

so that:

tribunals overall constitute a coherent structure for the delivery of administrative justice.

In short, that there should be a system with coherent structures that meets legal, political and managerial standards.

The title of the Report *Tribunals for Users: One System; One Service* neatly encapsulates the Leggatt vision of a user-focused systemic service. Perhaps only in one respect did the report and its recommendations stray outside its remit, in proposing that the Council on Tribunals should not only continue to oversee tribunals but also become responsible for upholding the system of administrative justice and keeping it under review.[5] The White Paper, which followed three years after Leggatt, outlined the new policy on tribunals within the wider context of the agenda of improving public services.[6]

[3] See Bell (1969) and Wraith and Hutcheson (1973), and, for late-20th century developments, the annual reports of the Council on Tribunals.
[4] Leggatt (2001), hereafter referred to as Leggatt.
[5] Leggatt: para 7.54.
[6] Department for Constitutional Affairs (2004), hereafter referred to as White Paper.

This chapter begins with an outline of the tribunal reforms, tracking it from Leggatt through the White Paper to the legislation, and then moves outwards towards the wider ideas of proportionate dispute resolution and the administrative justice system. Consideration is paid to developments in Scotland, Wales and Northern Ireland. The development of systemic oversight, proportionate dispute resolution, the preference for alternative dispute resolution including factors favouring the use of particular techniques and whether representation is needed in hearings will then be analysed.

Tribunals

At the time of the Leggatt review there were some 70 different tribunals[7] whose annual caseload ranged from zero to 274,472.[8] Leggatt identified three tests which would point to the use of tribunals rather than courts deciding cases.[9] First, where participation by the user in the proceedings is desired; secondly, where expertise or accessibility to users is a major issue in the resolution of the relevant disputes; and thirdly, where in the decisions of the administrative or regulatory authorities to be considered there is a mixture of fact and law.

Administrative efficiency, user-friendliness and legal principle were factors that, in combination, led to the proposals for structural change. These were intended to streamline the number of tribunals, remove them from the sponsoring policy departments that administered them and place them in an executive agency in which there was both judicial leadership and civil service management and administration.

The timescale of the reforms was that Leggatt reported in 2001 and his proposals were circulated for consultation. In 2003 the Government announced its acceptance of the principles that informed the proposals and in 2004 a White Paper was published. A draft Bill was published for consultation in the summer of 2006 and subsequently the Tribunals, Courts and Enforcement Act 2007 (TCEA 2007) was passed with different provisions coming into force from 2007 to 2009. The bulk of this implementation in relation to tribunals happened in two phases, on 3 November 2008 and in April 2009.

Structure

Leggatt proposed that the various tribunals, whether they were dealing with disputes between the citizen and the state, or between party and party, could

[7] Leggatt: paras 1.9.

[8] For the Appeals Service (social security), see Council on Tribunals (2001: 63). The statistics are for calendar year 2000. The next highest were Employment Tribunals with 114,983 and School Admission Appeals Panels with 89,182 applications received.

[9] Leggatt: paras 1.10–1.13.

be brought together in one overarching structure in which tribunals dealing with similar subject matter would be grouped into nine divisions.[10] These were social security and pensions, immigration, employment, health and social services, financial, land, transport, education and regulatory matters. This type of structural change had previously been implemented on a smaller scale when five tribunal jurisdictions dealing with appeals in separate social security and child support benefits were merged to form the Appeals Service.[11] This organisation was an executive agency in which there was a Chief Executive responsible for administration and a President who exercised judicial leadership and was responsible for training, deployment and the appraisal of legally qualified and specialist members.[12] Leggatt proposed that there should be a Senior President of Tribunals (SPT) who would be supported by Presidents in each of the divisions.[13] The government accepted the streamlining structure but did not initially see the need for divisions, as they proposed to create a Tribunals Service (TS) comprising the 10 largest tribunals.[14] The TCEA 2007, however, provides for chambers[15] and on its implementation on 3 November 2008 the First-tier Tribunal had three chambers, Social Entitlement; Health, Education and Social Care; and War Pensions and Armed Forces Compensation, with two further chambers planned to be introduced in 2009, Lands, Property and Housing, and Tax; and with a General Regulatory Chamber likely to be established in late 2009 early 2010.[16]

Leggatt also sought to rationalise the 'hotchpotch'[17] of various ways in which tribunal decisions could be challenged. He proposed a general right of appeal from a first-tier tribunal on a point of law, with permission, to an appellate tribunal.[18] This was straightforward but the linked proposal was controversial, that the right to seek judicial review could be removed. He suggested this because there would be a right to an appeal from every tribunal on a point of law to a specialist tribunal. The retention of judicial review would have complicated matters and could have undermined the development of a coherent body of law by experts.[19] This was accepted in the White Paper[20] but the legislation went further by not only creating an Upper Tribunal to hear appeals on a point of law from the First-tier Tribunal,[21] but also by providing for the transfer to it from the

[10] Ibid paras 6.2–6.5, 6.41 and Table C.
[11] Social Security Act 1998.
[12] Leggatt: 133–39.
[13] Ibid para 6.37.
[14] White Paper paras 6.37–6.38.
[15] TCEA 2007 s 7, Sch 4.
[16] Senior President of Tribunals (2008: paras 5, 32–38 and Annex 6).
[17] Woolf (1988).
[18] Leggatt paras 6.9–6.13.
[19] Ibid paras 6.31–6.36.
[20] White Paper paras 7.14–7.28.
[21] TCEA 2007 ss 5, 11.

Figure 1: Structure of First-tier and Upper Tribunal

FIRST-TIER TRIBUNAL

Chambers launched 3 November 2009			Launched 1 April 2009	Sept 2009/Jan 2010	15 Feb 2010
Social Entitlement	Health, Education and Social Care	War Pensions and Armed Forces Compensation	Taxation	General Regulatory	Immigration and Asylum
Asylum Support Social Security and Child Support Criminal Injuries Compensation	Care Standards Mental Health Review Special Education Needs and Disability	War Pensions Armed Forces Compensation	Tax and Duties	*Launched 1 Sept 2009* Charities Consumer Credit Estate Agents	Immigration and Asylum
				Launched 18 Jan 2010 Gambling Claims Management Information Immigration Services Transport Adjudication Panel for England	

UPPER TRIBUNAL

Chamber launched 3 November 2008	Chamber launched 1 April 2009	Chamber launched 1 June 2009	Chamber launched 15 Feb 2010
Administrative Appeals Chamber	Finance and Tax Upper Chamber Renamed Tax and Chancery Chamber Sept 2009	Lands Chamber	Immigration and Asylum
Social Entitlement Health, Education and Social Care War Pensions and Armed Forces Compensation	Tax and Duties (appeals)	Lands Tribunal (mixture of first instance and appeals)	Immigration and Asylum
Added Sept 2009 and Jan 2010 General Regulatory *Includes* some first instance Transport	*First Instance Jurisdictions April 2010* Financial Services and Markets Pensions Regulator	*Proposed for a Land, Property & Housing Chamber in First-tier* Agricultural Lands Residential Property *possibly* Valuation	
	Possible Chancery Appeals Charities Land Registry Adjudicator		

courts of classes of judicial review.[22] The Upper Tribunal had an Administrative Appeals Chamber on its launch and, as planned, two further chambers, Finance and Taxation, and Lands were added in 2009.[23] The two classes of judicial review transferred in directions made by the Lord Chief Justice were: (1) appeals against decisions on review under the Criminal Injuries Compensation Scheme; and (2) reviews of decisions of the First-tier Tribunal made under the new Tribunal Procedure Rules for the Tribunal where there is no right of appeal to the Upper Tribunal against the decisions.[24]

This structure and its administration clearly improved the perception of independence of tribunals that had been a concern.[25] Not only did it remove the tribunals from a sponsoring department and its administrative support, funding and in some cases appointment of wing members, but it treated like them like the courts by putting them into a similar 'arms length' relationship with a department that would not be a party to any of the disputes.[26] Such an arrangement would also ensure that the requirements of the European Convention on Human Rights would be met, particularly those on independence and impartiality in Article 6(1), and on procedural equality between the parties, or 'equality of arms', in Article 6(3).[27]

The arrangements for the appointment of the legally qualified and specialist members of tribunals were brought in ahead of the implementation of the other tribunal reforms in the Constitutional Reform Act 2005, which placed them within the remit of the Judicial Appointments Commission that makes recommendations to the Lord Chancellor.[28]

The rest of Leggatt's structural reforms were not adopted in their entirety. It was decided that the Employment Tribunals (ET) should not be brought into the First-tier Tribunal but that their administration would be incorporated into the TS,[29] and that ET judges and members would be subject to the overall judicial leadership of the Senior President of Tribunals, while retaining their own president.[30]

The situation has been more complicated with asylum and immigration appeals. Here there used to be a two tier structure but concerns about the very sizeable recourse to appeals and challenges to decisions by the asylum and immigration decision-making and appellate bodies led to the creation of a single-tier Asylum and Immigration Tribunal (AIT) in 2004.[31] In light of this, it was

[22] TCEA 2007 ss 15–21.
[23] Senior President of Tribunals (2008: paras 7, 27–31 and Annex 6).
[24] Lord Chief Justice (2008).
[25] Leggatt para 2.2.
[26] Ibid paras 2.5–2.6.
[27] Ibid paras 2.11–2.16.
[28] Constitutional Reform Act 2005 Pt 4, Sch 12.
[29] Leggatt para, 6.37.
[30] Ibid paras 6.59–6.60.
[31] Asylum and Immigration (Treatment of Claimants etc) Act 2004 s 23, Sch, which amended Nationality, Immigration and Asylum Act 2002 s 81, Sch 4.

not thought appropriate to include the AIT in the generic tribunal structural change.[32] As with ETs, the AIT is administered by the TS and its judiciary are subject to the SPT.

Although the intention behind policy and legislation was to reduce challenges, opportunities were widely used with the result that the Administrative Court was overwhelmed by applications to reconsider decisions of the AIT, and, in 2007, applications for permission for a judicial review of immigration and asylum decisions amounted to 8,078 out of 11,293 applications, that is, to 71.5 per cent of applications.[33] A review was conducted in 2008 and it was proposed that an asylum and immigration chamber should be inserted into the First-tier Tribunal, with the Upper Tribunal taking over onward appeals and challenges from the Administrative Court.[34] This enjoyed support from officials and the judiciary, and met ministerial concerns about 'abuse' associated with appeals and challenges. It was announced in May 2009 that it would be implemented in 'early 2010'.[35]

Other tribunals, particularly those administered by local government have not been included in the new structure. These include educational matters, appeals against schools admissions and exclusions, car parking and aspects of housing matters which are currently dealt with by the Residential Property Tribunal Service.

Judicial Leadership

The range of duties and responsibilities of the office of SPT were not fully spelled out in the Leggatt proposals, although it was suggested that the office holder should be a High Court judge. There were slightly more details on the role of the presidents of each of the divisions. As presidents of jurisdictions, they would have an important role in the transition to and operation of the individual tribunals as they were incorporated into the chambers in the new structure, particularly in the first tier. The 2004 White Paper gave more detail about the SPT but the passage of the Constitutional Reform Act 2005, which introduced a greater separation of the judiciary from the executive and the legislature, in particular with the redistribution of powers held by the Lord Chancellor in his former role as head of the judiciary, played a major role in shaping the provisions concerning the SPT in the TCEA 2007. In effect, the TCEA 2007 gives to the SPT in relation to tribunal judges and members, a similar range of powers, duties and responsibilities, as the 2005 statute gives to the Lord Chief Justice in relation to the judges in the courts. Sir Robert Carnwath, a Lord Justice of Appeal was appointed SPT Designate in autumn 2004 and so was able to play a major role in shaping policy

[32] White Paper: para 7.18.
[33] Ministry of Justice (2008: Tables 1.12–1.14).
[34] UK Border Agency (2008).
[35] UK Border Agency and Tribunals Service (2009).

and influencing the 2007 Act, under which he was formally appointed SPT in November 2007.

The TCEA 2007 not only specifies functions given to the SPT but also matters which must be taken into account when exercising those functions. These matters are:

— the need for tribunals to be accessible;
— the need for proceedings before tribunals to be fair and handled quickly and efficiently;
— the need for the members to be experts in the subject matter or law to be applied in cases; and
— the need to develop innovative methods of resolving disputes that might be brought before tribunals.[36]

The SPT's functions include: providing for the training, guidance and welfare of the tribunal judiciary and members; in concurrence with the Lord Chancellor determining the allocation of functions between chambers; prescribing the qualifications for appointment to the First-tier and Upper Tribunals; assigning tribunal judges and members to tribunals in accordance with a published policy agreed with the Lord Chancellor; administering oaths to tribunals judges and members; serving on or nominating a person to the Tribunal Procedure Committee; requesting that Circuit and High Court judges serve as tribunal judges with the relevant Chief Justice's consent.[37]

Each chamber is to have a President and the Presidents of the three First-tier Chambers were appointed following competitions run by the Judicial Appointments Commission (JAC).[38] The President of the Lands Chamber in the Upper Tribunal was also appointed following a JAC competition, but the Presidents of the Upper Tribunal's Administrative Appeals Chamber and the Finance and Tax Chamber are both High Court judges and were assigned to become Chamber Presidents without JAC involvement.

The everyday judicial administration in chambers will be delegated by the SPT to the Chamber Presidents. This will include the deployment of judges and members to meet the demands of that Chamber's work. As each Chamber, other than the War Pensions and Armed Forces Compensation Chamber, will have a number of similar subject matter jurisdictions, there is the possibility that judges and members may, if they have suitable qualifications be 'ticketed' not only to deal with cases in jurisdiction(s) to which they were initially appointed but also to other jurisdictions.

There is also the possibility of 'assigning' judges and members from another chamber. For this to happen the SPT has to publish a policy on assignment that has

[36] TCEA 2007 s 2(3).
[37] TCEA 2007 Sch 1.
[38] TCEA 2007 s 7, Sch 4, Senor President of Tribunals (2008: paras 19–20).

been agreed by the Lord Chancellor. The principles that the policy will implement are that:

— the judge or member has the necessary skills and ability to hear cases within the Chamber to which they are assigned;
— the assignment process is open and transparent;
— assignment will be based on merit, with a link to judicial appraisal where appropriate;
— the assignment process will not be used for promotion—promotion opportunities will be advertised and subject to the JAC processes; and
— subject to business need, the process must also balance opportunities for judges and members to develop their judicial careers while at the same time retaining their skills and expertise.[39]

The SPT is responsible for training and has established a Tribunals Judiciary Training Group which plans, costs and reviews training that will usually be provided by the Tribunals Committee of the Judicial Studies Board, whose Tribunals Judicial Training Strategy also caters for tribunals outside the TS.[40]

Users

Leggatt had adopted an approach which focused upon the needs of the user. The major concern which he identified was the need for the provision of high quality information through the whole length of the tribunal process, beginning with the decisions that individuals were dissatisfied about and which gave rise to an appeal, through advice about and support for appeals, to the tribunal decision and any onwards appeals.[41] He also argued that it is important that decision makers state their decisions and supporting reasons clearly.[42] If a user is considering an appeal then the information should set out the jurisdiction, the possible remedies and their limits, and indicate other possible means of redress. Users should be informed about what they would be required to prove, the evidence needed and how it should be presented, what they may expect the department to provide. Other procedural information should include scheduling, whether there will be pre-hearing meetings and the procedure to be followed at those meetings, as well as and the procedure to be followed at the hearing. Users should also be told about the venue, how to get to it, whether, if there are travel expenses, they may be claimed, what facilities and services are available, such as photocopying. The nature of tribunal decisions should also be explained, as should their expected timing and further appeals options.[43] This information should be available in

[39] Tribunals Service (2007).
[40] Senior President of Tribunals (2008: Annexes D and G).
[41] Leggatt paras 4.1–4.14.
[42] Ibid para 4.10.
[43] Ibid para 4.12.

different media and languages to cater for the diversity of users and their needs.[44] Leggatt was impressed that the Special Educational Needs Tribunal had a video on appeals which could be sent to users.[45]

Leggatt also emphasised the importance of independent help and advice for users[46] and this will be considered below in the section on Proportionate Dispute Resolution.

As well as users receiving information, they are also the source of information which should be tapped through user groups. These can provide feedback both on specific issues in the various jurisdictions as well as on system-wide matters.[47]

The White Paper accepted the analysis and most of the recommendations relating to users[48] but some significant differences emerged over hearings which will be explored next.

Proportionate Dispute Resolution

Perhaps the most controversial of Leggatt's proposals was the expectation that users should represent themselves at hearings,[49] a view that Leggatt acknowledged was contrary to the research findings that users were more likely to succeed before a tribunal if they were represented.[50] Leggatt took the view that user participation was very desirable and that enabling it would mean achieving one of the special characteristics of tribunals, that users could access them without lawyers.[51] Leggatt did have conditions for users' self-representation. First, users should have good pre-hearing advice and assistance. Secondly, the tribunal should conduct the hearing in an enabling fashion that facilitates self-representation.[52] Leggatt thought that the Community Legal Service and its legal assistance scheme could help users prepare for their hearing.[53]

The White Paper took a different view, with the Lord Chancellor asserting in the foreword that 'the public do not want to go to a Tribunal', rather, 'they want their complaint or dispute resolved quickly and fairly'. The White Paper agreed with Leggatt about the importance of advice and support for citizens aggrieved with a public body or an employer, but placed more emphasis on the development of redress mechanisms that would enable more disputes to be resolved without a

44 Ibid para 4.5.
45 Ibid para 4.2.
46 Ibid paras 4.15–4.20.
47 Ibid paras 4.29–4.32.
48 White Paper paras 10.1–10.9.
49 Leggatt para 4.21.
50 Ibid para 4.21, citing Genn and Genn (1989).
51 Ibid para 4.21.
52 Ibid para 4.21.
53 Ibid para 4.18.

hearing.[54] A significant factor behind this new approach, known as proportionate dispute resolution (PDR), is that the delivery of fair resolutions in disputes between citizens and public bodies should be part of the government's reform of public services.[55] The key aspects of PDR seek to:

— minimise the risk of people experiencing legal problems by ensuring that the framework of law defining people's rights and responsibilities is as fair, simple and clear as possible, and that State agencies, administering systems like tax and benefits, make better decisions and give clearer explanations;
— improve people's understanding of their rights and responsibilities, and the information available to them about what they can do and where they can go for help when problems do arise. This will help people decide how to deal with the problem themselves if they can, and ensure they get the advice and other services they need if they cannot;
— ensure that people have ready access to early and appropriate advice and assistance when they need it, so that problems can be solved and potential disputes nipped in the bud long before they escalate into formal legal proceedings;
— promote the development of a range of tailored dispute resolution services, so that different types of dispute can be resolved fairly, quickly, efficiently and effectively, without recourse to the expense and formality of courts and tribunals where this is not necessary; but also
— deliver cost-effective court and tribunal services, that are better targeted on those cases where a hearing is the best option for resolving the dispute or enforcing the outcome.[56]

The White Paper's discussion of justice in the relationship between individuals and state bodies also noted that it was important in disputes about public services that the resolution feeds back into the decision-making process so that there is less error in the future.[57] This was something which Leggatt wished to see expanded, having been influenced by British and Australian experience.[58] The domestic examples were the annual reports by the President of the Appeals Service (social security and child support tribunals) on the standards of decision making, and the meetings between the Criminal Injuries Compensation Appeal Panel and decision makers in the Criminal Injuries Compensation Board. In Australia, successive Presidents of the Commonwealth (federal) Administrative Appeals Tribunal (AAT) had established links with departments so as to be able to identify systemic problems and weaknesses in cases that came before the tribunal. At the time of the review, the AAT President held biannual meetings with heads of agencies.[59] Leggatt suggested that feedback from tribunals had been under-developed

[54] White Paper para 2.3.
[55] Ibid paras 1.7, 1.14, 3.9–3.11.
[56] Ibid para 2.3.
[57] Ibid para 1.7.
[58] Leggatt paras 9.12–9.14.
[59] Ibid para 9.12.

as not all tribunals had a presidential structure, or the resources to be able to devote to the necessary analysis. The feedback process should be transparent to guard against any concern that it might have an impact on individual decisions. While Leggatt wanted to separate the management of tribunals from the departments whose work they considered, he did not think that this independence and their impartiality would be compromised by tribunals having a relationship with the departments that fostered the learning of lessons.[60]

These two aspects can be summarised as 'putting it right' and 'getting it right'. In dealing with the tribunal procedure for 'putting it right' Leggatt looked to the Woolf reforms of civil procedure[61] where a similar problem and response were to be found. The common problem was that some parties had not fully prepared their cases for the initial listed hearing, which resulted in adjournments and an inefficient use of court and tribunal time.[62] The solution—active case management—was adopted, resulting in the court taking charge and setting out a timetable stipulating which actions by the parties are to be carried out.[63] Some tribunals used pre-hearing reviews to identify issues, and made directions about evidence and how it should be presented. Leggatt's proposals were modelled, in part, on the Lands Tribunal, where legally qualified registrars would conduct pre-hearing screening that could also decide whether cases should be referred back for review, or suggest alternative dispute resolution (ADR).[64] For example, Leggatt stated that some of the disputes raised by citizens with departments and tribunals were really disputes about the procedure, rather than about outcomes, and, as such, were more properly to be regarded as maladministration for which some compensation might be an appropriate remedy.[65] Party versus party tribunals, such as the ET, should have rules similar to the Civil Procedure Rules (CPR) in the courts.[66]

Leggatt also wanted agencies to conduct reviews of cases lodged for appeal as errors could be corrected without putting the citizen to the trouble of attending a hearing.[67] In the White Paper, case management was extended beyond those tribunals that currently used it.[68] There would be a Tribunal Procedure Committee, modelled largely on the committee responsible for developing the CPR, and the aim would be to seek harmonisation of the different tribunal procedural rules, with new rules approved by the Lord Chancellor.[69] The rules would be supplemented by jurisdiction-specific Practice Directions issued by the SPT.[70]

60 Ibid para 9.14.
61 Woolf (1996).
62 Leggatt paras 8.2–8.3.
63 Ibid paras 8.5–8.7.
64 Ibid para 8.8.
65 Ibid para 8.18.
66 Ibid para 8.13.
67 Ibid para 8.7.
68 White Paper para 7.10.
69 Ibid paras 7.5–7.6.
70 TCEA 2007 s 23.

A Tribunal Procedure Committee was established and conducted a rather quick consultation on procedural rules for each of the chambers launched in November 2008. These rules, in the main, established common provisions for the different jurisdictions in each chamber. The Health, Education and Social Care chamber has special provision for mental health cases. The SPT issued both practice directions and practice statements just before the launch of the new chambers.[71] The practice directions included the circumstances and manner in which evidence should be given by child, vulnerable adult and sensitive witnesses in both the First-tier and Upper Tribunals. The practice statements dealt with the composition of various jurisdictions in the First-tier Tribunal chambers, and the delegation of some tasks to legally qualified staff in the Administrative Appeals Chamber of the Upper Tribunal, such as exercising some case management powers, striking out and reinstating cases, and summarily assessing costs.

System Review

Just as Leggatt sought to systematise the 70 plus different tribunals, he was also alive to the consideration that tribunals were only one of the dispute resolution processes to which citizens who are aggrieved with public bodies could have recourse. This awareness is reflected in his proposals to move to ADR some cases that begin as appeals before a tribunal, and in the rationalisation of onward appeals where judicial review rights would be restricted in order to allow a specialist appellate tribunal to develop a coherent body of law. The Council on Tribunals had the task of keeping under review the composition and working of tribunals (and inquiries).[72] Leggatt suggested that it might become the hub of the wheel of administrative justice and not just tribunal justice.[73] Accordingly it should keep under review developments in administrative law.[74]

The White Paper developed Leggatt's thinking, accepting that it should have a wider advisory role beyond tribunals across the administrative justice landscape.[75] It would embrace the users' perspective in its work, both in the overseeing of the tribunal reform programme and in its proposed wider remit.[76] The White Paper did not accept Leggatt's proposal that the Council, which would be renamed the Administrative Justice Council, should be able to commission research; rather it should make proposals for research.[77]

[71] These are all published on the Tribunals Service website www.tribunals.gov.uk/Tribunals/Rules/directions.htm, as are Practice Statements at www.tribunals.gov.uk/Tribunals/Rules/statements.htm.

[72] Tribunals and Inquiries Act 1992 s 1.

[73] Leggatt para 7.49.

[74] Ibid para 7.54.

[75] White Paper paras 11.12–11.13.

[76] Ibid paras 11.12–11.13.

[77] White Paper para 11.10; Leggatt para 7.54.

The TCEA 2007 abolished the Council on Tribunals and created in its place the Administrative Justice and Tribunals Council (AJTC),[78] the title deriving from the fact that its supervision not only included administrative justice but party versus party tribunals, in particular the ET. The AJTC was to keep under review the administrative justice system, consider ways of making it more accessible, fair and efficient, advising ministers and the SPT, and making proposals for research.[79] The administrative justice system was defined as:

> the overall system by which decisions of an administrative or executive nature are made in relation to particular persons, including—(a) the procedures for making such decisions, (b) the law under which such decisions are made, and (c) the systems for resolving disputes and airing grievances in relation to such decisions.[80]

The AJTC would, like its predecessor, have a Scottish Committee[81] but, taking into account the new devolution arrangements, would also have a Welsh Committee[82] Its remit, like that of its predecessor, did not to extend to Northern Ireland, where competence had been devolved to the Northern Ireland Assembly.[83] The membership was to be a minimum of 10 and a maximum of 15 plus the Parliamentary Ombudsman,[84] who in addition was also an *ex officio* member of the Scottish and Welsh Committees. These committees also had as *ex officio* members the relevant public services ombudsman.[85]

Devolution

The asymmetric nature of the devolution settlement in the UK does make it a little difficult to grasp who is responsible for which tribunals. Only tax, and asylum and immigration tribunals are organised throughout the UK. A large number traverse England's land borders with Scotland and Wales. Only a small number of tribunals in Wales are devolved but, in Scotland, rather more tribunals are part of the devolved responsibility of Scottish authorities.

In Wales, devolution has not included justice functions, and many tribunals with jurisdiction in Great Britain operate in Wales. In addition to these non-devolved tribunals, there are also some 14 tribunals that are devolved, as Welsh Ministers are the 'authority responsible'. The criteria for tribunals being within this category are that a tribunal's functions are only exercisable in Wales and

78 TCEA 2007 ss 43–44.
79 TCEA 2007 Sch 7, para 13(1).
80 TCEA 2007 Sch 7, para 13(4).
81 TCEA 2007 Sch 7, para 4(1).
82 TCEA 2007 Sch 7, para 7(1).
83 TCEA 2007 Sch 7, para 24.
84 TCEA 2007 Sch 7, para 1(1).
85 TCEA 2007 Sch 7, paras 4(2), 7(2).

Welsh Ministers have the power either to appoint members to the tribunals and/or to make procedural rules.[86]

There also appear to be two tribunals that are not quite in either of those categories: the Agricultural Land Tribunal for Wales and the Mental Health Review Tribunal for Wales. These tribunals operate only in Wales and are supported by the Welsh Assembly Government, but Welsh Ministers have no power either to appoint members to the tribunals or to make procedural rules.

The Welsh Committee of the AJTC announced in late 2008 that it would undertake a review of all tribunals in Wales. It is expected that it will report in late 2009.

In both Scotland and Northern Ireland there are tribunal reform proposals that are in keeping with the Leggatt proposals. In Scotland the Administrative Justice Steering Group has reported on tribunals, dividing them into three groups: (1) the Great Britain (GB)-wide tribunal in the TS; (2) Scottish tribunals existing before 1998; and (3) Scottish tribunals established after devolution.[87] The steering group's concerns related to:

— independent and impartial processes;
— an independent and skilled judiciary; and
— a coherent system.[88]

In the AJTC's view, Scottish tribunals in groups (2) and (3) were not sufficiently independent of the Scottish Government.[89] Whilst some had independent administration, all were funded by directorates within the Scottish Government.[90] Scottish Ministers also made some appointments to them.[91] The training arrangements for these tribunals varied in their quality and had no single body supervising them.[92] Overall across the three groups the tribunals operated in isolation from each other.[93]

The report contains five options for reform:

1. Retain the status quo.
2. Secure better co-operation between the TS and Scottish tribunals.
3. Bring all Scottish tribunals within the remit of the existing TS.
4. Establish a new Scottish Tribunals Service to support all Scottish tribunals.
5. Establish a new Scottish Tribunals Service to support both GB tribunals within Scotland and all Scottish tribunals.[94]

[86] Administrative Justice and Tribunals Council (Listed Tribunals) (Wales) Order 2007, SI 2007/2876 (W250).
[87] Administrative Justice Steering Group, hereafter referred to as AJSG.
[88] AJSG (2008: para 49).
[89] Ibid paras 53–54.
[90] Ibid para 55.
[91] Ibid para 55.
[92] Ibid paras 60–61.
[93] Ibid para 66.
[94] Ibid para 73.

Option 1 is not recommended by the report.[95] Options 3 and 5 have opposite constitutional effects with 3 'undoing' devolution by putting Scottish tribunals into a GB body and 5 putting GB-wide tribunals into a Scottish body.[96] Therefore option 4, which would retain GB-wide tribunals in the Tribunal Service and establish a devolved body for devolved tribunals, is perhaps the option which causes least constitutional problems,[97] whilst not being the most economic course. The report points out that, to meet its concerns about independence and skills, tribunal appointments could be made by the Judicial Appointments Board for Scotland[98] and that the Scottish Courts Service seemed a sensible candidate for accommodating a Scottish Tribunals Service that would be sufficiently independent of the Scottish Government.[99] Training should co-ordinated for Scotland and it would be prudent, whichever option was adopted, to explore co-operation with the SPT and the Judicial Studies Board.[100]

In welcoming the AJSG Report, the Minister for Community Safety (Fergus Ewing MSP) said that '[t]he report rightly concludes that the status quo is no longer an option' and '[t]he distinctiveness of the Scottish legal system means that it makes much more sense for all these bodies to be administered in the future from within Scotland, rather than from London'. This is widely thought to rule out Options 1 and 4.

The report also considered the role of the Scottish Committee of the AJTC. If options 2 and 3 were implemented then the current committee could carry on or a separate AJTC for Scotland be created.[101] This new institution would probably be necessary for option 4 and probably essential for option 5, given the number of tribunals which would be incorporated in the new devolved Scottish Tribunals Service.[102] The argument in the AJSG Report was that it would make little sense to maintain the present structure because the majority of administrative justice would have been devolved in Scotland.[103]

In Northern Ireland attention had been directed towards tribunal reform following Leggatt and the White Paper. Here the situation has been complicated by the 'on-off' nature of devolution since the Belfast Agreement and the Northern Ireland Act 1998, which implemented the agreement and made provision for a devolved government for Northern Ireland, and also because the controversial functions of policing and justice will only be devolved after further negotiation. An inter-departmental review had led to the announcement in March 2006 by the Northern Ireland Secretary during 'direct rule', that administrative support for the Northern Ireland tribunals would be undertaken by the Northern

[95] Ibid para 75.
[96] Ibid paras 90, 98–101
[97] Ibid para 97.
[98] Ibid para 80.
[99] Ibid para 94.
[100] Ibid paras 96, 105.
[101] Ibid paras 106–108.
[102] Ibid para 110.
[103] In June 2009, the Administrative Justice Steering Group published a second, broader report entitled 'Administrative Justice in Scotland—The Way Forward' (AJSG 2009).

Ireland Court Service (NICtS), which was an agency of a UK government department (the Department for Constitutional Affairs). This would become a unified courts and tribunals service. The NICtS already serviced a few tribunals and any newly established tribunals would be administered by it. The preparations for transfer were suspended to allow the devolved institutions to decide what to do when devolution was re-established in 2007. The broad thrust of tribunal reform was accepted and another inter-departmental body was asked to arrange for the transfer of responsibility for the administration of NI tribunals to the NICtS, to identify the financial and non-financial benefits and to report on these before implementation.[104] Implementation is planned to take place on a phased basis so that by the Spring of 2010 the majority of NI tribunals will be administered by the NICtS. Prior to devolution of policing and justice and the transfer of administrative responsibility to the NICtS, implementation will be way of agency arrangements under section 28 of the Northern Ireland Act 1998. The devolution of policing and justice provides an opportunity to transfer such responsibility statutorily, but, while the main political parties in Northern Ireland now agree that policing and justice is to devolve, there is no agreement yet as to its timing.

Following devolution of policing and justice there will be an opportunity for local ministers to consider the reform of tribunals in a more fundamental way, including their structure, leadership, appointments, training and oversight.[105]

Since the devolved tribunals in Northern Ireland were not under the supervision of the old Council on Tribunals,[106] it is likely that an oversight body will be created. Two likely options are to create a Northern Ireland Committee of the AJTC or a freestanding AJTC for Northern Ireland.

Analysis

The theme that underpins the reform of tribunal and administrative justice is system-building. Most UK and GB tribunals have been systematised into the two-tier structure and are now a part of the newly recognised administrative justice system. This system is to be subject to oversight and the twin concerns are to put things right and get things right first time.

Systemic Oversight

It is somewhat surprising that it has taken quite so long to progress from an appreciation that tribunals and inquiries, ombudsmen and public bodies' internal complaints

[104] Northern Ireland Court Service (2008: 10, 34). See, also Broderick (2008) available at: www.ajtc.gov.uk/adjust/articles/SiobhanBroderickSpeech2008.pdf.

[105] Some tribunal posts, mostly for legally qualified chairing positions, are currently listed judicial offices within the remit of the Northern Ireland Judicial Appointments Commission. See Justice (Northern Ireland) Act 2002 Sch 3.

[106] They were not listed in Tribunals and Inquiries Act 1992 Sch 1, or its predecessors.

systems and courts are all involved in providing redress for people aggrieved with public bodies, to the realisation that the adoption of a holistic approach was logical and desirable. From the individual's perspective it was not clear what they could do about their grievance with a public body, a point verified by the research into citizen redress that was conducted for the National Audit Office[107] (see Dunleavy's chapter in this volume). This report was a first attempt to quantify the volume and costs of redress mechanisms by central government departments. It noted that, although there are two separate channels of redress (appeals and complaints), the distinction between them was not understood by people who were simply concerned that something had gone wrong and wished to remedy it.[108] The situation may sometimes be even more complicated as the episode giving rise to the grievance may be one to which different public services have contributed, and the outcomes that are sought may vary. For example, the episode might have included inputs from both medical and social care that caused harm through acts of commission and omission, as well as an unhelpful attitude when the individual or relatives asked questions of those providing the care. A court action could secure damages whereas a complaint might secure an apology and an explanation of what went wrong and why, as well as an account of what is being done to prevent a recurrence. Human rights infractions can be remedied in the courts or through a finding of maladministration by an ombudsman. Indeed, both ombudsmen and the courts have rules which tend to set each up as a last resort, proposals for dealing with this are considered below. Accordingly citizens need assistance to help them understand what their situation is, to decide what might be their preferred outcome and how best that might be achieved, and to prepare or support them as users of a method of redress.[109]

The position of citizens needs to be considered at two levels, the micro and the macro or strategic. It is that latter role which the AJTC has been charged to review, as it will consider how the components of the administrative justice system relate to each other so as to ensure that the system is accessible, fair and efficient. The AJTC will seek to achieve that purpose by playing a pivotal role in the development of coherent principles and good practice; promoting understanding, learning and continuous improvement and ensuring that the needs of users are central.[110] The AJTC's first work programme is aligned to its strategic objectives, which are:

— keeping under review and influencing the development of administrative justice and tribunals;
— keeping under review the work of the TS, the tribunals within it and other tribunals; and
— responding authoritatively to emerging issues and proposals that affect or involve administrative justice, tribunals or inquiries—more generally.[111]

[107] National Audit Office (2005: para 4.19).
[108] Ibid para 4.17.
[109] See discussion in Adler (2008b).
[110] Administrative Justice and Tribunals Council (2008a: iv).
[111] AJTC (2008b: 10).

Under 1, the AJTC will produce a paper on the administrative justice system and begin work on generally applicable principles of administrative justice with a 'scoping paper' that will be followed up in a paper applying the principles to particular aspects of the administrative justice system, and will work with the Ministry of Justice in identifying collaborative opportunities for the promotion of PDR techniques across the administrative justice system.[112] The AJTC has published a survey that indicates that there is not much evidence of the use of ADR techniques.[113] ADR is included in a consideration of PDR below.

The work of its predecessor (the COT) in dealing with tribunals will continue, but with a reduced frequency of visits to individual tribunals both within and outside the TS, and the provision of feedback from those observations. Two strands of work will encompass procedure and users. The AJTC is statutorily represented on the Tribunal Procedure Committee and will consider updating its guide to drafting tribunal rules. The AJTC will engage with the TS Consumer Champion, and follow up its survey of user groups to ensure that there is an effective network of user groups in the new structure. It will work with the TS and the SPT to ensure that their annual reports to the Lord Chancellor provide an adequate account of the tribunals from the user's perspective.[114] In responding to consultations the AJTC will use research evidence and while the AJTC is not funded to commission research, it will, in addition to its statutory function of making proposals for research to ministers, also seek to promote research by co-operating with others who are interested in funding research. A paper has been produced which outlines sources of funding, gives examples of research that has been carried out on administrative justice and suggests priorities for research.[115]

The Scottish and Welsh Committees' work programmes are similar, and they will continue to report on their observations of devolved and non-devolved tribunals. Both seek to be the facilitators of increased awareness and understanding of their administrative justice systems. The Scots wish to act with organisations using new approaches to dispute resolution so as to promote the exchange of information and best practice and to play roles within the Administrative Justice Steering Group and the First Minister's Review of Tribunals, and to identify and improves link with the academic research community.[116] In Wales the Committee was established in June 2008 and so there is necessary work to be done to promote awareness of its role and remit as well as on mapping the interface between Wales, England and the UK. They will also map the provision of support, information and advice to users in Wales and continue work that the former Council on Tribunals undertook in relation to Welsh language issues.[117]

112 Ibid 3–4.
113 AJTC (2008a: App F).
114 AJTC (2008b: 5–6)
115 AJTC (2008c).
116 AJTC (2008b: 9–11).
117 Ibid 12–14.

Feedback

The AJTC takes seriously learning the lessons from putting things right in order to get things right first-time. It has taken an interest in feedback from tribunals to initial decision makers and has included this as one of its research priorities. It supported the annual reports made by the President of the Appeals Service on standards of decision making but noted that points were being repeated, apparently to no avail. The AJTC has therefore engaged with the Department of Work and Pensions, informing itself about their training in decision making and the qualification that its staff can obtain as well as considering the work of the reformed departmental 'Standards in Decision-making Committee'. The AJTC was consulted by the Parliamentary Ombudsman on her three sets of guidance: *Principles of Good Administration, Principles for Remedy and Principles of Good Complaint Handling*[118] and will be reviewing the work of ombudsmen and independent complaints handlers in making suggestions for improving administration.

The AJTC publicised a research report on feedback by Partington and Kirton-Darling commissioned by the SPT.[119] This study suggested that there were three types of reporting mechanism: official reports; direct communication with the decision maker and informal feedback to the department or agency.[120] The official reports included those from the President of the Appeals Service, the Internal Review Service for the Social Fund, and reports by the National Audit Office (several of which were on social security), the Parliamentary and Health Service Ombudsman, and the Local Government Ombudsmen.[121] The report did not specifically mention the Public Services Ombudsmen in Scotland and Wales and Northern Ireland. The broad conclusion on these reports is that their impact appears to be limited on a stand-alone basis but they may be able to support other forms of feedback.[122]

The second category of direct communication between the tribunal and the decision maker provides examples of two ways in which this could happen. The first was a trial in which the DWP sent a Presenting Officer to represent it at all appeals in Incapacity Benefit.[123] After the trial, it was decided not to send a Presenting Officer to appeals as a matter of course. The internal research report on the study was not formally published but its findings were uncovered by Kirton-Darling. The report concluded that it was not feasible to send a Presenting Officer to every appeal, they attended 68 per cent. The benefit of having the officer there was mainly for the appellant who would obtain at a hearing a full explanation

118 Parliamentary Commissioner for Administration (2008).
119 Partington and Kirton-Darling (2007), hereafter referred to as Feedback.
120 Feedback para 1.6.
121 Ibid paras 1.8–1.31.
122 Ibid para 1.36.
123 Ibid paras 1.39–1.40.

of the decision. Usually the outcome of the appeal did not change and, where it did, it was because of additional evidence presented by the appellant.

The report found that, after an appeal was lodged, the reconsideration usually did not change the decision as no new information was available. While the report justified on cost effectiveness not sending Presenting Officers, it is unclear if it noted that initial decision making could be improved so as to secure important information at that stage rather than at the appeal hearing.[124]

The other approach discussed is where the initial decision makers are met by the feedback reporter, which happens in the Social Fund. The Social Fund Commissioner and his staff visit each region to discuss their annual report on decision making. It seems, however, that this is limited in impact as points are repeated from year to year.[125]

This section also contains a note about the situation before the (Australian) AAT, where a 2005 amendment to the principal 1975 statute imposes a duty on first instance decision makers to assist the tribunal.

> In a proceeding before the Tribunal for a review of a decision, the person who made the decision must use his or her best endeavours to assist the Tribunal to make its decision in relation to the proceeding. The President of the AAT hopes that this will help agencies avoid adopting an overly adversarial approach and it will remind them that they have an obligation to assist the tribunal to reach the right answer by:
>
> reconsidering their initial decision to ensure it is still their position,
> providing evidence and submissions, particularly where the claimant is unrepresented, and
> responding to requests for assistance on particular issues from the Tribunal.[126]

Partington and Kirton-Darling note that these points are very similar to the President of the Appeals Service's identification of the 'vital dual role' of decision-takers, who 'should both represent the agency in explaining the decision made and act as *amicus curiae* in assisting the tribunal to come to the correct legal decision'.[127]

Their conclusions on direct communication are that, as presenting officers are unlikely to be present at all appeals, research could focus on identifying those types of case where such a presence would be useful. Guidance, or a statutory requirement, could be developed to require initial decision makers to help the tribunal reach the legally correct decision and Australian practice may be helpful in this regard. More efficient ways should be identified to acquire additional evidence or information more quickly, thereby reducing the need for tribunal hearings.[128]

[124] Ibid para 1.40.
[125] Ibid para 1.41.
[126] Ibid paras 1.42–1.43.
[127] Ibid para 1.44.
[128] Ibid paras 1.45–1.47.

The final category is informal feedback to initial decision makers from review bodies, which can take the form of written recommendations passed through senior management or liaison officer, bulletins sent directly to initial decision makers, and regular high-level meetings between officials and review or appeal bodies, as well as regular training provided by the appeal or review body to the initial decision makers.[129] One or more of these methods are used by the Social Fund Commissioner (who conducts training), the Parliamentary Ombudsman and the complaint handlers who are intermediate between the Parliamentary Ombudsman and the departments' own complaints schemes. These include the Adjudicator, whose biggest jurisdiction is tax (Her Majesty's Revenue and Customs), who meets senior officials and distributes material through a liaison officer; the Independent Complaints Reviewer, whose reports for the Land Registry are considered by a specially constituted body; and the Local Government Ombudsmen who produce annual letters to chief executives reporting on any trends arising out of complaints handled by the LGO against that council.[130] The conclusions on the effectiveness of these informal methods are that feedback is taken seriously by the decision maker if there is trust between them and the review or appeal body; there is scope for the communication to be two-way and not just from the review or appeal body; and effective communication may not be achieved simply through written material but through meetings and training sessions.[131]

Falling short

Although the AJTC was created to provide oversight of the 'joined-up' administrative justice system, the bodies to which it reports have some distance to travel as neither the departments nor the parliamentary select committees in London, Edinburgh and Cardiff have re-organised in a complementary fashion. There are separate arrangements for putting it right and getting it right. The Whitehall departmental leads are respectively, the Ministry of Justice and the Cabinet Office, and the Westminster Select Committees are, respectively, the Justice Committee and the cross-cutting Public Administration Committee, to which the Parliamentary Ombudsman reports. England does not have a 'one-stop ombudsman', retaining separate statutory offices for central government, the National Health Service, local government and public sector housing. In Scotland and Wales devolved public services are overseen by their national public services ombudsman, a merger that was initially suggested for England but not implemented. However, the Parliamentary, Health Service and Local Government Ombudsmen in England have been authorised to work collaboratively with each other.[132]

129 Ibid para 1.48.
130 Ibid paras 1.49–1.70.
131 Ibid paras 1.72–1.76.
132 The Regulatory Reform (Collaboration etc between Ombudsmen) Order 2007 SI 2007/1889.

Another deficiency in the tribunal reform process has been that the Tribunal Service as an Executive Agency has a limited policy role. Its task is operational, preparing for generic tribunals by bringing together the different tribunal jurisdictions with their varying administrative processes, IT platforms and estates, and the different terms and conditions of their legally qualified and expert members. While there has been a user focus, it has been fragmented in that their concern is with the user experience once the user has engaged with a tribunal, its information and processes. It has not been its function to oversee the framework for advice that users might receive prior to approaching a tribunal or indeed to divert them elsewhere to other remedies. Such policy matters should have been the concern of the parent department but it seems that administrative justice reform was focused on tribunal reform which was left to the TS, leaving a policy vacuum at the Department for Constitutional Affairs and its hastily created successor, the Ministry of Justice. This has potentially been addressed by the creation of a new Access to Justice Directorate which brings together civil, family and administrative justice in the one policy section, which can encompass awareness, advice, and support throughout the courts and tribunals services.

An example of the slippage from the ideals of the White Paper is the failure to develop the promised Enhanced Advice Project with the Legal Services Council (LSC).[133] It may be that the LSC's policies for Community Legal Advice Centres (CLACs) and Community Legal Advice Networks (CLANs) could play a role similar to that envisaged in the White Paper's Enhanced Advice Project. The CLACs and CLANs are intended to deal with social welfare law issues including social security, debt, housing, employment, family and community care problems. They would be a 'one-stop shop' for social welfare problems, providing advice and support, including representation, and they would be expected to link with providers of those services not covered, such as mental health, immigration and education, and deal with clinical negligence, personal injury, actions against the police and crime. Five CLACs have been established and negotiations are underway in eight areas to commission jointly with local authorities so as to be operating by April 2010.[134]

In Scotland the Justice Directorate has also re-organised and, like its Whitehall counterpart, will lead on putting it right with the getting it right being part of public service reform which is in the remit of the Finance and Sustainable Growth Directorate. While there is a Justice Committee in the Scottish Parliament, public services are not overseen by a specific committee and neither is the Scottish Public Service Ombudsman, although the Local Government Committee has considered its annual reports to the Scottish Parliament.

[133] White Paper para 10.10.

[134] Legal Services Commission (2006). See, in particular, the section of the Legal Services Commission's website dealing with Community Legal Advice Centres and Networks (CLACs and CLANs), available at www.legalservices.gov.uk/civil/innovations/community_legal_advice_centres_and_networks.asp. See also discussion in Adler (2008b).

In Wales it could be said that devolution may have provided the seed for what might be termed a nascent Welsh legal system in the England and Wales jurisdiction but justice is not a devolved function. There is a Department for Public Service Reform, which is part of the responsibility of the Minister for Finance and Public Service Delivery, and the department is scrutinised by the National Assembly's Health, Well-being and Local Government Committee. Although this committee would be the logical one to deal with the Public Services Ombudsman for Wales, it does not appear in the remit document prepared for the committee's first meeting in July 2007. The Ombudsman reports to the Assembly.

Propotionate Dispute Resolution

PDR can be regarded as a system or framework which is a logical joining-up of putting it right across civil, family and administrative justice. It is a structured approach to disputes by seeking to avoid them through building awareness of rights, then reducing their escalation with advice, and, finally, resolving them with a range of tailored techniques. The White Paper indicated that the PDR approach would focus on the individual's desired outcomes and then match this with a dispute resolution process that emphasises alternatives to tribunal hearings, which should only be used where they are the best means of resolving the dispute.[135]

Preferring ADR

Given the policy preference of avoiding hearings, which has its counterpart in the avoidance of litigation in the courts following the Woolf reforms, what has been done to take it forward? In the legislation, provision has been made for ADR and pilot studies for two different early resolution techniques have been conducted. Under section 24 of TCEA 2007, principles are stipulated for those making tribunal procedural rules or practice directions in relation to mediation. First, mediation can only take place where the parties agree, and secondly, where the parties do not mediate or the mediation fails to resolve the dispute, this failure does not affect the outcome of tribunal proceedings. All of the procedural rules for the First-tier and Upper Tribunal chambers have a common provision rule 3, which allows the tribunal, where appropriate, to indicate the availability of appropriate ADR and to facilitate it if the parties so wish and provided it is compatible with the overriding objective of dealing fairly and justly with the case. There have been two early resolution pilots.[136] The first ran for a year from August 2006 until July 2007. It was a type of judicial mediation in ETs, and was used in race, sex and disability

[135] White Paper ch 2. The conflict between choice and justice is discussed by Clarke, McDermont and Nerwman's (in their chapter in this volume) and by Adler (2008b).

[136] Tribunals Service (2007: paras 86–96).

discrimination cases. The second pilot saw Early Neutral Evaluation being used in Disability Living Allowance and Attendance Allowance cases. A full-time tribunal judge (then called a District Chairman) considered the case papers and formed a view on the likely outcome. The party that was thought likely to lose would be contacted. If it was the department, they might re-consider their decision, and the appellant would be warned that the appeal would be likely to fail. The appellant might be given other suggestions, including submitting further evidence, seeking advice or perhaps focusing on specific issues that the tribunal could consider. If the case was complex or evenly balanced, and the judge could not form an opinion on the likely outcome, then neither party would be contacted and the case would proceed to a hearing in the normal way, although the judge could issue directions in the interests of having to avoid an adjournment. This pilot began in one office for six months and it was planned to extend it to another office. The evaluations of these pilots had not been published by the end of 2009.

These initiatives seem somewhat weak compared to the emphasis placed on the preference for avoiding hearings in the White Paper. One factor is perhaps the impact of the Court of Appeal's decision in *Halsey v Milton Keynes General NHS Trust*,[137] which made it clear that the possibility of not following the normal rule on costs where the losing party pays those of the successful party could only happen where there had been an unreasonable refusal to mediate. This was perceived as a brake on judicial encouragement of ADR due to conflicting interpretations of the decision.[138]

Section 24 itself has an unusual legislative history. It appeared as a clause in the draft Bill which was subjected to a consultation exercise,[139] but was removed when the Bill was introduced into Parliament. It was reinserted following an opposition amendment. The Minister said that it had been removed because the Government had been advised that they did not need the provision to conduct mediation.[140] Another point that may be made is that section 24 deals with mediation and not other ADR processes, yet the procedural rules do specify ADR. A contrast may be made with the AAT that had influenced Leggatt. Amending legislation was passed in 2005 which extended its ADR provision that comprise conferences, mediation, conciliation, neutral evaluation and case appraisal.[141] The AAT's definitions of mediation and conciliation[142] are broadly similar to those in the White Paper,[143] in that the disputing parties are assisted to come to their own settlement. However, the AAT's definition allows for a conciliator to be more interventionist

137 [2004] EWCA Civ 576, [2004] 1 WLR 3002.

138 Genn et al (2007), Ministry of Justice (2007) and literature cited therein.

139 The draft Tribunals, Courts and Enforcement Bill (Cm 6885, 2006).

140 Baroness Ashton of Upholland, Hansard HL vol 689 col 258 (31 January 2007). See also House of Lords Select Committee on the Constitution (2008: 13).

141 Administrative Appeals Tribunal Amendment Act 2005 (Cth), which amends Administrative Appeals Tribunal Act 1975 (Cth) s 3(1).

142 See website for both definitions and factors favouring the use of these and other ADR processes at www.aat.gov.au/ApplyingToTheAAT/AlternativeDisputeResolution.htm.

143 White Paper para 2.11.

in making suggestions and actively encouraging the parties to settle on terms compatible with the statute. Neutral evaluation is the same in both sets of definitions with the evaluator giving a non-binding opinion on the likely outcome based on a consideration of the facts and law. The AAT's case appraisal process produces a non-binding opinion based on the facts. In the AAT procedure, the first stage is the conference which is conducted by a tribunal member or official enabling the parties to

> describe and define the issue(s), identify further evidence that needs to be gathered, explore whether the matter can be settled, discuss further progress of the matter, including referral to an ADR process or going to a hearing if a settlement is not possible.[144]

While the White Paper was positive about a role for ADR in cases set down for determination by tribunals, others were not. The AJTC survey of ADR provision showed not only that it was minimal but that those consulted, who included tribunal members, advisers, regulators and legal practitioners, were sceptical about its possible scope.[145] If the case was about rights, then the scope for negotiation is limited since an individual is either entitled or not to a right, for example a social security benefit.

There are also criticisms about the principle of ADR. In their literature review, Harris et al highlight transparency and fairness.[146] In citizen versus state disputes, ADR is thought to be inappropriate because of its confidentiality, which is an essential aspect of mediation and conciliation. It is argued that citizen versus state disputes should be in the public domain, for example in determining a point of law and establishing a precedent. Particular concern has been raised about cases involving fundamental rights not being determined in public. It has also been pointed out that, in ADR, individuals might settle for less than their entitlement which they could expect to be awarded following a hearing.[147]

Factors Favouring Particular Resolution Processes

The AJTC has listed among its research priorities, research on the 'principles [that] should guide the policy maker when matching a redress mechanism to a dispute?'[148] Its predecessor, the Council on Tribunals, conducted a survey on *The Use and Value of Oral Hearings in the Administrative Justice System*,[149] which was considered along with other studies by Richardson and Genn in their recent article on tribunals.[150] They noted that there were instrumental reasons for supporting oral hearings in both the law (in the common law and in the jurisprudence

144 Administrative Appeals Tribunal (2006: 1).
145 AJTC (2008d and 2008e).
146 Harris, Ridell and Smith (2008: 29–31).
147 Adler (2006: 978).
148 AJTC (2008c: 28).
149 Council on Tribunals (2007).
150 Richardson and Genn (2007).

on Article 6(1) of the European Convention on Human Rights) and the research literature, to the effect that oral hearings can improve the accuracy of decisions, enhance transparency and improve public confidence.[151] There are other factors, independent of the outcome of the decision, which may favour oral hearings such as the dignity of the individual, democratic legitimacy and participation.[152] Richardson and Genn also referred to the research on tribunal users' experiences, highlighting the work of Tyler, who identified four primary factors: 'opportunities for participation (voice), the neutrality of the forum, the trustworthiness of the authorities, and the degree to which people are treated with dignity and respect'.[153] The disadvantages of oral hearings included stress caused to citizens who have to appear at an oral hearing, especially where the hearing is regarded as daunting and legalistic,[154] delays and difficulties in securing attendance and finding suitable venues. The approach adopted by Richardson and Genn was to differentiate categories of claim against the state.[155] They suggest it is essential to have independent adjudication by means of an oral hearing where fundamental rights are at stake, for example, in mental health reviews and in asylum and immigration cases which concern liberty of the person. They argue that, as the relevant tribunals are not simply applying the individual's fundamental rights but determining their boundaries, which must be done in an independent and authoritative manner, such disputes are not appropriate for negotiation. At the opposite end of the spectrum lie claims to assessments or consideration, such as provision for children who have special educational needs. Such provision is a social right that is heavily constrained, notably by resources. There is not a right to a particular provision but a right to have an assessment. Given that there will usually be a continuing relationship between the parents and their education authority, a negotiated outcome might be in everyone's interests. Where the parent rejects an offer, then an oral hearing should only be used if all other attempts at resolution fail. Placed between these two points are claims involving entitlements to material benefits such as social security or criminal injuries compensation. Richardson and Genn distinguish between eligibility and quantum. Adjudication is appropriate in eligibility cases because there is not a range of outcomes which can be negotiated and so the role of the tribunal is to decide the issue. Where this has been established, they argue that whether the citizen's factual circumstances meet the specified level of benefit or award it is again a question of eligibility. Is an oral hearing required for entitlement to a material benefit? The key point is the testing of evidence and while this points to an oral hearing, it does not conclusively require one. In their consideration of this issue they refer to the wider context of

[151] Ibid 129, citing Galligan (1996), Fuller (1978) and Bayles (1990).

[152] Ibid 129–30, citing Mashaw (1981) and Barber (1984). See also discussion in Richardson (1994).

[153] Tyler (2000).

[154] Richardson and Genn (2007: 129), citing Council on Tribunals (2007) and Genn, Lever and Gray (2006: 197).

[155] Ibid 133–41.

economy and convenience. An individual would prefer an accurate decision to having to make an appeal, but it may cost more to provide more accurate initial decision making than to provide error-correction through an appeal.

Should Appellants be Represented in Hearings?

Having established some criteria which would guide the types of dispute that are most appropriately directed towards an oral hearing, the question then arises as to whether or not users should be represented. Leggatt recommended that, except in complex cases or where the user was vulnerable or did not have English as a first language, self-representation should be expected. This was regarded as controversial as research had indicated that representation was a factor which increased the success rate in tribunals. However, Adler's recent study of Criminal Injuries Compensation Appeal Panels, Employment Tribunals, Social Security and Child Support Appeal Tribunals, Special Educational Needs and Disability Tribunals and Additional Needs Support Tribunals (Scotland) indicates that the 'representation premium' of 15 to 18 per cent that Genn and Genn identified 20 years ago in their research on Immigration Hearings, Industrial Tribunals, Social Security Appeal Tribunals and Mental Health Review Tribunals[156] has been reduced to 5 per cent overall and to only 4 per cent where the unrepresented tribunal user has had pre-hearing advice.[157] Adler attributes this to the ways in which tribunal hearings are now conducted. He devised a set of indicators to measure the 'activism' of tribunal chairs and members, the extent to which they are generally 'enabling' and the extent to which they adopt 'inquisitorial' methods, for example in their questioning of users. He concludes that the decline in the 'representation premium' in citizen versus state tribunals is due to the fact that the active, enabling and inquisitorial methods that most tribunals use make it easier for unrepresented users to put their case and achieve a successful outcome.

This research, which has been presented in seminars but has not yet appeared in a peer reviewed publication, seems to vindicate Leggatt's position.

It also seems to fit in with the annual reports on standards of decision making by the President of the Appeals Service which consistently record that the two most common reasons why a social security or child support appeal is successful is that new information is uncovered or that the tribunal takes a different view of the evidence from that of the initial decision maker.

Exchanging Cases between Ombudsmen and the Courts

Another example of the matching of disputes to the most appropriate dispute resolution procedure is to be found in the Law Commission for England

[156] Genn and Genn (1989).
[157] Eg Adler (2008a).

and Wales' consultation paper on *Administrative Redress: Public Bodies and Redress*.[158] It identifies four pillars of redress: complaints, ombudsmen, tribunals and the courts, and examines their advantages and disadvantages.[159] It considers the statutory bar on ombudsmen accepting complaints that could have had, or did have, recourse to the courts.[160] This bar is subject to a proviso that, if the ombudsman thinks that it was unreasonable to expect the complainant to have or have had recourse to a legal remedy, the case may be accepted for investigation. The bar is a particular problem where the complainant did have recourse to a court or a tribunal and, on the same facts, complained to the ombudsman. The bar has been interpreted differently by the Local Ombudsmen, the Public Service Ombudsman for Wales and the Parliamentary Ombudsman.[161] The Law Commission is proposing that an ombudsman may conduct an investigation notwithstanding the fact that the complainant has or has had a legal remedy if, in all of the circumstances, it is in the interests of justice to investigate.[162] This provisional view was reached because it was felt to outweigh the fact that delay and duplication of effort could be caused by allowing 'repeated consideration of the same issues in different legal contexts', and that inconsistent results may bemuse claimants and be undesirable for public bodies who have used public resources in defending litigation.[163] The Law Commission is also proposing that it should be open for a court to refer a case to an ombudsman and for the ombudsmen to be able to refer an issue in a complaint for a court ruling.

What might be the factors that can be taken into account in determining the appropriate means of redress? The Law Commission makes four suggestions. The first factor is the availability of statutory procedures for a particular grievance which should ordinarily be used. The Local Government or Health Service Ombudsman might take a case that had not exhausted the statutory complaints procedure because there had been a breakdown of trust between the complainant and the authority.[164] The second factor is the nature of the complaint. The crux of a complaint of maladministration might be a contested legal issue that should therefore be determined by a court or tribunal.[165] The third factor relates to the characteristics of the parties. The complexity of the issues, the lack of available resources and the limited ability and degree of vulnerability of the complainant might indicate that the free investigative service of the ombudsman is preferable to expensive adversarial proceedings. This would also be the case if there is an ongoing relationship between the parties which, it is feared,

[158] Law Commission (2008).
[159] Ibid paras 3.1–3.5.
[160] Ibid Pt 5.
[161] Ibid paras 5.63–5.67.
[162] Ibid paras 5.69–5.73.
[163] Ibid para 5.74.
[164] Ibid paras 5.10–5.12.
[165] Ibid paras 5.13–5.14.

could be adversely affected, such as that between landlord and tenant or between healthcare professional and patient.[166] The fourth factor is the claimant's objectives. Recourse to an ombudsman might be preferred if the claimant is seeking an apology or wishes to maintain privacy as complainant identities are not revealed. On the other hand, if a prerogative order or interim relief are sought, then the court is the only recourse. Although it might be thought that, if a monetary remedy is sought. the court would be more appropriate, there are certain types of loss, which include distress, hardship or pure economic loss, which are not recognised by law but may be remedied on the recommendation of an ombudsman.[167]

Conclusions

It has taken seven years from the publication of the Leggatt Report to the launch of phase one of the First-tier and Upper Tribunals. The new structure will take some time to be implemented fully and to 'bed in'. Although the environment in which the First-tier and Upper Tribunals were launched has become a financially restrictive one that may curb innovation, it is suggested that the underlying policy is sound. The idea of PDR, of matching disputes to the appropriate resolution process is a good one, more work needs to be done on identifying criteria to make the appropriate allocation. While Leggatt followed the Franks Report in modelling tribunals on the courts, he did think that they were different in possessing expertise which enables them to deal with their jurisdictions in a way that should facilitate citizens accessing them without the need for representation. Leggatt's conditions for self-representation were pre-hearing advice and the tribunal conducting its proceedings in an enabling fashion. It seems that recent research has vindicated this position, that the improvements in training and the appraisal of tribunal personnel have equipped them to facilitate self-representation whilst maintaining their impartiality. It is to be hoped that there will be adequate provision of pre-hearing advice. The AJTC, with its users' focus across the administrative justice system, has a very important role to play if it is to become an authoritative adviser to ministers, not only on putting things right, but also on getting things right first time. It will need to work well with all the stake-holders in the system, including the research community, in order to provide the evidence base to make its advice compelling. Not only will it be reviewing the administrative justice system but contributing to its realisation as the different redress elements and initial decision makers appreciate that they are all inter-connected and seek to become, accessible, fair and efficient.

166 Ibid paras 5.15–5.18.
167 Ibid paras 5.19–5.24.

Disclaimer

Although Brian Thompson is a Member of the Administrative Justice and Tribunals Council, he has written this chapter in his personal capacity and his views should not be taken to be those of the AJTC.

References

Abel-Smith, B and Stevens, R (1968) *In Search of Justice: Law, Society and the Legal System* (Harmondsworth, Penguin).

Adler, M (2006) 'Tribunal Reform: Proportionate Dispute Resolution and the Pursuit of Administrative Justice' (2006) 69 MLR 958.

—— (2008a) 'Can Tribunals Deliver Justice in the Absence of Representation?' unpublished paper presented at the Legal Services Research Centre conference, University of Greenwich, 18–20 June.

—— (2008b) 'The Idea of Proportionality in Dispute Resolution' 30 *Journal of Social Welfare and Family Law* 309.

—— (2009) Tribunals ain't what they used to be', *Adjust Newsletter*, March 2009, available at www.ajtc.gov.uk/adjust/09_03.htm.Administrative Appeals Tribunal (2006) *Conference Process Model, available at* www.aat.gov.au/docs/ADR/ConferenceProcessModel.pdf.

Administrative Justice and Tribunals Council (2008a) *Annual Report for 2007/2008* (London, The Stationery Office).

—— (2008b) *Work Programme*, available at www.ajtc.gov.uk/docs/First_WP_accessible.pdf.

—— (2008c) *Developing Administrative Justice Research*, available at www.ajtc.gov.uk/docs/researchdoc-plain.pdf.

—— (2008d) *Survey Report: The Use of Proportionate Dispute Resolution in Tribunals*, available at www.ajtc.gov.uk/adjust/articles/feature_use_of_pdr.htm.

—— (2008e) *Adjust* (Special PDR edition) February, available at www.ajtc.gov.uk/adjust/08_02.htm.

Administrative Justice Steering Group (2008) *Options for the Future Administration and Supervision of Tribunals in Scotland* (Glasgow, Consumer Focus Scotland) available at www.ajtc.gov.uk/docs/Tribunals_in_Scotland.pdf.

—— (2009) *Administrative Justice in Scotland—The Way Forward* (Glasgow, Consumer Focus Scotland, available at www.consumerfocus.org.uk/assets/3/files/2009/11/AdministrativeJusticeinScotlandTheWayForwardFullReport.pdf.

Barber, B (1984) *Strong Democracy: Participatory Politics or a New Age* (Berkeley and Los Angeles, University of California Press).

Bayles, M (1990) *Procedural Justice: Allocating to Individuals* (Dordrecht, Kluwer).

Bell, K (1969) *Tribunals in the Social Services* (London, Routledge and Keegan Paul).

Broderick, S (2008) Speech to Administrative Justice and Tribunals Council Conference, *Adjust Newsletter*, available at www.ajtc.gov.uk/adjust/articles/SiobhanBroderickSpeech2008.pdf.

Council on Tribunals (2001) *Annual Report 2000/2001* HC 343 (London, HMSO) available at www.council-on-tribunals.gov.uk/docs/ar_01.pdf.

—— (2007) *Consultation on the Use and Value of Oral Hearings in the Administrative Justice System: Summary of Responses*, available at www.council-on-tribunals.gov.uk.

Department for Constitutional Affairs (2004) *Transforming Public Services: Complaints, Redress and Tribunals* Cm 6443 (London, The Stationery Office).

Franks, Sir Oliver (1957) *Report of the Committee on Administrative Tribunals and Enquiries* Cmnd 218 (London, HMSO).

Fuller, L (1978) 'The Forms and Limits Adjudication' 92 *Harvard Law Review* 392.

Galligan, D (1996) *Due Process and Fair Procedures* (Oxford, Clarendon Press).

Genn, H and Genn, Y (1989) *The Effectiveness of Representation before Tribunals* (London, Lord Chancellor's Department).

Genn, H, Lever, B and Gray, L (2006) *Tribunals For Diverse Users* DCA Research Series (London, Department for Constitutional Affairs).

Genn, H, Fenn, P, Mason, M, Lane, A, Bechai, N, Gray, L and Vencappa, D (2007) *Twisting Arms: Court Referred and Court Linked Mediation Under Judicial Pressure* (London, Ministry of Justice).

Harris, N, Ridell, S and Smith, E (2008) 'Special Educational Needs (England) and Additional Support Needs (Scotland) Dispute Resolution Project Working Paper 1: Literature Review', available at www.creid.ed.ac.uk/adr/pubs/adr_workingpaper1.pdf.

Law Commission (2008) *Administrative Redress: Citizens and Public Bodies* (Law Com CP 189) (London).

Legal Services Commission (2006) *Making Legal Rights a Reality: The Legal Services Commission's Strategy for the Community Legal Service 2006–2011* (London).

Leggatt, Sir Andrew (2001) *Tribunals for Users: One System; One Service* (London, Lord Chancellor's Department) available at www.tribunals-review.org.uk/.

Lord Chief Justice (2008) *Direction—Classes of cases specified under section 18(6) of the Tribunals, Courts and Enforcement Act 2007*, available at www.tribunals.gov.uk/Tribunals/Rules/directions.htm.

Mashaw, J (1981) 'Administrative Due Process: The Quest for Dignitary Theory' 61 *Boston University Law Review* 885.

Ministry of Justice (2008) *Judicial and Court Statistics 2007* Cm 7467 (London, The Stationery Office).

National Audit Office (2005) *Citizen Redress: What citizens can do if things go wrong with public services* HC-21 (London, The Stationery Office).

Northern Ireland Court Service (2008) *Annual Report for 2007–2008* (Belfast) available at www.courtsni.gov.uk/en-GB/Publications/Targets_and_Performance/Annual+Report+2007-2008.htm.

Parliamentary Commissioner for Administration (2008) *Principles of Good Administration, Principles for Remedy and Principles of Good Complaint Handling*, available at www.ombudsman.org.uk/improving_services/principles/index.html.

Partington, M and Kirton-Darling, E (2007) *Research Issues Paper: Feedback* (London, Tribunals Service).

Richardson, G (1994) 'The Legal Regulation of Process' in G Richardson and H Genn (eds), *Administrative Law and Government Action* (Oxford, Oxford University Press).

Richardson, G and Genn, H (2007) 'Tribunals in Transition: Resolution or Adjudication?' PL 116.

House of Lords Select Committee on the Constitution (2008) *Report on Tribunals, Court and Enforcement Bill* (Fifth Report 2007–08).

Senior President of Tribunals (2008) *Second Implementation Review,* available at www.tribunals.gov.uk/.

Tribunals Service (2007) *Transforming Tribunals, Implementing Part 1 of the Tribunals, Courts and Enforcement Act 2007* (London).

Tyler, T (2000) 'Social Justice: Outcome and Procedure' 35 *International Journal of Psychology* 117.

UK Border Agency (2008) *Consultation Paper: Immigration Appeals—Fair Decisions; Faster Justice* (London) available at www.ukba.homeoffice.gov.uk/sitecontent/documents/aboutus/consultations/immigrationappeals/immigrationappealsconsultation?view=Binary.

UK Border Agency and Tribunals Service (2009) *Immigration Appeals, Response to Consultation—Fair Decisions; Faster Justice* (London) available at www.ukba.homeoffice.gov.uk/sitecontent/documents/aboutus/consultations/immigrationappeals/immigration-appeals-response.pdf?view=Binary.

Woolf, LJ (1996) *Access to Justice: Final Report on the Civil Justice System in England and Wales* (London, Lord Chancellor's Department).

—— (1988) 'A Hotchpotch of Appeals—the need for a blender' 7 *Civil Justice Quarterly* 44.

Wraith, RE and Hutcheson, PG (1973) *Administrative Tribunals* (London, Allen and Unwin).

INDEX

Introductory Note

References such as '178–9' indicate (not necessarily continuous) discussion of a topic across a range of pages. Wherever possible in the case of topics with many references, these have either been divided into sub-topics or only the most significant discussions of the topic are listed. Because the entire volume is about 'administrative justice', the use of this term (and certain others which occur constantly throughout the book) as an entry point has been minimized. Information will be found under the corresponding detailed topics.

Index

Index

THIS BOOK COMPRISES a definitive collection of papers on administrative justice, written by a set of very distinguished contributors. It is divided into five groups, each of which contains articles on a particular aspect of administrative justice. The first group deals with the impact of 'contextual changes' on administrative justice and considers the implications of changes in governance and public administration, management and service delivery, information technology, audit and accounting, and human rights for administrative justice. The second group deals with conceptual issues and describes a number of competing approaches to administrative justice. The third group deals with the application of administrative justice principles to private law disputes while the fourth group deals with the distinctive characteristics of administrative justice in three other jurisdictions. The final group deals with current developments in administrative justice and the book concludes with a discussion of legislative and policy developments in the UK.

The general approach of the book is socio-legal and interdisciplinary. The chapters adopt a variety of disciplinary perspectives, including those derived from political science, public policy, social policy, accounting and information technology as well as from law. Although most of the contributors are academics, some are practitioners. For these reasons, the book should be of interest to lawyers, particularly those with interests in administrative law, and to social scientists, particularly those with interests in public administration, public policy and public management.

MICHAEL ADLER is Emeritus Professor of Socio-Legal Studies and Leverhulme Emeritus Fellow in the School of Social and Political Science at Edinburgh University.

COVER IMAGE: AMBROGIO LORENZETTI, *THE ALLEGORY OF GOOD GOVERNMENT* : FOTOGRAFIA LENSINI, SIENA